EAST ANGLIA AND ITS NORTH SEA WORLD
IN THE MIDDLE AGES

EAST ANGLIA AND ITS NORTH SEA WORLD IN THE MIDDLE AGES

Edited by
David Bates and Robert Liddiard

THE BOYDELL PRESS

© Contributors 2013

All Rights Reserved. Except as permitted under current legislation
no part of this work may be photocopied, stored in a retrieval system,
published, performed in public, adapted, broadcast,
transmitted, recorded or reproduced in any form or by any means,
without the prior permission of the copyright owner

First published 2013
The Boydell Press, Woodbridge
Paperback edition 2015

ISBN 978 1 84383 846 3 hardback
ISBN 978 1 78327 036 1 paperback

The Boydell Press is an imprint of Boydell & Brewer Ltd
PO Box 9, Woodbridge, Suffolk IP12 3DF, UK
and of Boydell & Brewer Inc.
668 Mount Hope Ave, Rochester, NY 14620–2731, USA
website: www.boydellandbrewer.com

A CIP catalogue record for this book is available
from the British Library

The publisher has no responsibility for the continued existence or accuracy of URLs for
external or third-party internet websites referred to in this book, and does not guarantee
that any content on such websites is, or will remain, accurate or appropriate

Designed and typeset by Tina Ranft, Woodbridge

— CONTENTS —

List of Illustrations vii
Preface xiii

INTRODUCTION: The North Sea 1
Robert Liddiard

PART I: EAST ANGLIA AND THE NORTH SEA WORLD: OVERVIEWS

1   The Origins of East Anglia in a North Sea Zone 16
    John Hines

2   East Anglia's Character and the 'North Sea World' 44
    Tom Williamson

3   Cities, Cogs and Commerce: Archaeological Approaches to the 63
    Material Culture of the North Sea World
    Brian Ayers

4   Medieval Art in Norfolk and the Continent: An Overview 82
    David King

PART II: TRADE AND ECONOMY

5   The Circulation, Minting, and Use of Coins in East Anglia, 120
    c.AD 580–675
    Gareth Williams

6   Coinage in Pre-Viking East Anglia 137
    Rory Naismith

7   The Castle and the Warren: Medieval East Anglian Fur Culture 152
    in Context
    Aleksander Pluskowski

8   Economic Relations between East Anglia and Flanders 174
    in the Anglo-Norman Period
    Eljas Oksanen

9   East Anglia's Trade in the North Sea World   188
    Wendy R. Childs

10 Iceland's 'English Century' and East Anglia's North Sea World   204
    Anna Agnarsdóttir

PART III: CASE-STUDIES: INFLUENCES AND LINKS

11 Ipswich: Contexts of Funerary Evidence from an Urban Precursor   218
    of the Seventh Century AD
    Christopher Scull

12 Imports or Immigrants? Reassessing Scandinavian Metalwork   230
    in Late Anglo-Saxon East Anglia
    Tim Pestell

13 Stone Building in Romanesque East Anglia   256
    Stephen Heywood

14 Romanesque East Anglia and the Empire   270
    Richard Plant

15 All in the Same Boat? East Anglia, the North Sea World and   287
    the 1147 Expedition to Lisbon
    Charles West

16 The *Liber Celestis* of St Bridget of Sweden (1302/3–1373) and   301
    its Influence on the Household Culture of Some Late Medieval
    Norfolk Women
    Carole Hill

17 Flemish Influence on English Manuscript Painting in East Anglia   315
    in the Late Fourteenth Century
    Lynda Dennison

    Index   337

— LIST OF ILLUSTRATIONS —

The editor, contributors and publishers are grateful to all the institutions and persons listed in the captions for permission to reproduce the materials in which they hold copyright. Unless indicated, all other images are copyright the author. Every effort has been made to trace the copyright holders; apologies are offered for any omission, and the publishers will be pleased to add any necessary acknowledgement in subsequent editions.

CHAPTER 1. The Origins of East Anglia in a North Sea Zone

Map 1	Cross-North Sea connexions.	20
Figure 1	Wrist-clasps. A: Class A; B: Class B.	23
Figure 2	Eriswell, Suffolk (ERL114), grave 405.	26
Figure 3	Eriswell, Suffolk (ERL114), grave 405: the wrist-clasps.	27
Figure 4	Domed silver buttons.	30
Plate 1	Great square-headed brooches of Group IV.	34
Plate 2	Gilt silver great square-headed brooches.	35
Plate 3	Gilt silver great square-headed brooch.	37
Table 1	The results of analysis by X-ray fluorescence of two great square-headed brooches of Group IV and the Mundham clasp button.	31

CHAPTER 2. East Anglia's Character and the 'North Sea World'

Map 1	East Anglia and its continental neighbours.	45
Map 2	Principal Danish strongholds, Danish place names, and the 'North Sea Province'.	54
Map 3	The distribution of cremation cemeteries and 'Anglian' artefacts.	55

CHAPTER 3. Cities, Cogs and Commerce: Archaeological Approaches to the Material Culture of the North Sea World

Plate 1	Reconstruction of the Bremen cog.	66
Plate 2	Casks of Baltic timber c.1490.	72
Plate 3	Fourteenth-century pilgrim badge mould, Norwich.	75

viii LIST OF ILLUSTRATIONS

CHAPTER 4. Medieval Art in Norfolk and the Continent: An Overview

Plate 1	Norwich cathedral, figure of St Felix, 1096–1119.	85
Plate 2	Norwich cathedral, capital, twelfth-century.	86
Plate 3	Merton, Norfolk, parish church of St Peter.	87
Plate 4	The Carrow Psalter and Hours, scenes from the Life of St Olaf, c.1250–60.	88
Plate 5	Heddal, Norway, altar frontal, c.1250.	89
Plate 6	Saxlingham Nethergate, Norfolk, window, medallion with Apostles, c.1250.	90
Plate 7	Figure of Beatrix of Valkenburg, window, c.1293.	91
Plate 8	Gorleston Psalter, Crucifixion, c.1320–30.	93
Plate 9	Monumental brass of Robert Braunche, d. 1364.	96
Plate 10	Attleborough church, west window, angel playing rebec, c.1340–60.	99
Plate 11	Crucifixion, panel painting, c.1410–20.	100
Plate 12	Norwich cathedral, Annunciation, c.1430–40.	102
Plate 13	Salle church, prophets, patriarchs and cardinals, window, c.1440.	103
Plate 14	St Peter Mancroft, Norwich, Crucifixion and Entombment, window, c.1450–55.	104
Plate 15	North Tuddenham church, Norfolk, Olybrius' squire, window, c.1420–30.	106
Plate 16	St Gregory, Norwich, St George and the dragon, c.1500.	108
Plate 17	Hans Holbein the Younger, *A Lady with a Squirrel and a Starling (Anne Lovell?)*, c.1527.	110
Plate 18	The Ashwellthorpe Triptych, c.1519.	111
Plate 19	St Andrew, Norwich, the Sacrifice of Isaac, window, 1510–20.	112
Plate 20	St Stephen, Norwich, the Sacrifice of Isaac and part of a Crucifixion, window, 1533.	113
Plate 21	St Andrew, Norwich, the Dance of Death, window, c.1506–10.	114
Plate 22	St Clement, Outwell, figure of St Stephen, window, c.1515–25.	115
Plate 23	Arms of the City of Norwich, c.1531–40.	116

CHAPTER 5. The Circulation, Minting, and Use of Coins in East Anglia, c.AD 580–675

Plate 1	Coins, blanks and ingots from the Sutton Hoo purse.	121
Plate 2	The Oxborough hoard.	126
Plate 3	Wilton Cross-pendant, Norfolk.	130
Plate 4	Gold solidi.	132
Plate 5	Gold shillings.	133

LIST OF ILLUSTRATIONS ix

CHAPTER 6. Coinage in Pre-Viking East Anglia

Plate 1	Continental *sceattas*, Series D, E and X.	143
Plate 2	East Anglian *sceattas*, Series R and Q.	143
Plate 3	Coins inscribed with the names of kings and moneyers.	145
Graph 1	Numbers of single-finds of *sceattas* from various counties.	140
Graph 2	Series/types of *sceat* represented in Norfolk and Suffolk.	142
Graph 3	Rate of productivity in dies per annum at Ipswich.	146

CHAPTER 7. The Castle and the Warren: Medieval East Anglian Fur Culture in Context

Figure 1	Main categories of fur in medieval northern Europe.	154
Map 1	Sites documented in the text.	158
Map 2	Documented rabbit warrens in East Anglia c.1200–1540.	170
Plate 1	Figures wearing robes lined with various pelts, c.1160–80.	166

CHAPTER 8. Economic Relations between East Anglia and Flanders in the Anglo-Norman Period

| Map 1 | England and Flanders in the Anglo-Norman period. | 175 |

CHAPTER 9. East Anglia's Trade in the North Sea World

Table 1	Annual averages of imports and exports, 1303–7 and 1308–9.	191
Table 2	Annual averages of imports and exports, 1390–1400.	194
Table 3a	Annual averages of imports and exports, 1460–70.	197
Table 3b	Annual averages of imports and exports, 1470–80.	197

CHAPTER 12. Imports or Immigrants? Reassessing Scandinavian Metalwork in Late Anglo-Saxon East Anglia

Figure 1	Trefoil mounts and brooches.	234
Map 1	Distribution of (a) Borre knotwork and (b) 'backward-facing beast' brooches in England.	237
Map 2	Distribution of Viking-type ingots in England and Wales.	247
Plate 1	Carolingian metalwork from Norfolk, ninth–tenth century.	232
Plate 2	Borre-style metalwork and 'backward-facing beast' brooch.	236
Plate 3	Thor's hammer pendants from Norfolk.	241
Plate 4	'Rider and Valkyrie' mounts from East Anglia.	243
Plate 5	Penny of King Æthelred of East Anglia.	245
Plate 6	The Hindringham silver ingot hoard.	248
Plate 7	Bronze ingot from Roman sestertius coin.	250

Plate 8	Fused silver pennies from Norfolk.	251
Table 1	A provisional handlist of fused silver pennies, arranged chronologically	251

CHAPTER 13. Stone Building in Romanesque East Anglia

Figure 1	Bury St Edmunds abbey church, reconstruction drawing.	266
Figure 2	Norwich cathedral, reconstruction drawing.	267
Plate 1	Greenstead-next-Ongar, church of St Andrew.	257
Plate 2	Urnes, Norway, stave church.	258
Plate 3	Urnes church. Interlace on north nave wall.	259
Plate 4	Hammarlunda church, Scania.	261
Plate 5	Herringfleet church.	264
Plate 6	Haddiscoe church.	265

CHAPTER 14. Romanesque East Anglia and the Empire

Figure 1	Bury St Edmunds abbey church, plan of surviving fabric.	276
Figure 2	Cologne cathedral, reconstruction of *c*.1100.	283
Plate 1	Peterborough abbey church (now cathedral), west front.	273
Plate 2	Ely cathedral, west front, lower parts.	274
Plate 3	Bury St Edmunds abbey church, remains of west front.	277
Plate 4	Hildesheim, church of St Michael.	282
Plate 5	Cologne, church of St Pantaleon, interior.	284
Plate 6	Hildesheim, church of St Michael, interior.	285

CHAPTER 17. Flemish Influence on English Manuscript Painting in the Late Fourteenth Century

Plate 1   318–19
a Oxford, Bodleian Library, MS Douce 131, Psalter, fol. 96v, detail of miniature.
b Brescia, Bibliteca Queriniana, MS A. V. 17, Psalter, fol. 7r, Psalm 1, detail of miniature.
c Oxford, Bodleian Library, MS Bodley 264, 'Romance of Alexander', fol. 51v, miniature.

Plate 2   320–1
a Oxford, Exeter College, MS 47, Psalter, fol. 33v, Psalm 51, initial and border.
b Church of St Mary Magdalene, Newark, Nottinghamshire, Alan Fleming, brass rubbing.

Plate 3   322
a Cambridge, Fitzwilliam Museum, MS 38-1950, Psalter, fol. 29r, detail, Psalm 26, miniature.
b St Margaret's Church, King's Lynn, Robert Braunche, detail, brass rubbing.

Plate 4   323–4
a The Hague, Rijksmuseum Meermanno-Westreenianum, MS 10. A. 14, Missal, fol. 143v, Crucifixion miniature.
b Paris, Bibliothèque nationale, MS latin 765, Fitzwarin Psalter, fol. 14r, Crucifixion miniature.

Plate 5   325
a Oxford, Bodleian Library, Lat. liturg. f. 3, Book of Hours, fol. 118v, detail, minor initial.
b Cambridge, Fitzwilliam Museum, MS 38-1950, Psalter, fol. 49v, detail, minor initial.
c London, British Library, MS Royal 13 D. 1*, Psalter, fol. 20v, Psalm 68, detail, border.
d Leça do Balio, Estêvão Vasques Pimentel, detail, heads of Christ and two Apostles, brass rubbing.

Plate 6   326
a Oxford, Bodleian Library, MS Auct. D. 4. 4, Psalter-Hours, fol. 234r, detail, initial of the Evangelist Matthew.
b Leça do Balio, Estêvão Vasques Pimentel, detail, the Evangelist Matthew, brass rubbing.

Plate 7   327
a Brussels, Bibliothèque royale de Belgique, MS 6426, Antiphonary, fol. 26r, detail, initial of the Nativity of Christ.
b Lübeck cathedral, Bishops Burchard von Serken and Johann von Mul, detail, background pattern of grotesques and butterflies, brass rubbing.

Plate 8   328
a Brussels, Bibliothèque royale de Belgique, MS 6426, Antiphonary, fol. 188r, detail, pen initial of female drollery.
b Oxford, Bodleian Library, MS Bodley 264, 'Romance of Alexander', fol. 108r, detail, initial of female drollery.

— PREFACE —

THIS BOOK sets out to discuss medieval East Anglia in a way not often attempted before, not so much as a distinctive English region, but rather as one that had strong and enduring links with its maritime neighbours across the North Sea. It starts from the well known premise that travel by sea was often easier in the Middle Ages than travel by land and recognition of the importance for the region of such well known phenomena as Sutton Hoo, the Viking invasions and settlements, and late medieval trade with the Low Countries. What, however, is ultimately very striking is the range and diversity of the contacts. Relations between East Anglia and its North Sea world have for the most part been peaceful, involving migration and commercial, artistic, architectural and religious exchanges, but have also at times been characterized by violence and contestation. All these elements have played a significant role in processes of historical change that have shaped the history both of East Anglia and its North Sea world.

The chapters in this book are based on papers delivered at the 'East Anglia and its North Sea World' conference held at the University of East Anglia, Norwich, in April 2010. The conference was an international event and a deliberately interdisciplinary affair. It featured contributions from scholars working in Iceland, Denmark, the Netherlands, Belgium and the United Kingdom and brought together specialists from many disciplines who share a common interest in East Anglia's medieval past. At the end of three days of discussion and debate there was a strong feeling that we had all been involved in the development of a new and scarcely studied subject and that a publication was a necessary outcome.

In organizing the conference and bringing this collection to publication we have incurred many debts. We would particularly like to express our thanks for the generous financial support given to the conference by the British Academy, which was instrumental in bringing together a host of international scholars. Further support was provided by the Centre of East Anglian Studies at the University of East Anglia, both in terms of financial assistance and by the attendance of so many associate members, who contributed enormously to the success of the conference. We would like to thank in particular John Alban, County Archivist at the Norfolk Record Office, who curated an exhibition 'Norfolk and its North Sea World' at the Norfolk Record Office to coincide with the conference, and also the staff of Norwich Cathedral, whose refectory provided a splendid backdrop for a plenary lecture and the conference dinner.

We would furthermore like to express our gratitude to Lucy Marten, who was a co-organizer of the conference and whose dedication underpinned much of the organizational work, in which she and the editors of this volume were ably supported by Natalie Mitchell and Natalie Orr from the University of East Anglia's Arts and Humanities Events Office.

During the preparation of the introduction Susan Raich provided invaluable bibliographical assistance and Wendy Davies kindly allowed the text of her unpublished introductory keynote address on the place of regions in the medieval world to be consulted. Finally, we must thank the anonymous reviewer who commented on an early draft of the proposal and Caroline Palmer at Boydell & Brewer for her customary efficiency and patience while this volume was brought to publication.

— Introduction —

THE NORTH SEA

Robert Liddiard

AT MORE THAN 970 kilometres long and 580 kilometres wide, encompassing an area of some 750,000 square kilometres and a volume of some 94,000 cubic kilometres, the North Sea is the largest body of water in Northern Europe. The North Sea is one of seven 'British Seas' as defined by modern oceanographers, all of which are linked via the continental shelf to the North Atlantic, but it is one given a certain geographical unity by virtue of the relatively shallow seabed framed by the east coast of Britain, by the northern coastline of Continental Europe and by Scandinavia.[1] This area forms the drainage basin for the Baltic Sea and for historically significant river systems such as the Rhine, Meuse, Scheldt and Elbe. When viewed as a connector, rather than as a barrier, the maritime geography of the North Sea helps to explain some of the long-term themes in its history, especially as a movement corridor for people, goods and ideas for those communities along its rim.[2] Today, awareness of the North Sea is chiefly connected with economic exploitation, principally for oil and gas, but also in periodic concerns about overfishing and, more recently, in attempts to harness the power of winds and waves for renewable energy. For historians, such concerns are arguably modern manifestations of much longer struggles for control of the sea and its resources, both natural and commercial.[3]

While the idea of a 'Northern Sea' or a 'Northern Ocean' or 'German Ocean' existed as far back as Antiquity, the first cartographic use of the term 'North Sea' dates from the early sixteenth century, when Dutch cartographers differentiated it from the east, west and middle seas that lay on its periphery.[4] As the name for the

---

[1] J. Hardisty, *The British Seas*, London 1990, 3–24.
[2] For an extended introduction to the region, see R. Van de Noort, *North Sea Archaeologies*, Oxford 2011.
[3] Echoed in contemporary politics over the fate of North Sea oil in the event of Scottish Independence: M. Keating, *The Independence of Scotland: Self-Government and the Shifting Politics of Union*, Oxford 2009.
[4] Today the Baltic, English Channel and southern North Sea, and the now reclaimed area of Friesland respectively. To this can be added the southern sea that is now the inland lake of the Ijsselmeer (Lake Yssel) in the Netherlands, Van de Noort, *North Sea*, 4–10.

area to the north of Dogger Bank, it probably had common currency in the late Middle Ages; *die Nordsee*, for example, is mentioned in the fifteenth-century *Booke of Margery Kempe*.[5] As was the case with other seas in the Middle Ages, the North Sea was both an obstacle and a unifier for those communities for whom it represented a shared frontier. The extent to which either predominated at any given time was subject to a number of factors, such as political and military control of the open sea (or more usually inshore coastlines or coastal ports), economics, and climatic and tidal conditions, all of which could operate together or independently to promote or inhibit movement and exchange.[6] Surveying the medieval period as a whole, however, the sense of connectivity is most immediately obvious, something best seen in the movements of Germanic and Scandinavian peoples across it during the early Middle Ages. Although perhaps less dramatic, but cumulatively just as significant, were the myriad of trading networks that came to be fully established from around the year 1000 onwards and which blend seamlessly with those of the Early Modern Period.

These travel and exchange routes were, however, hard won. During the Middle Ages, the North Sea had a fearsome reputation for violent storms and treacherous currents.[7] Crossing it required investment in technology, skill in seamanship, physical endurance and at times a significant level of courage.[8] Beyond the entrances to the Baltic and the English Channel were known waters and shipping lanes to Russia, Biscay and beyond, but to the north where it bordered the Atlantic the geography was less well known and to the medieval voyager represented the edge of the world. Here was a place where the sea was haunted by dragons and demons and the land inhabited by Nomads who lay beyond the bounds of Christendom.[9] The physical risks that sea travel represented lie behind the numerous instances in medieval writing where ships in distress were miraculously saved by the interventions of saints. Bede, for example, recounts how in 651 Utta the priest, recalling the teaching of Bishop Aiden, prevented his ship from capsizing by literally pouring oil on stormy waters while travelling back from Kent with the

---

[5] Van de Noort, *North Sea*, 4; J. Hsy, 'Lingua franca: Overseas Travel and Language Contact in *The Book of Margery Kempe*', in *The Sea and Englishness in the Middle Ages*, ed. S. Sobecki, Cambridge 2011, 159–78, at 170.

[6] For discussion of sea power and control of the North Sea, J. Haywood, *Dark Age Naval Power: Reassessment of Frankish and Anglo-Saxon Seafaring*, London 1991; J. Pullen Appleby, *English Sea Power, c.871–1100*, Hockwold-cum-Wilton 2005; for the role of the sea as defining the effective reach of military power, J. H. Pryor, *Geography, Technology and War: Studies in the Maritime History of the Mediterranean, 649–1571*, Cambridge 1988.

[7] Pryor, *Geography*, 12; some measure of the violence of storms is given in H. Lamb, *Historic Storms of the North Sea, British Isles and Northwest Europe*, Cambridge 1991.

[8] N. Ohler, *The Medieval Traveller*, trans. C. Hillier, Woodbridge 1989.

[9] P. Brown, *The Rise of Western Christendom*, Cambridge, MA 1996, 300–1. R. Muir Wright, 'The Rider on the Sea-monster: *Quid gloriaris in militia…*', in *The North Sea World in the Middle Ages: Studies in the Cultural History of North-west Europe*, ed. T. R. Kiszka and L. E. M. Walker, Dublin 2001, 70–87; I. Zachrisson, 'The Sámi and Their Interaction with the Nordic Peoples', in *The Viking World*, ed. S. Brink, Oxford 2008, 32–9.

future bride of the Northumbrian King Oswy.[10] The frequency of such stories in hagiographical literature is a reminder of the hazards faced by those crossing the sea throughout the Middle Ages, while at the same time unwittingly helping to point up the fact that, for all its dangers, such journeys were routine.

This collection of essays takes the North Sea during the Middle Ages as its central theme, albeit from the perspective of one of the many regions that lies along its edge: East Anglia. It seeks to investigate the place of East Anglia within a geographical context in which it has always been known to have played a part, but which has seldom been directly explored. As such it seeks to make a contribution not just to the understanding of one English region, but also to add to the substantial body of material on the study of seas and oceans, and to the history of north-western Europe as a whole.

STUDYING THE SEA

Any consideration of the role and the significance of seas in history is dominated by the work of Fernand Braudel, whose 1949 classic *La Méditerranée et le monde méditerranéen à l'époque de Philippe II* remains a landmark (or perhaps seamark) in historical study, stressing as it did the central role of the Mediterranean sea as a structuring force for human activity over the *longue durée*.[11] Two generations of scholars have followed Braudel's lead and what has come to be recognised as 'maritime history' has been a fertile area for multi-national research.[12]

Other than the Mediterranean, perhaps the clearest example of the advantages of foregrounding seas and oceans for the purposes of historical analysis is to be seen in the study of 'Atlantic history', which as a concept has acquired considerable currency and consequently a substantial bibliography.[13] A summary of the approach

---

[10] *Bede's Ecclesiastical History of the English People*, ed. B. Colgrave and R. A. B. Mynors, Oxford 1969, 260–1.
[11] F. Braudel, *The Mediterranean and the Mediterranean World in the Age of Philip II*, trans S. Reynolds, London 1975.
[12] The literature on the Mediterranean is vast, but key texts include: P. Horden and N. Purcell, *The Corrupting Sea, a Study of Mediterranean History*, Oxford 2000; D. Abulafia (ed.), *The Mediterranean in History*, London 2003; D. Abulafia, *The Great Sea: A Human History of the Mediterranean*, London 2011. For a historiographical survey, G. Harlaftis and C. Vassallo, 'Maritime History since Braudel', in *New Directions in Mediterranean Maritime History*, ed. G. Harlaftis and C. Vassallo, Research in Maritime History, 28, St John's, Newfoundland 2004, 1–19.
[13] For a recent overview, see D. Egerton, A. Games, J. Landers and K. Lane, *The Atlantic World: A History, 1400–1888*, New York 2007, with key texts; B. Bailyn, *Atlantic History: Concept and Contours*, Cambridge, MA 2005; N. Canny, 'Atlantic History: What and Why?', *European Review* 9, 2001, 399–411; H. Pietschmann (ed.), *Atlantic History: History of the Atlantic System, 1580–1830*, Göttingen 2002; E. Manke and C. Shammas (eds), *The Creation of the British Atlantic World*, Baltimore 2005; J. Canizares-Esguerra and E. Seeman (eds), *The Atlantic in Global History, 1500–2000*, Upper Saddle River, NJ, 2007; A. Games, 'Atlantic History: Definitions, Challenges and Opportunities', *American Historical Review* 111, 2006, 741–57; J. Greene and P. Morgan (ed.), *Atlantic History: A Critical Appraisal*, Oxford 2009; D. Armitage and M. Braddick (eds), *The British Atlantic world, 1500–1800*, 2nd edn, Basingstoke 2009.

is that it discusses 'the creation, destruction, and re-creation of communities as a result of the movement, across and around the Atlantic basin, of people, commodities, cultural practices and values', but such a comment could apply equally well to the study of other seas and oceans.[14] Cumulatively, scholars of the Atlantic have come close to the 'total history' practised by Braudel and the *Annales* School and have succeeded in writing multi-period histories from a variety of geographical perspectives. The interaction between otherwise remote and scattered communities in Sub-Saharan Africa, western Britain and the eastern seaboard of the United States has been key to understanding of the development of each constituent part – and the whole – over several hundred years of inter-connected history. In addition to studies of the Mediterranean and Atlantic, the field of maritime history now boasts biographies of seas across the globe, ranging from the Irish Sea to the Indian and Pacific Oceans.[15]

Although 'maritime history' is a catch-all term for a variety of distinctive sub-disciplines, a certain unity of approach is provided by the principle that seas can be the central point of analysis.[16] Human beings create regions, but those regions are often facilitated and structured by patterns of movement across bodies of water. Seas need not be seen simply as entities only to be 'viewed from the shore' and solely in economic terms; rather, they can be both enablers and structuring forces for human activity and also as distinctive places in the cultural imagination.[17] Underpinning numerous studies of what are, superficially at least, bodies of water with little to connect them are a series of recurring themes that provide a framework for analysis: diaspora and migration, connectivity, economic and cultural exchange, contestation and control. Seas were at the same time both connectors and dividers, but with the balance favouring the former over the *longue durée*.[18] When seen in conjunction with tributary rivers that were navigable inland, seas were potential super-highways for long-distance movement of goods, people and ideas with a reach far beyond the coastline itself.[19] In such analyses the strict

---

[14] J. H. Elliott, quoted in P. D. Morgan and J. P. Greene, 'Introduction: The Present State of Atlantic History', in *Atlantic History: A Critical Appraisal*, 2–33, at 3.

[15] The 'Seas in History', a series published by Routledge is most relevant here: P. Butel, *The Atlantic*, London 1999; M. Pearson, *The Indian Ocean*, London 2007; D. Freeman, *The Pacific*, London 2009, and the most relevant for the present study, D. Kirby and M. Hinkkanen, *The Baltic and North Seas*, London 2000. See also, P. Squatriti, 'How the Irish Sea (May Have) Saved Irish Civilisation', *Comparative Studies in Society and History* 43, 2001, 615–30.

[16] Most clearly seen in archaeological approaches, Van de Noort, *North Sea*, and the dedicated volume in the journal *World Archaeology*, G. Cooney (ed.), 'Seascapes', *World Archaeology* 53, 2003.

[17] See the excellent introduction by R. Gorski, 'Roles of the Sea: Views from the Shore', in *Roles of the Sea in Medieval England*, ed. R. Gorski, Woodbridge 2012, 1–23; S. Rose, *The Medieval Sea*, London 2007.

[18] Gorski, 'Roles of the Sea', 10, the cumulative body of research points to the fact that, as far as the British Seas are concerned 'over the long term they have connected more than they have isolated'; in an eleventh-century context see M. Gardiner, 'Shipping and Trade between England and the Continent during the Eleventh Century', *Anglo-Norman Studies* 22, 2000, 71–93.

[19] In an English context see J. Blair (ed.), *Waterways and Canal-building in Medieval England*, Oxford 2007; for the role of the ship see R. W. Unger, *The Ship in the Medieval Economy, 600-1600*, London 1980.

divide between sea and land is broken down and as a result conventional geographical boundaries (and histories) may become incidental or tangential to the central narrative. Thus it becomes possible to write about the existence of communities that cut across the established structures and borders of land-based lordships or nation states and discuss instead maritime societies with 'oceanic mentalities'.[20] Such mentalities represented, to some extent, common cultures based upon a shared experience and understanding of the sea, its exploitation and the dynamics of travel and exchange, often over very long distances.[21] While this might seem obvious for 'self-contained' seas such as the Mediterranean, it is also true for much larger bodies of water. Cunliffe, for example, has argued for the existence of a northern Atlantic 'maritime zone' best thought of as an 'arc of peninsulas' that stretched from Spain to Ireland. Such zones may have very deep routes: in the case of the European Atlantic, scientists have suggested a prehistoric origin on the basis of genetic markers in modern populations.[22]

A 'NORTH SEA WORLD'?

Turning to the North Sea, it has long been known that there were significant and enduring links between the coastlines and archipelagos scattered around its rim, and for which the sea represented a shared frontier.[23] At the beginning of the Middle Ages this was most obviously reflected in migration of people, with the Saxon and then Viking settlement, and by the end in well established trade networks, seen particularly clearly in the activities of the Hanseatic League. While contacts and exchanges have been the subject of numerous studies, the question whether they amount to a phenomenon that can be called a 'North Sea World', which might bear comparison with other well documented maritime cultures, has rarely been seriously tackled.

Reasons for scepticism are not hard to find. Defining the geographical extent of any such North Sea World is difficult. As a marginal sea, in places its boundaries lack clear definition. While the Straits of Dover and the Skagerrak represent obvious cut off points with neighbouring bodies of water and have been points of contes-

---

[20] B. Cunliffe, *Facing the Ocean. The Atlantic and Its Peoples, 8000 BC–AD 1500*, Oxford 2001.
[21] The phrase is taken from Cunliffe, *Facing the Ocean*, 565.
[22] B. McEvoy, M. Richards, P. Forster and D. Bradley, 'The *longue durée* of Genetic Ancestry: Multiple Genetic Marker Systems and Celtic Origins of the Atlantic Façade of Europe', *American Journal of Human Genetics* 75, 2004, 693–702.
[23] Kirby and Hinkkanen, *Baltic and North Seas*, passim; M. M. Postan, 'The Trade of Medieval Europe: The North', in *The Cambridge Economic History of Europe, vol. 2. Trade and Industry in the Middle Ages*, ed. M. M. Postan and E. Miller, 2nd edn, Cambridge 1987, 196–204; T. Lloyd, *England and the German Hanse, 1157-1611: A Study of Their Trade and Commercial Diplomacy*, Cambridge 1991; A. Pedersen, 'Anglo-Danish Contact across the North Sea in the Eleventh Century: A Survey of the Danish Archaeological Evidence', in *Scandinavia and Europe, 800–1350: Contact, Conflict and Coexistence*, ed. J. Adams and K. Holman, Turnhout 2004, 43–67; K. Friedland and P. Richards (eds), *Essays in Hanseatic History*, Dereham, Norfolk 2005; U. Fransson et al (eds), *Cultural Interaction between East and West: Archaeology, Artefacts and Human Contacts in Northern Europe*, Stockholm 2007.

tation for centuries, the boundary with the North Atlantic is more arbitrary. In his study mentioned above, Cunliffe's 'Atlantic Zone' cuts the North Sea in half, with the northern and southern portions both having their own slightly different historic trajectories. The inclusion of the Baltic in any North Sea World also presents difficulties, with arguments for and against its status as a separate entity. Moreover, known movements of people did not always respect what would seem to be the obvious geographical boundaries. The Norwegian Vikings are a case in point. As raiders or traders, their activities took them across the North Sea either to primary destinations or as stepping stones to places further afield, but they were not confined to its bounds; numerous expeditions, to the Irish Sea and to Iceland and Greenland, took them away from the North Sea and into other maritime geographies.

Furthermore, historiographical trends within national histories have not always been receptive to the idea of a shared narrative for those areas on the North Sea rim. In German historical writing the focus has tended to look southwards to Italy and the Empire's relationship with the papacy, while in England the Norman Conquest has long been seen as shifting England's national view away from the north in favour of more mainstream European culture centred on France. For Scandinavian historians the trend unsurprisingly has, however, been more towards a holistic view, principally as the gateway by which the Vikings had their impact upon European events, but here also the tendency has been towards national histories, rather than maritime cultures.[24]

Despite its lack of general appeal to historians, the existence of a 'North Sea World' that might bear comparison with the Mediterranean and Atlantic has attracted a degree of scholarly attention. As far back as 1985 a collection of essays discussing the North Sea over the *longue durée* drew attention to a shared history.[25] A similar collection, published in 2001, focussing on the Middle Ages and taking a more literary and cultural perspective, again has the idea of such a world as implicit.[26] The existence of a 'North Sea World' in the Early Modern period has, however, been the subject of a detailed discussion, where it is explicitly argued that many of the characteristics of the Mediterranean World find similar expression in the North Sea.[27] If judged by the yardstick set down by studies of more demonstrable maritime cultures, then the idea of a North Sea World clearly has merit. A certain 'fuzziness' of borders is not in itself problematic; indeed, is to be expected. As many historians have stressed, regions were themselves made up of constituent sub-regions, frequently connected by bodies of water, so there is no difficulty, for

---

[24] For the political histories of the major players at this time, R. McKitterick (ed.), *The New Cambridge Medieval History II c.700–c.900*, Cambridge 1995; S. Imsen (ed.), *Norwegian Domination and the Norse World 1100–1400*, Trondheim 2011.

[25] A. Bang-Anderson, B. Greenhill and E. Grude (eds), *The North Sea: A Highway of Economic and Cultural Exchange*, Oslo 1985.

[26] T. R. Kiszka and L. E. M. Walker (eds), *The North Sea World in the Middle Ages: Studies in the Cultural History of North-West Europe*, Dublin 2001.

[27] L. Van Ross and J. Roding (eds), *The North Sea and Culture (1550–1800)*, Hilversum 1996.

example, in the inclusion of the Baltic in such a 'North Sea' World.[28] Within the North Sea rim, it has been suggested that it was the combination of trade links, high levels of urbanization and areas of relatively weak lordship that contributed to a vibrant maritime culture.[29] While not attempting to play down political, linguistic and cultural differences that of course remained, a certain unity based upon family structure, inheritance custom and connectivity provided by the North Sea existed up to the nineteenth century, and only came to an end with the rise of the nation state.[30] Although primarily concerned with developments post-1500, many of these observations are suggestive of a similar situation at the end of the Middle Ages and probably earlier; it seems impossible that such a 'world' appeared fully-fledged out of nothing at the beginning of the sixteenth century. Further contributions have come from archaeology, most notably Robert Van de Noort's *North Sea Archaeologies*, which sets out clear evidence for a particular cultural unity to the North Sea rim from prehistory.[31] In short, there seems enough evidence already in existence to make the idea of a 'North Sea World' in the Middle Ages at least one worth exploring.

But it is the relationship between one region bordering the North Sea – East Anglia – and its larger maritime hinterland that is the subject of this collection. It should be noted that the essays presented here are not intended to argue definitively for or against the existence of a 'North Sea World' in the Middle Ages (although it will immediately become apparent to the reader that this is the thrust of many of the contributions); rather, they represent an attempt to place East Anglia in the broader geographical and social context within which it has long been recognized to have played a part. The title of this volume has been carefully chosen to reflect this fact. In placing the relationship between a region and the sea at the foreground of the discussion it is hoped not only that a more nuanced picture of East Anglia emerges, but that at the same time it serves a broader function of demonstrating that the North Sea can be profitably studied in the same way as the Mediterranean or Atlantic. If we were to borrow one term suggested by historians of the Atlantic, the approach here would be 'cis-Atlantic': that is, the study of one region – in this case East Anglia – in relation to its wider North Sea World, keeping in mind the proviso that any comparisons 'can be meaningful without being quite so literal'.[32]

---

[28] Braudel, *Mediterranean*, 276; Horden and Purcell, *Corrupting Sea*, 463–523; Pearson, *Indian Ocean*, 1–12.
[29] W. Blockmans and L. van Voss, 'Urban Networks and Emerging States in the North Sea and Baltic Areas: A Maritime Culture?', in *The North Sea and Culture (1550–1800)*, ed. Van Ross and Roding, 10–20.
[30] Ibid.
[31] Van de Noort, *North Sea Archaeologies*, passim.
[32] D. Armitage, 'Three Concepts of Atlantic History', in *The British Atlantic World*, 2nd edn, ed. D. Armitage and M. Braddick, Basingstoke 2009, 11–27, at 22; quotation from Gorski, *Roles of the Sea*, 10.

MEDIEVAL EAST ANGLIA: REGIONALISM AND IDENTITY

The distinctive character and identity of what was later to become East Anglia can be seen long before the Middle Ages. The Icenian revolt against the Romans in AD 60 is perhaps the first recorded instance of East Anglia as a regional polity impacting upon the wider stage.[33] Although today the term East Anglia is applied to Cambridgeshire, Essex and occasionally parts of the adjoining county of Lincolnshire, during the Middle Ages it was more closely defined and referred chiefly to what is now Norfolk and Suffolk. The 'East Angles' are first encountered in the historical record in Bede's *Ecclesiastical History* and East Anglia was an important player in national politics during the period of the Heptarchy. Some sense of the geographical extent of the kingdom can be gauged from the boundaries of the diocese of Norwich, which probably preserve the territorial limits as they existed at some point in the later Middle Saxon period.[34] The sense of an independent identity outlived the Danish and West Saxon conquests of the ninth and tenth centuries and the administrative unity of Norfolk and Suffolk persisted until relatively late; the two counties were only shired during the reign of Cnut, but even then held a joint shrievalty until the final quarter of the sixteenth century.[35]

There is little doubt that medieval East Anglians had a strong awareness of their own identity and that it found expression in art, architecture and in a sense of a common past.[36] The image of King Edmund, the last king of an independent East Anglia, was of particular resonance and manifested itself in the 'memorial coinage' issued only a few decades after his death.[37] The cult of St Edmund was one of the chief mechanisms by which the history of East Anglia was articulated and as a means by which to exercise control over the saint's former kingdom in subsequent centuries it was crucial: as Simon Yarrow has commented, St Edmund occupied 'a pivotal position between East Anglia as a discrete political entity and those outsiders seeking to consolidate their authority over it'.[38]

Contemporaries were also well aware of regional characteristics. Throughout the Middle Ages, it was East Anglia's great wealth that consistently drew comment. As a monk of Peterborough put it, 'Whoever once enters Norfolk, will not wish to

---

[33] The picture of a culturally distinct Iceni is confirmed by archaeology, see J. A. Davies, 'Where Eagles Dare: the Iron Age of Norfolk', *Proceedings of the Prehistoric Society* 62, 1996, 63–92.

[34] For discussion, T. Pestell, *Landscapes of Monastic Foundation: The Establishment of Religious Houses in East Anglia, c.650–1200*, Woodbridge 2004.

[35] L. Marten, 'The Shiring of East Anglia: An Alternative Hypothesis', *Historical Research* 81, 2008, 1–27.

[36] A. Bale (ed.), *St Edmund, King and Martyr: Changing Images of a Medieval Saint*, Woodbridge 2009, 299; for the most detailed discussion of the cult of St Edmund, see R. Pinner, 'St Edmund, King and Martyr: Constructing His Cult in Medieval East Anglia', unpublished PhD thesis, University of East Anglia, 2011.

[37] C. Blunt, 'The Saint Edmund Memorial Coinage', *Proceedings of the Suffolk Institute of Archaeology* 31, 1969, 234–55.

[38] S. Yarrow, *Saints and Their Communities: Miracle Stories in Twelfth-Century England*, Oxford 2006, 34.

leave it as long as he lives, for once he has seen so good a land he will declare it a little Paradise.'[39] Such sentiments were echoed by Jordan Fantosme who, in his account of the rebellion of 1173–4, asserted that he was prepared to swear on oath that, apart from London, 'there is no clerk in all the world ... who could tell me of or name me any land between here and Montpellier as good as the county of Norfolk, of which you hear me talk, or more honourable knights or a more fruitful soil or more gracious ladies adept at open-handed generosity', although he later added that there was nowhere more prosperous than Bury St Edmunds.[40] Modern historians have offered more sober, but nonetheless equally striking, impressions of the region's affluence.[41] From the eleventh to the fifteenth century and beyond, East Anglia was the wealthiest and most heavily populated region of the kingdom, with the walled circuit of its regional capital, Norwich, encompassing a greater area than that of London.[42] In the countryside, the fields of East Anglia were something of an agrarian powerhouse; in places output was to reach levels not seen elsewhere in England until the agricultural revolution.[43] The most visible legacy today of medieval economic success is the region's built environment, much of which is of national or international importance. Secular buildings such as the royal castle at Norwich represented cutting edge designs for their day and exhibit significant regional characteristics.[44] Some one in ten of all monastic foundations in England in the period 1066–1200 took place within the diocese of Norwich and places such as Bury St Edmunds, Castle Acre priory and Binham retain important examples of ecclesiastical architecture, again much of it regionally distinctive.[45] East Anglia's stock of late medieval parish churches is equally significant, with the campaign of church building that took place on the back of the burgeoning wool trade resulting in cathedral-like structures at places like Lavenham and Salle which remain a tangible reminder of East Anglia's status as England's economically pre-eminent region at the end of the Middle Ages.

The economic and cultural identity of East Anglia is intimately connected to its topography, something that inevitably draws attention not so much inland to the south and west, but to the North Sea rim. Perhaps the most dramatic evidence for this being the case is Sutton Hoo, where the ship burial given to King Rædwald is undeniably Scandinavian in character.[46] The Anglo-Saxon kingdom's physical

---

[39] A remark by John of St Omer, cited in C. Harper-Bill, 'Searching for Salvation in Anglo-Norman East Anglia', in *East Anglia's History, Studies in Honour of Norman Scarfe*, ed. C. Harper-Bill, C. Rawcliffe and R. G. Wilson, Woodbridge 2002, 19–39, at 20.
[40] *Jordan Fantosme's Chronicle*, ed. R. C. Johnston, Oxford 1981, 67–9.
[41] M. Bailey, *Medieval Suffolk, 1200–1500*, Woodbridge 2007.
[42] B. Ayers, *Norwich*, London 1994.
[43] B. Campbell, 'Agricultural Progress in Medieval England: Some Evidence from East Norfolk', *Economic History Review*, 2nd series 36, 1983, 24–46.
[44] T. A. Heslop, *Norwich Castle Keep: Romanesque Architecture and Social Context*, Norwich 1994.
[45] Pestell, *Landscapes of Monastic Foundation*, passim.
[46] M. Carver, *Sutton Hoo: A Seventh-Century Princely Burial Ground and Its Context*, Reports of the Research Committee of the Society of Antiquaries, London 2005.

boundaries came to be represented by natural or semi-natural features – the North Sea to the east and north, the fens to the west, with the Stour valley to the south the dividing line between East Anglia and the kingdom of Essex. When viewed as a means of communication, the bodies of water on each side, in particular the long northern and eastern coastline, became the means by which East Anglia related to a much wider world. The potential speed of such connections should not be underestimated; despite the attendant dangers, the distances that could be travelled by sea were considerable. It has been suggested that in the seventh century an oar-powered ship could perhaps travel 36 nautical miles per day and a sailing vessel 72 nautical miles, compared with some 15 miles on foot. This would mean that a sea journey from Ipswich to the major Frankish port of Quentovic bore some kind of equivalence to an overland journey to Bury St Edmunds, and that in the time it took to travel overland from Ipswich to Winchester or Tamworth, the sea-borne traveller could expect to reach Bamburgh in Northumberland or Esbjerg in Jutland.[47] It may not therefore be entirely without coincidence that St Edmund's power in particular was requested by those experiencing dangers on the sea.[48]

There can be little doubt that the economic advantages of proximity to the resources offered by the sea and by trading contacts that resulted were in part responsible for East Anglia's wealth as a region. The fact that during the twelfth century East Anglia was seen by contemporaries to be doing particularly well at a time of generally favourable economic conditions was in no small part connected with the phenomenon known to scholars as 'the AD 1000 fish event horizon', which saw marine fish consumption outstrip that of fresh-water fish. Species such as herring become a staple foodstuff, with the increased catches feeding rapidly increasing populations.[49] Within East Anglia exploitation of North Sea fish was connected to a burgeoning internal economy of peat digging and mixed farming inland, a combination that led to dramatic growth.[50] For most of the Middle Ages international trade was integral to the regional economy, providing markets for export and the importing of specialized goods.[51]

---

[47] M. Carver, 'Pre-Viking Traffic in the North Sea', in *Maritime Celts, Frisians and Saxons*, ed. S. McGrail, Council for British Archaeology Research Report 71, London 1990, 117–25.

[48] Yarrow, *Saints*, 54–5.

[49] J. H. Barrett, A. M. Locker and C. M. Roberts, 'Dark Age Economics Revisited: The English Fish Bone Evidence AD 600–1600', *Antiquity* 78, 2004, 618–36; J. H. Barrett, A. M. Locker and C. M. Roberts, 'The Origins of Intensive Marine Fishing in Medieval Europe: The English Evidence', *Proceedings of the Royal Society B: Biological Sciences* 271, 2004, 2417–21.

[50] For a historical discussion of the herring industry in the eleventh century, J. Campbell, 'Domesday Herrings', in *East Anglia's History*, 5–17.

[51] N. J. M. Kerling, *Commercial Relations of Holland and Zeeland with England from the Late 13th Century to the Close of the Middle Ages*, Leiden 1954; G. V. Scammell, 'English Merchant Shipping at the End of the Middle Ages: Some East Coast Evidence', *Economic History Review* 2nd series, 13, 1961, 327–41; N. Williams, *The Maritime Trade of the East Anglian Ports, 1550–1590*, Oxford 1988; C. Barron and N. Saul (eds), *England and the Low Countries in the Late Middle Ages*, Stroud 1995.

The contacts made through economic exploitation also served to connect communities in other ways. It was via the North Sea that news and events on the wider international stage frequently made themselves felt. Matthew Paris reported that in 1238 herrings were unusually cheap in England because the men of Gothia and Frisia had not come to Yarmouth as usual because they feared to leave their families as Genghis Khan's Mongol hordes approached.[52] Although yet to be fully explored, there is also evidence for shared cultural practices. The cult of the little-known East Anglian saint Botolph, for example, is well attested in Scandinavia, so much so that it 'is one of the most enduring signs of the English role in the Christianising process in the Nordic lands'.[53] There were also sometimes close comparisons between standing buildings. As Heyward has consistently argued, the closest parallel to East Anglia's round-towered churches are those in Schleswig-Holstein, a pattern which demands some kind of cross-sea influence.[54] As important as close connections were, they often help to point up differences. Familiarity could also breed a certain amount of contempt for near neighbours and the strong relationship between East Anglia and Flanders led to a certain degree of stereotyping. It was clearly with some relish that the chronicler Ralph Diceto related that there had never been such as harvest of Flemings as there had been in the aftermath of the royal victory over the rebel army outside Bury St Edmunds in the rebellion of 1173, a rebel army which, in any event was made up of men who were described with derision as Flemish 'weavers', rather than fighters.[55]

In conjunction with economic advantage, the sea also brought with it a constant threat of misadventure or disaster. For all the benefits brought by maritime contact there was the disadvantage that the same shipping lanes could be used for altogether more hostile purposes. The various threats of sea-borne raiding, piracy or invasion were almost a constant in the history of East Anglia during the Middle Ages. For centuries Scandinavia represented the most serious threat and Danish military intervention in English politics via the North Sea was the nightmare scenario for numerous Anglo-Saxon kings. On frequent occasions Danish incursions had a specifically East Anglian dimension and the major urban centres of Norwich, Ipswich and Thetford were all sacked during the late pre-Conquest period. The Scandinavian threat did not cease until well into the eleventh century. It was the thought that the rebels had secured Danish help that so concerned Lanfranc, archbishop of Canterbury, following the siege of Norwich castle in 1075 in the end-game in the rebellion of the three earls. The *Anglo-Saxon Chronicle*'s comment that in 1085 William the Conqueror ordered land near the sea to be wasted in order to deny supplies to an invader probably included parts

---

[52] Matthew Paris, *Chronica Majora*, ed. H. R. Luard, 7 vols, Rolls Series, London 1872–84, 3, 488–9.
[53] J. Toy, 'St Botulph: An English Saint in Scandinavia', in *The Cross Goes North: Processes of Conversion in Northern Europe AD 300–1300*, ed. M. Carver, York 2003, 565–70.
[54] S. Heywood, 'The Round Towers of East Anglia', in *Minsters and Parish Churches: The Local Church in Transition, 950–1200*, ed. J. Blair, Oxford 1988, 169–77.
[55] Jordan Fantosme, *Chronicle*, 79.

of East Anglia.[56] The foundation myths of several East Anglian towns claimed a Roman provenance that originated in the defence of the coastline and memories of Viking attacks seemed to have lingered in the collective memory of East Anglian men and women long into the twelfth century.[57]

On other occasions it was the violence of the sea itself that had a direct impact on those living on its shores. This is famously demonstrated at Dunwich, where a series of ferocious storms washed away parts of the thriving port and by 1328 had irrevocably blocked the harbour mouth with sand and shingle, precipitating irreversible economic decline.[58] Events like those at Dunwich, together with what must be a host of unrecorded losses of vessels and ship wrecks, act as a reminder that the sea could be a hostile environment and as such was the seedbed for myth and legend. In Norse mythology the chief enemy of Thor was the serpent Jörmungandr who lived at the bottom of the ocean and in the pair's final battle during Ragnarok it was the sea, along with fire, that consumed the earth.[59]

The past two decades have seen a large corpus of material devoted to aspects of the region during the Middle Ages and as a result a much clearer picture of the internal dynamics and idiosyncrasies has emerged.[60] It now seems clear that one of the ways in which the subject can be taken forward is to examine East Anglia's relationship with the North Sea. It is hoped that by foregrounding the North Sea and placing it at the centre of the narrative, this volume furthers our understanding of *both* East Anglia and its wider world.

* * *

The following essays are by scholars from a range of backgrounds, with expertise drawn from the disciplines of history, archaeology, literary studies and historic architecture. Each contribution adds something to our understanding of East Anglia's relationship with its North Sea World during the Middle Ages, be it taken from a particular geographical view point (either from East Anglia looking out or looking towards it from elsewhere), a specific historic event, or through exami-

---

[56] *The Letters of Lanfranc Archbishop of Canterbury*, ed. H. Clover and M. Gibson, Oxford 1979, 126–7; D. Whitelock and D. C. Douglas (eds), *The Anglo-Saxon Chronicle*, London 1961, 161 ('E' Chronicle, *sub anno* 1085).

[57] J. Weiss, 'East Anglia and the Sea in the Narrative of the *Vie de St Edmund* and *Waldelf*' in *The Sea and Englishness in the Middle Ages*, ed. S. Sobecki, Cambridge 2011, 103–11. In the later Middle Ages, the main enemy was France and elaborate arrangements were in place for coastal defence: J. Alban, 'Early Fourteenth-Century Coastal Watches in Norfolk', *The Quarterly. The Journal of the Norfolk Archaeological and Historical Research Group* 48, 2002, 3–9; idem, 'A Fourteenth-Century Array in Norfolk', *The Annual. The Bulletin of the Norfolk Archaeological and Historical Research Group* 14, 2005, 3–17.

[58] M. Bailey, '*Per impetum maris*: Natural Disaster and Economic Decline in Eastern England, 1275–1350', in *Before the Black Death. Studies in the Crisis of the Early Fourteenth Century*, ed. B. M. S. Campbell, Manchester 1991, 184–208, at 195–6.

[59] H. R. Ellis Davidson, *Gods and Myths of Northern Europe*, London, 1964.

[60] Concisely summarized in C. Harper-Bill (ed.), *Medieval East Anglia*, Woodbridge 2005.

nation of particular source material. Four overviews give general assessments of important themes, a section on trade examines contact and exchange, and a series of case studies shed light on particular issues.

What emerges strongly from a number of contributions is a reassertion of the idea of important movements of people across the sea, especially during the early Middle Ages. The essays by Hines, Pestell and Scull all draw attention to how the archaeology of East Anglia during the Migration and Viking periods can only be explained with reference to the physical movement of individuals and groups. Frequency of contact stimulated economic growth and, as essays by Naismith and Williams explain, the numismatic evidence shows clear evidence that East Anglia's monetary exchange system was established early and was particularly vibrant up to the first Viking age.

Discussions of connectivity raise questions over the extent of the 'North Sea World' and the 'big geography' forms the basis of a number of contributions. As Williamson explains, East Anglia is best thought of as two regions: 'Northern East Anglia', which displays more cultural affinities with the Scandinavian north, and 'Southern East Anglia', which in turn looks towards parts of northern France, Flanders and the Netherlands. Taken together, East Anglia is best thought of as a peninsula (an observation that finds immediate affinity with Cunliffe's Atlantic zone) but it is one that lies at the juncture between the North Sea and the Channel worlds, something which in part explains its peculiar identity and cultural landscape.

An awareness of the geographical subtleties of East Anglia's location aids an understanding of trading networks and points of contact. Contributions by Ayers, Childs and Oksanen illuminate the reach of trading connections in the later Middle Ages. In the eleventh and twelfth centuries East Anglia had the advantage of geography when it came to channelling trade between England and Flanders, particularly the export of wool and grain, and this laid the foundations for the region's celebrated wealth. East Anglia's head ports of Lynn, Yarmouth and Ipswich all had subtly different contacts across the North Sea rim. Lynn tended to look north to Norway, the Baltic and northern Germany, Yarmouth to Germany, Friesland and the Low Countries, while Ipswich looked south to Flanders and northern France. While cargoes and destinations fluctuated in accordance with broader economic trends, the core of East Anglia's trade was always centred on the southern North Sea, with the distant markets of Bordeaux and Norway inclining to be squeezed out in difficult periods. The denial of opportunities in some regions did, however, lead to the opening up of others. As Agnarsdóttir explains, the opening up of a lucrative trade with Iceland by the late fourteenth century paved the way for the 'English Century' in which commercial links were heavily exploited.

Trading contacts and shipping routes brought wealth, and also provided opportunities for the exchange of cultural ideas. As King shows, foreign influences on East Anglian art could sometimes be instant and direct, but were also frequently remote, watered down and brought through intermediaries. Here too, movement of people could be important. Lynda Dennison, for example, shows that the Flemish influence on English manuscript painting in the late fourteenth century was in large part down to Flemings working in England. The influence of individuals was not just, of course, dependent upon one person moving from one location to another, but could be transmitted through texts. As Hill shows, the writings of St Bridget of Sweden were highly influential in late medieval Norfolk. East Anglia was not simply the recipient of influences, however, but also an exporter of ideas. Heywood suggests that the prevalence of round-towered churches in East Anglia took inspiration from Norwich cathedral and Bury St Edmunds abbey and that the same idea also found expression across the North Sea in church building in northern Germany. Something of the complexity of such ties is illustrated by Plant, whose discussion of the great East Anglian churches of the Anglo-Norman period shows that in turn some aspects of their design almost certainly came from the Holy Roman Empire.

If discussions of artistic influence and modes of cultural dissemination are, out of necessity, often nebulous, then the motivations behind political events can sometimes be equally obscure. This is true of the Lisbon expedition of 1147 during the Second Crusade, an episode whose origins have long been something of a puzzle. As West explains, what is significant about the expedition that left Dartmouth that year is that it is one of a number of seemingly autonomous responses to the Latin crisis, but one which proves the existence of strong politico-maritime links across the southern North Sea at that time, as it brought together men from England, Flanders and the Rhineland. Here the commercial links forged from economic exploitation of the sea seem to have developed (and the constituent links been strong enough) to sustain a substantial military operation hundreds of miles away. Although such instances show demonstrable connections and normally unseen networks, part of any North Sea identity was bound up in differences, as well as shared affinities. Pluscowski's analysis of the fur trade points up the differences between the societies of the North Sea World and those of Siberia and Russia. The Baltic and North Seas may have been the conduit that brought prestige furs to East Anglia, but both its production and its cultural meaning were very different to the home-bred rabbit for which East Anglia is noted.

Taken together, these essays show that the idea of a 'North Sea World' in the Middle Ages has merit and that studying the North Sea in the same manner as other maritime communities is a profitable way forward. This volume will have succeeded in its aim if it helps to promote the study of the North Sea in the same way as the Mediterranean and Atlantic and in so doing sheds light on the development of one of its most important sub-regions. What seems clear from this collection is that there were many North Sea *Worlds* during the Middle Ages, which overlapped in space and time. Unpicking the geographies and chronologies will be a worthwhile undertaking for future research.

PART I

EAST ANGLIA AND THE NORTH SEA WORLD: OVERVIEWS

— Chapter 1 —

THE ORIGINS OF EAST ANGLIA IN A NORTH SEA ZONE

John Hines

AS A GEOGRAPHICALLY distinct part of Britain, it is unsurprising that East Anglia should have had a cultural character and identity of its own from prehistoric times. When Britain emerged into the part-light of ancient history in the first century AD, this was the heartland of the powerful *Iceni*, who spearheaded the major revolt against Roman imperial rule and colonization under their queen Boudicca in AD 60 or 61. This region or *civitas* territory saw curiously little urbanization in the succeeding three and a half centuries of the Roman Period in Britain,[1] although it is fairly rich in the Romanized rural homesteads classified as villas, and treasures such as the Hoxne hoard reflect the wealth of the late Romano-British social elite here.[2] In the Anglo-Saxon period, East Anglia emerged not merely as a clearly defined and independent political unit, but also as a significant player in the struggles and alliances that characterize this stage in the story of the construction of England. The aim of the present chapter is to show how the North Sea connexion played a major role in the foundation of the kingdom of the East Angles, and concurrently to demonstrate the essential place that archaeology occupies in affording us such insights.

Although we can talk with confidence of an East Anglian kingdom that existed from at least the mid-sixth century AD to the year 869, this polity is famously bare of historical records.[3] We have to track its history through a series of less direct references in the histories of other kingdoms or of the Church, to whom East Anglia was intermittently a matter of concern. Under King Rædwald, for a few years at least, the king of the East Angles reportedly enjoyed overlordship amongst the English kings south of the Humber: according to Bede, Rædwald was already making the East Angles pre-eminent before the death of Æthelberht of Kent in

---

[1] J. Wacher, *The Towns of Roman Britain*, 2nd edn, London 1995; B. C. Burnham and J. Wacher, *The Small Towns of Roman Britain*, London 1990.
[2] P. Guest, *The Late Roman Gold and Silver Coins from the Hoxne Treasure*, London 2005.
[3] B. Yorke, *Kings and Kingdoms of Early Anglo-Saxon England*, London 1990, 58–71.

AD 616.⁴ The date and circumstances of Rædwald's death are unknown, although it is highly probable that the famous ship-grave under Mound 1 at Sutton Hoo, excavated in 1939, is his burial.⁵ Bede traces Rædwald's paternal descent back to a grandfather, Wuffa, and notes that the East Anglian royal line is known as the *Uuffingas*.⁶ References to a cognate royal kindred, the *Ylfingar*, in Old Norse eddic poetry, and to a people of the same name, the *Wylfingas* or *Wulfingas*, in the Old English poems *Beowulf* and *Widsith*, have attracted attention in this context, but the reproduction of a name based upon such a common root as 'wolf' may be sheer coincidence.⁷ By the mid-seventh century, East Anglia was faced with a more powerful rival to the west, Mercia, and the historical records imply that at best East Anglia could continue to exercise some power or influence within the Middle Anglian zone that lay between these two kingdoms. In the reign of Offa of Mercia (758–796), East Anglia fell under Mercian subjection, which apparently continued to the 820s, when the East Angles, probably under their King Æthelstan, killed Beornwulf, king of the Mercians.⁸ The East Anglian kingship was extinguished by Viking invaders, who put King Eadmund, rapidly venerated as a saint and martyr, to death in the year 869.

It would appear at least in part to be the paucity of historical records that has encouraged archaeological modelling of the steady and successful evolution of a stratified Anglo-Saxon polity in East Anglia,⁹ although the fact that this emerges also as such a thoroughly anglicized area of Britain must also be a major factor. In terms of the quality, quantity and diversity of known Early Anglo-Saxon archaeological sites, the region of East Anglia is second to none in England. Such were also the circumstances that made East Anglia a key focal point for my own doctoral research into the relationship(s) between England and Scandinavia in the earliest centuries of the Anglo-Saxon Period – before the already familiar Viking expeditions and incursions across the North Sea.¹⁰ The present chapter has been conceived essentially as a critical review of the data, style of interpretation, and

---

4 Bede, *Historia Ecclesiastica Gentis Anglorum. Bede's Ecclesiastical History of the English People*, ed. and trans. B. Colgrave and R. A. B. Mynors, Oxford 1969, II.5, 148–9.
5 R. L. S. Bruce-Mitford, *The Sutton Hoo Ship-Burial*, 3 vols, London 1975–83, esp. Vol. I, at pp. 683–717; J. Hines and A. Bayliss (eds.), *Anglo-Saxon Graves and Grave Goods of the 6th and 7th Centuries AD: A Chronological Framework*, Society for Medieval Archaeology, Leeds, forthcoming.
6 Bede, *Historia Ecclesiastica*, II.15, ed. Colgrave and Mynors, 188–91.
7 Cf. S. Newton, *The Origins of Beowulf and the Pre-Viking Kingdom of East Anglia*, Cambridge 1993, 105–31.
8 Yorke, *Kings and Kingdoms*, 62–4; *The Anglo-Saxon Chronicle: A Collaborative Edition. Vol. 3: MS A*, ed. J. M. Bately, Cambridge 1986, s.a. 823.
9 See especially, M. Carver, 'Kingship and Material Culture in Early Anglo-Saxon East Anglia', in *The Origins of Anglo-Saxon Kingdoms*, ed. S. Bassett, London 1989, 141–58; C. J. Scull, 'Before Sutton Hoo: Structures of Power and Society in Early East Anglia', in *The Age of Sutton Hoo*, ed. M. Carver, Woodbridge 1992, 3–23; and most recently, A. Hutcheson, *The Origins of East Anglian Towns: Coin Loss in the Landscape, AD 470–939*, BAR, British Series, Oxford, forthcoming.
10 J. Hines, *The Scandinavian Character of Anglian England in the Pre-Viking Period*, BAR, British Series, 124, Oxford 1984; J. Hines, 'The Scandinavian Character of Anglian England: An Update', in *The Age of Sutton Hoo*, ed. Carver, 315–29.

conclusions drawn from that research, rooted as it was over thirty years ago in the approaches and evidence of the later 1970s. Amongst the positive facets of the experience of looking back from a full generation later is that of being able to see much more clearly than was possible then how one's work conformed or adapted to the nature of its own scholarly circumstances: to appreciate how much of what one strove to do was actually a process of extemporizing within the confines of a self-directing drama that offered one a certain range of roles to play, and encouraged one to adapt and to hybridize them as best one could. It is nevertheless reassuring to discover that, despite great changes in the empirical evidence over thirty years, partly as a result of excavations and publication, but not least as a result of the transformation of small finds recording through metal-detecting and the Portable Antiquities Scheme, the arguments made and conclusions drawn in the early 1980s still stand up. It is undoubtedly true, though, that at the time of writing, in 2012, much more than a mere re-statement of the propositions of thirty years ago is required.

THE SCANDINAVIAN CHARACTER OF ANGLIAN ENGLAND: IDEAS AND APPROACHES

Tum erumpens grex catolurum ... primum in orientale parte insulae ... terribiles infixit ungues
Then an erupting pack of dogs first fixed its dreadful claws in the eastern part of the island.[11]

Writing probably in the first half of the sixth century, the British Christian polemicist Gildas was clear that the Saxons (as he names them indiscriminately) had invaded Britain from over the seas to the east. Bede, in the eighth century, followed Gildas' account, although he also differentiated between three invading Germanic peoples, the Angles, Saxons and Jutes, and indicated that he understood the first invasion, led by Hengist and Horsa, to have been located in Kent.[12] By the 1970s, such a historical view was a sitting duck for attack as exemplifying the unmodern and simplistic assumption that the spatial expansion of material and other cultural attributes such as language or identity must be explained through the movement – probably by means of conquest and colonization – of peoples who could not but bring those characteristics with them as outward reflexes of who they were. The issue remains a sensitive one;[13] nonetheless, even Grahame Clark,

---

[11] *De excidio Britanniae. Gildas: The Ruin of Britain and Other Works*, ed. and trans. M. Winterbottom, Chichester 1978, 23.
[12] Bede, *Historia Ecclesiastica*, I, 15, ed. Colgrave and Mynors, 48–53; cf, *Historia Brittonum. Nennius: British History and the Welsh Annals*, ed. and trans. J. Morris, Chichester 1980, 31, 36.
[13] N. J. Higham, *Rome, Britain and the Anglo-Saxons*, London 1992, 1–16; C. J. Arnold, *An Archaeology of the Anglo-Saxon Kingdoms*, 2nd edn, London 1997, 1–32; S. Lucy, *The Anglo-Saxon Way of Death: Burial Rites in Early England*, Stroud 2000, 1–15.

launching the self-consciously enlightened attack on the 'invasion hypothesis' as a mode of archaeological explanation in 1966, apparently accepted the *adventus Saxonum* as a true explanation of the transition from Roman Britain to Anglo-Saxon England.[14] The positive outcomes of this controversy have been not only to compel much more careful evaluation of a range of possible explanations of cultural diffusion – amongst which dogmatic 'migration-denial' becomes an impossibility – but also with that to encourage an increasingly nuanced attention to the details of typology, chronology, function and contexts of the material in question. The passing phase of 'Theory' in British and European archaeology has shaken out many easy assumptions, but it was no revolution.

In the early 1980s it did indeed appear rather unsophisticated to attempt nothing more than to map out as accurately as possible certain parallels between England and Scandinavia in the Early Anglo-Saxon Period – that is, the fifth to seventh centuries AD – and then to try to account for them. Some of those archaeological similarities had already been noticed, or at least suspected;[15] that was the context in which the project was formulated. Other material parallels remained unnoticed or uninvestigated. Through a series of female dress-accessories – wrist-clasps; great square-headed, cruciform and plain equal-armed brooches; and bracteates and scutiform pendants – it proved possible to confirm that there were true and direct connexions between Scandinavia and what Bede identified as the Anglian area of England; moreover that in certain cases it was possible to locate the lines of connexion very closely indeed, and also to date them quite precisely.[16] Even without exploring in any detail the specific links between Kent and Jutland,[17] the sum total of these connexions points to quite a diffuse range of links between areas around the east coast of England and western Scandinavia, from Jutland up to Sogn og Fjordane in Norway, which were also spread in time from the later fifth century to the early seventh (Map 1). In the earliest stages, a source in Scandinavia for influences crossing the North Sea in a westerly direction to England is beyond doubt. In the middle and later sixth century, conversely, we encounter parallel developments either side of the North Sea that we cannot confidently assign to influence running in one direction rather than the other, while by the early seventh century (although probably earlier) the movement of material from England eastwards into Scandinavia becomes a proven fact.

If it was an affront to the sophisticated 'hypothetico-deductive' approach to archaeology cheerfully to spend a lot of time and effort ascertaining what the

---

[14] G. Clark, 'The Invasion Hypothesis in British Archaeology', *Antiquity* 40, 1966, 172–89, at 173.

[15] H. Shetelig, *The Cruciform Brooch in Norway*, Bergen Museums Årbok, Bergen 1906, 97–114; E. T. Leeds, 'The Distribution of the Angles and Saxons Archaeologically Considered', *Archaeologia* 91, 1945, 1–108, at 111–15; H. E. F. Vierck, 'Some Leading Types of the Anglian Province of Culture, Fifth to Seventh Century A.D., with Their Oversea Connections' unpublished BLitt thesis, University of Oxford, 1966.

[16] See Hines, *Scandinavian Character*, esp. 270–85.

[17] Cf. P. Kruse, 'Jutes in Kent? On the Jutish Nature of Kent, Southern Hampshire and the Isle of Wight', *Probleme der Küstenforschung im südlichen Nordseegebiet* 31, 2007, 243–376.

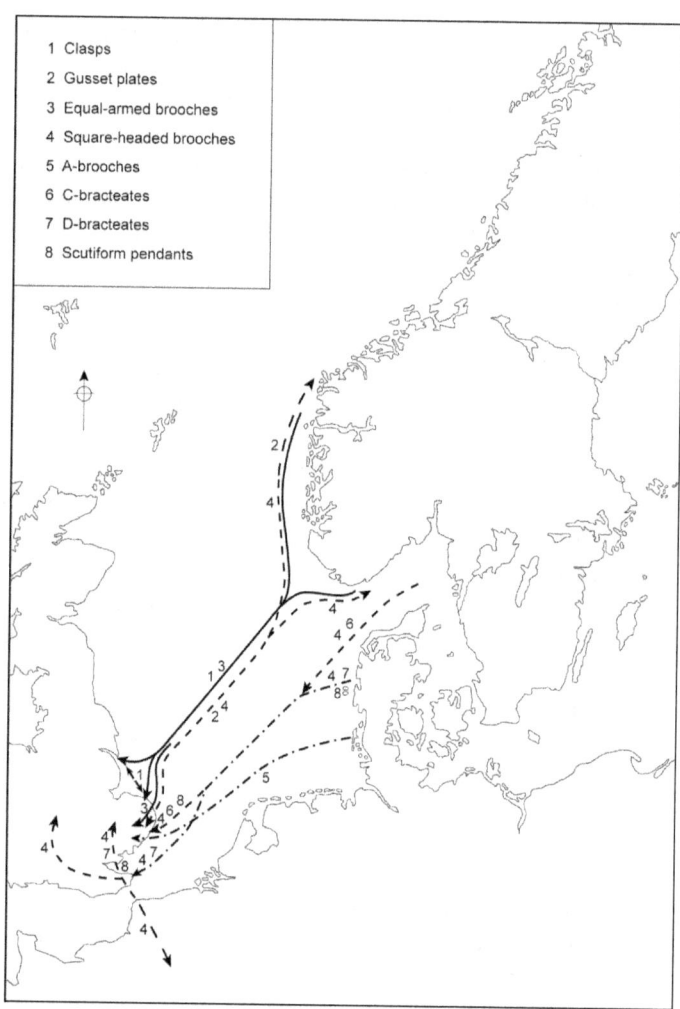

MAP 1 Cross-North Sea connexions evidenced by archaeological material of the late fifth and sixth centuries (after Hines, *Scandinavian Character*, Map. 6.1).

archaeological facts were before considering what explanations there might be for them, it was even more egregious in the early 1980s to infer that for *some* (though by no means all) of the earliest influence from western Norway on eastern England around the Wash and the Humber estuary, dating to the second half of the fifth century, a migration was the best explanation. In fact, even that was rather apologetically presented as an explanation of last resort, although it was fairly rooted in the argument that the adoption of wrist-clasps as a feature of women's dress in Anglian England represented the acceptance of a style of costume characteristic of

Scandinavia, and not just of a certain distinctive class of artefacts.¹⁸ At the time, this argument was underpinned by a more general proposition, that costume, and especially female costume, is commonly a strong identity-bearing aspect of material culture: this perception continues to be widely held, and the argument remains valid.¹⁹ In a minor but explicit and significant way, what in effect this does is to transfer the evidential dependency from specific typological details of artefacts to what is fashionably called the *habitus* in which those artefacts play a role.²⁰ When the inferences were first drawn, I was concerned that the migration hypothesis for explaining the diffusion of the wrist-clasp-wearing habit across the North Sea from Scandinavia was weakened by the absence of many other signs of the transference of material culture from the relevant parts of Norway to eastern England, and certainly a lack of any other influence that was comparably widespread.²¹ Subsequently this disquiet could partly be stilled by a greater confidence in the importance of the model of the combinative reconfiguration of identity in Anglian England, in preference to simpler concepts of inheritance and slow evolution.²²

In the concluding discussion of the 1984 publication, the cross-North Sea connexions attributed to migration (in other words, primarily to the movement of people, carrying material culture) were contrasted with other links which seemed better attributed to 'trade and exchange' as a general concept representing what was primarily the movement of material culture, passed from person to person. At the time there was already quite a considerable array of relevant historical models available as a framework for a discussion focussed relatively impersonally on material exchange: ranging from traditional interpretations of the Frisians as a maritime people, operating a strong trading network around the North Sea, to German economic geographical models of largely stable settlement districts and communications networks (*Siedlungs*- and *Verkehrsräume*), and to politically influenced models then recently encapsulated in Richard Hodges's *Dark Age Economics*.²³ If anything, it is all of these approaches to the production and distributional practices around the North Sea in the very early Middle Ages that now appear over-simplified: and I shall try and give a better representation below.

This introductory section, however, is also the appropriate place in which to summarize another group of major advances in empirical archaeological under-

---

¹⁸ Cf. J. Hines, *Clasps-Hektespenner-Agraffen: Anglo-Scandinavian Clasps of the 3rd to 6th Centuries A.D.*, Stockholm, 1993, 76–82, 87–9.
¹⁹ K. Høilund Nielsen, 'The Real Thing or Just Wannabes? Scandinavian Style Brooch in the Fifth and Sixth Centuries', in *Foreigners in Early Medieval Europe: Thirteen International Studies in Medieval Mobility*, ed. D. Quast, Mainz 2009, 51–111, at 102–06; cf. M. Martin, 'Ethnic Identities as Constructions of Archaeology(?): The Case of the Thuringi', in *The Thuringi: An Ethnographic Perspective*, ed. H. Steuer, Studies in Historical Archaeoethnography, Woodbridge, forthcoming.
²⁰ P. Bourdieu, *Outline of a Theory of Practice*, trans. R. Nice, Cambridge 1977, esp. 17–22, 72–87.
²¹ Hines, *Scandinavian Character*, 272–7.
²² Hines, 'The Scandinavian Character of Anglian England: An Update'; cf. Hines, *Scandinavian Character*, 300.
²³ R. Hodges, *Dark Age Economics*, London 1982.

standing, which now promise to provide much more detailed insights in the near future into the direct relationship between East Anglia and the lands across the North Sea in the fifth to seventh centuries. Firstly, there is new scope for both a more reliable and a more precise chronology of Early Anglo-Saxon material culture than we have ever before had at our disposal. A long-term English Heritage-funded project, initially targeted at the chronology of later furnished burials from c.AD 570 to the early eighth century, will publish its final report very soon, in fact providing a detailed chronological scheme from c.AD 520/530 and across the seventh century, and a general framework into which further detail from the fifth and early sixth centuries can be fitted.[24] East Anglia has been and will remain very much at the forefront of Anglo-Saxon archaeological research to fill out this earliest area of the sequence. Analysis of the finds from four East Anglian inhumation cemeteries excavated in the 1970s has defined a set of phases covering the period c.AD 480–530.[25] From the huge cremation cemetery at Spong Hill, Norfolk, we shall soon have a substantial and detailed study of fifth-century burials and their associated artefacts,[26] while from southern Essex the rather delayed publication of the cemeteries at Mucking also now provides us with further important comparative material.[27] At the same time, chronological detail and precision for the fifth-century sequences in northern Germany and southern Scandinavia have improved dramatically, through the study of weaponry and dress-accessories in sacrificial votive deposits, building on the earlier work of Horst Wolfgang Böhme.[28]

A second source of new data that we can be sure will yield significant results is biochemical analysis of the human skeletal remains themselves. Oxygen and strontium isotopes in the teeth or bones can provide information on the locality in which an individual grew up, while we now appear finally to be on the verge of being able systematically and consistently to extract sufficient samples of preserved human DNA from inhumed populations to start tracing genetic relationships within the communities, and possibly, eventually, to compare and contrast population genetic profiles between different parts of both Britain and Europe in a meaningful way. In relation to all of our inferences concerning long-distance connexions and relationships, those will be invaluable data.

---

[24] Hines and Bayliss (eds.), *Anglo-Saxon Graves*, forthcoming.
[25] K. Penn and B. Brugmann, *Aspects of Anglo-Saxon Inhumation Burial: Morning Thorpe, Spong Hill, Bergh Apton and Westgarth Gardens*, East Anglian Archaeology 119, Gressenhall, Norfolk 2007.
[26] C. Hills and S. Lucy, *The Anglo-Saxon Cemetery at Spong Hill, North Elmham, Vol. IX*, McDonald Institute, Cambridge, forthcoming.
[27] S. Hirst and D. Clark, *Excavations at Mucking: Volume 3, The Anglo-Saxon Cemeteries*, 2 vols, London 2009.
[28] A. Rau, *Nydam Mose: Die personengebundene Gegenstände*, 2 vols, Aarhus 2010; R. B. Iversen, *Kragehul Mose: Ein Kriegsbeuteopfer auf Südwestfünen*, Aarhus 2010, 25–9; H. W. Böhme, *Germanische Grabfunde des 4. bis 5. Jahrhunderts zwischen unterer Elbe und Loire*, 2 vols, Munich 1974; idem, 'Gallien in der Spätantike: Forschungen zum Ende der Römerherrsdraft in den westlichen Provinzen', *Jahrbuch des Römisch-Germanischen Kommission Mainz*, 34, 1987, 469–574.

NEW FINDS AND NEW VIEWS

There is, of course, both new evidence and new studies now available which modify and improve our understanding of the early direct relationships between East Anglia and Scandinavia. It makes sense to start a closer re-assessment of this topic with the empirical evidence that continues to prove the clearest picture of the introduction of Scandinavian habits and styles across the North Sea – as I would still argue, by migration: the wrist-clasps. These are hook-and-eye fasteners, whose history can be traced back, with great confidence and considerable precision, to around the beginning of the fourth century AD in southern Scandinavia. One class, Class A, formed of wire spirals, was always and only a feature of female costume: used to fasten the cuffs of a sleeved undergarment, but occasionally, it appears, for the front of some sort of blouse or jacket (Figure 1A). A different class, Class B, constructed of hammered metal plates and cast rivets or bars, was worn originally by men: either on shirt sleeves, as in the women's dress, or for the legs of breeches (Figure 1B). Scandinavian male costume never adopted the female Class A clasps, while up to the middle of the fifth century there is just a handful of examples of women buried with the predominantly male Class B clasps. In the later fifth century in Scandinavia, however, there was a dramatic shift, as that class of clasps was adopted wholesale into the inventory of women's dress-accessories.

During the fourth and fifth centuries, the geographical range in which clasps were used was steadily expanding northwards too, from southern Scandinavia into Norway and further north in Sweden, and eastwards over the Baltic into Finland and Estonia. What is most remarkable is that the last major stage of expansion in Scandinavia, which can still be characterized there as a step in a steady process of diffusion, is concurrent with a dramatic leap across the North Sea into Britain. While the expansion of the range of this class of artefacts north into the Arctic and east across the Baltic is not at the expense of its internal typological consistency of form and function within the Scandinavian zone, the expansion to England

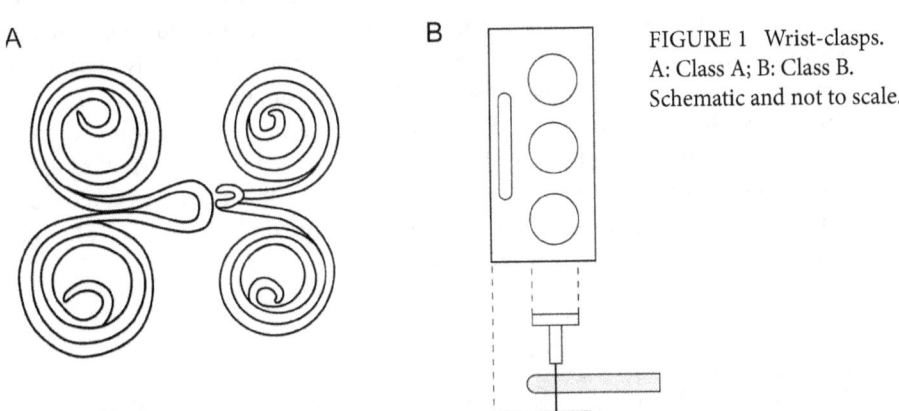

FIGURE 1 Wrist-clasps. A: Class A; B: Class B. Schematic and not to scale.

involved considerable shifts both in those respects. Firstly, clasps appear in England *only* as an element of female costume. Thus, a process of change within Scandinavia was amplified in England: the female costume was altered to adopt previously male clasp-types in Scandinavia, but that change was not an option, rather the rule, in England. Concurrently, and most significantly in archaeological terms, the forms, types and designs of clasps that appear in England comprise details that are extremely rare in Scandinavia, with the consequence that their Scandinavian prototypes can be very precisely located in both place and time. From such initial elements and models, the Anglian English series developed a completely new and highly varied range of forms – which nevertheless continued to be restricted to the role of sleeve-fasteners in women's dress.

Class A clasps seem to have been introduced to England as early as any habit of wearing wrist-clasps was, in or at least by the last quarter of the fifth century. Typologically and contextually it is not really possible to identify both the earliest examples in England and how then they subsequently spread out, although an example from grave 155 at Sleaford on the fen edge in southern Lincolnshire can still confidently be identified as one of the earliest datable specimens on the basis of the small size of the spirals of the clasps and the type of cruciform brooch also included in this woman's costume. More recent finds have not significantly altered the quite compact distribution of Class A clasps in England: around the Fens and the mouth of the Humber, and spreading inland, via the Trent or the Foss Way, to Leicestershire and Rutland.[29]

The profusion and diversity of formal changes within the range of Class B clasps makes it much more practical to track their introduction, chronological development, and diffusion within England. The form with the plate buttoned to the garment with round-headed rivets is represented by just a few finds, distributed down the fen edge in Norfolk, and once in the Yorkshire Wolds; its immediate derivatives, which are sewn to the garment but which preserve the rivets as a purely decorative feature, confirm this distribution. A very rare form in Scandinavia, found only in western Norway, with the plate pinned to the garment, also occurs, along with its immediate derivatives, in exactly the same area of England. Evidently, the Wash, and especially the East Anglian side of it, and/or the Humber were the points of entry for these items.[30] We cannot determine if they arrived at those landing points from Scandinavia independently, or came first into one area and then moved to the other because of some close but secondary connexion between those areas on the coast of eastern England. When we can look at a wider range of sixth-century material evidence it becomes very clear that there was some close relationship between East Anglia and Humberside, and probably through a coastal connexion rather than via an overland route.[31]

---

[29] Hines, *Clasps-Hektespenner-Agraffen*, 9–11.
[30] Hines, *Clasps-Hektespenner-Agraffen*, 33–55, *passim*.
[31] J. Hines, 'The Archaeology of the Cambridge Region and the Origins of the Middle Anglian Kingdom', *Anglo-Saxon Studies in Archaeology and History* 10, 1999, 135–49, at 136–41.

There have, of course, been further finds of clasps in Scandinavia which modify matters of detail in my earlier arguments – although there too, in broad terms, the new evidence largely confirms the main lines of the history and significance of this class of artefacts previously inferred. The most significant new discussion is based upon the relatively large collection of clasps more recently excavated from discrete fourth- and fifth-century depositions in the votive lake, now a bog, at Nydam in Als, southern Jutland.[32] Rau rightly notes that my own classificational scheme and emphases were shaped by a particular concern to explore the Migration-period expansion of the clasp-habit, and thus the parallelism between England and Scandinavia, separated by the North Sea, by the sixth century; his focus, complementarily, prioritizes the contexts and sources of the special deposits at this unusual but not unique site. In this regard, however, the particular value of the Nydam material as assessed by Rau is to provide a much more detailed view of the range of sub-types and -forms of clasps that I assigned to Forms B1 and B2 in southern Scandinavia, within the period when those forms were still primarily a feature of male costume (which explains why they should occur in votive hoards dominated by male and military equipment).

This new work of Rau's becomes particularly interesting to us in assessing an exceptional new find from a site on the fen edge in north-western Suffolk, in grave 405 within burial ground ERL114 at RAF Lakenheath in the parish of Eriswell. This woman was buried with relatively few dress-accessories: a small long brooch (Figure 2A) at one shoulder and single large bead under her chin (Figure 2B); she also had an unusual twisted copper-alloy wire finger ring on one hand (Figure 2C). She also appears to have been buried wearing wrist-clasps of hitherto unparalleled form at each wrist (Figure 3): possibly two pairs at the left wrist (Figure 2D). Each clasp-piece comprised a cast copper-alloy bar, about 32 mm long, with a small panel containing Style I zoomorphic ornament in cast relief at each end. The zoomorphic motif is smart and legible as a profile head above a figure-2-shaped limb. The functioning clasp was created by soldering these bars to small sheet metal plates, of which only five were recovered from the grave, although there ought originally to have been at least twelve and perhaps as many as eighteen for the six bars in the assemblage. Three of the surviving plates have perforated holes through which the item was to be sewn on to a garment, and two are the functioning hook- and catch-elements of the clasps. We should expect the hook- and catch-plates to have been attached to the underside of the bars in the middle with, most likely, an attachment plate at either end.

Strictly, these clasps belong to no form previously defined, since neither the plate nor the bar can function on its own as the body of the clasp and they are separate elements, not cast as one piece. In principle they are closest to Form B14a: clasps consisting of a bar soldered to a plate which is not rectangular (= Form B13a) but rather has individual projecting, perforated lugs through which it was sewn to

---

[32] Rau, *Nydam Mose*, 125–45.

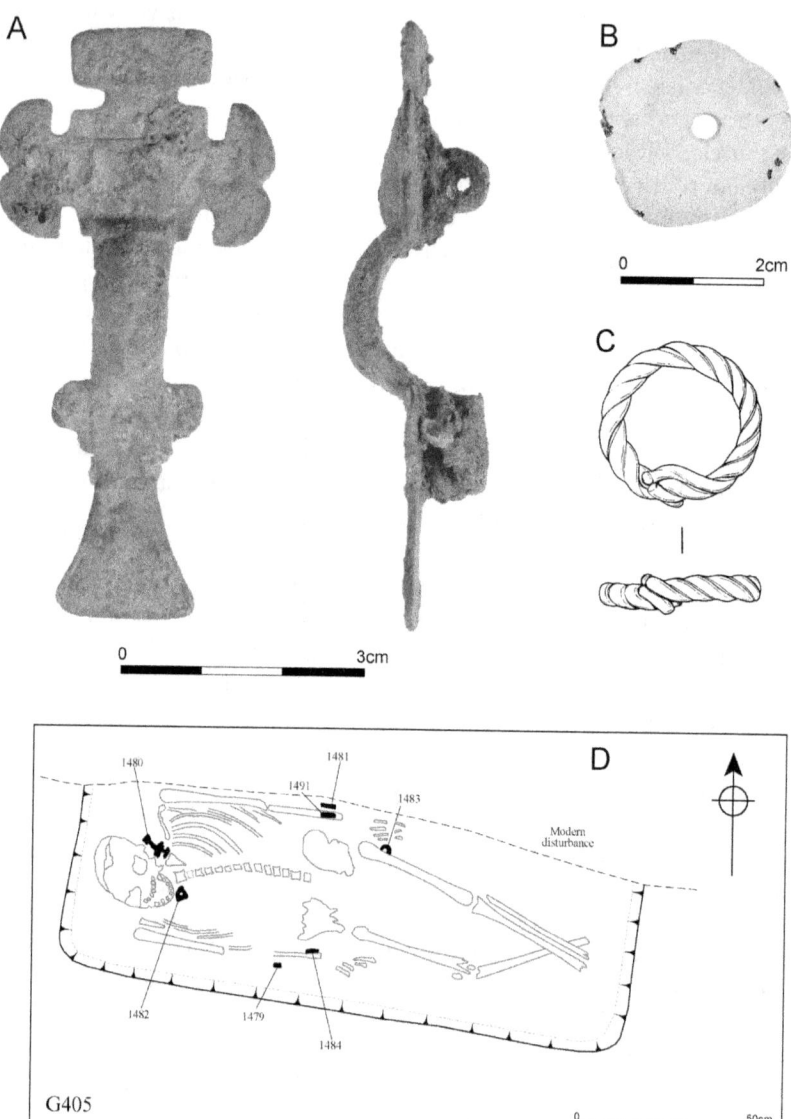

Above:

FIGURE 2 Eriswell, Suffolk (ERL114), grave 405. A: small long brooch (SF1480); B: amber bead (SF1482); C: finger ring (SF1483); D: grave plan. (A, B and D photographed and drawn by Gemma Andrews; C drawn by Donna Weatherall, Suffolk Archaeology).

Right:

FIGURE 3 Eriswell, Suffolk (ERL114), grave 405. The wrist-clasps (SF1479, 1481, 1484, 1491 and 1536). Scale 3:2 (drawn by Donna Weatherall, Suffolk Archaeology).

THE ORIGINS OF EAST ANGLIA IN A NORTH SEA ZONE

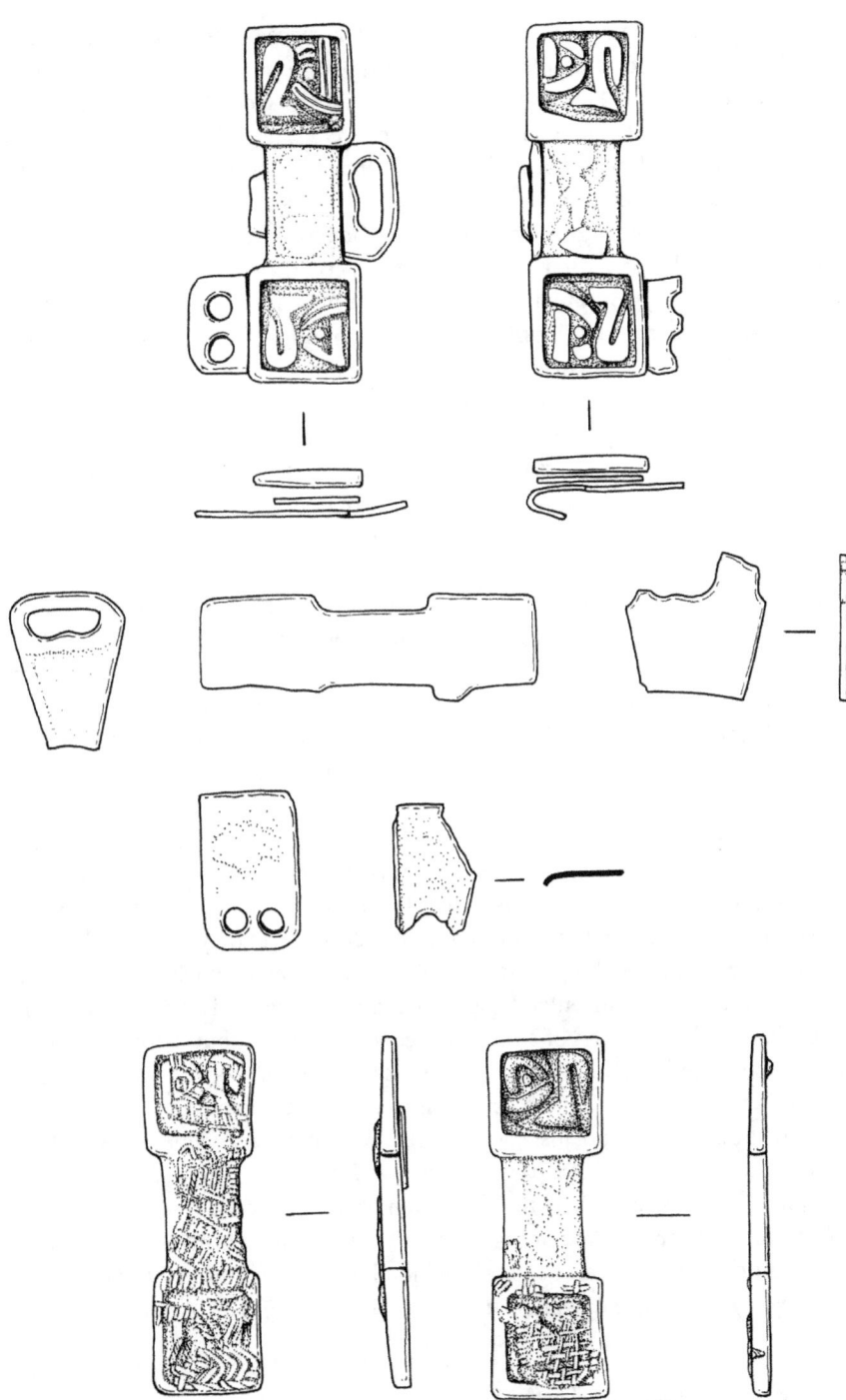

the garment. This plate is also the hook- or catch-piece of the clasp, so that a pair of plates could function on their own as a clasp without the bars.[33] As part of the discussion of Form B14a written twenty years ago, the scope for a straightforward pattern of development of forms of Class B clasp in England was discussed, given that the elements of plate, bar and buttons were all introduced from Scandinavia, albeit normally to rivet the clasp-halves to the cloth of a garment, not to be attached by sewing. It could be argued then that once the modification of sewing as a presumably easier alternative to riveting was introduced, the emergence of sewn plates, sewn bars, and any combination of sewn plate plus bar, could proceed directly, without any necessary developmental sequence amongst those derivative forms. It was noted, however, that Form B12, the bar with lugs or spigots for sewing directly to the cloth, appeared to be very well represented amongst earlier finds: an observation corroborated by Penn and Brugmann's analysis of the four East Anglian cemeteries using a finer classification and chronology of the glass beads common in women's graves than was available in the early 1990s.[34]

If the wrist-clasps in grave 405 at Eriswell can be regarded merely as an idiosyncratic design composed out of the same elements, then the typological-developmental argument just summarized can remain unaltered. What may cause one to hesitate in drawing that simple and comfortable conclusion is the fact that the small plates that are part of the clasp-pieces in this grave are so similar to the forms reviewed amongst the small Form B1 clasps of southern Scandinavia of the fourth and fifth centuries by Rau.[35] They are not identical: few of those Scandinavian specimens need provision for sewing, and none separates the arrangements for attachment from the hook- or catch-element. Nonetheless, on clasps dated to the fourth century from graves in the cemetery at Sejlflod, northern Jutland, such plates are associated with a double-headed rivet that is the earliest form of bar, and this form appears to continue to develop as Form B2 not only at Sejlflod but also to spread throughout Scandinavia during the fifth century and into the sixth. It is never a numerous form, but examples of it appear very widely.[36] The form might, of course, be re-invented separately in different parts of Scandinavia during that relatively long period of some 150 years if not more, but if we allow for at least some underlying relationship amongst the examples of the form there, we cannot exclude extending the connexions to these unusual pieces from Eriswell.

If so, the site at Sejlflod, just south of the Limfjord in Jutland, provides both the most proximate geographical parallel as well as formally the most similar plates. It is appropriate to reiterate here how important it would appear, typologically, to be able to account for the predominance of the bar amongst earlier English Class B clasps: an element that can be paralleled in all parts of Scandinavia. The critical discrepancy between the Sejlflod finds with the most similar plates and Eriswell

---

[33] Hines, *Clasps-Hektespenner-Agraffen*, 53–5.
[34] Penn and Brugmann, *Aspects of Anglo-Saxon Inhumation Burial*, 28–9.
[35] Rau, *Nydam Mose*, Abb. 46–7 & Tafn. 1–4.
[36] Hines, *Clasps-Hektespenner-Agraffen*, 34–7.

grave 405 is that of date. The small long brooch (Figure 2a) in this grave-assemblage is a type with projecting lappets below the bow, classified as *sm3* by Penn and Brugmann and found by them to occur primarily in their Phase FA2a, which starts in the late fifth century but falls primarily within the first half of the sixth.[37] Although the woman buried in grave 405 was curiously accoutred, the Style I motifs in the panels on the bars of her wrist-clasps confirm that these items were not themselves exceptionally old when buried, and so a direct artefactual connexion between the smaller and earlier Sejlflod clasps of Form B2 and Eriswell cannot be argued for in this case. But this does not mean that the parallelism that has been identified is any less significant. On the contrary, it reveals the structural relationship to have been one between the populations and their material cultures – the rules and practices of craft-production as well as costume – rather than something that was contained within the artefacts themselves, however they moved, along with people or from hand to hand. Complementing the more recent finds from Nydam, the Eriswell grave 405 clasps suggest there is still much to learn about the range and diversity of clasp-types in fifth-century Scandinavia.

Another exciting recent find from Norfolk had its background further east, in the Baltic zone. This is a metal-detected item uncovered in the 1980s, and first recognized by Christopher Scull, but then put to one side only to come to wider attention again thanks to Tim Pestell of the Castle Museum in Norwich. This is a silver domed button (Figure 4A) found at Mundham, Norfolk, which looks very much like a type that we know was made on the island of Helgö and and a site called Bäckby in the Mälar region of central Sweden (and no doubt elsewhere too), and which is common on women's dress in east central Sweden and across the Baltic both in Finland and Estonia. These Form B1, Type vi, domed buttons are datable to the late fifth and first half of the sixth centuries.[38] The specimen found in Norfolk is not identical in design with any counterpart in Scandinavia, although with its Style I masks in three fields dividing the hemispherical face of the dome it is quite closely paralled in central Sweden, for instance in clasp buttons from Viken on Lovö in Uppland (Figure 4b).[39] We must note that Rau argues that a domed button of similar form but different design from the Nydam deposits is a sword button rather than a clasp button.[40] The domed button illustrated here from grave 3 at Viken on Lovö is also from a weapon grave – unfortunately a badly disturbed one. The presence of woven woollen textile on the underside of the button supports its identification as a clasp button in this case.

Assuming that it *is* a clasp button, formally the Mundham specimen is so unparalleled in design within England, and so similar to the Swedish prototypes, that we could believe that it had been made in Scandinavia and imported across the North Sea. In that respect, however, the results of metallurgical analysis of the body of the

---

[37] Penn and Brugmann, *Aspects of Anglo-Saxon Inhumation Burial*, 24–5 and 48–73, *passim*.
[38] Hines, *Clasps-Hektespenner-Agraffen*, 28–30.
[39] J. P. Lamm, *Undersökningar på Lovö 1958–1966*, Stockholm 1972, 30–44.
[40] Rau, *Nydam Mose*, 142–3.

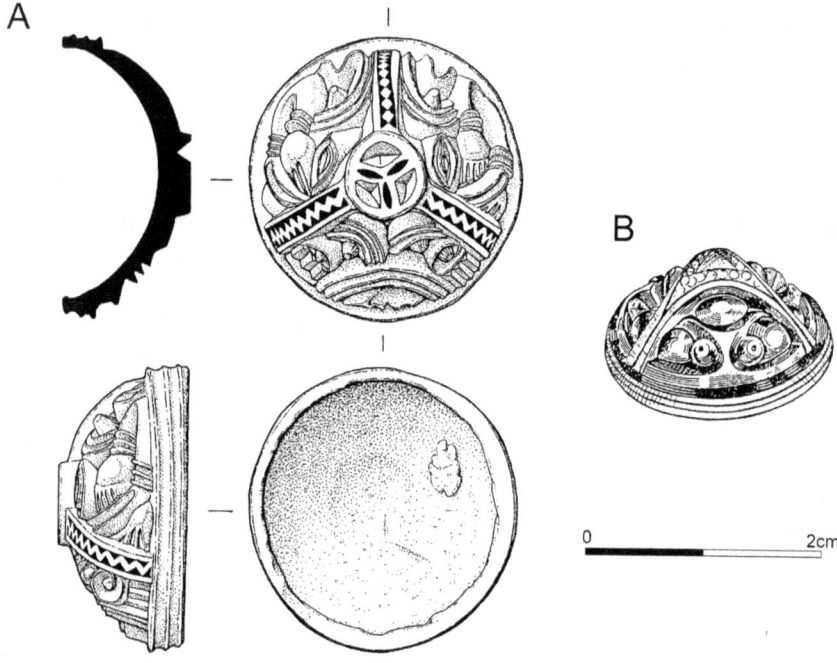

FIGURE 4 Domed silver buttons. A: Mundham, Norfolk; B: Viken, Lovö, Uppland, Sweden, grave 1.

item undertaken for the Castle Museum are truly startling. Although the button appears to be good quality silver, its silver content is low: analyses of different areas of the piece reveal a silver (Ag) content of about 32% and that the metal is made up of around 57% copper (Cu). These proportions are in fact strikingly similar to those found in two great square-headed brooches dated to the very early sixth century and found in Suffolk (Table 1).[41]

There are differences between the objects: in particular the markedly small quantity of zinc (Zn) detected in the Mundham clasp button and the correspondingly higher levels of iron (Fe) and lead (Pb) in it. We can compare this further with the Form C1-Norwegian Type clasps found at Broughton Lodge, Willoughby-on-the-Wolds, Notts. These are utterly Norwegian in design, but it was argued on the basis of contents of 45–64% Ag and 30–50% Cu, contrasted with the 80–90% Ag of their Norwegian twins, that they were produced in England.[42]

[41] R. Brownsword and J. Hines, 'The Alloys of a Sample of Anglo-Saxon Great Square-Headed Brooches', *Antiquaries Journal* 73, 1994, 1–10.
[42] J. Hines, 'A "Norwegian-type" Wrist-Clasp from Willoughby-on-the-Wolds, Nottinghamshire, England', *Universitetets Oldsaksamlingen Årbok 1984/1985*, 1986, 87–98; idem, *Clasps-Hektespenner-Agraffen*, 67–8.

TABLE 1 The results of analysis by X-ray fluorescence of two great square-headed brooches of Group IV (Brownsword and Hines, 1994, see note 41) and the Mundham clasp button by Jane Kershaw and Adrian Allsop of the Oxford University Research Laboratory for Archaeology and the History of Art.

		Cu	Ag	Sn	Fe	Pb	Zn
Holywell Row 11	Great square-headed brooch	57.7	30.7	5.83	1.36	1.29	3.23
Suffolk [IV]	Great square-headed brooch	55.6	32.0	5.83	0.08	1.68	4.81
Mundham (body)	Clasp button	56.4	32.7	4.67	3.37	2.86	0.12
Mundham (rim)	Clasp button	57.3	30.4	6.34	1.87	3.43	0.27

Note: Trace measurements of antimony (Sb), arsenic (As) and nickel (Ni) were recorded by Brownsword for the great square-headed brooches (totalling 0.27 and 0.23% of the metal of the brooches respectively) but not for the Mundham clasp. The figures published by Brownsword and Hines for copper (Cu), silver (Ag), tin (Sn), iron (Fe), lead (Pb) and zinc (Zn) for the brooches have been rescaled accordingly.

Unfortunately, we lack adequate comparative analyses of silver alloys of the relevant period and in the relevant part of Sweden. The relatively small collection of this material from the famous site of Helgö, for instance, has not been examined.[43] Birgit Arrhenius (pers. comm.) draws attention to belt-fittings from a grave from the cusp of the Migration and Vendel Periods (middle to late sixth century) at Tune in Alsike, Uppland, Sweden, as items with relatively high copper levels, but in these cases the lowest Ag reading is 77.7% and the highest Cu level 17%.[44] We do not have sufficient evidence on which to draw even provisional conclusions, but one can nevertheless observe a pattern here and note it as worthy of further investigation. It is conceivable that the similarity between the Mundham clasp button and the early Group IV great square-headed brooches from East Anglia represents a situation in an area where silver was in short supply, and base-silver artefacts were consequently produced from a mixture of around one part of silver to two parts of copper.

If so, the Mundham clasp button is a truly extraordinary copy of a Swedish artefact prototype; just as extraordinary and special as the Broughton Lodge Class C clasps, but no more so, as copies of the prototype also represented by two pairs of clasps from a grave at Ommundrød in Vestfold, Norway. Comparative work by Swedish and Norwegian archaeologists in the 1990s and 2000s, however, had made the case that there was a profound difference in the production and distribution of good-quality metalwork between western and eastern Scandinavia in the fifth and

[43] K. Lamm, 'Non-ferrous Metal Objects and Scrap: The Archaeological Context', *Excavations at Helgö XVII: Workshop, Part 3*, Stockholm 2008, 21–37, at 24–5.

[44] B. Arrhenius, 'Die Zeitstellung des Grabs XIV von Tune, Kirchspiel Alsike, Uppland', *Prähistorisches Zeitschrift* 55, 1980, 228–58, and especially at 253–6.

sixth centuries.⁴⁵ Apparently typical of the area of Norway and Early Anglo-Saxon England was production in the hands of itinerant craftsmen, whose 'workshops' constantly moved with them from customer or patron to customer.⁴⁶ In the eastern or even specifically Swedish zone, by contrast, such metalwork was produced primarily at regular, centralized production sites such as Helgö and Bäckby. A small site at Gene in Ångermanland, relatively far north in Migration-period Sweden, has produced evidence of more regular production than any Anglo-Saxon settlement site of the same period,⁴⁷ even the large and thoroughly excavated sites of Mucking in Essex and West Heslerton, North Yorkshire. Long-distance distribution of goods associable with a single production centre is thus characteristic of the east rather than the west, and with that a material culture in which *exchange*, as characterized above, has to be a more palpable feature. Had it not been for the metallurgical analysis, we would easily have been convinced that the Mundham button was an imported object that represented a direct connexion between Norfolk and the Baltic zone. That it represents – albeit from the end of the line – a network of relationships that did not just extend so far to the east but actually originated somewhere in central Sweden *is* something we can claim with confidence. What is more, it adds to the evidence that Scandinavian craft models and practices not only stood behind key developments in Anglian England but were necessarily, practically, transformed in their execution on this side of the North Sea.

It was, in fact, in respect of the second major category of artefacts that represent a specifically Scandinavian element in the material culture of Early Anglo-Saxon England – what is known as the 'great square-headed brooch' – that the idea of high-quality and comprehensive itinerant craftwork had initially to be developed. Unlike the wrist-clasps, the detailed analysis of these much larger pieces of dress-jewellery, which are correspondingly more complex in design, faces us with a remarkable diversity of separate influences that appear to have made entrances all the way around eastern and southern England; and then indeed to provide evidence of reverse influence, returning from England across the North Sea into Scandinavia.⁴⁸ This widespread pattern of relationships seems to have begun around the end of the fifth century – quite likely, in light of the improving chronological definition of this period discussed above, starting a little later than the earliest evidence of connexions provided by the wrist-clasps – and then to have continued well into the second half of the sixth century. Again, out of more than two hundred known specimens, there are just two that might have been made in Scandinavia and imported to England: both are of silver; one from grave 1 at Empingham

---

⁴⁵ E. Hjärthner-Holdar, K. Lamm and B. Magnus, 'Metalworking and Central Places', in *Central Places in the Migration and Merovingian Periods*, ed. B. Hårdh and L. Larsson, Uppåkrastudier, 6, Lund 2002, 159–83.

⁴⁶ Hines, *Clasps-Hektespenner-Agraffen*, 83–6; idem, *A New Corpus of Anglo-Saxon Great Square-Headed Brooches*, Reports of the Research Committee of the Society of Antiquaries of London, 51, Woodbridge 1997, 205–22.

⁴⁷ P. H. Ramqvist, *Gene*, Archaeology and Environment, 1, Umeå 1983, esp. 177–82.

⁴⁸ Hines, *A New Corpus*, especially, 223–34.

(cemetery I), Rutland, again a very eastern Scandinavian style of brooch,[49] and one from Dartford in Kent which has significant parallels in design in counterparts of similar date in Denmark.[50] One of the differences between the wrist-clasps and the great square-headed brooches is that major brooches of this kind were already, functionally, a key part of women's costume, and the new type was indeed simply a new shape of brooch used to fulfil an existing function. Where a migration hypothesis appeared the best explanation of the introduction of wrist-clasps to Anglian England, the diffuse nature of influence represented by the great square-headed brooches would point to a myriad of migrations and settlements of colonists if that were the underlying cause. All things considered, it seemed most reasonable (as well as, ideologically, safest in the early 1980s) to attribute the personal movement and contacts implied by the diffusion of the great square-headed brooches to an economically specialized group, the travelling craftsmen, rather than to organic populations.

It was an exciting development when, in the early 1990s, metallurgical analysis by Roger Brownsword of Coventry University confirmed a direct and very close link between the two otherwise individualistic brooches that design relationships assign to the very beginning of the East Anglian sequence: one from grave 11 at Holywell Row and the other from an unknown site within the same county of Suffolk.[51] The metallurgical composition of these two brooches is so similar that Brownsword concluded they must have been cast from the same melt at exactly the same time (see Table 1). In design, they display Scandinavian details in different combinations: both, for instance, with a pair of inset garnet roundels in the headplate inner panel, but Holywell Row 11 with a human mask between these and at the apex of the footplate frame, while the Suffolk brooch (Suffolk [IV]) has a more linear style here, filling the headplate inner panel with running spirals (Plate 1). The latter brooch, however, has mirrored masks in the footplate inner panel frame, where Holywell Row 11 only has spirals.

Since 2010 two new finds have been made that provide important new information but at the same time only add to the complexity of the network of relationships the designs of these brooches fall into. From Snetterton, Norfolk, have come two joining fragments of a very fine and small gilt silver brooch that was originally only some 61–62 mm long (Plate 2B). In size, quality and shape, this brooch immediately reminds one of the brooch from grave 1 at Empingham I just referred to (Plate 2A).[52] The Empingham brooch is larger, 83 mm long. On both brooches the un-gilt silver frames are enhanced with black niello inlay: a characteristic but not common feature of fifth- and sixth-century metalwork. The Mundham button has cells that appear designed for niello inlay, but no niello has been put in them. In the decorative design of the surface and body of the brooches,

---

[49] Ibid., 175–8, pl. 90b.
[50] Ibid., 28–30, pl. 2a.
[51] Above, Table 1; Brownsword and Hines, 'Alloys'.
[52] Hines, *A New Corpus*, 175–8, pl. 90b.

PLATE 1 Great square-headed brooches of Group IV. A: Holywell Row, Suffolk, grave 11; B: unknown find-place, Suffolk.

however, the only closely related feature between the Snetterton and Empingham brooches one can identify is the linear moulded footplate terminal lobe, below a full-face mask, which is within the footplate inner panel on the Snetterton brooch but part of the terminal lobe itself on Empingham I 1.

The Snetterton brooch has several other features that have closer relatives and

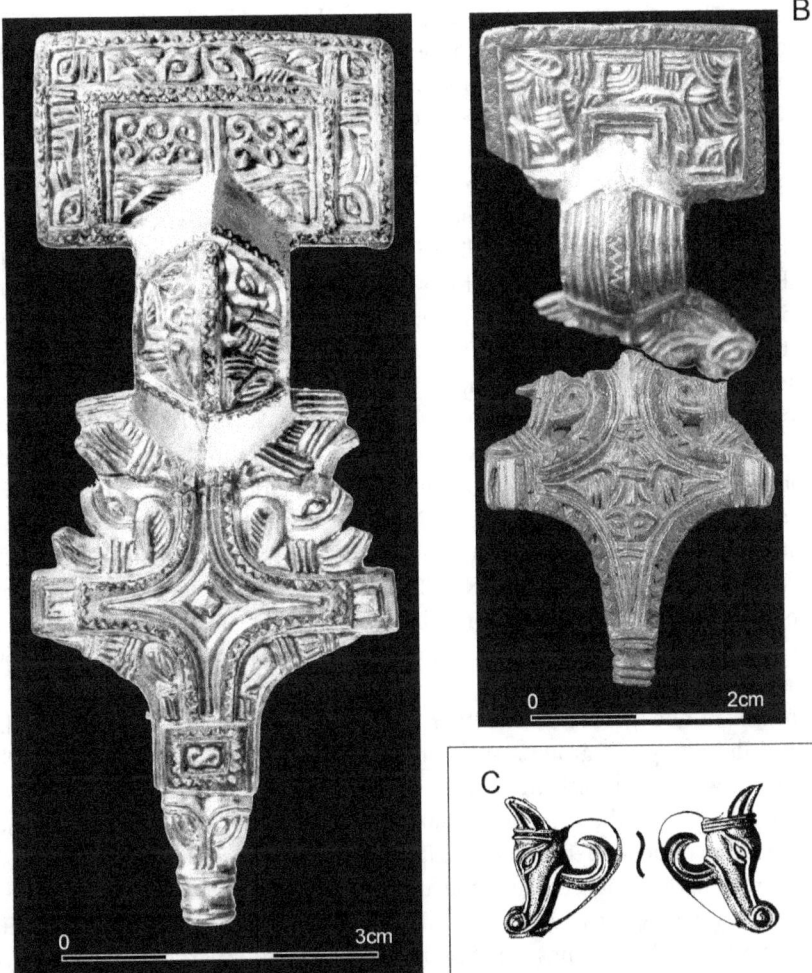

PLATE 2 Gilt silver great square-headed brooches. A: Empingham I, Leics (Rutland), grave 1; B: Snetterton, Norfolk. With the footplate upper border design from the Gummersmark brooch (C) for comparison. (B: courtesy of the Portable Antiquities Scheme; C: drawn by Howard Mason).

parallels elsewhere in the south of England. The disposition of the jaws on the downward-facing profile animal heads in the footplate upper borders is very similar to that on the earliest Group II great square-headed brooches, which are Kentish, and behind that on a Jutlandic brooch from Gummersmark (C on Plate 2).[53] There is a general similarity in the Style I animal ornament in the headplate second panel

---

[53] Hines, *A New Corpus*, 32–41, esp. figs. 15b and 16c.

between the Snetterton and the early Group II brooches as well, but no definite relationship of design can be identified here. The symmetrical stylized forward-facing Style I human motif in the footplate inner panel, meanwhile, is more similar to that of Group III great square-headed brooches, the earliest of which is from grave 22 at Chessell Down, Isle of Wight, although a simpler version of the same motif also appears on a brooch from Paglesham, Essex.[54]

In the case of great square-headed brooches of both Groups II and III, origins in England represented by the earliest-looking forms in the historically 'Jutish' areas of Kent and the Isle of Wight are followed by derived stages in the history of these brooch-groups where the design is adopted and flourishes in eastern England north of the Thames – particularly in Essex, Cambridgeshire and Norfolk and Suffolk. The overall distribution of Group II is extraordinary, with a lead model of this brooch-form even having been unearthed in Geneva, Switzerland, but the second stage of this group is now represented by five brooches in those eastern counties north of the Thames, plus two in adjacent Northamptonshire: at Edix Hill and Linton Heath in Cambridgeshire,[55] Mucking in Essex, and at West Stow and Witnesham (alias Westerfield) in Suffok – the latter a recent metal-detector find (Treasure Annual Report 2003, No. 72). The brooch Empingham I 1 can also be grouped with another brooch from Chessell Down, Isle of Wight (Chessell Down [uc]), in an informal sub-group (i) of two brooches less formally and consistently related to one another than those within the defined Groups, while the Snetterton brooch can be regarded as a further example of the same general relationship, although linking sub-group i with Group II of the great square-headed brooches as well as with Groups III and IV. And yet we have to regard the Snetterton brooch as independent of those major Groups: where we can properly trace derivation, rather than independent relationship, it is back to a Jutlandic model on the Gummersmark brooch, through the footplate upper borders.

Here we may also briefly introduce and discuss another recently found fragment, from Wetheringsett in Suffolk (Plate 3). This is part of the footplate of a great square-headed brooch, with a footplate inner panel frame again very close in design to that on Chessell Down [uc] and Empingham I 1 of informal sub-group i, while the footplate inner panel has a spiralled swastika also found on Chessell Down [uc] as well as one a pair of small silver square-headed brooches from Barrington, Cambs.[56] The plain side lobes on this footplate are sufficiently similar to those on Empingham I 1 and Suffolk [IV] to be counted as related,[57] while the crouched profile animal in the footplate lower borders derives originally from Scandinavian models, and appears a slightly simplified form of close parallels on Chessell Down 22 (Group III) and Suffolk [IV].

---

[54] Hines, *A New Corpus*, 42–8, fig. 20b.
[55] See also, T. Malim and J. Hines, *The Anglo-Saxon Cemetery at Edix Hill (Barrington A), Cambridgeshire*, CBA Research Report, 112, York 1998, 202–3 & fig. 3.65 no. 18).
[56] G. Haseloff, *Die Germanische Tierornamentik der Völkerwanderungszeit*, 3 vols, Berlin 1981, 288–325.
[57] Cf. Hines, *A New Corpus*, fig. 91.

PLATE 3 Gilt silver great square-headed brooch. Wetheringsett, Suffolk (Courtesy of the Portable Antiquities Scheme).

The cultural connexions and relationships revealed by the great square-headed brooches have been rendered even more complex by the new finds. There is undoubtedly evidence within Group IV of this brooch-class of independent Scandinavian influence on eastern Anglian England, especially around the Fens,[58] while at the same time the primacy of the southern specimens of Groups II and III from Kent and the Isle of Wight continues to imply a supplementary but highly significant strand of influence either overland or around the coast from the Jutish south-east of England. It is certainly possible, though, that all of the related elements on the Snetterton and Wetheringsett brooches compared with Groups II and III in that southern zone are the products of independent derivation from Scandinavian models.

Such a possibility adds a new nuance to our understanding of East Anglia's use of its overseas connexions across the North Sea rather than subverting them. It is useful here to refer to the recent work of Karen Høilund Nielsen, who has looked at the occurrences of such 'Nordic' brooches on the Continent, and in one case was able to show, looking at different generations in a single buried community, how women could be claimed to have been continuing to wear such brooches as badges of identity and even as claims to a particularly Scandinavian ancestry.[59] A critical matter to emphasize, however, is that the situation on the Continent was different from that anywhere in England, except Kent in certain respects: this Scandinavian-derived material is less common and less influential on the Continent than it is in England. If it did represent an assertion of a specific identity or connexion in

---

[58] Hines, *A New Corpus*, 48–58.
[59] Høilund Nielsen, 'The Real Thing or Just Wannabes?', especially 90–106.

Alamannic Germany then it could do so by displaying one unusual Germanic identity in the context of several which were available there. In England, by contrast, the great square-headed brooch became so widespread and diverse that, although socially exclusive in the sense that it was largely associated with relative wealth and high status, in itself it expresses simply a general Germanic – or by now English – identity. This is not to say, though, that the sort of regional links already noted between East Anglia and Humberside were merely accidental and insignificant: the product of practical relationships but of no symbolic salience. In fact one of the reasons we can recognize them so clearly is that just to the south-west of East Anglia, along the Icknield Way and across a series of fifth-century ditches and banks, in Cambridgeshire we enter a culturally distinct zone, where connexions to the west, in Bedfordshire, Oxfordshire, Northamptonshire and Warwickshire, were reflected and cultivated instead. In the seventh century that whole region briefly found political expression as the short-lived kingdom of Middle Anglia.[60]

The distinction between Middle Anglia and East Anglia in the sixth century is as clearly embodied in the distribution of different types of great square-headed brooch as anything else. The great, serially reproduced, designs of Groups XVI and XVII characterize the East Anglian/Humberside zone; at the same time the latest descendants of the earliest Group IV types just discussed, including brooches with a spiralled swastika in the footplate inner panel, characterize Cambridgeshire and Northamptonshire: Group XV.[61] Scandinavian links continue to play an important role to the end of these series; however here there is one marked difference. The Middle Anglian brooches appear to incorporate individual Scandinavian design elements almost as artistic 'quotations' within a composition.[62] The Group XVI and XVII brooches, by contrast, rather show a continuing general trend of development in the whole design or composition with Scandinavia; even, it appears, stimulating the adoption or mutation of a Bichrome Style, contrasting gilded relief with plain silver zones, in mid-sixth-century Norway. The situation implies a better case for conscious, deliberate assertion of connexions in the more inland, Middle Anglian, area, in contrast to the coastal zone where the links and their products continued to develop and appear more naturally within a practical, cultural whole.

THE CONSTRUCTION OF AN ANGLO-SAXON KINGDOM

We move finally on to the emergence of an East Anglian kingdom, summarily to consider how that might be related to this historical and archaeological context. East Anglia undoubtedly saw Germanic settlement from across the North Sea in the fifth century. Happily we can now *discuss* the many great uncertainties of demographic history in this period rather than having defensively to apologise for even talking in terms of population change. The Germanic cultures appearing in East

---

[60] Hines, 'The Archaeology of the Cambridge Region'.
[61] Hines, *A New Corpus*, 111–41; idem, 'The Archaeology of the Cambridge Region', fig. 7.
[62] Hines, *A New Corpus*, especially, 116–17; cf. also ibid., 62, 80.

Anglia come from right around the North Sea, from the southern littoral – the areas of Frisia and Saxony – to Jutland and well up the west coast of Norway. Quantitatively, though, the core of the Germanic culture that appears in East Anglia as the basis of the Anglo-Saxon culture points to the Anglian homelands, north of the Elbe in Germany, primarily in what is now Schleswig-Holstein.[63] From there, indeed, the Angles took their name; generally, however, and especially in the sixth century, their material culture was blended and reconstructed, as indeed were their identities, to become Anglian in an English sense and context and even specifically East Anglian. There does appear to be a pattern whereby 'minority' constituents in the cultural hybrid were assigned to women's and children's spheres: a nice example is the regular survival of Romano-British bracelets as children's anklets at Great Chesterford,[64] a feature that recurs amongst the more recently excavated burials at Eriswell. We may never precisely know what the proportions of indigenous and settler populations were in these contexts, but there is plenty for us to work on and learn from the processes that we can observe without getting pessimistic about those details of the background that we struggle to infer.

The North Sea was also a zone of considerable, long-distance material exchange, certainly from early in the sixth century; possibly earlier. We are gradually improving our understanding of production, distribution, exchange and trade from the Migration Period right through to the Viking Age. Where our grasp of the role and organization of agrarian production beyond subsistence strategies is still weak, studies of trading ports and social and economic central places have burgeoned since the 1980s. The results of excavations, and publication, have been rich in the cases of Southampton and London; not quite so much from York for this period.[65] In the case of Ipswich we wish more of the evidence were available, and Norwich remains enigmatic – but even that is beginning to change.[66]

A seventh-century development across a band of coastal Europe from the

---

[63] C. Hills, 'Did the People of Spong Hill Come from Schleswig-Holstein?', *Studien zur Sachsenforschung* 11, 1998, 145–54; J. Hines, 'The Anglian Migration in British Archaeological Research', *Studien zur Sachsenforschung* 11, 1998, 155–65.

[64] Malim and Hines, *The Anglo-Saxon Cemetery at Edix Hill*, 325–6.

[65] See in general, G. Astill, 'Overview: Trade, Exchange and Urbanisation', in *The Oxford Handbook of Anglo-Saxon Archaeology*, ed. H. Hamerow, D. A. Hinton and S. Crawford, Oxford 2011, 503–14; T. Pestell, 'Markets, *emporia*, *wics*, and "Productive" Sites: Pre-Viking Trade Centres in Anglo-Saxon England', in ibid., 556–79. For London, L. Blackmore, 'The Origins and Growth of Lundenwic, A Mart of Many Nations', in *Central Places*, ed. Hårdh and Larsson, 273–301; G. Malcolm, J. Bowsher and R. Cowie, *Middle Saxon London: Excavations at the Royal Opera House 1989–99*, London 2003. For Southampton, V. Birbeck et al., *The Origins of Mid-Saxon Southampton: Excavations at the Friends Provident St Mary's Stadium 1998–2000*, Salisbury 2005, 190–205. For York, R. Kemp, *Anglian Settlement at 46–54 Fishergate*, The Archaeology of York 7i, York 1996; C. A. Spall and N. J. Toop, 'Before *Eoforwic*: New Light on York in the 6th–7th Centuries', *Medieval Archaeology* 52, 2008, 1–25.

[66] K. Wade, 'The Urbanisation of East Anglia: The Ipswich Perspective', in *Flatlands and Wetlands: Current Themes in East Anglian Archaeology*, ed. J. Gardiner, East Anglian Archaeology, 50, Scole, Norfolk 1993, 142–51; C. J. Scull, 'Ipswich: Development and Contexts of an Urban Precursor in the Seventh Century', in *Central Places*, ed. Hårdh and Larsson, 303–16; Hutcheson, *The Origins of East Anglian Towns*.

English Channel to the Baltic is the centralization of economic functions that were previously dispersed across the settled landscape, and even shifted around, at permanent ports – the sites known as *wīcs*. What is especially frustrating about the fact that less of the urban settlement evidence from early Ipswich is as yet available compared with that from London, Southampton and York is the fact that at Ipswich we have especially good evidence of what looks like a sequence of relocation of functions and a gradually increasing focus on the port site. From as early as the fifth century there is a rich clustering of finds around the formerly Roman small town at Coddenham – a crossing point of the Gipping. The cemetery sequence of Hadleigh Road, Boss Hall and Buttermarket effectively marks stages both preceding and within the emergence of the east coast port.[67] It must be implicit in this, as indeed in the contemporary growth of London and Southampton, that overseas contacts were attracting attention, power and wealth (to speak of abstractions) to these land-sea gateways, and people and activity in concrete terms. Continuing the Scandinavian connexion visible in earlier contexts, a piece of knotted repp fabric that had somehow come from Scandinavia has been identified overlying a buckle in a grave at Buttermarket, Ipswich.[68]

However one of the abiding puzzles concerning the flourishing of the seventh- and eighth-century Anglo-Saxon ports is exactly what their economic function was. That trade was crucial is obvious; but trade in what? We know something of commodities that were being both imported and exported to and from England, but in no one case can we say that there is evidence for particularly high demand – like the later medieval wool trade, or steel and coal in the nineteenth century – that we could identify as the prime cause. Perhaps we must, then, conclude that there was a steady increase in general trade, and both a desire to channel that through particular ports and the authority to enforce that. Similarly with production: the *wīcs* were sites where crafts were practised, but again (with the possible exception of tanning) not in any one case at a level that goes any way towards explaining their existence. One consideration that we can accept, however, virtually as an *a priori* truth, is that the *wīcs* were too large, stable and economically dynamic not to sit squarely in the focus of interest and attention of those with political power in the relevant community – the kings of the kingdoms in which they were located.

Ideas have, of course, moved on from the relatively simple 'argument from design' that proposed the *wīcs* were created as administered depots for royally controlled trade in prestige goods – a view that concurrently emphasized evidence for 'planned' layouts such as regular street patterns.[69] Possibly one of the crucial con-

---

[67] C. J. Scull, *Early Medieval (Late 5th–Early 8th Centuries AD) Cemeteries at Boss Hall and Buttermarket, Ipswich, Suffolk*, Society for Medieval Archaeology Monograph, 27, Leeds 2009, 305–19.

[68] P. Walton Rogers, untitled contribution in Scull, *Boss Hall and Buttermarket*, at 231.

[69] Hodges, *Dark Age Economics*; cf. D. Skre, 'Post-Substantivist Towns and Trade AD 600–1000', in *Means of Exchange*, ed. D. Skre, Kaupang Excavation Project Publication Series, 2, Aarhus 2009, 327–41; idem, 'Dealing with Silver: Economic Agency in South-Western Scandinavia AD 600–1000', in ibid., 343–55; Astill, 'Overview: Trade, Exchange and Urbanisation'.

ceptual issues whose case still has to be fully and effectively presented is the desirability of moving away from an anarchic and primeval view of the Roman to Anglo-Saxon transition in England, where virtually everything had to be re-established following a systemic collapse, to a greater appreciation of cultural inheritance and the progressive reconfiguration of its practices in the development of new institutions. In respect of the economic dimension of social power, for example, I have recently argued that a combination of historical, linguistic and archaeological evidence indicates that early Anglo-Saxon culture saw the systematic use and display of precious metals (gold and silver) in a bimetallic system which incorporated exchange-rates encoded in fifth-century Roman law.[70] Within that case, the famous royal ship-burial under mound 1 at Sutton Hoo is a key reference point. The Sutton Hoo great gold buckle contains an amount of gold that is very close indeed to three hundred *tremisses* or early English gold shillings: the *wergild* or life-price of a nobleman according to contemporary Kentish and West Saxon laws.

In that case, then, we have an insight into a mode of exchange of valuables that is high-value, and not subject to the fluctuations of a free market, precisely because it is 'socially embedded'. It represented the use of what was, in effect, a currency, both to express and to enact the relations of power amongst and between the various ranks of a hierarchical society: ranks that were fundamental to the political definition of that society and community as a kingdom. A corollary of this, then, is that we can understand the emergence of ports such as Ipswich in more informative terms than merely as the products of virtually natural evolution and economic growth in liberal circumstances: of entrepreneurial trade which the kings took control of as they could. Generally in England by the late sixth century we have clear and repeated evidence of the growing interest of the southern and eastern, coastal, kingdoms in cultivating overseas connexions: Kent with Merovingian Gaul; Essex with Kent in turn; East Anglia with the North Sea zone and not least Scandinavia. In the case of the northernmost east-coast kingdom, meanwhile, Northumbria, the evidence is rather of interest in connexions with the north and west within the British Isles. To put a hypothesis succinctly: the dynamics of political development contrast the three major inland kingdoms of Early Anglo-Saxon England, Wessex, Mercia and Northumbria, with the smaller coastal kingdoms, but in both cases in a constructive manner. While the former could expand territorially over British territory, the social elite in the former had primarily to look beyond their coastal frontiers to overseas links for the support of additional resources and alliances. East Anglia had to respond to the power and influence of Mercia to the west by exploiting connexions via the North Sea: to Northumbria and Kent within England, and overseas to Frisia and Scandinavia.

If this is the case, the eclectic display character of the wealth in Mound 1 at Sutton Hoo is by no means just a reflection of the acquisitive ambitions of an early seventh-century king. Nor are its Scandinavian features merely a late, if spectacular,

---

[70] J. Hines, 'Units of Account in Gold and Silver in Seventh-Century England: *scillingas, sceattas* and *pæningas*', *Antiquaries Journal* 90, 153–73; Erratum, *Antiquaries Journal* 91, 397–8.

echo of a Scandinavian background, although that undoubtedly is a feature of their context. The Sutton Hoo mound 1 ship burial is as much East Anglian and at home as it is Scandinavian and exotically out of place. Yet curiously – and so often there are ways in which a key historical trend in one direction is accompanied by a counter movement – the growth of social and political control over contacts and trade led to the establishment not only of dominant ports but also of trading monopolies that in the end promoted localism in culture rather than internationalism. In such a way, for instance, the *sceatt* coinage of the eighth century was an international common currency at one level, and yet is represented in a wide range of regionalized forms at another.

The links with Scandinavia that I explored at the beginning of my research career in the late 1970s and early 1980s and so have concentrated on again in this review were certainly not the only, nor even, looking at the entirety of the history of the East Anglian kingdom from the sixth century to the ninth, the most important of East Anglia's transmarine connexions. They can, however, be shown to have been intimately involved in the definition of East Anglian identity, both cultural and political. The link between East Anglia and Scandinavia appears to have been the farthest horizon for direct overseas connexions of early Anglo-Saxon England, and that position is not to be treated lightly.

Careful attention to the archaeologically essential details of types, dates, distributions and contexts allows us to produce a comprehensive historical reconstruction. In the case of East Anglia, the story that emerges is one of demographic change and movement, of contact and adaptation, and of a dynamic and productive material life that truly mattered to the population of what was a nodal region seen in the context of England's relationships with continental Europe and Scandinavia. East Anglia achieved a strong place for itself in the international and overseas networks of the pre-Viking period. Having had to defend their coasts in the south and south-west of England against Viking attacks from the late eighth century to the early tenth, the West Saxon rulers who became the kings of a united England appreciated very well both the opportunities and the threats posed by access and openness to the sea, from where both powerful allies and powerful enemies could come. Politically, as a result, we can better understand why it also mattered to the tenth-century West Saxon monarchy to write East Anglian kingship out of the script of continuing history with the hagiographical legend of a model Benedictine end for Eadmund, last king of East Anglia, virgin martyr, and saint.

Whatever relative weights we attribute to migration and colonization on the one hand, or to trade and exchange on the other, in the establishment of East Anglia as a distinctly North Sea kingdom from early in the Anglo-Saxon period, we must not fail to recognize how much a historically new and greater a level of confidence in exploiting the sea-routes across the North Sea is implied by the evidence of the connexions reviewed above. The barbarian threat that led to the southern and eastern shores of Late Roman Britannia being designated the *litus Saxonicum* shows that regular Germanic navigation of these seas had been developed by the fourth century AD.[71] For four centuries after the Germanic conquest of what was to become England, the sea-board itself and the lands and peoples across the seas became the hinterland and resources that could be used by the coastal Anglo-Saxon kingdoms of the south and east to maintain their autonomy and distinctiveness. In the Viking period, however, the direct North Sea connexion with southern Scandinavia was to become a threat again – although then again we see violence and disruption give way before long to mutual influence and assimilation.[72] The early medieval history and archaeology of East Anglia provides a fascinating case-study in a regional strategy to exploit and to balance competing associations with neighbours: the powerful south-east, with its cross-Channel links to the Continent, the north-eastern English kingdoms, the mighty Mercians to the west, and Scandinavia across the North Sea. In the direction of three of the four quarters of the compass, such relationships were dependent upon maritime connexions, and the practical way in which such communications were maintained is therefore an essential element to a full understanding of Anglo-Saxon East Anglia's fortunes and success.

ACKNOWLEDGEMENTS

Excavations and further research at RAF Lakenheath have been funded by the UK Ministry of Defence and the author is most grateful for the opportunity and permission to present results from post-excavation analysis in progress in this paper. Warmest thanks to Dr Tim Pestell, Castle Museum Norwich, for the information on and drawings of the Mundham clasp button; to Dr Helen Geake, Portable Antiquities Scheme, for information on and illustrations of the Snetterton and Wetheringsett great square-headed brooches; and to Ian Dennis, Cardiff University, for his invaluable assistance with the illustrations.

---

[71] D. E. Johnston (ed.), *The Saxon Shore*, CBA Research Report, 18, York 1977; J. C. Mann, 'The Historical Development of the Saxon Shore', in *The Saxon Shore: A Handbook*, ed. V. A. Maxfield, Exeter Studies in History, 25, Exeter 1989, 1–11.

[72] See the chapter in this volume by Tim Pestell.

— Chapter 2 —

EAST ANGLIA'S CHARACTER AND THE 'NORTH SEA WORLD'

Tom Williamson

EAST ANGLIA: CHARACTER AND LOCATION

My title begs a question: what do we mean by the 'character' of a region or place? For the purposes of this chapter I will use this term simply to describe those distinctive features of landscape and social institutions which make a particular tract of territory different from its neighbours. In terms of East Anglia we might thus draw attention to such things as idiosyncrasies in social structure – the large numbers of free men recorded in Domesday Book, and to some extent in later periods; in architecture – round-towered churches in the Middle Ages, pantiles in the post-medieval period; or in the landscape, especially the character of field systems and settlement, most notably the absence, from many parts of the region in the medieval period, of closely nucleated villages and highly communal open-field systems. I shall attempt to examine the extent to which aspects of East Anglia's identity can be attributed to its place within the North Sea World, to the contacts which its geographical position engendered with areas on the shores of Continental Europe. But I shall also look more generally at how the region's relationship with the North Sea helped to forge its distinctive character, a concept which is subtly but significantly different.

To understand the influence of the 'North Sea World' we need to define it, to decide which countries and regions formed its constituent elements: and defining any geographical entity usually involves the imposition of firm lines on a shifting and subjective reality. Denmark, Norway and Sweden clearly need to be included within this 'world', the first perhaps more than the others; so too must Frisia and parts of north Germany. But as Map 1 perhaps emphasizes, the Netherlands would lie towards its peripheries, while modern Belgium would be better included, together with northern France, within a maritime region focused on the English Channel, rather than on the North Sea. Hard lines are difficult to draw and seldom very meaningful in discussions like these but for convenience we may assume that the 'North Sea World' embraces the continental littoral to the north and east of the

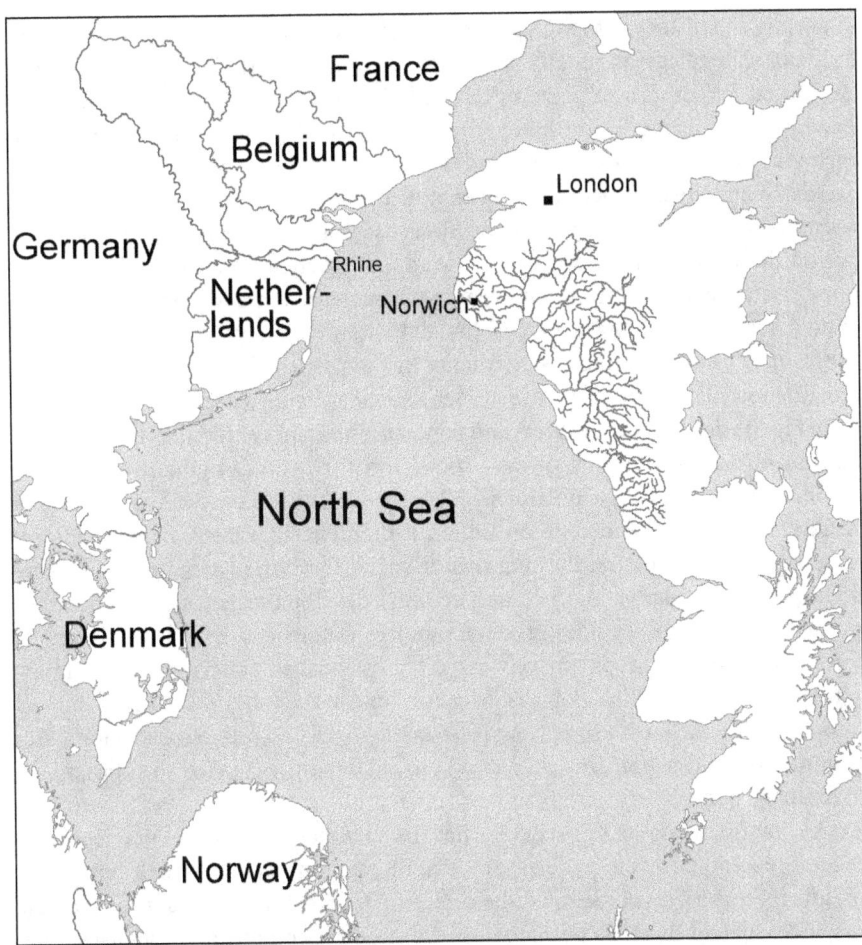

MAP 1 East Anglia and its continental neighbours, with the English rivers whose drainage basins constitute the 'North Sea Province'.

Rhine-Meuse-Scheldt Delta. The Rhine formed, of course, the north-eastern boundary of the Roman Empire, and perhaps the most important defining feature of the 'North Sea World' in its early history is that it lay outside and beyond the classical world. It was, in essence, the 'barbarian' north, where Christianity and all that was associated with it, including written history itself, only arrived at a relatively late date.

Understanding how location and topography shape the character of place necessitates some consideration of the nature of boundaries, and of patterns of social and cultural contact. Historians in general have not been good at thinking about such matters, with the notable exception of local and regional historians, especially those of the 'Leicester School'. It was Alan Everitt who first emphasized the importance in history of topographic regions, based on drainage basins and defined by major watersheds, although his concept of 'region and wold' was elaborated and developed in important ways by Harold Fox and Charles Phythian-Adams.[1] According to this model, the main settlements even in lowland districts tended, in early Anglo-Saxon times, to be found within major river valleys, with the upland 'wolds' lying between them initially exploited for grazing and pannage, and as a source of wood and timber. As population rose in the course of the Anglo-Saxon period these woodland pastures were gradually opened up for cultivation, temporary settlements within them became permanent, and additional ones proliferated. However, such places continued to be dependent upon or tenurially subservient to the 'primary' settlements in the principal valleys, and generally remained smaller in size. Everitt's model, as well as being a useful way of conceptualizing the development of local and regional landscapes and economies, can also help in our understanding of past social territories. As Phythian-Adams has emphasized, because the upland wolds between the valleys were at best only sparsely settled, they tended to constitute cut-off points in patterns of human interaction – to form, that is, the margins of social territories. Communities were focused on particular valleys, or valley systems, developing identities distinct from those dwelling the other side of the surrounding watersheds. Even when the interfluves came to be more intensively exploited established patterns of social interaction tended to continue, not least because some of the valley settlements evolved into market centres, with important roles as the social and economic foci for wider communities. Over time, in other words, social territories tended to approximate to drainage basins.

As Phythian-Adams in particular has urged, upland 'wolds' do not represent the only cut-off points in patterns of social interaction.[2] While in their upper and middle reaches rivers constituted the centres of territories, as they approached the sea and widened they too became obstacles to daily contact, and estuaries often constituted major territorial boundaries, with that of the Thames for example separating the Anglo-Saxon kingdoms of Essex and Kent. It is noteworthy that the boundaries of our oldest administrative units, those of the hundreds, tend to follow the interfluves between major rivers but only until these approach the sea. They then leave the higher ground, following one or other of the rivers as it begins to widen into an estuary.

Yet this last observation immediately raises a problem with the familiar and useful 'river and wold' model: it takes little account of different modes of contact,

---

[1] A. Everitt, 'River and Wold: Reflections on the Historical Origins of Regions and Pays', *Journal of Historical Geography* 3, 1977, 1–19; H. S. A. Fox, 'The People of the Wolds', in *The Rural Settlements of Medieval England: Studies Presented to Maurice Beresford and John Hurst*, ed. M. Aston, D. Austin and C. Dyer, Oxford 1989, 77–104; C. Phythian-Adams, *Re-Thinking English Local History*, Leicester 1987.

[2] C. Phythian-Adams, 'Introduction: an Agenda for English Local History', in *Societies, Cultures and Kinship, 1580–1850: Cultural Provinces in English Local History*, ed. C. Phythian-Adams, Leicester 1993, 1–23.

or of the differences in the kinds of contact enjoyed by members of different social groups. It deals in essence with patterns forged through the everyday interactions between the broad mass of an agrarian population. The paths trod and contacts made by more mobile elites, on an intermittent basis, could take different paths and different patterns. So too could sporadic, yet culturally important, trading contacts. Well into the post-medieval period goods and people were more easily and more rapidly moved by water – by sea or, inland, along navigable rivers – than by land. As Martin Carver has reminded us, it would have been easier for the East Anglian kings at Rendlesham to reach Denmark than it would have been for them to visit Tamworth in the west Midlands.[3] We might thus expect East Anglia's position, on the eastern side of England and facing towards those parts of the European mainland just discussed, to have ensured that its character was indeed forged, in part, by contacts and connections with such foreign lands. The North Sea was, for much of history, a highway which brought influences, goods or people from the continent, and then along major rivers, with the degree of contact fading as the upper reaches of their tributaries, the margins of their drainage basins, were reached. Looked at in this way much of East Anglia formed part of a 'North Sea Province' which extended northwards through the east Midlands and northeast England, and which was defined by the drainage basins of rivers with outfalls into those part of the North Sea lying to the north of the mouth of the Rhine on its opposite shore. The south of East Anglia, in contrast – that is, southern Suffolk and Essex – did not really form part of this world. In this district, rivers like the Colne and Blackwater, and even the Stour and the Gipping/Orwell, entered the sea opposite the Belgian coast, into what was effectively the northern edge of a wider Thames estuary.

There is another way of thinking about these matters. As well as being a highway, the sea was also a barrier to movement. It allowed important yet essentially intermittent contact over long distances, but curtailed everyday intercourse. With the Fenland – watery and sparsely-settled for much of history – to the west, East Anglia thus becomes a peninsula. Its southern portions lie closer to the political and cultural heart of the medieval and post-medieval nation, London. But its northern parts – north east Suffolk and Norfolk – are always more remote, more cut off from currents of ideas and fashions which spread, as it were, at 'vernacular' level, exchanged face to face, through regular daily contacts. Even today, no-one really visits Norwich *en route* to somewhere else. For both of these reasons the south and west of East Anglia faced away from the North Sea World, towards the southeast of the country. Its European contacts came via this latter area, and ultimately from those parts of Europe on the far side of the English Channel. The north and east of the region, in contrast, was more remote from the 'core' areas of southern England yet at the same time more open to influences emanating from northern Europe. Looked at in both

---

[3] M. Carver, 'Pre-Viking Traffic in the North Sea', in *Maritime Celts, Frisians and Saxons*, ed. S. McGrail, London 1990, 117–25.

ways, however, the low watershed running across Suffolk, separating rivers draining into the North Sea as defined above from those with outfalls into the Thames or its greater estuary, formed a significant if permeable barrier.

THE COMPLEXITY OF CHARACTER

When considering the extent to which its place in the 'North Sea World' shaped East Anglia's character we need to be aware of two key problems. Firstly, we have to be on our guard against a tendency to exaggerate similarities between the two sides of the North Sea, and of mistaking *influence* for *parallel development*: that is, the similar responses of communities developing in broadly similar geographic and environmental zones to the same, or similar, challenges and possibilities. Visitors from southern Scandinavia or the Low Countries to northern East Anglia – to Norwich in particular – will immediately recognize parallels between the land they have left, and that which greets them. Some are architectural, most obviously the fact that many vernacular (and some elite) buildings are roofed with pantiles, distinctive tiles with a section like a shallow 'S' and which are not nailed or pegged into the roof battens, like plain tiles, but kept in place by their weight. Pantiles were introduced into England from the Low Countries – the Dutch word 'pan' means 'tile' – although they are not evidence of some ancient cultural connection, having only been imported from the late seventeenth century and only manufactured locally from the start of the eighteenth.[4] This is, nevertheless, clearly an aspect of 'character' which the region does owe directly to its contacts with a wider 'North Sea World', although such tiles are not of course restricted to East Anglia, or even to the eastern coast of England, being used for example in the Somerset levels. But other apparent similarities are more complicated. A visit to the Castle Museum in Norwich would allow our notional tourists to enjoy the unparalleled collection of the paintings produced by members of the early nineteenth-century Norwich School, with their views of marshlands drained by windmills, level landscapes, sandy heaths, wide skies – and pantiled, 'Dutch'–gabled buildings. The Norwich Society of Artists was founded in 1803, its inception reflecting in part the continuing economic vitality of the city and its hinterland in the early nineteenth century, and hence the market presented by wealthy businessmen who (together with owners of landed estates in the surrounding countryside) were important collectors of works by Netherlandish artists, especially of landscapes.[5] In part this preference was simply a manifestation of East Anglia's strong trading connections with the Low Countries. But it also reflected similarities in the landscapes of Holland and East Anglia, both characterized by broad waterways, wide valleys, prosperous

---

[4] R. W. Brunskill, 'Distributions of Building Materials and Some Plan Types in the Domestic Vernacular Architecture of England and Wales', *Transactions of the Ancient Monument Society* 23, 1978, 41–65, at 46–7.

[5] A. Moore, *Dutch and Flemish Painting in Norfolk: A History of Taste and Influence, Fashion and Collecting*, London 1988; A. Moore, *The Norwich School*, Norwich 1985.

yet ancient towns, muted terrain. Such visual echoes made Dutch art appealing to East Anglian consumers. The paintings produced by John Crome, and subsequently by James Stark, Henry Bright, the Stannard family and others, were of similar scenes: some, indeed, are closely comparable to works by Dutch seventeenth-century masters like Hobbema, Hondecoeter, or Cuyp.[6] Yet it is a moot point how far we are dealing here with direct influence, how far with parallel development: how far the artists in question were directly influenced by Dutch models, and catered for the taste in them of local patrons; and how far resemblances in scale and subject matter reflect real similarities in the landscape of the two regions. Windmills are thus a common motif, and in the words of one art historian, one 'no doubt learnt from the Dutch'.[7] But windmills were also a quintessential part of the East Anglian scene, given the fact that muted terrain and sluggish rivers with wide valleys made water power less important – for grinding grain, or for much else – than in more westerly districts of England. Expanses of heath and wide, slow-flowing rivers are likewise a feature of both regions, while in both level terrain ensured the overwhelming importance of the ever-changing sky as a key element in the composition.

Windmills, and especially drainage windmills, appear an obvious candidate for close and direct cultural influence between East Anglia and the Netherlands. But although Dutch engineers advised on the draining of the East Anglian Fens, and perhaps on the reclamation of the Broadland marshes, drainage mills themselves followed different and divergent paths of development in the two countries in the course of the post-medieval period, with those in Holland more likely to power Archimedean screws than scoop wheels, to lack fantails and to display a range of distinctive features quite foreign to the East Anglian and English traditions, many for example having thatched external walls. Broad visual similarities in landscape are thus not necessarily the result of 'influence', of a shared 'culture', but may instead reflect parallel developments or similarities of environment, exaggerated in some cases by our own subjective perceptions of these things.[8]

The second difficulty we need to consider is the very real problems involved in distinguishing those aspects of East Anglia's character which are a consequence of foreign influence, coming via the North Sea, from those which are simply a function of the region's location on the eastern side of England. The counties of eastern and north-eastern England share a number of important features which are directly or indirectly the result of climatic factors – their location in the drier side of the country. The distribution of arable land use, for example, has been strongly concentrated in these areas for several centuries in part because of soils but mainly because a relatively dry climate makes for a larger and more reliable grain harvest. The distribution of a particular social or economic phenomenon along the eastern seaboard is not, therefore, necessarily evidence of any 'North Sea

---

[6] Ibid., 58–9.
[7] P. Howard, *Landscapes: the Artists' Vision*, London 1991, 74.
[8] R. Hills, *Power from the Wind: A History of Windmill Technology*, Cambridge 1996.

connection', but of environmental factors born of an eastern location, and it is arguable that historians have sometimes confused the two.

The most deeply entrenched example is perhaps the traditional interpretation of the numerous 'free peasants' recorded by Domesday Book. These are thick on the ground, not only in East Anglia but also in the two other key 'North Sea' counties, Lincolnshire and Yorkshire, gradually fading in numbers in counties lying towards the south and west. Their presence here has often been explained as the consequence of the Viking invasions of the ninth century. In Stenton's words, it was no accident that 'a social organisation to which there is no parallel elsewhere in England occurs in the one part of the country in which the regular development of native institutions had been interrupted by a foreign settlement'.[9] One suggestion is that the free men and socmen of Domesday represented the lineal descendants of de-mobbed Viking armies, or of Scandinavian peasants who migrated in the wake of conquest. Another is that the disruptions brought about by raiding and conquest allowed the inhabitants of the Danelaw to escape the increasing oppression suffered by their fellows in areas which remained under Saxon control.[10] Yet there is very little evidence that early medieval social and tenurial patterns, and Viking settlement, were in fact causally connected, and many good reasons for believing that the former had other explanations.[11] Socmen, and to a lesser extent free men, are commonly recorded across much of northern Essex and eastern Hertfordshire where Scandinavian place names are unknown, and in general 'free peasants' are found far to the west of any of the suggested boundaries of Danish settlement; 'soc' is an English not a Scandinavian term; and socmen are better understood as the survivors of the free *ceorls* of the middle Saxon period, and the sokelands on which they dwelt as the tattered remnants of ancient territories focused on royal *tuns*.

There was, it is important to note, a general coincidence between areas in which free men and socmen comprised more than 25 per cent of the population, and areas with recorded Domesday population densities of ten or more per square mile. Both distributions, moreover, correspond closely with the distribution of arable land as recorded by the Land Utilisation Survey in the 1930s,[12] at a time when enclosure, the widespread adoption of improvements like marling and under-drainage, and the continued elaboration of the transport infrastructure had ensured that arable land use was generally concentrated in those parts of the country best suited to the cultivation of cereals.[13] In the later Anglo-Saxon period reliable harvests clearly

---

[9] F. M. Stenton, *Anglo-Saxon England*, Oxford 1943, 519.
[10] B. Dodwell, 'The Free Peasantry of East Anglia in Domesday', *Norfolk Archaeology* 27, 1941, 145–57; F. M. Stenton, 'The Historical Bearing of Place Name Studies: the Danish Settlement of Eastern England', *Transactions of the Royal Historical Society* 4th ser., 24, 1942, 1–24; R. H. C. Davis, 'East Anglia and the Danelaw', *Transactions of the Royal Historical Society* 5th ser., 5, 1955, 23–39.
[11] D. Hadley, *The Northern Danelaw: Its Social Structure, 800–1100*, Leicester 2000, 91–2.
[12] L. Dudley Stamp, *The Land of Britain: Its Use and Misuse*, London 1950, 85.
[13] T. Williamson, *The Transformation of Rural England: Farming and the Landscape 1700–1870*, Exeter 2002, 158–75.

encouraged both a greater rate of population growth in the east than in the west of the country, where it would be unchecked by periodic harvest failure and dearth, and the survival, or enhancement, of peasant freedoms. To judge from ethnographic parallels, frequent crop failures may have obliged peasant cultivators to fall into dependence on social superiors with greater command of resources, and greater facilities for the storage of surpluses. Moreover, although rapid demographic growth would have ensured that peasant holdings shrank in size, through the workings of partible inheritance to a greater extent than in western districts, small farms were more viable in the drier east, while in a populous and wealthy district, with a highly monetarized economy, income could be supplemented through various forms of by-employment. The result was that the east of England, East Anglia included, developed a more fluid, complex and market-orientated society than the west, a characteristic which was maintained into the Middle Ages and which, while strengthened no doubt by the intensity of trade within the North Sea basin, was not fundamentally caused by it.[14] Many other aspects of East Anglia's character are, perhaps, similarly best understood in terms of the region's location in the drier east of England, combined with particular features of its soils and natural topography. Distinctive features of East Anglia's settlement patterns and field systems have been seen as cultural imports from Frisia or Denmark but they, too, are more likely to have had environmental causes.[15]

SETTLEMENT AND ETHNICITY

To suggest that the 'free peasants' of eastern England were not the simple consequence of Scandinavian settlement is not, of course, to deny that there were significant contacts between the Scandinavian world and eastern England in the ninth and tenth centuries, involving some degree of population movement.[16] Scandinavian place-names, and other evidence for Viking activity, extend from East Anglia, northwards through Lincolnshire and Yorkshire, and westwards into the neighbouring counties. But such evidence is not equally strong in all parts of East Anglia. Scandinavian terms are thus found, if in limited numbers, in the place-names of the north and east of the region, and especially in minor names, such as the use of the word *bekkr*, 'beck', for a small stream. But in south-west Suffolk they are rare,

---

[14] An argument developed at greater length in my *Environment, Society and Landscape in Early Medieval England: Time and Topography*, Woodbridge 2012.
[15] The Frisians were seen as a major influence on the development of East Anglian field systems by Homans: Martin has argued that the Vikings were a formative influence, at least on the agrarian landscapes of the north and east of the region. G. C. Homans, 'The Explanation of English Regional Differences', *Past and Present* 42, 1969, 18–34; E. Martin and M. Satchell, *Wheare Most Inclosures Be. East Anglian Fields, History, Morphology and Management*, published as *East Anglian Archaeology* 124, Ipswich 2000, 226–8. See Williamson, *Environment, Society and Landscape*.
[16] S. Margesson, 'Viking Settlement in Norfolk: a Study of New Evidence', in *A Festival of Norfolk Archaeology*, ed. S. Margesson, B. Ayers and S. Heywood, Norwich 1996, 47–57: D. Hadley, *The Vikings in England*, London 2006.

as they are in neighbouring Essex where names show 'but slight traces of any Scandinavian settlement'.[17]

The main centres of Scandinavian military power – as indicated by the strongholds mentioned in the Anglo-Saxon Chronicle – have a slightly different distribution to that of major Scandinavian place-names, concentrated more in the east Midlands, but they nevertheless fit neatly enough into this same overall east Midlands/north-east England/East Anglian pattern. This, it should be noted, is slightly different from the configuration of the 'Danelaw' as usually presented in text books dealing with the period. These usually show a 'Danish' territory defined by the frontier established by a treaty drawn up between Guthrum and Alfred, probably at Wedmore in 879, as David Dumville and others have argued, although Stenton and Davis favoured a date in the late 880s.[18] This apparently fixed the boundary between Saxons and Danes along the line of the Thames as far as its confluence with the Lea; then up the Lea to its source, near Leagrave in Bedfordshire; from there in a straight line to Bedford; and then along the river Ouse to Watling Street. According to this, 'Danish' territory thus embraced not only the east Midlands and the *whole* of East Anglia, but also the modern county, and the Anglo-Saxon kingdom, of Essex.

Dumville, however, has provided a radical reinterpretation of this frontier. He has drawn attention to the fact that the Anglo-Saxon Chronicle, while making it clear that eastern Mercia and East Anglia were over-run by the Danes, is less clear in its treatment of Essex: 'Essex was territory that was being debated.'[19] The Chronicle never actually tells us that Essex as a whole was occupied by Danish armies, and an entry for 896, looking back to events earlier in the 880s and 890s, recalled the deaths of 'many of the king's best thegns' – including Brihtwulf, ealdorman of Essex.[20] So far as the evidence goes, Essex had been effectively incorporated into the West Saxon kingdom in the 820s, and it would appear that control was never subsequently relinquished, except in the north-east of the present county, in the area around Colchester, which was seized and occupied by Danish forces.

This of course raises problems with the boundary described in the Alfred/Guthrum treaty, which appears to place Essex firmly within the 'Danelaw'. As noted, Dumville and others have argued that this dates to 879 – that is, before Alfred's occupation of London, and of the territories in south-eastern Mercia seized by the Danes, in 886. In other words, according to Dumville, the conventional reading of the treaty must be the wrong way round: it was territory to the *south and west* of the line, in Mercia, which was at this time in Danish hands, while Essex was still, at this time, controlled by the English. Dumville has also argued, surely

---

[17] A. Mawer and F. M. Stenton, *The Place-Names of Essex*, Cambridge 1935, p. xxviii.
[18] Stenton, *Anglo-Saxon England*, 260-1; R. H. C. Davis, 'Alfred and Guthrum's Frontier', *English Historical Review* 9, 1982, 803–10; D. Dumville, *Wessex and England from Alfred to Edgar: Six Essays on Political, Cultural and Ecclesiastical Revival*, Woodbridge 1992, 14–15.
[19] Dumville, *Wessex and England*, 8–9.
[20] *The Anglo-Saxon Chronicle*, trans. M. Swanton, London 1996, 90.

EAST ANGLIA'S CHARACTER AND THE 'NORTH SEA WORLD'

correctly, that the treaty did not create some kind of lasting peace which fixed the cultural and ethnic geography of England with a measure of permanence, but was instead a temporary agreement which must have become irrelevant with the occupation of London and the neighbouring lands in 886.

The way in which Danish influence, cultural and political, seems to have declined sharply across the middle of greater East Anglia is superficially strange, given the long, vulnerable coastline of Essex, and the distance of this territory from the main centres of West Saxon power. Yet as so often, distribution maps of dots and symbols make little sense unless further detail, and in this case topographic detail, is added. It then becomes immediately apparent that Scandinavian influence, and presumably settlement, were nested within what I defined earlier as a 'North Sea Province' – within the drainage basins of the rivers with their outfalls into the North Sea – and stopped at its boundaries (Map 2).

What makes this correlation more striking is that the same spatial pattern can be discerned in a rather earlier period. The archaeology of early Anglo-Saxon settlement, especially as manifest in the cemeteries which are still our main source of knowledge, displays a marked pattern of regional variation which follows rather similar lines. In particular, cremation cemeteries, and especially those large cemeteries in which cremation is the sole or overwhelmingly dominant rite, are thus a feature of northern East Anglia, the Midlands, and north-east England (especially Yorkshire), although inhumation was also practised in these regions and became more important with the passing of time. While cremation was practised in the south of the country and in the Thames valley, inhumations with grave goods was always here the dominant rite: cremation cemeteries are much rarer and generally small in size.[21] Once again, Essex can be seen allying itself with the counties lying to its south, rather than north, and south-west Suffolk with it. The north of East Anglia thus followed, in the periods of both 'settlements', a different path to the south (Map 3).

An earlier generation of archaeologists interpreted the distribution of different Anglo-Saxon funerary practices as a reflection of the geography of ethnic settlement outlined by Bede in the early eighth century. In a famous passage Bede described how the settlers:

> ... came from three very powerful Germanic tribes, the Saxons, the Angles, and the Jutes. The people of Kent and the inhabitants of the Isle of Wight are of Jutish origin, and also those opposite the Isle of Wight, that part of the Kingdom of Wessex which is still today called the nation of the Jutes. From the Saxon country, that is, the district now known as Old Saxony, came the East Saxons, the South Saxons, and the West Saxons. Besides this, from the country of the Angles,

---

[21] C. Hills, 'Early Historic Britain', in *The Archaeology of Britain: An Introduction from the Upper Palaeolithic to the Industrial Revolution*, ed. J. Hunter and I. Ralston, London 1998, 176–193, at 183–4.

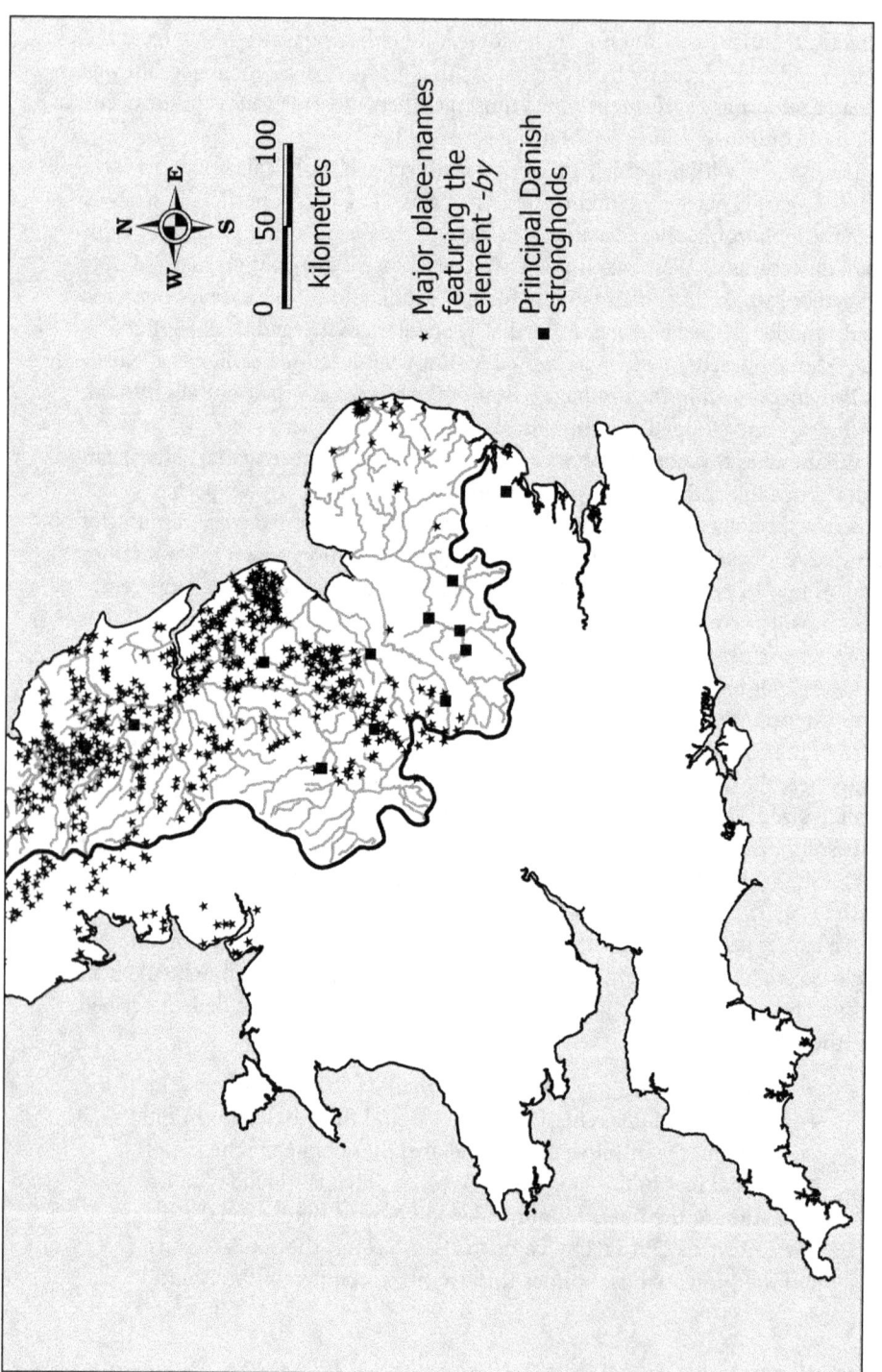

MAP 2   Principal Danish strongholds, Danish place names, and the 'North Sea Province'.

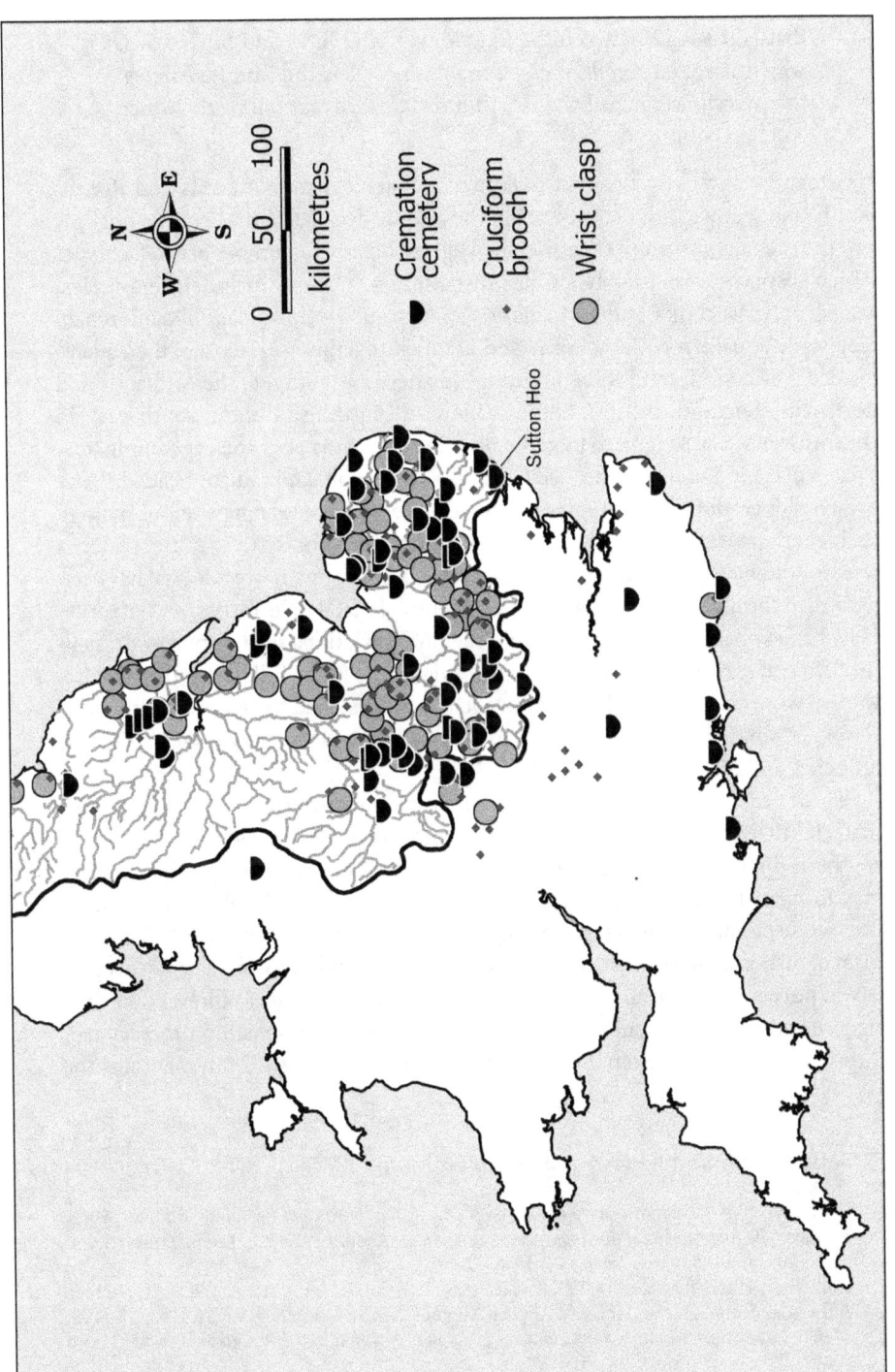

MAP 3 The distribution of cremation cemeteries and selected 'Anglian' artefacts (after S. Lucy, *The Anglo-Saxon Way of Death: Burial Rites in Early England*, Stroud 2000), and the 'North Sea Province'.

that is the land between the kingdoms of the Jutes and the Saxons, which is called *Angulus*, came the East Angles, the Middle Angles, the Mercians, and all the Northumbrian race, as well as the other Anglian tribes.[22]

Nineteenth- and early twentieth-century archaeologists like Leeds and Roach-Smith, and many of their successors in the middle decades of the century, not only saw the rite of cremation as specifically 'Anglian' but also a number of artefact types which display a remarkably similar distribution.[23] These include the artefacts known as 'wrist clasps' and particular styles of brooch – those classified by archaeologists as 'equal armed', 'cruciform', and 'annular', together with most of the 'square-headed' variety. All tend to be found in northern East Anglia, the Midlands and north-east England. In the Thames valley, and in the south and south-east, in contrast, wrist clasps tend to be rare and different forms of brooch predominate – a particular kind of square-headed ('Group VIII'), quoit, and radiate-headed.[24] The present generation of archaeologists are, on the whole, less happy about making such easy correlations between material culture and ethnicity.[25] But the patterns remain, and have not been significantly eroded as more and more material has been recovered through excavations and the activities of metal detectorists. As Catherine Hills has explained, there clearly were regional variations in the style of dress in the fifth and early sixth centuries: 'In East Anglia, the East Midlands and Yorkshire, women wore cruciform and annular brooches, and fastened their sleeves with metal clasps. In southern England, in Sussex, Wessex and Essex, they preferred round brooches and did not use clasps.' (Map 3).[26]

These various 'Anglian' artefacts have their closest affinities with contemporary material in Denmark and Sweden. The round forms of brooch fashionable in southern districts, in contrast, are rare in Scandinavia, have debated origins and may in part at least represent a development of Roman traditions.[27] In a similar way, while cremation cemeteries are unquestionably an intrusive, north European form of disposal, this is less certainly the case with the other form of 'pagan' Anglo-Saxon burial, inhumation with grave goods, which may in fact represent, not the signature of 'invaders', but an indigenous development of existing funerary traditions. Although late Roman burials were mostly unfurnished inhumations, the

---

[22] Bede: *The Ecclesiastical History of the English People*, ed. J. McClure and R. Collins, Oxford 1994, 27.
[23] C. Roach-Smith, *Collectanea Antiqua: Etchings and Notices of Ancient Remains*, London 1850; E. T. Leeds, *The Archaeology of the Anglo-Saxon Settlements*, Oxford 1913; E. T. Leeds, 'Denmark and Early England', *Antiquaries Journal* 26, 1946, 22–37.
[24] Hills, 'Early Historic Britain', 184; M. Parker Pearson, R. van de Noort, and A. Woolf, 'Three Men and a Boat: Sutton Hoo and the East Anglian Kingdom', *Anglo-Saxon England* 22, 1993, 27–50, at 34–6; J. Hines, *The Scandinavian Character of Anglian England in the Pre-Viking Period*, Oxford 1984.
[25] S. Lucy, *The Anglo-Saxon Way of Death*, Stroud 2000, 4.
[26] Hills, 'Early Historic Britain', 184.
[27] Lucy, *Anglo-Saxon Way of Death*, 34–7.

later fourth century saw the appearance across both Britain and Gaul of inhumations which were equipped with weapons and elaborate belt fittings, which may – as Hills has suggested – have developed into the wider fashion for burial accompanied by grave goods.[28] There are hints here of important differences between south-east England and areas adjacent to the North Sea in the character of the transition from Roman Britain to Anglo-Saxon England. In the former, social and economic developments may have been more akin to those in northern France and other areas lying within the Roman *limes*, areas with which, as Evison argued long ago, these districts continued to maintain close contacts through the 'invasion' period. It is in this region, focused on the English Channel, that we also find sporadic evidence for the survival of Christianity through the fifth and sixth centuries, most strikingly at Verulamium/St Albans in west Hertfordshire;[29] a town which lies within an extensive area, including much of Hertfordshire, Middlesex and Essex, in which an almost complete absence of even inhumation cemeteries of the fifth and sixth centuries has encouraged a succession of scholars to posit the survival of some kind of sub-Roman population, culture and perhaps administration.[30] In the north of East Anglia, the east Midlands and Yorkshire, in contrast, cultural influences came direct from the barbarian north, and the transition to Anglo-Saxon England may have been more traumatic.

There is no space here to explore the implications which these spatial patterns may have for our understanding of either the Anglo-Saxon or the Scandinavian 'settlements', beyond noting that the fact that they tend to cut off at relatively minor topographic features – the boundaries of the 'North Sea Province' are, for the most part, marked by muted terrain – makes it hard to see them as marking the arbitrary limits of military conquest. This may suggest that both distributions must, to some extent at least, reflect patterns of contact and emulation, rather than simply of settlement and conquest. The crucial point in the present context is that while greater East Anglia lay, for the most part, within the 'Anglian' and 'Scandinavian' zones of influence – and clearly formed a part of the 'North Sea World' – it did not do so in its entirety. Instead, not only Essex, but also the south and south-west of Suffolk, appear to have had affinities with the south-east of England, and with the areas of northern France on the far side of the English Channel.

[28] Hills, 'Early Historic Britain', 184.
[29] M. Biddle and B. Kjolbye-Biddle, 'England's Premier Abbey: the Medieval Chapter House of St Albans and its Excavation in 1978', *Hertfordshire's Past* 11, 1981, 3–29, at 26; R. Niblett and I. Thompson, *Alban's Buried Towns: an Assessment of St Albans' Archaeology to AD 1600*, Oxford 2005, 145; M. Biddle and B. Kjolbye-Biddle, 'The Origins of St Albans Abbey: Romano-British Cemetery and Anglo-Saxon Monastery', in *Alban and St Albans: Roman and Medieval Architecture, Art and Archaeology*, ed. M. Henig and P. Lindley, Leeds 2001, 45–77.
[30] K. Brannigan, *The Catuvellauni*, London 1985, 175–92; K. Dark, *Civitas to Kingdom: British Political Continuity 300–800*, Leicester 1994, 87–8; P. Drury and W. Rodwell, 'Settlement in the Later Iron Age and Roman Periods', in *The Archaeology of Essex to AD 1500*, ed. D. G. Buckley, London 1980, 59–75, at 71; K. Rutherford Davis, *Britons and Saxons: the Chiltern Region 400–700*, Chichester 1973; R. E. M. Wheeler, *London and the Saxons*, London 1935, 59–74.

A LAND OF TWO HALVES

This division within greater East Anglia between the north and east – Norfolk and north-east Suffolk – and the south and south-west – southern and south-western Suffolk and Essex – reappears in a number of other contexts, the two parts of the region sometimes forming part of the wider cultural 'provinces' already described, and sometimes not. In the later Iron Age, for example, the material culture of southern Suffolk, like that of the adjacent areas of Essex and Hertfordshire, indicates contacts with the Roman world. It features wealthy burials, furnished with grave goods including amphorae and other exotic imports; wheel-turned pottery; and the early use of coinage. All these areas were evidently linked to exchange networks which connected the south-east of England with Gaul, and ultimately with the Mediterranean. In central and northern Suffolk and in Norfolk, in contrast, wheel-thrown pottery did not really become current until after the Claudian conquest, wealthy burials with rich foreign imports are virtually unknown, and few if any sites of 'oppida' type existed. This difference in culture and economics is associated, although just how closely is uncertain, with a political division. Northern East Anglia was the land of the Iceni, whose leading families remained hostile to the Roman world even after the Conquest – famously mounting, under the leadership of Boudicca, the great revolt of AD 61. Southern East Anglia – Essex, and south-western Suffolk, together with the eastern parts of Hertfordshire – was the land of the Trinovantes.[31] In the middle Saxon period, too, the same division appears. The distribution of Ipswich Ware – made at Ipswich and probably distributed through some kind of controlled exchange system, rather than via a true market economy – also excludes southern and south-western Suffolk, as well as Essex, thus displaying a distribution curiously asymmetrical in relation to its source, perhaps suggesting that in middle Saxon times south/south-west Suffolk was not only culturally distinct from the rest of East Anglia but also *politically* separate, and part of the kingdom of Essex.

The distinction continued to appear through the Middle Ages, and well into the post-medieval period. In particular, such quintessential 'East Anglian' phenomena as round church towers, a tradition probably derived from north Germany and southern Scandinavia, as Heywood has argued;[32] or the habit of placing two or more parish churches in the same or adjacent churchyards; are most common in the north and east of the region, relatively rare in the south and west.[33] Aspects of medieval and post-medieval vernacular architecture display broadly similar

---

[31] E. Martin, 'Suffolk in the Iron Age', in *Land of the Iceni: the Iron Age in Northern East Anglia*, ed. J. Davies and T. Williamson, Norwich 1999, 44–99, at 83–90; C. Haselgrove, 'Wealth, Prestige and Power: The Dynamics of Late Iron Age Political Centralisation in England', in C. Renfrew and S. Shennan, *Ranking, Resources and Exchange: Aspects of the Archaeology of early European Society*, Cambridge 1982, 79–88; B. Cunliffe, *Iron Age Britain*, London 1995, 58–97

[32] S. Heywood, 'The Round Towers of East Anglia', in *Minsters and Parish Churches: The Local Church in Transition*, ed. J. Blair, Oxford 1988, 169–77.

[33] T. Williamson, *England's Landscape: East Anglia*, London 2006, 90–1.

patterns. Late medieval houses with queen post (as opposed to crown post) roofs, or the tendency – when open halls were being floored over during the sixteenth century – to place the chimney stack between the hall and the parlour, rather than at the lower end of the hall, are thus a feature of both northern and eastern Suffolk and of Norfolk, but are much less common in south-west Suffolk and Essex.[34] And pantiles, although discussed earlier as if they were a quintessential feature of East Anglia as a whole, have in fact a distribution which again excludes the far south and south-west of Suffolk, as well as Essex.[35]

In recent years a number of archaeologists, encouraged in part by national 'characterization' policies developed by English Heritage, have argued for the existence of long-term 'cultural provinces' in England, spanning many centuries, and manifested in a wide range of artefacts, practices and aspects of social organization. In the case of East Anglia Edward Martin, perhaps our greatest Suffolk archaeologist, has likewise drawn attention to many of the distributions mentioned above, but has argued that they represent a deeply-entrenched cultural division, stable over the centuries, which followed closely the line of the rivers Lark and Gipping – the 'Lark-Gipping Divide'.[36] Martin's work is interesting and stimulating, but – concentrating *only* on East Anglia – tends to ignore the fact that some of these distributions, such as that exhibited by 'Anglian' material culture, form part of rather wider cultural zones. It also plays down the more straightforward possibility that topographic structures and constraints may simply have shaped and funnelled patterns of exchange and interaction in a broadly similar manner in a number of different chronological contexts. In fact, rather than exhibiting a hard 'line' following the two rivers, this division between the north and south of East Anglia is better understood as a broader zone or band of discontinuity. Many of the cultural and economic distributions noted above, moreover, seem to cut off not along the line of the two river valleys but instead along the high watershed which runs to the north of the Gipping (separating its drainage basin from that of the Deben), and which continues as the watershed between the Gipping and the Blackbourne, and the Gipping and the Lark. The Lark valley and Breckland, that is, rather than forming part of 'southern' East Anglia, fall firmly within the northern portion of the region.[37]

The distinction between the two East Anglias, in other words, was thus not some arbitrary yet immobile cultural frontier, but a more general contrast between those parts of the region most deeply and regularly influenced by contact and exchange with the North Sea World (directly or via rivers draining into the Wash)

---

[34] S. Coleman and M. Barnard, 'Raised-Aisled Halls and Queen-Post Roofs', in *An Historical Atlas of Suffolk*, ed. D. Dymond and E. Martin, Ipswich 1999, 180–1.
[35] For a more detailed discussion of these patterns, Williamson, *East Anglia*, 98–106.
[36] Martin and Satchell, *Wheare Most Inclosures Be*, 214–28.
[37] As indicated, for example, in the distribution of Iron Age coins, or early Anglo-Saxon cremation cemeteries: Martin, 'Suffolk in the Iron Age', 85–91; S. West, 'The Early Anglo-Saxon Period', in *Historical Atlas*, ed. Dymond and Martin, 44–5.

and most isolated from the main currents of national life and fashions coming by land, and those parts which looked more to the south and south-east of England – to London, the Home Counties, the Channel, and ultimately northern France and Belgium. It was a division shaped both by the way that the configuration of coasts, rivers and watersheds channelled movement by water – by 'river and wold' writ large. But it was also a consequence of more basic topographic patterns, of the character of East Anglia as a peninsula, with a northern end relatively remote in terms of land contact, and of ideas exchanged face to face, from the main centres of medieval and post-medieval cultural life.

THE ORIGINS OF EAST ANGLIA

East Anglia was thus always a divided world, looking both ways. How then did it ever come to be considered as a single entity, within its current boundaries? This is a complex question which can only be considered briefly and partially here. If by East Anglia we mean, in strict terms, the lands of the North Folk and the South Folk, and exclude the land of the East Saxons, then we have the additional problem of not knowing when these territories actually achieved their modern limits. Even at the time of Domesday anomalies on the county boundaries suggest recent definition: the vill, and later parish, of Bures St Mary thus lies on the Suffolk side of the Stour, but Mount Bures lies on the Essex side, as does Bures Hamlet – although it is part of the parish of the Bures St Mary.[38] Ultimately, the roots of our modern concepts, and of our administrative divisions, lie in the political arrangements of the middle Saxon period, in the kingdom of the East Angles. Yet the kingdom of the Wuffingas, before absorption and unification in later Saxon times, may also have had uncertain boundaries, fluctuating with the fortunes of war and the vagaries of dynastic policy, embracing at times Ely and its dependencies in the Fens, but perhaps excluding – at least initially – the south-west of Suffolk, to judge from the distribution of Ipswich Ware already noted. These problems accepted, the broad lines of political geography, and how they were related to topographic structures, seem tolerably clear.

Most historians would today accept that state formation occurred, in the course of the sixth and seventh centuries, through the gradual amalgamation of a number of smaller and less hierarchical or sophisticated territories, as small tribes successively conquered and absorbed their neighbours in what Steven Bassett has aptly described as a 'glorious knock-out competition'.[39] Yet here we are faced with a conundrum, seldom addressed in the historical literature: for the core of the kingdom, the homelands of the *Wuffingas*, did not lie in the centre of East Anglia, but on its extreme southern margins. Their palace at Rendlesham, their burial ground at Sutton Hoo, and various other places associated with the first kings, such

---

[38] J. H. Round, *Victoria County History of Essex*, vol. 1, London 1902, 408.
[39] S. Bassett, 'In Search of the Origins of Anglo-Saxon Kingdoms', in *The Origins of Anglo-Saxon Kingdoms*, ed. S. Bassett, Leicester 1989, 3–27, at 26.

as the monastery at *Dommoc*, within the Roman fort at Walton, all lie at the far southern end of the Sandlings, so close to the boundary with Essex that some archaeologists have gone so far as to argue that Sutton Hoo was the burial ground of the East Saxon rather than of the East Anglian kings.[40] This territory lay, moreover, not merely on the extreme southern fringes of what was to become the East Anglian kingdom, but more importantly on the extreme southern edge of the 'Anglian' zone – of the North Sea World. In their material culture the affinities of the Wuffingas and their people lay with the north; and the earliest burials at Sutton Hoo, dating to the later sixth century, are in a style which clearly signals, in Martin Carver's words, 'affiliation to the cultural practices of Scandinavia and north Germany'.[41] More specifically, the rite of ship burial evident in Mounds 1 and 2 has its closest parallels in southern Scandinavia, in the rather similar burials thinly scattered along the coast of the Baltic and the North Sea.

But by the very time that these burials were made, at the end of the sixth centuries, as the Wuffingas were rising to dominance in the region, there was an increasing interest on the part of elites throughout England in the styles and fashions emanating not from the north, but from the land of the Franks and from the Mediterranean world.[42] In the words of John Blair, 'Suddenly, the English turned their backs on a range of cultural markers from their Germanic inheritance, and replaced them with new ones redolent of Frankish and eventually Mediterranean culture.'[43] In this context the Wuffingas were better placed geographically than any other petty dynasty with its roots in the north to control access to exchange networks with that other, more southerly world, that of the Franks and the south. They would thus have had easier access to, and greater control over access to, the kinds of prestige goods which were now increasingly in demand than could be enjoyed by neighbouring groups in East Anglia: a geographical advantage which was subsequently developed further with the growth of the great emporium at Ipswich on the river Orwell. Such an advantage would have ensured that the Wuffingas were well supplied with warriors, thus allowing their military domination of surrounding territories and also, for a short while under Rædwald, a wider political supremacy in England.

So far, perhaps, so good. But accepting this model raises some more interesting and fundamental questions about regionality, identity and the character of early state formation. If their geographical position allowed the Wuffingas to enjoy economic and therefore military advantages over their neighbours, Bassett's 'knockout competition' model would imply that the outlines of the kingdom they

---

[40] T. Williamson, *Sutton Hoo and Its Landscape: The Contexts of Monuments*, Macclesfield 2008, 17–21; Parker Pearson *et al*, 'Three Men and a Boat'.

[41] M. Carver *et al*, *Sutton Hoo: A Seventh-Century Princely Burial Ground and Its Context*, London 2005, 490.

[42] H. Geake, *The Use of Grave Goods in Conversion Period England*, Oxford 1997; idem, 'Invisible Kingdoms: The Use of Grave Goods in Seventh-Century England', *Anglo-Saxon Studies in Archaeology and History* 10, 1999, 203–15.

[43] J. Blair, *The Church in Anglo-Saxon Society*, Oxford 2005, 40.

gradually assembled ought to have been essentially unpredictable in character, the consequence of random outcomes on the battlefield. Their territory, that is, could have come to extend southwards into what is now Essex, rather than northwards into East Anglia: or could have expanded, more plausibly, to an equal extent both to the north and the south of the Deben. Yet it grew only to the north and west, into that portion of East Anglia which formed a part of the North Sea World. Such an asymmetrical pattern of growth may be telling us something important. The Wuffingas, in effect, *only* rose to supremacy over people of their own kind. This in turn may provide hints that the process of state formation in the sixth and seventh centuries was more subtle and more complex than a simple military model, or territories forged by the outcome of military battles, might suggest. Privileged access to prestige goods was used to achieve political dominance not only by attracting a body of warriors, but though gifts, dowries, bribes and other ways which worked most effectively on dynasties with whom Rædwald and his kin shared familial links and certain aspects of a common culture, and which were correspondingly less effective in maintaining an ascendancy over neighbours with a different cultural background dwelling to the south.

The coherent kingdoms which emerged in the middle Saxon period, and the administrative units which developed as England became unified, generally had boundaries which followed not sparsely-settled interfluvial zones, but the hard, definable lines provided by rivers. We do not know when southern and south-western Suffolk became fully incorporated into East Anglia – whether it was before or (more probably) after the reconquest from the Danes. But its distinctive, 'south-eastern' character was perpetuated through the medieval and post-medieval period, and survives today. 'Constable Country', the Stour valley with its textile towns trading with northern France and Belgium, their late medieval wealth proudly displayed in huge churches and in flamboyant timber-framed buildings roofed with plain tiles, is a world away from the land of Norwich, or even that of the Suffolk 'Sandlings'. East Anglia has always been a land divided between the North Sea World and the Channel-focused south-east of England. Yet this, paradoxically, in large part explains the fact that it *is* a recognizable entity: it owes its very existence to the peculiar advantages which its first rulers gained from living close to the junction of both.

— Chapter 3 —

CITIES, COGS AND COMMERCE: ARCHAEOLOGICAL APPROACHES TO THE MATERIAL CULTURE OF THE NORTH SEA WORLD

Brian Ayers

THIS CHAPTER EXPLORES the potential of disparate material culture to increase understanding of the medieval North Sea world, be it in the form of topography, buildings, excavated structures and features, artefacts or palaeo-environmental data. It concentrates on the high medieval period, that is from approximately 1200 to 1500, and, perhaps inevitably, focuses on the evidence for commerce, and particularly the greatest product of that commerce, the urban medieval trading community. Hence its title which, although deliberately alliterative, is designed to highlight the main argument: that while the physical expression of medieval communities can obviously be explored archaeologically, so too can interaction between communities and thereby the economic and even social underpinning of those communities.

While a range of archaeological examples are drawn upon, these cannot pretend to be all-embracing or even representative of the approaches currently in train. Archaeology is the great bridge discipline; it is concerned with the humanities, social sciences and sciences. It can address issues of ethnicity, migration, state formation, social organization and technological development. New methodologies appear constantly, such as, for example, isotope analysis, which can now identify the locality wherein an individual spent his or her formative years, and application of which in large enough numbers to reliably dated medieval graveyard assemblages would have a profound effect upon our understanding of population movements. Archaeologists are studying urban and rural landscapes on the margins and hinterlands of the North Sea and even recovering data for prehistoric landscapes on the sea bed.[1]

Medieval archaeologists, however, do have a problem, which Tim Champion

---

[1] V. L. Gaffney, S. Fitch and D. N. Smith, *Europe's Lost World: The Rediscovery of Doggerland*, CBA Research Report 160, York 2009.

has, perhaps unkindly, characterized as 'the tyranny of the historical record'.[2] Medieval archaeology is still a young discipline (it is only a little over fifty years since the launch of the journal of that name) and, while its practitioners would ignore historical evidence at their peril, it has been claimed that engagement with historians can be an exercise where 'the debate between documentary and archaeological history is more a monologue than a dialogue'.[3] This is probably as much the fault of archaeologists as historians in that archaeologists constantly strive to fit their data to the historical framework, often inevitably failing to do more than illustrate the past, rather than recognizing that both archaeological methodologies and archaeological results are frequently better placed to address such big themes as ethnicity or spatial organization of settlement. Here they can bring new and different information, rather than merely complementing existing frameworks established through use of historical data.

Although, therefore, this chapter is keen to demonstrate that the archaeological approach is one that can make a major contribution to medieval studies in general – and that of the North Sea world in particular – it could still be argued that much of what follows may nevertheless *seem* like mere historical illustration. However, there is a point here too. Archaeological study of material culture brings direct contact with the *physicality* of the medieval world, enabling a more acute awareness of the resource needs and the living conditions of ordinary people in the Middle Ages as well as often providing a greater understanding of the environmental, economic and social contexts within which much decision-making must have been made. It is this physicality which is explored here, using the themes of cog, city and commerce to highlight certain archaeological approaches to the medieval North Sea world. By way of conclusion the paper suggests some potential research areas, of interest to both archaeologists *and* historians.

COGS

It is necessary at the outset to consider the sea itself and the obstacles and opportunities presented by that sea. It is important to recognize the technological challenges faced by peoples wishing to move and trade across the waters between continental Europe and the British Isles. That such movement and commerce had been undertaken for millennia does not negate the continual innovation needed to progress towards the maritime bulk carrier that was the cog of the late Middle Ages. Two ways in which archaeology contributes to the study of such technological innovation is firstly through the examination of largely undocumented medieval trading boats and ships while, secondly, offering a critique of information drawn from historical sources. Thus, ship development can be charted through physical

---

[2] T. C. Champion, 'Medieval Archaeology and the Tyranny of the Historical Record', in *From the Baltic to the Black Sea: Studies in Medieval Archaeology*, ed. D. Austin and L. Alcock, London 1990, 79–95.

[3] D. Austin, 'The "Proper Study" of Medieval Archaeology', in ibid., 9–42.

examination of the remains of a variety of vessels: the Viking Age *karv* (used for cargo but originally a warship and exemplified by the Gokstad ship now in Oslo[4]), for instance, was followed by the eleventh-century *knarr*, perhaps a more purpose-built Scandinavian cargo ship as in the example recovered from Skuldelev fjord in Denmark.[5] Archaeologists still have a problem identifying the *hulc*, apparently a keel-less vessel, its earliest form perhaps dating from the eighth century as in the famous example of the Utrecht ship.[6] A brick from mid fifteenth- century deposits at Brinkum, Lower Saxony, appears to show a *hulc*,[7] and the likely importance of such vessels to North Sea communities is shown by many towns seemingly using them as illustrations in stylized form on their seals, as depicted on the thirteenth-century seal of New Shoreham in Sussex.[8] Numerous illustrations of other ships are known – examples being graffiti depicting ships which appear on buildings such as Norwich cathedral or Wiveton church, Norfolk[9] – but, until the wreck of a *hulc* is recovered, its form and indeed very existence as a type remains unproven.[10] Archaeology can nevertheless characterize the most developed merchant ship of the high medieval period which was the cog.

Cogs were high-deck, flat-bottomed trading vessels which, because of their design, had an enhanced cargo capacity. However, unlike more shallow draft Scandinavian-style vessels, they required deep water quayside facilities. Although the origins of the cog may well date to the Carolingian period, the fully-developed trading vessel, capable of transporting bulk goods across the North Sea, only came into being in the thirteenth century. Unfortunately, while cogs could be seen on town seals (such as that for Stralsund of 1329),[11] it was difficult to understand their capacity, structure,[12] or indeed, seaworthiness without a vessel to study.

This deficiency was remedied in 1962 with the fortuitous discovery of an almost intact cog in the muds of the River Weser at Bremen in Germany. Initially uncovered by machine excavation, the ship proved to be one lost due to an exceptional flood which washed it from its moorings as it neared completion in a Bremen shipyard in 1380 (shipwrights' tools were found on board but the boat had yet to be

[4] R. W. Unger, *The Ship in the Medieval Economy 600–1600*, London and Montreal 1980, 88 and fig. 7.
[5] Ibid., 91 and fig. 10.
[6] Ibid., 58ff and fig. 4.
[7] R. Bärenfänger and D. Ellmers, 'Der Backstein und das Schiff', *Archäologie in Niedersachsen* 2, 1999, 124–6, fig. 1.
[8] Ibid., fig. 2.
[9] M. Champion, 'Reading the Writing on the Wall: the Norfolk Medieval Graffiti Survey', *Current Archaeology* 256, 2011, 36–41.
[10] '...many now refute that such a distinctive [hulc] tradition ever existed', Joseph Flatman, review of O. Crumlin-Pedersen, *Archaeology and the Sea in Scandinavia and Britain: A Personal Account*, Copenhagen 2009, *Medieval Archaeology* 55, 2011, 357.
[11] Unger, *The Ship in the Medieval Economy*, 161.
[12] Archaeological examination of actual cogs was necessary in order to refute the historical thesis that cogs were essentially a German, frame-led innovation rather than a development of the clinker, shell-first tradition. See summary in R. van de Noort, *North Sea Archaeologies: A Maritime Biography 10,000 BC-AD 1500*, Oxford 2011, 172.

PLATE 1 Reconstruction of the Bremen cog (photograph: Betty Arndt).

fitted out for a voyage). Heeled over in the mud, the starboard side survives almost to its full height, including stern-castle, enabling full-scale reconstruction (Plate 1). While attractive and interesting for an assessment of seagoing quality, the extraordinary preservation of the cog meant that its carrying capacity could also be established, this 60-ton ship, some 23 metres long and 7.6 metres wide, being able to hold between 143 and 160 cubic metres of cargo depending upon the load.[13]

Subsequent discoveries, although not as well preserved as the Bremen example, suggest that 80 tons was about average for such a seagoing vessel in the fourteenth-century North Sea.[14] This meant that it could penetrate the wider and deeper rivers of towns inland from the coast, as at Bremen, but also such ports as Boston on the

[13] K.-P. Kiedel and U. Schnall (eds), *The Hanse Cog of 1380*, Bremerhaven 1985. See also D. Ellmers, 'The Cog of Bremen and Related Boats', in *The Archaeology of Medieval Ships and Harbours in Northern Europe*, ed. S. McGrail, BAR, International Series, no. 66, 1979, 1–15.

[14] Examples include those recovered in excavations in 1976–78 at Vejby and Kollerup in Denmark which, together with a discovery at Kolding, enable a chronological series of cogs ranging from c.1200 to c.1375 to be determined, O. Crumlin-Pederson, 'To Be or Not To Be a Cog: The Bremen Cog in Perspective', *International Journal of Nautical Archaeology* 29.2, 2000, 230–46. This paper includes a useful survey of cog finds.

Witham or Lübeck on the Trave. Trade could therefore be conducted between entrepôts with extensive local and regional networks (King's Lynn alone served at least eight counties of central and eastern England)[15] without the need for transhipment.[16]

So far, so obvious perhaps. However, the point of this paper is to try to show how such archaeological discoveries not only provide information otherwise not recoverable, but also, given emerging archaeological methodologies, can pose questions, and suggest answers, both to short-term innovation and long-term trends. A good example of archaeological research throwing up new ideas is the notion of 'the AD 1000 fish event horizon' whereby a combination of techniques (analysis of fish bones from large urban assemblages together with stable isotope analysis of human bones recovered from sites in the coastal zone) shows a marked shift at this time from consumption of freshwater to marine fish.[17] The work, when allied to the growth in bulk carriers such as the emerging cog, enables argument that about AD 1000 there was therefore a change from transport of prestige goods between élites to carriage of more bulk commodities such as fish, grain, timber and wool, in part addressing the needs of growing urban communities. Multi-disciplinary investigation, of which the fish bone analysis is but one example, of the complex archaeology of these towns and cities within the North Sea region, both above and below ground, together with an increasing awareness of the potential of the rural landscape (particularly the changing coastal zone) to provide information, therefore offers much new evidence for an increased historical understanding.

ENVIRONMENTAL AND TOPOGRAPHICAL CHANGE IN CITIES, TOWNS, PORTS AND THE WIDER LANDSCAPE

Human exploitation of the North Sea zone changed with the growth of towns, especially those established around the turn of the first millennium in marginal estuarine or coastal locations – places on the east coast of England such as King's

---

[15] Lynn was chosen as a staple port in the later fourteenth century principally because 'various streams ran through the counties of Warwick, Leicester, Northampton, Rutland, Bedford, Bucks., Huntingdonshire and Cambridgeshire, by which wool and other goods could be conveyed more easily and cheaply to Lynn than to any other port', *Rotuli Parliamentum* quoted in H. Clarke, 'The Town's Hinterland and Trade Connexions', in H. Clarke and A. Carter (eds), *Excavations in King's Lynn 1963-1970*, Society for Medieval Archaeology Monograph 7, 444-49.

[16] Some Nordic vessels could carry as much cargo as – or even more than – early cogs. The so-called 'Big Ship of Bergen', found in 1955, excavated in 1962 and dating to 1188, was one of these, Crumlin-Pederson, 'To Be or Not To Be a Cog', 244.

[17] Van de Noort, *North Sea Archaeologies*, 86-7, summarizing the work of J. H. Barrett, A. M. Locker and C. M. Roberts, '"Dark Age Economics" Revisited: The English Fish Bone Evidence AD 600-1600', *Antiquity* 78, 2004, 618-36. Barrett et al go so far as to conclude that 'this intensification in marine fishing [herring and cod] probably ran counter to climatically determined patterns in fish abundance. As the naissance of intensive, probably commercial, marine fishing, the century between AD 950 and 1050 can now be pinpointed as the ultimate origin of today's fishing crisis ...', in J. H. Barrett, A. M. Locker and C. M. Roberts, 'The Origins of Intensive Marine Fishing in Medieval Europe: The English Evidence', *Proceedings of the Royal Society B*, 2004, 2417-21.

(formerly Bishop's) Lynn (by about 1100), Boston (about the same time or soon thereafter) and Hull (before 1200).[18] Each of these towns needed to control and exploit the water which provided its commercial *raison d'être*, leading to activities the investigation of which, over the last fifty years, has not only opened up an entirely new area for study – that of waterfront archaeology – but, in so doing, has provided insights into the physical growth of towns, has enhanced awareness of technological innovation in the Middle Ages, has illuminated the use and organization of urban space, has uncovered raw material which gives a greater understanding of the economics of medieval trade and, lastly but importantly, has enabled development of methodologies.

These seem like wide-ranging assertions but there is now considerable evidence for all of them from a range of excavations on both sides of the North Sea, supported by allied studies such as buildings' archaeology. Exploration of the urban waterfront can be said to have started in Norway in 1955 when, in the aftermath of a disastrous fire through a large part of the surviving hanseatic warehousing of *Bryggen* in Bergen, excavations by Asjbørn Herteig were able to demonstrate that the distinctive urban geography of the port owed its existence to the manner in which port facilities had developed from the Viking Age onward.[19] In addition, work subsequently has established that the organized system of double tenements in Bergen, separated by a common passageway and leading to a common wharf, was originally created in the first part of the twelfth century.[20] It was already known from the surviving Urban Code or Town Law of Bergen that streets were supposed to be of certain widths but it became clear from archaeological evidence, where timber-laced roads survived to be measured, that these norms were not implemented.

This mismatch between documentary and physical evidence was complemented by the insights gained into the growth of Bergen out into the harbour of Vågen. Here, excavation showed that the town had advanced considerably into the water, gaining ground which was subsequently developed. It was a process which soon became apparent elsewhere. The first such work in England was a relatively minor excavation by Helen Parker (subsequently Helen Clarke) in the courtyard of Thoresby College, King's Lynn, in 1963 which nevertheless found evidence for an early fourteenth-century wharf nearly 60 metres east of the present-day bank of the River Ouse.[21] This was followed by massive campaigns in London[22] as well as

---

[18] For Boston and King's Lynn, M. Beresford, *New Towns of the Middle Ages*, London 1967, 463, 467. For Hull, E. Gillett and K. A. MacMahon, *A History of Hull*, Oxford 1980, 2.

[19] A. Herteig, 'The Excavation of Bryggen, Bergen, Norway', in *Recent Archaeological Excavations in Europe*, ed. R. Bruce-Mitford, London 1975, 65–89.

[20] I. Øye, 'The Infrastructure of Bergen in the Middle Ages and Early Modern Period to c.1700', in *Lübecker Kolloquium zur Stadtarchäologies im Hanseraum IV: Die Infrastruktur*, ed. M. Gläser, Lübeck 2004, 513–29.

[21] H. Parker, 'A Medieval Wharf in Thoresby College Courtyard, King's Lynn', *Medieval Archaeology* 9, 1965, 94–104.

[22] Much of the work is synthesized in G. Milne, *The Port of Medieval London*, Stroud 2003, with details of numerous reports in the bibliography.

work in ports such as Hull, Dordrecht, Utrecht and Trondheim. The work at Hull, for instance, produced exceptional survival of timber revetments used for wharfage alongside the haven of the River Hull, together with evidence for a relatively rapid infilling of the river edge east of High Street.[23]

The infilling, necessitated by a combination of greater draught of shipping requiring deeper water for anchorage together with rivalry for prime commercial positions, led to substantial urban topographic change, nowhere better seen than in London.[24] It also led to a reverse archaeological stratigraphy – as tenements extended by infilling the water's edge, greater and greater amounts of infill material were used, the latest deposits therefore being the deepest. The large timber revetments, as well as providing wharves, separated these deposits while the revetments themselves, constructed of wood, were capable of close dating by dendrochronological analysis. In Hull, for example, such analysis of timbers for the largest of the revetments recovered suggested a construction date of 1323 ± 9.[25]

This precision, within a context of frequent rebuilding, means that assemblages of waste material, which are both profuse and well preserved in the waterlogged conditions, can be dated much more closely than on other sites, with consequent refinement of typologies elsewhere. While this does little to enlighten those historians who find archaeological data too imprecise, it does enhance understanding of that area of chronological development for which archaeological material is particularly good, namely long-term structural change. Trends can be identified, isolated, defined and characterized. As Grenville Astill has observed, careful assessment and questioning of rubbish can yield important results, as at Lincoln where sixteenth-century waste assemblages indicate 'a pronounced change in the conformation of sheep and cattle: the muscle-bearing parts of the animal seem to have increased, while other parts of the body, such as the skulls, remained the same size. Such evidence is thought to indicate attempts at selective breeding, and predates the well-documented attempts during the "Agricultural Revolution".'[26]

Towns, of course, did not grow in isolation; they were often first and foremost commercial entities, responding to developing economic circumstances. Such is the argument put forward for the development of 's-Hertogenbosch in the Netherlands, a *novum oppidum* which grew from 'an insignificant settlement around a ducal court around 1200 to a middle-sized European town of ... between 13,000 and 14,000 inhabitants around 1350', a development recognized by historians, who nevertheless remain 'unsure about the details and causes, partly due to the scarceness of written evidence. The archaeological evidence is able to fill

---

[23] B. Ayers, *Excavations at Chapel Lane Staith 1978*, East Riding Archaeologist 5, Hull Old Town Report Series 3, Hull 1979.
[24] Milne, *Port of Medieval London*, fig. 7.
[25] J. Hillam, 'Tree-Ring Analysis of the Timbers', in Ayers, *Excavations at Chapel Lane*, 38.
[26] G. Astill, 'Archaeology and the Late-Medieval Urban Decline', in *Towns in Decline AD 100-1600*, ed. T. R. Slater, Aldershot 2000, 214-234

this gap ...'.[27] The importance of commerce, exploiting the productivity resulting from the new agricultural system of 'plaggen wirtschaft' (massive manuring of previously poorly-performing soils), led to infrastructural development in the town such as 'canalising of watercourses, the use and adaptation of the natural rivers as town moats ... and the construction of well-organised waterfronts' (evidence for the last being uncovered in some of the staggering number of 120 large rescue excavations since 1977).[28]

Engineered change did not just take place in towns. Archaeological survey and excavation on both sides of the North Sea is demonstrating how marginal landscapes were protected from the sea and exploited. A section through the seabank at Clenchwarton in Norfolk recovered pottery of eleventh-century date but detailed analysis of foraminifera and mollusca also showed that the bank was constructed in sections between low tides.[29] Similar dates have been recorded for the construction of such sea defences in Flanders and Zeeland with twelfth-century dates for structures in northern and southern Holland. Dates in the eleventh century have been established for seabanks in the Wadden Sea area and Niedersachsen.[30] The dating is interesting because, although the role of major institutions (notably the Church) in building and maintaining these defences is known from documentation, initiation of the works often predates ecclesiastical involvement, implying locally-derived solutions in many instances, only subsequently regularized through institutional activity.

Protected land could thereafter be colonized or 'socialized', sometimes through the construction of further monuments such as the *terpen* still extant in Friesland in the Netherlands. Archaeological work indicates that the origin of these dwelling mounds can date to the middle of the first millennium BC although establishment of mounds continued until the beginning of the second millennium AD. Simplistic models relating terp development to periods of marine regression have now been replaced by recognition of a more complex series of factors. Van de Noort points out that 'the availability of saltmarsh for stockbreeding, alongside local fluctuations in sea-levels and the occurrence of storm floods, as well as socio-political and economic choices to enlarge the terp to increase the size of the village and arable land, all played their role in the evolution of the terpen.'[31]

The use of environmental data, as at Clenchwarton, can be extended to examination of waste assemblages recovered from port excavations, to explore evidence

---

[27] H. Janssen, "'s-Hertogenbosch, a "novum oppidum" and Its Hinterland, 1200–1350 – The Archaeological Evidence for Growth and Stagnation of Medieval Towns', in *Archaeology of Medieval Towns in the Baltic and North Sea Area*, ed. N. Engberg et al., National Museum Studies in Archaeology and History 17, Copenhagen 2009, 27–49.

[28] Ibid., 36.

[29] A. Crowson, T. Lane and J. Reeve (eds), 'Fenland Management Project Excavations 1991–1995', *Lincolnshire Archaeology and Heritage Reports Series* 3, 2000.

[30] Summarized in van de Noort, *North Sea Archaeologies*, 118.

[31] Ibid., 115.

for environmental change or exploitation. England, isolated from the continent by the North Sea, has useful archaeology for the study of environmental change. The advent of the rabbit to these shores has recently been established by work in Norfolk as occurring unequivocally during the Roman period (rabbit skeletons were found in a Roman context; the animals had been butchered with their paws removed – pawless rabbits cannot burrow and therefore were not intrusive animals from contexts of later centuries).[32] Work in Norwich has recovered walnut shells in eleventh-century contexts, predating the earliest recorded walnut trees in the country by five centuries, and seeds of grape, the earliest post-Roman record for the area.[33]

Surprisingly precise data is available from work in towns for obtaining a greater understanding of local environmental changes. In London, for instance, sediments of two successive fourteenth-century deposits showed that the later material had a marked increase of those diatoms (microscopic unicellular algae) associated with polluted water, suggesting increasing pollution in the adjacent River Fleet. It may be coincidence but this observation dovetails neatly with known demands by Edward III to the mayor of London for cleansing of the area.[34]

Good survival of organic material can be indicative of both trade and environmental management. Casks recovered at Blaydes Staith in Hull and dating to 1490 (Plate 2) were shown to be made of Baltic timber, while forty-three out of forty-four fourteenth-century coffins recovered from the cemetery of the Augustinian friary in the same port were made from Baltic oak.[35] Buildings archaeology at the Guildhall in Boston in 2006 demonstrated that the roof timbers of the building date from c.1390 and are also of Baltic oak.[36] Coppicing is frequently evident from examination of excavated timbers, implying sourcing of wood from managed forests.

Even social differentiation can be determined by environmental material. An interesting study in Amsterdam (in seventeenth-century deposits) was able to suggest identification of Jewish-owned or occupied properties compared with non-Jewish ones, a non-Jewish property being defined as one with 5 per cent or more of pig bones in the animal bone assemblages recovered from its cesspits.[37]

---

[32] Anon, 'Unearthing the Ancestral Rabbit', *British Archaeology* 86, 2006, 7. See also N. Sykes and J. Curl, 'The Rabbit' in *Extinctions and Invasions: A Social History of British Fauna*, ed. T. O'Connor and N. Sykes, Oxford 2010, 116–126.

[33] P. Murphy, 'Plant Macrofossils' in B. Ayers and P. Murphy, *A Waterfront Excavation at Whitefriars Street Car Park, Norwich, 1979. East Anglian Archaeology* 17, 1983, 40–44.

[34] J. Schofield and A. Vince, *Medieval Towns*, London 2003, 213.

[35] Ibid., 171, 275.

[36] K. Giles and J. Clark, 'St Mary's Guildhall, Boston, Lincolnshire: The Archaeology of a Medieval "Public" Building', *Medieval Archaeology* 55, 2011, 226–256. I am grateful for the observation concerning the Baltic provenance of the timber to a personal communication from Paul Richards.

[37] F. G. Ijzereef, 'Social Differentiation from Animal Bone Studies', in *Diet and Crafts in Towns*, ed. D. Serjeantson and T. Waldron, BAR British Series 199, 1989, 41–53.

PLATE 2 Casks of Baltic timber c.1490 perhaps used for storing live fish, Blaydes Staith, Hull (photograph: Bill Marsden, Humberside Archaeology).

TECHNOLOGICAL INNOVATION

While examination and consideration of waste, linked to ever tighter chronologies, is therefore an increasingly informative archaeological approach, so too is the study of technological innovation. The potential of archaeological discovery to increase understanding of when new ideas and processes were implemented is illustrated well by the work of Gustav Milne and others on the timbers recovered from various excavations at the London Thames waterfront. Clear statements, with obvious implications for understanding of the history of technology, can now be made as in: 'Neither the saw nor the standard mortise and tenon joint were known before the Norman Conquest; nor were they in common use until over a century later. As such, they do not therefore represent features directly introduced by the Normans in the late eleventh century.'[38] Other observations include a typology of revetment construction which noted an increasing medieval awareness of the stresses to which such structures were subjected and thereby the development of constructional techniques which resisted pressure of infilled earth on one side and differential tidal pressure on the other (perhaps best exemplified by the features recorded at Trig Lane, London[39]). Reuse of house timbers in waterfront revetments has also enabled a study of the development of domestic timber-framing from the eleventh century onward,[40] a study impossible to conduct with standing structures as such early examples no longer exist.

Technological innovation was not confined to revetting of banks but extended to harbour construction. Wooden caissons were manufactured on dry land in Bergen in the thirteenth century and sunk, weighed down by stones, to form foundations for harbour walls.[41] In Lübeck, very much part of the North Sea world even if on the Baltic, the lack of urban development space led to specific infilling of an embayment of the River Trave with deliberate dumping on a hill-slope towards river meadows at the foot of St Peter's Hill, an area of some 13 hectares.[42] This extensive location required some 3 to 5 metres depth of material in order to provide for housing and an extension of the commercial waterfront. Difficult excavations in 1978 at Große Petersgrube within standing buildings uncovered evidence for a deliberate policy of thirteenth-century land reclamation, material being carefully deposited and held in place by horizontal lacing timbers.[43] This astonishing procedure, over a period of some forty years, is completely undocumented, but its effects can be seen in the standing structures where, notwithstanding the care taken with the infilling, subsidence during construction for a seventeenth-century house led to straightening of the gable as work progressed.

SOCIAL IDENTITY

Lübeck is a town where the impact of archaeology has been very great over the last thirty-five years. It is also one where, since 1997, the local archaeological organi-

---

[38] G. Milne, 'Timber Building Techniques in London c.900–1400', *London & Middlesex Archaeological Society Special Paper* 15, 1992, 131.
[39] G. and C. Milne, 'Medieval Waterfront Development at Trig Lane, London', *London & Middlesex Archaeological Society Special Paper* 5, 1982.
[40] T. Brigham, 'Reused House Timbers from the Billingsgate Site, 1982-3' in *London & Middlesex Archaeological Society Special Paper* 15, 86–105.
[41] S. Myrvoll, 'Vågen and Bergen: The Changing Waterfront and the Structure of the Medieval Town', in *Waterfront Archaeology: Proceedings of the Third International Conference on Waterfront Archaeology held at Bristol 23–26 September 1988*, ed. G. L. Good et al, CBA Research Report 74, 1991, 150–161. See fig. 19.4.
[42] M. Gläser, 'The Emergence of Lübeck as a Medieval Metropolis' in *Archaeology of Medieval Towns*, ed. Engberg, 79-92. See fig 8.
[43] W. Erdmann, 'Hochmittelalterliche Baulandgewinnung in Lübeck und das problem beider Gründungssiedlungen: Erste Befunde aus den Gebieten Große Petersgrube und An der Untertrave', *Lübecker Schriften zur Archäologie und Kulturgeschichte* 6, 1982, 7–31.

zation, Bereich Archäologie, has organized a biennial conference entitled *Stadtarchäologie in Hanseraum*. Eight conferences have been held so far, in English and German, with representatives of some forty towns invited to address themes chosen by the organizers, publication of the proceedings following promptly at each successive meeting. The definition of *Hanseraum* is generous – it includes places such as Cork, Norwich and, on one occasion, even Tours, which were hardly hanseatic cities. Topics for discussion have been as wide-ranging (trade, housing, urban infrastructure, for instance) and can, on occasion, lead to repetition ('defences' was a subject where photographs of usually restored walls were all too common). Each of these topics also runs the risk of characterization as stereotypically archaeological – one can count the pots, draw the houses and photograph the fortified gateways.

However, a recent conference discussed 'luxury and lifestyle' and not only resulted in some of the sprightliest debate but also one of the largest publications.[44] The problem, of course, was one of definition, particularly when it came to luxury. While various historical sources testify to luxurious living (and sometimes legislated against it or for its control) and while numerous high-status buildings survive in towns throughout northern Europe indicating an urban affluence at least amongst the élite, it is exceptionally difficult to determine how far through society a feeling of luxury permeated. Time itself is a luxury for those who do not have any, such as hard-pressed servants, and yet the provision of a small room for such a servant in the garret of a grand mercantile house might, within such a context, constitute a luxurious existence for that individual. In addition, the archaeological recovery of luxurious items frequently does not accord with known historically affluent locations – excavations in Bruges, for instance, at the *Prinsenhof* site in 2004, the location of the fifteenth-century court of the count of Flanders, were remarkable for revealing ceramic and other finds of a type common to other sites in the city. Here, apart from a few stove-tile fragments, known throughout northern Europe, there was little to suggest high-status living.[45] This necessarily raises one question: what exactly *did* constitute a high-status site in the Middle Ages? Were expressions of such status confined to outward demonstrations of show – structural materials and clothing, for instance – rather than through more quotidian existence?

However, notwithstanding such awkward questions, it became self-evident at the Lübeck conference that the matter of lifestyle in the medieval period, far from being a difficult subject with which to engage using archaeological evidence, was actually significantly enhanced by questioning of material culture. In Hull, for instance, work within the medieval town has been extensive enough to enable mapping of key artefacts such as domestic painted window glass, stone architectural features (in a region devoid of building stone) and fine vessel glass, the results being

---

[44] M. Gläser (ed.), *Lübecker Kolloquium zur Stadtarchäologie im Hanseraum VI: Luxus und Lifestyle*, Lübeck 2008.

[45] H. de Witte, 'Lifestyle! Luxury in Medieval Bruges. The Value of the Archaeological Contribution', in *Lübecker Kolloquium VI: Luxus und Lifestyle*, ed. Gläser, 105–120.

compared, in true interdisciplinary fashion, with records of taxable wealth.[46] This traditional methodological approach was complemented by more advanced concepts such as that adopted with material from Schleswig. Here, it was argued that the sampling methodology enabled sufficient differentiation of goods to suggest both personal preference and cultural norms. Thus, perhaps unsurprisingly, it was postulated that luxurious items not only enabled individuals to mark out their own status but also that groups could similarly use goods to demonstrate their heterogeneity to the outside world. Luxurious items could be both 'markers and makers'.[47]

Archaeological study of the use of goods to express social identity is a mechanism that enables assessment of medieval society without the biases inherent in documentary evidence. The data has its own biases of course: differential survival rates of differing materials; intrusive mixing of deposits and their contents; truncation by later development; the sampling policies of archaeologists themselves. Nevertheless, pertinent questions can be asked, especially when set against the context of discovery and examination of locally-available resources, questions which can seek to explore the likely social composition of locations, the richness or otherwise of the inhabitants, and their likely actions as determined by their environment, its structures and their contents.

Even individual discoveries can suggest significant implications. Work at Cinema City in Norwich in 2005 uncovered part of a fourteenth-century stone mould for the manufacture of large openwork bronze pilgrim badges showing the Annunciation, almost certainly for the pilgrim market in Walsingham (Plate 3). Not only has an intact badge made from this very mould been found in London but the style of the craftsman, presumably one based in Norwich, shows that he (or she) was also making moulds for the shrine of St Thomas at Canterbury.[48] The likelihood of regional centres of industrial production by a few craftspeople, rather than localized production by many, is thus heightened by this discovery.

The Schleswig methodology mentioned above seeks to use archaeological material to enter the minds of urban people in the Middle Ages. Is this

PLATE 3 Fourteenth-century pilgrim badge mould depicting the Annunciation, Norwich (© NPS Archaeology).

---

[46] D. H. Evans, 'Luxury in the Medieval Town? Reflections on the Evidence for Lifestyles and Wealth Distribution in Hull from 1300 to 1700', in ibid., 63–94. See figs. 3, 7 & 8.
[47] U. Müller, 'Luxus und Lifestyle – Konzepte, Funde und Befunde zum Beispiel von Schleswig', in ibid., 357–76, at 357–61.
[48] Personal communication from the late Geoff Egan.

valid? Can inanimate objects be used in such a manner? The answer to both questions is almost certainly yes provided that the context of the material is also recorded and, if not fully understood, at least considered from as broad a basis as possible. In support of this argument are two pieces of recent research from Norwich, one involving later medieval work at the cathedral, and the other an analysis of mercantile buildings in the city.

The Carnary College at Norwich cathedral was founded by Bishop Salmon in 1316 immediately west and north of the west front of the great church. Eric Fernie has demonstrated that its designer drew inspiration from imperial architecture, notably a palatial lineage starting at Charlemagne's chapel in Aachen (c.800) and proceeding through later buildings such as Sainte-Chapelle in Paris (1240s) and St Stephen's chapel, Westminster (1292).[49] Roberta Gilchrist has acknowledged the 'imperial imagery' so used, but also suggests that the building draws upon the 'iconography of death'. She argues that the 'proportions and form of the Carnary chapel are strongly reminiscent of a reliquary or a saints' shrine', being an architectural expression of an artefact familiar to people at the time of its construction.[50] The implication that can be drawn, therefore, from this surviving example of material culture, is one of a popular sensibility rich in awareness and understanding of visual allusion, a sensibility that inhabited a built environment which could be 'read' by much of the population. In a similar manner, and again following archaeological analysis of a building, it could be argued that the reuse of smashed stone coffins in the structure of the (now ruined) carnary at Bury St Edmunds was designed to foster mental association of the burial of the body with the structure housing the institution which prayed for the soul.

Similarly, an archaeological examination by Chris King of the surviving mercantile houses of Norwich has produced most interesting results. At the level of individual houses, he can suggest, for instance, that Agnes, the widow of Nicolas Sotherton who died shortly before the completion of the 15th-century works at Strangers Hall, placed her own head on the central boss of the entrance porch to her hall, thus indicating that she was now mistress of the estate (the head is carved with a widow's veil). More generally, he also concludes that the surprising profusion of somewhat anachronistic great halls in surviving large 15th-century merchants' houses goes a long way towards explaining factionalism in late medieval Norwich. The city was a notoriously disputatious place, perhaps fostered by the need for the various mercantile guilds to meet in private houses rather than common halls as in London or York. The opportunities for exclusion and favouritism were that much greater, an archaeological assessment of physical evidence thus suggesting, at least partially, causes for social strain in the city.[51]

---

[49] E. Fernie, *An Architectural History of Norwich Cathedral*, Oxford 1993, 182.
[50] R. Gilchrist, *Norwich Cathedral Close: The Evolution of the English Cathedral Landscape*, Woodbridge 2005, 250.
[51] C. King, *House and Society in an English Provincial City: The Archaeology of Urban Households in Norwich, 1370–1700*, unpublished University of Nottingham PhD thesis, 2006.

COMMERCE AND THE TRANSMISSION OF IDEAS

It could be argued that these examples of possible approaches to the construction of monuments within the urban environment stray from a consideration of East Anglia and the North Sea. The use of iconography, however, was not exclusively English and must have been influenced by the movement of ideas, a movement facilitated by vessels such as the cog. It is a movement whose occurrence is suggested by archaeological analysis as well as historical research. As an example, a religious impetus which is otherwise only known on the continent, that of the followers of Lambert de Beguin, the *beguines*, can be suggested in at least one English location by examination of physical evidence in Norwich. Beguinages are extant in places such as Bruges and Ghent and were known in northern France but are undocumented in England. However, the eighteenth-century historian Blomefield records (from a lost source) that a medieval community of women lived in a house in the corner of the churchyard of St Peter Hungate. A fifteenth-century building survives here, known now as the Briton's Arms and with direct access to the churchyard. Chris King, once again, has examined the building and determined that, although small, it was organized with numerous heated rooms in the manner of a hostel or a small monastic community.[52] Buildings' archaeology here can imply a commonality of religious sensibility with continental Europe that is otherwise missing from the historical record.

Thus far, this article has sought to indicate that it is possible to explore aspects of the physical environment in such a manner as to view medieval urban society and intellectual contact across the North Sea in ways not necessarily readily available to the historian. However, currently developing archaeological methodologies also enable the acquisition of both new information for, and new insights into, the past.

Perhaps some of the most exciting archaeological research is that which is engaging with state and urban formation in the first millennium across northern Europe. This is outside the temporal scope of this paper but it is worth noting in passing its influential emphasis upon gaining an understanding of rural hinterlands, their developing economies, their commercial contacts and their growing need for urban centres.[53] Within eastern England formative work has been undertaken by Andy Hutcheson providing a pre-Conquest context for the later development of King's Lynn. His assessment of the data from a range of so-called 'productive sites', notably his use of coin evidence, has enabled discussion of early medieval settlement and governance.[54] Across the North Sea, similar work exploring archaeological evidence for economic growth and thereby market sites is also being undertaken, as at Groß Strömkendorf on the north German Baltic coast.[55]

---

[52] Ibid., 156–7.
[53] D. Perring, *Town and Country in England: Frameworks for Archaeological Research*, CBA Research Report 134, York 2002.
[54] A. R. J. Hutcheson, 'The Origins of King's Lynn? Control of Wealth on the Wash Prior to the Norman Conquest', *Medieval Archaeology* 50, 2006, 71–104.
[55] A. Tummuscheit, 'Groß Strömkendorf: a Market Site of the Eighth Century on the Baltic Sea Coast',

This work on the rural context of towns is as pertinent for the high medieval period. While most studies of hinterlands have been based upon documentary evidence (a recent assessment by Galloway is a case in point)[56] data can be drawn increasingly from archaeological material to amplify study of both the economic viability of hinterlands and their influence upon and from urban centres. Archaeological methodologies are being developed which enable examination of settlement hierarchies, rural production and exchange, social contexts and environmental impact.[57] A range of questions can be formulated addressing consumerism, craft specialization, regional differentiation and communication networks. Albarella has recently illustrated how animal bone assemblages can inform understanding of changes in animal husbandry, the likely hinterland areas drawn upon by different towns for their animal resources and the changing nature of consumption over time,[58] while Ervynck, studying archaeological evidence for late medieval sheep around Ypres, was able to establish from kill-off rates that wool production was far more important than that of mutton to the local community.[59]

The North Sea province is therefore an encouraging one for archaeological work. Not only is it frequently possible to uncover diagnostically identifiable material but the sheer range of maritime and riverine contacts engenders considerable research potential. This potential, however, remains compromised by the nature of the material itself and the analytical challenges posed thereby. As an example, medieval ceramics are durable and ubiquitous artefacts, found throughout the North Sea world. Traditionally, typologies of pottery wares have been used to establish broad dating chronologies and to characterize trade. Yet, as Frans Verhaeghe has summarized, different mechanisms of trade and approaches to distribution can severely impact upon the usefulness of pottery as a reliable indicator of commercial contacts.[60] Veeckman has noted, for instance, that in the county of Flanders English pottery wares are discovered regularly and yet, in Antwerp on the other side of the River Scheldt, 'not a single sherd of earthenware ... has been recognised as an English product'.[61]

Caution is therefore needed when using such archaeological evidence to char-

---

in *Markets in Early Medieval Europe: Trading and 'Productive' Sites, 650–850*, ed. T. Pestell and U. Ulmschneider, Macclesfield 2003, 208–20.

[56] J. Galloway, 'Urban Hinterlands in Late Medieval England', in *Town and Country in the Middle Ages*, ed. K. Giles and C. Dyer, Society for Medieval Archaeology Monograph 22, 2005, 111–30.

[57] Perring, *Town and Country*, 12ff.

[58] U. Albarella, 'Meat Production and Consumption in Town and Country', in *Town and Country in the Middle Ages*, ed. Giles and Dyer, 131–48.

[59] A. Ervynck, 'Wool or Mutton? An Archaeozoological Investigation of Sheep Husbandry around Late Medieval Ypres', in *Ypres and the Medieval Cloth Industry in Flanders*, ed. D. Dewilde, A. Ervynck and A. Wielemans, Archeologie in Vlaanderen monografie 2, 1998, 77–86.

[60] F. Verhaeghe, 'Trade in Ceramics in the North Sea Region, 12th to 15th Centuries: A Methodological Problem and a Few Pointers', in *Lübecker Kolloquium zur Stadtarchäologie im Hanseraum II: Der Handel*, ed. M. Gläser, Lübeck 1999, 139–67.

[61] J. Veeckman, 'Trade in Antwerp from the 12th to the 17th Centuries: Archaeological Data in a Historical Context', in ibid., 123–37 (quotation p. 126).

acterize commerce and perhaps it should not be characterized with regard to specific sites and chronologies but more in terms of general trends. Verhaeghe again, having seriously questioned the trustworthiness of ceramic finds, believes nevertheless that there is sufficient ceramic data to state with confidence that, within the North Sea region and its river systems, two major commercial subregions are identifiable: a southern one comprising southern England, Flanders, parts of northern France and parts of the Netherlands; and a northern one, extending from Flanders and England to Scandinavia, Germany and the Baltic. In the latter, for instance, 'Rhenish products dominate the trade, accompanied by a far less important but still fair amount of English and Low Countries products.'[62]

Within such a broad framework, it then becomes possible to study other trends: the range of ceramics which crossed the North Sea; specific trade in ceramics such as that of English wares to Scandinavia; mechanisms of distribution which seem to indicate the primacy of water routes even for inland towns of continental Europe; redistribution networks from major ports such as Southampton, Amsterdam and Bremen; regional variation, specialization and competition. Each of these themes can be addressed by archaeological methodologies, adding to broad understanding of North Sea commercial activity.

One mechanism for such study might be to explore the nature, durability and extent of a specific hanseatic culture given the trading influence of the Hanseatic League itself.[63] At one level, such a culture seems self-evident when consideration is given to the almost ubiquitous houses and warehouses of northern Europe[64] or the evidence for sophisticated stoves in the homes of wealthier merchants. Such civilized features of comfort reached Finland[65] and Russia but until recently were a rare find in Britain (although fragments of stove-tile have now been recovered from major cities such as London and Norwich and, in Scotland, from Edinburgh, Perth, St Andrews and Stirling[66]). Gaimster has considered both stove tiles and ceramics and concluded that, by the end of the fifteenth century, the importation of pottery to England represented 'not only the adoption of a new set of material goods, but also a new lifestyle, based essentially on Continental (Hanseatic) culture and its aspi-

---

[62] Verhaeghe, 'Trade in Ceramics', 155.

[63] The concept of an overarching hanseatic 'power' has been strongly attacked in a recent paper which claims that the 'role of the hanseatic League was totally over-estimated in the older historiography', C. Jahnke, 'The Influence of the Hanseatic League on the Cities in the North Sea and Baltic Sea Area', in *Archaeology of Medieval Towns*, ed. Engberg et al, 51–63.

[64] M. Gläser (ed.), *Lübecker Kolloquium zur Stadtarchäologie im Hanseraum III: Der Hausbau*, Lübeck 2001, especially the later medieval buildings of Germany, the Netherlands and Flanders.

[65] K. Majantie (ed.), *Pots and Princes: Ceramic Vessels and Stove Tiles from 1400 to 1700*, Archaeologia Medii Aevi Finlandiae XII, Turku 2007.

[66] D. Gaimster and B. Nenk, 'English Households in Transition 1400–1600: The Ceramic Evidence', in *The Age of Transition. The Archaeology of English Culture 1400–1600*, ed. D. Gaimster and P. Stamper, Society for Medieval Archaeology Monograph 15, 1997, 171–96. Also G. Haggarty and D. Hall, '"Throw Some More Fuel On The Fire". The Stove Tiles of Medieval Scotland', in *Exchanging Medieval Material Culture: Studies in Archaeology and History Presented to Frans Verhaeghe*, ed. K. de Groote, D. Tys and M. Pieters, Brussels 2010, 67–74.

rations'.[67] Oddly though, the Hanse merchants resident in Britain seem to have failed to import their own architectural culture. The only surviving hanseatic warehouse in England (at King's Lynn) is predominantly a stubbornly English timber-framed structure[68] while even the Steelyard in London seems to have been insular in its design,[69] despite the archetypical hanseatic appearance of its most famous denizen, Georg Giese.[70]

The *limits* of material culture as a signifier ought therefore to be explored by archaeologists as much as the potential. Georg Giese demonstrates that there was a hanseatic presence in England – does the archaeology illustrate that this presence was perhaps more superficial in its impact than is apparent from the documentary record? Or was perhaps England always a more conservative country with regard to innovation? Brick, for instance, is used surprisingly late and sparingly in England with locations such as Hull and Beverley being among the few to show relatively rapid adoption of the medium (assisted by a complete lack of local building stone). While brick became a more common building material within English towns of the fifteenth century, its use in rural contexts remained extremely limited. This cannot have been merely a matter of wealth or opportunity. Comparable contemporary settlements on the continent appear to have had brick structures as the norm, such as the comprehensively excavated Flemish village of Walraversijde on the coast near Brugge in Belgium (and now rebuilt in part as a tourist attraction).[71] Brick villages of the fifteenth century in England are hard to find.

In summary, therefore, while the North Sea was clearly an important trading conduit with material evidence which can be charted archaeologically, so it is necessary to remember that it also divided communities and that development across such an expanse of water did not always lead to a common culture. The differences that can be observed in the physical remains of North Sea communities have as much potential to inform as do cultural linkages.

FUTURE RESEARCH

This chapter has been something of a ragbag collection of archaeological approaches to the North Sea world. Omissions are legion, in terms of themes, subjects, methodologies and theories. Some omissions are dreadful – apart from referencing urban hinterlands, advances in the understanding of the medieval rural

---

[67] D. Gaimster, 'Cross-Channel Ceramic Trade in the Late Middle Ages: Archaeological Evidence for the Spread of Hanseatic Culture to Britain', in *Archäologie des Mittelalters und Bauforschung im Hanseraum*, ed. M. Gläser, Rostock 1993, 251–60.
[68] V. Parker, *The Making of King's Lynn*, Chichester 1971, 115–17, fig. 26 and plate 30.
[69] See detail of Hollar's prospect of 1647 illustrated as fig. 97 in J. Schofield, *The Building of London*, London, 1984.
[70] Painted by Hans Holbein the Younger in 1537. Now housed in the Gemäldegalerie, Berlin. See http://www.smb.museum/smb/sammlungen/details.php?lang=en&objID=5&p=24
[71] C. Kightly, *Walraversijde 1485*, Ostend 2003.

environment have been largely ignored. Discussion of élite culture has been very limited, castles have not been mentioned and the Church only glanced at obliquely.

Where can archaeology of the medieval North Sea go? There is considerable potential for an archaeological contribution to greater understanding of the economies of regions and states around the North Sea basin. Within such a framework, enhanced knowledge of the role of commerce in urban development can be sought as can better awareness of hierarchies of both urban and rural settlements. The organization and use of space, a particularly interesting area of study, is one that invites comparison between different societies.

At a local level, exploration of buried horizons can be developed. The potential of new analytical processes can be garnered, such as that offered by geochemical signatures within buried silt deposits whereby it is probable that activities such as an intensification of industrial processes can be recorded. Mapping using GIS systems is already being used to marked effect in both urban and rural landscapes while traditional techniques such as borehole investigation can yield fresh information through digital plotting, either of specific sites or entire towns. Coastal survey work could be expanded as could awareness of changes wrought by the sea and the potential for preservation beneath the sea.

Genetic studies, allied to archaeological chronologies, could revolutionize understanding of population growth and movement. New dating technologies should increasingly refine those chronologies. Palaeo-environmental studies will undoubtedly continue to provide fresh information on change in both urban and rural societies. Analysis of resource acquisition, utilization and discard, particularly of food resources, is already transforming knowledge of both trade and husbandry.

Perhaps what is needed is an interdisciplinary Research Strategy for the North Sea basin. Archaeological research strategies now exist for regions such as the East of England,[72] sub-regions such as the Thames estuary,[73] and cities such as London.[74] The North Sea conference was a commendably broad-based event. It demonstrated that research into the medieval North Sea world is vibrant and dynamic. Publication is a landmark (or, more appropriately, a seamark). Like the seamark which was provided by the tower of the Greyfriars at King's Lynn, however, use of this publication needs to consider the direction of future travel for study as much as an appreciation of recorded travel in the past.

---

[72] M. Medlycott (ed.), 'Research and Archaeology Revisited: A Revised Framework for the East of England', *East Anglian Archaeology Occasional Paper* 24, 2011.

[73] E. M. Heppell, *The Greater Thames Estuary Historic Environment Research Framework: Update and Revision of the Archaeological Research Framework for the Greater Thames Estuary 1999*, English Heritage 2010, http://www.english-heritage.org.uk/publications/greater-thames-estuary-res-framework-2010/gt-research-framework-2010-pt1.pdf.

[74] T. Nixon et al, *A Research Framework for London Archaeology*, London 2002.

— Chapter 4 —

MEDIEVAL ART IN NORFOLK AND THE CONTINENT: AN OVERVIEW

David King

INTRODUCTION

Any attempt to assess the nature and extent of contacts between medieval art in Norfolk and the North Sea World is immediately faced with a conceptual problem. In art-historical terms contacts are usually thought of as influence, or at least potential influence, and influence is a much-used but problematic term which encompasses very different and often intangible movements the perception of which is essentially subjective.[1] Style, design, iconography and technique were all subject to developments coming from both inside and outside the workshop or studio and it is very difficult to differentiate the processes that went into the creation of a work of art made usually by an anonymous artist or artists working in an ill-defined location at an uncertain date. The problems are magnified when the role of mutual interaction with other countries is being considered. As will be seen, foreign influence can be direct and immediate, but is often distant, diluted and transmitted by a number of intermediary agencies. For the purposes of the present chapter it means that a fluid and loose definition of the North Sea World must be used which includes not only countries bordering directly on the ocean, but also those that sent and received people, ideas and objects to and from Norfolk via the sea. In practice, this means that as well as northern France, the Netherlands, Germany and Scandinavia, we must also take into account the rest of France, the Baltic lands and also Italy with passing mentions of Bohemia and Austria.[2]

---

[1] Margit Thøfner's plenary lecture at the East Anglia and North Sea World conference made this point very effectively. Although it has not been possible to publish the lecture in this volume, I must acknowledge how helpful her discussion of influence was to the writing of this chapter.

[2] A number of studies of the connections between the medieval art of England as a whole and the Continent have been consulted for this chapter: M. Rickert, *Painting in Britain in the Middle Ages*, 2nd edn, Harmondsworth 1965, 3–6, 145, 179, 198; J. Mitchell (ed.), *England and the Continent in the Middle Ages: Studies in Memory of Andrew Martindale*, Harlaxton Medieval Studies, 8, Stamford 2000; C. Reynolds, 'England and the Continent: Artistic Relations', in *Gothic: Art for England 1400–1547*, ed. R. Marks and P. Williamson, London 2003, 76–85; K. Woods, 'Immigrant Craftsmen and Imports', ibid., 91–4; U. Engel, 'British Art and the Continent', in *The History of British Art 600–1600*, ed. T. Ayers, London 2008, 53–67.

Definitions of what constitutes the medieval period vary widely. It has been said that in the British Isles medieval art began in the late sixth century with Celtic and Saxon work and continued to just before 1500.[3] Here, a fairly brief treatment of the evidence from the mainly archaeological record for Celtic, Saxon and Viking art will be attempted. Rather more needs to be said about the Norman contribution, of which important examples survive in the county, but in order to take account of the relative quantities of material the bulk of this chapter will deal with the art of Norfolk in the late Middle Ages up to the Reformation.

THE EARLY PERIOD – SAXONS AND VIKINGS

By 420 Britain was no longer part of the Roman Empire. It is not known if there had been any Saxon immigration from what is now Germany during the Roman occupation, but over a period from about the middle of the fifth century there was a substantial inflow.[4] Although these early Saxon migrants possessed artistic skills far inferior to earlier Celtic and Roman invaders, by the seventh century the court craftsmen of Kent and East Anglia were making jewellery of a quality unrivalled in Europe.[5] The Sutton Hoo burial treasure from Suffolk, probably from the grave or cenotaph of Rædwald, overlord of southern Britain, who died c.627, demonstrates in a spectacular way the artistic skills of the Anglo-Saxons, but also shows how they deliberately borrowed elements from foreign cultures, including Celtic, Roman, but also Scandinavian art.[6] Of sculpture from this period little has been found.[7]

The Christianization of East Anglia was begun by Rædwald's father, King Sigeberht, in the seventh century. In 680 the East Anglian see was divided and the northern bishopric was based at Elmham, almost certainly North Elmham. Viking raids on England began in the late eighth century, preceded in Norfolk by incursions from Mercia to the west. By the middle of the ninth century Norfolk was being seriously harassed by the Danes and in 869 Thetford was occupied. Much art must have been lost in the resultant destruction of Anglo-Saxon monasteries and the abolition of the East Anglian sees. After the death of St Edmund, king and martyr, in 870, East Anglia was ruled by the Vikings until 920. The Danish leader Guthrum, who became a Christian, and King Alfred finally made a treaty in 886 dividing England between them.[8]

Evidence for the material culture of the Vikings in Norfolk remained very exiguous until the advent of metal-detecting, which has in recent years made many small finds, increased by field work and excavations, the combined effect of which has altered our perceptions of this period. The spread and quantity of these finds point to a far greater population than was realized, but one consisting of peasant

[3] Rickert, *Painting in Britain*, 1.
[4] S. W. Martins, *A History of Norfolk*, Chichester 1984, 23.
[5] L. Stone, *Sculpture in Britain in the Middle Ages*, Harmondsworth 1955, 8.
[6] J. Hawkes, 'Art at Sutton Hoo', in Ayers (ed.), *The History of British Art*, 44–5.
[7] Martins, *History of Norfolk*, 26, where a carving from Thetford grammar school is illustrated.
[8] Ibid., 24–8.

farmers rather than wealthy raiders. Many of the finds consist of low-grade decorative items of jewellery and domestic items decorated with Viking ornament. Although the settlers soon converted to Christianity, both pagan and Christian artefacts were used. By 917 most of Norfolk was back under Anglo-Saxon control after the defeat of the Danes by Edward the Elder; however, widespread finds of Viking metalwork from the tenth and eleventh centuries have been made. Illustrating the complexities of foreign influences on English art, several items of Celtic metalwork have been found in Norfolk which may have been looted from Ireland, taken back to Denmark or Sweden, and then brought to Norfolk. In 1004 Norwich and Thetford were sacked by the Vikings and from 1016 to 1042 England was ruled by the Danish king Cnut and his sons. This period saw a fusion of Scandinavian and Anglo-Saxon styles with objects manufactured in England rather than brought by the settlers.[9]

This renewed Danish control did not lead as before to a breakdown of the structures of the Church, as the Vikings had converted to Christianity. From the eleventh century on many fine stone churches were built by the Anglo-Saxons all over the county, a few with surviving sculptural decoration. A fragment of a tenth-century cross from the now lost church of St Vedast in Norwich bears animal ornament in Viking style.[10]

THE NORMANS

After the Norman Conquest in 1066, the Normans both used the work of Anglo-Saxon craftsmen and artists and were themselves influenced by them.[11] The most obvious signs of Norman rule in the county were of course the castles and Norwich cathedral, built to impress and subdue the local populace, together with parish churches and stone houses. The present castle at Norwich, replacing an earlier wooden one, was built at the same time and by the same craftsmen as those who built the cathedral, using stone imported from Caen in Normandy.[12] The see was transferred to Norwich in 1094 by Bishop Herbert Losinga, building work starting two years later.

The story of the construction of the cathedral has been much discussed in recent years and will not be repeated in detail here; a few comments will suffice to set it in the context of our theme. The importance of Saint-Étienne in Caen as a model for both other large churches in Normandy and late eleventh-century architecture in eastern England, including Norwich cathedral, has been stressed. Comparisons

---

[9] S. Margeson, 'Viking Settlement in Norfolk: A Study of New Evidence', in *A Festival of Norfolk Archaeology*, ed. S. Margeson, B. Ayers, and S. Heywood, Norwich 1996, 47–57; T. Pestell, 'Viking Settlement in Norfolk', in *An Historical Atlas of Norfolk*, ed. T. Ashwin and A. Davison, 3rd edn, Chichester 2005, 36–7.

[10] Martins, *History of Norfolk*, 29.

[11] S. Margeson, F. Seillier and A. Rogerson, *The Normans in Norfolk*, Norwich 1994, 2–3.

[12] Other castles were built at Wormegay, Horsford, Denton, Middleton, Raveningham, Quidenham, Castle Acre, New Buckenham, Weeting and Castle Rising.

for the eastern arm at Norwich have been drawn with Cerisy-la-Forêt in Normandy, but also with Méhun-sur-Yèvre near Bourges and Soignies Abbey in Belgium. In the nave, both German and French sources are cited and the columns with helical grooves derive from Durham via other sources going back to Rome. The transepts, while relating to Ely and Bury St Edmunds, also refer to Speyer cathedral and other buildings in the Holy Roman Empire.[13]

Some of the original Norman sculptural decoration survives in the cathedral. The figure now in the south choir ambulatory depicting a standing saint in a niche was made for Bishop Herbert between 1096 and 1119 and originally placed in an arched niche above the doorway into the north transept; it is now thought to represent St Felix, the missionary and native of Burgundy, who brought Christianity to East Anglia, rather than the bishop himself (Plate 1). In the presbytery the Norman corbel heads display a surprising affection for rather ancient prototypes from some minor churches in Normandy. Perhaps the most interesting, and certainly the finest, Romanesque sculpture from the cathedral is the collection of reused capitals from the original Norman undated twelfth-century cloister. These sculptures vary widely in technique and quality, but the work of a gifted sculptor can be seen on a group of eight capitals, including one with a design of adorsed and interlaced dragons, a well-known Scandinavian motif (Plate 2).[14] The few remains of a high-quality scheme of wall painting in the south nave aisle, which include roundels depicting the story of the foundation of the cathedral by Losinga, date from c.1190–1200, but no Continental influences have been discerned in these very fragmentary scenes other than the fact that they depict a Norman bishop.[15]

PLATE 1   Norwich cathedral, south choir ambulatory, figure of St Felix, 1096–1119 (© UEA WAM).

[13] E. C. Fernie, *An Architectural History of Norwich Cathedral*, Oxford 1993; *Norwich Cathedral. Church, City and Diocese, 1096–1996*, ed. I. Atherton, E. Fernie, C. Harper-Bill and H. Smith, London and Rio Grande 1996; S. Heywood, 'The Romanesque Building', in ibid., 73–115; idem, 'Romanesque Architecture in Norfolk', in *A Festival*, ed. Margeson *et al*, 72–85.

[14] G. Zarnecki, catalogue entries 126, 134, *English Romanesque Art*, ed. G. Zarnecki, J. Holt and T. Holland, London 1984, 167, 175; Fernie, *Norwich Cathedral*, 84–7; J. A. Franklin, 'The Romanesque Sculpture', in *Norwich Cathedral*, ed. Atherton *et al*, 116–35.

[15] D. Park and H. Howard, 'The Medieval Polychromy', in *Norwich Cathedral*, ed. Atherton *et al*, 379–409.

PLATE 2 Norwich cathedral, capital from Norman cloister, twelfth century (© UEA WAM).

Leaving the cathedral and moving on to Norman parish churches in Norfolk, we find a feature very close to our subject in the ubiquitous western round towers (Plate 3). These have often been dated too early and assigned to the pre-Conquest period, but they were in fact a standard feature in Norman times. Their significance is iconographic, being a small-scale version of the round towers seen on many major north European churches. Their influence has been described thus: '[They illustrate] the strong cultural common ground of the North and Baltic seas where the bordering countries of Poland, Germany and Sweden also constructed round towers at the west ends of their parish churches.'[16]

THE THIRTEENTH CENTURY

Relatively little architecture and little work in other media are extant from the thirteenth century in the county, largely because of the dissolution of the monasteries and the late-medieval rebuilding of the great majority of churches. The dearth of locally illuminated manuscripts is harder to explain, although the cathedral scriptorium would have been disrupted by the events of 1272 when many of the

---

[16] Heywood, 'Romanesque Architecture', 76–9.

PLATE 3   Merton, Norfolk, parish church of St Peter (photograph: Mike Dixon).

PLATE 4 Baltimore, USA, Walters Art Gallery MS W. 34, the Carrow Psalter and Hours, f. 42. Scenes from the Life of St Olaf, c.1250–60 (© Walters Art Gallery).

monastic buildings were destroyed. The iconographic influence of Norway is detectable in one thirteenth-century illuminated manuscript which does have connections with Norfolk. The Carrow Psalter and Hours, Baltimore, Walters Art Gallery MS W.34, of 1250–60, owned by Carrow priory just outside Norwich by at

PLATE 5 Oslo University, Kulturhistorik museum, altar frontal from Heddal, c.1250 (© Oslo University).

least the fifteenth century, has on f. 42 a series of six medallions illustrating the Life of St Olaf (Plate 4).[17] He was the sainted king of Norway martyred in 1030 whose cult spread to England, where it was strongest in areas occupied by the Vikings.[18]

The loss of almost all panel painting in England of this period is to a small extent compensated for by the survival of several altar frontals of the late thirteenth and early fourteenth century in Norway painted by artists trained in England or under strong English influence.[19] The frontal at Heddal in eastern Norway of c.1250 has been compared to English and French stained glass (Plate 5).[20] It shows to left and right a series of seated Apostles grouped in threes with lively gestures, each group

[17] The six episodes from the life of Olaf are within the Beatus initial on f. 42r, which can be seen on http://www.flickr.com/photos/medmss/6165862427, accessed 26 January 2012. Paul Binski leaves open the possibility of a later date for the Psalter: P. Binski, 'The Ante-Reliquary Chapel Paintings in Norwich Cathedral: The Holy Blood, St Richard, and All Saints', in *Tributes to Nigel Morgan. Contexts of Medieval Art: Images, Objects and Ideas*, ed. J. M. Luxford and M. A. Michael, Turnhout 2010, 241–61.

[18] For the cult and iconography of St Olaf in Norfolk, see A. E. Nichols, *The Early Art of Norfolk*, Kalamazoo 2002, 223–4.

[19] For the Norwegian altar frontals, *Painted Altar Frontals of Norway 1250–1350*, 3 vols., vol. 1, *Artists, Styles and Iconography*, ed. E. B. Hohler, N. J. Morgan and A. Wichstrøm; vol. 2, *Materials and Technique*, ed. Unn Plahter; vol. 3, *Illustrations and Drawings*, ed. Unn Plahter, London 2004.

[20] *Altar Frontals*, ed. Hohler et al, I, 25; *Altar Frontals*, ed. Plahter, III, 23 (illustration).

PLATE 6 Saxlingham Nethergate, parish church of St Mary the Virgin, medallion with Apostles, window sII, c.1250 (photograph: Mike Dixon).

except one with a blank scroll. They can be compared with a medallion from a window of c.1250 now in Saxlingham Nethergate which is part of a series of seated Apostles in pairs (Plate 6), although a closer comparison for the placing of seated Apostles in pairs is seen on the metal altar frontal of c.1150 from Brodetopp, itself made under strong English influence.[21] These are generic comparisons helping to fill the gap left by English losses, rather than suggestions of immediate connections with Scandinavian work.

[21] For the Saxlingham Nethergate glass, http://www.cvma.ac.uk/publications/digital/norfolk/sites/saxlinghamnethergate/history.html, accessed 31 January 2012; for the Brodetopp frontal, now in Stockholm, Statens Historika Museet, see P. Lasko, *Ars Sacra 800–1200*, Harmondsworth 1972, 171–2, pl. 180; a painted altar frontal of c.1200–25 from Baltarga (Cerdagne) in Catalonia, now in the Museu d'Art de Catalunya in Barcelona, has the seated Christ blessing in a mandorla flanked by seated pairs of Apostles. See *Altar Frontals*, ed. Hohler et al, I, 39–65 (39, fig. 5.1).

PLATE 7 Glasgow, The Burrell Collection, figure of Beatrix of Valkenburg, *c*.1293 (© CGS CIC Glasgow Museums Collection).

One other panel of glass of thirteenth-century date which was almost certainly made for a Norfolk building is the figure in the Burrell Collection, Glasgow, of Beatrix of Valkenburg, third wife of Richard of Cornwall, king of the Romans. Beatrix died in 1272 and the panel has been thought to come from the church of the Greyfriars in Oxford, where she was buried (Plate 7). There are, however, good reasons for thinking that it is from the Norwich Franciscan house and dates from around 1293, when the construction of the church had just begun. The reason for it having been given to the friary at this time may be linked with a visit made by Edward I, Beatrix's nephew, to Norfolk at Lent in 1293. He was accompanied by Henry, count of Bar, who married the king's daughter Eleanor in September of that year. Beatrix provided a genealogical link between Edward I and Henry. The style of the glass shows the influence of the Court style which spread from France and the Rhineland to England at this time and suggests that it may even have been made in Lorraine from where the count of Bar hailed. A further continental link with the friary is that one of the citizens who donated or sold land on which it was built in the 1290s was Giles the Painter of Bruges.[22]

---

[22] D. King, 'Mendicant Glass in East Anglia', in *The Friars in Medieval Britain*, Harlaxton Medieval Studies, XIX, ed. N. Rogers, Donington 2010, 169–84.

THE FOURTEENTH CENTURY

The first half of the fourteenth century is perhaps the best known period for medieval art in Norfolk. During this time were made the illuminated manuscripts associated with Norwich and much admired for their lively decoration with rich borders inhabited by grotesques and other figures. These include the Gorleston, Bromholm, Douai, Macclesfield and St Omer Psalters and the styles and iconography of some of them betray Italian influence, mainly from Siennese art (Plate 8).[23] The main promoters of such influence were high-status court and ecclesiastical patrons and the principal routes of transmission were the trade routes and political and intellectual exchange coming from Italy to England via Avignon. One such protagonist may well have been John Salmon, bishop of Norwich from 1299 until 1325. It was during his episcopacy that Italian influence arrived in the city. His family had been hereditary goldsmiths to Ely priory since the twelfth century and he clearly had an interest in artistic matters, giving many vestments and ornaments to his cathedral, including a *tabula preciosissima* for the high altar in 1314. This was probably a painted retable and had been made ready (*comparatam*) in London.[24] This was probably too early for the Italian influence which seems to have arrived in the 1320s, but Salmon was a much travelled man and particularly after he became Chancellor of England in 1320 he would have had access to all that was most fashionable in importations of Italian art and the artists from that country who had arrived in London.[25]

One art historian has described how a new figure style which emerged on the Continent in the 1340s derived from a combination of an English approach to depicting the human figure and the new Italian awareness of the interconnectedness of figure and setting. The English origins of this style can already be seen in East Anglian manuscripts of *c.*1300, with the first developed form of the new style being seen in the late 1320s and early 1330s in such manuscripts as the Ormesby and St Omer Psalters, both connected with Norwich and including the imported Italianate elements in these paintings. The new style spread to Flemish manuscripts and thence to Cologne and other parts of Germany, France, and even Austria.[26]

Many of the artists of the first half of the fourteenth century in England, including Norfolk, would have had their careers cut short by the Black Death in 1348–9. The successors to the great East Anglian manuscript illuminators were the

---

[23] The best introductions to the East Anglian manuscripts remain P. Lasko and N. J. Morgan (eds), *Medieval Art in East Anglia 1300–1520*, Norwich 1973, and L. F. Sandler, *Gothic Manuscripts 1285–1385*, 2 vols, London and Oxford 1986. For the more recently discovered Macclesfield Psalter, see S. Panayotova, *The Macclesfield Psalter*, London 2008.

[24] C. Norton, D. Park and P. Binski, *Dominican Painting in East Anglia. The Thornham Parva Retable and the Musée de Cluny Frontal*, Woodbridge 1987, 79.

[25] For John Salmon, see M. C. Buck, 'Salmon, John (d. 1325), administrator and bishop of Norwich', ODNB, http://www.oxforddnb.com/view/article/24553, accessed 5 December 2011.

[26] G. Schmidt, 'England and the Emergence of a New Figure Style on the Continent during the 1340s', in Mitchell, *England and the Continent*, 129–36.

PLATE 8 London, British Library MS Additional 496, the Gorleston Psalter, f. 7, Crucifixion, c.1320–30 (© British Library).

artists who worked for the Bohun family over a number of decades. These were not based in Norfolk, as far as is known, but one of them was Flemish and his work is closely linked in style and design to some of the group of monumental brasses imported into England from Flanders in the second half of the fourteenth century, some of which are in the county.[27]

We return to Norwich for more direct links with our subject and continue with goldsmiths, whose works have always been particularly prone to loss. In 1306 there is in the city records the first mention of an important figure, Henry de Trith of Brabant. In that year a leading local craftsman, Robert de St Edmund, goldsmith, conveyed a property in 'le Welleyard' to Henry, who was married to Robert's daughter. Trith-Saint-Léger is today in northern France near Valenciennes. Between 1310 and 1335/6 Henry conducted frequent property transactions, mostly with his wife and in the parish of St Peter Mancroft. He appears to have been a well established member of the Norwich goldsmiths' community.[28]

Another goldsmith whose name reveals a probable Flemish origin was Edmund Lamberd, first mentioned in 1312/13, when he bought with his wife Joan a property in St Peter Mancroft from Henry de Trith, a transaction perhaps confirming his Low Countries origin. He continues to be mentioned in the property deeds until 1339.[29]

Our final foreign worker in gold brings us back to Norway. In 1317 John de Norweye, goldsmith, and Margaret his wife sold a property in the parish of St Mary the Less, and in 1323/4 there were three more transactions enrolled on the city court rolls marking the sale by the same John and his wife to John de Ramseye, son of Richard Curteys, in St Mary the Less. Other references to John de Norweye may or not be related to the goldsmith.[30] It is tempting to think that these continental arrivals in the early fourteenth century may have been encouraged by Bishop Salmon, who as has been stated above, came from a long-established family of goldsmiths.

John de Ramsey, mason, was an important figure in the history of English architecture. His father was probably the Richard le Machun who worked for the cathedral from 1285 to 1290. John was part of a family of masons responsible for much work at the cathedral and elsewhere in Norfolk, but also in Ely and London. He was probably also a sculptor.[31] The Ramseys were of course English, but it has been suggested that one of their number called William (there were three of that name) may have been Guillaume de Nourriche (William of Norwich), a sculptor

---

[27] L. Dennison, 'The Artistic Context of Fourteenth Century Flemish Brasses', *Transactions of the Monumental Brass Society*, 14, part 1, 1986, 1–38.

[28] W. Rye, *A Calendar of Norwich Deeds Enrolled in the Court Rolls of that City, Norwich 1307–41*, Norwich 1915, 24, 29, 38, 77, 84, 87. Another Flemish goldsmith, who is recorded in 1325/6 and 1333/4, is called Henry Flemyng, but could be the same person as Henry de Trith, ibid., 130, 178.

[29] Rye, *A Calendar*, 39, 143, 171, 181, 198, 200, 219.

[30] W. Rye, *A Short Calendar of the Deeds Relating to Norwich Enrolled in the Court Rolls of that City 1285–1306*, Norwich 1903, 9, 19, 22, 51, 79, 86, 112; Rye, *A Calendar*, 20, 74, 118, 120.

[31] J. Harvey, *English Medieval Architects. A Biographical Dictionary down to 1550*, revised ed., Gloucester 1987, 239–45.

who carved two figures of Apostles in 1319–24 for the Apostolic College of the church of Saint-Jacques-l'Hôpital in Paris. The statues are now in the Cluny Museum in Paris.[32]

One important type of metalwork was the monumental brass. Arguably the most outstanding example of English origin in the fourteenth century is that of Sir Hugh Hastings (died 1347) at Elsing in Norfolk. The provenance of this brass is disputed; London has been suggested, but convincing arguments have been made for an East Anglian origin, with Norwich, King's Lynn and Cambridge in the field, with strong stylistic connections to stained glass at Ely and some illuminated manuscripts. Continental stylistic influence from Flanders and France has also been mooted, but this may derive from English manuscript painting itself produced under Flemish influence. The Elsing brass displays more than most works of art the ways in which the discrimination of continental influences on English art is riven with complexity and ambiguity.[33]

A few other brasses and an indent have been ascribed to the same workshop as the Hastings brass, but the work of this high-quality enterprise appears to have been cut off by the Black Death in 1348–9. This coincides with the start of the importation of large monumental brasses of impressive quality from Flanders, two of which can still be seen in Norfolk. It has been suggested that this development had something to do with a decline in quality of native brasses because of the loss of craftsmen in the plague. The Flemish brasses are quite unlike English work, being very large and consisting of contiguous plates of metal with no gaps revealing the underlying marble. They are also very detailed, with large central figures and complex inhabited architectural canopies and often scenes at the bottom. The Flemish brasses in Norfolk are both in the parish church of St Margaret in King's Lynn; one is to Adam de Walsokne, died 1349, and the other to Robert Braunche, who died in 1364 (Plate 9).[34] Both men were mayors of Lynn; another mayor, William de Bittering, was buried in the chapel of St Nicholas in Lynn in the eastern part of the south aisle, 'under a very large fair stone, ten feet long, and six broad, all covered with brass, having their effigies cut in the middle upon the same, neatly engraven, and embellished with fine decorations round the verge';[35] this eighteenth-century description is surely of a third, sadly now lost, Flemish brass in Lynn, the port into which these items would have been imported.

---

[32] For Guillaume de Nourriche, *Les fastes du gothique. Le siècle de Charles V*, ed. F. Baron, Paris 1981, 68–9; J. Alexander and P. Binski (eds), *Age of Chivalry*, London 1987, 418. The identification of Guillaume de Nourriche with William Ramsey was suggested by T. A. Heslop (private communication).

[33] P. Binski, 'The Stylistic Sequence of London Figure Brasses', in *The Earliest English Brasses. Patronage, Style and Workshops 1270–1350*, ed. J. Coales, London 1987, 69–130; L. Dennison and N. Rogers, 'The Elsing Brass and its East Anglian Connections', *Fourteenth Century England*, 1, ed. N. Saul, Woodbridge 2000, 167–93.

[34] Dennison, *Flemish Brasses*.

[35] F. Blomefield and C. Parkin, *An Essay towards a Topographical History of the County of Norfolk*, London 1805–10, 8, 511.

PLATE 9 King's Lynn, parish church of St Margaret, monumental brass of Robert Braunche, d. 1364, brass rubbing (reproduced by courtesy of H. Martin Stuchfield).

One interesting footnote to both the Hastings brass and the imported Flemish memorials is that in 1349/50 Gilbert de Coy, marbler, was enrolled as a freeman of Norwich.[36] Coye-la-Forêt is in northern France about 25 kilometres north of Saint-Denis and not far from Tournai, where most of the Flemish brasses were made at this time. We do not know how important he was, but if he was Flemish or Franco-Flemish, the question arises as to his influence on the local production of brasses in Norwich. He may have worked in the county before taking up the freedom, but the date of his appearance in the documentary record may suggest that he had sensed the opening in England for Flemish work and was aiming to try his fortune here, rather than making brasses in Flanders and exporting them. The fact that he came to Norwich, where no imported brasses are known, also suggests that he saw the importations at Lynn as restricting the potential for his trade. If his skills were related more to manufacture rather than design, he may have been quickly absorbed into the local milieu.

Norfolk is the original home of some of the very rare survivals of English panel painting from the fourteenth century. The most important is the set of altar paintings consisting of a frontal, now in the Cluny Museum in Paris, and a retable, now in Thornham Parva church in Suffolk. They date from c.1335–40, or possibly a little later, and have been shown to have been made for the Dominican friary in Thetford, but their style betrays no influence from foreign sources. A distinguishing feature of these panels is the background, where both painted motifs and motifs stamped in *pastiglia* are used. The latter feature is the earliest known example in the west of this technique of panel painting. This points to the origin of this technique in goldsmiths' work, and we have already noted that that craft was thriving in Norwich at this period, with goldsmiths from Flanders and Norway working in the city as well as the local workers, although the place of production of the paintings remains disputed. Although stylistically independent of artistic currents on the Continent, the Thetford panels were a harbinger of the fashion for *pastiglia* grounds seen in German, Bohemian and Netherlandish, but also in England, in work after 1350.[37]

If the Thetford altar paintings hinted at later technical developments in continental painting, the Despenser Retable in Norwich Cathedral of c.1380–1400 was by general agreement the recipient of some European stylistic input, but there is little consensus as to the exact source. Bohemia, France and North Germany, in particular the work of Meister Bertram of Hamburg, have been mooted. What may have been the previous high altarpiece in the cathedral, that given in 1314 by Bishop Salmon, mentioned above, was got ready in London, but the despite the foreign

---

[36] J. L'Estrange, *Calendar of Freemen of Norwich from 1317 to 1603*, ed. Rye, London, 1888, 38. Marblers produced monumental brasses.

[37] Norton, Park and Binski, *Dominican Painting*; A. Massing (ed.), *The Thornham Parva Retable. Technique, Conservation and Context of an English Medieval Painting*, Painting and Practice 1, Turnhout 2003; D. King, 'John de Warenne, Edmund Gonville and the Thetford Dominican Altar Paintings', in *Tributes to Nigel Morgan*, ed. Luxford and Michael, 293–306.

influences discerned in the Despenser Retable, its stylistic resemblance to some of the painted panels from the parish church of St Michael at Plea, now in the cathedral, may suggest that it was the work of local painters.[38]

In comparison with the following century, there is little extant fourteenth-century stained glass made in Norfolk. Some of the glass can be linked to the general stylistic milieu of the East Anglian manuscripts, but that at Attleborough parish church, for example, is reminiscent of York glass of the 1330s and 40s, such as that of c.1338 in the west window of the Minster, whose style has been seen to have been influenced by French work such as that in Rouen (Plate 10).[39] As is the case with later glass in the first half of the fifteenth century, we have here a case of an influential local style developed under foreign influence which spreads over a wide area, so that the original continental input becomes very diluted. There is even less glass in Norfolk from the second half of the fourteenth century. A small amount from an excavation in Norwich and the churches of Poringland and Pulham St Mary was probably made in the city and a painted head found during the excavation is comparable in general terms to the style of the Bohun manuscripts, which was in turn influenced by Flemish art of the period.[40]

INTERNATIONAL GOTHIC

Towards the end of the fourteenth century there developed a style of painting over large parts of Northern and Central Europe and England known as the International Style. Its origins have been seen in Bohemian art of the 1350s and 1360s, but also in Parisian art, and it appears in a variety of forms in different countries. Its penetration of England occurred from the 1380s onward, with influences from Flemish art on its manifestation in manuscript painting and from German art in stained glass and wall painting. Little remains from the main phase c.1400 in Norfolk, but the style lingered here into the second half of the fifteenth century and can be seen in many examples of stained glass and screen painting in the county.[41] Here again, the foreign influence is diluted and its exact extent cannot be determined.

T. A. Heslop has drawn attention to an early fifteenth-century panel painting

---

[38] A. H. R. Martindale, catalogue entry 51, in Lasko and Morgan, *Medieval Art*, 36–7; P. Tudor-Craig, catalogue entry 711, in Alexander and Binski, *Age of Chivalry*, 516–17; D. J. King, 'The Panel Paintings and Stained Glass', in *Norwich Cathedral*, ed. Atherton et al, 410–30.

[39] For the York west window, see T. French and D. O'Connor, *York Minster. A Catalogue of Medieval Stained Glass. Fascicule 1, The West Windows of the Nave*, Corpus Vitrearum Medii Aevi, Great Britain, 3, Oxford 1987.

[40] For the late fourteenth-century glass at Poringland, see Nichols, *Early Art*, 55, 97; for that at Pulham St Mary, ibid., 104. The dating of all this glass is the author's. For the influence of Flemish brasses on the Bohun manuscripts, see Dennison, *Flemish Brasses*, 3–12. The excavated glass is unpublished.

[41] For a discussion of International Gothic glass in Norfolk, see D. King, *The Medieval Stained Glass of St Peter Mancroft, Norwich*, Oxford 2006, cvii–cxxiii, and for manuscripts and other media, Lasko and Morgan, *Medieval Art*, 29–43.

PLATE 10 Attleborough, parish church of St Mary, west window, angel playing rebec, c.1340–60 (photograph: Gordon Plumb).

PLATE 11 Denver Art Museum, Colorado, Berger Collection, panel painting of the Crucifixion, *c.*1410–20 (Eckart Lingenauber).

in the Art Museum in Denver, Colorado.[42] It has been attributed to a Westfalian artist working in England and depicts a Crucifixion (Plate 11). Heslop argues for a date of c.1410 and a possible provenance in Norfolk. Some iconographical elements have English antecedents (although German and French models are also evoked) and the form of the panel matches that in the few panel paintings from altarpieces from Norfolk of this date. The question of continental influence on the style is not taken further in the article, but in general terms a northern German input would be possible. Nothing is known from sources other than the object itself of the provenance of the painting, but two details may provide clues. On the dexter side of the cross behind the Virgin, St John and one of the Marys stand two nuns in black habits, and on the other side the centurion has a patterned tunic decorated with pairs of seated talbots under a coronet. The (unusual) presence of the nuns combined with the talbots suggests that a possible patronage by an abbess or prioress in Norfolk called Talbot might be worth investigating. These clues lead to Crabhouse priory in the parish of Wiggenhall St Mary Magdalen, south of King's Lynn, the only house of Augustinian canonesses in the county, where in 1395 Matilda Talbot was elected prioress.[43] Little is known of Matilda, but in 1420 she resigned and was succeeded by Joan Wiggenhall, of whom much more is known and under whose leadership the convent was much rebuilt and refurbished. Since there are two nuns depicted on the altarpiece, it is possible that Joan was responsible for the painting, which was perhaps intended to be a memorial for both herself and her long-serving predecessor, which would date it to some time soon after 1420. Joan's extensive programme of renewal of buildings and furnishings suggest strongly that it was she rather than Matilda who had the Crucifixion panel painted, but the possibility must not be rejected that Matilda was the donor during her period as prioress from 1395 to 1420, perhaps also depicting her predecessor, Cecilia Beaupre.[44] It may be relevant that there is evidence of a number of campaigns of church decoration during the 1420s and 30s in the Marshland area of west Norfolk.[45] The proximity of the port of King's Lynn may explain any northern German influence on the style, as it was a conduit of foreign goods, people and influence.[46]

---

[42] T. A. Heslop, 'Attending at Calvary: an Early Fifteenth-Century English Panel Painting', in *Tributes to Nigel Morgan*, ed. Luxford and Michael, 278–92.

[43] *The Victoria History of the County of Norfolk*, ed. W. Page, 2, London 1906, 408–10.

[44] M. Bateson, 'The Register of Crabhouse Nunnery', *Norfolk Archaeology* 11, 1892, 1–71.

[45] The chancel of Walpole St Peter was glazed in the early 1420s; see Blomefield and Parkin, *History of Norfolk*, 9, 117. The north aisle, and possibly the south aisle, of Wiggenhall St Mary Magdalen received its glazing in c.1430-40, D. King, 'The Stained Glass of Wiggenhall St Mary Magdalen, Norfolk', *King's Lynn and the Fens. Medieval Art, Architecture and Archaeology*, British Archaeological Association Conference Transactions, 31, ed. J. McNeill, Leeds 2008, 186–98. Glass now at North Tuddenham of c. 1420-30, including scenes from the lives of St Margaret and St George, has been shown to be from Wiggenhall St Peter (to be published in the CVMA Summary Catalogue for Norfolk). Joan Wiggenhall paid half of the cost of rebuilding the chancel there in 1420 (Bateson, 'Register', 58).

[46] In the time of Matilda the convent owned a tenement in the Gresmarket in Lynn lived in by Symon Sadler. In an alien subsidy roll of 1439/40 it was lived in by John Sadiler, Dutchman; his servant William is also listed as an alien. People called Saddler were often painters (wooden saddles were

PLATE 12 Norwich cathedral, panel painting of the Annunciation, from the parish church of St Michael at Plea, Norwich, c.1430–40.

Some of the panel paintings now in Norwich cathedral which came from the church of St Michael at Plea in the city are later than the late fourteenth-century works which have been compared to the Despenser Retable (Plate 12). Although now assembled into a composite altarpiece, they are from more than one context in the church and are of different dates. The Annunciation, with a Visitation as *Nebenszene*, has been compared to the work of Melchior Broederlam from Ypres and the Resurrection has echoes of the Bohemian Trebon altarpiece of the 1380s. The date of these panels has never been satisfactorily fixed, suggestions ranging from c.1420 for the Annunciation to the late fifteenth century for both.[47]

As stated above, some aspects of International Gothic style lingered on in Norfolk well beyond their appearance in most other places. The prophets and patriarchs of the side windows of the c.1440 chancel glazing at Salle are still in the soft style and may have been painted by John Wighton, the head of the leading mid fifteenth-century workshop in Norwich (Plate 13). Wighton employed several other glaziers in his workshop, including a

highly decorated objects), and in late fourteenth-century Norwich Gilbert and Henry Sadler were glaziers. So it is possible that a German or Dutch painter was a tenant of Crabhouse nunnery. For the Sadlers of Norwich, D. King, 'Glass-Painting in Late-Medieval Norwich: Continuity and Patronage in the John Wighton Workshop', in *Patrons and Professionals in the Middle Ages*, Harlaxton Medieval Studies 22, ed. P. Binski and E. A. New (forthcoming).

[47] J. Mitchell, catalogue entry 277, Marks and Williamson, *Art for England*, 392–3.

PLATE 13   Salle, parish church of St Peter and St Paul, prophets, patriarchs and cardinals, window nII, *c*.1440.

Dutchman called William Mundeford, originally from Montfoort in the diocese of Utrecht, who is documented in the city from 1436. Mundeford's son John became the head of the workshop after the death of Wighton in 1458; another son, Henry, trained as a glazier with a Franco-Flemish glazier called Henry Piers who worked in the city and had received the freedom in 1427. A body of work in the county has been attributed to William Mundeford on the basis of his sketchy and fluid style with fully characterized faces, very different from that of his own son John, who was trained by Wighton and whose painting became increasingly linear. No precise comparisons have been found, but his style can be compared in general terms to Dutch art of the early fifteenth century, although the almost total loss of Dutch and Flemish stained glass of this period makes the finding of parallels with glass impossible.[48]

Another member of the Mundeford family, Robert, is recorded in 1455 as a carver and an alien.[49] A set of carved wooden 'bosses' in the chancel at Salle of

---

[48] For the John Wighton workshop and its oeuvre, D. J. King, 'A Glazier from the Bishopric of Utrecht in Fifteenth-Century Norwich', in *Utrecht: Britain and the Continent. Archaeology, Art and Architecture*, The British Archaeological Association Conference Transactions 18, ed. E. de Bièvre, Leeds 1996, 216–25; King, *St Peter Mancroft*, cxxiv–clii; King, 'Glass-Painting in Late-Medieval Norwich'.

[49] King, 'A Glazier from the Bishopric of Utrecht', 218.

PLATE 14 Norwich, parish church of St Peter Mancroft, Crucifixion and Entombment, attributed to William Mundeford, window I, *c*.1450–*c*.1455.

c.1440 or later, depicting the Life of Christ, include a Circumcision scene based on the same model as that in the Toppes window of c.1450-55 in the church of St Peter Mancroft in Norwich (Plate 14). This window was almost certainly painted by John Mundeford and it can reasonably be suggested that Robert may have been the sculptor of the bosses.[50] An earlier Dutch carver had been employed at the cathedral in 1415-16.[51] Two other carvers at work in Norwich in the fifteenth century have names which may indicate a foreign origin in Norway and Germany or Flanders, but no other evidence is available.[52]

Other continental influences have been perceived in the work of the John Wighton workshop, particularly in that at St Peter Mancroft. The style of the mid fifteenth-century glass, notably the Toppes Window, is again a late derivation from International Gothic, with the addition of an essentially English linearity and a rejection of spatial perspective, depth being conveyed by the overlapping of pictorial elements. However, the landscape elements such as trees and cliffs which appear frequently show an awareness of French manuscript painting from earlier in the century. Indeed already in the fine panels of classical International Gothic glass now at North Tuddenham of c.1420-30 (Plate 15), but originally almost certainly from Wiggenhall St Peter, these elements were seen, and have been compared to the work of the celebrated Franco-Flemish illuminators the Boucicaut Master and the Limbourg brothers.[53]

The mid-century glass reveals hints of iconographic borrowings from earlier sources in France, and in one case an actual model from a French manuscript of c.1424-35 may be posited, perhaps arriving in England with the entourage of Sir John Fastolf. The well known soldier and landowner from Norfolk was steward for a time to the duke of Bedford in France and a bibliophile. He had access to the duke's library, which contained many French illuminated manuscripts, and brought a French illuminator known as the Fastolf Master to England. On his return in 1439 he built a fine castle at Caister near Yarmouth where he had many priceless tapestries, presumably from France or Flanders. He also had a house in Norwich decorated with stained glass which survived until the eighteenth century. Fastolf's many links with prominent Norfolk families such as the Pastons and his membership of the elite guild of St George in Norwich may explain much of the French influence seen in Norfolk at this time.[54]

After the death of John Mundeford in 1481 the Wighton workshop may have

---

[50] For the bosses, see W. L. E. Parsons, *Salle. The Story of a Norfolk Parish. Its Church, Manors & People*, Norwich 1937, 59 and plates between pp. vi and vii; King, *St Peter Mancroft*, lxxxiv. For the Toppes Window, ibid., clxix-cxcvii.
[51] E. C. Fernie and A. B. Whittingham, *The Early Communar and Pittancer Rolls of Norwich Cathedral Priory, with an Account of the Building of the Cloister*, Norfolk Record Society, 41, 1972, 41.
[52] They are Thomas Alman, free as a carver in 1437-40, and Robert Hakun, free as a carver in 1445-6. L'Estrange, *Calendar of Freemen*, 3, 66.
[53] R. Marks, *Stained Glass in England during the Middle Ages*, London 1993, 184; King, *St Peter Mancroft*, cv.
[54] King, 'A Glazier from the Bishopric of Utrecht', 224-5; King, *St Peter Mancroft*, ciii-civ.

PLATE 15 North Tuddenham, parish church of St Mary, west window, formerly Wiggenhall, parish church of St Peter, Olybrius' squire invites St Margaret to follow him, c.1420–30. (photograph: Mike Dixon).

been taken over by a nephew and name-sake of John Wighton.[55] A window of the Life of St John the Evangelist painted probably in 1487 for the church of St Peter Mancroft is in a style which both looks back to the mid-century Wighton workshop windows, but also begins to respond to the growing fashion for more realistic painting under the influence of Flemish painting.[56]

This glass may be by the latest phase of the Wighton workshop, but the historical evidence suggests that it was in decline by this time and was being overtaken by another workshop which was soon to be producing work in a number of media. The craft genealogy of this enterprise begins with a rather shadowy figure, Thomas Goldbeater, who died in 1467 and had apprentices who became glaziers and painters, one of whom was the glazier Nicholas Heyward, who took over a property belonging to his master after the latter's death. Nicholas' younger brother William became a freeman in 1485 and is known to have been active as a glazier and as a producer of monumental brasses, and it has recently been suggested that his workshop was also responsible for some of the best-known Norfolk screen painting, including that at Ranworth, and also possibly the magnificent wall-painting in St Gregory's church in Norwich. It has often been said that fifteenth-century painting in England after the International Gothic phase was story of decline, with a constant repetition of old designs and a painting style which hardened and refused or was unable to adapt to the new currents of realism from the Continent, until it was totally submerged by work by or influenced by them later in the century. The glass, brasses, screen and wall paintings attributed to the Heyward workshop at first sight would appear to fit this description, but closer examination of the oeuvre suggests that the situation was rather more complex. Some of the work is of high quality, such as the Ranworth screen and the St Gregory's wall-painting. The Ranworth style has been described as a 'late but elegant and surprisingly refined version of the International Gothic "soft" style'. As such, it is an even paler reflection of continental stylistic influences going back to the beginning of the century.[57]

The wall-painting of St George and the Dragon in the Norwich parish church of St Gregory is reminiscent of the flamboyant late-Gothic mannerism of the Ranworth screen (Plate 16). Its iconography depicts a very common subject, which must have been even more frequent than surviving works reveals in Norwich, where there was a special devotion to this saint.[58] The ubiquity of the subject makes

---

[55] King, 'Glass-painting in Late-Medieval Norwich'.
[56] King, *St Peter Mancroft*, clii–clv, ccvii–ccxiv.
[57] For the Heyward workshop, see D. King, 'A Multi-Media Workshop in Late Medieval Norwich – A New Look at William Heyward', in *Lumière, formes et couleurs. Mélanges en hommage à Yvette van den Bemden*, ed. C. De Ruyt, I. Lecocq, M. Lefftz and M. Piavaux, Namur, 193–204; idem, 'The Indent of John Aylward – Glass and Brass at East Harling', *Monumental Brass Society, Transactions*, XVIII (3), 2011, 251–67; for the glaziers involved, see King, St Peter Mancroft, 140–1; for the style of the Ranworth group of screens, J. Mitchell, 'Painting in East Anglia around 1500: The Continental Connection', in *England and the Continent in the Middle Ages: Studies in Memory of Andrew Martindale*, 365–80.
[58] For the iconography of St George in Norfolk with a list of extant and lost imagery, see Nichols, *Early Art*, 196–200.

PLATE 16 Norwich, parish church of St Gregory, wall painting of St George and the dragon, *c.*1500 (© Victoria and Albert Museum).

the tracing of iconographic sources difficult, as two images which show similarities may come from a remote and lost common source. With this caveat, it is still worth pointing to the repetition in the wall-painting of several iconographical details seen for example in a much earlier depiction, that in the Boucicaut Hours, painted by the Boucicaut Master, credited with the Limbourg brothers with the invention of naturalistic landscape and mentioned above in connection with the North Tuddenham glass.[59] As in the case of the Wighton workshop glass, the continental influence is discernible, but the route travelled has long since been erased.

A more immediate iconographical model has been suggested for some of the screens of the Ranworth group attributed to the Heyward workshop: early copies after Martin Schongauer's engravings from the late 1470s. The advent of readily accessible engravings provided a much more rapid way of disseminating new designs, foreshadowed in the 1460s by the block-book edition of the *Biblia Pauperum*. This possibility becomes a reality in the next generation of screen painters in Norfolk in the early sixteenth century who have been shown to have made frequent use of engravings by a number of Flemish, Dutch and North German artists, including Schongauer. Furthermore, the screen paintings based on continental designs, principally those at Cawston, Aylsham, Tacolneston, Marsham and Worstead, also show an awareness of new developments from the Continent in painting technique, especially for drapery.[60]

THE END OF THE MIDDLE AGES

There is a variety of other works in different media made for high-status patrons in Norfolk in the first half of the sixteenth century either by foreign artists or under their strong influence; it is sometimes impossible to say where they were produced. Two high-status productions are associated with East Harling, where Sir Thomas Lovell had bought the manor and rebuilt the hall, bequeathing it to his nephew Sir Francis Lovell when he died in 1524. From Sir Thomas's lifetime and made, it is assumed, *c.*1516 for the gateway of the new hall, is the bronze plaque depicting the bust of Sir Thomas set in the Garter. It is ascribed to the Italian sculptor Pietro Torregiano (1472–1528), who came to England to work in the English court.[61] The second work made for East Harling is the portrait by the German painter Hans Holbein the Younger, *c.*1527, of Anne Lovell, the wife of Sir Francis Lovell. Holbein also painted the portraits of a number of other people associated with the county (Plate 17).[62]

One of these was Thomas Howard, third duke of Norfolk. He had a palace at

---

[59] For the Boucicaut Master, E. Panofsky, *Early Netherlandish Painting*, Harvard 1953, 1, 53–61, and M. Meiss, *French Painting in the Time of Jean de Berry. The Boucicaut Master*, London 1968. The St George miniature is illustrated at pl. 10.
[60] Mitchell, 'The Continental Connection', 373–80.
[61] P. Motture, catalogue entry 9, in Marks and Williamson, *Art for England*, 152, and pl. 13.
[62] D. King, 'Who was Holbein's Lady with a Squirrel and a Starling?', *Apollo* 159, May 2004, 42–9.

PLATE 17 London, National Gallery, Hans Holbein the Younger, *A Lady with a Squirrel and a Starling (Anne Lovell?)*, c.1527 (© National Gallery).

PLATE 18 Norwich Castle Museum, The Ashwellthorpe Triptych, c.1519 (© UEA WAM).

Kenninghall in the south-west of the county and the family mausoleum was in the Cluniac priory of nearby Thetford. The duke lived through the dissolution of the monasteries and when the Thetford house was dissolved, the tombs intended for himself and his son-in-law were unfinished. Some of the completed parts dating from c.1536–9 were subsequently incorporated into new tombs built in 1555–9 in Framlingham church in Suffolk. The original tombs were conceived after the model of contemporary French monuments which were in turn inspired by Italian sculpture.[63]

A number of altarpieces by Flemish painters were imported into England from the late fifteenth century onwards. One of these was made for the Knyvett family of Ashwellthorpe in about 1519 by the Master of the Magdalen Legend, a painter active in Brussels c.1490–1525. Sir Christopher, the likely donor, was a member of the royal household and also owned land in Tournai (Plate 18).[64]

With stained glass made for churches the situation is less clear. Two churches in Norwich have related sixteenth-century pre-Reformation glass which may have been made locally by one or more of the glaziers working in the city at the time,

[63] R. Marks, catalogue entry 336, in Marks and Williamson, *Art for England*, 446–7.
[64] A. Martindale, 'The Ashwellthorpe Triptych', *Early Tudor England*, Proceedings of the 1987 Harlaxton Symposium, Woodbridge 1989, 107–23.

PLATE 19 Norwich, parish church of St Andrew, The Sacrifice of Isaac, window sV, originally in east window of chancel, 1510–1520 (photograph: Mike Dixon).

but whose style suggests a strong foreign input. The east window of the parish church of St Andrew dates from c.1510–20 and had a large Crucifixion scene with typological Old Testament scenes in the outer lights, as did that at St Stephen's, dated 1533 (Plates 19 and 20). In both cases, parts of the outer scenes survive, the Crucifixion having been lost through iconoclasm.[65] No sign of any Flemish or other foreign glaziers working in Norwich has been found yet in the documentary record and it remains an open question as to who made the windows and where.

In the north clerestory windows at St Andrew's church was a long series depicting the Dance of Death, dating to c.1506–10. One panel survives, now in a south aisle window (Plate 21). The style is local, but the iconography is French in origin and although earlier English examples are known, the design source for this series may well have been a printed French book. Several such series were produced by the French publishers Guy Marchant and Anthoine Vérard from 1485 onwards, and the figure of the bishop here is very similar to that in a hand-coloured version by Vérard which has thirty pairs of figures.[66] A more accessible model, however, would have been a printed primer, which sometimes included this iconography.[67]

In the parish church of St Clement at Outwell is glass in two different styles, both showing Flemish or German characteristics. A figure of Balthazar in the Fincham chapel on the north side of the chancel is from a depiction of the Adoration of the Magi. The adjacent window had figures of three English sainted kings: St Æthelbert, St Edmund and St Edward the Confessor (Plate 22). The glass dates from c.1520–30 and was probably given by John Fincham the younger, who died

[65] King, *St Peter Mancroft*, clvi–clix.
[66] For the St Andrew's panel, King, *St Peter Mancroft*, clix, clxi and fig. 143; for the Vérard Dance of Death series, R. Hammerstein, *Tanz und Musik des Todes: die mittelalterliche Totentanz und ihr Nachleben*, Bern 1980, 174–5 and figs. 49–53.
[67] See E. Duffy, *The Stripping of the Altars*, New Haven and London 1992, 227–8, 304, pl. 111.

PLATE 20 Norwich, parish church of St Stephen, The Sacrifice of Isaac and part of a Crucifixion scene, east window of chancel, 1533 (photograph: Mike Dixon).

114   *David King*

Above:

PLATE 21   Norwich, parish church of St Andrew, scene from the Dance of Death, window sVII, formerly in north clerestory, *c.*1506–1510.

Right:

PLATE 22   Outwell, parish church of St Clement, window sIII, St Stephen, *c.*1515–1525. (photograph: Mike Dixon).

PLATE 23 Melton Constable, parish church of St Peter, arms of the City of Norwich, window nIII, c.1531–1540. (photograph: Mike Dixon).

in 1527. Outwell is just south of King's Lynn, which had close links with Cologne. The style of the glass suggests German, perhaps Rhenish, influence. The combination of the Three Kings, the centre of whose cult was Cologne, with other kings, may be compared with the iconography of the upper choir windows of Cologne cathedral.[68] The glass in the east window of the Beaupré chapel also has iconographical links with Cologne and the Continent, with Saints Ursula, Olaf and Martina being present, but also, as in the Fincham chapel, with English saints. The style of the glass is unusual, combining a certain naivety in technique and design with realistic modelling and facial types and continental figure types. It was probably painted in King's Lynn under German or Flemish influence.[69]

The arrival of the Renaissance in Norfolk art cannot be dated precisely. The St Stephen's glass of 1533 includes part of a donor panel with a Renaissance architectural setting. Just a year before, the screen at Wellingham had been painted in the old style, the St George and Dragon being based on the design of the wall-painting at St Gregory's Church.[70] Only a few fragments of the 1534 glazing of the Mayoral Council Chamber of the Guildhall in Norwich survive. The style as far as can be discerned shows a general affinity with Flemish painting, but in a local version, as might be expected of

---

[68] H. Rode, *Die mittelalterlichen Glasmalereien des Kölner Domes*, Corpus Vitrearum Medii Aevi, Deutschland, IV:1, Berlin 1974, 98–140.

[69] For the glass at Outwell, http://www.cvma.ac.uk/digpub/norfolk/sites/outwell/history.html, accessed 27 January 2010; C. Daunton, 'The Patronage and Iconography and Iconography of Stained Glass in Late Medieval Norfolk: An Historical Analysis', unpublished PhD thesis, University of East Anglia (2009), 160–208.

[70] For an image of the St George panel at Wellingham, http://norfolkchurches.co.uk/wellingham/images/dscf2211.jpg, accessed 31 January 2012.

a civic programme. The iconography of the windows was recorded in the eighteenth century and reveals a series of Justice paintings with texts, such as were to be found all over northern Europe in town halls.[71] The fragments of the Howard tomb of 1536–9 intended for the Thetford Cluniac house confirm the arrival of the Renaissance style, however. A number of ex-situ panels of glass associated with Norwich have a local interpretation, with ornament and putti associated with heraldry and merchant's marks. They date from *c*.1540. The most complete examples are the coat of arms of Norwich now at Melton Constable church (Plate 23), almost certainly from the Norwich house of a goldsmith, and the shields of arms now in the Marble Hall building of Aviva Insurance but made for Surrey House, one of the city houses of Thomas Howard, third Duke of Norfolk.[72]

CONCLUSION

This survey of continental influence on the art of medieval Norfolk is necessarily incomplete. Much of the material culture of the county at this period has been lost, but this is compensated for to a certain extent by the documentary record. The picture that emerges is of frequent but sporadic interchange with the North Sea world. It is often impossible to distinguish between connections with northern France and Flanders, since boundaries changed and the whole area was a cultural unit at certain periods. Scandinavia plays a more important part in the earlier period and Germany in the later period. The Baltic countries with no direct North Sea link are nevertheless worthy of consideration because the route of transmission of influence came via Norfolk's North Sea ports, although it is usually impossible to be sure of this. In fact after the Viking period their role seems to have been confined to the provision of raw materials. Overall links are predominantly from the Continent towards Norfolk and vary greatly in intensity, duration and route of access. Some changes such as the pervasive influence of the International Gothic style in its many different forms (which nevertheless do have an underlying commonality) were mostly mediated via other English art; others were immediate and local, particularly where the immigration of a particular artist or a particular work of art was concerned. The port of King's Lynn appears to have played an important part in providing an access point for works of the art, influence and craftsmen, judging by the style of some of the surviving art connected with the town and its hinterland, and Norwich was understandably a focus of immigration for foreign artists in many periods, although the lack of early sixteenth-century examples is

---

[71] For the Guildhall glazing, http://www.cvma.ac.uk/publications/digital/norfolk/sites/norwich guildhall/history.html; for continental town hall glazing, see U. Lederle, *Gerechtigkeits-darstellungen in deutschen und niederländischen Rathäusern*, doctoral dissertation, Heidelburg, Philippsburg, 1937.

[72] These remain largely unpublished. They include fragments in the Castle Museum, Norwich, Foulsham church and there are some drawings by G. A. King in the Norfolk Record Office. For the Surrey House glass, see E. A. Kent, 'The Houses of the Dukes of Norfolk in Norwich', *Norfolk Archaeology* 24, 1932, 73–87.

puzzling. Further research may show that what was thought to be foreign influence was in fact the result of local development and may shed more light on the role of workshop practice and the interplay between style and design. It must not be forgotten that although foreign influences, whether direct or mediated via other parts of England, were important for art in Norfolk, the county was always open to developments from within the country, particularly from London, although its geographical position made it especially prone to the influences coming from the sea.

PART II

TRADE AND ECONOMY

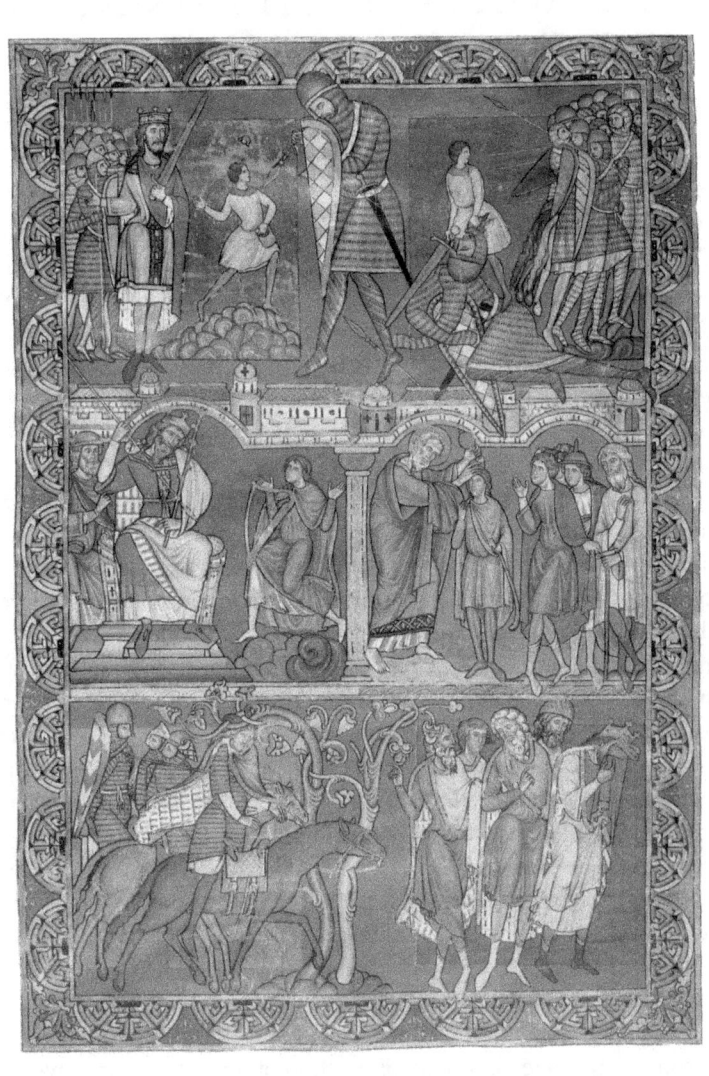

— Chapter 5 —

THE CIRCULATION, MINTING, AND USE OF COINS IN EAST ANGLIA, c.AD 580–675

Gareth Williams

AMONG THE MANY FINDS in the famous Sutton Hoo ship burial was a purse. This contained thirty-seven tremisses, three blank gold discs the size, shape and weight of tremisses, and two slightly larger ingots (Plate 1), with a total weight of 61.11 g, equivalent to just over forty-eight tremisses or sixteen solidi.[1] Both denominations survived the collapse of the western Roman Empire, and continued to be used in the eastern Roman (or Byzantine) coinage, as well as in various successor kingdoms in western Europe, including the Anglo-Saxon coinage which emerged around the end of the sixth century.

All of the Sutton Hoo coins were imported, although the blanks and ingots were probably produced locally. The coins are predominantly Frankish, from mints across France, Belgium, western Germany and Switzerland. The main concentration comes from north-eastern Frankish and Frisian mints, concentrated between the Seine valley and the Rhine, and thus from an area separated from (or connected to) East Anglia by the North Sea. The presence of these coins close to the Suffolk coast, in what is generally seen as an East Anglian royal grave, thus invites interpretation of East Anglia's monetary connections across the North Sea. Given the unique character of the Sutton Hoo burial as a whole, and given also the paucity of other coin finds from the early East Anglian kingdom, it has hitherto been difficult to ascertain whether or not Sutton Hoo presents a representative picture of monetary circulation. However, the corpus of coin finds from the region has grown substantially over recent decades, and the aim of this chapter is to reconsider against the background of this new evidence both the Sutton Hoo coins and the wider pattern of the importation, circulation and production of coinage in early East Anglia in relation to its place in the wider North Sea world.

Interpretations of the Sutton Hoo coins have varied, but there is no doubt that the coins only made up a small proportion of the gold in the grave.[2] This limited

---

[1] A. M. Stahl, 'The Nature of the Sutton Hoo Coin Parcel', in *Voyage to the Other World: The Legacy of Sutton Hoo*, ed. C. B. Kendall and P. S. Wells, Minneapolis 1992, 3–14.

[2] E. Schoenfeld and J. Schulmann, 'Sutton Hoo: An Economic Assessment', in *Voyage to the Other World*, ed, Kendall and Wells, 15–27.

PLATE 1 The coins, blanks and ingots from the Sutton Hoo purse. BM 1939.1003.1-42 (© Trustees of the British Museum).

value for the coins accords well with the established view of coin circulation in early Anglo-Saxon England developed in the 1960s and 1970s. According to this view, coin use had been widespread in late Roman Britain, but came to a halt in AD 410 when Rome abandoned Britain to its own devices. There was then a complete break in coin use until *c.*AD 600, when coinage was reintroduced in the kingdom of Kent, with further coin types following in London and York during the first half of the seventh century, with the beginnings of coinage in Kent linked both with the Augustinian mission and with a perception that Kent has closer ties with the Continent than was the case for other Anglo-Saxon kingdoms. On this interpretation, Sutton Hoo, and East Anglia more generally, lay completely outside the circles of monetary circulation at the time of the burial, and no coin type was attributed to East Anglia during the period of the early Anglo-Saxon gold coinage, which lasted until the late seventh century.[3]

THE CIRCULATION OF IMPORTED COINAGE IN THE FIFTH TO SEVENTH CENTURIES

There is no doubt that the early fifth century saw a fundamental break in the importation of coinage to Britain, and consequently to the nature of coin circulation. Coins were imported in large numbers until around AD 407–8, briefly supplemented on a smaller scale by coins of the usurper Constantius III

---

[3] J. P. C Kent, 'From Roman Britain to Anglo-Saxon England', in *Anglo-Saxon Coins: Studies Presented to F. M. Stenton on the Occasion of his 80th Birthday 17 May 1960*, ed. R. H. M. Dolley, London 1961, 1–22.

(407–11).⁴ However one interprets the end of Roman Britain, it seems clear that the decision was taken at this time to stop paying Roman troops in Britain with imported Roman coinage. Furthermore, there is no additional evidence to suggest that Anglo-Saxon minting began before the very end of the sixth century. The association of the beginning of minting with the conversion of Æthelberht of Kent by St Augustine in 597 still seems more likely than not. This appears to be consistent with a broader correlation across Europe between minting and a concept of Romanized Christian kingship,⁵ and provides a historical context for the introduction of minting in different Anglo-Saxon kingdoms. Thus far, the traditional interpretation holds good. However, when considering coin circulation rather than the official issue of coinage, the gap between the beginning of the fifth century and the end of the sixth century has now been partially filled in two ways.

Firstly, the coinage already in circulation at the beginning of the fifth century apparently continued in use for some time, supplemented to some extent by older coins brought back into use, although this does not mean that the character of monetary circulation remained unchanged. A large number of hoards are known with *tpqs* at the very beginning of the fifth century. These are dominated by silver siliquae, including both official issues and imitations of uncertain origin. Many of these are clipped, a phenomenon which is rarely observed on the Continent, and seems to a great extent to reflect the shortage of coins available in Britain. This probably took place with increasing severity over an extended period, with the final stage of clipping and deposition potentially taking place several decades after the date of issue, and thus well into the fifth century. Interestingly, even in the final stage of clipping, the centre of the coin, showing the imperial bust, survived.⁶ This interpretation of the chronology of clipping and hoarding is reinforced by analysis of the proportions of different coin types within the hoards, using hoards containing the comparatively rare coins of Constantine III as a reference point for the mixture of coins in other hoards.⁷ Recent analysis of single finds of siliquae also supports progressive clipping, and the continued use of clipped siliquae for some decades into the fifth century, although the exact duration of this sub-Roman coinage remains uncertain.⁸

Some clipping may be associated with unofficial abuse of the coinage, but it is also possible that much of the clipping of the fifth century was carried out officially, as a means of extending the limited coin stock, while enabling the clippings to be

---

4   R. A. Abdy, 'After Patching: Imported and Recycled Coinage in Fifth- and Sixth-Century Britain', in *Coinage and History in the North Sea World, c.500–1200. Essays in Honour of Marion Archibald*, ed. B. J. Cook and G. Williams, Leiden and Boston 2006, 75–98, at 80.
5   G. Williams, 'The Circulation and Function of Gold Coinage in Conversion-Period England, c.AD 580–680', in *Coinage and History in the North Sea World*, ed. Cook and Williams, 145–92.
6   P. Guest, 'Hoards from the End of Roman Britain', *Coin Hoards of Roman Britain* X, London 1997, 411–23; idem, *The Gold and Silver Coins from the Hoxne Treasure*, London 2005.
7   I am grateful to Nick Wells for useful discussion of this point.
8   T. S. N. Moorhead, R. Bland, and P. Walton, 'Finds of late Roman silver coins from England and Wales', in *The Traprain Law Hoard*, Society of Antiquaries of Scotland Monograph, ed. F. Hunter and K. Painter, Edinburgh, forthcoming.

recycled, either as further imitative siliquae or as bullion.⁹ The possibility of late locally produced imitative siliquae has yet to be studied in any detail, but even if no siliquae were produced, recycling clippings into ingots or some other form of bullion seems a strong possibility, since the late Roman economy was structured towards payment by weight, both within the empire and especially beyond the frontiers, even when payments were made predominantly in coin.¹⁰ This would also fit with the apparent resumption of use of earlier and obsolete coinage, as shown in some hoards.¹¹ These early coin types had little intrinsic value, and can perhaps be interpreted as reflecting the official sanction of re-use of earlier coins with a nominal value above the intrinsic value of their metal content.

None of this indicates complete continuity either in the nature of authority or of monetary circulation. Without the regular influx of coinage from the Continent, the monetary system of late Roman Britain could not survive, and the absence of a Roman army with coin to spend must also have had a wider impact on coin-use. Presumably the nature of taxation also changed, again with an impact on coin-use, although the exact nature of the change is not documented. However, what seems clear is that the changes in coin-use as represented in the hoards indicate a struggle to maintain a coin-based economy in the absence of continued imports of current coinage, and that the volume of currency in active circulation dramatically decreased. The re-introduction of obsolete coinage and prevalence of clipping could point to a complete breakdown of control, or to authorities controlling and sanctioning the use of currency which would not have been tolerated prior to the cessation of large-scale coin supply. The fact that clipping consistently respects the imperial bust, and that the clippings themselves are not found, for me suggests that a degree of control is more likely than a collapse into completely uncontrolled bullion. Either way, continued use of coin indicates a continued need for currency, even if we can only speculate about both the nature and the volume of that currency.

An interesting question here is the extent to which bronze coins continued to be used in the fifth century. Unlike gold and silver, these largely ceased to be hoarded. However, the presence of Roman bronze coins re-used as weights and pendants in Anglo-Saxon graves points to their availability in the settlement period, even if the coins in question were again recycled 'obsolete' types.¹² Furthermore,

---

9   Abdy, 'After Patching'; idem, 'Patching and Oxborough: The Latest Coin Hoards from Roman Britain or the First Early Medieval Hoards from England?', in *Coin Hoards in Roman Britain* XII, Collection Moneta 97, ed. R. A. Abdy, E. Ghey, C. Hughes and I. Leins, Wetteren 2009, 394–5; idem, 'The Patching Hoard', in *The Traprain Law Hoard*, forthcoming.
10 J. P. C. Kent, and K. S Painter, *Wealth of the Roman World AD 300–700*, London 1977; P. Guest, 'Roman Gold and Hun Kings: The Use and Hoarding of Solidi in the Late Fourth and Fifth Centuries', in *Roman Coins outside the Empire: Ways and Phases, Contexts and Functions*, Collection Moneta 82, Wetteren 2008.
11 Williams, 'Circulation and Function', 160.
12 For a useful and comparatively recent review of this material, T. S. N. Moorhead, 'Roman Bronze Coinage in Sub-Roman and Early Anglo-Saxon England', in *Coinage and History in the North Sea World*, ed. Cook and Williams, 99–109. Moorhead here rejects the idea of continuity in the use of Roman bronze coins in the fifth century, but for a position more broadly in agreement with that

Roman bronze coins of the fourth century, typically heavily worn, are among the most common stray finds to be discovered today, and without context many of these could also have been deposited post-410.[13] Only the excavation of more in the way of tightly dateable fifth-century sites, and the presence (or absence) of earlier coins in fifth-century layers will resolve this.

Returning to the gold and silver, if the interpretation suggested above is correct, it suggests that some element of sub-Roman authority survived the official withdrawal of Roman troops in the early fifth century, an interpretation which has been explored in a number of variations by both historians and archaeologists since the 1970s. What is striking about this is that both hoards and single finds suggest that coin use remained most widespread in southern and eastern Britain, although coins seem to have largely disappeared in the West Midlands and the North-West. Coins had previously circulated across Roman Britain, even if with a greater concentration in the east.[14] Thus, post-Roman coin use is not concentrated in the British west, but in the primary areas of Anglo-Saxon settlement, including East Anglia, with the largest and best known of these fifth-century hoards coming from Hoxne in Norfolk.[15] This eastern focus may also relate to a comparatively short-lived burst of hoarding of both coins and bullion in the Anglo-Saxon homelands, beyond the frontiers of the Roman Empire, but clearly indicating economic interaction, although this need not have been limited to military service and/or plunder.[16] In this phase of activity, we may therefore perhaps even see monetary movement from East Anglia (and elsewhere in south-eastern Britain) eastward across the North Sea. Establishing a causal link between the continued availability of precious metal in eastern England and the intensification of Anglo-Saxon migration and eventual settlement lies beyond the scope of this chapter, but presents an interesting line of enquiry for future research.

The second element which helps to fill the gap *c*.AD 410–600 is a growing body of evidence which indicates continued importation of coinage, albeit on a rather smaller scale than during the preceding period. Here the picture has changed substantially as a result of the growth of metal detecting as a hobby since the 1970s. Prior to this, only a very small number of imported coins were recorded, mostly from Kent (exceptions including Sutton Hoo, and a seventh-century hoard from Crondall in Hampshire, containing both imported and Anglo-Saxon coins), mostly

---

presented here, see idem, 'Early Byzantine Copper Coins Found in Britain: A Review in the Light of New Finds Recorded by the Portable Antiquities Scheme', in *Ancient History, Numismatics and Epigraphy in the Mediterranean World: Studies in Memory of Clemens E. Bosch and Sabahat Atlan and in honour of Nezahat Baydur*, ed. O. Tekin, Istanbul 2009, 263–74.

[13] Williams, 'Circulation and Function', 160.
[14] For a recent study of changing patterns of coin circulation in Roman Britain, P. Walton, *Rethinking Roman Britain: Coinage and Archaeology*, Collection Moneta 137, Wetteren 2012.
[15] Guest, *Hoxne Treasure*.
[16] H. W. Horsnæs, 'Late Roman and Byzantine Coins Found in Denmark', in *Byzantine Coins in Central Europe between the 5th and 10th Century*, Moravia Magna, Seria Polona, vol. III, ed. M. Woloszyn, Kraków 2009, 231–70; idem, *Crossing Boundaries. An Analysis of Roman Coins in Danish contexts*. Vol. 1. *Finds from Sealand, Funen and Jutland*, Copenhagen 2010.

from graves, and mostly showing secondary usage as pendants.[17] These pendants clearly represent demonetization of the coins, but nevertheless relied on the presence of coins for re-use. However, the finds record is now dominated by metal-detected single finds, and the majority of these show no signs of secondary usage, whereas the coin-pendants are largely (though not exclusively) confined to graves, presenting a pattern of casual loss of coins through use, in contrast to the deliberate deposition of coin-jewellery in graves.[18] In fact, a small number of coins without secondary treatment are also recorded from seventh-century graves, with a purse typically containing one or two coins perhaps a symbolic representation of moneyed wealth.[19] Here the Sutton Hoo purse simply reflects the atypical wealth of the grave in other respects.

The supply of coins comes from a variety of sources, including late Roman/Byzantine, 'Gallic' pseudo-Imperial, Merovingian, Visigothic, Burgundian, and even a couple of Sasanian coins.[20] Imported coins can be traced from the early fifth century through to the seventh, with a number of peaks and troughs. The supply of Byzantine and sub-Byzantine coins dried up in the reign of Heraclius (610–40), but Merovingian coins continued to be imported well into the seventh century, although the majority of these were of the mint-and-moneyer type, and cannot be precisely dated. No large hoards are known from after the mid-fifth century, but a mixed hoard of gold and silver coins and hack-silver from Patching, West Sussex (tpq 470), points to the use of both imported coin and bullion, while a small hoard of fragmented coin jewellery from Oxborough, Norfolk (tpq 475) (Plate 2), shows both the secondary treatment of coins as jewellery and subsequent re-use as bullion.[21]

The location of these hoards reflects the widespread distribution of the single finds of imported coins. Kent still has by far the largest concentration of imported coins in this period, but no longer completely predominates, with an overall distribution of imported single finds much the same as the hoards and single finds of the early fifth century, with coins distributed across much of eastern and southern England, with a particular concentration in East Anglia, as well as in Essex, Lincolnshire and Kent. In addition to hoards, grave finds and individual stray finds, we now also have increasing numbers of single finds from so-called 'productive sites', which show evidence of trade and exchange, including imports, well before the establishment of the *wics* of the late seventh and eighth centuries.[22] These are

---

[17] S. E. Rigold, 'The Sutton Hoo Coins in the Light of the Contemporary Background of Coinage in England', in *The Sutton Hoo Ship Burial*, vol. 1, *Excavations, Background, the Ship, Dating and Inventory*, ed. R. Bruce-Mitford, London 1975, 653–77.
[18] Williams, 'Circulation and Function', 162–4.
[19] R. A. Abdy and G. Williams, 'A Catalogue of Hoards and Single Finds from the British Isles, c.AD 410–680', in *Coinage and History in the North Sea World*, ed. Cook and Williams, 11–74, at 21–2.
[20] Abdy and Williams, 'Catalogue', *passim*.
[21] Abdy, 'After Patching', 'Patching and Oxborough', 'The Patching Hoard'.
[22] T. Pestell and K. Ulmschneider, (eds), *Markets in Early Medieval Europe: Trading and 'Productive' sites, 650–850*, Bollington 2003; T. Pestell, 'Markets, emporia, wics, and "Productive" Sites: Pre-Viking Trade Centres in Anglo-Saxon England', in *The Oxford Handbook of Anglo-Saxon Archaeology*, ed. D. Hamerow, D. A. Hinton and S. Crawford, Oxford 2011, 556–79.

PLATE 2 The Oxborough hoard, *tpq* AD 475. BM 2003.0713.1-4 (© Trustees of the British Museum).

again focused in the east, with three of the most important being at Rendlesham and Coddenham in Suffolk, and Heckington (also known as the 'South Lincolnshire productive site'), in Lincolnshire.[23]

This distribution should come as no surprise. While the post-war generation of scholars who originally interpreted Sutton Hoo were inclined to see Britain's island status as something which isolated it from the Continent, more recent approaches have stressed the importance of maritime contacts in this period, and (as reflected in the theme of this volume) particularly the importance of the North Sea as a connecting route rather than a barrier.[24] At the same time, there is increasing evidence of continued trade with the Byzantine empire, as well as with closer neighbours across the North Sea and along the Atlantic seaboard.[25]

---

[23] M. A. S. Blackburn, '"Productive" Sites and the Pattern of Coin Loss in England, 600–1180', in *Markets in Early Medieval Europe*, ed. Pestell and Ulmschneider, 20–36; A. Daubney, 'Heckington', in N. Christie, 'Medieval Britain and Ireland in 2006', *Medieval Archaeology* 51, 40–54; Pestell, 'Markets, *emporia*, *wics*, and "Productive" Sites'.

[24] E.g. I. Wood, *The Merovingian North Sea*, Alingsås 1983; M. O. H. Carver (ed.), *The Age of Sutton Hoo: The Seventh Century in North-Western Europe*, Woodbridge 1992; E. Kramer, I. Stoumann and A. Greg (eds), *Kings of the North Sea, AD 250–850*, Assen 2000.

[25] E. Campbell, 'Trade in the Dark-Age West: A Peripheral Activity?', in *Scotland in Dark-Age Britain*, ed. B. E. Crawford, St Andrews 1996, 79–91; J. Wooding, *Communication and Commerce along the Western Sealanes AD 400–800*, Oxford 1996; K. R. Dark (ed.), *External Contacts and the Economy of Late Roman and Post-Roman Britain*, Woodbridge 1996; A. Harris, *Byzantium, Britain & the West: The Archaeology of Cultural Identity, AD 400–650*, Stroud 2003.

Two trade routes into Britain can be observed, one across the North Sea to Frisia and northern Francia (connecting via the Rhine valley to southern Europe and the Mediterranean) and the other via the English Channel and the Atlantic to southern Francia, Spain and beyond. Given the location of East Anglia, one would expect that it would be supplied primarily via the direct North Sea route. In fact, the single finds from East Anglia (as well as the Sutton Hoo purse) include a number which could well have come via the western route, since these include both Visigothic and Provençal pseudo-Imperial issues which are more likely to have circulated in south-west France and Spain than in the north. However, a gradual shift northward overland cannot be excluded, since Continental hoards also show a relatively uncontrolled circulation of coins from different mints. It is therefore unclear whether these southern issues came directly to East Anglia via the western seaboard and then the North Sea, or overland to northern Francia/Frisia and then via the North Sea, or (less probably) whether they entered circulation in southern England and then made their way north to East Anglia overland. Nevertheless, although finds of the mint-and-moneyer type reflect a random distribution of Frankish mints, there is a definite tendency among East Anglian finds towards coins from north-eastern mints, including the major trading centres of Dorestad and Quentovic as well as mints such as Chalons-sur-Saône and Cologne, indicating trade along the Rhine valley to the North Sea. There are also East Anglian finds of the Frisian 'Nietap' and 'Dronrijp' types.[26] All of this points to strong monetary links across the North Sea.

A further link with Frisia may be suggested by the three blank flans in the Sutton Hoo purse. Parallels are known from the Frisian Dronrijp hoard, as well as from the Crondall hoard, which contained blank flans as well as Anglo-Saxon, Frankish, Frisian and Byzantine coins.[27] However, there is increasing single-find evidence for a bullion economy in East Anglia and Essex in this period. Just since 2010, detectorists have discovered a tremissis-sized blank flan from near Woodbridge, a cut fraction of a Frankish tremissis from near Colchester, a whole tremissis with a cut fraction of another attached to it (presumably to increase the weight), again from Rendlesham, and another whole tremissis with a fragment of a second attached from Beachamwell, Norfolk.[28] Without the evidence of the single finds, the blanks in both Sutton Hoo and Crondall could be seen as make-weights to round up the total to a nominal total weight, or total number of 'coins', reflecting a symbolic function for the entire hoard rather than a genuinely monetary role within it.[29] By

---

[26] Catalogues of the recorded (to 2009) examples of imported gold coins of the fifth to seventh centuries, organized by ruler or, in the case of the mint-and-moneyer coinage, first by mint then by moneyer, are provided in G. Williams, 'Anglo-Saxon Gold Coinage, Part 1: The Transition from Roman to Anglo-Saxon coinage', *British Numismatic Journal* 80, 2010, 51–75.

[27] C. H. V. Sutherland, *Anglo-Saxon Gold Coinage in the Light of the Crondall Hoard*, Oxford 1948, 8, 67–8; P. Grierson and M. A. S. Blackburn, *Medieval European Coinage*, vol. I, *The Early Middle Ages*, Cambridge 1986, 125.

[28] Treasure cases 2010 T649; 2011 T202; 2011 T704; 2011 T199.

[29] E.g., P. Grierson, 'The Purpose of the Sutton Hoo Coins', *Antiquity* 44, 1970, 14–18. However, Grierson's interpretation was based on a round number of 100 coins in the hoard, which was not the case (Williams, 'Circulation and Function', 173–7).

contrast, the single finds suggest a circulating currency which included bullion alongside minted coin, in which case the Sutton Hoo and Crondall bullion can also potentially be interpreted in the same way.

Against this background, the coins from Sutton Hoo seem less exceptional, although they remain one of the largest groups of coins deposited in England in the sixth or seventh centuries to be discovered so far, and the mixture of coins in the purse reflects a wider pattern of the circulation of coins and related currency in East Anglia in the sixth and early seventh centuries, with the coins in the purse probably representing continental contacts both via the North Sea and perhaps also, directly or indirectly, the western sea-lanes.

PRODUCTION AND CIRCULATION OF ANGLO-SAXON GOLD COINS

What are we to make, however, of the absence of native Anglo-Saxon coins in the Sutton Hoo purse? Here it is important to remember that seventh-century England was politically fragmented, with a number of independent kingdoms, although individual kings might temporarily exercise a degree of overlordship over others.[30] A broad correlation between minting and a concept of Romanized Christian kingship has been noted as a feature of post-Roman European coinage, and this seems to apply to Anglo-Saxon kingdoms as well as to their continental counterparts, with no substantive Anglo-Saxon types which can be convincingly interpreted as predating Augustine's mission.[31] This correlation only applies to a particular form of Romanized Christian kingship, not to Christian kingship *per se*, and minting was not introduced in Ireland, Scotland and Wales until much later.[32] This is of course an over-simplified view of the political-religious context, and it may be argued that minting owes as much to economic/fiscal factors as to different models of kingship, but given the demonstrable use of imported gold coin across much of England prior to the commencement of minting, and the continued usage of imported coins and bullion after minting was introduced, it is difficult to see that purely economic needs for currency required localized minting, and conversion seems to have been the major spur.

Since different kingdoms converted to Christianity at different times, it is only to be expected that they also began minting at different times, and this appears to

---

[30] J. Campbell, *Bede's Reges and Principes*, Jarrow Lecture 1979; B. A. E. Yorke, 'The Vocabulary of Anglo-Saxon Overlordship', *Anglo-Saxon Studies in Archaeology and History* 2, 1981, 171–200; D. N. Dumville, 'The Terminology of Overkingship in Early Anglo-Saxon Kingship', in *The Anglo-Saxons from the Migration Period to the Eighth Century: An Ethnographic Perspective*, ed. J. Hines, Woodbridge 1997, 345–73.

[31] Sutherland, *Anglo-Saxon Gold Coinage*; P. Grierson, *The Coins of Medieval Europe*, London 1991, *passim*; Williams, 'Circulation and Function', 187; idem, 'Kingship, Christianity and Coinage: Monetary and Political Perspectives on Silver Economy in the Viking Age', in *Silver Economy in the Viking Age*, ed. J. Graham-Campbell and G. Williams, Walnut Springs, CA 2007, 177–214, at 206.

[32] Williams, 'Circulation and Function', 187.

be the case, in so far as individual types can be attributed to particular kingdoms, and in so far as a relative chronology of coin- types can be established. Unfortunately, Sutton Hoo, with no local coins, cannot be precisely dated in relation to the documented conversion of East Anglia. The burial has been associated with King Rædwald (died c.625), largely on the basis of a particular interpretation of the dating of the coins.[33] However, while this interpretation has been repeated so often that it is frequently presented as if it were a fact, the method and interpretation have been repeatedly questioned, and a broader dating of c.610–640 seems a more realistic view, at least as far as any dating is based on the Sutton Hoo coins themselves.[34]

An important forthcoming article by Marion Archibald on the Wilton Cross pendant (Plate 3) may help to narrow this down again, as it seeks to provide an entirely independent means of dating the Sutton Hoo burial. The Wilton Cross incorporates a solidus of Heraclius and Heraclius Constantine minted in c.623. The solidus was mounted once in a gold collar, originally looped for suspension, and then re-used without the loop as an inner collar within a more elaborate gold and garnet cross, which has been linked stylistically by other archaeologists with the gold and garnet ornaments from Sutton Hoo, to the extent to which it has been seen either as a (possibly later) product of the same workshop, or as a product of a broader 'school' of associated metalwork. Archibald argues that the coin is unlikely to have been mounted in the cross before the mid 630s, and that if the attribution of the pendant itself as a late product of the Sutton Hoo workshop is accepted, this would then be consistent with the traditional date of c.625 for the Sutton Hoo burial, although she cautiously notes that slightly later dates for both cross and burial are also possible.[35] Rædwald thus remains a very strong possibility, both within the wider dating proposed for the Sutton Hoo coins, and on the tighter dating proposed by Archibald, but the possible date range continues to span Rædwald's own conversion and apostasy, through to the more lasting adoption of Christianity in East Anglia in the 630s.

---

[33] R. L. S. Bruce-Mitford, 'Introduction and Observations on the Dating of the Hoard and the Burial', in *The Sutton Hoo Ship Burial*, vol. 1, ed. Bruce-Mitford, 578–88; J. P. C Kent, 'The Date of the Sutton Hoo Hoard', in ibid., 588–607.

[34] D. Brown, 'The Dating of the Sutton Hoo Coins', in *Anglo-Saxon Studies in Archaeology and History* 2, BAR British Series 92, Oxford 1981, 71–86; A. M. Stahl and W. A. Oddy, 'The Date of the Sutton Hoo Coins', in *Sutton Hoo: Fifty Years After*, ed. R. Farrell and C. de Vegvar, Kalamazoo 1992, 129–47; G. Williams, 'Sutton Hoo: The Coins', in *Hoops-Reallexikon der Germanischen Altertumskunde* 30, 2005, 150–3.

[35] M. M. Archibald, 'The Wilton Cross Coin Pendant: Numismatic Aspects and Implications', in *Early Medieval Art and Archaeology in the Northern World*, ed. A. Reynolds and L. Webster, Leiden and Boston, forthcoming. It should be noted that this paper was originally completed in 2005, but publication was delayed for reasons beyond its author's control. The article thus predates the discovery of the Staffordshire hoard in 2009. The large quantity of gold and garnet work in that hoard, including some very close in style to both the Sutton Hoo ornaments and the Wilton Cross, raises important questions both about the attribution of all such work to a single workshop, and about both the geographical attributions and dating of the styles. These questions are unlikely to be resolved quickly, but the *tpq* for the Wilton Cross provided by the solidus means that it will be central to this discussion.

PLATE 3 Cross-pendant from Wilton, Norfolk, incorporating a light-weight gold solidus of Heraclius and Heraclius Constantine. BM 1859.0512.1 (© Trustees of the British Museum).

One of the problems here is that the early Anglo-Saxon coin types are largely anonymous, with either no inscriptions at all, or inscriptions which are either blundered or enigmatic. Only one coinage can be attributed with any certainty. Semi-literate coins attributed to Eadbald of Kent (616–40) suggest that he minted in both London and Canterbury.[36] Another type, with a facing bare-headed bust which may represent an episcopal rather than a royal coinage, has an inscription LONDVNIV, and can reasonably be attributed to London. Other types with less literate London inscriptions cannot be so safely attributed, since they could equally well be coins minted elsewhere, but imitating London issues.[37]

[36] M. A. S. Blackburn, 'A New Coin of King Eadbald of Kent (616–40)', *Chris Rudd List* 34,1998, 2–4; idem, 'Two New Types of Anglo-Saxon Gold Shillings', in *Coinage and History in the North Sea World*, ed. Cook and Williams, 127–40; G. Williams, 'The Gold Coinage of Eadbald, King of Kent (AD 616–40)', *British Numismatic Journal* 68, 1998, 137–40; P. Shaw, 'Orthographic Standardisation and Seventh- and Eighth-Century Coin Inscriptions', in *Studies in Early Medieval Coinage. Two Decades of Discovery* 1 ed. T. Abramson, Woodbridge 2008, 97–112.

[37] Sutherland, *Anglo-Saxon Gold Coinage*, 41–5, 856; A. Gannon, *The Iconography of Early Anglo-Saxon Coinage. Sixth to Eighth Centuries*, Oxford 2003, 25–6; Williams, 'Anglo-Saxon Gold Coinage. Part 2'.

Other coin types can be attributed purely on the basis of their distribution, with varying degrees of certainty. For example, a group of related types found predominantly in Yorkshire but with a few outlying examples in Lindsey, can reasonably be interpreted as products of the kingdom of Northumbria or of the smaller Northumbrian kingdom of Deira.[38] Other types are more problematic, either because they are rare and unique (and therefore statistically meaningless), or because most or all of the known examples come from a hoard found at Crondall in Hampshire. This hoard contains a wide variety of imported and Anglo-Saxon issues, indicating a lack of control over the circulation of coinage at the place and time in which the hoard was gathered together. Coins within the hoard could therefore potentially come from several different Anglo-Saxon kingdoms, including East Anglia. Since the hoard was probably deposited around AD 640, with the general correlation of minting and Christian kingship mentioned above, types within the hoard might reasonably be assumed to come from kingdoms which had already converted by that time, although one must be wary of circular arguments here.

There are no hoards of any size for the remainder of the gold series, which probably continued into the 670s, with pale gold (i.e. more silver than gold) types succeeding the earlier gold issues, and being supplanted in turn by transitional types with only minimal gold content, and eventually c.675–80 by a purely silver coinage.[39] Despite the lack of hoards, these later issues seem to have been struck in larger quantities, as they are found more frequently as single finds than most of the earlier gold coins, and typically seem to have been struck from a greater number of dies. While none of the pale gold or transitional types can be attributed to individual kingdoms on the basis of literate inscriptions, the greater numbers do permit a study of the distribution.

IDENTIFYING EAST ANGLIAN COINAGE

Against this background, what can we say about East Anglia? There are no coin types that carry inscriptions which can be linked plausibly either with a known East Anglian ruler, or with any East Anglian mint. However, if the suggested link between Christianization and minting holds good, one might expect there to have been East Anglian issues as early as the 620s, and more probably from the 630s, but this is only expectation rather than fact. Since the majority of early Anglo-Saxon coin-types lack inscriptions, it is certainly possible that one or more of these originated in East Anglia, but this can only be argued for individual coin-types on the basis of distribution. In 1993, with the exception of the productive site at Coddenham, finds of Anglo-Saxon gold coins in East Anglia were 'virtually absent' (in contrast to finds of imported Merovingian tremisses, and later Anglo-Saxon

---

[38] G. Williams, 'The Gold Coinage of Seventh-Century Northumbria Revisited', *N Circ* cxv, no. 1, February 2007, 6–8; Williams, 'Anglo-Saxon Gold Coinage. Part 2'.
[39] Williams, 'Anglo-Saxon Gold Coinage. Part 2'.

PLATE 4
4.1 Gold solidus, Helena type
4.2 Gold solidus, Two Emperors type
(both © Trustees of the British Museum)

silver coins),[40] but a steady increase in the number of East Anglian finds means that our understanding of the distribution of several types has changed. Anglo-Saxon issues included both tremisses/shillings and the larger solidi. In the latter denomination, two have possible East Anglian assocations. Both imitate earlier Roman types, one (from Chapel Hill, near Markshall, Norfolk) of Helena, mother of Constantine the Great, the other (from Merton, Norfolk) a type showing two emperors on the reverse, and shared by several fourth-century emperors, although most closely related to designs of Valentinian I and Magnus Maximus (Plate 4).[41] Each is currently known only from a single example, which is statistically insignificant, and the fact that the Two Emperors coin has effectively been demonetized by mounting it as a pendant makes it even less reliable for interpretation of minting and monetary circulation. However, the fact that both types derive from Roman rather than Frankish prototypes (unlike most tremisses) is an interesting coincidence. Continuing that line of coincidence (and perhaps pushing it too far), one may note that one of the types currently known only from the Crondall hoard is derived from a type of Licinius.[42] An attribution to East Anglia is currently no more than a matter of speculation, and one which will be increasingly difficult to sustain in the absence of East Anglian finds, as the total number of coin-finds from the region steadily increases. However, there are no other coin-types represented in Crondall which have a distribution which points to East Anglia, although on the arguments given above, one might expect minting to have begun there before the hoard was deposited.

One type known from Crondall is also recorded from East Anglia. This is a type with a blundered inscription, derived from a more literate type with the inscription WITMEN MONITA (either 'Witmen the moneyer' or possibly 'money of Witmen'). The literate example cannot be attributed, since it is known only from a single example with an unrecorded find-spot (Plate 5.1),[43] but an example of the Witmen-derivative 1 is known from the productive site at Rendlesham, Suffolk. However,

---

[40] D. M. Metcalf, *Thrymsas and Sceattas in the Ashmolean Museum, Oxford*, Royal Numismatic Society Special Publication no. 276, vol. 1, London 1993, 33, 43.
[41] Sutherland, *Anglo-Saxon Gold Coinage*, nos. 20–21; Abdy and Williams, 'Catalogue', nos. 276, 270.
[42] Sutherland, *Anglo-Saxon Gold Coinage*, 39–41, 81–2.
[43] Ibid., no. 57.

PLATE 5
5.1 Gold shilling, Witmen prototype
5.2 Gold shilling, Witmen-derivative 2
5.3 Pale gold shilling, Crispus type
5.4 Pale gold shilling, Constantine type.
5.5 Pale gold shilling, Two Emperors type
5.6 Transitional shilling, Vanimundus type (all © Trustees of the British Museum)

this is one of the most common types in the Crondall phase, and has a distribution across much of south-east England.[44] The fact that there are four separate find-spots in Kent, and no more than one find (counting Crondall as one find, although it contained twenty-one coins of the type) in any other county, points towards a Kentish origin, suggesting that the Rendlesham example indicates the circulation of imported coin rather than a local issue. This contrasts with a second related type (Witmen-derivative 2), with a blundered inscription with variants around a form WVNNEETON (Plate 5.2). It does not appear in Crondall, although the metal content suggests that it may have been contemporary with the later types in the hoard, including Witmen-derivative 1.[45] The absence of the type from the hoard could indicate no more than an element of geographical separation. Again there is only a single East Anglian example, from near Ufford in Suffolk, but the absence of any examples from Kent (or Crondall) and the presence of other examples in Essex, Buckinghamshire, Gloucestershire, South Lincolnshire and 'the Thames river' makes an origin north of the Thames probable, even if the evidence is currently too weak to suggest a more specific attribution.[46]

[44] Williams, 'Anglo-Saxon Gold Coinage. Part 2'.
[45] D. Hook and G. Williams, 'Analysis of Gold Content and Its Implications for the Chronology of the Early Anglo-Saxon Coinage', in A. Gannon (with contributions by M. M. Archibald, D. Hook and G. Williams), *Sylloge of Coins of the British Isles, 63. British Museum. Anglo-Saxon Coins. Part I. Early Anglo-Saxon Coins and Continental Silver Coins of the North Sea, c.600–760*, London, forthcoming.
[46] Williams, 'Anglo-Saxon Gold Coinage. Part 2'.

Matters become clearer in the group of pale-gold types which are normally taken to post-date the Crondall hoard, although recent analysis of metal content suggests that the beginning of this phase may have overlapped with the later types represented in Crondall. The phase contains four main types, all of which are derived from Roman designs. Of these, one, which imitates the *Concordia militum* type of Carausius, can plausibly be attributed to Kent, despite the small sample.[47] Another comparatively rare type, imitating a type of Crispus, but with a runic inscription *delaiona* or *desaiona* (Plate 5.3), can probably be attributed to East Anglia, with three examples from Suffolk (two from Coddenham and one from Eyke, near Woodbridge), with a single outlier near St Albans in Hertfordshire, although the inscription may represent a corrupted version of *De Lundona*.[48] An even stronger case can be made for a rather more numerous type copying a type of Constantine (Plate 5.4). Although there are outliers (one in each case) from London, Essex and Lincolnshire, a concentration of five in Norfolk and four in Suffolk, together with the spread of the outliers, now leaves little doubt of the East Anglian attribution, although Peterborough was earlier proposed, when the number of finds was smaller.[49] A further sub-type derived from this one, with a star rather than a hand in front of the imperial bust, also appears to be East Anglian, with two examples from Suffolk, and one from Norfolk.[50]

The most intriguing type in this phase is the most common, a shilling (Plate 5.5), with the same Two Emperors design as the Merton solidus. The distribution is widespread, with six examples from Suffolk, four from Norfolk, and one from Cambridgeshire, but also six from Kent, two from Essex, and one each from Buckinghamshire, Lincolnshire and London.[51] While the overall distribution appears to favour East Anglia, the presence of so many examples from Kent as well as East Anglia raises an interesting question. Is this genuinely a single type, in which case we have clearer evidence for monetary interaction between East Anglia and Kent (the type is also recorded on the Continent) than appears to have been typical in the seventh century? Alternatively, can this type be divided into distinct sub-types, with separate areas of circulation? A more detailed study of the type would help to resolve this, and such a study is planned, but has not yet taken place. Minting was thus firmly established in East Anglia in the pale gold phase, and the total numbers of finds currently suggest a greater volume of coin use in East Anglia than in any other kingdom, including the previously dominant Kent, although figures here are slightly distorted by the fact that the Coddenham and Rendlesham productive sites were both active in this phase, and a greater body of evidence will be required before this can be accepted as more than a trend.

---

[47] Ibid.
[48] Ibid.;Metcalf, *Thrymsas and Sceattas*, 44.
[49] Metcalf, *Thrymsas and Sceattas*, 49; Williams, 'Anglo-Saxon Gold Coinage. Part 2'.
[50] Williams 'Anglo-Saxon Gold Coinage. Part 2'.
[51] Ibid. Here again the balance of evidence has shifted towards East Anglia only recently, whereas in 1993 the evidence still pointed towards Kent (Metcalf, *Thrymsas and Sceattas*, 46).

With minting already established in this phase, one would expect to find East Anglian minting in the transitional phase that followed. The types in this phase began in pale gold but declined relatively quickly to contain only minimal traces of gold, thus forming a transition into the more extensive silver coinage. There are two main types within this phase. The rarer of the two, copying the name of a continental moneyer, Vanimundus, appears to be East Anglian, with a distribution dominated by Norfolk, Suffolk and Cambridgeshire, with outliers in neighbouring counties and only a single example from Kent (Plate 5.6).[52] The more common type in this phase, which carries the runic inscription *pada*, is more complicated. Like the Two Emperors type, distribution of the Pada coins is widespread, with examples from both East Anglia and Kent, as well as from Essex and several other counties/kingdoms, and the overall distribution points to monetary circulation and interaction across the borders of the different kingdoms. As with other types, the increase in East Anglian finds is relatively recent, with the distribution previously pointing much more strongly towards a Kentish origin.[53] The Pada coinage is further complicated by the fact that the series has three main sub-types, normally interpreted as struck consecutively at the same mint. However, recent analysis of the metal content suggests that they could be contemporary (or at least overlapping) rather than consecutive, wherever they were minted.[54] All three main sub-types are represented both in East Anglia and elsewhere, pointing to extensive circulation, and further work is needed before any of these can be attributed with any certainty.[55]

SUMMARY AND CONCLUSIONS

In the fifth and sixth centuries, East Anglia fits a wider pattern of coin circulation in eastern and south-eastern England, with continued use over some decades, on a decreasing scale, of the coin stock already available in England at the beginning of the fifth century, including both current and curated obsolete coinage. This was supplemented, and eventually entirely replaced, by a continued influx of coin from the Continent, although on a much reduced scale. While some of the imported coins may reflect use of the western sea-lanes, it appears that the bulk of the imported coin reached East Anglia via the North Sea from Frisia and northern Francia. The same period also saw a flow of coinage eastwards across the North Sea into the Anglo-Saxon homelands, and this may also have passed through East Anglia and other parts of eastern England en route.

The seventh century saw continued monetary imports across the North Sea and beyond, reflected increasingly through single finds of coins showing no sign of sec-

---

[52] Ibid. This represents a shift from an earlier suggestion of London/Essex (Metcalf, *Thrymsas and Sceattas*, 44).
[53] Metcalf, *Thrymsas and sceattas*, 44; Williams, 'Anglo-Saxon Gold Coinage. Part 2'.
[54] Hook and Williams, 'Analysis of Gold Content'.
[55] Discussed further in Williams, 'Anglo-Saxon Gold Coinage. Part 2'.

ondary usage. These were supplemented for monetary purposes by bullion, now known from single finds as well as from Sutton Hoo. This, together with the wide range of imported types, suggests that coins themselves functioned partly as bullion rather than solely as regulated currency, while the existence of such a symbolically neutral bullion currency suggests that the coins had an economic function rather than functioning within purely social 'special purpose' exchanges. Again, parallels in Frisia point to continued economic contact across the North Sea.

Minting began in East Anglia at some point in the seventh century, probably following the adoption of Christianity, and therefore no later than the 630s, although no coins can yet be firmly attributed to East Anglia in the phase of 'good' gold coinage up to c.650. However, there are several unattributed types within this phase which may yet turn out to have East Anglian origins. Within the pale gold phase that followed, the Crispus and Constantine types can be attributed to East Anglia, and perhaps also some or all of the Two Emperors type, although this is less certain. In the transitional stage that followed that, the Vanimundus type is almost certainly East Anglian, and this may also be true of one or more of the main varieties of the Pada type. The uncertainty concerning the attribution of some of the types with widespread distribution, and the presence of outlying finds both of East Anglian coins found elsewhere and Kentish coins in East Anglia, together with the wider concentration of coin finds in eastern England, provide a useful reminder that the North Sea provided an important alternative to overland travel for contacts between the eastern Anglo-Saxon kingdoms. An interpretation of early East Anglia as an area isolated from coin use is no longer tenable, either before or after the introduction of Anglo-Saxon minting c.600, even if there is not yet sufficient evidence in place for a detailed interpretation of the coin-based economy. However, as the volume of evidence grows, we may reasonably expect to develop an ever clearer picture both of how coins were used within East Anglia itself, and of how the coin finds reflect wider economic connections with neighbours on both sides of the North Sea.

ACKNOWLEDGEMENTS

I am grateful to Marion Archibald for helpful comments on this paper, and for permission to discuss her then unpublished article on the Wilton Cross. I have also benefited in developing the ideas expressed here from discussion with Richard Abdy, Anna Gannon, Peter Guest, Duncan Hook, Helle Horsnæs, Sam Moorhead, Philippa Walton and Nick Wells. Any mistakes are of course my own.

— Chapter 6 —

COINAGE IN PRE-VIKING EAST ANGLIA

Rory Naismith

COINS ARE one of the most important types of evidence for anyone seeking to find out about East Anglia and its place in the North Sea World during the Anglo-Saxon period. Where the sparse testimony of chronicles and charters peters out, and other material evidence is unavailable, coins provide a comparatively plentiful and reliable source for all kinds of purposes. Indeed, such is the political obscurity of East Anglia in the period running up to the Viking invasions of the later ninth century that there are even times when knowledge of regnal succession relies heavily or entirely on the coins.[1] Several kings otherwise known solely from problematic, late, or uninformative sources are also attested by contemporary coins, raising them in historians' estimation. Among such rulers are Beonna (c.749–60?) and Æthelberht I (fl. 749), the first East Anglian kings to place their names on coins in the middle of the eighth century;[2] the royal saint Æthelberht II (d. 794), slain by Offa of Mercia's command; and, another saint, Edmund (c.855–69), martyred by the Vikings. Others would have been completely forgotten were it not for their coins. These unlucky figures include Eadwald (796–c.800), who rose up against Mercian control following King Offa's (757–96) death; Æthelstan (c.825–45) and Æthelweard (c.845–55), the first two kings of an independent East Anglian kingdom established in the teeth of Mercian resistance; and Oswald and Æthelred, who probably ruled as Viking quislings after Edmund's martyrdom in the 870s.[3]

East Anglia hence enjoyed a rich numismatic history which complements the narrative that can be derived from written sources alone. But the 'sad stories of the

---

[1] For a general overview of East Anglia during this period, see S. Plunkett, *Suffolk in Anglo-Saxon Times*, Stroud 2005.
[2] The coinages of these rulers have been thoroughly analysed in M. Archibald, 'The Coinage of Beonna in the Light of the Middle Harling Hoard', *British Numismatic Journal* 55, 1985, 10–54, and 'A *Sceat* of Ethelbert I of East Anglia and Recent Finds of Coins of Beonna', *British Numismatic Journal* 65, 1995, 1–19.
[3] The coins of most of these rulers after the time of Beonna and Æthelberht I are collected in D. Chick, *The Coinage of Offa and His Contemporaries*, ed. M. Blackburn and R. Naismith, London 2010; and R. Naismith, *The Coinage of Southern England 796–865*, 2 vols, London 2011. For Æthelred and Oswald see below, p. 149.

deaths of kings' constitute just one aspect of the numismatic evidence. To take, quite literally, the flip side of the coin, the reverses of all these rulers' coins carried the names of the moneyers: the men responsible for running the business of receiving, melting and re-minting silver as it was brought in by customers. Where they worked is less clear, as no mints were named on East Anglian coins before the tenth century, though it is likely that Ipswich was always the leading centre of minting, and probably the only one for the century after about 760. Approximately thirty-five moneyers were named on East Anglian coinage down to the end of independent native coinage in the 870s, and in contrast to the swift, bloody succession of kings, these moneyers show a high degree of continuity.[4] To take one example, the moneyer Lul began his career during the 780s or 790s when Offa of Mercia held control over East Anglia. A few years later, he started producing coins for the local pretender Æthelberht, probably not long before his death in 794. Then it was back to Offa – until 796, when Lul's coins began instead to name the obscure local king Eadwald. Then, probably around 800, Eadwald was ousted in favour of another Mercian overlord, this time Coenwulf, for whom Lul struck coins for the rest of his career.[5] Lul had survived no fewer than four changes of ruler, and there were many other moneyers who had similar experiences. These moneyers seem not to have been members of any political establishment tied to the fortunes of a particular royal house, but were probably canny men of means and influence in the mercantile and artisanal community of the day. Indeed, they played an important part in the process of coin production, up to and including aspects of design. Kings at this time probably did not deal with 'the mint(s)' as a whole, but more often with individual moneyers, sometimes on a very personal level, as in the case of Lul, who was the sole moneyer responsible for Æthelberht II's coinage. Royal control, in other words, took diverse forms and must not be overestimated.[6]

The focus in this case will not be primarily on the stories of either kings or moneyers, fascinating though they are. The primary aim of this chapter is, rather, to look at why the kingdom of East Anglia did so well out of the coinage – that is, the economic and monetary role of coinage down to the Viking conquest, and how far it shows integration with other areas around the North Sea. What was it that kept Lul and others like him in business, and drew kings to take a hand in minting?

The answers lie in the scale and circulation of currency within East Anglia, and how the region related to the rest of England and other areas around the North Sea. This currency was, with very few exceptions, one of silver. Instituted in England and Frankia in the 670s, silver pennies weighing between one and one and a half grams came to dominate currency throughout northern Europe for over five centuries. Even within the years before 900 this currency saw a number of important

---

[4] Cf. the tables in Chick, *Coinage of Offa*, 178–81; and Naismith, *Southern England*, I, 144.
[5] For Lul's coins see Chick, *Coinage of Offa*, types 171–3, 186 and 251; and Naismith, *Southern England*, types E3 and E10.
[6] For further discussion of this theme see R. Naismith, *Money and Power in Anglo-Saxon England: the Southern English Kingdoms 757–865*, Cambridge 2012, 87–155.

changes. The first incarnation of the silver pennies looked very different to the broad, thin, inscribed coins on which Offa, later kings and their moneyers inscribed their names. Often known as *sceattas*, these first silver pennies were much smaller and thicker.[7] They rarely carried an inscription, making their dating and attribution problematic. This is compounded by the bewildering array of types produced between the inception of this coinage in the 670s and its end in southern England around 750. Over 200 varieties are recorded, probably made at thirty or more minting-places across England and at many more locations all around the North Sea, in what is now France, the Low Countries and even Denmark.[8] There has been a veritable transformation in knowledge of this coinage since the advent of metal-detecting as a hobby in the 1970s, and thanks to the detailed record-keeping of projects like the Corpus of Early Medieval Coin Finds and the Portable Antiquities Scheme, this period is now recognized as probably the richest in terms of coin-use between the end of the Roman Empire and the thirteenth century.[9]

Within this wealth of silver coinage, East Anglia figures prominently. Graph 1, based on the data available on the Corpus of Early Medieval Coin Finds, shows the distribution by modern counties of almost 3,000 single-finds of seventh- and early eighth-century silver pennies known to February 2012. Note that it excludes all coins known to have been found as part of hoards.[10]

The East Anglian counties of Norfolk and Suffolk, along with their neighbours Cambridgeshire, Hertfordshire, Essex and Lincolnshire, all do extremely well in terms of the national distribution of these finds. To some extent this is a perennial feature of the distribution of coin-finds throughout the Middle Ages: they tend to be concentrated in the eastern half of England from Yorkshire down to Kent and Hampshire, which hints at the association of coin-use with generally more densely settled lowland areas, and also at the principal source of bullion being silver brought across the Channel and the North Sea. Norfolk and Suffolk stand out even within this group of more richly represented areas, in part because they have both benefited from particularly active and well recorded metal-detecting activity in

---

[7] There is strong evidence that the small silver coins were already known as *denarii* or *pæningas* ('pennies') by the end of the seventh century. The term *sceat* may have come to be equated with these coins, although it probably emerged as a label for fractions of the gold *scilling*: see now J. Hines, 'Units of Account in Gold and Silver in Seventh-Century England: Scillingas, Sceattas and Pæningas', *Antiquaries Journal* 90, 2010, 153–73.

[8] The best survey of this rich period – though already out of date in some particulars – is D. M. Metcalf, *Thrymsas and Sceattas in the Ashmolean Museum, Oxford*, 3 vols, London, 1993–4. For its iconographical dimensions, A. Gannon, *The Iconography of Early Anglo-Saxon Coinage (Sixth to Eighth Centuries)*, Oxford 2003.

[9] Corpus of Early Medieval Coin Finds (based at the Fitzwilliam Museum, Cambridge): www.fitzmuseum.cam.ac.uk/emc/; Portable Antiquities Scheme (based at the British Museum): www.finds.org.uk.

[10] Hoards of *sceattas* are relatively scarce, in contrast to the volume of single-finds. For a list see http://www-cm.fitzmuseum.cam.ac.uk/dept/coins/projects/hoards/index.list.html; a recent and important addition is the Aldborough (Norfolk) hoard of sixty-five *sceattas*; a publication is currently being prepared by Adrian Marsden. For the small number of ninth-century East Anglian hoards see also Naismith, *Southern England* I, 59–82.

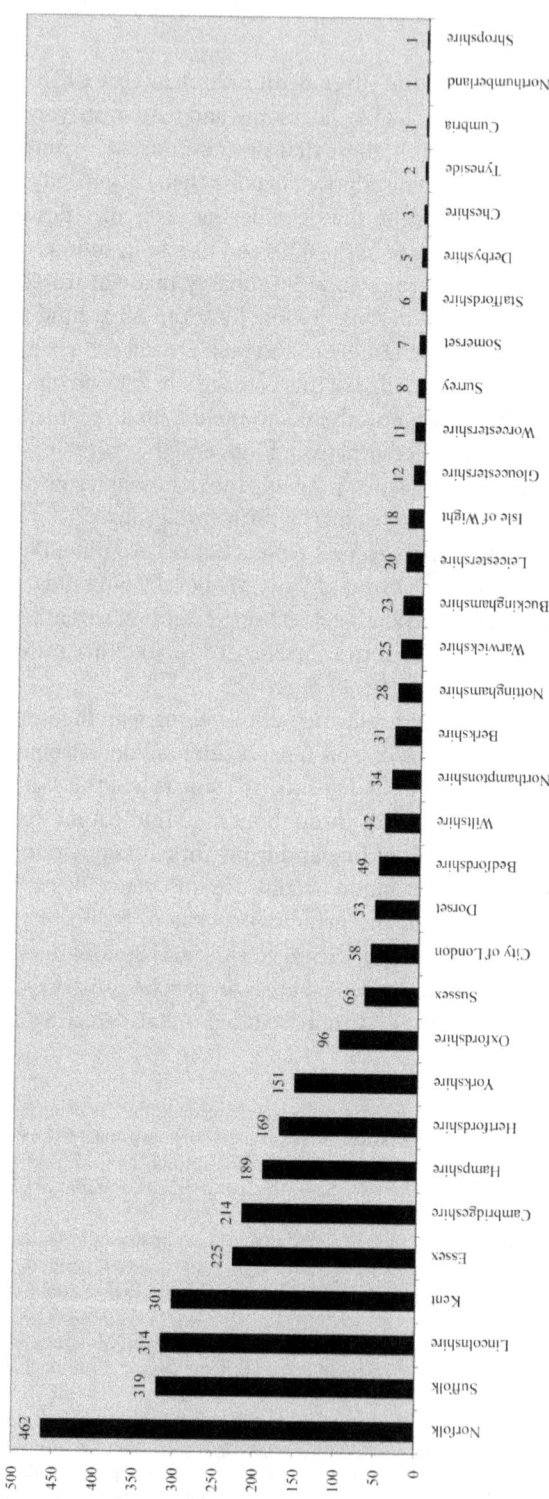

GRAPH 1 Numbers of single-finds of *sceattas* from various counties recorded on EMC (February 2012).

recent decades,[11] and partly because the use of coinage genuinely was especially intense within them.

The natural question is what kind of coins out of the many varieties available made up this vibrant East Anglian currency, and how its makeup differed from other parts of the country. Graph 2 shows the various types that have been found among 757 identifiable single-finds from Norfolk and Suffolk. The complex range of types and variants among the early pennies are here broken down into lettered series first laid out by Stuart Rigold in the 1970s, although there are some which do not fit so easily into these series and so are still numbered according to the typology instituted with the catalogue of the British Museum collection in the 1880s.[12] Naturally there is a huge amount of variation, and many types are known from only a handful of finds. The best represented types, by quite a substantial margin, are those which are known by the modern labels Series E and Series R, which represent about 20 per cent and 18 per cent of East Anglian finds, respectively. Series E is to some extent best treated as a pair with Series D, since these are the principal types from the Low Countries which circulated in England.[13] D was an early series, while E began at a relatively early date but continued for much of the eighth century. Their distribution is plentiful across eastern England; East Anglia does not stand out as having a higher proportional concentration of them than other areas. This is a reflection of the degree of economic and cultural interaction between England and the area of the modern Low Countries in the decades around 700 (even if the opposite leg of the journey is much less well represented among Dutch finds).[14] There are also other types, numerically fewer, which likewise originated abroad and which enjoyed a relatively significant representation in East Anglia. Series X, for example, occurs at several widely scattered pockets of concen-

---

[11] For an investigation of the pattern of searching within Norfolk see M. Chester-Kadwell, *Early Anglo-Saxon Communities in the Landscape of Norfolk*, British Archaeological Reports: British Series 481, Oxford 2009. See also J. Richards, J. Naylor and C. Holas-Clark, 'Anglo-Saxon Landscape and Economy: Using Portable Antiquities to Study Anglo-Saxon and Viking England', *Internet Archaeology* 25, 2009 (www.intarch.ac.uk/).

[12] S. Rigold, 'The Two Primary Series of Sceattas', *British Numismatic Journal* 30, 1960–1, 6–53, and 'The Principal Series of English Sceattas', *British Numismatic Journal* 47, 1977, 21–30. The British Museum scheme is expanded in B. H. I. H. Stewart, 'The Early English Denarial Coinage, c.680–c.750', in *Sceattas in England and on the Continent: the Seventh Oxford Symposium on Coinage and Monetary History*, ed. D. Hill and D. M. Metcalf, British Archaeological Reports: British Series 128, Oxford 1984, 5–26.

[13] For recent discussion see D. M. Metcalf and W. Op Den Velde, 'The Monetary Economy of the Netherlands, c.690–c.715 and the Trade with England: a Study of the Sceattas of Series D', *Jaarboek voor Munt- en Penningkunde* 90, 2007 for 2003, 1–211, and 'The Monetary Economy of the Netherlands, c.690–c.760 and the Trade with England: a Study of the "Porcupine" Sceattas of Series E', 'Series E Reconsidered', *Jaarboek voor Munt- en Penningkunde* 96 and 97, 2 vols., 2009–10, 1–506.

[14] Among more than 1,000 *sceattas* found at Domburg and Westenschouwen, for example, only 8 per cent (84 coins) were of English types (among them six specimens of the East Anglian Series Q and R), while Series D and E accounted for 22 and 47 per cent respectively: W. Op Den Velde and C. J. F. Klaassen, *Sceattas and Merovingian Deniers from Domburg and Westenschouwen*, Middelburg 2004.

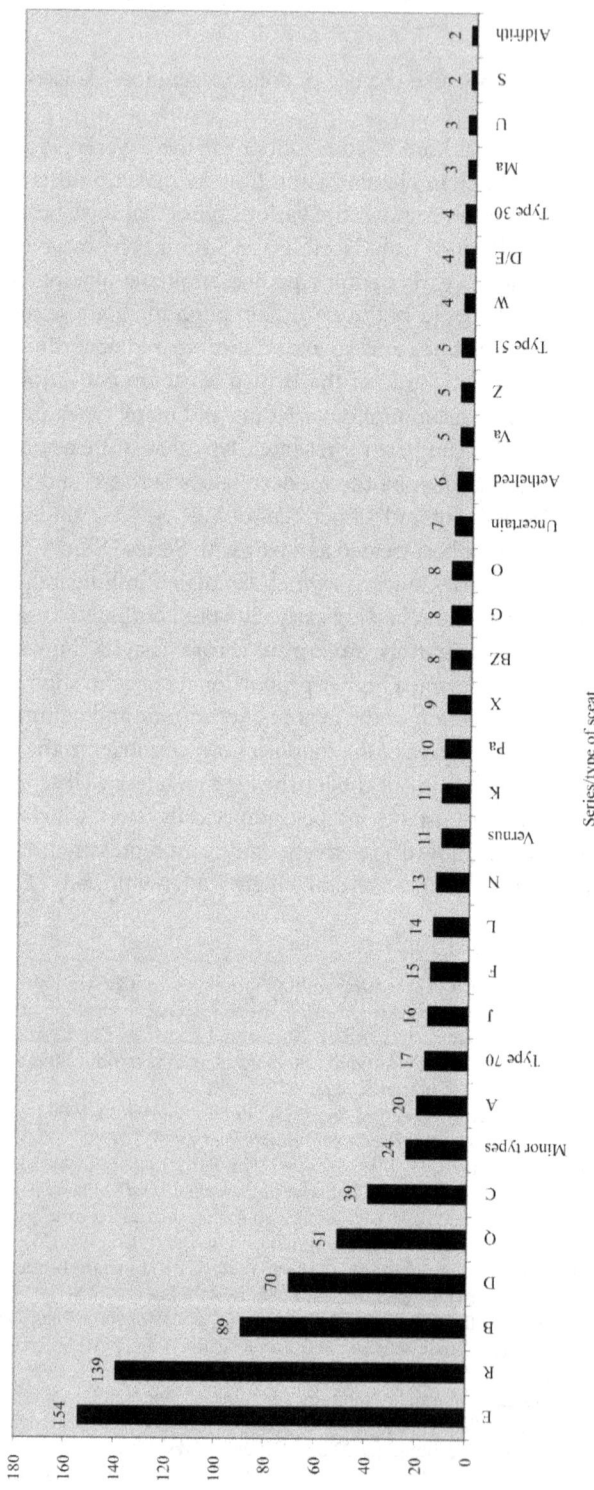

GRAPH 2 Series/types of *sceat* represented in Norfolk and Suffolk, according to EMC (February 2012).

PLATE 1 Continental *sceattas* of Series D, E and X
(© The Fitzwilliam Museum, Cambridge).

PLATE 2 Two specimens each of East Anglian *sceattas* of Series R and Series Q
(© The Fitzwilliam Museum, Cambridge).

tration across East Anglia, Mercia, Kent and elsewhere. Michael Metcalf has associated these 'hot spots' with the destinations favoured by traders from Series X's home mint of Ribe in modern Denmark.[15] Coins constitute one of the best pieces of evidence for interactions across the North Sea at this time: in a very real sense, therefore, East Anglia was a full participant in the North Sea world of coin circulation in the seventh and eighth centuries (see Plate 1).

The leading native type was Series R (Plate 2).[16] This was very much a local coinage: over 60 per cent of all single-finds of this series have occurred in East Anglia, 45 per cent in Norfolk and 24 per cent in Suffolk. The leading mint was probably Ipswich, perhaps with one or two smaller mints further up the coast in Norfolk. Series R had grown out of Series C, which was issued in Kent in the late seventh century.[17] Both types were characterized by a reverse design based ultimately on a standard used in late Roman coin designs, while the obverse showed an increasingly stylized crowned bust. Alongside this bust was a runic inscription. The exact form of this varied considerably, but was usually some variant of *epa*. These letters may initially have had some significance, such as the name of a moneyer, but soon seem to have become a formalized part of the design devoid of any specific meaning.

Series R was a long-running type, beginning about 710 and lasting for around forty years. About a dozen sub-varieties can be discerned within it which can be roughly grouped into three associated units (R1–14/8/10, R5/9/11 and R7), perhaps representing different mints. The very latest sub-types, which were rare and of low weight and poor metal quality, replaced the now immobilized obverse runes with

---

[15] D. M. Metcalf, 'Single Finds of Wodan/Monster Sceattas in England and their Interpretation for Monetary History', *Nordisk Numismatisk Årsskrift* 2000–2002, 109–48.

[16] For detailed discussion of this series and its many permutations, see Metcalf, *Thrymsas and Sceattas* III, 502–23.

[17] Ibid., I, 106–16.

longer inscriptions naming the moneyers responsible for production: Wigræd and Tilbeorht. Naming the moneyers responsible for production was probably a measure intended to help boost confidence in an increasingly dubious coinage, and it prefigures the appearance of the king's name for similar reasons a short time later.[18]

Series R was the dominant East Anglian coinage, but it was not the only issue from the kingdom. Series Q is the other main type associated with East Anglia (Plate 2). This was a much smaller type, known from about a third as many finds overall as Series R, and was probably not struck over as long a period. Most of Series Q – the sub-types QI–III – probably belongs to a mint or mints located in west Norfolk, perhaps reflecting a division within the kingdom and/or a different economic centre.[19]

Unlike the visually rather dull Series R, Series Q is among the most iconographically rich segments of early Anglo-Saxon coinage. Its array of birds, beasts and human figures invites speculation as to their meaning, which Anna Gannon has proposed should often be seen in theological terms.[20] One important new specimen makes this religious significance unambiguous by showing a facing bust superimposed on a cross. This form of crossed halo identifies the figure as Jesus Christ. Representation of Christ on coins was a relatively new development when this coin was made around 720. They had been introduced in Visigothic Spain and Byzantium in the 680s, but this was apparently the first time Christ had been shown on a coin anywhere north of the Alps. It marks an important first for Anglo-Saxon coinage, and gives some clue to the artistic influences and piety that penetrated Anglo-Saxon society during the century after conversion to Christianity.[21]

So, even in this formative era of Anglo-Saxon coinage East Anglia figures prominently both in economic and cultural terms. Iconographic inspiration came more from the Christian world of the Mediterranean and local English tradition than from the lands east across the sea. But monetarily East Anglia was, along with the rest of eastern England, integrated with the North Sea regions of Frisia and Denmark, all of which saw proliferation of silver *sceattas* in the late seventh and early eighth centuries.[22] East Anglia at this time was a powerhouse of minting and

---

[18] The end of the period of the early pennies/*sceattas* is discussed in R. Naismith, 'Kings, Crisis and Coinage Reforms in the Mid-Eighth Century', *Early Medieval Europe* 20, 2012, 291–332.

[19] D. M. Metcalf, *Thrymsas and Sceattas* III, 483–501, and 'Determining the Mint-Attribution of East Anglian Sceattas through Regression Analysis', *British Numismatic Journal* 70, 2001, 1–11. A mint at or in the vicinity of Ely was suggested by John Newman ('Wics, Trade, and the Hinterlands – the Ipswich Region', in *Anglo-Saxon Trading Centres: Beyond the Emporia*, ed. M. Anderton, Glasgow 1999, 32–47, at 43–4). There was also one other sub-type of Series Q, QIV, which was probably produced in the Ipswich area.

[20] A. Gannon, *Iconography*, esp. 28–9, 130–1, 154–6 and 188–92.

[21] B. H. I. H. Stewart and D. M. Metcalf, 'The Bust of Christ on an Early Anglo-Saxon Coin', *Numismatic Chronicle* 167, 2007, 179–82. For more general discussion see A. Gannon, 'Coins, Images and Tales from the Holy Land: Questions of Theology and Orthodoxy', in *Studies in Early Medieval Coinage 2: New Perspectives*, ed. T. Abramson, Woodbridge 2011, 88–103.

[22] It should be noted that monetary evidence of interaction with the Merovingian kingdom is much weaker: just eight Merovingian *denarii* are recorded as having been found in East Anglia on the Corpus of Early Medieval Coin Finds (as of March 2012).

PLATE 3 Coins inscribed with the names of kings and moneyers: Beonna, moneyer Efe; Offa of Mercia, moneyer Eadnoth; Eadwald of East Anglia, moneyer Lul; and Edmund of East Anglia, moneyer Beornferth (© The Fitzwilliam Museum, Cambridge).

coin circulation, home to a large local currency but also receptive to other coinages coming in from abroad and from elsewhere in England. What this suggests is that the impetus which kept Series Q and Series R circulating mostly within East Anglia was economic, not governmental: there was no formal requirement to use a specific type of coin for all purposes within the kingdom. Rather, it looks like the extent of coin-use and general exchange within East Anglia itself was sufficiently dynamic and self-contained to draw in the bulk of local currency.[23] East Anglia was part of the North Sea economy, and of wider patterns of exchange within England, but it was also in many ways already a separate and distinct entity.

In the middle of the eighth century the silver coinage of England went through a period of crisis and transformation. This was an English and (to some extent) Frankish phenomenon, not a facet of broader North Sea developments: both Frisia and Ribe in Jutland maintained relatively healthy output and circulation of *sceattas* for much longer than the lands to their west.[24] In England, on the other hand, the volume, weight and fineness of later *sceattas* all declined, and in no fewer than five kingdoms in England and Frankia the local monarchs supervised reforms of the currency which sought to restore reliable standards. This started in Northumbria under King Eadberht (737–58) around 740, and was followed next by Beonna in East Anglia, who came to the throne around 749.[25] Beonna's coinage was influenced by that of Northumbria and by the latest East Anglian *sceattas*. In turn, it served as one inspiration for the new Carolingian coinage of the 750s. As in the 670s, changes in the monetary system of Frankia exerted strong influence in Southern England, where the model of broader, thinner coinage instituted by Pippin III (751–68) was adopted by Mercian and Kentish rulers. All of these new coinages reflect a new and generally higher level of royal involvement in minting, founded on a partnership between the king and moneyers (Plate 3). It should be stressed that the latter were very much the key unit of production: minting towns did not always operate as a

[23] Cf. Naismith, *Money and Power*, 230–1.
[24] For the later phases of Series E see Op Den Velde and Metcalf, 'Series E', pp. 52–60. Continued production and use (down to the ninth century) of Series X within Ribe is discussed in C. Feveile, 'The Coins from 8th–9th Centuries Ribe – Survey and Status 2001', *Nordisk Numismatisk Årsskrift* 2000–2002, 149–62.
[25] On Beonna's coinage see Archibald, 'Coinage of Beonna', and 'A *Sceat* of Ethelbert I'.

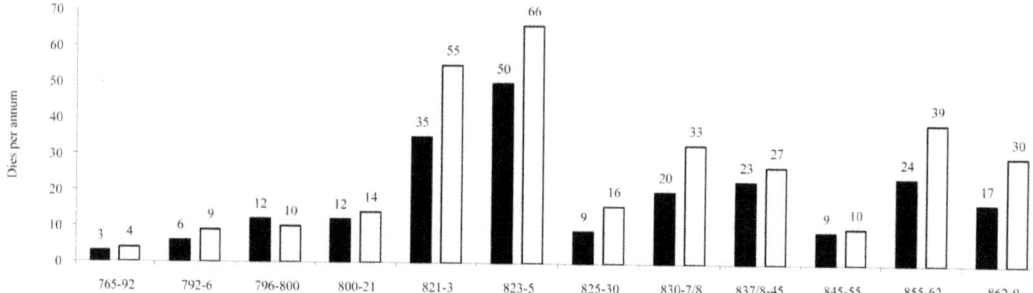

GRAPH 3 Rate of productivity in dies per annum at Ipswich (black column in each period indicates obverse dies; white column reverse dies).

single unit, while lay elites had no direct influence over coin production, and ecclesiastical powers relatively little.[26]

Although kings and moneyers were now named as standard, mints were not, and so there is some uncertainty about how many mint-places were active and where some of them were located. In the case of East Anglia, similarities of style and political affiliation suggest that most or all the late eighth- and ninth-century moneyers worked in a single location, and given the general association of minting with important centres of trade, Ipswich stands out as the most likely possibility.[27] Overall there was a substantial decline in the number of locations where coinage was issued: only six locations across England can be confidently identified as mints in the period from Offa to Alfred. Based on a recent die-study of all c.4,000 known specimens of southern English coins struck at these locations during the years 760–865, it is possible to follow their productivity in some detail.[28] Graph 3 shows how the rate of productivity, in terms of number of dies per year, changed at the East Anglian mint. It started out relatively small compared with the other southern English mints, but its output began to expand rapidly from about 800, coinciding closely with a sudden and serious decline in output at London. By about 830 Ipswich was the second most important mint in southern England behind Canterbury: a position it retained until the end of the 860s. Both were comparable in output to the larger mints of late Anglo-Saxon and Norman England.[29]

About 1,000 of the king- and moneyer-signed pennies of this period have been found as single-finds, and allow the movement of money once it left the mint to be followed in some detail. Foreign silver was no longer a substantial element of the currency, but was probably still coming in: presumably it was being handed

[26] Naismith, 'Kings, Crisis and Coinage Reforms'.
[27] Naismith, *Money and Power*, 128–9, and *Southern England*, I, 35.
[28] Chick, *Coinage of Offa*; Naismith, *Southern England*.
[29] Detailed commentary may be found in Naismith, *Money and Power*, 188–92. The relevant coins are listed and illustrated in Chick, *Coinage of Offa*; and Naismith, *Southern England*.

over and re-minted on entering the kingdom. The nature and origins of these incoming coins had, however, changed. As far as can be seen, links were now much stronger with the Carolingian empire (incorporating Frisia) than with Scandinavia and the rest of the North Sea area. East Anglian moneyers of the ninth century were influenced by the largely aniconic contemporary Carolingian coin-issues, and one of the rare figural coin designs of the period imitated the famous ship coins from Dorestad.[30]

Even if the closely integrated North Sea monetary economy was largely at an end, however, a lot more leniency was shown to coins from various Anglo-Saxon kingdoms. That is to say, there does not seem to have been any obstacle to using coins struck in Kent in East Anglia, or *vice versa*. This system is best explained as originating at a time when all the mints of southern England lay under the control of a single ruler, Offa of Mercia, who oversaw three reforms of the coinage during his long reign.[31] But even after Offa's death and into the early ninth century, when the south-east and East Anglia were intermittently under Mercian, West Saxon or independent control, the coinages remained similar and continued to circulate interchangeably. This was facilitated by the use of a common weight and metal standard at all the mints, at least until debasement began in about the 840s. There was one important exception to this zone of common circulation in England: Northumbria, where the coinage had retained the smaller, thicker format of earlier issues and was also severely debased from early in the ninth century. Southern coins circulated on only a limited scale north of the Humber, while Northumbrian coins in the south were slightly more numerous, but probably functioned as fractional currency.[32]

The crucial point for present purposes is how these important changes in the nature of minting organization affected the monetary economy of East Anglia. Already in the second half of the eighth century there was a stronger tendency for coins from Ipswich to be lost within East Anglia than was the case with products of the south-eastern mints in their own hinterlands. That is to say, Canterbury and London catered more to long- and middle-distance exchange extending fairly evenly across England south of the Humber.[33]

Although it would be several centuries before the volume of minting and coin circulation in England returned to the levels seen in the early eighth century, from about the 780s there was a substantial revival of the fortunes of the southern English currency which continued until approximately the 830s. During this time, East Anglia again appears to have been a generally rich area in terms of circulation. Moreover, despite Ipswich's expansion in output from around 800, it retained a

[30] G. Williams, 'The Influence of Dorestad Coinage on Coin Design in England and Scandinavia', in *Dorestad in an International Framework: New Research on Centres of Trade and Coinage in Carolingian Times*, ed. A. Willemsen and H. Kik, Turnhout 2010, 105–11, at 109–11.
[31] R. Naismith, 'The Coinage of Offa Revisited', *British Numismatic Journal* 80, 2010, 76–106.
[32] Naismith, *Money and Power*, 207–8, 210, 246–9.
[33] D. M. Metcalf, 'The Monetary Economy of Ninth-Century England South of the Humber: a Topographical Analysis', in *Kings, Currency and Alliances: History and Coinage of Southern England in the Ninth Century*, ed. M. Blackburn and D. N. Dumville, Woodbridge 1998, 167–97.

more localized focus: half or more of finds of coins from Ipswich continue to be found within East Anglia, whereas Kent never provided more than 26 per cent of all finds of coins from Canterbury.

From the 830s this buoyant currency of broad silver pennies bearing the names of king and moneyer fell on harder times. Across southumbrian England, the number of single-finds declined by about half: only some 180 are known of coins minted between about 830 and 865, as opposed to 386 of coins minted between about 796 and 830. This decline hit the south-eastern mints hardest, although the actual spread of circulation never contracted substantially, and their hinterlands experienced the same level of decline as distant areas. Neither did the middle of the ninth century witness any major visible contraction in output, implying that the change was associated with the way in which coins were being used.[34]

Ipswich and East Anglia present a somewhat different story. The overall number of finds of coins minted after 830 falls slightly in East Anglia, because the volume of coins entering from the south-east declines. Similarly, fewer coins from Ipswich are found outside East Anglia than in earlier years. But the number of coins from Ipswich lost in East Anglia actually remains the same as in the preceding thirty years. The increased activity of the mint doubtless contributed to this rise in the proportion of local coins among finds from East Anglia. In the period from *c*.830 to 865, some 62 per cent of finds of Ipswich pennies occurred in East Anglia, which now represent 75 per cent of all finds from that area. In other words, East Anglia and its mint of Ipswich seem to have been insulated from the decline in coin-use which affected the rest of southern England in the middle of the ninth century. This was largely thanks to persistently intense use of local coins within the kingdom of East Anglia. As in the early eighth century, it again looks like this should be seen as a factor of economics rather than any governmental monetary policy. Sometimes specific moneyers seem to have played a particularly prominent role in the trade between, for example, East Anglia and Mercia. Thanks to them, pennies from Ipswich always circulated outside as well as inside East Anglia, while a significant proportion of the currency in East Anglia always came from mints other than Ipswich. But it is the close tie between successful mint and vibrant local economy which is so striking.[35]

What was it that made East Anglia remarkable from the point of view of coin-circulation in this period, and indeed earlier in the eighth century? As we have seen, possession of a substantial mint with connections to the outside world was an important factor, because the life-blood of minting in pre-Viking England seems to have been foreign trade. Other commodities, not least pottery, bear witness to East Anglia's overseas links, while the opposite leg of the journey – what it was that traders took away with them, and where they went – is harder to pin down. Finds of Anglo-Saxon coins abroad provide some hint, and East Anglian coins have turned up from sites in the Netherlands, Italy and Scandinavia: North Sea monetary

---

[34] Naismith, *Money and Power*, 209–18.
[35] Ibid., 218–23.

exchange may have been curtailed, but it was not completely stifled. The background to this must be the vitality of East Anglia itself as the region which provided Ipswich with its wealth and furnished the market for most of its coin production. It emerges consistently as the most highly monetized part of pre-Viking England, and also one of the most tightly focused, in contrast with the Thames estuary, which functioned as a monetary *entrepôt* for the rest of southumbrian England. The likelihood is that East Anglia's population, markets and production grew to be dense at an early stage, and combined to provide a fertile context for coin-use. Evidence for this might lurk in the precocious development of local ceramics during the eighth century,[36] in the investigation of physical remains left by different kinds of settlement and also in documentation for settlement and agriculture which emerges in the tenth and eleventh centuries.[37]

The coinage thus seems to pose as many questions as it answers, yet provides an undoubtedly useful window onto the otherwise obscure history of East Anglia in the eighth and ninth centuries. It sheds light onto political history, society, international relations and the nature of at least one aspect of the economy. There are many further avenues that should be pursued. How, for example, does the distribution of different coin-types within East Anglia relate to the organization of the kingdom? Where were all the mints, and how were they and the moneyers and die-cutters structured? And for what purposes were all these coins used?

To conclude, just one of these additional questions will be discussed: that of how the arrival of the Vikings and renewed links across the North Sea affected the coinage in East Anglia. The first point to be noted is that minting and coin-use never actually ceased altogether. The Vikings were used to an economy based on silver bullion rather than coinage as such, and carried on this practice to some extent within East Anglia.[38] But Viking rulers also inherited and developed the same basic model of making and using silver pennies that had prevailed since the seventh century. Minting in East Anglia fell to a low ebb in the decade after Edmund's martyrdom at the hands of the Vikings in 869. Just eight coins are known in the names of the obscure kings Æthelred and Oswald who ruled at this time, probably under Viking suzerainty, in contrast to over 200 surviving coins in Edmund's name, some of whose moneyers survived to work in the 870s. Thereafter the coinage of East Anglia consisted of two elements: some coins imitated the so-

---

[36] Above all Ipswich ware: see P. Blinkhorn, 'Of Cabbages and Kings: Production, Trade and Consumption in Middle-Saxon England', in *Anglo-Saxon Trading Centres*, ed. Anderton, 4–23.

[37] Naismith, *Money and Power*, 230–1.

[38] M. Blackburn and A. Rogerson, 'Two Viking-Age Silver Ingots from Ditchingham and Hindringham, Norfolk: the First Ingot Finds from East Anglia', *Medieval Archaeology* 37, 1993, 222–4. This form of silver economy is vividly illustrated by the recently published finds of coins and metalwork from the trading settlement of Kaupang in Norway: D. Skre, ed., *Means of Exchange: Dealing with Silver in the Viking Age*, Kaupang Excavation Project Publication Series 2, Aarhus 2008; and, in England, from the finds made at Torksey, Lincolnshire: M. Blackburn, 'The Viking Winter Camp at Torksey, 872-3', in his *Viking Coinage and Currency in the British Isles*, London 2011, 221–64. Also important are the papers in *Silver Economies, Monetisation and Society in Scandinavia AD 800–1100*, ed. J. Graham-Campbell, S. M. Sindbæk and G. Williams, Aarhus 2011.

called two-line coinage of Alfred of Wessex (871–99), instituted *c*.880, and others named the local Viking ruler Guthrum (879/80–after 890), whose army settled East Anglia in 879, under his baptismal name Æthelstan. Some of these used a Carolingian-inspired design of a temple, which had already been adopted in the time of Æthelred and Oswald, and built on a particularly East Anglian tradition of Frankish influence on design going back to the 830s.[39] But the bulk of the coins in the name of Guthrum also use the two-line design of Alfredian type. While Alfred's new coinage was associated with a reform in which the weight of each penny was raised substantially, in East Anglia the standard seems to have remained as it was under Edmund and earlier kings, providing another element of continuity.[40]

Yet in other respects the arrival of the Vikings brought fundamental changes. These are most manifest in the next and much larger Viking coinage, the so-called St Edmund Memorial issue, which was struck from about 895 until the conquest by Edward the Elder in the 910s. On the face of it this coinage was not at all Viking, and very much East Anglian: it perpetuated the memory of the now sanctified local martyr, and was inspired by the design of his pennies. It constitutes the first source for his cult, and powerful evidence for the progress of Christianity in the Danelaw.[41] But under the skin it was quite a different entity to Edmund's original coinage, and reveals reinforced links with other areas of England and even with continental Europe. This overseas link is shown by the names of the men responsible for the coinage. Among about eighty known moneyers, Veronica Smart has shown that over sixty bear names indicating continental Germanic origin, up to eleven may be Old English and only two or three might be Scandinavian. The likelihood is that the Frankish men behind this coinage – a few of whom had already appeared in the earlier coinage of Guthrum – were brought or invited in under Viking influence, as may also have been done in York. Also, although the St Edmund Memorial coinage remained most concentrated and dominant in East Anglia, it was not solely an East Anglian coinage, as the pattern of modern single-finds shows. Finds from other Viking-held areas like Cambridgeshire, Lincolnshire and Northamptonshire are relatively numerous, and there are hints that multiple mints were involved in its production. Some at least of these were probably outside East Anglia, and may have been in places such as Stamford.[42]

---

[39] Williams, 'Influence of Dorestad'.

[40] These coinages are discussed in M. Blackburn, 'Currency under the Vikings. Part I: Guthrum and the Earliest Danelaw Coinages', *British Numismatic Journal* 75, 2005, 18–43, at 22–5. Important additions and discussion can be found in addenda to the reprint of this paper in Blackburn, *Viking Coinage*.

[41] See (*inter alia*) L. Abrams, 'The Conversion of the Danelaw', in *Vikings and the Danelaw: Selected Papers from the Proceedings of the Thirteenth Viking Congress, Nottingham and York, 21–30 August 1997*, ed. J. Graham-Campbell et al, Oxford 2001, 31–44.

[42] C. E. Blunt, 'The St Edmund Memorial Coinage', *Proceedings of the Suffolk Institute of Archaeology and History* 31, 1967–9, 234–55; P. Grierson and M. Blackburn, *Medieval European Coinage, with a Catalogue of the Coins in the Fitzwilliam Museum, Cambridge*, vol. 1: *the Early Middle Ages (5th–10th Centuries)*, Cambridge 1986, 319–20; C. E. Blunt, B. H. I. H. Stewart and C. S. S. Lyon, *Coinage in Tenth-Century England: from Edward the Elder to Edgar's Reform*, Oxford 1989, 100–2;

Conquest by the Vikings in 869 thus did, over the next half-century, bring about important changes to the monetary life of East Anglia, including renewal of some links across the North Sea, albeit not with Scandinavia itself. Designs and the personnel behind minting in particular were affected, the former showing more influence from West Saxon models for a time, while the local kings and moneyers named on coins before 869 were replaced by a Viking ruler, a local martyr and a coterie of largely foreign moneyers. The region's position as a leading centre of minting and above all coin-use was shaken but never stirred, not even by the Vikings, who maintained local practices long after taking over. Viking East Anglia thus was, in many respects, firmly a part of the North Sea world, as it had been to a greater or lesser extent for two centuries. But this had never been the sole outside market or community in which East Anglia was involved: it also enjoyed strong links to Frankia and to the other Anglo-Saxon kingdoms, links which often had more of an effect on local conditions than the influence of other areas around the North Sea.

M. Blackburn and H. Pagan, 'The St Edmund Coinage in the Light of a Parcel from a Hoard of St Edmund Pennies', *British Numismatic Journal* 72, 2002, 1–14; and V. Smart, 'The Moneyers of St Edmund', *Hikuin* 11, 1985, 83–90.

— Chapter 7 —

THE CASTLE AND THE WARREN: MEDIEVAL EAST ANGLIAN FUR CULTURE IN CONTEXT

Aleksander Pluskowski

INTRODUCTION

Fur is one of the most striking luxury commodities associated with medieval European societies. Over the course of the latter centuries of the first millennium AD, it emerged as the focus of an international trade linking the worlds of the North Sea, the Baltic and the Black Sea. By the mid twelfth century, fur was associated with the very identity of Christian aristocracies, not only through the wearing of fur-lined garments, but also with its incorporation into heraldry. Different regions became specialized producers of specific peltries and East Anglia became known for its rabbit fur. Rabbits, housed in carefully guarded warrens, only became widely established in the thirteenth century, prompting the development of a significant and regionally distinct fur industry, sourced from aristocratic estates. The role of élite groups in the organization of fur acquisition was mirrored across northern Europe, but where woodlands supported abundant and diverse populations of fur-bearing mammals, pelts were obtained through more complex networks linking trappers with merchants and consumers. The fur trade has been extensively studied, but more recently there has been growing interest in its cultural and ecological impact on source regions. The burgeoning demands of the fur trade, particularly the overemphasis on particular species, prompted the development of specialized infrastructure, colonization in some areas, landscape re-organization in others, and ultimately resulted in local ecological shifts. In Eastern England, this saw the 'indigenization' of the once exotic rabbit; in Scandinavia and north Russia sustained trapping would lead to the collapse of local fur-bearing mammal populations. This chapter situates the acquisition, production, dissemination and conceptualization of fur – broadly defined as 'fur culture' – in medieval East Anglia with the broader context of northern Europe, and particularly through a comparison with the Scandinavian Peninsula. Both regions were linked by water and commerce throughout the Middle Ages; both shared comparable 'European' power structures which extended to the structured exploitation of natural resources, especially wild animals, although their development and characteristics varied. Both were transformed by the widespread acceptance of Christianity, which include a reconsideration of the value of other species. Superficially then, these regions were part of a pan-European whole: medieval Christendom. However, their cultural heterogeneity – and the specific character of East Anglian fur culture – arose from the interaction of diverse cultural and ecological contexts. Moreover, before the twelfth century, evidence for the use of fur as a luxury commodity in England is sporadic, and so it is essential to situate this within the broader context of the North Sea world.

FUR AS AN AESTHETIC COMMODITY

Fur consists of layers of hair forming a thick insulating covering over the bodies of certain species of mammals. The thicker, outer layers are referred to as 'guard hairs', protecting the 'underfur' which provides insulation. These hair fibres rarely survive in the archaeological record. An exceptional example was excavated in Kołobrzeg (German Kolberg, Pomerania), where at the back of a property of a shoemaker, an assemblage of 50,000 leather objects (mostly off cuts) dating to the early fourteenth century included a small amount of beaver, otter and sheep/buck leather tanned, fur side up, probably for the production of hats, collars and linings.[1] Waste bone fragments from the fur working process are encountered more often, although direct evidence of skinning – in the form of observable cut marks – is relatively infrequent. More detailed evidence for the movement and handling of furs can be found in a diverse range of written and artistic sources, the former most comprehensively studied by Robert Delort.[2]

Fur cannot be understood as a commodity in isolation. It is derived from a specific group of animals with distinct ecological niches, and therefore its acquisition is closely related to how people exploited particular environments. In medieval Europe there was a dynamic hierarchy of furs linked to consumer demand and cycles of fashion, although mustelids (e.g. marten, stoat) and squirrels consistently fetched the highest prices (Figure 1). The possession and public display of fur-lined garments became more than simply a reflection of wealth, for by incorporating furs into the earliest Western European heraldic charges from the mid twelfth century, these products became visual classifiers of nobility.[3] Within a few

---

[1] M. Rębkowski, 'Remarks on Handicraft in Medieval Kołobrzeg', in *Lübecker Kolloquium zur Stadtarchäologie im Hanseraum V: das Handwerkeds*, ed. Ilka Hillenstedt, Lübeck 2006, 449–57 at 451–2.

[2] R. Delort, *Le commerce des fourrures en Occident à la fin du Moyen Age (vers 1300–vers 1450)*, 2 vols., Rome 1978. See also E. M. Veale, *The English Fur Trade in the Later Middle Ages*, 2nd edn, London 2003, and J. Martin, *Treasure of the Land of Darkness: the Fur Trade and its Significance for Medieval Russia*, Cambridge 1986.

[3] M. Pastoureau, *Traité d'Héraldique*, Paris 1997. See also A. G. Pluskowski, 'Communicating through Skin and Bone: the Appropriation of Animal Bodies in Medieval Western Seigneurial Culture', in *Breaking and Shaping Beastly Bodies: Animals as Material Culture in the Middle Ages*, ed. A. G. Pluskowski, Oxford 2007, 32–51.

SMALL WOODLAND MAMMALS

| Squirrel | Stoat | Sable | Pine marten |
| (*Sciurus vulgaris*) | (*Mustela erminea*) | (*Martes zibellina*) | (*Martes martes*) |

WETLAND AND AQUATIC MAMMALS   MEADOW AND UPLAND MAMMALS

Beaver (*Castor fiber*)   Otter (*Lutra lutra*)   Hare (*Lepus* genus)   Reindeer (*Rangifer tarandus*)

DOMESTICATES AND SEMI-DOMESTICATES

Lamb (*Ovis aries*)   Cat (*Felis s. catus*)   Rabbit (*Oryctolagus cuniculus*)

LARGER WILD CARNIVORES

Wolf (*Canius lupus*)   Bear (*Ursus arctos*)   Lynx (*Lynx lynx*)   Fox (*Vulpes vulpes*)

FIGURE 1 Main categories of fur in medieval northern Europe.
There is a broad correlation between body size and value; the most desirable furs came from squirrels and mustelids, whilst the pelts of larger carnivores rarely feature in commercial documents and their remains are infrequently found on medieval archaeological sites.

decades a standardized fur hierarchy had developed and as upwardly mobile social classes sought to emulate the aristocracy, this prompted the introduction of sumptuary laws in some regions, regulating the wearing of such powerful visual identifiers. By this time the choice of furs was extensive, facilitated by an increasingly complex trading network stretching beyond the frontiers of Christendom. The medieval fur trade had a significant ecological dimension, for the exploitation of habitats which supported abundant communities of fur-bearing animals was in many regions facilitated by colonization.

It is instructive to outline briefly the acquisition and processing of furs.[4] Access to domesticated or managed populations was straightforward, whereas the most valuable furs were derived from small mammals which had to be hunted or trapped in their natural habitats, using techniques that avoided significant damage to the pelt. Squirrels, for example, were shot down from trees with blunted arrows.[5] The season of acquisition was important in determining the quality of the hide. The awareness of differential quality, evident in the documentation of the fur trade, can explain the regional preferences that become increasingly evident in northern Europe over the course of the twelfth century. Rather than a purely subjective process, fur standards within and across species became internationally recognized. The thickest pelt is grown in the winter months and aside from its effectiveness as an insulating material, more relevant to the use of fur as a luxury commodity in medieval Europe is the aesthetic concept of 'luster' – the reflection of light on the 'guard hairs', which fades as the hairs lose their natural oils and become brittle. Colour – pigmentation in the case of fur, linked to fibre density – was singularly important within the visual culture of medieval society. Different regions became known for the distinct pelts of the same species. In the case of the squirrel, for example, hanseatic merchants distinguished Masovian (*Massouvesches werkes*), red Russian (*rosyteschwerk*), Hungarian, Lithuanian, Finnish, Swedish and Slovakian black (*swartewerk*).[6] Both the seasonal acquisition and subsequent treatment of the fur was therefore important for producing high quality garment trimming – the primary use of luxury fur in medieval Europe. In the case of the beaver, its fur is at its prime in late spring when the water is at its coldest, and the fur fibres and guard hairs are thoroughly and evenly distributed. The quality of fur also changes during the course of hibernation. Bear pelts taken after hibernation appear off-coloured and the fibres matted and dull, although the lowest quality furs were derived from animals caught in the late spring and summer. Animal hides and skins were often delivered with heads, feet and tails still attached. These unwanted attachments were often removed and discarded, typically recognizable as concentrations of limb

---

[4] For detailed guides to fur terminology, typology and preparation, M. Bachrach, *Fur: A Practical Treatise*, 3rd edn, London 1953, and J. C. Sachs, *Furs and the Fur Trade*, 3rd edn, London 1933.

[5] A widespread practice discussed in detail in J. Sztetyłło, 'Wokół snycerki ze Stralsundu (Strzałowa) zdobiącej stalle hanzeatów kupczących w Nowogrodzie', in *O rzeczach minionych*, ed. M. Młynarska-Kaletynowa and J. Kruppé, Warsaw 2006, 319–27.

[6] Sztetyłło, 'Wokół snycerki ze Stralsundu'.

bones and cranial elements exhibiting skinning marks in places where the skin was most tightly attached to the bone.[7] In some cases these extremities may have been deliberately left on; both ermine and fox tails were incorporated into dress.[8] Fatty tissues would then be scraped off from the interior, and the peltries would be dressed by tanning them with vegetable oils and alum tanning agents, preventing the adhesion and putrefaction of the fibres. After tanning, the furs would be washed, dried and passed onto textile workers for incorporation into garments. In some cases they may have been dyed. This was a way of increasing the value of lower-priced pelts by making them resemble more prestigious furs; an alternative was to breed animals such as cats to grow coats with specific colours. The selective breeding of cats for white fur is documented in Sweden from the sixteenth century, reflecting the well established demands of the fur industry.[9] Poor quality pelts could also be shredded and mixed with other fibres to create felt, as suggested for two pieces excavated in London and made from a combination of mustelid hairs (possibly weasel or stoat) and wool, with the aim of producing a noticeable sheen.[10]

The basic tenets of fur acquisition and preparation demonstrate the role of specialized knowledge and skill at all points on the 'assembly line'. The primary market was the aristocracy, in turn emulated by upwardly mobile groups including the merchants handling the furs. The pivotal role of merchants in bringing products from source to consumer shaped and defined the fur trade. Sources of fur were, in one sense, widely available at the European scale. The pine marten's range, for example, extended over much of continental Europe and the British Isles. Beavers were also widely distributed. Indeed, each region saw the opportunistic harvesting of a diverse range of species, but only a few came to dominate exports. In order to meet demand there had to be a regular supply linked to an effective infrastructure. International fur markets emerged in the Viking Age and developed significantly with the opening up of the eastern Baltic trading networks in the later twelfth and thirteenth centuries. At this point hanseatic merchants drove the movement of furs across northern Europe, successfully linking the diversity of producers and consumers across the North Sea and Baltic worlds.[11] In England, hanseatic contacts were strongest in the south-east with the *kontor* based in London, and in the ports of East Anglia. The rabbit, more than any other animal, provided the staple fur exported from this region, but this invariably developed as a by-product of farming the animals for exclusive meat consumption. On the other side of the North Sea, in a completely different social and ecological context, the northern taiga saw

---

[7] Discussed in detail in relation to the faunal material from Birka, Sweden, in B. Wigh, *Animal Husbandry in the Viking Age Town of Birka and its Hinterland*, Stockholm 2001.
[8] M. Jones. *The Secret Middle Ages*, Stroud 2002.
[9] Wigh, *Animal Husbandry*, 119–20.
[10] E. Crowfoot, F. Pritchard and K. Staniland, *Textiles and Clothing c.1150–c.1450: Finds from Medieval Excavations in London*, Woodbridge 2004, 75.
[11] U. C. Ewert and S. Selzer, 'Bridging the Gap: the Hanseatic Merchants' Variable Strategies in Heterogeneous Mercantile Environments', International Economic History Congress, Helsinki, 2006, 1–16. www.helsinki.fi/iehc2006/papers3/Ewert.pdf.

reindeer hunted for their fur by the indigenous Saami. In contrast at the fifteenth-century site of Geahčeváinjárga in East Finnmark, the large quantities of surplus meat became the staple food for the community as a result of commercial hunting.[12] Both regions participated in the international fur trade facilitated by the Hanse, and a comparison of the development of fur culture in East Anglia – and more broadly in Scandinavia – leads to a much more nuanced understanding of how the heterogeneous cultures and environments around the North Sea and Baltic worlds, including the value attached to different species, were bridged through the language of commerce.

THE DEVELOPMENT OF FUR CULTURE IN PRE-CHRISTIAN SCANDINAVIA

The extensive belt of boreal and mixed woodlands of Norway, Sweden and Finland, denser before the gradual colonization of the Peninsula's interior in the high medieval period, supported abundant and diverse populations of wild, fur-bearing mammals. Compared with other regions, the pelts of these animals have much longer hair growth, a silkier texture and on average they are bigger than those of southern species; northern Norwegian and Swedish pelts, in particular, tend to be comparatively larger and heavier.[13] Colonization of the interior began in earnest in the twelfth century, accompanied by deforestation and the extension of the cultivated area which in a number of instances brought people closer to wild mammals, as reflected in the palaeoenvironmental profiles of Norwegian and Swedish sites.[14] Sustained episodes of hunting had a dramatic impact on wild ungulate populations a century later, such as reindeer in the southern Norwegian mountains and elk in central eastern Sweden, but it is difficult to quantify the impact of hunting and trapping on mustelids and squirrels which provided sources of luxury fur, especially given the sensitivity of these species to habitat change.[15]

It is possible to see two distinct responses to wild mammals in Scandinavia developing from the Migration Period, which can be linked to the development of fur as a commodity. The northern regions of the Peninsula were occupied by the Saami, who developed a strong relationship with reindeer, elk and other species from at least the fifth century AD, and included them within mortuary

[12] K. Odner, 'Trade, Tribute and Household Response,' *Acta Borealia* 18/1, 2001, 25–50.
[13] Bachrach, *Fur*, 43.
[14] D. Moe, 'The Utilisation of Un-Cultivated Rural Land in Southern Norway during the Last 2500 Years – from the Coastal Areas to the Arctic-Alpine Zone: A Pollen Analytical Survey', in *Proceedings. Ve Congrès international d'archeologie médiévale (Grenoble) 1993*, ed. M. Colardelle, Paris 1996, 122–8; K.-Å. Aronsson, *Forest Reindeer Herding, A.D. 1–1800: An Archaeological and Palaeoecological Study in Northern Sweden*, Umeå 1991; J-E, Wallin, 'History of Sedentary Farming in Ångermanland, Northern Sweden, during the Iron Age and Medieval Period Based on Pollen Analytical Investigation', *Vegetation History and Archaeobotany* 5/4, 1996, 301–12.
[15] G. Proulx *et al*, 'World Distribution and Status of the Genus *Martes* in 2000', in *Martens and Fishers (Martes) in Human-Altered Environments: An International Perspective*, ed. D. J. Harrison, A. K. Fuller and G. Proulx, New York 2004, 21–76.

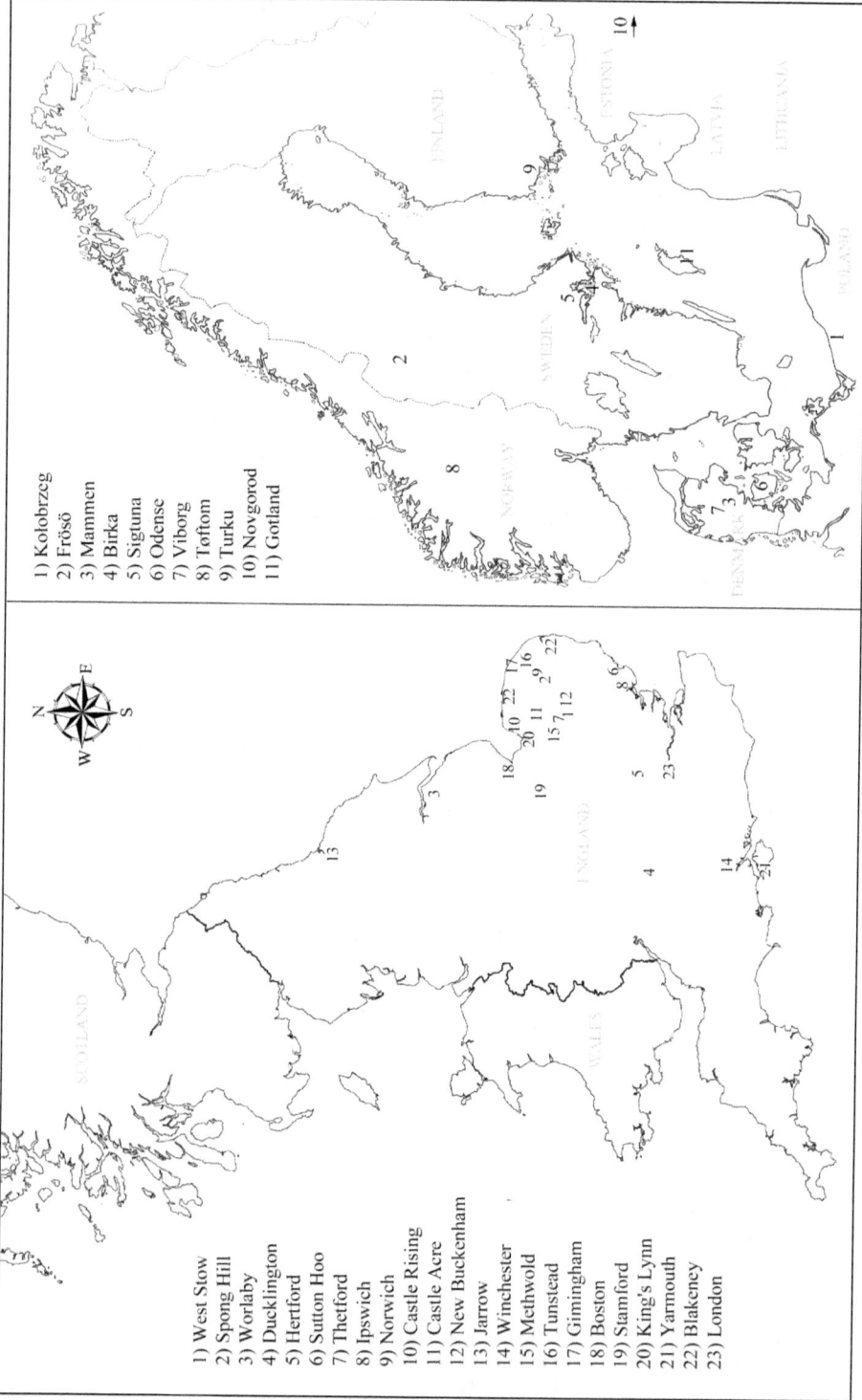

MAP 1 Map of Britain, Scandinavia and the Baltic region showing sites mentioned in the text.

rituals.[16] The bear became the most important carnivore in Saami culture, as particularly evidenced by the burial of whole animals from the Late Iron Age into the modern period.[17] The southernmost expression of this culture in the Viking Age and its influences on Nordic society is represented by a ritual deposit of bear bones and those of other species, scattered around the remains of a tree stump and C14 dated to AD 920 in Frösö (Jamtland, Sweden; for the location of this and other sites see Map 1). A church was subsequently built directly on top of this cult site.[18] The popularity of the bear in southern Scandinavian culture – represented by the widely documented presence of bear pelts in graves (with no evidence of bear burials) – may have been another Saami influence, or may have developed completely independently. The use of bear skins may have had a strong cultic dimension and ritual animal disguise, particularly associated with large carnivores, is an evident feature of Scandinavian public and martial culture.[19] Significance has been attached to the use of cat fur (and most likely wild cat and lynx; claws – presumably linked to pelts – of the latter are also sometimes found as grave goods) by its association with the goddess Freya, and described in *Eiríks saga rauða* as elements of the costume of the vǫlva or sorceress.[20] Furs may well have been widely worn within Scandinavian society by both men and women, although the evidence is largely derived from cemeteries where they may have fulfilled a distinct mortuary role. Not all animal-related garments in southern Scandinavian society were derived from those species most closely associated with the ritual sphere. The richly furnished grave at Mammen (north Denmark) contained a cloak which was either fur or fur-lined, with the long-haired fibres resembling those from a beaver or marten.[21] On the other hand, more complex roles assigned to both the beaver and marten are evident in areas of Finno-Ugrian settlement as well as Scandinavian colonization in the eastern Baltic and western Russia.[22] The relationship between the Norse and Saami in the Viking Age is the subject of ongoing and somewhat controversial debate, but one of the main interfaces of this relationship would have been access to fur.[23]

---

[16] C. Olofsson, 'Making New Antlers: Depositions of Animal Skulls and Antlers as a Message of Regeneration in South Sámi Grave Contexts', *Norwegian Archaeological Review* 43/2, 2010, 97–114.

[17] I. Zachrisson and E. Iregren, *Lappish Bear Graves in Northern Sweden: An Archaeological and Osteological Study*, Stockholm 1974.

[18] B.-M. Näaström, 'Offerlunden under Frösö kyrka', in *Jämtlands Kristnande*, ed. S. Brink, Uppsala 1996, 65-86.

[19] N. S. Price, *The Viking Way: Religion and War in Late Iron Age Scandinavia*, Uppsala 2002, 374.

[20] Ibid., 108 (incorporating Davidson's observations).

[21] E. Munksgaard, 'The Embroideries from Bjerringhoj, Mammen', in *Festskrift til Thorleif Sjovold pa 70-arsdagen*, ed. M. Hogestol et al, Oslo 1984, 169–70.

[22] H. Luik, 'Beaver in the Economy and Social Communication of the Inhabitants of South Estonia in the Viking Age (800–1050 AD)', in *Bestial Mirrors*, ed. A. G. Pluskowski, G. K. Kunst, M. Kucera, M. Bietak and I. Hein, Vienna 2010, 46–54.

[23] See works by Inger Storli, e.g. 'Sami Viking Age Pastoralism – Or the Fur Trade Paradigm Reconsidered', *Norwegian Archaeological Review* 26/1, 1993, 1–20 (and the follow up commentary), and by Bjørnar Olsen, e.g. 'Belligerent Chieftains and Oppressed Hunters? Changing Conceptions of Interethnic Relationships in Northern Norway during the Iron Age and Early Medieval Period', in *Contact, Continuity and Collapse*, ed. J. Barrett, Turnhout 2003, 9–31.

Irrespective of whether southern Scandinavian merchants acquired their own fur, or more likely acquired it from Saami traders and trappers,[24] Scandinavian trading centres begin to process furs for international export.

The eighth century saw the rise of proto-urban trading centres or *emporia* across the North Sea and Baltic region. Excavations at the Swedish settlement of Birka recovered 2534 bones from nineteen different wild mammal species (representing 7.4 per cent of the total faunal assemblage) of which 90 per cent derived from red squirrel, red fox and pine marten. The highest proportion was found in two refuse deposits containing several complete squirrel and marten paws (485 pine marten bones were identified, but mustelids also included ermine, polecat, badger, otter and non-specific *Martes*), representing pelt dressing waste. In town, paws were cut off and finished furs made into clothing or exported, and at this point the grey or white winter furs of the red squirrel and ermine appear to have commanded a high price, although two centuries earlier Jordanes had recorded that the Svear had traded in black fur (perhaps marten) with the Romans.[25] In the later eleventh century, Adam of Bremen had referred to Birka as an important centre of fur production, succeeded by Sigtuna where there is also evidence of diverse fur working (although not as abundant as in Birka), and later by medieval Stockholm. Scandinavian merchants reached the eastern Mediterranean and Black Sea regions, bringing furs with them and fostering a completely new market. Animal skins had generally been shunned in the Greco-Roman world, but fur became a popular luxury item of dress in the Islamic Caliphates from the eighth century.[26] This commercial demand may have prompted changes in how northern areas used and perceived furs. What it certainly resulted in was the association of fur with high fashion that subsequently proliferated in European Christian courts.

It is clear that the biodiversity of the Scandinavian Peninsula stimulated the development of a fur culture which included a significant cultural dimension expressing complex notions of social and metaphysical identity, particularly amongst Saami groups. The conversion to Christianity eroded this dimension, although it remained amongst the Saami who represented important providers of furs to both Norwegians and Swedes in the high medieval period. This interface between Christians and pagans represents one of the significant aspects of the fur trade in the North Sea and Baltic regions, breaching the boundaries of an idealized Christendom.

---

[24] The volume of scholarship on the Norse fur trade is extensive, but particularly pertinent studies include: I. Bergman, L. Östlund, O. Zackrisson and L. Liedgren, 'Stones in the Snow: a Norse Fur Traders' Road into Sami Country', *Antiquity* 81/312, 2007, 397–408.

[25] Wigh, *Birka*, 120, 123.

[26] J. Howard-Johnson, 'Trading in Fur, from Classical Antiquity to the Early Middle Ages', in *Leather and Fur: Aspects of Early Medieval Trade and Technology*, ed. E. Cameron, London 1998, 65–79 at 76; G. R. Owen-Crocker, *Dress in Anglo-Saxon England*, Woodbridge 2004, 244.

THE CHARACTER OF THE LATER MEDIEVAL SCANDINAVIAN FUR TRADE

With the collapse of the Viking Age *emporia*, new towns grow up in close proximity to the abandoned trading centres, and took on their former role as centres exporting luxury commodities. Specialized economies developed catering for particular markets and included the selective exploitation of wild mammals. Indirect evidence for the establishment of a social and commercial fur hierarchy comes from the remains of skinned cats, evident in urban sites such as Odense and Sigtuna, but interestingly not in Viking Age Birka.[27] Scandinavian towns – like many European towns – developed sizeable populations of feral cats, which were sometimes harvested for their fur. Excavations at Viborg (Søndersø I and II; dating from the eleventh to fourteenth century) recovered bones from polecats with skinning marks, but the remains of domestic cats, fox, dogs and hares were represented in much higher proportions. Cats had been skinned aged between two and seven months – before they were sexually mature and tearing at their coats.[28] The remains of wild mammals found in medieval towns can be associated with the expansion of urban economic hinterlands and provide only hints of fur-working in these centres, but locally sourced products were dominated by reindeer. Excavations of dwellings and accumulations of bones at Tøftom in Grimsdalen (around 1130 metres above sea level) revealed an extensive reindeer trapping system which operated particularly intensively from c.1000 to 1280, though the Tøftom area had been in use from the fifth/sixth century AD. The majority of the c.56,000 fragments of bones recovered during the excavations came from reindeer, whilst other fur-bearing species were represented by mountain fox and red fox. The system was no longer in use in the fourteenth century, most likely because of its devastating effect on the migrating reindeer population.[29] When permanent Norwegian settlement expanded into Finnmark in the fifteenth century, the region attracted the interest of fish and fur merchants, although the influence of the Hanse had already prompted the local Saami to hunt reindeer on a commercial basis. But with its thinly populated swathes of boreal woods and wetlands, Fennoscandia remained a reliable source of smaller, more valuable furs. Historians regard the fur trade as one of the foundations of the economic and political positions of the north-Norwegian chiefs, partly through collecting tributes from local Saami population and trading with Finns.[30] The *Historiae Norvegiae* (c.1195) describes how the country of the Finns was full of fur-bearing animals – bears, wolves, lynx, foxes, sables, otters,

---

[27] L. Jonsson, 'Massfångst av sjöfågel och pälsdjursjakt', in *Avstamp – för en ny Sigtunaforskning*, ed. S. Tesch, Sigtuna 1989, 54–7.

[28] J. Hjermind, 'Craftwork in Viborg from the 11th–18th century', in *Lübecker Kolloquium zur Stadtarchäologie im Hanseraum V: das Handwerk*, ed. I. Hillenstedt *et al*, Lübeck 2006, 625–639, at 631.

[29] E. Mikkelsen, *Fangstprodukter i vikingtidens og middelalderens økonomi. Organisering av massefangst av villrein i Dovre*, Oslo 1994.

[30] P. Urbańczyk, *Arctic Norway*, Warsaw 1992, 55.

badgers and beavers. *Egil's Saga* (14, 17), written *c*.1230, associates grey squirrel, beaver, sable and marten fur with Finnmark.[31] However, taxes to the Norwegian king were paid specifically in the most commercially valuable furs – squirrel and ermine hides – this *Finneskat* was last collected in 1310–11.[32] The Swedish kings also collected tribute in the form of hides from the Saami, referred to as the *Lappskatten*. Stockholm's traders sailed out in summer to markets held along the coast to the north to procure goods such as furs, salmon, seals and butter. Furs would then be exported.[33]

The woods and wetlands of Finland remained important sources of fur-bearing animals throughout the Middle Ages. The so-called 'Swedish crusades' against the Finns and the accompanying process of colonization saw the establishment of new political centres and settlements in the southern part of Finland. The economic network established by the Swedish Crown in the Gulf of Bothnia in the fourteenth century, with the so-called 'bircarlians' (*birkarlar*) as middlemen in contacts with the interior parts of northern Fennoscandia, appears to have been fundamental in moving products such as furs.[34] In Turku (Swedish Åbo), one of the most important centres founded in the late thirteenth century, the faunal assemblage recovered from the bishop's castle in Kuusisto included mountain hare, squirrels, a bear, an unidentified mustelid, roe deer, falcons and goshawks; hare and squirrels were also found in the town quarter of Åbo Akademi.[35] The élite controlled the acquisition of furs, as they did in the principality of Novgorod, and Magnus Eriksson's regulations encouraged the hunting of wolves, but forbade hunting squirrels, marten or stoat before 1 November, a direct and seasonal means of regulating populations of the most valuable fur-bearers.[36] As elsewhere in contemporary Europe, there is little archaeological evidence from high-status sites to suggest these were major centres of fur production. As in the case of Novgorod, the comparatively limited presence of bones from fur-bearing species points to a different organization of fur-working and dressed pelts remain intangible. Fur-bearing animals were instead acquired in the wooded estates by tenants who would present them as taxable goods, and so the acquisition and movement of furs was more or less comparable across the taiga biome of north-western Europe. South-east of Finland, in the frontier region of Karelia, subjects of Novgorod also collected hides from the Saami to pay their tributes to the city state. The principality of Novgorod would itself come to be defined by the systematic exploitation of fur-bearing mammals in the

---

[31] H. Pálsson and P. Edwards. *Egil's Saga*, Harmondsworth 1976, 44, 49–50.
[32] Ibid, 56.
[33] K. Söderlund, 'Trading City Stockholm – from the Thirteenth to Seventeenth Centuries. Topography and Catchment Area', in *Lübecker Kolloquium zur Stadtarchäologie im Hanseraum II: der Handel*, ed. R. Dunckel, M. Gläser, and U. Oltmanns, Lübeck 1999, 505–11, at 506.
[34] T. Wallerström, 'The Saami between East and West in the Middle Ages: An Archaeological Contribution to the History of Reindeer Breeding', *Acta Borealia* 17/1, 2000, 3–39.
[35] V. Immonen and M. Hiekkanen, 'Luxuries in the Town of Turku during the Middle Ages', in *Lübecker Kolloquium zur Stadtarchäologie im Hanseraum VI: Luxus und Lifestyle*, ed. C. Kimminus-Schneider *et al*, Lübeck 2008, 609–25, at 616.
[36] Law of Settlement XIX; R. Donner, *King Magnus Eriksson's Law of the Realm*, 2000, 55.

Russian taiga and tundra.³⁷ The inevitable conflict between the Scandinavian kings and Novgorod was resolved through the official designation of territorial rights in 1326, and Norwegian taxable territory stretched as far as the White Sea. But despite widespread access to fur, the trade became polarized. Novgorod would come to dominate the acquisition and export of fur, whilst the Norwegians concentrated on stockfish.³⁸ The final phase of the medieval fur trade, now dominated by Russian suppliers, is associated with pine marten and sable, which became particularly fashionable in the fifteenth and sixteenth centuries.³⁹ The acquisition and movement of these *Martes* is testimony to the extensive networks of supply and demand that characterized the organization of the late medieval fur trade. The situation in East Anglia was comparable in the way that fur was driven by export, but very different in terms of its ecological context and the acquisition of major fur-bearing species.

EAST ANGLIA AND THE SYMBOLIC USES OF FUR

The use of fur in early medieval England remains obscured by very limited and fragmentary data. In East Anglia, nucleated villages developed in the Middle and Later Saxon periods, with further settlement complexity unfolding from the eleventh to thirteenth century, resulting in a distinct dispersed pattern.⁴⁰ Most districts had an abundance of woodland and wood-pasture, grazing and hedges, although in the western parts of the region there were loosely clustered villages with extensive areas of open, intermixed arable. Particularly large areas of woodland are recorded in Hertfordshire and Essex, whilst the Fens remained an extensive area of wetland.⁴¹ These habitats supported a diverse range of fur-bearing wild mammals, which in the various categories of woodlands included foxes, wolves, squirrels and small mustelids, in more open environments hares, and in wetlands beavers and otters. However, wild mammals make up a tiny proportion of faunal assemblages from pre-Conquest sites across England, including settlements in East Anglia.⁴² At West Stow, where wild species make up less than one per cent of the substantial faunal assemblage, fur-bearers include hare, badger, fox and bear – the last most likely an import.⁴³ Evidence of bears is restricted to claws recovered from

---

37 M. Maltby, 'From *Alces* to Zander: a Summary of the Zooarchaeological Evidence from Novgorod, Gorodishche and Minino', in *The Archaeology of Medieval Novgorod in its Wider Context*, ed. M. Brisbane, E. Nosov and N. Makarov, Oxford 2012, 361–91; N. Makarov, 'Traders in the Forest: the Northern Periphery of "Rus" in the Medieval Trade Network', in *Pre-Modern Russia and Its World: Essays in Honor of Thomas S. Noonan*, ed. J. Tracy, K. Reyerson, T. Noonan and T. Stavrou, Wiesbaden 2006, 115–34.
38 J. Martin, *Treasure of the Land*.
39 Veale, *English Fur Trade*, 133–41.
40 T. Williamson, 'Explaining Regional Landscapes: East Anglia and the Midlands in the Middle Ages', in *Medieval East Anglia*, ed. C. Harper-Bill, Woodbridge 2005, 11–32, at 18.
41 T. Williamson, *Shaping Medieval Landscapes: Settlement, Society, Environment*, Macclesfield 2003, 33.
42 N. Sykes, *The Norman Conquest: A Zooarchaeological Perspective*, Oxford 2007.
43 P. Crabtree, *West Stow. Early Anglo-Saxon Animal Husbandry*, Ipswich 1989.

male graves indicating the presence of pelts, however, it is not clear whether these were imports or acquired locally. A relatively commonly exploited fur-bearer appears to have been the beaver; burial with beaver incisor artefacts is documented at thirteen English cemeteries, with two East Anglian burial sites producing other types of beaver remains.[44] Most are described as pendants consisting of lower incisors dating from the late fifth (e.g. Worlaby, Lincolnshire) to seventh century (Ducklington, Oxon). Whilst pendants were also made from the teeth and claws of canids and wild boar, only those of beaver were set in gold (making them particularly valuable) whilst their actual meaning must remain speculative.[45] Beaver teeth can be linked to the exploitation of the species, but even with the cemetery data the extent is very limited compared with, for example, sites in north-eastern Europe. More convincing evidence of the social and commercial value of beaver fur is derived from Sutton Hoo. Here, fragments of the lyre recovered from Mound 1 had patches of animal skin and hair identified as *Castor fiber*.[46] These have been interpreted as the remains of a beaver-skin bag used for displaying the lyre, but again it is difficult to ascertain whether this was imported, as other objects in the assemblage had been, or obtained locally. Furs clearly played an important role in Anglo-Saxon culture, but fur acquisition itself appears to have been relatively localized or reliant on imports.[47]

Beaver fur can be linked to the East Anglian élite in the seventh century – there is no zooarchaeological evidence that fenland beavers were exploited at settlement sites (in contrast to eastern Baltic and Russian sites) – all point to infrequent acquisition and use of fur in the context of gift exchange. This is certainly the case in later documented instances of skin garments; goat hair bedclothes and a cloak of silk and goat hair were sent to England by the missionary Boniface in the eighth century, whilst Boniface's colleague Lull received an otter skin robe from the Northumbrians. In 1075 marten skin garments were given by King Malcolm of Scotland and Queen Margaret to her brother Edgar Ætheling of England, along with imported grey squirrel and ermine (*hearma scyenne*) fur garments. This form of gift-giving may have prompted the development of fur wearing as a fashionable expression of aristocratic identity in the later eleventh century. Edgar's gift represents the earliest evidence for combining good quality cloth and fur to make a lined garment.[48] The earliest zooarchaeological evidence for more systematic fur exploitation in East Anglia has, to date, been found in Hertford. Here an assemblage dominated by domesticates included fragments of pine marten, otter, red squirrel, hare, rabbit, mole and cat, along with thirty-six bones of several red foxes was found in a tenth to twelfth century context; unfortunately the dating is

---

[44] B. Coles, *Beavers in Britain's Past*, Oxford 2006, 130.
[45] A. L. Meaney. *Anglo-Saxon Amulets and Curing Stones*. Oxford 1981, 171.
[46] Coles, *Beavers*, 134.
[47] J. Bond, 'The Cremated Animal Bone', in *The Anglo-Saxon Cemetery at Spong Hill, North Elmham, Part 8: The Cremations*, ed. J. McKinley, Norwich 1994, 121–35.
[48] Owen-Crocker, *Dress*, 181–2.

no more precise.[49] Fur-working as a specialized industry appears to have been established in English towns by the mid eleventh century, although quantities of recovered animals are very small.[50] Certainly by the late Anglo-Saxon period there is increasing evidence for the treatment of wild species as something that could be exploited and owned, whilst urban biological profiles represent an increasingly remote relationship with the countryside. Their populations were not actively engaged in hunting, but took advantage of provisioning networks connected to rural suppliers. This would be re-iterated following the Norman Conquest.[51] By the twelfth century the wearing of pelts had become popularly associated with the visual identity of secular lordship, and robes lined with fur panels, including ermine, are represented on high status figures in the Winchester Bible (Plate 1).[52] The development of a fur hierarchy must have been relatively organic and dependent on the re-organization of networks of international suppliers following the collapse of the earlier *emporia*. But by the end of the twelfth century, stylized furs had begun to be used in heraldry suggesting that such a hierarchy was already in place.

There is a time lag between the early evidence and the recorded use of named furs. *Miniver*, referring to spotted or variegated fur, is first documented in English at the start of the fourteenth century.[53] The first documented use of the word *sable* is in the mid fourteenth century, a Romanic derivative from a Slavonic word (Russian, Polish, Czech *sobol*, whence German *zobel*; Danish/Swedish *sobel*).[54] In English the heraldic term came to be synonymous with black, perhaps because it was customary to dye sable-fur black to heighten its contrast with ermine, when both were worn together.[55] *Ermine* is first documented in English in *c*.1200, whilst the first reference to it being worn dates from 1297. The term may be Armenian in origin, although some scholars believe the Romanic rendering may derive from Old High German *harmîn*, synonymous with Old English *hearma* already referred to above. The first reference to squirrel fur, with a distinction between a grey back and a white underside, is rendered as *vair* in 1300, whilst the term appears in English heraldry as bell-shaped spaces of two or more tinctures (usually azure and argent) in imitation of small skins sewn together, in Legh's *Armorie* in 1562.[56] In England, the use of heraldic furs from the thirteenth century was relatively limited: *vair* features in just 3 per cent of English and Scottish armorials from the thirteenth

---

[49] I. L. Baxter and S. Hamilton-Dyer, 'Foxy in Furs? A Note on Evidence for the Probable Commercial Exploitation of the Red Fox *(Vulpes vulpes L.)* and other Fur Bearing Mammals in Saxo-Norman (10th–12th century AD) Hertford, Hertfordshire, U.K.', *Archaeofauna* 12, 2003, 87–94.

[50] E. Fairnell, 'The Utilisation of Fur-bearing Animals in the British Isles: A Zooarchaeological Hunt for Data', unpublished MSc dissertation, York 2003.

[51] Sykes, *Norman Conquest*.

[52] G. Zarnecki, J. Holt and T. Holland, *English Romanesque Art 1066–1200*, London 1984, cat. 65.

[53] *Oxford English Dictionary* (henceforth abbreviated to OED) 9, 821.

[54] OED 14, 322.

[55] Ibid., 323.

[56] Ibid., 19, 402.

PLATE 1 Figures wearing robes lined with various pelts individually stitched together, c.1160–80. Loose folio associated with the Winchester Bible showing the story of David from the Book of Samuel: New York, Pierpont Morgan Library, M.619 verso (© The Morgan Library and Museum).

to fifteenth centuries, whilst ermine is represented in just 5 per cent, being most popular in western France (Normandy, Brittany, Poitou, Anjou, Maine) where it is represented in 8 per cent of armorials. The use of sable is significantly higher, consisting of 23 per cent (as tinctures or *emaux*), where the term denotes the heraldic colour. The association may have been particularly striking in the milieu of the tournament, where heraldic emblems, garments and fabrics were combined, exaggerated and highly stylized.[57] Whilst there is a chronological disparity between the development of fur wearing and its documented use, the synchronicity between heraldic tinctures and ranked costume appears to be fully developed by the end of the thirteenth century/start of the fourteenth century,[58] after which the first sumptuary laws regulating fur wearing appear in the reign of Edward III.[59] The popularity of dark furs coincides with the fashion for dark silks, replacing the fourteenth and fifteenth century high fashion trend for lighter, reddish furs.[60] However, this was not simply a matter of colour co-ordination: clothing was interpreted as a key to an individual's identity which was strategically and consciously constructed. Fur fulfilled the practical requirements of insulation, noted by contemporaries, and an expression of rank linked directly with commercial and aesthetic values.[61] The development of the fur culture in East Anglia coincides with the standardization of aristocratic identity following the Norman Conquest, an identity partly – but strikingly – embedded in the physical control of the landscape and its natural resources.

CULTURAL CHANGE AND FUR PRODUCTION IN MEDIEVAL EAST ANGLIA

Following the Norman Conquest the élite of the new regime constructed castles as visible bases of authority and administration, founded churches and monasteries and developed an exclusive hunting culture. East Anglia saw relatively little castle building; a royal castle was constructed in Norwich in 1067 and other towns such as Thetford and Ipswich, followed by major baronial foundations at Castle Acre, Eye, Haughley and Clare in the 1070s.[62] There was a subsequent phase of castle building and re-building in the 1140s (e.g. Castle Rising and New Buckenham) as visible indicators of political competition between local baronial families. The small number of castles (one of the smallest clusters in England) probably reflects the fact that only a few baronial families possessed enough land in the region to justify their construction. One of these families was the Warennes. Their fief, like those

---

[57] Pastoureau, *Traité*, 117.
[58] F. Piponnier and P. Mane, *Dress in the Middle Ages*, New Haven 2000, 74.
[59] J. Crawford, 'Clothing Distributions and Social Relations c.1350–1500', in *Clothing Culture, 1350–1650*, ed. C. Richardson, Aldershot 2004, 153–64.
[60] M. Hayward, *Rich Apparel: Clothing and the Law in Henry VIII's England*, Farnham 2009, 102.
[61] Ibid., 103.
[62] R. Liddiard, 'The Castle Landscapes of Anglo-Norman East Anglia: A Regional Perspective', in *Medieval East Anglia*, ed. C. Harper-Bill, Woodbridge 2005, 33–51.

of other Anglian barons, had at its core a collection of Old English estates that were procured more or less intact, and saw the direct replacement of late Anglo-Saxon/Anglo-Danish high status building with castles. Castle Acre, belonging to the Warennes, was raised on a late Anglo-Saxon manor house (or hall), as were at least six other castles in Norfolk and Suffolk.[63] This was a very visible and deliberate process of legitimizing the authority of the new regime. However, there is little to suggest these locations had any military significance. Instead they mirrored the existing settlement pattern, with a large number of castles being constructed on the edges of common land or on large expanses of heath or wood pasture, suggesting their location was dictated by ease of access to estates and resources. The biological profile of these castles is comparable across Anglo-Norman England (and indeed other regions of Europe), characterizing them very much as 'consumers' of natural resources.[64] Analysis of faunal assemblages from these sites underlines the change in hunting practices that is expressed through the documents of a rapidly burgeoning governmental bureaucracy. Hunting deer, especially the native red and recently imported fallow, became the very definition of lordship. These animals were kept in enclosed hunting grounds or parks, structures that were seen as increasingly attractive elements in the unfolding vision of a seigneurial landscape.[65]

Castle Acre is often cited as a classic example of the Anglo-Norman impact on the English countryside, closely associated with the Cluniac monastery (the church was dedicated in the mid 1140s), a planned settlement and deer park. A substantial pond was also situated to the south of the outer bailey. During the excavations of the castle in the 1970s, food refuse accumulated no later than the 1140s consisted of skeletal fragments from fallow deer and another imported and enclosed animal: the rabbit, which comprises 2.3 per cent of the total assemblage.[66] Two beaver mandibles were also recovered, interpreted at the time as foreign or residual, but it seems far more likely that these derived from a local population living in the Fens, some fifteen kilometres downstream of the castle.[67] In fact, all of these animals were probably obtained directly from the Warenne estates. Beaver bones have been recovered from two other high medieval English sites belonging to religious communities where they may represent remains of Lenten food (at Jarrow, among fallow deer, rabbit, red and roe deer there was a beaver ulna and humerus, and from the Bishop's Palace at Winchester part of a beaver cranium was recovered). In Wales beaver fur was valued above all other furs in the late twelfth-century laws of Hywel

---

[63] Ibid., 36.
[64] A. Ervynck, 'Medieval Castles as Top-Predators of the Feudal System: An Archaeozoological Approach', *Château Gaillard* 15, 1992, 152–9.
[65] The literature on this topic is significant; for a compilation see R. Liddiard (ed.), *The Medieval Park, New Perspectives*, Macclesfield 2007; also Sykes, *Norman Conquest*.
[66] P. Lawrance, 'Animal Bones', in 'Excavations at Castle Acre Castle, Norfolk, 1972-77: Country House and Castle of the Norman Earls of Surrey', ed. J. G. Coad and A. D. F. Streeten, *Archaeological Journal* 139, 1982, 138–301.
[67] Coles, *Beavers*, 163.

Dda, perhaps a reflection of its rarity, and laws in Newcastle and Perth a few centuries later demonstrate the continuing value of beaver pelts.[68] But the evidence for beaver hunting in East Anglia is elusive – perhaps the population was indeed too fragmented and small – and the new élite came to focus on more reliable sources of wild products.

In the process of reshaping English society, the Normans initiated a protracted restructuring of the indigenous ecology. However rabbits (or *coneys*) were not part of the initial 'package' and only became popular during the later Angevin period. Initially located on islands, by the late twelfth century rabbits had been moved inland and were housed in enclosed *coneygarths* or warrens.[69] Documentary sources for the establishment of warrens are limited before the middle decades of the thirteenth century,[70] and by the 1270s several had been constructed in East Anglia, particularly in Breckland where the sandy soils were ideally suited for breeding rabbits. Many warrens were founded by ecclesiastical lords – bishops and monasteries – whilst the two main secular foundations were pioneered by the earls of Norfolk and by the Warenne family – the earls of Surrey.[71] The Warennes maintained several of these exclusive farms in Methwold, Thetford, Tunstead and Gimingham in Norfolk and in Surrey; in 1240, the earl was ordered to supply two hundred rabbits for Henry III's Christmas feast. The earls expressed their control of wild resources through personal seals, and the association was so strong that it inspired artists decorating the Gorleston and Macclesfield Psalters – books commissioned by the Warennes. In the Gorleston Psalter, warrens repeatedly appear in line endings and margins as self-contained emblematic images and in both works there are explicit heraldic renderings of rabbits.[72] The *coneygarths* of the Warennes, so close to the very identity of the family, represented an accessible supply of exclusive meat for gift giving and personal consumption. The motivation for introducing the rabbit can be situated within the development of a post-Norman aristocratic culture, and the species rapidly acquired multiple layers of social meaning. Alongside the rabbit came the proliferation of domesticated ferrets, trained to hunt within the confines of the warrens, as well as ferreters, warreners, warren lodges and the infrastructure forming an elaborate 'coney culture'.[73] Initially access to rabbit meat was most likely more important than its fur, although the sale of rabbit pelts to furriers became an obvious means of meeting the high running costs of warrens

---

[68] Ibid, 54–5.
[69] N. Sykes and J. Curl, 'The Rabbit', in *Extinctions and Invasions: A Social History of British Fauna*, ed. T. O'Connor and N. Sykes, Oxford 2010, 116–26.
[70] Veale, *English Fur Trade*, 88.
[71] M. Bailey, 'The Rabbit and the Medieval East Anglian Economy', *Agricultural History Review* 36, 1988, 1–20, at 4.
[72] M. M. Nishimura and D. Nishimura, 'The Patronage of the Gorleston Psalter', in *Tributes to Lucy Freeman Sandler: Studies in Illuminated Manuscripts, 2008*, ed. K. A. Smith and C. Krinsky, London 2008, 205–18 at 13.
[73] P. van Dam, 'Voracious Rabbits. Shaping European Landscapes, 1300–1600', Paper for the Conference 'Nature, Society and History' Vienna, 30 September–2 October 1999. Available at: http://www.univie.ac.at/iffsocec/conference99.

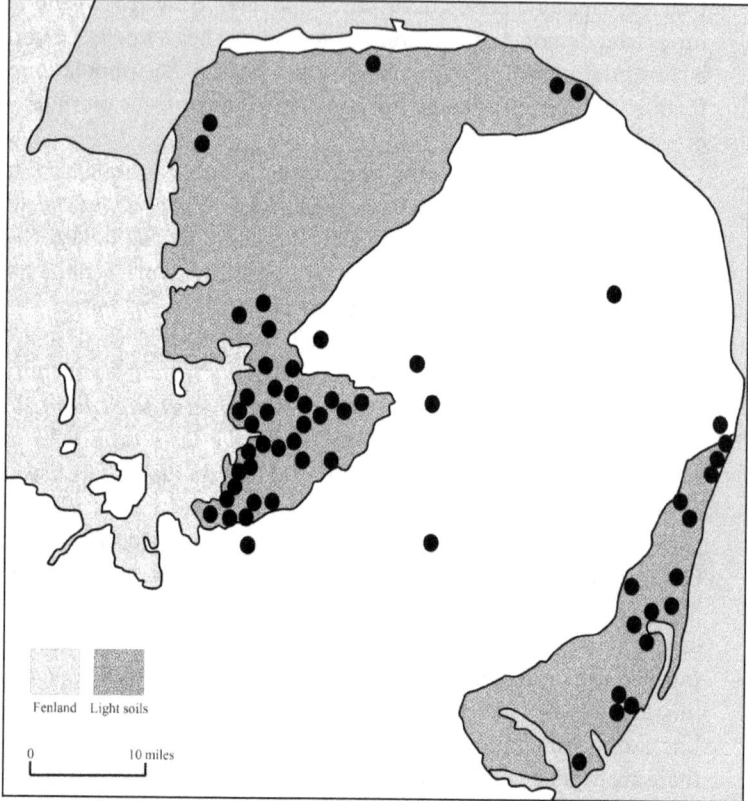

MAP 2 Documented rabbit warrens in East Anglia from c.1200 to 1540 (redrawn after M. Bailey, 'The Rabbit and the Medieval East Anglian Economy', *Agricultural History Review* 36, 1988, 1–20 at 3)

and was readily incorporated into the demesne economy. This developed into a major commercial enterprise and several different colours of pelt were bred. Between 1270 and 1460, there were over fifty warrens in East Anglia, each producing up to 3000 rabbits every year (Map 2).[74] As the international market for rabbit fur developed in the later fourteenth century, it appears that the animal began to be bred for fur in England and in other western European regions with a 'coney culture' such as Flanders.[75]

In East Anglia one of the most important outlets for this fur was Norwich, which was not only home to the odd warenner but also to many furriers or skinners (*peliparrii*); ninety are listed from the period 1275–1348.[76] The growth of towns such as Norwich saw the diversification of specialist trades relating to handling animal related products, and the development of inter-related industries. The largest group in the late thirteenth century *Enrolled Deeds* were the leatherworkers; butchers

[74] Bailey, 'The Rabbit', 6.
[75] van Dam, 'Voracious Rabbits'.
[76] E. Rutledge, 'Economic Life', in *Medieval Norwich*, ed. C. A. Rawcliffe, London 2004, 157–88, at table 2.

supplied a group of tanners, curriers, tawyers, cordwainers (fine leather workers), shoemakers, saddlers, glovers and parchment makers.[77] They also supplied bone and horn to a further group of artisans. Furriers would have been recipients of the growing concentration of warrens belonging to secular and ecclesiastical lords in East Anglia from the mid thirteenth century. Rabbits were procured from warrens on estate land for consumption and their furs would then be sold on. The city's main exports in the thirteenth and fourteenth centuries were fish, wool and cloth, however it is likely that furs and other luxury goods found an early market amongst the twenty-nine members of knightly and baronial families in high medieval Norwich, not to mention the increasingly prosperous community of merchants. Fur wearing was an established social custom amongst the urban élite; the Composition of 1415 called for the mayor and aldermen to be arrayed in clothes worthy of their estate, enabling the former to wear a furred and lined cloak appropriate to the season of the year.[78] By the mid fourteenth century these key industries had declined, and Norwich changed from a prosperous city with a wide industrial and commercial base to one with a high influx of rural poor, heavily dependent on weaving.[79] After the Plague, levels of prosperity increased so much that Norwich was the largest and wealthiest provincial city in England by 1525, second only to London.[80] Many Norwich tradesmen invested in fur, either as a business staple or occasional sideline. For example, William Sporle was a pelter who exported thousands of rabbit, lamb and cat skins in the 1380s and 1309s. Richard Purdans, who served as mayor in 1420 and 1433, exported rabbit skins and 500 otter skins.[81] These skins represented the cheaper end of the fur trade, although quality and commercial value would be based on seasonality with full winter-caught skins fetching the highest prices. Business was brisk. In December 1388, a consortium of Norwich exporters arranged for the shipping of a cargo of rabbit skins, along with worsted (yarn) and cheese from Yarmouth to the Continent – the vessel was back in port in eighteen days.[82] The other major fur export was lamb fur (*budge*), consisting of hair attached to a pelt rather than shorn fibres. In the later fourteenth and fifteenth century this was a relatively low quality fur; the sumptuary laws of Henry V, for example, forbade scholars at the University of Cambridge to wear any fur except *budge*.[83]

Beyond the export of locally produced furs, East Anglia supplied imported furs to local clients, including royalty. Henry III thought nothing of spending £100 on furs in a single season, and between 1250 and 1259 he bought from one English

---

[77] B. Ayers, 'Archaeological Evidence for Trade in Norwich from the 12th–17th centuries', in *Lübecker Kolloquium zur Stadtarchäologie im Hanseraum II: der Handel*, 25–35 at 34–5.
[78] R. H. Frost, 'The Urban Élite', in *Medieval Norwich*, ed. C. A. Rawcliffe, London 2004, 235–253 at 238.
[79] Rutledge, 'Economic Life', 188.
[80] P. Dunn, 'Trade', in *Medieval Norwich*, ed. Rawcliffe, 213–234 at 214.
[81] Ibid., 220.
[82] Ibid., 224–5; Bailey, 'The Rabbit', 1–20.
[83] C. H. Cooper, *Annals of Cambridge*, 1, Cambridge 1842, 156–7.

merchant alone furs to the value of £1200. Almost all his purchases were made at the East Anglian fairs of Boston, Stamford, and St Ives, or at Lynn, sometimes from English traders, sometimes from Norwegian or Gotlandic merchants. The king's tailor journeyed to Lynn in 1245 and there spent £1747 17*d.* on 'greywork' purchased from Edmund of Gotland and others, and we read of payments being made at Boston in 1250 to six merchants of Norway and to Ledbroc of Gotland for 'greywork' for the king. Norwich, like other key trading towns such as Lynn and Yarmouth, imported foreign furs.[84] By the late fourteenth century Flemish cloth had completely disappeared, and so had squirrel skins, for fashions in dress had altogether changed; furs of any kind were no longer the status symbol they had once been, and the fur market, such as it was, had moved to London. St Ives and the other, once famous, international fairs of East Anglia vanished. However, rabbit exports continued, as at Blakeney in Norfolk in the sixteenth century.[85] The sumptuary law of 1510 restricted the use of imported furs to the ranks of the gentry and nobility; everyone else had to make do with locally available lamb, rabbit, fox and squirrel.[86] The value of rabbit fur did not change as animals began to escape from warrens, for demand was highest in the 1370s, and only with the later proliferation of feral populations came a downgrading of the animal's status. But even in the mid fifteenth century, rabbit appears to have replaced squirrel as the staple fur of north-western Europe and London remained an important market for East Anglian warrens.[87] However, the ecological shift was so drastic that complaints begin to be documented about coneys being a nuisance.[88] Rabbit pelts became considered to be particularly lowly, and along with cat skins they continued to play a commercial role as the quintessential imitation fur, requiring dyeing, treatment and manipulation.[89] In a parallel development the status of the once prized pine marten changed in Scandinavia. Increasingly perceived as a pest from 1600, this animal became perennially hunted in contrast to earlier seasonal regulations, leading to a rapid depopulation of the species.[90]

CONCLUSION: SITUATING EAST ANGLIA IN THE WORLD OF MEDIEVAL FUR

The commercial exploitation of fur in medieval northern Europe emerged within the Scandinavian Peninsula under virtually unique conditions during the Viking Age. Subsequently it became the economic lynchpin for the rise of the Russian prin-

---

[84] E. M. Carus-Wilson, 'The Medieval Trade of the Ports of the Wash', *Medieval Archaeology* 6/7, 1962-3, 182–201, at 192.
[85] Bailey, 'The Rabbit', 15.
[86] Hayward, *Rich Apparel*, 103.
[87] Bailey, 'The Rabbit', 12.
[88] Sykes and Curl, 'Rabbit', 125.
[89] Sachs, *Furs*, 82.
[90] J.-O. Helldin, 'Population Trends and Harvest Management of Pine Marten *Martes martes* in Scandinavia', *Wildlife Biology* 6, 2000, 111–20, at 113.

cipalities, and regional suppliers developed alongside the infrastructure of international commerce in the twelfth and thirteenth centuries. The Saami, with their intimate understanding of the wilderness, represented essential suppliers of fur for southern Scandinavian merchants. The southern Scandinavian élite sought to control the supply, but did not promote an exclusive hunting culture on the Peninsula. In contrast, the development of the fur trade in East Anglia, which became particularly noted for its rabbits, was a very different process linked to the seigneurial and commercial culture developing over the course of the twelfth and thirteenth centuries, where the visual language of authority became fused with the management of natural resources and the conspicuous consumption of luxuries. The Anglo-Saxon legacy is limited in this respect; whilst some contact with wild species is evident in settlement (e.g. West Stow) and cemetery sites (e.g. Spong Hill), there is no evidence for the systematic exploitation of local (and relatively limited) woodlands for fur-bearers either before or after the Conquest.[91] Indeed, whilst this lack of wild species in early Anglo-Saxon assemblages has been interpreted as an absence of suitable habitats,[92] it is also clear that such animals were conceptualized differently than in the late Anglo-Saxon period.[93] The development of a new élite culture saw an emphasis on the management of natural resources, particularly game. Unlike the squirrels and martens of the northern Fennoscandian woods, rabbit fur, as with fallow-deer venison which became the most popular wild meat in late medieval England, was effectively farmed. Occasional hunting of wild fur-bearers such as fox, hare and marten, came to be governed under the 'right of warren'. The prevalence of these animals is very difficult to reconstruct, but the high density of *coneygarths* in East Anglia may suggest that numbers of potential predators – such as foxes and mustelids – were limited. Where they were an evident threat, these carnivores were hunted to protect the prized rabbits.[94] In this respect, the ecology, experience and organization of the fur trade in eastern England was very different to that of the main source of luxury furs: the belt of taiga covering much of the Scandinavian Peninsula, Finnmark and northern Russia. The changing prices and popularity of furs from these regions must be situated within the broader context of the international fur trade, and the regional vicissitudes that in the case of East Anglia ensured the profitability of breeding rabbits as a staple fur into the early modern period.

---

[91] For a summary of fur-bearers in assemblages, see D. Yalden, *The History of British Mammals*, London 1999, 144.
[92] Ibid., 139.
[93] N. Sykes, Wild Animals in Anglo-Saxon Archaeology handbook.
[94] Bailey, 'The Rabbit'.

— Chapter 8 —

ECONOMIC RELATIONS BETWEEN EAST ANGLIA AND FLANDERS IN THE ANGLO-NORMAN PERIOD*

Eljas Oksanen

REFLECTING ON the recent civil war of 1173–4, which pitted King Henry II of England (1154–89) against the supporters of his son Young King Henry, the English poet Jordan Fantosme described the character and aspirations of the foreign mercenary soldiers brought into East Anglia by the prince's supporter Earl Robert of Leicester:

> Soon you could have heard the Flemings from Flanders and French and Picards shouting aloud: 'We have not come to this country to hang around but to destroy the king, Henry, the old warrior, to get for ourselves the wool of England that we so much desire.' My lords, the truth is that most of them [the soldiers] were weavers, they do not know how to bear arms like knights, and why they had come was to pick up plunder and the spoils of war, for there is no more prosperous region on earth than Bury St Edmunds.[1]

Leicester and his mercenaries were defeated by forces loyal to Henry II at the battle of Fornham, near the abbey-town of Bury St Edmunds, on 16 October 1173, and whatever plundering they may have had the time to partake in was brought to an end. Fantosme's account of the war, in which he dealt primarily with military operations in northern England and East Anglia, sought to alleviate the lingering post-

---

* I would like to thank M. David Martin, Jenny Benham, Charles West, Philip Poole and Helen Keeble for their valuable comments and corrections to an earlier draft of this paper. All mistakes remain mine.

[1] 'Tost i purrïez oïr e bien en halt crier / entre Flamens de Flandres et Franceis e Puier: / "Nus n'eimes pas en cest païs venuz pur sujorner, / mes pur lu rei destruire, Henri, le vielz guerier, / e pur aver sa leine, dunt avum desirier." / Seignurs, ço est la verité: li plus furent telier, / ne sevent porter armes a lei de chevalier, / mes pur ço furent venuz, pur aver guain e guerre, / kar n'ad meillur vïandier de Saint Edmund en terre.', Jordan Fantosme, *Jordan of Fantosme's Chronicle*, ed. and trans. R. Johnston, Oxford 1981, 72, lines 991–9.

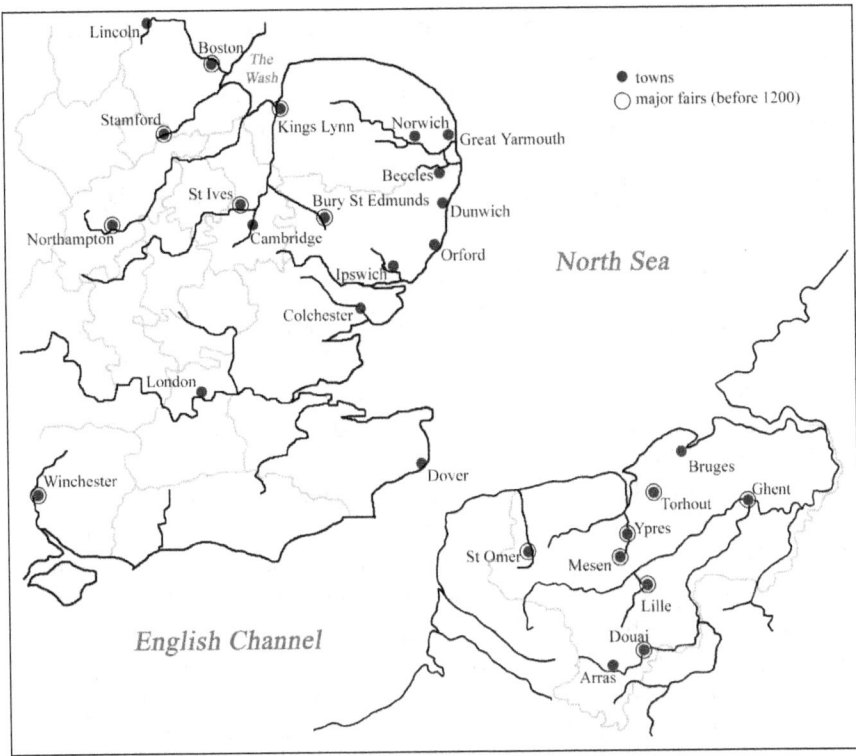

MAP 1 England and Flanders in the Anglo-Norman period

war domestic tensions by recasting the conflict not in terms of an inter-dynastic civil war but an invasion of England by opportunistic foreign forces. His East Anglian episode, in particular, focuses on the brutality of the Flemish mercenaries. A clever re-interpreter of recent history, Fantosme worked with the grain of his audience's expectations and cultural biases, and with prevailing literary tropes, to create a powerful image of a barbaric, dishonourable foreign foe.[2] His materials were drawn from the exceptional economic developments that were transforming the societies and politics of north-western Europe, a central feature of which was the growth of textile industries and overseas trade. Over the course of this period wool became England's chief export and Fantosme's belligerent weavers had resonance as a distorted inversion of the multitude of peaceful Flemish merchants who, during the

[2] The Flemish soldiers are also referred to in Roger of Howden, *Gesta Regis Henrici Secundi Benedicti Abbatis*, ed. W. Stubbs, Rolls Series, London 1867, I, 60–2; Jocelin of Brakelond, *The Chronicle of Jocelin of Brakelond*, ed. and trans. H. Butler, London 1949, 1. For scholarship on the chronicle, see Jordan Fantosme, *Chronicle*, ed. Johnston, xi–xlix; L. Ashe, *Fiction and History in England, 1066–1200*, Cambridge 2007, 81–120; R. Johnston, 'The Historicity of Jordan Fantosme's Chronicle', *Journal of Medieval History* 2, 1976, 159–69; M. Strickland, 'Arms and the Men: War, Loyalty and Lordship in Jordan Fantosme's Chronicle', *Medieval Knighthood* IV, 1990, 187–220.

poet's lifetime, were a frequent sight in English towns, markets and fairs. Nationality ultimately divided the Flemish and English in Fantosme's chronicle. In this chapter, however, I shall investigate Flanders and East Anglia from the late eleventh to the early thirteenth centuries not primarily as disparate regions belonging to different realms, but rather as two parts of a single economic organism whose internal interests often stood in opposition to the political will of their rulers (Map 1).

ECONOMIC GROWTH AND TRADE NETWORKS

The Central Middle Ages was a period of tremendous economic expansion both in England and among its continental neighbours. The county of Flanders, a territorial princedom whose counts were functionally independent of the French crown in the eleventh and twelfth centuries, was the dominant political force in the southern Low Countries. By the twelfth century it had developed into one of the pre-eminent economic regions in Europe with a higher degree of industrialization and urbanization than anywhere else north of the Alps. The greater part of Flemish industrial wealth was founded on the enormous cloth-manufacturing and trading sectors controlled by the county's urban merchants. Flemish textiles enjoyed significant market penetration both geographically and socio-economically throughout medieval Europe. Surviving records show that they were traded from northern France to Novgorod and the Mediterranean basin alike, and that their range varied from high-quality luxury textiles to cheap low-grade cloths.[3]

Political, social, economic and cultural exchanges between the southern Low Counties and England were extensive through the Anglo-Norman period.[4] In the sphere of commerce, Flanders and its urban centres and great fairs constituted a major nexus linking the nearby North Sea shores to trade routes and networks in mainland Europe. The vibrancy of trade between these maritime regions by the eleventh century is suggested by such references as the mention of the Flemish seaport of Wissant thronging with merchants waiting to cross into England in 1068.[5] Mark Gardiner's investigation of English seaborne trade in the eleventh century shows that the eastern and south-eastern seaports, fuelled by overseas commerce, were the kingdom's fastest growing towns. Given their geographical orientation Flanders was most probably England's chief trading partner at this

---

[3] P. Chorley, 'The Cloth Exports of Flanders and Northern France during the Thirteenth Century: a Luxury Trade?', *Economic History Review* 40, 1987, 349–79; H. Krueger, 'The Genoese Exportation of Northern Cloths to Mediterranean Ports, Twelfth Century', *Revue Belge de Philologie et d'Histoire* 65, 1987, 722–50; D. Nicholas, *Medieval Flanders*, London and New York, 1992, 112–15; H. Pirenne, 'Draps d'Ypres à Novgorod au commencement du XIIe siècle', *Revue Belge de Philologie et d'Histoire* 9, 1930, 563–6.
[4] See E. Oksanen, *Flanders and the Anglo-Norman World 1066–1216*, Cambridge 2012.
[5] Hariulf, *Chronique de l'Abbaye de Saint-Riquier*, ed. F. Lot, Paris 1894, 241. More broadly on pre-Conquest commerce, P. Grierson, 'The Relations between England and Flanders before the Norman Conquest', *Transactions of the Royal Historical Society*, 4th ser., 23, 1941, 71–112; P. H. Sawyer, 'The Wealth of England in the Eleventh Century', *Transactions of the Royal Historical Society*, 5th ser., 15, 1965, 145–64.

time.[6] English trade patterns grew and diversified in other directions during the twelfth century, especially south towards Normandy, but eastern trade remained important. The tax records for the one-fifteenth levied by King John (1199–1216) on the value of English imports and exports in 1203–4 puts Boston (£780 15s. 3d.) after London (£836 12s. 10d.) as the kingdom's second busiest trading port. Altogether, the ports from Boston down to Colchester along the East Anglian coastline contributed a third of the total £4,958 7s. 3.5d. raised.[7]

Along with port towns the great seasonal fairs that convened at Boston, Stamford, King's Lynn, Northampton, St Ives, Bury St Edmunds and Winchester were principal centres of English foreign trade. The annual cycle of fairs, each lasting up to a few weeks at a time, brought together merchants from around England and the North Sea littoral.[8] The broader East Anglian economic zone – which, for the purposes of this paper, comprises not only Norfolk, Suffolk and Essex, but also extends through Cambridgeshire and Huntingdonshire into eastern Northamptonshire and southern Lincolnshire – was the heartland of these fairs and by virtue of their scale the nexus of English commerce over the North Sea. Sensitivity towards Flemish trade appears to have prevailed from the earliest days of the fair network: the timing of the fair of St Ives, established by Ramsey Abbey in 1110, at the feast of Easter may have been deliberately chosen to synchronize with the older Lenten fair of Ypres, later a major event on the commercial circuit of north-western Europe.[9]

The impact of geography on English and Flemish commercial development is clear in the pattern of trading networks. It is notable that six of the seven major Anglo-Norman fairs, excepting only Winchester near the south coast, were all located within a hundred kilometres of each other. A central position both within England and in relation to North Sea shipping, along with the high agricultural productivity of the region, must have contributed to East Anglia's success as a trading hub. Yet what is most striking about this network of fairs is their common position along waterways that discharged into the Wash. The medieval East Anglian economic zone was defined first and foremost by its natural transport network, and water transport remained the cheapest and most efficient way of moving bulk goods over long distances.[10] Bulk quantities of many goods such as foodstuffs were rarely sold at a distance of more than fifteen kilometres via an

[6] M. Gardiner, 'Shipping and Trade between England and the Continent during the Eleventh Century', *Anglo-Norman Studies* 22, 1999, 71–93. More generally on the development of towns on the eastern seaboard, see the following chapters in *The Cambridge Urban History of Britain vol. 1 600-1540*, ed. D. Palliser, Cambridge 2000: D. Keene, 'The South-East of England', 545–72; C. Dyer and T. Slater, 'The Midlands', 609–22; B. Brodt, 'East Anglia', 639–55.

[7] N. Gras, *The Early English Customs System*, Cambridge, MA 1918, 221–2.

[8] E. Moore, *The Fairs of Medieval England. An Introductory Story*, Toronto 1985, especially 9–23.

[9] Ibid., 14. On Flemish fairs, Nicholas, *Medieval Flanders*, 111–13; M. Yamada, 'Le mouvement des foires en Flandre avant 1200', in *Villes et campagnes au Moyen Âge. Mélanges Georges Duby*, ed. J.-M. Duvosquel and A. Dierkens, Liège 1991, 773–89.

[10] M. M. Postan, 'The Trade of Medieval Europe: the North', in *The Cambridge Economic History of Europe vol. 2. Trade and Industry in the Middle Ages*, ed. M. M. Postan and E. Miller, 2nd edn, Cambridge 1987, 196–204.

overland route.¹¹ Thus grain grown in Cambridgeshire and the adjacent regions, a bread basket of medieval England, for sale in London was usually not taken south directly. It was shipped north-east down the rivers Welland, Nene, Ouse and their tributaries to the grain depot of King's Lynn, and from there along the coast southwards towards its eventual destination.¹²

Like the basin of the Wash, Flanders was a land of waterways that provided exceptional access to inland markets and agricultural regions. From the eleventh century on its natural transport infrastructure was improved through dredging of the rivers, the construction of canals and the establishment of coastal outports for inland towns.¹³ The particular demands posed by water transport are reflected in the technologies that arose in these maritime regions. The favoured cargo carrier on the continent's Atlantic seaboard was the cog, a spacious and box-like ship with steep sides that rode low in the water. By virtue of its superior capacity its development in the Central Middle Ages had a crucial impact on the growth of overseas bulk trade. It had a rival in the hulk, however, a ship-type of which no physical remains survive but whose rounded, crescent-shaped hull is preserved through illuminations, carvings and seals. While the cog reigned on the seas, the hulk appears to have developed as a shallow draught ship that could traverse not only the seas but also the inland waterways that the cog could not enter. Boats of similar construction are even today favoured as people and goods carriers in the great river deltas of south-eastern Asia. Some of the earliest surviving records of the hulk are from the southern Low Countries and there is a strong possibility that the ship-type was developed for domestic trade there.¹⁴ The similar geography of the adjacent eastern England, where all the major fairs and many of the important towns lay by river routes, must have enhanced its popularity as an international trading vessel.

TRADE GOODS

Goods carried by cogs and hulks from the southern Low Countries to England include textiles, woad and wines, in particular French wines, a trade in which Flemings occupied the lucrative position of the middle man.¹⁵ Overall, however,

---

[11] R. Britnell, *The Commercialisation of English Society, 1000–1500*, 2nd edn, Manchester 1996, 82–4.
[12] Ibid., 87–8; N. Gras, *The Evolution of the English Corn Market from the Twelfth to the Eighteenth Century*, Cambridge 1915, 48–9, 62–4; E. Miller and J. Hatcher, *Medieval England: Rural Society and Economic Change 1086–1343*, London and New York 1978, 78–9. On transport and waterways by the Wash, see H. Darby, *The Medieval Fenland*, Newton Abbot 1974, 93–118.
[13] J. Dhondt, 'Développement urbain et initiative comtale en Flandre au XIᵉ siècle', *Revue de Nord* 30, 1948, 133–56; Nicholas, *Medieval Flanders*, 100. For an overview of Flemish urban development, A. Verhulst, *The Rise of Cities in North-Western Europe*, Cambridge 1999, 68–118.
[14] B. Greenhill, 'The Mysterious Hulk', *The Mariner's Mirror* 86, 2000, 3–18; G. Hutchinson, *Medieval Ships and Shipping*, London 1994, 15–20; R. Unger, *The Ship in the Medieval Economy 600–1600*, London 1980, 133–9. On ships, see also above Chapter 3.
[15] *The Great Rolls of the Pipe for the 19ᵗʰ Year of the Reign of King Henry II (1172–73)*, Pipe Roll Society, London 1895, 29, 165; *Pipe Roll 1 John (1198-9)*, 182; Moore, *Fairs of Medieval England*, 30–5; H. Pirenne, 'Un grand commerce d'exportation au moyen âge: les vins de France', *Annales; économies, sociétés, civilisations* 5, 1933, 231–5.

the greater volume of the flow of goods across the Channel was west-to-east. As the chronicler Henry of Huntingdon wrote in c.1130: 'Silver is brought from the nearest part of Germany, along the Rhine, in exchange for a wonderful abundance of fish and meat, of costly wool and milk, and cattle without number, so that the wealth of silver [in England] seems greater than in Germany.'[16] Detailed information on the volume of trade is elusive, but the emerging picture is that of an export-oriented English economy that was enriched by inflows of silver from the Continent, especially through the Flemish trade nexus.[17]

Documentary sources from Flanders add other goods such as hides, cheese and rock coal to Huntingdon's list of English exports.[18] In the context of Anglo-Flemish commerce the most important exports were wool and grain. 'Costly wool' had by the thirteenth century become the chief English export, and in the Late Middle Ages the importance of the Anglo-Flemish wool trade to both economies approached interdependence.[19] While the vital importance of this trade to the Flemish textile industry before the thirteenth century is contested, it is generally accepted that a commercially important volume was being shipped across the Channel already in the twelfth century.[20] A well-known account in the 'Miracles of St Mary of Laon' relates a tale of an ill-starred group of Flemish merchants who crossed to England with 300 marks of silver in 1113, travelling the markets and fairs of the country and finally assembling at Dover for a return journey, only to have the warehouse containing their precious wool burn down.[21] Their more fortunate successors brought to Flanders the English wool mentioned a few generations later in the charters and customs lists of Nieuwpoort and Bruges.[22]

---

[16] 'Aduehitur autem argentum a proxima parte Germanie per Renum pro mira fertilitate piscium et carnium, lane pretiossisme et lactis, armentorumque absque numero, ut maior ibi videtur copia argenti quam in Germania.' Henry of Huntingdon, *Historia Anglorum*, ed. and trans. D. Greenway, Oxford 1996, 10.

[17] P. Harvey, 'The English Trade in Wool and Cloth, 1150-1250: Some Problems and Suggestions', *Prodizione, commercio e consumo dei panni di lana nei secoli XII-XVII*, ed. M. Spallanzani, Florence 1976, 369–75; E. Miller and J. Hatcher, *Medieval England. Towns, Commerce and Crafts 1086–1348*, London and New York 1995, 187–97.

[18] *Cartulaire de l'ancienne estaple de Bruges*, ed. L. Gilliodts-van Severen, Bruges 1904, I, 19; *De oorkonden der graven van Vlaanderen (juli 1128 – september 1191)*, ed. T. de Hemptinne, L. de Mey and A. Verhulst, Brussels 1988, I, 346; G. Dept, *Les influences anglaise et française dans le comté de Flandre au début du XIIIe siècle*, Ghent and Paris 1928, 70; J. Lestocquoy, *Patriciens du Moyen-Âge. Les dynasties bourgeoises d'Arras du XIe au XVe siècle*, Arras 1945, 27.

[19] J. Munro, *Wool, Cloth, and Gold. The Struggle for Bullion in Anglo-Burgundian Trade, 1340–1478*, Brussels and Toronto 1972, 1–9. More broadly on the evolution of the trade in the Middle Ages, T. Lloyd, *The English Wool Trade in the Middle Ages*, Cambridge 1977; E. Power, *The Wool Trade in English Medieval History*, Oxford 1941.

[20] G. Dept, 'Les marchands flamands et le roi d'Angleterre (1154–1216)', *Revue du Nord* 12, 1926, 311–13; Lloyd, *English Wool Trade*, 4–7; Harvey, 'English Trade in Wool and Cloth', 369–73. But for a reminder on the importance of the native Flemish wool production, A. Verhulst, 'La laine indigène dans les Pays-Bas entre le XIIe et le XVIIe siècle. Mise en œuvre industrielle production et commerce', *Revue historique* 248, 1972, 281–97.

[21] Herman the Monk, 'De Miraculis S. Mariae Laudunensis', ed. J.-P. Migne, *Patrologia Latina* 156, Paris 1853, cols 975–7.

[22] *Cartulaire de l'ancienne estaple de Bruges*, I, 19; *De oorkonden*, I, 346.

It is possible to reconstruct a more comprehensive picture of wool sales to Flemings in East Anglia from the thirteenth century onwards thanks to the significant increase in transaction records. The fair of Boston, which also drew in sellers from Lincolnshire and south-eastern Yorkshire, emerged in this period as the leading wool market in eastern England, but all the great fairs attracted wool sellers and buyers.[23] The roots of this trade were older: Jordan Fantosme's wool-hungry Flemish soldiers of 1173 were not an exercise in mere poetic licence. Periods of war between Flanders and the Anglo-Norman realms provide us with evidence on the Anglo-Flemish trade from confiscation records and fines. Count Philip of Flanders (1168–91) had supported the Young King Henry in his rebellion against Henry II and the Pipe Rolls for that year record the sale of £39 worth of wool, wine and other goods confiscated by royal officials from Flemings in Suffolk, and also the seizing of a Flanders-bound shipment of Essex wool worth £4 18s. 8d.[24]

Studies of medieval sheep breeds and wool retail records show that wool produced in medieval East Anglia and the eastern Midlands varied from coarse and low-cost to the middling sort, but what it lacked in quality it made up in volume.[25] Sheep were reared in most parts of these counties but, just as with fields recently reclaimed from the sea across the Channel in Flanders, the salt marshes along the coasts from Essex to Norfolk and the fenlands of Cambridgeshire and southern Lincolnshire were particularly well suited to the task. It was difficult to grow grain in salty and marshy areas, and heavier livestock would have found it difficult to graze on the soft terrain.[26] Already by 1086 there were flocks totalling some 14,400 sheep belonging to the abbey of Ely and its dependants in the north Cambridgeshire fenlands, in the region that was to become the geographical heartland of the network of international fairs in the twelfth century.[27] Little Domesday Book of 1086 records 46,458 sheep in demesne farms in Norfolk, 37,522 in Suffolk and 46,095 in Essex. Sheep enjoyed an unchallenged prominence in the region's animal husbandry. In Suffolk and Essex there were over twice as many sheep as all other recorded livestock animals, and in Norfolk the ratio was over three-to-one.[28] It is difficult to estimate the market price of wool in the eleventh century, but in 1200 the Little Domesday numbers would have represented roughly £5,100 worth of flocks producing roughly £1,400 worth of wool,

---

[23] Moore, *Fairs of Medieval England*, 47–50.
[24] *Pipe Roll 19 Henry II* (1172–3), 13, 29; *Pipe Roll 20 Henry II* (1173–4), 14.
[25] N. Heard, *Wool. East Anglia's Golden Fleece*, Lavenham 1970, 43, 47; J. Munro, 'Medieval Woollens: Textiles, Textile Technology and Industrial Organisation, c.800–1500', in *The Cambridge History of Western Textiles* vol. 1, ed. D. Jenkins, Cambridge 2003, 186–7; M. Ryder, *Sheep and Man*, London 1983, 449, 463.
[26] H. Hallam, 'Farming Techniques. Eastern England', in *The Agrarian History of England and Wales vol. II. 1042–1350*, ed. H. Hallam and J. Thirsk, Cambridge 1988, 293–321; R. Trow-Smith, *A History of British Livestock Husbandry*, London 1957, 76.
[27] Power, *Wool Trade*, 21.
[28] H. Darby, *The Domesday Geography of Eastern England*, Cambridge 1971, 142, 199, 255.

or a sum approximately equivalent to the annual revenues of the archbishop of Canterbury.[29]

A second significant English export to Flanders was grain, a commodity that much like wool was tied to the urban and industrial make-up of the county. David Nicholas has argued that the commercial fortunes of the Flemish cloth towns were initially founded on interregional trade in foodstuffs. The great towns developed by major trading routes, typically rivers, at the juncture between two agricultural zones, with the wealth created by the bulk movement of foodstuffs and other raw materials providing the capital for later industrial development. As the towns grew beyond the agricultural capacity of their hinterlands, urban merchants reached out into international markets. By the Late Middle Ages the urban merchants' capacity to import cheap foreign produce in bulk allowed them to dominate the local foodstuff market to the point of depressing the native Flemish agricultural economy.[30] The paucity of records makes it difficult to estimate the extent to which Flemish towns were already dependent on foreign food exports during the Anglo-Norman period, although Galbert of Bruges' contemporary account of a famine in Flanders in 1124–5 does show that towns did act as grain depots and that during the crisis urban merchants had a key role in supplying the county with imported produce.[31] The nearby East Anglia was one of the most fertile regions in medieval England, and manorial records from the thirteenth and fourteenth centuries show that wheat, rye, oats and especially barley were grown there.[32] Trade in grain was certainly established between Flanders and eastern England before the war of 1173–4. Along with wool and wine cargoes as mentioned above, a ship carrying grain to Flanders was seized off the coast of Essex in 1173, and the 1177 Pipe Roll entry for Cambridgeshire records that fines valued between 6s. 8d. and £6 13s. 4d. were levied on sixty-one individuals, presumably merchants, for breaking the royal justiciar's war-time ban on the sale of grain. The toponymics of these merchant's names shows that the majority hailed from Cambridgeshire, Norfolk, Suffolk, Essex and Kent.[33]

---

[29] Britnell, *Commercialisation*, 39; Trow-Smith, *History of British Livestock Husbandry*, 135–42; D. Farmer, 'Prices and Wages', in *The Agrarian History of England and Wales vol. II 1042–1350*, ed. Hallam and Thirsk, 748, 757.

[30] D. Nicholas, 'Settlement Patterns, Urban Functions, and Capital Formation in Medieval Flanders', in *Trade, Urbanisation and the Family*, Aldershot 1996, IV, 1–30; D. Nicholas, 'Of Poverty and Primacy: Demand, Liquidity and the Flemish Economic Miracle, 1050–1200', *American Historical Review* 98, 1991, 17–41. The topic is contested, however, and for alternative views on Flemish urban development and the size of the county's agriculture, A. Verhulst, 'The Alleged Poverty of the Flemish Rural Economy as Reflected in the Oldest Account of the Comital Domain Known as "Gros Brief" (A.D. 1187)', *Studia historica œconomica. Liber amicorum Herman van der Wee*, Louvain 1993, 369–82; C. Verlinden, 'Marchands ou tisserands? À propos des origines urbaines', *Annales. Économies, sociétés, civilisations* 27.2, 1972, 396–406.

[31] Galbert of Bruges, *De Multro, Traditione, et Occasione Gloriosi Karoli Comitis Flandriarum*, ed. J. Rider, Corpus Christianorum Continuatio Mediaevalis 131, Turnhout 1994, 9, 11.

[32] Hallam, 'Farming Techniques. Eastern England', 293–307.

[33] *Pipe Roll 19 Henry II* (1172–3), 13; *Pipe Roll 23 Henry II* (1176–7), 183–4. For a similar list of fines from 1198 for breaches of a ban on Flemish grain trade, see below p. 184.

MARKET ECONOMY

Growing international trade in wool, grain and other goods was a feature of the expansion of the market economy in Anglo-Norman England.[34] We naturally have most information on the activities and possessions of the élite. Little Domesday Book records 8,110 sheep on manors owned by Earl William I de Warenne and his under-tenants in Norfolk, Suffolk and Essex, 3,307 of which were reared on demesne estates.[35] William was married to the Flemish noblewomen Gundrada of the important Oosterzele family in western Flanders, and the Warennes held the advocacy of the monastery of St Bertin by St Omer in the late eleventh century and again in the late twelfth.[36] Their great wealth in wool must have made its way to the market, and it is hard to believe that the Warenne family would have considered their political connections and commercial interests to be separate spheres. Sheep flocks were common on aristocratic estates. The *Rotuli de Dominabus et Pueris et Puellis*, a record of aristocratic manors held by the king for widows and underage heirs in 1185, records sheep flocks on nearly all of the listed large manors to a total of some 15,000 animals. Roughly 3,500 were reared on thirty-three estates in Norfolk, Suffolk, Essex and Cambridgeshire.[37] Even as the Anglo-Norman period was coming to a close, financial pressures stemming from the increasing commercialization and monetization of the English economy led many manorial lords to reorganize their estates from a dispersed system of rental properties farmed out to under-tenants to a more centrally managed estate structure. One outcome of this restructuring was that it made for the production of larger quantities of goods for markets.[38] Though the trend was not universal, it pushed lords towards greater involvement with the kingdom's developing financial infrastructures. Wool's position as the chief overseas export made it a convenient product around which to structure large transactions. The Flemish financier William Cade of St Omer who operated in King Henry II's court is known to have made loans against wool payments. A document listing debts amounting to a total of roughly £5,000 owed to Cade at the time of his death in *c.*1166 survives. The largest concentration of his debtors was in Essex (39 out of 198), followed by

---

[34] The scholarship is considerable. For an introduction, see J. Bolton, 'What is Money? What is a Money Economy? When Did a Money Economy Emerge in Medieval England', in *Medieval Money Matters*, ed. D. Wood, Oxford 2004, 1–15, and more broadly Britnell, *Commercialisation*, and J. Masschaele, *Peasants, Merchants and Markets. Inland Trade in Medieval England 1150–1350*, New York 1997.

[35] *Alecto Edition of Little Domesday Book*, ed. A. Williams and G. Martin, 6 vols, London 2001, fols 36–38, 157–172v, 398–400v.

[36] E. van Houts, 'The Warenne View of the Past 1066–1203', *Anglo-Norman Studies* 26, 2003, 103–21, especially 116–19.

[37] *Rotuli de Dominabus et Pueris et Puellis*, ed. J. H. Round, Pipe Roll Society 35, London 1913, 47–64, 68–87; Dept, 'Les marchands flamands', 312–13.

[38] Miller and Hatcher, *Medieval England. Rural Society and Economic Change 1086–1348*, 198–239.

London (31) and Kent (22), which shows that at least this Flemish mercantile tycoon had heavy dealings in East Anglia and the south-east.[39]

The Warenne family's keen interest in North Sea trade was furthered by Earl William V de Warenne's acquisition of the seasonal fair of Stamford in 1206. Contemporary market institutions in England were private franchises typically controlled by local magnates who drew an income through tolls, stall rents and other transactions arising from the event, and were thereby enmeshed in the fabric of regional commerce. The owners of the large seasonal fairs in East Anglia were all important figures, some, like Earl Warenne, magnates of international stature.[40] Fair ownership was lucrative: between 1175 and 1181 the fair of Boston, in royal hands due to the minority of its owner Constance, the daughter of Conan IV, duke of Brittany and earl of Richmond (1156–71), yielded Henry II an average of £70 per annum, or a sum equivalent to the annual rents of a very large aristocratic manor. In 1183, before the fair passed to king's third son Duke Geoffrey of Brittany, Constance's new husband, the income had jumped to as high as £104 19s. 5d.[41]

The large seasonal fairs were the heavy-weights of the medieval commercial circuits, but the framework of local trade was actually founded on numerous weekly markets. Local markets may have originated as informal gatherings, but by the eleventh century magnates were already taking a keen interest in the economic opportunities they represented. By then lords often founded markets on their own initiative; the king's right to award market charters or to suppress unlicensed ones was not respected until the thirteenth century.[42] Control over markets was a strategy pursued by many lords to consolidate their power. The relocation of a weekly market by Geoffrey de Mandeville, earl of Essex, to his manor at Saffron Walden in southern Cambridgeshire in 1141 was clearly calculated to take advantage of his control over a key link in the major commercial

---

[39] E. Amt, *The Accession of Henry II in England. Royal Government Restored 1149–1159*, Woodbridge 1993, 94–8; H. Jenkinson, 'William Cade, a Financier of the Twelfth Century', *English Historical Review* 28, 1913, 209–27, and see 220–7, nos. 6, 17, 36, 43, 115 for transactions involving wool. Cade probably started his career during the reign of King Stephen (1135–54), who was also the count of Boulogne in south-western Flanders, near St. Omer, and whose predecessors as counts of Boulogne had held the vast honour of Boulogne in Essex. We need not invent a direct connection between Cade and Stephen, but their overlapping fields of operation illustrate the variety of not only economic but political relations that existed between the southern Low Countries and the eastern regions of England. On England and the counts of Boulogne, see E. King, 'Stephen of Blois, Count of Mortain and Boulogne', *English Historical Review* 115, 2000, 271–96; H. Tanner, 'The Expansion of the Power and Influence of the Counts of Boulogne under Eustace II', *Anglo-Norman Studies* 14, 1991, 251–86; ibid., *Families, Friends and Allies. Boulogne and Politics in Northern France and England c.879–1160*, Leiden and Boston, 2004, 128–243.

[40] Moore, *Fairs of Medieval England*, 12–17, 21–2.

[41] *PR 21 Henry II* (1174–5), 4; *PR 22 Henry II* (1175–6), 121; *PR 23 Henry II* (1176–77), 80; *PR 24 Henry II* (1177–8), 73; *PR 25 Henry II* (1178–9), 24; *PR 26 Henry II* (1179–80), 75; *PR 27 Henry II* (1180–1), 47; *PR 28 Henry II* (1181–2), 47; *PR 29 Henry II* (1182–3), 57.

[42] R. Britnell, 'English Markets and Royal Administration before 1200', *Economic History Review*, 2nd series, 31, 1978, 183–96.

routes that tied the East Anglian fair network with London.[43] Throughout his life Geoffrey was known for his connection with Flanders: he employed Flemish retainers and sent his son William, later King Henry II's chief liaison with Count Philip of Flanders, to be raised at the Flemish court.[44] A great nobleman's political and military status was inextricably tied to his wealth, and a rich market added a desirable economic dimension to the Mandevilles' dealings with the southern Low Countries. As the inclusion of a clause in Magna Carta of 1215 for the safe conduct of foreign merchants shows, the profitable foreign trade was of concern to the élite at large.[45]

Magna Carta reflected a past history of royal policies hostile to foreign powers which had seriously disrupted local commercial interests. Following Henry II's example, King Richard I (1189–99) instituted a trade ban against the continental allies of King Philip II of France in the mid-to-late 1190s. In 1197 Flemish merchants were imprisoned at the fair of King's Lynn in Norfolk,[46] and the Pipe Roll for 1198 lists amercements against those that sold grain 'to the king's enemies in Flanders'. Fines were levied on thirty-three individuals in Norfolk and Suffolk, and nineteen in Essex, most ranging between half a mark and five marks, but now entire urban communities were also subjected to sanctions. All were coastal townships: in East Anglia Dunwich was fined 1,060 marks, the great grain depot of King's Lynn 1,000 marks, Ipswich and Great Yarmouth 200 marks each, Beccles 60 marks and Orford 15 marks, in Kent Dover 100 marks and Hythe 20 marks, and in Sussex Rye and Winchelsea 100 marks each.[47] Count Baldwin IX of Flanders (1194–1206) concluded a treaty with Richard in 1197,[48] and it has often been observed that Richard's trade ban must have resulted in a great deal of domestic pressure on Baldwin to change sides in the conflict[49] – no less so if the county had already become partially dependent on foreign food exports. Faced with a similar ban in 1208 the burghers of the leading Flemish towns of Ypres, Lille, St Omer, Bruges, Ghent and Douai rebelled against the Francophile regent Philip of Namur and swore allegiance to King John.[50] But the Pipe Roll fines are equally suggestive of the importance of Flemish trade to the East Anglian economy, and the pressure that individual entrepreneurs and urban communities alike were under to break the royal ban.

---

[43] *Regesta Regum Anglo-Normannorum 1066–1154*, ed. H. A. Cronne, R. H.C. Davis and H. W. C. Davis, Oxford 1968, III, 99, no. 274.

[44] *The Book of the Foundation of Walden Monastery*, ed. and trans. D. Greenway and L. Watkiss, Oxford 1999, xxiv–xxvii, 44, 80; *The Waltham Chronicle*, ed. and trans. M. Chibnall and L. Watkiss, Oxford 1994, 80–2.

[45] J. C. Holt, *Magna Carta*, 2nd edn, Cambridge, 1992, 460–2, §41.

[46] *Pipe Roll 8 Richard I* (1196–7), 226.

[47] *Pipe Roll 9 Richard I* (1197–8), 92–3, 137–8, 209–10.

[48] *Diplomatic Documents Preserved in the Public Records Office*, ed. P. Chaplais, London 1964; Roger of Howden, *Chronica*, IV, 20.

[49] For example, Dept, *Les influences*, 24–32; J. Gillingham, *Richard I*, New Haven and London 1999, 307–10; Lloyd, *English Wool Trade*, 8–9.

[50] *Rotuli Chartarum in Turri Londinensi Asservati*, ed. T. D. Hardy, London 1837, 182; Dept, *Les influences*, 69–73.

The tendrils of international trade thus wound their way well below the level of the manorial lords. Weekly markets are often considered primarily for their role in distributing and redistributing local goods, services and cash, but they, and by extension the market owners and the local peasants who frequented them, were tied into the broader patterns of commerce in England. From this period onwards the influence of the growing overseas trade can be seen in new market foundations along important routes used by foreign merchants.[51] The English countryside market network in the Central and Late Middle Ages was unusually extensive and well developed, and provided the opportunity for market participation to a broad section of the populace. Though individual magnates could reap great profits, the estates of small-time local nobles such as knights, much smaller than those of the manorial lords but far greater in numbers, contributed in total far more goods for sale in the economy. Yet more important in terms of the volume of trade were the upper ranks of the peasantry. The agricultural income of a wealthy peasant household might be on average only a third of that of a knight, but their numbers were greater by an order of magnitude. The contribution of the lower nobility and the peasantry was not limited to domestic trade. In the early fourteenth century ecclesiastical estates, usually referenced as the primary producers of wool for the market, accounted for only a sixth of the total volume of wool exported from England, in contrast to an estimated one half produced by the peasantry.[52] It is difficult to estimate how accurately these figures can be mapped onto earlier times, but, given the introduction of large monastic flocks on formerly marginal lands and the intensification of the exploitation of manorial estates from the thirteenth century onwards, it is unlikely that the earlier ratio would be more favourable to the large estates.

The peasantry's contribution to the Anglo-Flemish grain trade may have been even more important than to the wool trade. Grain, like wool, was sometimes sold in bulk directly from large estates – customers of the archdeacon of Wells, near Bristol in Somerset, sought and received special permission to export 600 sacks of grain to Flanders in 1208 as an exception to the royal ban on shipping[53] – but most of the grain on the market was not transacted in such centralized fashion.[54] As noted, the list of fines for contraband corn from 1198 includes not only individual merchants but coastal towns through which the grain trade must have been conducted; their distribution suggests that at this time the majority of Anglo-Flemish grain trade was conducted from or through East Anglia. Norfolk, Suffolk and Essex enjoyed in the Anglo-Norman period the highest concentration of recorded markets in England, probably due to the high population density of these counties. A total of thirty-three markets are recorded in the sources as having been founded

---

[51] R. Britnell, 'The Proliferation of Markets in England, 1200–1349', *Economic History Review* 2nd series, 34, 1981, 213–14.
[52] Masschaele, *Peasants, Merchants, and Markets*, 48–53.
[53] *Rotuli Litterarum Patentium in Turri Londinensi Asservati*, ed. T. D. Hardy, London 1835, 78–9.
[54] Britnell, 'Proliferation', 214.

there before 1200 (the actual number is very likely higher), with a further sixty market charters issued over the following half a century.[55] The involvement of East Anglian town communities in the Flemish grain trade and the high density of countryside markets suggests a possible model for Anglo-Flemish commerce. It may have been the English urban merchants from the maritime towns who took on the key role of linking Flemings with agricultural producers by travelling a circuit in the urban hinterland, purchasing grain and other produce not only from large estates but also from small-scale farmers at the markets, collecting it in depots in the towns and then either shipping it to Flanders in bulk or selling it to Flemish merchants who visited their ports.[56] Such middle-man strategies were later employed by Cistercian and Gilbertine monks in the wool trade.[57] Though many of the specific transaction patterns that obtained in Anglo-Flemish trade still elude us, the existence of trade in foodstuffs surely established a direct connection between these regions that involved not only the specialized textile industries but the day-to-day livelihoods of a wide range of urban and rural peoples.

CONCLUSION

In his poem Jordan Fantosme evinced nothing but contempt for low-born Flemish soldiers, but in 1173–4 King Henry II had faced down his challengers thanks to a similar force of Brabanter mercenaries drawn from the Franco-German marches of the southern Low Countries. The royal clerk and chronicler Roger of Howden wrote: '[they] served him faithfully, but not without the large pay which he gave them'.[58] The logistics of warfare are governed by contemporary economic realities; in the 1170s they favoured the use of mercenary troops. The growth of the English economy in the Central Middle Ages, of which the great wealth generated by overseas commerce was a vital part, had a tremendous impact on the political, military and social history of the kingdom. I have attempted here to highlight the position and to describe the particular contribution of the East Anglian region to these developments. Flanders was during this period the premier economic and industrial region in western Europe, and the commercial connection that it shared with eastern England was vital to both regions. East Anglia, with its fairs and busy ports, occupied a central role in channelling English trade to and from the southern Low Countries. The distance from the Wash to the Flemish coast is some 300 kilometres, half again as much as the breath of England at that latitude. Yet the two coasts, at less than two days sailing from each other, were much closer to each other

---

[55] Britnell, 'English Markets', 188 fig. 7; idem., 'Proliferation', 210.
[56] On links between urban communities on both shores of the North Sea in the twelfth century, see Chapter 15 by Charles West in this volume.
[57] *Rotuli Hundredorum vol. 1*, ed. W. Illingworth, London 1812, 317; Masschaeles, *Peasants, Merchants, and Markets*, 133.
[58] Roger of Howden, *Chronica*, II, 47; J. Boussard, 'Henri II Plantagenêt et les origines de l'armée de métier', *Bibliothèque de l'École des Chartes* 106, 1945–6, 189–224; J. Hosler, *Henry II. A Medieval Soldier at War*, Leiden 2007, 119–23.

in terms of their mutually shared livelihoods than the eastern and western shores of England. Here physical geography played a key role. Flanders and East Anglia were twinned by their landscapes, both afforded exceptional transport opportunities by the waterways that penetrated deep into their interiors. If the North Sea was the ultimate connecting element, the binding medium that enabled efficient communication and the transport of cargoes from one shore to another, it was the rivers and canals that massively broadened the scope of commerce and allowed for the creation of an extraordinary wealth of markets and industries. This rich exchange encompassed within its sphere the economic fortunes of a great multitude of merchants, manorial lords, textile workers, urban craftsmen and agricultural producers of high and humble status alike.

— Chapter 9 —

EAST ANGLIA'S TRADE IN THE NORTH SEA WORLD

Wendy R. Childs

I

FOR CENTURIES migration, conquest, mission and trade had tied the regions of the North Sea together, so East Anglia's North Sea trade at the end of the Middle Ages was in an area long familiar. East Anglian ports traded directly all around the North Sea from Bergen to Calais and also beyond, into the Baltic and down to Bordeaux. Their busiest commercial associations were, unsurprisingly, with their nearest neighbours in the Low Countries, where populous areas provided good export markets in themselves and access to a wide hinterland. The Low Countries also offered opportunities for English merchants to buy a wide range of goods in return – raw materials for English industries, victuals, manufactured goods and luxuries. A great advantage of dealing in the Low Countries was Bruges and, to a lesser extent, smaller entrepôts such as Middelburg and Dordrecht and (in the fifteenth century) the great marts of Bergen-op-Zoom and Antwerp. Here the English bought goods from all over Europe. To Low Country goods such as Flemish cloth, Holland linen, Zeeland madder, tiles, cabbages, garlic, onions they could add Norwegian stockfish, Baltic timber, osmund, herring, and wax, German beer, Rhenish and Iberian wines, Spanish iron and olive oil, Mediterranean and Eastern spices, silks and many other goods. Trade also offered many opportunities for the exchange not only of artefacts but also of people, ideas, and commercial and industrial techniques.

Commercial ties were not of course the only ones linking England and East Anglia to continental Europe. Dynastic marriages, diplomacy, the church and universities were also potent stimuli to travel and accounted for most exchanges in ideas, literature, painting, and architecture at a higher cultural level, but merchants and seamen undoubtedly formed the largest group of regular travellers. Merchants travelled when young to learn their business and later maintained contacts abroad through junior partners, factors and agents and periodic visits to the major fairs. They had to operate within the language, legal framework, money and measurements of their customers. Seamen were more transient, staying only as long as the ship was in harbour, but they visited regularly and also became familiar with the language, law and customs of port towns. Trade also provided most of the transport for other travellers. A few nobles owned their own ships and the rich might hire vessels for specific voyages, but most others – messengers, pilgrims, friars, and scholars – took passage on the hundreds of trading vessels that crossed the North Sea. The largest numbers left from London, which might see between 450 and 750 ship movements a year,[1] but in their busiest years Lynn, Yarmouth or Ipswich could provide nearly fifty to seventy departures a year. While some made voyages to Gascony, Norway, the Baltic and Hamburg, normally more than half went to Calais and the Low Countries. People using the short crossing of the North Sea could expect to find a ship within a week or ten days all year round.

This commercial contact was very important for the spread of awareness and knowledge of other communities around the North Sea, but it did not necessarily bring liking. At the personal level, merchants built up solid and friendly relationships with the individuals they traded with. At the more general level, attitudes varied according to region and time. Even when trade was good, the English resented the Hansards for their customs privileges and refusal of reciprocal duties, and the Flemings for their intermittent political hostility. During the Peasants' Revolt, Flemish immigrants were murdered in London, and the author of *The Libelle of Englyshe Polycye* illustrates the ambivalent attitudes probably common among many merchants: while acknowledging the vital importance of Low Country trade, he denounced the Flemings as drunken cowards.[2] His views of other communities across the North Sea were not so passionate.

Many documents illustrate the breadth of England's overseas trade, but the national customs accounts allow assessment of the direction, strength, regularity and frequency of contacts to be more precise. Trade was funnelled through designated ports to clear customs, and the Exchequer monitored customs income keenly. Its final enrolled accounts (which survive almost unbroken) indicate the overall scale of trade through summaries of the tax collected, and the particulars of account sent up from the ports (on which the enrolled accounts were based) provide details of merchants, ships, and goods. Particulars survive less well than the enrolled accounts but in sufficient numbers to show patterns of trade in East Anglia and changes over time.

The three designated head ports in East Anglia, each with jurisdiction over adjacent coasts and smaller ports, were King's Lynn, Great Yarmouth, and Ipswich, whose jurisdiction spread into Essex.[3] The three ports naturally had much in common. As Tables 1–3 show, their trade was of similar size. None reached the

---

[1] V. Harding, 'Cross-Channel Trade and Cultural Contacts: London and the Low Countries in the Later Fourteenth Century', in *England and the Low Countries in the Late Middle Ages*, ed. C. Barron and N. Saul, Stroud 1995, 153–68, at 155.

[2] *The Libelle of Englyshe Polycye. A Poem on the Use of Sea-Power 1436*, ed. G. Warner, Oxford 1926, 4–9, 13–17, 26–9.

[3] E. M. Carus-Wilson and O. Coleman, *England's Export Trade 1275–1547*, Oxford 1963, 175–93.

level of London and the major provincial ports, but Lynn was the third largest importer of Low Country cloth in the early fourteenth century, and Lynn and Yarmouth ranked fifth and sixth for the value of general foreign-owned goods handled in the same period. All experienced broadly similar ups and downs over the centuries, in line with European economic movements. All handled broadly similar exports: fish, grain, ale, and England's most important exports – wool and cloth. Wool tied them tightly to the Low Countries, mainly to Flanders but increasingly to Holland and Zeeland, at first directly and then through Calais. Not all wool merchants were keen on the Calais Staple, which added transport costs and in 1366 some Dutch merchants (probably with the connivance of Yarmouth officials, although this was denied) continued to export wool and fells directly from Yarmouth to Rotterdam, selling them in a tavern called 'Calais', and joking between themselves that 'ore nous avons esté à Caleys'.[4] The temporary shift of the wool staple to Middelburg in 1384–88, when Flemings could not use Calais, acknowledged the potential of the northern wool markets and undoubtedly pleased East Anglian wool merchants. Chaucer's merchant probably echoed many East Anglians when he said:

> He wolde the see were kept for any thyng
> Bitwixe Middelburgh and Orewelle.[5]

However, the Calais staple was there to stay and hard-bargaining merchants from Holland regularly bought there.[6]

All the ports also took part in the cloth trade, changing in the course of the fourteenth century from major importers of Flemish cloth to exporters of English cloth. This opened up many more markets, but brought a more competitive note to the relationship with the Low Countries. These populous areas offered potentially large markets for English cloth, but Flanders, seeing it as a threat to its own industries, forbade sales within its borders and allowed only limited transit to Germany. The other provinces accepted English cloth and allowed access to Germany, and became even more useful markets when English merchants lost ground in the Baltic and Gascony in the fifteenth century. Unfortunately, by then the northern provinces were themselves cloth producers and all under Burgundian control. They increasingly willingly accepted ducal attempts to enforce uniform trade policies.[7] Embargoes on cloth imports eventually had a major impact on the

---

[4] TNA PRO SC 1/55/66–70; printed in H. J. Smit, *Bronnen tot de geschiedenis van den handel met Engeland, Schotland en Ireland*, 's Gravenhage 1928, I, nos. 515–19.
[5] Chaucer, 'Canterbury Tales: General Prologue', ll. 276–7, in *The Complete Works of Geoffrey Chaucer*, ed. F. N. Robinson, 2nd edn, Oxford 1957, 20.
[6] E. Power, 'The Wool Trade in the Fifteenth Century', in *Studies in English Trade in the Fifteenth Century*, ed. E. Power and M. M. Postan, London 1933, 60–2; N. J. M. Kerling, *Commercial Relations of Holland and Zeeland with England from the Late 13th Century to the Close of the Middle Ages*, Leiden 1954, 60–7; A. Hanham, *The Cely Letters 1472–1488*, Early English Text Society, 273, Oxford 1975, no. 34.
[7] Kerling, *Holland and Zeeland*, 72–83.

cloth industry of the eastern counties, as English merchants accommodated Low Country demands and increasingly exported unfinished cloth. The three East Anglian ports were at times badly hit by difficulties in the eastern cloth markets and their troubles were exacerbated by London's growing dominance in the area.

II

Alongside these similarities, the ports also had distinctive characteristics in both exports and areas of trade. A more detailed examination of the customs accounts for three periods (the early fourteenth century, the late fourteenth century, and the mid fifteenth century) illustrates their varied patterns and the changes in them over the centuries.

In the first decade of the fourteenth century our picture of their trade is partial because only foreign merchants paid duties on all their goods and trade in English hands (apart from wool, fells and hides) was unrecorded in these records. However, information on the patterns of trade of foreign merchants still provides valuable indications of the frequency and directions of trade in the three ports.

As Table 1 shows, Lynn was possibly the busiest of the three ports with the highest cloth imports and foreign-owned exports and second-highest foreign-owned imports. Apart from wool, exports were mostly grain and ale, which made up 70 to 80 per cent of non-wool exports by value.[8] Ale is particularly interesting to a study of transport and contact, because it is perishable within a fortnight and getting it from manufacturers to drinkers in good condition was only possible given dependable, regular, fast journeys. At Yarmouth wool exports were the highest of the three and foreign-owned general exports ran second to Lynn, although foreign-owned imports were the lowest of the three. Here, apart from wool, exports were

TABLE 1 Annual averages of imports and exports, 1303–7 and 1308–9[1]

	wool exports (in sacks)	value of other foreign-owned exports (in £)	cloth imports by foreign merchants (in cloths)	value of foreign-owned imports (in £)
Lynn	957	2197	747	2465
Gt Yarmouth	1129	1740	332	2197
Ipswich	1075	158	629	2757

1. The figures for wool exports include those for English and foreign merchants; cloth imports and the value of general goods are for foreign-owned trade only. For wool exports see Carus-Wilson and Coleman, *Export Trade*, 40–1; for other trade see Lloyd, *Alien Merchants*, 216–18.

[8] TNA PRO, E122/93/2, 3, 4; see also E. M. Carus-Wilson, 'The Medieval Trade of the Ports of the Wash', *Medieval Archaeology* 6–7, 1962–3, 182–201, at 185.

mainly herring and English cloth, very different from Lynn. In 1310–11 nearly 500 lasts of herrings made up 53 per cent of export values and English cloth, including worsteds, made up 34 per cent of values. Ale made up just one per cent of export values.[9] Ipswich's trade looks more asymmetrical. Foreign-owned cloth imports were twice those of Yarmouth, the value of foreign-owned goods was the highest of the three, and wool exports were only a little less than at Yarmouth, but the value of other foreign-owned exports (mainly grain and ale, like Lynn) was surprisingly low.[10] This probably indicates a higher level of English exporters.

This scale of trade demanded considerable shipping. Quite apart from the wool shipments to the Low Countries, ship movements (in and out) at Lynn averaged around 180 a year and in the busiest year (1303–4) reached around 275. At Yarmouth in 1310–11 movements were similar at 182. Ipswich numbers appear to be lower, but damage to the rolls makes assessment difficult. Total movements at all three ports were higher than this, as ships carrying goods exclusively for English merchants (who did not pay tax on general goods) were not recorded. The directions of trade are somewhat blurred because customs collectors also did not record destinations or last ports of call, but they attached place-names to ships or masters or merchants in about 50 per cent of cases. Ships often made complex voyages and toponyms are uncertain indicators, but nonetheless this information together with the nature of inward cargos probably reflects geographical links reasonably accurately. All the ports had strong links with the Low Countries through wool exports, but they showed distinct differences in other trade routes.

Lynn's main trade showed a distinctively northern bent. Between twenty and twenty-eight ships a year brought codfish, oil, timber, skins and butter from Norway, under masters and merchants of Trondheim, Bergen, Tønsberg and Lynn itself. Alongside these came a regular contingent of six to eight ships a year from the western Baltic (Gotland, Lübeck, and Stralsund) with boards, iron, wood ashes, wax, pitch and salt. Back in the North Sea, an occasional ship or merchant came from Jutland, a steady group of two to five Hamburg ships brought timber, pitch, iron and 'diverse goods', and a few ships and merchants came from Bremen and Kampen (Friesland). The Low Countries were, of course, also important to Lynn. Not only was wool sent there, but at least thirty to forty Low Country ships arrived each year loaded with cloth and varied goods. Flanders was the most frequent contact. Ships, masters and merchants from Axel, Blankenberge, Bruges, Diksmuide, Dunkirk, Lapscheure, Monnikerede, Ostend, Slepeldamme, Sluis, and others often accounted for well over twenty movements a year. Ships from Holland and Zeeland, from Cats, Deventer, Harderwijk, Kortegene, Middelburg, Renesse, Zierickzee, and Zutphen were fewer, but not far behind. Compared with Yarmouth

---

[9] TNA PRO E122/148/13, 15. For discussion of the herring trade, see A. Saul, 'English Towns in the Late Middle Ages: the Case of Great Yarmouth', *Journal of Medieval History* 8, 1982, 75–88; idem, 'The Herring Industry at Great Yarmouth c.1280–c.1400', *Norfolk Archaeology* 38, 1981, 33–43.

[10] TNA PRO E122/52/38, 50/8.

and Ipswich, Lynn's French contacts were low, although not absent. Merchants of Amiens (often bringing woad), Gravelines, Sangatte, and Wissant appeared; in 1308-9 some ships came from Normandy; and Lynn regularly sent three to five ships a year to Bordeaux for wine.[11]

The direction of Yarmouth's trade, as shown in the single detailed account that survives for 1310-11, was strikingly different. There were no recorded Norwegian links and only two ships with possible origins in the western Baltic. Much more important were North Sea ships from Germany (seven from Hamburg and Bremen with boards, iron, wax, eels, sturgeon and fruit), Friesland (ten from Stavoren and Kampen with boards and ashes), and the Low Countries. At least ten Flemish ships came from Axel, Blankenberge, Hulst, Iser, Ostend, Slepeldamme, and Sluis with cloth and various goods, and a similar sized group came from Holland and Zeeland (Dordrecht, Graveningen, Harderwijk, Medemblik, Waldercome). Yarmouth was also quite different from Lynn in its strong French connections. In 1310-11 the largest group of foreign ships and merchants came from northern France. At least twenty-two vessels came from Calais, Wissant, Boulogne, Etaples, Abbeville, Waben, Saint-Valéry, Dieppe, Caen, La Hogue, and Barfleur, and numerous English ships bringing woad for foreign merchants (probably from Picardy) strengthened this French connection. Yarmouth also played a major role in the Bordeaux wine trade. Each year between 1303 and 1309 thirty to fifty Yarmouth ships loaded wine there, providing by far the largest English contingent.[12]

Ipswich customs collectors more regularly recorded ships' home ports. This gives a sharper picture of its contacts. These were even more southern than those in Lynn and Yarmouth. Not only were there no links with Norway, but also not many with Germany, Holland and Zeeland. A few ships of Hamburg and Kampen arrived, but the strongest contingent came from Flanders (Blankenberge, Dunkirk, Iser, Lombaertsijde, Muiden, Nieuwpoort, Slepeldamme) with cloth. This was matched by a very strong link with northern France as far as Normandy (Gravelines, Sangatte, Saint-Valéry, Dieppe, Caen, Barfleur, La Hogue) for woad and canvas. In addition Ipswich also sent ten to fifteen ships a year to Bordeaux, fewer than Yarmouth, but considerably more than Lynn. With Gosford (Woodbridge Haven), which sent fifteen to twenty ships a year, and Harwich, which sent ten to thirteen, it formed an important ship-owning nucleus on the Suffolk-Essex border.[13]

East Anglian contacts in the 1300s were thus very wide and went far beyond the North Sea. The emphasis varied between ports, with Lynn showing strong interest in Norway and the Baltic and the others making strong French contacts all the way to Bordeaux, but overall in all of them very busy connections were maintained with their nearest neighbours and the greatest wool market – the Low Countries – and the ports were busy with ships coming and going all year round.

Seventy years or so on, in the late fourteenth century, there were significant

---

[11] TNA PRO E101/158/10, 160/3, 161/3, 162/1, 4, 5, 6, 163/1, 4.
[12] See note 11.
[13] See note 11.

TABLE 2 Annual averages of imports and exports, 1390–1400[1]

	wool exports (in sacks)	cloth exports (in cloths of assize)[2]	value of goods paying petty customs (in £)[2]	value of goods paying poundage (in £)
Lynn	2038	1542	907	9255
Gt Yarmouth	147	*1561*	*1928*	*13432*
Ipswich	285	*1181*	*1450*	*4185*

1. For wool and cloth see Carus-Wilson and Coleman, *Export Trade*, 53–5, 84–7. For the value of goods see Jenks, *Enrolled Customs Accounts*, part 2, 513–14, 516–27, 529–32, 534–5, 537, 539–40, 542, 544–8, 550; part 5, 1243–7, 1261–2, 1279–80.
2. The petty custom on cloth and the value of foreign-owned goods was farmed for much of the 1390s. Lynn's figures therefore cover only five years, 1394–9; those for Ipswich and Great Yarmouth cover only two years (one of which falls outside the decade), 1399–1401. These partial figures are in italics.

shifts in emphasis. The years of expansion were over and the ports were trading in very different circumstances. They faced European-wide problems of contraction after the Black Death, the impact of the French war, and early signs of bullion shortage, as well as locally specific problems of erosion and silting.[14] However, in England the major shift from wool to cloth exports and the disappearance of foreign cloth imports offered opportunities for expansion. As Table 2 shows, the ports still look quite buoyant (even allowing for the fact that figures now include all English trade following the imposition of new poundage charges), contacts abroad were still frequent and regular, and the directions of trade were changing as the ports adapted to new conditions.

Lynn was still doing well. Against the general trend, wool exports had risen to around 2,000 sacks a year, the highest level since the 1290s, strengthening links with the Low Countries via Middelburg (1384–88) and Calais. Cloth exports averaging around 1,500 cloths a year were healthy and diverse enough to suit a variety of overseas markets. In 1390–1 Lynn exported well over 1,000 standard broadcloths valued at £1,948, and also narrow cloths, white cloths, kerseys, damdoks, chalons, worsteds, Irish cloth, and 'English' cloth. Altogether cloth values reached around £4,600 that year, nearly 95 per cent of the total value of exports paying poundage.[15] Ale had disappeared and grain was insignificant this year, although licences show that grain could still be an important export to Holland and Zeeland.[16] Imports had changed too. Skånia herring, valued at £2,355 (42 per cent of import values) was three times more valuable than Norwegian cod, and beer imports indicate the reason for the decline of ale exports.

[14] For example, Saul noted four estuaries appearing and disappearing at Yarmouth, and high costs to keep the port open, 'English towns', 83.
[15] TNA PRO E122/94/13.
[16] Smit, *Bronnen*, I, no. 557.

Yarmouth's trade shows more difficulties. Unlike Lynn, its wool exports had seriously dropped away, but cloth exports and the value of goods paying poundage were healthy. Here too cloth exports showed a considerable variety: broadcloths, narrow cloths, kerseys, chalons, cloth for mantles, kerseys, damdoks, beaver and narrow beaver, but about half the exports were worsteds, for which Norfolk was particularly well-known. In 1388 cloth accounted for around half of export values, evenly balanced between worsteds and woollens, and herring exports were still strong, accounting for between 35 and 45 per cent of export values.[17] However, Yarmouth's fortunes were already sliding downwards, and the figures already hide severe problems of declining fish catches, decreased demand after the Black Death, war costs, silting and competition from Lowestoft.[18] One might add too, a change of taste to fresh fish and competition from the Skånia herring fairs where English merchants hoped to sell more cloth in exchange for herring.

The fortunes of Ipswich were more modest but followed similar trends. Again the drop in wool exports was balanced by promising exports of Ipswich-made narrow cloths and Colchester broadcloths.[19] The value of foreign merchants' trade shows their continued interest in Ipswich, and the poundage value, while not very high, was part of a steady increase from the 1370s.

Trade still demanded much shipping. Lynn still needed eighty-four inward and fifty-two outward movements in 1390–1, and seventy-eight outward in 1392–3.[20] One third of these were English (nearly all from Lynn itself), one third from Holland and Zeeland, and one third Hansard. Yarmouth still needed ninety-six movements (in and out) for nine months in 1388 and 179 movements for eleven months in 1392–3;[21] but this activity hides a significant crash in Yarmouth's own shipping. This made up just 12 per cent of movements. The exceptionally large merchant fleet that had dominated Bordeaux trade had disappeared. At Ipswich activity was lower at an average of sixty-three movements a year from 1396 to 1398, but English shipping was more important, providing 45 per cent of vessels.[22]

The directions of trade in all ports show considerable changes now. Lynn's distant routes still operated. Three to eight ships a year were still sent to Bordeaux but only two or three English and Hansard ships brought Norwegian cod, which Hansards increasingly channelled towards Germany. Lynn's trade showed a marked shift into the Baltic. The Skånia fisheries attracted many to the western Baltic and Skånia herring sometimes made up 40 per cent of Lynn's import values. There was also a dramatic growth in trade with the eastern Baltic. In 1390–1 twenty-three of the eighty-four incoming ships came from Baltic ports: seven from the west (the Sound, Lübeck, Wismar) and sixteen from the east (Stettin, Elbing and Danzig)

---

[17] TNA PRO E122/149/22, 27; P. Dunn, 'The Role of Norwich Merchants in Yarmouth', in *Medieval Norwich*, ed. C. Rawcliffe and R. Wilson, London 2004, 213–34, at 215–17, 219–20.
[18] Saul, 'English Towns', 79, 82–5.
[19] N. Amor, *Late Medieval Ipswich: Trade and Industry*, Woodbridge 2011, 58–9, 107–8.
[20] TNA PRO E122/94/12–14.
[21] TNA PRO E122/149/22, 27.
[22] TNA PRO E122/50/29–30, 33, 36, 193/33 (analysed by Amor, *Late Medieval Ipswich*, 52–3, 78–9).

with the overwhelming majority (fourteen) from Danzig. Lynn merchants (who used most of the capacity of these Hansard vessels) also used at least eight and possibly ten Lynn ships on the route. They formed the largest English group to suffer Baltic losses in 1385 and remained important in Danzig (where Margery Kempe's son lived and chose his bride) until Hull drew ahead in the 1430s.[23] Baltic trade was clearly Lynn's preference, but its North Sea trade was also lively. In 1390–1 five ships of Hamburg and Bremen and two of Kampen arrived with North German and Norwegian cargoes, but Low Country shipping was much busier. Thirty Holland and Zeeland vessels arrived. Ships of Dordrecht and Veer were particularly prominent with others from Brill, Middelburg, Schiedam, Vlissingen and Zierickzee.[24] The ships were small, inevitable given their shallow home waters, and their Low Country cargoes were of much lower value than Baltic cargoes, but they ensured frequent contact between East Anglia and the Low Countries, where the Middelburg staple also attracted wool ships.

The directions of Yarmouth's trade had changed even more dramatically with a collapse of French trade. A few Norman ships came for herring when truces allowed, an occasional Bayonne ship brought wine, and Yarmouth now sent only three to six ships a year to Bordeaux.[25] Yarmouth had refocused trade tightly to the North Sea. Hanse ships (seven to eleven a year, predominantly from Hamburg) were still important, but Flemish shipping had all but disappeared and the most regular and frequent shipping was from Holland and Zeeland. In the 1390s they provided up to 60 per cent of shipping at Yarmouth and were particularly numerous in 1392–3, when seventy-four ships arrived. The most frequent contacts were with Dordrecht, Rotterdam, Zierickzee, and Veer, but Schiedam, Middelburg, Brill, and Vlaardingen were also busy. As in Lynn, Dutch ships and cargoes were much smaller than Hanse ones, but the small ships sailed frequently – often once a week – ensuring strong contacts.

At Ipswich French and Hanseatic shipping was rare now and English and Dutch shipping predominated. In two years, 1396–98, 45 per cent of the ships were English, 45 per cent were Dutch and of the remainder 8 per cent were French and just 2 per cent (three ships) were Hansards. The frequency and constancy of Dutch activity is epitomized by Andrew Johnessone who sailed in and out of Ipswich and Harwich fifteen times in those two years.[26]

Thus, in all three ports geographical patterns had changed from the 1300s. Eastern Baltic trade was still growing at Lynn, but elsewhere merchants adapted to new developments. They pulled back to the core North Sea region as the Norway and Bordeaux trades were squeezed. In this trade, alongside Hanse and English

---

[23] *The Book of Margery Kempe*, ed. B. A. Windeatt, Harmondsworth 1985, 268–70; T. H. Lloyd, *England and the German Hanse 1157–1611. A Study of their Trade and Commercial Policy*, Cambridge 1991, 91–4, 169.
[24] TNA PRO E122/94/13.
[25] TNA PRO E101/179/10, 180/2, 182/5–6, 183/11.
[26] TNA PRO E122/50/29, 30, 33, 193/33; Amor, *Late Medieval Ipswich*, 78; Lloyd, *England and the German Hanse*, 94–5.

TABLE 3a Annual averages of imports and exports, 1460–70[1]

	wool exports (in sacks)	cloth exports (in cloths of assize)	value of foreign-owned goods in and out (in £)	value of goods paying poundage in and out (in £)
Lynn	0	400	648	899
Gt Yarmouth	3	255	726	1730
Ipswich	651	1512	1755	896

1. For wool and cloth figures see Carus-Wilson and Coleman, *Export Trade*, 53–5, 84–7. For the value of goods see Power and Postan, *Studies in English Trade*, 340, 348, 360.

TABLE 3b Annual averages of imports and exports, 1470–80[1]

	wool exports (in sacks)	cloth exports (in cloths of assize)	value of foreign-owned goods in and out (in £)	value of goods paying poundage in and out (in £)
Lynn	0	282	619	825
Gt Yarmouth	0	203	560	1517
Ipswich	642	567	656	1264

1. For sources see Table 3a.

shipping, the shipping of Holland and Zeeland became far more visible, due partly to the growth of their own economies, and also to difficulties in Flanders, whose shipping disappeared with the establishment of the Calais Staple, the silting of the Damme and competition from Holland and Zeeland.

Moving on another seventy years brings us to the mid fifteenth century, a period of substantial contraction in England's commercial activity. The problems of low populations and war dogged much of the century, and acute bullion and credit shortages made the 1440s particularly difficult. All the East Anglian ports suffered, and unlike the southern and western ports, who could look to Iberia and whose direct international trade recovered at the end of the century, theirs continued to languish, partly because of the dominance of London. Nonetheless there were some bright spots, their Low Country trade remained central, and again their individual fortunes varied.

As Tables 3a and 3b show, Lynn's wool exports dropped away entirely, cutting direct contacts with Calais, and average cloth exports of 282 cloths a year were a far cry from the 1,500 cloths earlier. Nonetheless, most remaining trade, including nearly 90 per cent of the cloth trade, was now in English hands and ships. The Hansards owned some 10 to 11 per cent of trade in the 1470s (a little more in the

1460s) and others, including the Dutch, were negligible merchants, although Dutch shipping remained busy.[27] Yarmouth had lost its former glory.[28] As at Lynn, wool had entirely disappeared and cloth exports and the value of goods had dropped, although the value of goods charged poundage was much higher than at the other two ports, which indicates higher English activity. The grain trade remained important,[29] as did the fish trade, which had adapted to a changed pattern: sprats were now often exported from member ports and herring was imported on Dutch ships.[30] What stands out here is the impact of the loss of Hansard trade in a small town: they had left Yarmouth after a case of customs corruption in 1414 and never returned.[31] Ipswich did better than the other two, even if its common quay fell into such disrepair that it was used as a 'rubbish tip and pigsty'.[32] Against the trend wool exports rose to levels of the 1300s, peaking in the 1420s at around 1,600 sacks a year and fluctuating but remaining buoyant for the rest of the century. Part of Ipswich's strength came from the arrival of Hanse merchants around 1417, although most actually traded through Colchester rather than Ipswich.[33] With their strong interest, cloth exports peaked in the 1440s at over 4,000 cloths a year, and remained healthy until the Hanseatic war in 1469.

Imports at all three ports show an interesting change at this time. Consumer goods had always been imported in commercial quantities to London, through which they were easily available to East Anglia. Small quantities of direct imports became visible in the late fourteenth century, such as haberdashery, scoops and mirrors at Lynn.[34] However, direct imports surged in quantity and variety only in the second half of the fifteenth century. This increase in consumer goods came despite the general decline in overseas trade in the ports, and indicates that international trade was not the sole factor in a port's prosperity. Citizens could prosper from property owning and industry, as Saul and Britnell have shown for Yarmouth and Colchester,[35] and coastal trade with London continued. Whether supply or demand led the surge in consumer goods is uncertain, but East Anglian buyers

---

[27] TNA PRO E122/97/4 (printed in D. Owen, *The Making of King's Lynn. A Documentary Survey*, Records of Social and Economic History, new series IX, London 1984, no. 410), 97/7, 8 (printed in N. S. B. Gras, *The Early English Customs System*, Harvard Economic Studies XVIII, Cambridge, MA 1918, 606–24), 97/9–11, 13.

[28] Saul, 'English towns', 85–6.

[29] T. R. Adams, 'Aliens, Agriculturalists and Entrepreneurs: Identifying the Market Makers in a Norfolk Port from the Water-Bailiffs' Accounts, 1400-60', in *Trade, Devotion and Governance. Papers in Later Medieval History*, ed. D. J. Clayton, R. G. Davies and P. McNiven, Stroud 1994, 140–57, at 146–8.

[30] TNA PRO E122/152/4–5, 9–10.

[31] S. Jenks, *England, die Hanse und Preussen. Handel und Diplomatie 1377–1474*, Quellen und Darstellungen zur Hansischen Geschichte, Neue Folge, Band XXXVIII, Teile 1–3, Cologne 1992, 411–15.

[32] Amor, *Late Medieval Ipswich*, 133.

[33] R. H. Britnell, *Growth and Decline in Colchester 1300–1525*, Cambridge 1986, 169–75.

[34] TNA PRO E122/94/12,16. For London's consumer imports, Harding, 'Cross-channel Trade and Cultural Contacts', 156–7, 163–5.

[35] Saul, 'English Towns', 81–2; Britnell, *Colchester*, 209–12.

clearly had spare money to pay for increasing comfort. Equally uncertain is whether East Anglian buyers sought a greater quantity than local industries could produce or better quality or cheaper prices or simply novelty. But whatever the stimuli, in all three ports buyers could now find earthen and stoneware pots, drinking glasses, glass beads, felt and straw hats (and straw to make hats), purses, gloves, featherbeds, bed ticks, cushions, painted cloths, linens, kettles, nails and shears, cupboards, trenchers, playing tables and many other small goods imported directly from abroad.

The overall decline in bulk trade is naturally reflected in shipping numbers, especially at Lynn where ship movements dropped as low as forty to eighty a year.[36] At Yarmouth and Ipswich movements stayed higher: at Yarmouth they sometimes reached between ninety and one hundred,[37] and at Ipswich in six winter months in 1465-6 they reached fifty-five.[38] With these numbers, contacts around the North Sea remained regular, but with an even closer focus on the Low Countries. At Lynn Norwegian trade had greatly diminished, perhaps because Icelandic voyages increased, despite Lynn's earlier prohibition of this trade.[39] Contact with Gascony also diminished after 1453 and West Country ships increasingly brought Gascon wine. On the other hand, Baltic trade remained steady with four to eight Hansard arrivals a year until the 1469-74 war.[40] England's improving political relations with Scotland allowed the odd Scottish ship to appear – opening up part of the North Sea World that had been difficult for a century and a half, but this new market was small. The main group of ships apart from those of Lynn itself were again Low Country vessels with Low Country cargoes, which normally accounted for between 30 and 50 per cent of arrivals. Low Country shipping was also high at Yarmouth where the Dutch were often the only foreigners to provide shipping, once the Hansards had left. For example in 1475-6 the Dutch provided 52 per cent of the shipping, the English 46 per cent; and in 1482-3 the Dutch provided 68 per cent, the English 25 per cent.[41] The beginning of a new economic expansion is visible in the arrival of a few ships from Spain and Brittany, but the main link was now overwhelmingly with the Low Countries. Ipswich too saw an occasional Spanish ship but Hansards, especially from Cologne, dominated Ipswich trade, handling 78 per cent of all import values and 88 per cent of cloth exports in their large ships until the war of 1469 upset their trade.[42] Nonetheless, alongside these sometimes up to 75 per cent of the ships were Dutch, shuttling back and forth to the Low Countries with small cargoes.

---

[36] TNA PRO E122/97/4, 7–10, 13, 17, 98/2, 5.
[37] TNA PRO E122/152/11, 13.
[38] TNA PRO E122/52/48.
[39] Carus-Wilson, 'Ports of the Wash', 199–200; Owen, *King's Lynn*, nos. 369–70, 376; TNA PRO 98/10, 11, 14, 16.
[40] TNA PRO E122/97/4 (printed in Owen, *King's Lynn*, no. 410), 97/7, 97/8 (printed in Gras, *Customs System*, 606–24), 97/9–13.
[41] TNA PRO E122/152/11, 13.
[42] TNA PRO E122/52/42–48; Carus-Wilson and Coleman, *Export Trade*, 101–3; Amor, *Late Medieval Ipswich*, 130, 135–6.

Customs accounts show just how closely integrated East Anglia was with the North Sea World throughout the fourteenth and fifteenth centuries. There were substantial differences between the ports and over time. Lynn had a clear preference for northern trade with Norway and then the eastern Baltic, while in the early fourteenth century Yarmouth had the strongest links with Gascony. Unsurprisingly, the most intense links were always with the Low Countries, their closest neighbours and vibrant commercial and industrial centres. Connections with Flanders changed shape with the establishment of the Calais Staple and contacts with Holland and Zeeland increased steadily in the fourteenth century; and when the more distant Scandinavian, Baltic and Gascon markets failed at various times in the fifteenth century, the East Anglian merchants fell back on to their closest markets.

III

Although it did not produce a homogeneous North Sea community, contact around the North Sea encouraged constant if variable changes within each community. Trade itself had the most obvious impact on the prosperity of East Anglian producers and port communities as fluctuations affected their livelihoods and they adapted their goods and markets to changing political and economic circumstances. The spread of goods and knowledge also made industrial and cultural impacts on East Anglians, but these are less easy to assess. Flows and dates of technological change can be difficult to chart; slow diffusion (sometimes from multiple centres) is more usual than dramatic change. However, the appearance of new goods spread knowledge of new techniques and immigrants also carried skills with them. Few English craftsmen seem to have migrated but numerous craftsmen left the over-populated Low Countries to find opportunities in England. 'Duche' people (a term that included Low Country and German immigrants) appeared all along the east coast.[43] The new industries of beer brewing and brick making certainly spread from the Low Countries. Beer brewing had a strong impact in East Anglia. First, it caused the collapse of East Anglia's ale exports, as beer drinking spread from Germany and destroyed ale markets in Holland and Zeeland. Then by the later fourteenth century beer was imported and soon imports of hops indicate the establishment of brewing in East Anglia. In the fifteenth century beer was exported from all three ports. Many of the brewers were immigrants and in Ipswich, where beer was brewed at least from 1416, the Dutch dominated the industry for years.[44] Imported Flemish bricks contributed to brick building in England in the thirteenth century, and again the craft was copied. English brick

---

[43] C. Barron, 'Introduction: England and the Low Countries 1327–1477', in *England and the Low Countries in the Late Middle Ages*, ed. C. Barron and N. Saul, Stroud 1995, 1–28, at 12–13; Kerling, *Holland and Zeeland*, 198–9; S. Thrupp, 'A Survey of the Alien Population of England in 1440', *Speculum* 32, 1957, 262–273, at 271.

[44] Kerling, *Holland and Zeeland*, 110–18; Amor, *Late Medieval Ipswich*, 154–6, 181–2.

kilns appeared by the early fourteenth century, sometimes run by immigrant Flemish brick makers. The new vogue for brick building in the early fifteenth century brought an increase of imported bricks and tiles in all the East Anglian ports, but by then the greatest impact of the Low Countries was probably less in the import of bricks and more in the continental workmen and architectural styles employed by the king, aristocrats and churchmen, who copied the buildings they admired on journeys abroad.[45]

The role of Flemish immigrants in the English cloth industry has provoked discussion over decades. They certainly did not initiate the English industry in the fourteenth century, but they came in large enough numbers to have their own guilds in London, and English weavers may well have learnt from them.[46] However, most English exports were still distinctively English, and when they did copy, English weavers copied the styles of Normandy (Montivilliers) rather than Flanders.[47] More obvious are Low Country impacts on the dyeing industry. On the one hand Zeeland helpfully supplied madder (giving English its descriptions of madder qualities: crap, mesne, and mull, drawn directly from the Dutch *krap*, *gemeene* and *mulle*).[48] On the other hand Low Country demands for unfinished cloth at the end of the fifteenth century cut work available for dyers in East Anglia as elsewhere.

The North Sea maritime community also had much in common. English fishermen absorbed new techniques through regular contact at fishing grounds and in 1394 Yorkshire fishermen at Scarborough and Whitby consciously adopted new techniques learnt in Skånia. These may have stemmed from Dutch practices, but clearly were not perceived as such by the Yorkshiremen.[49] Ship building techniques were broadly familiar all around the North Sea, through the constant movement of vessels, which were also bought and sold, repaired wherever they were, and worked by international crews. There remained a multitude of regional types with a multitude of local names. The Dutch are well known for innovations such as the herring buss in the fifteenth century and the *fluyt* in the sixteenth,[50] and their vessels were highly visible in East Anglian ports, but there is no evidence that their cargo ships were any more advanced than the English at this time or that they were consciously copied. The maritime community also shared many

---

[45] L. F. Salzman, *Building in England down to 1540*, 2nd impression, Oxford 1967, 141–4; N. J. Moore, 'Brick', in *English Medieval Industries*, ed. J. Blair and N. Ramsay, London 1991, 211–36, at 212–23.

[46] Heaton's remarks on Yorkshire stand for all England: H. Heaton, *The Yorkshire Woollen and Worsted Industries*, Oxford 1965, 9–20; Barron, 'Introduction', 13; Anne F. Sutton, 'The Early Linen and Worsted Industries of Norfolk and the Evolution of the London Mercers' Company', *Norfolk Archaeology* 40, 1989, 201–25, at 213–14.

[47] Britnell, *Colchester*, 165, 169.

[48] Kerling, *Holland and Zeeland*, 123–4.

[49] *Calendar of Fine Rolls 1391-9*, 116; R. W. Unger, 'The Netherlands Herring Fishery in the Late Middle Ages: the False Legend of Willem Beukels of Biervliet', *Viator* 9, 1978, 325–56.

[50] R. W. Unger, *The Ship in the Medieval Economy 600–1600*, London 1980, 206, 260–4; on the east coast use of small ships, G. V. Scammell, 'English Merchant Shipping at the End of the Middle Ages: Some East Coast Evidence', *Economic History Review* 2nd ser., 13, 1961, 327–41, at 329, 332–4.

operational practices. Seamen on both sides of the sea used rutters rather than charts for navigation;[51] the judgements of Oléron underpinned codes of conduct on the management of shipping in England, France and the Low Countries;[52] and law merchant, dispensed by panels of merchants of mixed nations, could supplement land law in commercial cases.[53]

Urban culture and everyday life was also influenced by foreign contacts. Brick buildings were erected not only by aristocrats but also in towns. Brasses in North German or Flemish style commemorated merchants in Lynn and Ipswich.[54] Urban public rituals of procession and the figures used in such processions, as in Ipswich, were influenced by Low Country practices, as were urban dramas such as morality plays, of which three of the four known survivals come from East Anglia.[55] No doubt immigrants kept their own social styles of life, at least in the first generation, and the private lives of merchants and their customers may have been influenced by the adoption of dress, foods, and life-styles they encountered abroad. Details of such private life-styles rarely leave traces in documents, but the exchange of consumer goods shows many points of similar material culture around the North Sea. East Anglian cloth and ale were familiar across the sea and people in East Anglia built with Flemish and Dutch bricks and tiles, drank German and Dutch beer in German and Dutch stone- and earthen-ware pots, cooked with Dutch onions and cabbages, wore imported linen, hats, purses and gloves, slept in imported featherbeds covered in imported bed ticks, and furnished their rooms with imported cushions, painted cloths, cupboards, trenchers, and playing tables.

IV

In the Late Middle Ages East Anglia's three head ports, King's Lynn, Great Yarmouth, and Ipswich, and their member ports were fully integrated into the trade routes of the North Sea area. Languages, political structures, legal frameworks and self-identities in the area remained distinct but had been familiar to other communities around the sea for centuries. The full complexity of East Anglian trading interests stretched beyond the North Sea to Danzig and Bordeaux, but the North Sea and

---

[51] G. A. Lester, 'The Earliest English Sailing Directions', in *Popular and Practical Science of Medieval England*, ed. L. M. Matheson, East Lansing, MI 1994, 331–67; K. Koppmann, *Das Seebuch*, Bremen 1876; A. Sauer, *Das 'Seebuch'*, Hamburg 1996.

[52] T. Kiesselbach, 'Der Ursprung der rôles d'Oléron und des Seerechts von Damme', *Hansische Geschichtsblätter* 33, 1906, 1–60; R. Ward, *The World of the Medieval Shipmaster*, Woodbridge 2009, 20–6, 183–205.

[53] C. Rawcliffe, '"That Kindliness Should be Cherished More, and Discord Driven Out": the Settlement of Commercial Disputes by Arbitration in Later Medieval England', in *Enterprise and Individuals in Fifteenth-Century England*, ed. J. Kermode, Stroud 1991, 97–117, at 97–104; Ward, *Medieval Shipmaster*, 15–20.

[54] Carus-Wilson, 'Ports of the Wash', 196; M. Clayton, *Catalogue of Rubbings of Brasses and Incised Slabs: Victoria and Albert Museum*, London 1968, 3–4.

[55] A. F. Johnston, 'Traders and Playmakers: English Guildsmen and the Low Countries', in *England and the Low Countries in the Late Middle Ages*, ed. Barron and Saul, 99–114, at 109–11.

especially the Low Countries always remained at the core. They became even more important when distant markets met trouble. Here East Anglians could always sell wool and cloth; here they could buy goods from all over Europe; and transport was particularly frequent. The spread of goods and new industries made material aspects of daily life similar on both sides of the sea; the mercantile and maritime communities absorbed knowledge and understanding of each other's commercial, industrial, cultural and social practices; and the frequent voyages also offered constant channels for the exchange of news, information and ideas at all levels.

— Chapter 10 —

ICELAND'S 'ENGLISH CENTURY' AND EAST ANGLIA'S NORTH SEA WORLD

Anna Agnarsdóttir

THE SUPERB FISHING banks off Iceland were attracting English seamen by the beginning of the fifteenth century, if not earlier. In 1436 *The Libelle of Englyshe Polycye*, one of the earliest English political poems, had this to say of Iceland:[1]

> Of Yseland to wryte is lytill need
> Save of stokfische…

So significant indeed was the English presence in Iceland during the fifteenth century that this period is known as 'The English Century'.[2] The English came not only to fish but also to trade, and Edward IV even went so far as to speak of 'terra nostra Island'.[3]

Icelandic scholars have long studied this period, but the most distinguished historian of the 'English Century' is Professor Björn Þorsteinsson (1918–1986) who in 1970 defended his doctoral thesis 'Enska öldin í sögu Íslendinga' [The English Century in the History of the Icelanders], which remains the definitive political and economic work on this subject. It was path-breaking in that he not only used the abundant Icelandic sources, but also English and Danish primary sources.[4] In

---

[1] *The Libelle of Englyshe Polycye*, ed. George Warner, Oxford 1926, 41.
[2] To Björn Þorsteinsson the English century spanned the years 1415–1475: Björn Þorsteinsson and Bergsteinn Jónsson, *Íslandssaga til okkar daga*, Reykjavík 1991, 149 (his last book, published posthumously). However, it must be noted that this statement is based on the fact that the English were the *only* foreign nation coming to Iceland at the time, the Hanseatic League arriving in the last quarter of the century.
[3] Þorsteinsson, *Enska öldin í sögu Íslendinga*, Reykjavík 1970, 178. He then went on to do further research on the sixteenth century and beyond. For example *Tíu þorskastríð*, Reykjavík 1976, in which he went on to identify ten cod wars between the Icelanders and English from 1415 to 1976.
[4] Volume XVI of the *Diplomatarium Islandicum* (a multi-volume collection of primary sources from the first extant documents regarding Icelandic history to the sixteenth century, published 1857–1972) [hereafter *D.I.*], was compiled by Professor Þorsteinsson. Most of the documents deal with foreign relations with the English and Germans (Hanse), the focus being on diplomatic and customs records from 1415 to 1589.

England E. M. Carus-Wilson wrote the pioneering work 'The Iceland Trade' in 1933,[5] while Evan T. Jones has focussed on the fisheries.[6] To them must be added studies of the maritime trade of the East Anglian ports.[7] However, the sources, for example customs records and port books, are imperfect; much went unrecorded and as much of what was recorded is no longer extant, scholars have repeatedly warned that only an incomplete picture at best can be given of the English fisheries and trade with Iceland. Another caveat must be added. To distinguish between those who were actually doggers and those who were merchants is, as Carus-Wilson stated, 'often...impossible',[8] and Þorsteinsson solved the problem by coming up with the term 'merchant adventure doggers'. In the early sixteenth century the fishing ship *James* from Dunwich carried one merchant with his wares. This may have been a pattern.[9] The point is that it is nigh impossible to make a distinction 'between those who traded for fish and those who themselves caught fish'.[10]

Anglo-Icelandic relations date back to the period of colonization in Iceland in the ninth century. Most of the Scandinavian settlers came from Norway, but some had lived for a long time in the British Isles, bringing their Celtic slaves with them. A commonwealth until 1262, Iceland came under the rule of the King of Norway until 1380 when the two monarchies of Denmark and Norway were united, with Denmark the dominant partner. At least since the early fourteenth century, if not before, the king of Norway had established a staple market for the trade of Iceland and other dependencies in Bergen, where the English had sought their stockfish. But little by little the merchants of the Hanseatic League tightened their grip on the Bergen market, the English lost out and around 1400 they were more or less forced to search for a new market. Fortuitously, it was at this point that they discovered Iceland, both the rich fishing grounds and the possibility of a direct trade with Iceland for the valued stockfish. During the late medieval period there were advances in shipbuilding techniques, in the rigging of the ships, number of masts and design of the sails. England's cloth industry was expanding, the population was growing, and thus there was an ever-increasing demand for stockfish as Lenten fish in Catholic England. The compass eventually superseded the lodestone

---

[5] E. M. Carus-Wilson, 'The Iceland Trade', in *Studies in English Trade in the Fifteenth Century*, ed. Eileen Power and M. M. Postan, London 1933, reprinted 1951, 155–182.

[6] Evan T. Jones, 'England's Iceland Fishery in the Early Modern Period', in *England's Sea Fisheries: The Commercial Fisheries of England and Wales since 1300*, ed. D. Starkey et al, London 2000, 105–10; idem, 'Charting the World of English Fishermen in Early Modern Iceland', *The Mariner's Mirror* 90, no. 4, 2004, 398–409.

[7] See e.g. N. J. Williams, *The Maritime Trade of the East Anglian Ports 1550–1590*, Oxford 1988, 95, and G. Alan Metters, to whom I am indebted for sending me the relevant part of his thesis on the Iceland trade from Lynn: 'The Rulers and Merchants of King's Lynn in the Early-Seventeenth Century', 2 vols. PhD thesis, University of East Anglia, Norwich, 1982.

[8] Carus-Wilson, 'The Iceland Trade', 173.

[9] Helgi Þorláksson, *Sjórán og siglingar. Ensk-íslensk samskipti 1580–1630*, Reykjavík 1999 [*Piracy and Navigation. Anglo-Icelandic Relations 1580–1630*], 280.

[10] Williams, *The Maritime Trade*, 87.

making navigation easier as the fifteenth century progressed.[11] To the English Iceland offered a new market.

The English were the first foreign nation to sail into the North Atlantic (following the Norwegians, who were not considered foreigners by contemporary Icelanders) – and the Icelandic waters became the 'training-grounds for a class of seamen who would in time create the British Empire', as Þorsteinsson worded it.[12]

THE ENGLISH DISCOVER THE ICELANDIC FISHING GROUNDS

A Cromer fisherman named Robert Bacon is said to have 'discovered Iceland' early in the fifteenth century,[13] thereby immediately linking Iceland to East Anglia. The first documentary evidence in Icelandic sources of Englishmen fishing off Iceland comes from the contemporary *Nýi annáll* [New Annal] for the year 1412: 'A ship came from England to the east of Dyrhólaey; men rowed out to them, they were fishermen from England.' The annal goes on to recount that five of them were separated from their companions and spent the winter in Iceland. They were rescued the following year by one Richard who came on a merchant ship from England, armed with a licence from the king of Norway permitting him to trade in all Norwegian dominions. The news soon spread and the following year there were thirty doggers or more.[14] The year 1414 saw a ship arriving carrying a letter from Henry V himself 'to the people and chief men of Iceland' asking that a trading licence be granted 'especially ... to the king's own ship'.[15]

To the consternation of the king of Denmark, the number of ships steadily increased. On Maundy Thursday in 1419 it snowed so much that *all around the coast* not less than twenty-five English ships were wrecked.[16] Thus before the end of the second decade of the fifteenth century trading relations had been introduced and the Iceland fisheries were well established all around the coast, destined to become one of England's major fisheries, at least until the seventeenth century.[17]

But did the English arrive earlier? According to two Icelandic annals an Icelander was slain by 'foreigners' in 1396–7, in all probability Englishmen.[18] And English sources indicate an earlier date. According to the antiquary John Leland (1503?–52) in his famous *Itinerary*, admittedly not a contemporary source, in the year 1312:

---

[11] Carus-Wilson, 'The Iceland Trade', 157–61; Björn Þorsteinsson and Guðrún Ása Grímsdóttir, 'Enska öldin', *Saga Íslands*, ed. Sigurður Líndal, V, 15–17.
[12] Þorsteinsson, *Tíu þorskastríð*, 7. See also Jones, 'England's Iceland Fishery', 105, and Jones, 'Charting the World', 398.
[13] Carus-Wilson, 'The Iceland Trade', 173. The source she and N. J. Williams give is F. Blomefield and C. Parkin, *An Essay Towards the Topographical History of the County of Norfolk*, viii, 104, but Carus-Wilson says 'no authority is given'.
[14] *Annálar 1400–1800*, Reykjavík 1922–7, I, 18–19.
[15] Quoted and translated by Carus-Wilson, 'The Iceland Trade', 162.
[16] *Annálar*, I, 22. My italics.
[17] Jones, 'England's Iceland Fishery', 110.
[18] Þorkell Jóhannesson, 'Plágan mikla 1402–1404', *Lýðir og landshagir*, Reykjavík 1965, I, 72.

'The first great increase of this Town [Kingston upon Hull] was by passing for Fish into Iceland from whence they had the whole Trade of Stock fish into England'. One could interpret this as Iceland fish coming through Bergen, but Leland then adds 'in such time as all the Trade of Stockfish for England *came from Iceland to Kingston* [my italics].'[19] Þorsteinsson declares the stones could be Icelandic.[20]

In Hakluyt's *The Principal Navigations, Voyages, Traffiques, and Discoveries of the English Nation*, there is a document from 1360 speaking of men sailing to Iceland 'from Linne in Norfolk' where there had 'bene of many yeeres a very common and usuall trade' and privileges were granted to the fishermen of Blakeney for freedom of service to Edward III 'in respect of their trade to Island'. An annotation in the margin dates the exemption to the years 1328–9, 1330–1 and 1357–8.[21] In a petition of the Commons in 1415, however, it is said that the English have been fishing off Iceland for (only) the last six or seven years, 'par sys ou sept ans', thus from 1408 at the earliest,[22] which tallies more or less with Icelandic sources. The evidence thus points to the fact that the English probably began fishing off Iceland during the last decade of the fourteenth century[23] and at the beginning of the fifteenth, but further research is needed into that neglected century, the fourteenth.

The king of Denmark was not happy with the English invasion of the fishing grounds off Iceland and even less so with the trading, but was powerless to stop them. The English century is a tale of disputes between the governments of England and Denmark and of frequent clashes between English merchants and royal officials on the island. Danish royal emissaries were constantly crossing the North Sea to England to complain about the behaviour of the English in Iceland. Negotiations were often successful, treaties were signed and both kings tried to profit by selling licences, though many seafarers dispensed with that formality. The Danish king, lacking a navy, was engaged in an impossible struggle to keep the English from sailing to Iceland. As early as 1415, King Erik sent two highly placed officials to London to complain to his brother-in-law Henry V about acts of violence committed by English subjects in Iceland. Henry was co-operative and forbade his subjects in sixteen ports, many of them in East Anglia, on the east coast of England from sailing to Iceland for a year 'except according to ancient custom' – *aliter quam antiquitus fieri consuevit*. And how ancient was that in 1415? This was clearly a

---

[19] From a memorandum by Sir Joseph Banks, 'Some Notes relative to the ancient State of Iceland, drawn up with a view to explain its importance as a Fishing Station at the present time, with comparative Statements relative to Newfoundland', 1813, The Natural History Museum, Botany Library, Dawson Turner Collection 17, 140–56. [Hereafter Banks's Memorandum]. Banks has modernized the English.
[20] Þorsteinsson, *Enska öldin*, 111.
[21] 'A Testimony of the Learned Mathematician Master John Dee, Touching the Foresaid Voyage of Nicholas De Linna', in Richard Hakluyt, *The Principal Navigations, Voyages, Traffiques, and Discoveries of the English Nation*, London 1598–1600, 122. See Mary C. Fuller, 'Where was Iceland in 1600?', *A Companion to the Global Renaissance*, ed. Jyotsna G. Singh, Chichester 2009, 155, where the authenticity of Dee's information is discussed.
[22] *D.I.*, XVI, no. 80, quote p. 227.
[23] Þorkell Jóhannesson, 'Plágan mikla', bls. 72.

navigation ban in disguise. The House of Commons strongly objected at the time. The realm would be laid waste.[24] Edicts were often issued such as one in 1450 which stated bluntly in Article 14 'we declare that all English and Irish men, who sail to Iceland without our licences, letters and seals, will be deemed outlaws and their ships and cargoes confiscated'.[25] But the English continued to sail to Iceland, undaunted.

THE ENGLISH FISHERIES

During the English century proper it is estimated that at least 100 English fishing vessels sailed annually to Iceland.[26] All scholars agree that though the fishing doggers came from 'a wide area', most hailed from the east coast of England.[27] The vessels came almost entirely from East Anglia, the major towns involved being King's Lynn and Yarmouth, while Ipswich, Blakeney, Burnham, Cley, Cromer, Dersingham and Orwell are among those mentioned in sources, as are more northern ports like Grimsby, Whitby, Boston, Hull and Scarborough, as well as London, Harwich and Cornish ports to the south and much further to the west.[28] Among the sixteen ports mentioned above in Henry V's 1415 prohibition were the East Anglian ports Yarmouth, Lynn, 'Gippenwich' (Ipswich), Orwell, Berwick, Blakeney, Burnham, Cromer and Dersingham,[29] whose fisheries must all have been pretty well established this early.

The vessels fished off the coast of Iceland more or less all the year except for the winter months. Most doggers were fairly small, between 30 and 100 tons.[30] The English caught the fish by using hand-lines and then salted them on board the vessel, while the preferred method of the saltless Icelanders was drying cod and the 'good Iseland ling'[31] into stockfish, a process practised well into the early nineteenth century. The English soon made themselves at home, mainly in the south and west of Iceland, where the best fishing grounds are to be found, especially in the Westman Islands. Forts were erected and Icelanders were employed. The fishing was lucrative: Þorsteinsson calculated that one successful voyage to Iceland, bringing back a full load of fish, could almost defray the costs of the ship itself and its outfitting.[32]

---

[24] D.I., XVI, nos. 78–80. Þorsteinsson, Enska öldin, 41–5.
[25] Þorsteinsson, Saga Íslands, V, the so-called Langaréttarbót, 73–8. D.I.,V, no. 55. Quote at p. 67.
[26] Björn Þorsteinsson, Tíu þorskastríð, Reykjavík 1976, 11, 16.
[27] Carus-Wilson, 'The Iceland Trade', 173; Jones, 'Charting English Fishermen', 398.
[28] Þorsteinsson has a list of all the major English towns and ports involved in the navigation to Iceland mentioned in fifteenth-century sources. He lists twenty-seven. See: Björn Þorsteinsson, Enskar heimildir um sögu Íslendinga á 15. og 16. öld, Reykjavík 1969, 27–8.
[29] D.I., III, no. 644.
[30] Jones, 'Charting English Fishermen', 398. Most scholars agree that the average size was about 50 tons.
[31] Quoted by Ethel Seaton, Literary Relations of England and Scandinavia in the Seventeenth Century, Oxford 1935, 29.
[32] Þorsteinsson, Tíu þorskastríð, 68–9.

Traditionally it has been assumed that there was a decline in the last quarter of the fifteenth century when the Hanse arrived in Iceland,[33] but this seems to be mainly the case as regards Bristol, where relations had begun to decline from about 1480,[34] the Bristol ships heading for Newfoundland. The oldest documentary evidence of convoys and naval protection is from the time of Richard III from 1484 for the sailors in Norfolk and Suffolk, with the requisite licences. The ships were convoyed past Scotland by English men of war from Hull,[35] surely a sign of the importance of the Iceland fisheries to East Anglia. The years 1490–1530 were in fact a major period of growth. This was mainly due to the 1489 treaty between Hans I and Henry VII, permitting English subjects to sail to Iceland and engage in fair trade and fish 'in all perpetuity' – on condition they pay customs dues and taxes and buy licences from the king of Denmark.[36] When Henry VIII succeeded to the throne in 1509, the first act of his reign permitted free voyages to Iceland, 'considering that Fysshe and other Commodities of that Cuntre [Iceland] be muche behovefull and necessarie toward the comen Weale of this Realme.'[37] During Henry's reign (1509–1547) he 'and his council had Iceland on their agenda more often than any English government down to our own time,' wrote Þorsteinsson, concluding: 'It is clear from the sources that English vessels sailed to Iceland to trade and to fish in greater numbers in the first decades of the sixteenth than at any other time down to the nineteenth century.'[38] Evan Jones agrees 'the English fishery developed into a major industry.'[39] And indeed in 1528, in a list compiled by Lord Cecil, there were no less than 149 ships along the east coast from London to Boston engaged in the fishery,[40] 'a sizeable proportion of England's total marine', or a fifth of England's total shipping tonnage.[41]

It seems clear that there was a decline in the English fisheries as the sixteenth century progressed. Jones explains this by detailing unwise acts of the English and Danish governments. In 1563, however, an act of parliament declaring Wednesday and Saturdays fish-days,[42] the hoped-for increase in demand may have had a hand in reversing the trend. At any rate, it seems clear that the Iceland fishery remained important. In the famous Anthony Parkhurst letter of 1578 to Richard Hakluyt it is asserted that there were not that many English vessels participating in the Newfoundland fishery compared with other nations because of the 'Trade our

---

[33] Carus-Wilson, 'The Iceland Trade', 181.
[34] David Quinn, *England and the Discovery of America 1481–1620*, London 1974, 49. Þorsteinsson, *Enskar heimildir*, 55.
[35] Þorsteinsson, *Saga Íslands*, V, 107. *D.I.*, XVI, no. 235.
[36] This is the first time that the English were legally permitted to fish in Icelandic waters, on condition they acknowledged Denmark's sovereignty of Iceland and renewed their licences at the end of seven years, Þorsteinsson, *Enska öldin*, 251–2.
[37] Quoted by Þorsteinsson, 'Henry VIII and Iceland', 73.
[38] Ibid., 67, 74.
[39] Jones, 'England's Iceland Fishery', 106.
[40] The list, with the number sailing from each port, is in *D.I.*, XVI, no. 283.
[41] Jones, 'Charting English Fishermen', 398; Jones, 'England's Iceland Fishery', 106.
[42] Jones, 'England's Iceland Fishery', 107.

Island has to Iceland'.[43] According to this most of England's cod was still coming from Iceland.

Professor Helgi Þorláksson of the University of Iceland has researched Anglo-Icelandic relations in the period 1580–1630. His study on English piracy and navigation during this period demonstrates quite clearly the importance of the Iceland fisheries and trade for this region. The main ports involved were Lynn, Yarmouth, Aldeburgh, Wells and Southwold, Walberswick and Dunwich. Bristol was quite out of the picture as already mentioned and Hull was almost exclusively sending its boats to Finnmark.[44] Both Þorláksson and Jones have demonstrated that it was around 1580 to 1630 that another resurgence of the English Iceland fisheries took place, due in part to a rise in population with a corresponding increase in food prices.

An interesting source is a pamphlet by Tobias Gentleman of Southwold, titled *England's Way To Win Wealth and To Employ Ships and Mariners*, printed in 1614, which enumerates the East Anglian ships sailing to Iceland annually: from Orford and Aldeburgh ten to twelve barks; Southwold, Walberswick and Dunwich had 'a very good Breed of Fishermen' and sent 'some 50 Sail' to Iceland for cod and ling; Great Yarmouth twenty barks to fish cod and ling; Wells and Blackeney together 'some twenty Sail of Barks'; and finally he mentions Lynn 'a proper gallant Town for Sea-faring Men, and for Men for *Iceland*; this is a rich Town, and they have some twenty Sail of *Iceland* ships, that they yearly send for Cods and Lings'. Accordingly there were around 120–125 ships sailing annually from East Anglia alone in the years before 1614.[45]

In 1628 the accepted number is 160, perhaps up towards 200 as the Icelandic annals state that there were 140 English doggers in the western fjords alone. John Coke, one of Charles I's principal secretaries of state, wrote in 1632, in his report 'Concerning the Fishing of Island', that the ships engaged in the Iceland fisheries were nearly 400, from 50 to 150 tons, bringing cod and ling to 'serve the whole kingdom',[46] though Þorláksson casts doubts on this figure, stating that they could hardly have been more than 200 around 1630.[47] The conclusion that must be drawn is that 'The English Century' in Icelandic history as regards the East Anglian ports was the early seventeenth century just as much as the fifteenth.

A. R. Mitchell's article on the early modern European fisheries in *The Cambridge Economic History of Europe* sheds a great deal of light on the seventeenth-century Yarmouth Iceland fishery. In a table for the Great Yarmouth fishing fleet 1594–1714 the Iceland ships have a separate column, demonstrating that

---

[43] Banks's Memorandum, year 1578.
[44] Þorláksson, *Sjórán og siglingar*, 225, 240.
[45] Tobias Gentleman, *England's Way To Win Wealth and To Employ Ships and Mariners*, London 1614, 384–5. Printed in volume III of *The Harleian Miscellany*, London 1745.
[46] Quoted by Jones, 'England's Iceland Fishery', 107. The original is on microfilm in TNA, SP 16/229, no. 82, p.194.
[47] Þorláksson, *Sjórán og siglingar*, 240.

throughout this period there was little let-up of the navigation to Iceland.[48] There were certainly fluctuations in their number, depending on the state of international relations or episodes like the Civil War. In the year 1634 Yarmouth sent out the largest fleet of the century to Iceland, sixty-three boats in all. According to Icelandic sources there were still significant numbers in the later years of the seventeenth century: in 1649 in the western fjords alone there were sixty doggers and the following year 1650 there were 140, accompanied by three naval vessels.[49] This could only have been part of the fleet. However, after that the number begins to decline: in the late 1650s there were over seventy ships. After the Restoration the fishery went into 'terminal decline', says Evan Jones, convincingly blaming the salt tax of Charles II.[50] By 1675 they were down to twenty-eight, but treatises were still being published as late as 1682 saying that in Icelandic waters were to be found 'multitudes of Fishery Vessels, both of Strangers and English there.'[51] And it is only after 1689 that the number of Iceland ships sailing annually from Yarmouth can be counted on one hand.[52] Jones quotes an English source from c.1680 that once 10,000 men had been engaged in the Iceland and 'Northern-Fishery' which now only employed 1,000.[53] This tallies with Icelandic sources. In *Eyrarannáll* for the year 1702 it is written: 'Danish merchantmen visited all the country's harbours; Dutch fishermen also came and French and Spanish whalers, but no English doggers.'[54] Indeed none came that year, but they were certainly expected and their non-appearance was a sign of the times.

THE ENGLISH TRADE

The Icelanders welcomed the English merchants, unlike their king. As early as 1413 a royal edict banned the Icelanders from trading with foreigners.[55] There was a good market in Iceland for foreign goods and best of all the English merchants offered a much better price for the fish than the Bergen traders had been willing to pay, about 70 per cent more for stockfish.[56] The English merchants sailed on large trading ships, of about 150–400 tons, and perhaps smaller ships of 70–170 tons were used to combine fishing and trade.[57]

The Icelandic produce sought by the English was first and foremost stockfish,

---

[48] A. R. Mitchell, 'The European Fisheries in Early Modern History', in *The Cambridge Economic History of Europe*, V, 161–6 (the table is on pp. 144–6).
[49] 'Vestfjarðarannáll yngri', *Annálar 1400–1800*, Reykjavík 1933–8, III, 123, 125.
[50] Jones, 'England's Iceland Fishery', 107–8.
[51] John Collins, *Salt and Fishery*, London 1682, 83, with a good description of Iceland at 75–90.
[52] See Mitchell's table (above, note 48).
[53] Jones, 'England's Iceland Fishery', 107.
[54] *Annálar*, III, 413.
[55] 'Nýi Annáll', *Annálar*, I, 20.
[56] Þorsteinsson, *Tíu þorskastríð*, 11.
[57] David Quinn says up to 300 tons, *England and the Discovery of America*, 48; Þorláksson, *Sjórán og siglingar*, 279.

woollen cloth called *vaðmál* and train oil. The Elizabethans were also fond of Icelandic dogs. In 1576 the scholar John Caius castigated these 'dogges of an outlandishe kinde ... I mean Iselande dogges, curled and rough al over'.[58] Woollen stockings and mittens were certainly imported into Lynn.[59] Hawks and falcons were also popular. James I wrote often to his brother-in-law requesting them, and English falconers such as Henry Buckston from Lynn were also merchants, taking dry saltfish, train oil, *vaðmál*, and of course falcons to England in 1608.[60]

What the English offered was an enticing array of goods. The English merchant ships were 'floating shops selling everything',[61] both necessaries and luxuries, first and foremost lengths of cloth and linen, even silk. England could supply grain, malt, beer, and honey, ironware such as horseshoes, swords and scissors, hats, shoes and thigh boots, glasses and combs, needles, and thread.[62] In short all that Iceland needed.

The actual trade in the fifteenth century appears to have been confined to relatively few ships. It was mainly a summer trade, quickly becoming a regular one with the same ships, masters and merchants engaged in it, as was the case in Hull.[63] While Bristol was pre-eminent at the beginning of the fifteenth century according to Carus-Wilson, and it must not be forgotten that *The Libelle of Englyshe Polycye* singles out Bristol,[64] Wendy R. Childs has shown that Hull 'played as great a role as Bristol in the early trade, and a greater one by far in the later fifteenth century', though the numbers of ships were small, only three to four, often sent by the mayor and burgesses. And occasionally ships came from London.[65] According to Þorsteinsson during the period 1439–73, when he deems licences reliable, thirty of the eighty ships were from Bristol.[66]

However, Þorsteinsson states emphatically that it *was* Lynn that became the main port of the Iceland trade early in the fifteenth century. By 1424 it had an acknowledged guild of merchants called the 'Merchants of Iceland', and, as in Hull, leading citizens were involved in the trade.[67] Unfortunately the records are patchy, though Þorsteinsson does not doubt that men from Lynn continued sailing to Iceland throughout the English century and beyond. From 1457 there are customs ledgers extant indicating the merchant ships sailing from Lynn and Yarmouth with ships, names of owners and the cargo, predominantly stockfish and 'wadmolle'. In 1465 Edward IV's negotiators with the royal Danish representative were five in all

---

[58] Seaton, *Literary Relations*, 32–5.
[59] Metters, 'King's Lynn Port Books'.
[60] Þorláksson, *Sjórán og siglingar*, 193, 196.
[61] Þorsteinsson, *Enskar heimildir*, 33.
[62] Childs, 'The Role of Hull', 15, 20; Carus-Wilson, 'The Iceland Trade', 175.
[63] Wendy R. Childs, 'England's Icelandic Trade in the Fifteenth Century: The Role of the Port of Hull', *Northern Seas Yearbook 1995*, Esbjerg 1995, 13.
[64] See E. M. Carus-Wilson, *The Overseas Trade of Bristol in the later Middle Ages*, New York 1937 and 1967 (2nd edn).
[65] Childs, 'Role of the Port of Hull', 11, 17–18, 27–8.
[66] Þorsteinsson, *Enskar heimildir*, 51.
[67] There were also 'merchants of Norway' and 'merchants of Prussia', *D.I.*, XVI, no. 229. Carus-Wilson, 'The Iceland Trade', 163.

and two came from Lynn – indeed negotiators often came from Lynn, indicating how important their interests in Iceland were.[68] And Lynn boasted a Stockfish Row, near the Tuesday Market.

Other East Anglian ports soon joined in. In 1433 a ship from Cromer belonging to Thomas Rudd arrived from Iceland and the stockfish had been smuggled into England, presumably because it did not have a licence. In 1438 Adam Horn from Cley and Roger Fouler from Cromer were accused of sailing to Iceland (instead of Bergen) where they loaded their ship with stockfish in exchange for barley and beer. In 1458 a licence for Richard Arnold from 'Crowemer' was issued at Westminster for a ship of 120 tons or less to sail to Iceland and return with a cargo of Iceland produce.[69] These are just a few examples.

By the 1500s the East Anglian ports had come into their own, according to the available documents. Customs records show for example that in 1519–20 Lynn sent seven ships, with extremely detailed lists of wares being sent to Iceland. By 1526–7 there are eleven, and thirteen in 1529–30.[70] Þorsteinsson identified a total of forty-two ships sailing to Iceland during the early sixteenth century from Lynn, one ship making the journey thirteen times.[71]

During the period from 1550 to 1590 'the Iceland voyage was almost entirely an East Anglian enterprise,' states N. J. Williams, though there was 'little trading on any but the smallest scale'. The majority of the ships sailing to Iceland were doggers not merchantmen carrying 'a few poundsworth of wares to sell in Iceland', even though the trade was thrown open mid-century.[72]

Little research has been done by Icelandic historians on the English trade during the period 1530–1580 but Professor Þorláksson's detailed study of Anglo-Icelandic relations in the subsequent decades 1580–1630, when the before-mentioned resurgence in the fisheries took place, shows that it was accompanied by a corresponding upswing in trade. In a letter to King Christian IV in 1595 Queen Elizabeth wrote that she was 'not unmindful of the value of the Iceland trade'.[73]

Ships from Blakeney brought back salted beef, butter and mutton in 1596, products not before seen in England as exports from Iceland. The following year two riding horses were imported and in 1601 falcons and twenty whale fins. Around 1600 sixteen to twenty merchants were going annually to Iceland from Buckston, Lynn, Wells, Southwold, Walberswick, Dunwich and Aldeburgh as well as London and Harwich.[74] The licensed English trade with Iceland was nearing its end. What seems to have led to a subsequent decline was the ever present threat of the pirates from Dunkirk. For instance Wells and Burnham were sending off thirty-

---

[68] Þorsteinsson, *Enska öldin*, 202.
[69] *D.I.*, XVI, nos. 95, 109, 167.
[70] *D.I.*, XVI, nos. 5, 49, 55, 57. The Customs records take up the first 220 pages of volume XVI of the *Diplomatarium Islandicum*.
[71] On Lynn see Þorsteinsson's detailed analysis, *Enskar heimildir*, 71–84.
[72] Williams, *The Maritime Trade*, 92–3, 95.
[73] Banks's Memorandum, year 1595.
[74] Þorláksson, *Sjórán og siglingar*, 65.

seven ships around 1588, but by 1603 the figure was down to twenty. Lack of naval protection vessels was blamed.[75] But the king of Denmark was also involved – preparing through legislation to make the Iceland trade a monopoly for his own subjects, as will be recounted shortly.

The Icelanders, as has been said, welcomed the English – but only if they engaged in some trade. They were never happy with foreigners fishing off the coast of Iceland, because they believed they were catching the best fish which thus never made it to the shallows where the Icelanders fished from their smaller rowing boats. When the Icelandic chieftains gathered at the *Alþingi*[76] to discuss the abovementioned 1489 peace treaty they made important changes, notably that they would not accept the right of foreigners to fish off the coast of Iceland. Further, foreigners were forbidden from wintering in the island and employing Icelanders, and all doggers found in Icelandic waters that did not engage in trade were condemned.[77] The only problem was that the Icelanders had no means to implement their ruling.

THE IMPACT OF THE ENGLISH ON ICELANDIC SOCIETY

There was of course a great deal of contact between Englishmen and Icelanders in the country itself. The seamen went ashore to get water and fresh food. Ships were frequently stranded or wrecked and then their English crews had to rely on the Icelandic farmers who strove to help them as the good Christians they were.[78] Relations often became violent but they were more often friendly and led to important cultural encounters.

'Many English who frequented Iceland were Pyrates as well as Fishermen; a minute account of the Enormities they committed is preserved', wrote Sir Joseph Banks to the British government in his memorandum on the Iceland fisheries in 1813. He is referring to the years 1415–1425, when men mostly from Hull and Lynn were accused of thirty-seven cases of dastardly crimes.[79] Perhaps the most serious case was when Björn Þorleifsson, the native-born and wealthy royal governor of Iceland, was killed along with seven of his men in 1467. The culprits were allegedly men from East Anglia, namely Lynn. His widow sailed to Copenhagen for an audience with Christian I. The 'Danish cannon at Copenhagen did not cover the Iceland seas', wrote Þorsteinsson, but the Danish supremacy over the Sound in the Baltic Straits was a potent weapon against England.[80] In revenge, the Sound was closed to English ships in 1468 and four ships from Lynn and two from Boston with valuable cargoes were captured.[81]

---

[75] Ibid., 219, 233–4, 290.
[76] *Alþingi* was the name of the Icelandic parliament that convened for two weeks each summer.
[77] *Píningsdómur* is the name of this famous ruling, *D.I.*, VI, no. 617. See Þorsteinsson, *Enska öldin*, 251–8.
[78] See e.g. ruling from the *Alþingi*, 1633, *Alþingisbækur Íslands*, Reykjavík, 1922, 1925–32, V, 301–2.
[79] Banks's Memorandum.
[80] Þorsteinsson, 'Henry VIII and Iceland', 98.
[81] Þorsteinsson, *Enska öldin*, 204–22.

During the sixteenth and seventeenth centuries relations were peaceful enough, except for one famous incident when William Clark and James Gentleman from Southwold, or *Jón Gentilmann*, as he was erroneously called in Icelandic sources, stole the church bell of the Westman Islands in 1614. However, it was marked and this had a happy ending when James I kindly had it returned.[82]

One question that has interested historians is whether Icelanders were forcibly taken by the English. Among the crimes listed in 1425 were accusations against the English for kidnapping Icelanders, among them children, and taking them to England to a life of servitude.[83] In August 1429 there is a well documented case pertaining to Lynn. An Iceland merchant attested to the fact that he and his companions had brought with them eight children, five boys and three girls, whom the Lynn Council ordered him to return. Furthermore, in 1432 the king of England told his subjects to return people they had taken from Denmark, Sweden and Norway 'but especially those from Iceland, Finnmark and Hálogaland [Norway]'.[84] This certainly suggests that the Lynn episode was far from being an isolated incident. And the problem seems to have persisted as a ruling from *Alþingi* in 1533 claimed that the doggers 'steal both money and people from this poor country'.[85]

Certainly quite a number of Icelanders left Iceland and are found in fifteenth-century sources living in English fishing ports. In Hull there were two Icelandic householders in 1443 and in 1465–6 two householders and nine other Icelanders.[86] In 1484 the Bristol alien subsidy roll lists fifty-one foreigners, forty-nine of them Icelanders, all but two men or boys. They were servants to Bristol burghers, though one William Yslond had become a Bristol merchant by 1492.[87] One can only imagine that similar numbers would appear regarding Lynn if similar records were extant. Carus-Wilson found terms such as 'Icelandman', 'Icelandwoman' or those 'born in Iceland' in the Subsidy Rolls.[88] In Southwold, Magnus 'Island man' was buried in 1603, along with others of his countrymen. Relations were often friendly, for example a Lynn skipper named Martin Gray stayed with the scholar Jón lærði Guðmundsson for three weeks in May 1623.[89] In Icelandic sources there are many Icelanders named who sailed with the doggers to England for a variety of reasons; to escape justice, seek adventure or to engage in trade themselves.

In the late sixteenth century the king of Denmark, buoyed up by a more powerful navy, began vigorously promoting exclusive Danish trade in Iceland.

---

[82] 'Fitjaannáll', *Annálar 1400–1800*, Reykjavík 1927–32, II, 98; Helgi Þorláksson, *Sjórán og siglingar*, 107–49.
[83] Þorsteinsson, 'Hannes Pálsson', 153; *D.I.*, IV, no. 381, especially 328.
[84] *D.I.*, IV, no. 558. Þorsteinsson, *Enska öldin*, 101–2. Þorláksson, 'Útflutningur íslenskra barna til Englands á miðöldum', *Sagnir*, Reykjavík 1983, IV, 48; Carus-Wilson, 'The Iceland Trade' 166–7.
[85] *D.I.*, IX, no. 550.
[86] Childs, 'The Role of Hull', 12–13.
[87] Helgi Þorláksson, 'Útflutningur íslenskra barna', IV, 47. See David Quinn's discussion of this question: *England and the Discovery of America*, 49–51.
[88] Carus-Wilson, 'The Iceland trade', 167.
[89] Þorláksson, *Sjórán og siglingar*, 141–2, 195, 277.

Initially the trade monopoly of 1602 did not put a stop to English ships, along with Scots, Irish, Dutch, Spanish (Basque) and French vessels, fishing off Iceland and illicitly trading with the natives when the opportunity presented itself. At the end of the eighteenth century (1786) the treasurer of Iceland Skúli Magnússon estimated there were 200–300 foreign ships fishing off Iceland, including English and Scottish.[90] Did English fishermen ever really leave the Iceland fishing grounds? In 1813, Sir Joseph Banks, naturalist, veteran of the *Endeavour* voyage and leader of the first British scientific expedition to Iceland in 1772, wrote a memorandum to the government extolling the advantages of the Iceland fisheries, remarking 'some English have at all time frequented it'.[91] It may well be that English fishermen continued to visit Icelandic waters until the last Cod War of 1976 put an end to the English Iceland fisheries.

During Iceland's 'English century' the Iceland fisheries were extremely important to the English economy and especially to the East Anglian ports of Norfolk and Suffolk. Robert Bacon of Cromer may or may not have 'discovered' the Icelandic fishing grounds and it is perhaps doubtful that the fishermen of Blakeney were trading with Iceland as early as 1328, but there is no doubt that by 1415 the Iceland fisheries of many East Anglian ports were well established. Lynn appears to have held pride of place, with Yarmouth second. It is significant that naval protection was first provided in 1484 especially to the 'mariners of the naveye of our countes of Norffolk and Suffolk, aswele fisshers as other, entending to departe into the parties of Island',[92] underlining the importance of the Iceland fisheries to East Anglia.

As to trade, Bristol, Hull and London all conducted a considerable trade with Iceland during the English century, but it was Lynn that became the main port of the Iceland trade early in the fifteenth century. By 1424 it had an acknowledged guild of merchants called 'Merchants of Iceland'. By the first decades of the 1500s extant documents demonstrate clearly that the East Anglian ports were preeminent at a time when a fifth of England's total shipping tonnage was engaged in the Iceland venture. And in the early seventeenth century John Coke in his report of 1632 concluded that Iceland 'is the greatest fishing in the Kingdom and exceedeth the Newfownd Land and hering fishings'.[93] The conclusion that must be drawn is that 'The English Century' in Icelandic history as regards the East Anglian ports was not only the fifteenth century but continued as such into the early seventeenth century.

---

[90] Gísli Gunnarsson, *Monopoly Trade and Economic Stagnation: Studies in the Foreign Trade of Iceland 1662–1787*, Lund 1983, 71.
[91] Banks's Memorandum.
[92] *D.I.*, XVI, no. 235.
[93] Quoted by Jones, 'England's Iceland Fishery', 107.

PART III

CASE-STUDIES: INFLUENCES AND LINKS

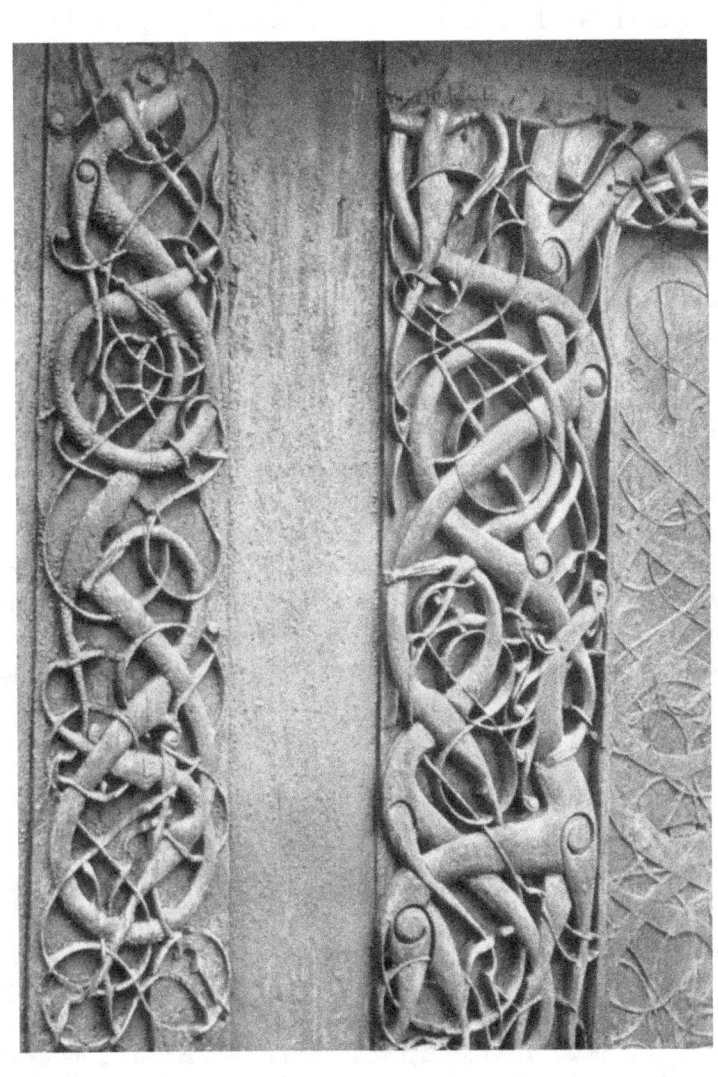

— Chapter 11 —

IPSWICH: CONTEXTS OF FUNERARY EVIDENCE FROM AN URBAN PRECURSOR OF THE SEVENTH CENTURY AD

Christopher Scull

IPSWICH, located at the head of the Orwell estuary in south-east Suffolk, is the site of one of the major trading and manufacturing settlements – the so-called *wics* or *emporia* – of seventh- to ninth-century England and is conventionally interpreted as the main port-of-entry for the East Anglian kingdom through which trade with the continent was directed and the benefits regulated and taxed.[1] Whether the major *emporia* ever enjoyed an exclusive monopolistic status is now open to question given the more recent recognition of considerable settlement complexity in Middle Saxon England which includes a range of sites, both coastal and inland, which were demonstrably connected to international exchange systems.[2] It is also important to draw a distinction between these settlements in their heyday and their seventh-century precursors.[3] Nonetheless, at the height of their development in the eighth and ninth centuries the major *emporia* stand out as more extensive and more densely occupied than other contemporary settlements, with evidence for a diversity and intensity of craft activity, and direct engagement in trade cross the

---

[1] R. Hodges, *Dark Age Economics: the Origins of Towns and Trade AD 600–1000*, London 1982, 67–74; H. Clarke and R. Ambrosiani, *Towns in the Viking Age*, revised edn, London 1995, 13–37; C. J. Scull, 'Urban Centres in pre-Viking England?', in *The Anglo-Saxons from the Migration Period to the Eighth Century: an Ethnographic Perspective*, ed. J. Hines, Woodbridge 1997, 269–310; D. Hill and R. Cowie (eds), *Wics. The Early Medieval Trading Centres of Northern Europe*, Sheffield 2001.

[2] K. Ulmschneider, *Markets, Minsters and Metal-Detectors: the Archaeology of Middle Saxon Lincolnshire and Hampshire Compared*, Oxford 2000; T. Pestell and K. Ulmschneider (eds), *Money and Markets in Early Medieval Europe: Trade and 'Productive' Sites, 650–850*, Macclesfield 2003; J. Naylor, *An Archaeology of Trade in Middle Saxon England*, Oxford 2004.

[3] C. J. Scull, 'Ipswich: Development and Contexts of an Urban Precursor in the Seventh Century', in *Central Places in the Migration and Merovingian Periods. Papers from the 52nd Sachsensymposium Lund, August 2001*, ed. B. Hårdh and L. Larsson, Lund 2002, 303–16; idem, 'Foreign Identities in Burials at Seventh-Century English Emporia', in *Studies in Early Anglo-Saxon Art and Archaeology: Papers in Honour of Martin G. Welch*, ed. S. Brookes, S. Harrington and A. Reynolds, Oxford 2011, 82–97, at 83.

Channel and the North Sea, on a scale rarely matched in the contemporary settlement record. The conclusion that they were major centres of population and major nodal places in regional and inter-regional economic networks remains unchallenged.

Consequently, these settlements have assumed a central place in debates over the nature of trade, urbanism and urban origins in post-Roman Britain, and are accorded an important role in the developing socio-economic complexity that governed the rise of the Anglo-Saxon kingdom structure.[4] Debate has focused on their economic function but much less attention has been paid to their social character. This is in part due to the fact that economics can be modelled from the ubiquitous debris of trade and manufacture, but evidence that might be brought to bear on social and demographic questions has been scarcer, more equivocal, and often fragmentary. This has begun to change, though, with the publication of synthesis and area excavations which give some idea of topography and built environment,[5] and a developing understanding of the burial record, in particular that associated with the earliest (seventh century) phases of these settlements.[6] It is now possible to investigate, at least for the seventh century, whether the exchange contacts focused on these places had discernible impacts on the cultural identities of their inhabitants. This chapter summarizes recently published burial evidence from seventh-century Ipswich,[7] and examines what it can tell us about social and community identities among the population of the settlement. In particular, it considers to what extent the people who lived and were buried here were culturally integrated with, or influenced by, a wider cross-Channel and North Sea cultural world.

Excavation has established the broad sequence of spatial development for the pre-Viking settlement at Ipswich which at its greatest extent covered around 50 hectares.[8] The crucial excavations for our understanding of the seventh and eighth centuries were undertaken at St Peter's Street/Greyfriar's Road close to the modern waterfront and on the site of the Buttermarket in the centre of the modern town.

---

[4] R. Hodges, 'The Evolution of Gateway Communities: Their Socio-Economic Implications', in *Ranking, Resource and Exchange. Aspects of the Archaeology of Early European Society*, ed. A. C. Renfrew and S. Shennan, Cambridge 1982, 117–23, and idem, *The Anglo-Saxon Achievement*, London 1989.

[5] A. D. Morton, *Excavations at Hamwic volume 1: Excavations 1946–83, excluding Six Dials and Melbourne Street*, London 1992; P. Andrews, *Excavations at Hamwic volume 2: Excavations at Six Dials*, York 1997; G. Malcolm, D. Bowsher, and R. Cowie, *Middle Saxon London: Excavations at the Royal Opera House 1989–99*, London 2003.

[6] Scull, 'Burials at Emporia'; idem, *Early Medieval (Late 5th–Early 8th Centuries AD) Cemeteries at Boss Hall and Buttermarket, Ipswich, Suffolk*, London 2009; and idem, 'Foreign identities'; V. Birbeck, R. Smith, P. Andrews and N. Stoodley, *The Origins of Mid-Saxon Southampton: Excavations at the Friends Provident St Mary's Stadium 1998–2000*, Salisbury 2005.

[7] Scull, *Early Medieval Cemeteries*. The discussion of the burials at Buttermarket and Boss Hall that follows is based on this publication which should be consulted for supporting data and analysis.

[8] K. Wade, 'The Urbanisation of East Anglia: the Ipswich Perspective', in *Flatlands and Wetlands: Current Themes in East Anglian Archaeology*, ed. J. Gardiner, Scole 1993, 142–51; Scull, 'Ipswich: Development and Contexts'. The archaeology of the seventh- and early eighth-century development of Ipswich is discussed by these authors in Scull, *Early Medieval Cemeteries*, 313–16.

At St Peter's Street/Greyfriar's Road, *Grubenhäuser* and pits were associated with ceramic assemblages of handmade wares and imported continental pottery which pre-date the production of Ipswich ware. At Buttermarket a sequence of activity from the seventh to the nineteenth centuries began with a cemetery in use during the seventh century. Together, the structural evidence from St Peter's Street/Greyfriar's Road and the distribution of residual pottery and other artefacts of the seventh and earlier eighth centuries suggest an initial settlement area of between 6 hectares and 30 hectares on the north bank of the River Orwell. Immediately to the north was the Buttermarket cemetery, which was almost certainly the main burial ground serving the settlement. The full area of the cemetery was not excavated, and within the excavated area there was much damage from later activity. It is however possible, with due caution, to estimate the minimum burial area and the original density of burial. This suggests that were originally at least 400–450 graves, of which at least seventy-one and possibly as many as seventy-eight were recorded (in some cases the remains were so damaged and fragmentary that secure identification of archaeological features as graves was not possible).

The material culture assemblage from early settlement contexts does not allow close dating. It belongs to a pre-Ipswich ware ceramic phase (that is, before AD 700–720), and it is seventh-century.[9] The cemetery, however, is dated both by grave goods and by radiocarbon, which agree well. The radiocarbon model gives us dates by which a community had started to bury here and so by extension the time by which a settlement with a permanent population had been established. Grave goods suggest that this was AD 610/20–640/50. The radiocarbon model gives *cal AD 595–640 (at 95% probability)* and *cal AD 610–635 (at 68% probability)*. The Buttermarket cemetery was abandoned by the end of the seventh century and it may have gone out of use as early as AD 680. The area was then given over to occupation and craft activity as part of a rapid expansion of the settlement to an area of 50 hectares, with streets laid out to an orthogonal pattern to the north of the original settlement nucleus and south of the River Orwell. During this phase production of Ipswich ware began north-east of the original seventh-century settlement area.

There is evidence for craft production and for overseas contacts from the earliest phases of the settlement. The ceramic assemblage is unique among contemporary (seventh-century) East Anglian sites for the high proportion (14 per cent) of imported wares. In the cemetery, the earliest graves include burials with material culture assemblages which suggest individuals from the Continent, discussed further below. The area of seventh-century settlement activity at Ipswich is larger than excavated contemporary rural settlements in Suffolk and the evidence suggests a substantially larger population and a higher population density. Because we have a radiocarbon model for the length of time the Buttermarket cemetery was in use, we can calculate (with due caution) the likely contributing population, which was probably in the low hundreds. By way of comparison, at a minimum estimate the

---

[9] P. Blinkhorn, *The Ipswich Ware Project: Ceramics, Trade and Society in Middle Saxon England*, Dorcester, 2012.

Buttermarket population was seven to eleven times greater than that at Bloodmoor Hill, Carlton Colville, Suffolk, where the cemetery is interpreted as representing a single household or the population of a single high-status establishment of the middle to later seventh century.[10]

What do the burials tell us about demography and social identity in the community or communities burying here? Men, women and children were all present. Only a very small proportion of burials could be sexed osteologically, but where we can make a judgement on biological sex or the expression of gender through the provision of grave goods the ratio is 2:1 men:women. This might be taken to suggest a permanent imbalance in the sex-structure of the population, such as might be expected if there were a preponderance of men involved in seasonal activity. The numbers, however, are too small to be taken as properly representative of the cemetery population as a whole.

Investment in burial suggests marked degrees of social differentiation. This is expressed in the provision of grave goods, and in the provision of structures, mounds and burial containers. Some of these aspects of burial practice tend to be mutually exclusive, and there appears to be some spatial (though not chronological) distinction between the provision of grave goods on the one hand and a limited suite of structures and containers (mounds and annular ditches, log coffins and boats) on the other. There is a sense that we are seeing here the remains of two competing, or at least distinctive, funerary languages. However, although there are some higher-status graves at Buttermarket, there is nothing outstanding. The status of the richer families burying here was not, on the evidence of the female graves, equal to those of the aristocratic women buried, for example, at Swallowcliffe Down, Wiltshire, or Desborough, Northamptonshire,[11] or elsewhere in East Anglia at Boss Hall, Ipswich, Harford Farm, Caistor St Edmund, Norfolk, or Coddenham, Suffolk.[12] The single outstanding burial at Buttermarket (grave 1306) is male, and continental, but it looks more impressive in England than it would on the Continent. The conclusion is that these are families of a local rather than a wider importance.

There is some evidence for burial plots. It is commonly argued that such patterning represents families or households, and this may well be so. The best evidence at Buttermarket, though, comes from an area used and maintained over two or perhaps three generations. This suggests that lineage, that is descent identity, was at least as important to the social foundations of the population burying here as the contemporary kindred relationships embodied in nuclear

---

[10] Scull, *Early Medieval Cemeteries*, 301–3, and 'The Human Burials', in S. Lucy, J. Tipper and A. Dickens, *The Anglo-Saxon Settlement and Cemetery at Bloodmoor Hill, Carlton Colville, Suffolk*, Cambridge 2009, 385–426, at 424–6.

[11] G. Speake, *A Saxon Bed Burial on Swallowcliffe Down*, London 1989; R. S. Baker, 'On the Discovery of Anglo-Saxon Remains at Desborough, Northamptonshire', *Archaeologia* 45, 1880, 466–71.

[12] K. Penn, *Norwich Southern Bypass, part 2: Anglo-Saxon Cemetery at Harford Farm, Caistor St Edmund*, Gressenhall 2000; and *The Anglo-Saxon Cemetery at Shrubland Hall Quarry, Coddenham, Suffolk*, Bury St Edmunds 2011.

family and household. This is a point worth emphasizing because both anthropological characterization of Anglo-Saxon kinship and social analysis of early Anglo-Saxon cemeteries have tended to play down the significance of the descent group even, in the latter case, when the groupings identified as family or household plots are archaeologically visible only because they have been used preferentially over several generations.[13] In addressing the cemetery evidence in this way there is perhaps a need to think in a more nuanced way about the dynamics of social reproduction and identity.

There are a few so-called deviant burials within the cemetery, including a possible execution victim. Following Andrew Reynolds,[14] we might interpret the presence of such a grave in a community cemetery rather than at a dedicated execution site as indicating a community where customary sanction rather than formal judicial authority operated. This would be interesting in the light of the role claimed for *emporia* in the rise of kingdoms and state structures. In particular, it may imply that even if the exchange activity focused on seventh-century Ipswich was regulated or taxed on behalf of a regional elite such oversight may not necessarily or universally have encompassed judicial authority.

To summarize, then, there is evidence at Buttermarket for social differentiation both within and between households and lineages or families, and for a balance between community identity (as implied by a single common burial ground) and the autonomy of household or kindred. It may also be possible to infer that the community, or elements within it, enjoyed a degree of judicial autonomy. The suggestion of some social competition in funerary practice between lineages reinforces the impression of segmentation and autonomy, and implies that this place had a permanence and integrity which made it the appropriate arena, and its inhabitants the appropriate audience, for such symbolic discourse.

The settlement at Ipswich was a new phenomenon of the earlier seventh century, although one which very probably developed in response to an intensification of pre-existing inter-regional exchange contacts focused on the head of the Orwell estuary.[15] It served to channel exchange with the Continent and the benefits in revenue, prestige and authority accruing from this, and it seems unlikely that it could have been established, functioned and developed without paramount sanction, although whether this amounted to more than the extraction of tolls and an understanding that the place was under royal protection remains open to question. It can be argued that the immediate property and economic interests were most likely vested in the magnates or magnate lineages able to extract and

---

[13] As examples, see L. Lancaster, 'Kinship in Anglo-Saxon Society', *British Journal of Sociology* 9, 1958, 230–250, 359–377; N. Stoodley, *The Spindle and the Spear. A Critical Enquiry into the Construction and Meaning of Gender in the Anglo-Saxon Burial Rite*, Oxford 1999, 126–35; D. Sayer, 'Death and the Family: Developing Generational Chronologies', *Journal of Social Archaeology* vol. 10, 2010, 59–91.

[14] A. Reynolds, *Anglo-Saxon Deviant Burial Customs*, Oxford 2009.

[15] Scull, 'Ipswich: Development and Contexts', 312; *Early Medieval Cemeteries*, 315–16.

redeploy landed surplus on the scale necessary to make long-distance bulk trade viable, and who constituted the market for elite and luxury imports. The day-to-day implementation, though, would have rested with officers, agents, middlemen and labourers.

Both socially and physically, therefore, the community burying at Buttermarket may be seen as an agglomeration of establishments and households, each a part of, or linked to, a discrete network of estates through which the surplus from extensive or multiple holdings could be redistributed or redeployed. Good candidates for the centres of such estates in the contemporary hinterland of Ipswich have been identified archaeologically at Coddenham and Barham in the Gipping valley.[16] Such 'productive' sites have been interpreted as inland *emporia* or periodic fairs. In these cases, though, the surface finds of elite metalwork and coinage present a material culture signature that is wholly different from that of the trading settlement at Ipswich, and both are more plausibly interpreted as centres of aristocratic consumption in the seventh and early eighth centuries: places where the material coming in through Ipswich ended up, fuelling the lifestyle that was one of the motors of elite social and political dynamics. At Coddenham, archaeology has demonstrated the existence of buildings, and part of a cemetery in use at the same time as Buttermarket has been excavated.[17] This includes aristocratic burials, with imported grave goods, of a status not seen at Ipswich: the difference in character between the two settlements at this time is thus reinforced by the differences in status and identity between their leading inhabitants.

We may envisage that each establishment at Ipswich would have a permanent complement, which might be augmented during the summer months when trading took place and which would embody the full range of skills needed to maintain household and buildings and to manage commodities and exchange. Some of those buried at Buttermarket may have been agents, dependants or retainers of the magnates buried at Coddenham. The settlement would also see a temporary population increase from elsewhere during the trading season. It is not impossible, in principle, that continental magnates, or their agents or middlemen, may have maintained permanent establishments here.

Some graves at Buttermarket contained assemblages or items of continental origin. For the most part the material culture types, their use, and other elements of burial practice sit happily within the range known from southern England at this time. However, some elements in a minority of burials express, more or less forcibly, continental identities or affiliations. This is seen at its strongest in a small number of graves with continental material culture assemblages or material culture types.

The clearest example is grave 1306, a continental assemblage which may be dated to the period AD 630/40–660/70. It was a coffined burial with a broad heavy

[16] S. E. West, *A Corpus of Anglo-Saxon Material from Suffolk*, Ipswich 1998; J. Newman, 'Exceptional Finds, Exceptional Sites? Barham and Coddenham, Suffolk', in *Money and Markets*, ed. Pestell and Ulmschneider, 97–109.

[17] Penn, *The Anglo-Saxon Cemetery*.

seax, a knife, a composite belt set, two spearheads, a shield, and two palm cups deposited in a wooden box. The seax and its sheath, belt set, shield boss and one spearhead are all continental types. The belt set finds it best parallels in examples from northern France, notably Armentières, and the shield boss appears to be a rare type otherwise unknown in England and represented on the continent by a few examples from the lower Rhineland and the Netherlands. It is highly probable that this is the burial of an individual from the Continent, probably from Frankish territory. There may of course be other explanations: ownership of imports need not denote a foreigner, and this may be a local buried with items acquired through exchange contacts or someone who had travelled to the Continent. Any such alternative interpretation, though, still requires an explanation of why there should be so strong and deliberate an expression of continental identity or affiliation in burial. Two further male graves (2297 and 3871), datable to the period AD 610/20–640/50, have continental belt sets and are also good candidates for burials of individuals from the Continent. Grave 2962, a female burial, included in an otherwise insular assemblage a chatelaine component of continental inspiration if not continental origin.[18]

There are also other aspects of burial at Buttermarket that are uncommon in contemporary England and may be best explained with reference to continental practice. One is burial in log coffins or dug-out coffins, something which is very rare in contemporary (seventh-century) East Anglia but is a widespread if minority practice on the contemporary continent from Switzerland to the Netherlands, Belgium and northern France. The other such feature is the provision of structures and linings in graves. Ten graves at Buttermarket had elaborate revetments and structures, including grave covers. Only two of these would be considered true chamber graves according to the archaeological criteria applied to the Merovingian-period continent, but both the complexity and frequency of structures and linings are unusual in south-east England and might be explained as a response to, or emulation of, the use of wooden structures and chambers in contemporary continental burial-practice, as can be seen in contemporary cemeteries in Belgium and in the Netherlands.[19]

Expressions of identity in burial at Buttermarket are multi-faceted and layered, and 'foreign' elements are only one part of a much more complex picture. Where such indications may be identified in the burial assemblages they are expressed through elements which represent the investment of portable wealth and which most emphatically symbolize gender-identity and associated social roles. They therefore symbolize a link (though not an exclusive one) between continental contacts and/or cultural affiliation and the position and identity of some higher

---

[18] Dating of, and comparanda for, these material culture items are discussed in detail in Scull, *Early Medieval Cemeteries*, 238–56.

[19] These elements of burial practice and their continental comparanda are discussed in detail in Scull, *Early Medieval Cemeteries*, 271–7.

status individuals or groups. This can be discerned at two levels within the small number of graves concerned: those that may be convincingly interpreted as the burials of individuals from the Continent, and those where the burial of individual pieces suggests some degree of cultural emulation or assertion of affiliation. Without seeking to draw precise individual parallels, or to identify specific graves as representing specific continental traditions, such circumstances might also explain other elements of burial-practice at Buttermarket which are uncommon in England: log-coffins or dug-out containers, and the frequent provision of substantial and elaborate structural features in the grave such as chambers, revetted wooden linings and grave-covers.

There is no reason to doubt that the majority of the population buried at Buttermarket was local, but a minority of furnished burials are either those of individuals from the Continent or express elements of identity or affiliation that look towards the Merovingian Continent. A larger number of burials, though again a minority of the excavated sample, have features that may be explained as adoptions or adaptations of aspects of burial practice on the other side of the North Sea and the Channel. This is best explained as a complex response by local groups and individuals to a range of cultural models and exemplars, accessible through the direct overseas exchange contacts focused on the settlement at Ipswich, with the probability that in some cases, as with grave 1306, we are seeing direct expression of continental identity. In this respect the diversity of burial practice at Buttermarket and the complexity and ambiguity of cultural expression may be taken as characteristic of a population of whom a significant proportion would have been directly engaged in the undertaking, mediation or control of overseas trade. By their nature as *foci* of long-distance exchange the seventh-century *emporia* would have been places of enhanced cultural interaction. Cognitive and cultural transactions arise from commercial contact, creating an environment in which the renegotiation of roles and identities – including the claim to a continental affiliation – might carry social and economic advantages, and in which other cognitive and cultural models were readily accessible.

The seventh-century community and settlement at Ipswich needs to be seen on its own terms, and should not be conflated with the rather different Ipswich of the eighth century and later. It included or accommodated people from the Continent, and the burial evidence suggests that some segments of the insular population were developing identities linked to but distinct from those of the immediate south-east Suffolk hinterland, looking to continental societies and cultural practices. In defining their identity in part by looking outwards towards the Merovingian Continent we must conclude that they consciously considered themselves socially and culturally, as well as economically, part of a wider Channel and North Sea world in ways and to an extent that were not true of communities further inland or places directly tied to the agrarian economy.

This should not necessarily come as a surprise. There is clear evidence from archaeology and textual sources for enduring and developing contacts around and across the North Sea and the Channel from the early fifth century and, by the later seventh century (at least in some latinate and ecclesiastical circles), a sense of shared ancestral identity with the inhabitants of the North Sea coastal areas of the Netherlands and Germany.[20] The similarities in material culture and burial practice that accord with the conventional narrative of migration from the North Sea coastal areas of what are now the Netherlands, Germany and Denmark are too well established to be discussed further here.[21] Both anthropological understanding of migration processes and recent archaeological studies confirm that this should not be viewed as a one-off event, but the outcome of a longer-term process that established and renewed contacts around and across the North Sea from the first half of the fifth century.[22] Hayo Vierck and John Hines have elucidated the part that cultural contacts between Eastern England and Scandinavia played in the emergence of insular material culture identities from second half of the fifth century.[23] Archaeological and numismatic evidence for burgeoning ties with the Frankish Continent and (at a remove) with the Mediterranean world in the sixth century includes strong indications that people from England settled in areas of northern France.[24] This is entirely consistent with the references in Procopius' *De Bello Gothico* which make it clear that Britain, though it may have been at the limit of Byzantine knowledge, was not isolated *terra incognita* in the sixth century, and that it figured in the political calculations of Merovingian monarchs.[25] The marriage of the Frankish princess Bertha and Æthelberht of Kent, which helped pave the

---

[20] See notes 21–25 below; H. Vierck, 'Zum Fernverkehr über See im 6. Jahrhundert angesichts angelsächsische Fibelsätze in Thüringen', in *Goldbrakteaten aus Sievern*, ed. K. Hauck, Munich 1970, 355–96; *Bede's Ecclesiastical History of the English People*, ed. B. Colgrave and R. A. B. Mynors, Oxford 1969, v. 9.

[21] See, for example, J. M. Kemble, 'On Mortuary Urns found at Stade-on-the-Elbe, and Other Parts of North Germany, now in the Museum of the Historical Society of Hanover', *Archaeologia* 36, 1855, 270–83; H.-W. Böhme, 'Das Ende der Römerherrschaft in Britannien und die Angelsächsische Besiedlung Englands im 5 Jahrhundert', *Jahrbuch des Römische-Germanischen Zentralmuseums Mainz* 33, 1986, 469–574; J. N. L. Myres, *The English Settlements*, Oxford 1986; J. Hines, 'Philology, Archaeology and the *adventus Saxonum vel Anglorum*', in *Britain 400–600: Language and History*, ed. A. Bammesberger and A. Wollmann, Heidelburg 1990, 17–36, and his essay in this volume.

[22] See, for example, D. Anthony, 'Migration in Archaeology: the Baby and the Bathwater', *American Anthropologist* 92.4, 1990, 894–914; S. Burmeister, 'Ursachen und Verlauf von Migrationen – Anregung für die Untersuchung prähistorischer Wanderungen', *Studien zur Sachsenforschung* 11, 1998, 19–41; C. J. Scull,, 'Approaches to Material Culture and Social Dynamics in the Migration Period of Eastern England', in *Europe between Late Antiquity and the Middle Ages: Recent Archaeological and Historical Research in Western and Southern Europe*, ed. J. Bintliffe and H. Hamerow, Oxford 1995, 71–83, at 75–79; C. M. Hills and S. Lucy, *The Anglo-Saxon Cemetery at Spong Hill, North Elmham*, volume 9, Cambridge, forthcoming.

[23] H. Vierck, 'Some Leading Types of the Anglian Province of Culture, Fifth to Seventh Century AD, with their Overseas Connections', BLitt thesis, University of Oxford, 1966; J. Hines, *The Scandinavian Character of Anglian England in the Pre-Viking Period*, Oxford 1984, and his essay in this volume.

[24] M. G. Welch, 'Contacts across the Channel between the Fifth and Seventh Centuries: a Review of the Evidence', *Studien zur Sachsenforschung* 7, 261–9.

[25] F. M. Stenton, *Anglo-Saxon England*, 3rd edn, Oxford 1971, 4–8.

way for the Augustinian mission, is unlikely to have taken place in a social and political vacuum, and links between East Anglia and Frankish Gaul saw Sigebehrt exiled there and Felix become his first bishop of the East Angles.[26] Ipswich's position in the seventh century developed from a complex and contingent web of existing regional and inter-regional contacts.

Loveluck and Tys have argued for the distinctive character and identity of coastal communities in the seventh to tenth centuries.[27] The cemetery evidence from Ipswich accords with this general proposition, and raises questions as to the diversity of otherwise unrecorded local identities and groupings that were subsumed with the extensive lordship of the regional kingdom, and the degrees of autonomy that might be enjoyed by such special-purpose settlements. It also serves to make the point that specific vectors of contact and configurations of identity were subject to change, and that such dynamism is itself a characteristic of coastal societies in the longer term.[28] The social character of the Ipswich settlement in the seventh century, and the identities expressed there in burial, may be characterized as responses to new circumstances brought about by the expansion and intensification of overseas contacts, a corresponding shift in the balance of socially embedded and commercial exchange, and the focus on a specific place. Interestingly, there is some evidence for an earlier local response to external contacts under the different conditions of the middle to later sixth century. At the cemetery at Hadleigh Road, Ipswich, which may plausibly be interpreted as that of an earlier community benefitting from socially-embedded long-distance contacts directed via the Orwell estuary, aspects of female burial may indicate a sense of specific local identity. In this case, though, the distinction lies in the way insular dress accessories were deployed in furnished burial, suggesting a sense of differentiation rooted firmly in insular identities rather than looking to a broader North Sea cultural milieu.[29]

From the late seventh or the early eighth century the settlement at Ipswich was radically transformed. The increase in area and population from c.AD 700 was accompanied by an intensification and diversification of craft production and economic activity, including the large-scale production and distribution of Ipswich ware. By the middle of the eighth century it is realistic to suggest that the greatly expanded settlement was linked to its insular hinterlands through markets with a significant element of monetary exchange. The evidence of coinage and imported pottery is that from the eighth century Ipswich's overseas trade contacts were

[26] *Bede's Ecclesiastical History*, iii. 18.
[27] C. Loveluck and D. Tys, 'Coastal Societies, Exchange and Identity along the Channel and Southern North Sea Shores of Europe, AD 600–1000', *Journal of Maritime Archaeology* 1, 2006, 140–69.
[28] B. Cunliffe, *Facing the Ocean – the Atlantic and Its Peoples*, Oxford 2001.
[29] Specifically, the high incidence of great square-headed brooches but the absence of other characteristic Anglian dress-accessories such as cruciform brooches and clasps. See Scull, *Early Medieval Cemeteries*, 312, 317; S. E. West, *A Corpus of Anglo-Saxon Material from Suffolk*, Ipswich 1998, 52–67, 275, figs. 58–95; J. Hines, *A New Corpus of Anglo-Saxon Great Square-Headed Brooches*, Woodbridge 1997, 304.

directed towards the Rhineland, Flanders and northern France.[30] This is consistent with the clearest expressions of foreign cultural identity at the Buttermarket cemetery but it is possible to argue that both the nature and focus of the contacts channelled through Ipswich in the eighth and ninth centuries differed from those of the seventh century, with a shift from socially and politically embedded links with northern France and Flanders to increasingly commercial contact on a larger scale with Rhineland via the Rhine mouths and the *emporia* at Domburg and then Dorestad. It may even be possible to seek in the broader economic and ideological tensions generated by territorial conflict between Frankish and Frisian rulers a context for contrasting mortuary vocabularies at Buttermarket, and in the fluctuations and eventual resolution of these conflicts a context for the expansion of the Ipswich settlement.[31]

The scale of expansion and the comprehensive re-configuration of social and physical space at Ipswich argue that this was planned and instigated by a central authority. It seems highly likely that this was a royal initiative, intended to regulate and exploit commercial activity on a new scale, and it is not implausible that it marks a watershed between a relatively light-touch extraction of dues and more structured oversight and taxation. The Buttermarket cemetery went out of use in the reign of Aldwulf (AD 663–713) and the remodelling of Ipswich may be attributed to him or possibly to his successor Ælfwald (AD 713–749). Interestingly, it is during the reign of Aldwulf that the wealthy female burial at Boss Hall gives us evidence for a high-status establishment close to Ipswich that might be a candidate for the seat of elite authority or control.[32]

The scale and nature of change also implies some social and economic realignment within the settlement population. It may be possible to infer a change in the social character and make-up of the settlement, perhaps with a greater proportion primarily involved in manufacture and with a lessening of magnate influence under royal oversight. It might even be argued that this in turn could bring about corresponding changes in perceptions of identity and affiliation as royal authority focused jurisdictional and social bonds, and as a larger permanent population with a greater element of craft manufacture looked more to local place than to foreign horizons. It is, however, extremely difficult to assess how things might or might not have changed in this respect. Aspects of identity and community are less clearly visible in the archaeology of the eighth and ninth centuries than in that of the seventh. This is partly because we still lack synthetic analysis

---

[30] K. Wade, 'Ipswich', in *The Rebirth of Towns in the West AD 700–1050*, ed. R. Hodges and B. Hobley, London 1988, 93–100, at 96–97; C. Coutts, *Pottery and the Emporia: Imported Pottery in Middle Saxon England with Particular Reference to Ipswich*, PhD thesis, University of Sheffield, 1991.

[31] Scull, *Early Medieval Cemeteries*, 318–19.

[32] The suggestion that Buttermarket grave 1306 is that of a royal official is implausible: see Scull, 'Foreign Identities' 86, *contra* D. Hinton, *Gold and Gilt, Pots and Pins: Possessions and People in Medieval Britain*, Oxford 2005, 75, and R. Hodges, 'Fifty Years after Dunning: Reflections on Emporia, Their Origins and Development', in *Studies in Early Medieval Coinage 1: Two Decades of Discovery*, ed. T. Abramson, Woodbridge 2008, 113–18, at 115.

and publication of excavations in Ipswich, and partly because changes in burial practice, and in particular the abandonment of formal furnished burial, mean that we cannot compare like with like. English Heritage is currently supporting work to consolidate and make accessible the Ipswich excavation archive preparatory to an expert synthesis of the town's archaeology. It is to be hoped that a definitive analysis of coins from Middle Saxon Ipswich, and a re-assessment of the imported pottery which draws upon the significant advances in understanding of contemporary continental ceramic traditions, will allow a more nuanced understanding of Ipswich's overseas trade, and that an understanding of settlement and craft activity, and material culture usage, will allow conclusions to be drawn about the social character and identity of the eighth-century community to complement or contrast our understanding of its seventh-century predecessor. It is, however, already clear that the Ipswich settlement of the seventh century differed in scale and character from its eighth-century successor. Ipswich of the eighth and ninth centuries has long been clearly understood as a major trading place of the thriving North Sea commercial network, but our evidence suggests that some inhabitants of its seventh-century precursor may have had even stronger outward-looking social links to the extent that they defined elements of their cultural identity through contacts across and around the Channel and North Sea.

— Chapter 12 —

IMPORTS OR IMMIGRANTS? REASSESSING SCANDINAVIAN METALWORK IN LATE ANGLO-SAXON EAST ANGLIA

Tim Pestell

UNDERSTANDING the issue of Scandinavian immigration and settlement in England has frequently been articulated in relatively straightforward terms, drawing upon two principal sources of evidence, namely existing historical sources and place-names.[1] But, was such Scandinavian character the result of their elite settling down with those women and children camp-followers that some contemporary sources noted?[2] Was it from taking English brides? Or was there an undocumented secondary mass migration following this initial conquest? As Lesley Abrams and David Parsons have pointed out, the lack of relevant historical sources in the late ninth and early tenth centuries has left scholars with 'an especially blank canvas on which to sketch out their hypotheses about settlement and society in Anglo-Scandinavian England'.[3]

However, in the last twenty years, a fundamental shift has occurred in the amount of new archaeological evidence that has a bearing upon the debate. As an example, rescue excavations have provided us with a far clearer understanding of the origins of England's urban centres and have tended to stress the role of Scandinavian settlers in stimulating trade in cities such as York, Lincoln and Norwich. More dramatically, there has been a boom in the number of archaeo-

---

[1] See for instance, F. M. Stenton, *Anglo-Saxon England*, 3rd edn, Oxford 1971, 254–7, and 'The Danish Settlement of Eastern England', *Transactions of the Royal Historical Society* 4th ser. 24, 1942, 1–24; P. H. Sawyer, *Kings and Vikings*, London 1982, 100, and for an overall summary D. Hadley, *The Vikings in England Settlement, Society and Culture*, Manchester 2006, 2–9.

[2] Thus the Anglo-Saxon Chronicle *s.a.* 893 records the storming of a fortification at Benfleet by English forces, during which the Vikings' women and children were seized, including their leader Hæsten's wife and two sons (D. Whitelock (ed), *English Historical Documents* I, 2nd edn, London 1979 (hereafter *EHD*), no. 1, 203.

[3] L. Abrams and D. Parsons, 'Place-Names and the History of Scandinavian Settlement in England', in *Land, Sea and Home*, ed. J. Hines, A. Lane and M. Redknap, Society for Medieval Archaeology Monograph 20, Leeds 2004, 379–431.

logical artefacts discovered through metal-detecting. Due to the discovery of these finds in random searching and with their detailed recording under the voluntary Portable Antiquities Scheme (hereafter PAS) only fifteen years old, these finds remain problematic to assess.

Nevertheless, these metal-detecting finds also have enormous potential. I wish to use this article as an opportunity to explore some aspects of this, not least as East Anglia has assumed an importance in wider debates over Viking settlement in Britain. This is largely because East Anglia's archaeologists were at the forefront of liaising with metal-detector users and established the mechanisms for the successful reporting of finds subsequently embodied in the PAS. As a result, Norfolk and Suffolk not only have records of metal-detected finds dating back over thirty years, they remain among the most prolific places in the UK for the discovery of metalwork.[4]

It is therefore perhaps unsurprising that one of the first scholars arguing for the presence of Scandinavian settlers based on finds of metalwork, the late Sue Margeson, worked in East Anglia. In two publications in 1996 and 1997, she outlined her belief that 'artefacts of the ninth and tenth centuries are the key to understanding the viking settlement of Norfolk'.[5] This contradicted Tom Williamson's earlier assertion that 'there is no documentary evidence to suggest a large-scale peasant immigration, and in Norfolk, as elsewhere in England, archaeological evidence for such a folk-movement is meagre'. He argued instead that Scandinavian artefacts found locally 'need indicate nothing more than trade with Scandinavia, or the presence of a Danish elite and the consequent prevalence of Danish taste'.[6] As the number of Scandinavian-style finds has continued to grow in England especially, so too has the influence of culture-historical arguments. In 2001 Kevin Leahy and Caroline Paterson considered such finds from Lincolnshire, a county producing a very similar range of metal-detected finds to Norfolk. They saw the majority of objects as 'cheap, mass-produced, copper-alloy artefacts of everyday usage and, with many pertaining to female adornment, they corroborate the notion of peasant-farmer settlers ... a major Scandinavian presence in Lincolnshire is undeniable'.[7] Most recently, similar conclusions have been drawn

---

[4] Thus Norfolk yields about 35–40 per cent of all UK portable antiquities and 20 per cent of all cases of Treasure reported under the 1996 Treasure Act; Norfolk recorded 'a relatively low total' of 17,700 finds in 2010–11 (A. Rogerson and S. Ashley, 'A Selection of Finds from Norfolk Recorded in 2011 and Earlier', *Norfolk Archaeology* 46 Pt.ii, 2011, 248–62) and Suffolk 4,034 in 2008 (*Portable Antiquities and Treasure Annual Report 2008*, London 2010, 26–7).

[5] S. M. Margeson, 'Viking Settlement in Norfolk: A Study of New Evidence' in *A Festival of Norfolk Archaeology*, ed. S. Margeson, B. Ayers and S. Heywood, Norwich 1996, 47–57 at 56. See also S. M. Margeson, *The Vikings in Norfolk*, Norwich 1997.

[6] T. Williamson, *The Origins of Norfolk*, Manchester 1993, 107.

[7] K. Leahy and C. Paterson, 'New Light on the Viking Presence in Lincolnshire: The Artefactual Evidence', in *Vikings and the Danelaw. Select Papers from the Proceedings of the Thirteenth Viking Congress, Nottingham and York, 21–30 August 1997*, ed. J. Graham-Campbell, R. Hall, J. Jesch and D. N. Parsons, Oxford 2001, 181–202 at 199.

PLATE 1 Carolingian metalwork of ninth- and tenth-century date from Norfolk, probably all horse-fittings. Found at (L-R) West Rudham, Great Dunham and Kilverstone (© Norwich Castle Museum and Art Gallery).

in Jane Kershaw's work on brooches, albeit adopting ideas of agency in the use of material culture to help shape social and cultural identities.[8]

As a museum curator seeing many Scandinavian finds emerging through the PAS, it might be too easy to look no further than metalwork and follow this simple correlation of brooches indeed equalling immigrant settlers, as first expounded by Margeson. However, despite Viking raids, there were also continuous trading contacts with both the Continent and Scandinavia, and on this basis caution is needed in the way we interpret material objects. For instance, Carolingian metalwork of the ninth and tenth centuries has often been viewed in the context of Viking *spolia*, brought with them after raiding on the Continent.[9] There are a number of high-quality examples from Norfolk (Plate 1), which may or may not have arrived through Scandinavian agency. However, Carolingian coinage was influential in Anglo-Saxon numismatic design, while the numbers of ecclesiastics with German names in early tenth-century England reminds us of the ongoing, peaceful, contacts with the Continent that there were at this time.[10] Similarly,

[8] J. Kershaw, 'Culture and Gender in the Danelaw: Scandinavian and Anglo-Scandinavian Brooches, 850–1050', 2 vols, unpublished DPhil thesis, University of Oxford, 2010, 37–47.

[9] For an overview of Carolingian metalwork, E. Wamers (ed.), *Die Macht des Silbers Karolingische Schatze im Norden*, Regensburg 2005. For a discussion of the English-found material, G. Thomas, 'Carolingian Culture in the North Sea World: Rethinking the Cultural Dynamics of Personal Adornment in Viking-Age England', *European Journal of Archaeology* (forthcoming).

[10] For Carolingian moneyers, P. Grierson and M. A. Blackburn, *Medieval European Coinage I: The Early Middle Ages*, Cambridge 1986, 320. For German ecclesiastics in England, D. Whitelock,

Ohthere and Wulfstan's appearance at King Alfred of Wessex's court, as traders rather than as raiders, reflects maintained commercial contacts with the Scandinavian world.[11] The discovery of a rare eighth-century Late Vendel style forerunner of a Scandinavian 'tortoise' brooch at Great Dunham likewise provides a reminder that Scandinavian material could end up in Norfolk as a result of pre-Viking Age North Sea trade.[12]

To what extent, therefore, may 'Viking' forms of metalwork be said to evidence the immigration and settlement of Scandinavians? I want to explore a selection of metalwork types that have been said to show Scandinavian influence, and examine the implications of their discovery, not only for assessing their place in an East Anglian context and its role in the North Sea world, but to show this may apply more widely to England.

DRESS FITTINGS AND JEWELLERY

Perhaps inevitably, items of jewellery have been most frequently examined for the influence or presence of Scandinavians in England. They were in everyday use, and their casual loss seems to provide a representative indication of what had been worn by society in life. The boom in metal-detecting has allowed the recording of a large number, and several studies have now been undertaken into specific object-types. For example, a characteristically 'Scandinavian' dress fitting is the trefoil brooch. Ultimately derived from Carolingian metalwork mounts used on sword baldrics (Figure 1a), in Scandinavian hands they became adapted into brooches worn by women and then copied, creating a new brooch type that was widely adopted and which came to employ a variety of decorative motifs.[13] A number of such Scandinavian-made brooches have been found in England, including examples from Colton and Hindringham in Norfolk (Figure 1b).[14] Of the seventy-four trefoil brooches catalogued in Kershaw's recent study, the largest number (47 or 63.5%) came from Norfolk, but interestingly, just three from Suffolk.[15] By far the most

'Some Anglo-Saxon Bishops of London', Chambers Memorial Lecture 4 May 1974, reprinted in D. Whitelock (ed.), *History, Law and Literature in 10th–11th Century England*, London 1980, 3–34 at 20. For a more general assessment of the links, J. L. Nelson, 'England and the Continent in the Ninth Century: I, Ends and Beginnings', *Transactions of the Royal Historical Society* 6th ser. 12, 2001, 1–21.

[11] M. J. Swanton, *Anglo-Saxon Prose*, London 1975, 32–7.
[12] A. Rogerson and S. Ashley, 'A Selection of Finds from Norfolk Recorded between 2006 and 2008', *Norfolk Archaeology* 45 pt. iii, 2008, 428–41, at 438–40, and fig. 7 no. 38.
[13] For a corpus of trefoil brooches see B. Maixner, *Die gegossenen kleeblattförmigen Fibeln der Wikingerzeit aus Skandinavien*, Universitätsforschungen zur Prähistorischen Archäologie 116, Bonn 2005.
[14] That from Colton is now in Norwich Castle Museum (hereafter NCM), accession 1993.201. The Hindringham brooch is from site 25997 on Norfolk's Historic Environment Record (hereafter HER).
[15] Kershaw, *Culture and Gender in the Danelaw*, cat. nos. 354–427. See also idem, 'Culture and Gender in the Danelaw: Scandinavian and Anglo-Scandinavian Brooches', *Viking and Medieval Scandinavia* 5, 2009, 295–325 at 314–15.

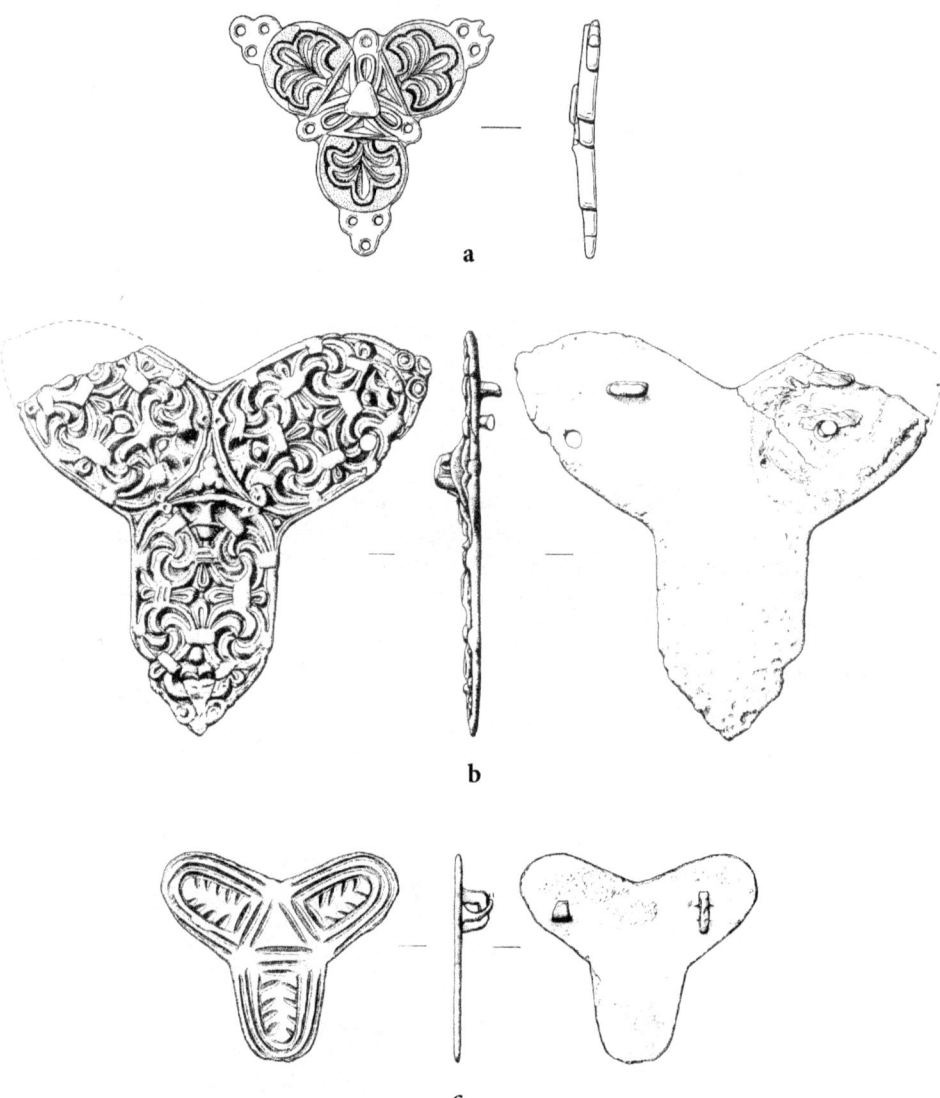

FIGURE 1 Trefoil mounts and brooches. (a) Carolingian mount from Great Barton, Suffolk (reproduced by kind permission of Suffolk County Council Archaeological Service); (b) Scandinavian trefoil brooch from Colton, Norfolk (© Norwich Castle Museum and Art Gallery); (c) trefoil brooch from Hindringham (© Norfolk County Council Historic Environment Service and David Gurney). All at 1:2.

commonly found are those whose 'English' pin arrangement shows they are of insular manufacture using a 'fir-tree' pattern derived ultimately from heavily-debased acanthus ornament (Figure 1c). It is therefore an open question as to whether such brooches represent their fashionable adoption by a local population rather than craftworkers providing jewellery for immigrants.

The obvious point that arises is one of social identity and what was being signalled in the wearing of jewellery. While there are many other examples of perfectly good Scandinavian metalwork forms being imported, for instance items bearing Borre ring-chain motifs (as with a strap-end from Congham and a peculiar animal-headed fitting from North Creake in Norfolk: Plate 2a and b),[16] it is in the replication of particular designs that we observe an almost standardized motif that might have represented a more structured range of meanings. Perhaps nowhere is this clearer than in East Anglia when considering two particular brooch types, the so-called 'Borre knotwork' and 'backward-facing beast' brooches (Plate 2c and d). Knotwork brooches have engendered much discussion considering whether they are of Insular or Scandinavian origin, Leahy and Paterson arguing that a recent find from Kalmergården in Denmark suggests the latter.[17] The beast brooches appear to have a ninth-century origin, quite possibly in East Anglia, and form a series analogous with the knotwork brooches, being of flat, cast, disc-shape virtually identical in size and pin arrangement.[18] Most striking is the sheer number regularly found: Kershaw noted 234 knotwork brooches, representing 47 per cent of her total English corpus of Scandinavian and Anglo-Scandinavian brooches, a dramatic increase on the 'over 50' that Leahy and Paterson recorded in 2001 (Map 1).[19]

More important, the relative proportions are dramatic within East Anglia, Cattermole noting eighty-one beast-type brooches in 2005, among 200 Anglo-Scandinavian brooches from Norfolk alone.[20] This is clearly significant. Not only was there a great variety of motifs and brooch types available in ninth- and tenth-century England, but Viking contacts brought a large number of new patterns. There was, therefore, a wide variety of types and designs of dress fittings which the occupants of eastern England could choose to wear. Despite this, two formulaic disc brooch types came to hold especial popularity. Moreover, thanks to Cattermole's

[16] Now NCM nos. 2009.113 and 1994.11.
[17] For discussion of the origin, D. M. Wilson, 'A Bronze Mounting from Oxshott Wood, Surrey', *Antiquaries Journal* 36, 1956, 70–1; V. I. Evison, 'A Group of Late Saxon Brooches', *Antiquaries' Journal* 37, 1957, 220–2; D. M. Wilson, 'The Borre Style in the British Isles', in *Minjar og Menntir*, ed. B. Vilhjálmsson, Reykjavík 1976, 502–9; I. Jansson, 'Kleine Rundspangen', in *Birka II:1. Systematische Analysen der Gräberfunde*, ed. G. Arwidsson, Stockholm 1984, 58–74; C. Richardson, 'The Borre Style in the British Isles and Ireland. A Reassessment', unpublished MLitt thesis, University of Newcastle 1993.
[18] Evison, 'A Group of Late Saxon Brooches', 220–2; B. J. Philp, 'Anglo-Saxon Animal Brooches from Burgh Castle and Brantham', *Proceedings of the Suffolk Institute of Archaeology* 27, 1958, 191–2; N. Smedley and E. Owles, 'Some Anglo-Saxon Animal Brooches', *Proceedings of the Suffolk Institute of Archaeology* 30, 1965, 166–74.
[19] Kershaw, *Culture and Gender*, 186; Leahy and Paterson, 'New Light', 196.
[20] A. M. Cattermole, 'Beasts and Brooches: A Study of Anglo-Scandinavian Disc Brooches Found in Norfolk', unpublished MA dissertation, University of Leicester 2005, 30.

PLATE 2 (a) Borre-style strap-end from Congham; (b) animal-headed terminal fitting from North Creake; (c) Borre-knotwork brooch from Anglia TV site, Norwich; (d) backward-facing beast brooch from Burgh Castle, Norfolk (all © Norwich Castle Museum and Art Gallery).

MAP 1 The distribution of (a) Borre knotwork and (b) 'backward-facing beast'-type brooches in England.

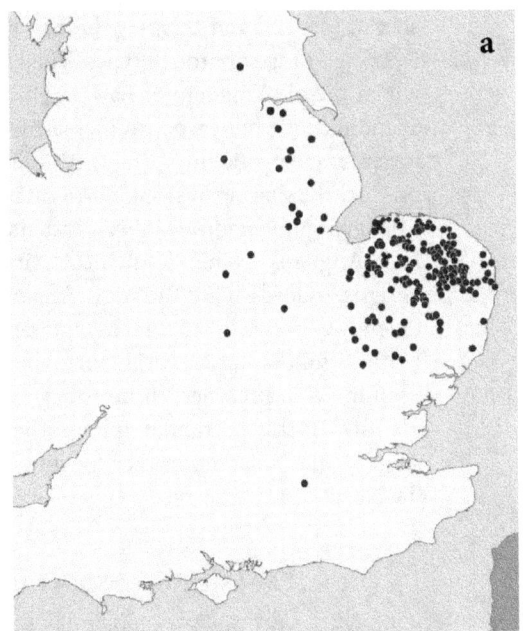

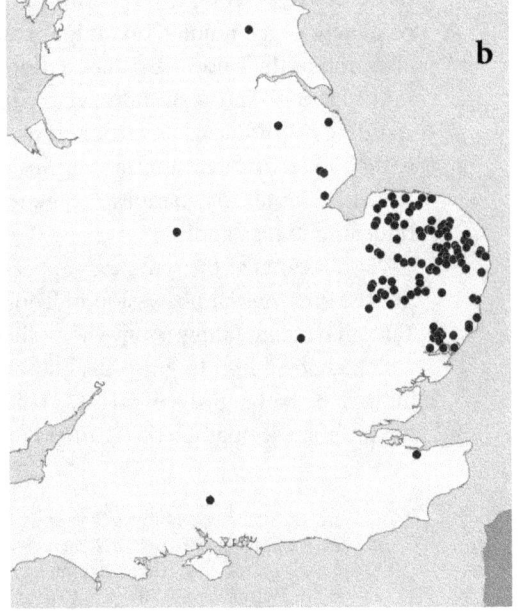

recent research on these types, a number of model-identical examples are emerging that illustrates their multiple production.[21]

This cannot be explained simply in terms of the cheapness of mass manufacture; the use of models and moulds could allow a wide variety of designs to be similarly replicated. Rather, a consumer-led choice is implied, indicating a deeper structuring to brooch-wearing habits, which particularly favoured two designs. Arguably, their use indicated a shared social identity. If this was a consequence of an underlying political orientation or ideology within East Anglia resulting from social change or tension, it would be interesting to date these brooches more closely. For Stanley West, the highly standardized design suggests the beast brooches 'must surely belong to a restricted time scale'.[22] Unfortunately, the few stratified examples of beast or knotwork brooches known usually cannot be dated any more closely than the tenth century, and some examples even appear to have been deposited (or re-deposited) in eleventh-century contexts.[23] Nevertheless, their *floruit* seems to belong to the tenth century, probably from the first half, their designs maturing from ninth-century antecedents.

Exactly what such brooches might have been viewed by their wearers as representing, and why, is less clear. Dress has historically formed a ready expression of

---

[21] Ibid., 8–10.
[22] S. E. West, *A Corpus of Anglo-Saxon Material from Suffolk*, East Anglian Archaeology 84, Bury St Edmunds 1998, 322.
[23] Cattermole, 'Beasts, Knots and Brooches', 13. For three examples from York, from tenth-century deposits, A. S. Mainman and N. S. H. Rogers, *Craft, Industry and Everyday Life*, The Archaeology of York 17/14, York 2000, 2571–2.

shared identity and this may be one reason for such widespread wearing of a restricted range of brooch types. Their appearance coincides with that period in which the old kingdom of East Anglia was finding a new identity as an Anglo-Scandinavian political entity, increasingly subject to external West Saxon political hegemony. Negotiating such identities in times of tension might be more likely to produce the sharing of group norms in reaction, and these brooches may represent a better argument for the impact and integration of Scandinavian immigrants with East Anglians, rather than locals simply adopting Scandinavian metalwork designs. Indeed, might this 'East-Anglo-Scandinavian' population have been sufficiently cohesive to offer a resistant identity to the West Saxon advance? We may, I think, follow up this argument about social identity, and in particular the Scandinavian presence, by considering artefact types associated with religious identity. In this particular sphere, the dominance of relevant finds from East Anglia reflects its importance for understanding Scandinavian migration across the North Sea.

THOR'S HAMMERS AND RELIGIOUS ITEMS

If brooches are more nuanced in their use by immigrants or locals, Thor's hammers represent a divergent form of jewellery, symbolic of belief. In being a resolutely pagan amulet, one might reasonably expect its wearer to be directing attention to their non-Christian outlook.[24] According to Snorri Sturlusson, Thor ranked second in the Scandinavian pantheon after Odin but was 'the most outstanding of [the Æsir] ... strongest of all the gods and men'.[25] He was associated with thunder and lightning: among his possessions was *Mjöllnir*, his hammer with which he smites his enemies and benefits from its convenient quality of always returning to his hand.[26]

Two aspects of the hammer's appearance as an amulet stand out. First, it was not the only special possession of Thor. Snorri records that Thor had two goats, Tanngnjost and Tanngrísnir, who pulled his chariot; he had a pair of iron gloves which enabled him to grasp his hammer; and perhaps most important to Thor himself, he had a 'girdle of might', a belt by which he doubled his strength. Unlike the prolific use of amuletic signifiers in Roman cultic practice, we do not appear

---

[24] E. Wamers, 'Hammer und Kreuz Typologische Aspekte einer nordeuropäischen Amulettsitte aus der Zeit des Glaubenswechsels', in *Rom und Byzanz im Norden I*, ed. M. Müller-Wille, Mainz 1999, 83–107; A.-S. Gräslund, 'Thor's Hammers, Pendant Crosses and Other Amulets', in E. Roesdahl and D. M. Wilson, *From Viking to Crusader: The Scandinavians and Europe 800–1200*, 22nd Council of Europe Exhibition, Copenhagen 1992, 190–1; J. Staecker, 'The Cross Goes North: Christian Symbols and Scandinavian Women', in *The Cross Goes North: Processes of Conversion in Northern Europe AD 300–1300*, ed. M. O. H. Carver, York 2003, 463–82; and S. W. Nordeide, 'Thor's Hammer in Norway. A Symbol of Reaction against the Christian Cross?' in *Old Norse Religion in Long-Term Perspectives Origins, Changes and Interactions*, ed. A. Andrén, K. Jennbert and C. Raudvere, Lund 2006, 218–23.

[25] A. Faulkes, *Snorri Sturluson Edda*, London 1987, 22.

[26] Ibid., 22–3, 97.

to have any belt, glove or goat amulets from the Scandinavian world.[27] At some point, therefore, the hammer appears to have become prominent both as a symbolic representation of Thor, and as an amulet invoking his protection. Second, while Snorri describes Odin as 'All-father, for he is father of all gods', so far as material evidence is concerned, there are few apparent amulets that were in use to celebrate Odin: this is despite his attributes of the hat and cloak of his wandering, his single eye or, equally visible as an amulet weapon, his spear Gungnir.[28] That invocations were made to him earlier is demonstrated by the eighth-century human skull fragment found at Ribe, Denmark, with a runic inscription including Odin's name.[29] It seems possible, therefore, that there may have been a shift in the culted popularity of Odin towards that of Thor.[30]

Indeed, the appearance of hammer amulets seems to coincide with the Viking Age, examples occurring in Scandinavian graves in the ninth and tenth centuries, for instance an iron neck-band with four small hammers, found in Ullna, in Uppland, Sweden.[31] This is also the period in which hammers are first seen at the aristocratic manor site of Tissø in Denmark, where a special fenced enclosure has been interpreted as a heathen cult area.[32] A mid- to late-ninth century date has also been suggested for an amber Thor's hammer found in a hearth from the earliest phase of a site at Temple Bar West in Dublin.[33]

---

[27] That there were some amulets like wheels (as also found in the Roman world) is true but despite having a wide distribution, their use seems to have been infrequent. For a discussion of these various types of amulet see B. Jensen, *Viking Age Amulets in Scandinavia and Western Europe*, BAR International Ser. 2169, Oxford 2010.

[28] Faulkes, *Edda*, 21, 54 and 69. Our knowledge of these mythological origins is extremely dependent upon Snorri's writings and Snorri seems to have expanded Odin's role in his writings, at times contradicting some of the surviving eddic sources in his accounts: A. Orchard, *Cassell's Dictionary of Norse Myth and Legend*, London 1997, 273. There are a few possible representations of Odin and weapon amulets, for example in J. Graham-Campbell, *Viking Artefacts A Select Catalogue*, London 1980, nos. 516 and 519, dating from the Middle Viking Period (late ninth–second half of tenth century). That other amulets certainly were made is shown by the amber leg of ninth- to eleventh-century date from Hedeby, one of a well known but restricted type: Roesdahl and Wilson, *From Viking to Crusader*, cat. no. 189. However, such items never seem to have gained widespread currency.

[29] Roesdahl and Wilson, *From Viking to Crusader*, cat. no. 178.

[30] A move perhaps witnessed by the prevalence across the northern world in the sixth and seventh centuries of horn-helmeted depictions that have often been take to represent Woden. These seem to disappear in the early ninth century. For a discussion and references see T. Pestell, 'Paganism in Early Anglo-Saxon East Anglia' in T. A. Heslop, E. A. Mellings and M. Thöfner (eds), *Icon? Art and Belief in Norfolk from Prehistory to the Present*, Woodbridge, 2012. For Thor's cult and its particular strength in Norway and the western Norse colonies, E. O. G. Turville-Petre, *Myth and Religion in the North*, London 1964, 75–105.

[31] Roesdahl and Wilson, *From Viking to Crusader*, cat. no. 179.

[32] In that site's Phase III: L. Jørgensen, 'Manor and Market at Lake Tissø in the Sixth to Eleventh Centuries: The Danish "Productive" Sites', in *Markets in Early Medieval Europe. Trading and 'Productive' Sites, 650–850*, ed. T. Pestell and K. Ulmschneider, Macclesfield 2003, 175–207 at 196–7.

[33] C. F. Johnson, 'Amber, Jet and Jet-like Materials from Excavations at Temple Bar West, Dublin' (unpublished stratigraphic report on excavations at Temple Bar West Dublin 2, Licence No. 96E245, vol. 4, 843).

As the corpus of Thor's hammers demonstrates, these amulets come in many different shapes and sizes, ranging from boat-shaped heads, to more rectangular forms, and with varying degrees of elaboration.[34] Of these, the most frequently illustrated in popular (and indeed scholarly) accounts of the Vikings tend to be elaborate hammers like the filigree-decorated silver example from Skåne in Sweden, or the punch-stamped hammer from Rømersdal in Denmark.[35] The majority are actually quite plain or simple.

Examples found in Norfolk illustrate this wide variety of types, ranging from an electrum hammer with punch-stamp decoration found at South Lopham, to an example from Babingley that could be considered questionable in its identification, so crude is its shape (Plate 3). Other Norfolk hammers include plain silver examples, a crisp lead piece that might arguably be a model, and an exceptional boat-shaped silver hammer, its head inlaid with gold filigree. Others like a lead example found near Attleborough do not appear especially hammer-like, and yet have perfectly good parallels with the Scandinavian material.[36] The fundamentally 'Viking' nature of the English hammers is most eloquently illustrated by the example found in Grave 511 at Repton. Buried at the neck of a man aged 35–40, the hammer was apparently deposited while Repton was being used as the base of the Viking Great Army which overwintered there in 873/4.[37] Another three or four have been found at the postulated overwintering site used by the Vikings at Torksey in 872/3.[38] In other words, there is a clear late ninth-century date and pagan context for the appearance of Thor's hammers in England.

The corpus of English hammers remains small, but some preliminary observations are possible. First, the materials utilized appear to be predominantly silver and lead. This is perhaps curious. The vast majority are made of silver, suggesting the special nature of such amulets, yet the use of lead would seem to undermine this. Furthermore, they do not generally seem to have used copper-alloy, the most logical choice for manufacture, considering its near all-pervasive use for most other items of jewellery in this period. The use of lead might be rationalized if such pieces were considered models. That from Thetford may indeed be so; it has a delicate

---

[34] F. W. Huber, 'Die wikingerzeitlichen Thorshammeranhänger zwischen Patreksfjord und Smolensk', unpublished MA dissertation, Christian-Albrechts-Universität, Kiel 2004.

[35] Roesdahl and Wilson, *From Viking to Crusader*, cat. nos. 180 and 181.

[36] For an illustration of the Attleborough hammer, sold since its discovery and whose whereabouts is now unknown, see T. Pestell, *Landscapes of Monastic Foundation. The Establishment of Religious Houses in East Anglia c.650–1200*, Woodbridge 2004, 71–2 and pl. 4. For parallels to this simple hammer see Huber, *Die wikingerzeitlichen Thorshammeranhänger*, Typ 4, Nr. 03; Typ. 3 Nr. 09 and Typ 2, Nrs. 6, 13, 14 and 16.

[37] M. Biddle and B. Kjølbye-Biddle, 'Repton and the "Great Heathen Army", 873–4', in *Vikings and the Danelaw*, ed. Graham-Campbell et al, 45–96, at 60–5. Further evidence of ritual or votive incorporations within the grave are a jackdaw's humerus and an adult wild boar's tusk that had been placed between the thighs of the man. For a (speculative) discussion of this particular grave's meaning, see also Jensen, *Viking Age Amulets*, 175–7.

[38] M. A. Blackburn, 'The Viking Winter Camp at Torksey, 872–3', in M. A. Blackburn, *Viking Coinage and Currency in the British Isles*, British Numismatic Society Special Publication 7, London 2011, 221–64 at 233.

SCANDINAVIAN METALWORK IN LATE ANGLO-SAXON EAST ANGLIA

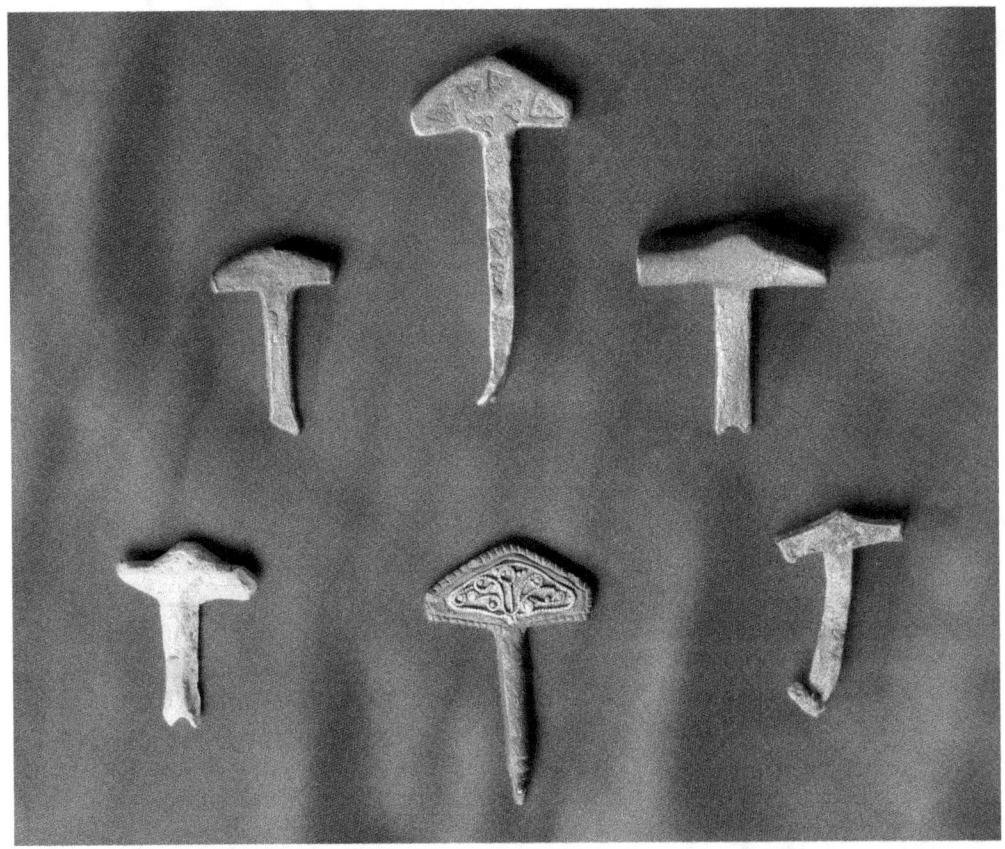

PLATE 3 A selection of Thor's hammer pendants from Norfolk (© Norwich Castle Museum and Art Gallery).

lead suspension loop that could surely never have survived long in everyday use. Recovered in excavations at St Nicholas' Street, this piece is so crisp in its execution and condition that it appears unlikely ever to have been used.[39] The Babingley example is so crude that it seems a real homemade effort, but it derives from a site yielding Late Anglo-Saxon material, suggesting it had indeed been worn. This point is made most forcefully for the Attleborough example. Not only was it found on a site producing other tenth-century items, but several of these were 'Scandinavian' in style, for instance a 'truncated spherical' Viking type weight, and a composite

---

[39] Curiously, the hammer was never published in the site excavation report (P. Andrews, 'Excavations at St Nicholas' Street, 1990, Site 1134', in P. Andrews and K. Penn, *Excavations in Thetford, North of the River, 1989–90* East Anglian Archaeology 87, Gressenhall 1999, 12–65). It was found by the present writer within the site archive, numbered smallfind 465. It derived from context *904* in Trench 2. It is accessioned as NCM L1994.1.465.

Borre-Jellinge-style brooch of Jansson's Type 1 A1.[40] More interesting, the site is on a green-edge, consonant with secondary, later, settlement, and thus perhaps the type of place an immigrant Scandinavian family might have been forced to settle, if colonizing an area marginal to already-established occupation centres.[41]

The distribution of known hammers in England is also perfectly consistent with their use within the Danelaw areas, meaning that they were probably not buried or dropped just by Vikings on campaign (as at Repton and Torksey), but by subsequent settlers both male and female. More difficult is to know how late these hammers continued in use in England. Given that they were worn as amulets around the neck, Thor's hammers indicate an outward display of non-Christian belief and, by implication, for the wearer to have been ethnically Scandinavian. Such outward displays would have been particularly sensitive to the subsequent and apparently fairly rapid Christianization of the Danelaw. By contrast, the longer timeframe taken to Christianize Scandinavia is presumably why artefacts such as the celebrated dual hammer and cross mould of the second half of the tenth century from Trendgården in Jutland were used.[42]

The decoration of the Great Witchingham Thor's hammer is of potential significance, as its gold filigree inlay is matched by another, said to have come from Norfolk, but which is known only from an artefact price-guide.[43] Silver hammers with gold insets are very rare within the overall corpus. Assuming the provenance to be reliable, it seems not unreasonable to suggest that the two pieces derive from the same workshop, and one that was possibly based in Norfolk. The implication is not simply that such idolatrous objects were being made in East Anglia, but that there was a large enough pagan clientele to commission them. The corpus is also of interest given the way that Thor's hammers have been interpreted by some. Staecker, for instance, has declared that 'it seems obvious that ... [hammers] must be regarded as a symbol of pagan reaction against Christianity'. He goes on to suggest that hammer pendants are typical of the tenth century in Scandinavia and help to show the influence of Christianity in the early part of that century through their adoption as a reaction to crucifixes and crosses.[44] While likely, the evidence of Tissø, Repton and Dublin shows that such pendants have a perfectly acceptable presence in the Viking culture of the ninth century. Although their increasing popularity may owe something to contact and familiarity with Christianity, this is clearly not the whole story.[45]

---

[40] I. Jansson, 'Kleine Rundspangen', in *Systematische Analysen der Gräberfunde* Birka II:1, ed. G. Ardwidsson, Stockholm 1984, 58–74.
[41] Pestell, *Landscapes*, 70–1.
[42] Roesdahl and Wilson, *From Viking to Crusader*, cat. no. 175.
[43] N. Mills, *Saxon and Viking Artefacts*, Witham 2001, 73 no. V198.
[44] Staecker, 'The Cross Goes North', 468.
[45] For the use of the Thor's hammer in a Christian context note its presence in the hand of a figure in a boat on the frieze fragment from Gosforth, Cumbria, which also shows Thor fishing: R. N. Bailey and R. Cramp, *Corpus of Anglo-Saxon Stone Sculpture II: Cumberland, Westmorland and Lancashire North-of-the-Sands*, Oxford 1988, 108–9 and R. N. Bailey, *Viking Age Sculpture in Northern England*, London 1980, 131–2.

PLATE 4 'Rider and valkyrie' mounts from (a) Bylaugh and (b) the Peterborough area; (c) a possible Viking votive figure from Colkirk. (a) and (c) © Norwich Castle Museum and Art Gallery; (b) © The Trustees of the British Museum).

Nor are Thor's hammers the only form of Scandinavian metalwork drawing upon non-Christian mythological origins to be found in England. At least five, and possibly six, figurative mounts or appliqués have now been recorded. Three, from Donington in south Lincolnshire, Exton in Rutland and Wickham Market in Suffolk, depict figures with trailing skirt-like costumes bearing shields, the Suffolk example with a sword, the others a spear.[46] They take their best parallels from ninth-century female figures from the Scandinavian world, usually identified as Valkyries, Odin's handmaidens who allotted victory on the battlefield, and chose slain warriors to join him in Valhalla.[47] Another three mounts or brooches, from Bylaugh in Norfolk, the Peterborough area and Winterton, Lincolnshire, have similar shield-bearing figures facing a horse with a mounted female warrior (Plate 4a and b).[48] The scene is exactly paralleled in Scandinavian imagery, the standing figure usually holding out a drinking horn or beaker as a sign of welcome, and again, generally interpreted as a

[46] For the Donington figure see Leahy and Paterson, 'New Light', 192 and pl. 10.1. The Wickham Market example is published in *Treasure Annual Report 2002*, 54–6, no 43.
[47] For a discussion of these figural objects see Jensen, *Viking Age Amulets*, 32–7.
[48] Now NCM 1990.199 and British Museum, P&E 1988, 4–7, 1. Interestingly, a silver-gilt brooch with this scene is also pictured in Mills, *Viking Artefacts*, 56 no. V120, sadly without provenance and not therefore certainly British. The Winterton example was apparently found but not recorded in the 1980s or 1990s and was recently sold by Timeline Auctions (15 March 2013, Lot 868).

Valkyrie.[49] One other figure, possibly male and surviving only as a head and torso, comes from Colkirk in Norfolk and is possibly mythological in origin (Plate 4c).[50]

Two features of this material stand out. First, with ten Thor's hammers from Norfolk alone, and five of the seven figural pieces from East Anglia or the Fens, the region is once again central to our understanding of Viking settlement.[51] Second, and more significant, such finds demonstrate the array of material relating to pre-Christian Scandinavian beliefs that were circulating in eastern England. Such fundamentally different religious views were unlikely to be adopted so readily by native populations compared with, for example, brooches. Such differences therefore provide a more reliable indicator of a foreign presence. We can continue this theme by examining the evidence for Viking economic exchange.

SILVER, INGOTS AND THE BULLION ECONOMY

The Vikings were, famously, attracted to England and the Continent by loot, but sought this wealth for a homeland without a monetized economy. Instead, their 'display' or 'status' economy based on gift-exchange evolved during the Viking Age to one using bullion as a medium for exchange.[52] In the course of adapting to English and Continental economic practices, the Vikings' encounters with coinage led them to undertake 'pecking', nicking the flat surface of coins with the point of a knife to see how soft, and therefore how pure, the silver was. Similar testing was performed by bending coins. Pecking appears to have started in England, beginning c.875, coincident with Alfred's coinage reforms that saw the reinstatement of a fine silver coinage.[53] Perhaps of more importance is the appearance in a Scandinavian

---

[49] For three examples from Denmark, P. V. Petersen, 'Valkyrier i Ribe', *By, marsk og geest* 5, 1992, 41–6. For another example, said to be a pendant, from Tissø, Denmark, see Jørgensen, 'Manor and Market', 197 and fig. 15.19.

[50] NCM 1997.86.5.

[51] Jensen, *Viking Age Amulets*, 37, comments that England is 'somewhat over-represented' with these figurative amulets in comparison with Scandinavia. While this may indicate their preferential use in a Christian land, perhaps as an active symbol of non-Christian belief as argued for the Thor's hammers, the number of finds is small and might simply reflect better recording of metal-detected stray finds in East Anglia.

[52] There has been much discussion over these economic models. For recent summaries and discussion, M. Gaimster, 'Money and Media in Viking Age Scandinavia', in *Social Approaches to Viking Studies*, ed. R. Samson, Glasgow 1991, 113–22; D. Skre, 'Dealing with Silver: Economic Agency in South-Western Scandinavia AD 600–1000', in *Means of Exchange. Dealing with Silver in the Viking Age* ed. D. Skre, Kaupang Excavation Project Publication Series 2, Aarhus 2007, 343–55; G. Williams, 'Silver Economies, Monetisation and Society: An Overview', in *Silver Economies, Monetisation and Society in Scandinavia, AD 800–1100*, ed. J. Graham-Campbell, S. M. Sindbæk and G. Williams, Aarhus 2011, 337–72; J. Graham-Campbell, 'Reflections on Silver Economy in the Viking Age', in *Silver Economy in the Viking Age*, ed. J. Graham-Campbell and G. Williams, Walnut Creek 2007, 215–23.

[53] M. Archibald, 'Pecking and Bending: The Evidence of British Finds', in K. Jonsson and B. Malmer (eds), *Proceedings of the Sigtuna Symposium on Viking Age Coinage, 1–4 June 1989* CNS Nova Series 6, London 1990, 11–24, superseded by her 'Testing' in J. Graham-Campbell, *The Cuerdale Hoard and Related Viking-Age Silver and Gold from Britain and Ireland in the British Museum*, British Museum Research Publication 185, London 2011, 51–64, esp. 62–4.

context of silver in the form of ingots and cut-up jewellery ('hacksilver'), evidence of economic exchange being undertaken based on the bullion value of the metal. Its emergence in the mid-ninth century at, for instance, Kaupang in Norway and arguably at Hedeby, was to be mirrored shortly afterwards in England as finds from Torksey seem to demonstrate.[54] The discovery of an increasing number of Viking hoards shows that bullion became an important medium for exchange in the northern Danelaw and especially the Hiberno-Norse sphere of influence well into the tenth century. The most famous expression of this Viking wealth in bullion is the Cuerdale hoard, deposited c.905–10 on the banks of the river Ribble in Lancashire, and which contained at least 8,500 pieces of silver, including over 7,500 coins, ingots and complete and cut-up jewellery, weighing over 40 kg.[55]

PLATE 5 Penny of King Æthelred of East Anglia (© Norwich Castle Museum and Art Gallery).

By contrast, the southern Danelaw appears to have seen far greater continuity in the production and use of coinage, even in its darkest days. In East Anglia for example, following Eadmund's death at the hands of the Vikings in 869, coinage of two English rulers in the kingdom, Æthelred and Oswald, was struck. These individuals, known only from their (exceptionally rare) coins (Plate 5), arguably acted as puppet rulers until Guthrum took up rule within East Anglia and minted coins in his own, baptismal, name of Æthelstan. Numismatic studies have also shown how the subsequent St Edmund memorial coinage was minted widely across the Danelaw, as were other coins imitating West Saxon designs and even weight standards.[56] The result of these different approaches is what has been described as the 'dual economy' in which both coinage and bullion were in circulation.[57] At issue

---

[54] J. Graham-Campbell, 'Silver Economies and their Ninth-Century Background', in *Silver Economies, Monetisation and Society in Scandinavia*, ed. Graham-Campbell *et al* 29–39 at 30–31; Blackburn, 'Viking Winter Camp at Torksey', 233–6.

[55] E. Hawkins, 'An Account of Coins and Treasure Found in Cuerdale', *Archaeological Journal* 4, 1847, 111–30. The non-numismatic material is comprehensively catalogued in Graham-Campbell, *The Cuerdale Hoard*.

[56] M. A. Blackburn and H. Pagan, 'The St Edmund Coinage in the Light of a Parcel from a Hoard of St Edmund Pennies', *British Numismatic Journal* 72, 2002, 1–14; M. A. Blackburn, 'Currency under the Vikings, Part I', reprinted in Blackburn, *Viking Coinage and Currency*, 2–31.

[57] M. A. Blackburn, 'Expansion and Control: Aspects of Anglo-Scandinavian Minting South of the Humber', in *Vikings and the Danelaw*, ed. Graham-Campbell *et al*, 125–42 at 134–5. See also J. Graham-Campbell, '"Silver Economies" and the Ninth-Century Background', in *Silver Economies, Monetisation and Society in Scandinavia, AD 800–1100*, ed. Graham-Campbell, Sindbæk and Williams, 29–40.

is the extent to which, and when, such a bullion economy existed in East Anglia, indicating Scandinavian economic practices. After all, large bullion deposits of the type known from Cuerdale, or more recently Silverdale, Huxley or the Vale of York hoards, have not been found in East Anglia. However, in recent years an increasing number of crudely-formed ingots of silver have been found.

One important caveat has first to be addressed. Dating an ingot as Viking Age is potentially problematic, especially if it was found in isolation. For example, a silver ingot from Ditchingham in Norfolk identified as of ninth- or tenth-century date in fact came from a field in which only one other find had been made – a sherd of Middle Anglo-Saxon Ipswich ware pottery.[58] In this case the stylistic attributes of the ingot seem to mark out its date: it had been shaped by a series of hammer blows forming a pattern of ridged parallel lines, known as 'transverse hammering', well attested on ingots from known Viking metalwork hoards whereas other hoards of Iron Age, Roman or Early Medieval date do not seem to exhibit this surface treatment.[59] Most problematic are those ingots with no such finishing but simply roughly cast. A silver ingot excavated from a fifth-century context in the Roman fort of Vindolanda looks (unsurprisingly) little different from many well dated Viking examples.[60] Despite this, as hoards show, 'the one period from which ingots are plentiful in Britain and Ireland is the late ninth and tenth centuries in the English Danelaw and Irish Sea littoral'.[61] Perhaps reassuringly, in the recent survey work undertaken at Rendlesham, Suffolk, a number of silver scraps associated with Anglo-Saxon settlement and possibly metalworking of seventh- to ninth-century date has not yielded ingots of the type more generally described as Viking. Rather, ingots seem most common in Viking Age hoards: but the caveat that they can and do occasionally appear in other datable contexts provides a caution.

If we accept that most of the ingots now being identified through the PAS do indeed date from the Viking Age, some interesting observations may be made. First, their distribution is far more widespread in England than that of bullion hoards, and broadly conforms to those areas that were part of the Danelaw (Map 2).[62] Single ingot finds, much like single coin finds, arguably help to show the normal circulation of silver and their loss while in everyday use. They therefore

---

[58] M. A. Blackburn and A. Rogerson, 'Two Viking Age Silver Ingots from Ditchingham and Hindringham, Norfolk: The First East Anglian Ingot Finds', *Medieval Archaeology* 37, 1993, 222–4.

[59] For instance, despite all the precious metal scrap and meltings recovered from the torc-rich site of Ken Hill, Snettisham, in Norfolk, none of the Iron Age bullion here could be mistaken for later Viking Age material. See R. R. Clarke, 'The Early Iron Age Treasure from Snettisham, Norfolk', *Proceedings of the Prehistoric Society* 20, 1955, 27–86.

[60] *Treasure Annual Report 2007*, 91 no. 153. Likewise, a gold bar from Brympton, Somerset, has been dated as possibly Iron Age on the basis of depletion gilding to the surface, a practice that also seems to have been undertaken at Snettisham in that period: *Treasure Annual Report 2008*, 78 no. 91.

[61] M. A. Blackburn and M. J. Bonser, 'A Viking Age Silver Ingot from near Easingwold, Yorks.', *Medieval Archaeology* 34, 1990, 149–50 at 149.

[62] Some outliers within West Saxon controlled areas may be anticipated given the peregrinations of the Viking armies.

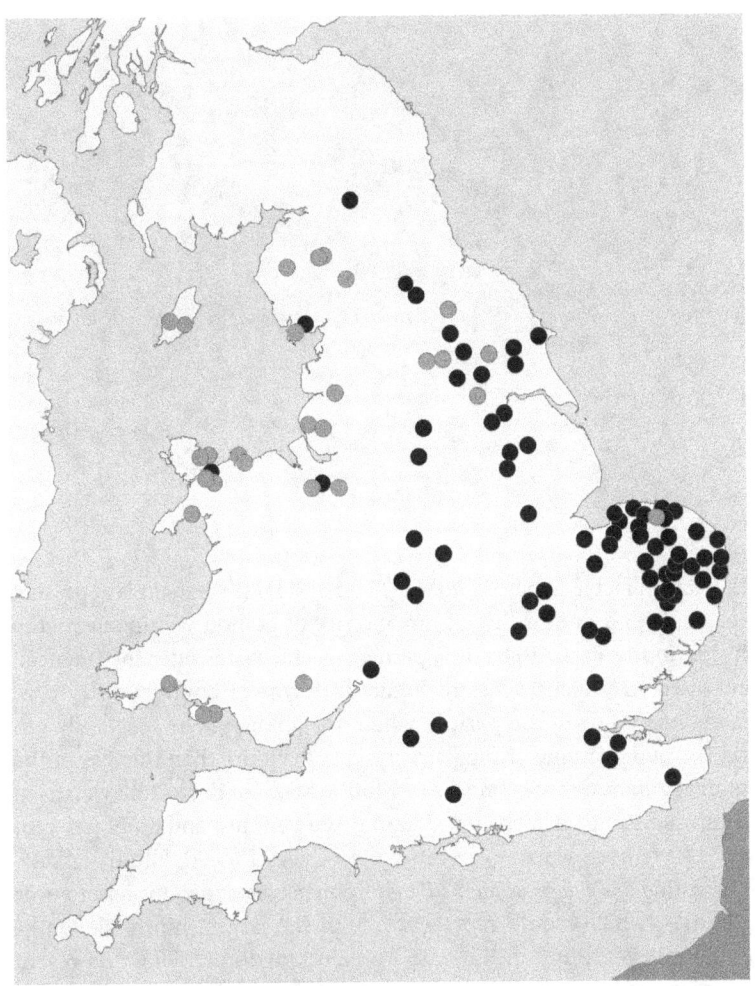

MAP 2 The distribution of Viking-type ingots in England and Wales based on data from the Portable Antiquities Scheme and Norfolk HER (dark dots). Viking bullion and ingot hoards are shown in light dots.

indicate the workings of the dual economy over far more of England than has hitherto been appreciated, and most especially within East Anglia.

Equally, it is clear that some hoarding of such bullion also occurred, countering the traditional view that hoards in the eastern regions were only of coin, as with the large Morley St Peter hoard of 883 pennies deposited c.924, or occasionally coins and jewellery.[63] At Hindringham in north Norfolk, a hoard of four silver ingots has now been recovered. The first ingot from the site, a long silver bar, was found in 1989, but it was only in 2002 that three more were identified from the site,

---

[63] R. R. Clarke and R. N. M. Dolley, 'The Morley St Peter Hoard', *Antiquity* 32, 1958, 100–03; T. H. McK. Clough, *Museums in East Anglia*, Sylloge of Coins of the British Isles 26, London 1980, 3–45.

PLATE 6 The Hindringham silver ingot hoard (© Norwich Castle Museum and Art Gallery).

indicating this was in fact a dispersed hoard (Plate 6).[64] Hindringham is at present an isolated example, but even if there is an absence of bullion within silver coin hoards at this period in East Anglia, it is perhaps useful to consider the financial wealth represented in the stray loss of ingots in terms of contemporary coin currency. Purse hoards from the period, while not unknown, are certainly not common and the bullion value of ingots represents far more than the loss of the odd coin. As an example, a recent find from Old Buckenham in Norfolk weighs in at 62.38 g, equivalent to over forty-four Viking Age pennies, and at 99 per cent purity, it would have been worth even more than that.[65] Indeed, Hindringham's four ingots, weighing 94.08 g or some 83.02 g of pure silver, are equivalent to over fifty-eight pennies, which would represent one of the largest ninth- or tenth-century coin hoards yet found in the East Anglian kingdom.[66] These represent serious losses of silver, and equally highlight the volume and value of silver that must have been circulating within the local economy.

Of equal interest is the number of gold ingots also being seen. It is clear that in this Late Anglo-Saxon period the economy was based fundamentally on the use of silver. Nevertheless, there is evidence for the use of gold in financial transactions both at a conceptual level and, as Blackburn has argued, probably through the production of a gold *mancus* coinage of highly restricted circulation.[67] A number of ingots have now been identified, stretching from Freshwater on the Isle of Wight

---

[64] *Treasure Annual Report 2002*, no. 37 and *Treasure Annual Report 2003*, no. 84. See also Blackburn and Rogerson, 'Two Viking Age Silver Ingots'. The ingots are now NCM 2004.25.1-4.
[65] *Treasure Annual Report 2005/6*, no. 229; now NCM 2006.993.
[66] After Morley St Peter stands a hoard of similar early tenth-century date from Brantham in Suffolk, found in 2003, which comprised ninety coins: *Treasure Annual Report 2003*, no. 390.
[67] M. A. Blackburn, 'Gold in England during the "Age of Silver" (Eighth–Eleventh Centuries)', in *Silver Economy in the Viking Age*, ed. Graham-Campbell and Williams, 55–98.

to Springthorpe in Lincolnshire. A particularly impressive example is the plain rough-cast gold ingot found at West Dereham in 2002.[68] We may never be able to prove that it is definitely of Viking Age date, although it is likely. At 58.2 g it represents by weight somewhere between eleven to fourteen Anglo-Saxon mancuses.[69] Perhaps the finest gold ingot yet found is that recovered from excavations at the Millennium Library site in Norwich. Sadly from an unstratified context, its elegant transverse hammering is suggestive of a Viking date.[70] Together, these hint at quite high values of bullion being in circulation, the West Dereham ingot being perhaps the equivalent of some 420 silver pennies.[71]

Perhaps the most interesting development is the very recent appreciation, first made in Norfolk, that there appear to be many copper-alloy ingots of Late Anglo-Saxon date. Lumps of bronze are common enough finds for metal-detector users and so the caveat expressed with the West Dereham gold ingot is especially pertinent here; context and treatment can be important. Yet when cast bronze ingots appear at sites like Bawsey in west Norfolk, best known for its aristocratic Middle Anglo-Saxon settlement, including an example with transverse hammering, the conclusion must be that these too are ingots in the image of bullion. Increasing numbers of similar finds are now known in East Anglia with examples from Wickham Skeith in Suffolk, Flitcham with Appleton, Keswick, Saham Toney, Scole and Wiveton in Norfolk, and they are joined by a growing number from elsewhere in England. Perhaps the most beguiling is that from Billingford in Norfolk. Displaying clear 'transverse hammering' on its surface, it was beaten from a second-century Roman sestertius coin of Faustina II or Lucilla, with *Luna Lucifera* the light bearer, still clearly visible at its centre (Plate 7). The extent to which copper-alloy ingots may have been part of a dual economy is uncertain. Possibly they were simply raw materials, but as Sindbæk has pointed out in discussing brass bar ingots from the Baltic, 'as material for recasting, bars are even less convenient than chips of scrap'. Such bars, he argues, are 'not just raw material; [they are] a tool facilitating exchange'.[72] Further research on the composition of the English ingots is now needed, but their appearance in such well shaped forms and appearing singly, rather than within obvious metalworking assemblages, makes it possible that they were

---

[68] *Treasure Annual Report 2002*, 49–50, no. 36 (now NCM 2004.44).
[69] The calculation is necessarily vague as the eight English mancuses known vary in weight between 3.34 and 4.80 g and in gold content between 83 per cent and 99 per cent pure gold; Blackburn, 'Gold in England', Appendix B; G. Williams and M. Cowell, 'Analysis of a Gold Mancus of Coenwulf of Mercia and Other Comparable Coins', *British Museum Technical Research Bulletin* 3, 2009, 31–6.
[70] NCM 2003.169.1
[71] Based on a mancus being the equivalent of some thirty silver pennies: Blackburn, 'Gold in England', 57–8.
[72] S. M. Sindbæk, 'An Object of Exchange. Brass Bars and the Routinization of Viking Age Long-Distance Exchange in the Baltic Area', *Offa* 58, 2001, 49–60. Although difficult to date on their own, one might note a bronze ingot from the Estonian fort at Rõuge, a site that has also yielded ten dirhams: A. Tvauri, *The Migration Period, Pre-Viking Age, and Viking Age in Estonia*, Estonian Archaeology 4, Tartu 2012, 230–1 and fig. 183.

PLATE 7 Bronze ingot from Billingford made from a refashioned Roman sestertius coin (© Norwich Castle Museum and Art Gallery).

indeed used as part of a three-tier bullion system of gold, silver and copper-alloy. As Blackburn noted when discussing various such copper-alloy ingots from Torksey, base Northumbrian stycas had been an accepted component of the Anglo-Saxon economy.[73]

An intriguing new possibility for silver used in financial transactions may be indicated by the discovery in recent years of a number of groups of silver pennies that have become fused together at high heat (Plate 8). Initial interpretations tended to suggest that they were the consequence of accidental mishaps. However, with the melting point of silver being 961.93 °C, the clumps demonstrate the very high temperatures required to fuse so many coins together by chance. Moreover, given the vast expansion in silver coinage output into the Middle Ages, if such fused pennies were simply the result of accidents, one would expect – all things being equal – that a correspondingly higher number should be of medieval date. They are not. Instead, the majority are tenth-century, with only a few earlier groups and a trickle of later ones (Table 1). Moreover, these later fused groups tend to be far larger, mostly of twenty coins or more, compared with the tenth-century groups typically of about two to nine coins. This suggests that their treatment in the tenth century differed. It seems possible, therefore, that the fusing of Anglo-Saxon pennies may represent something of a halfway house between a fully melted and cast ingot, and the carrying of smaller, loose 'purse hoards' of coins. Alternatively, a more complex (and destructive) method of analysis for testing silver quality was by cupellation (fire assay), in which coins were melted. Archibald has noted a

---

[73] As Blackburn noted when discussing copper-alloy ingots from Torksey, base Northumbrian stycas had been an accepted component of the Anglo-Saxon economy: Blackburn, 'Viking Winter Camp', 235–6. I hope to publish the results of metallurgical investigation into the Norfolk ingots in the near future.

PLATE 8 Fused silver pennies from Aylsham (left), Wymondham (top), Walsoken (bottom) and Barton Bendish (right) (© Norwich Castle Museum and Art Gallery).

TABLE 1 A provisional handlist of fused silver pennies, arranged chronologically (the start date for each dating bracket is used to position the grouping within the table).

Findspot	Date	No. coins	Weight (g)	Ref
Rendlesham, Suff	c.680–710	3	3.65	2010 T249
Tarrant Rushden, Dorset	c.840x852	3		TAR 2002 T20
Walpole St Peter, Norf	?c.848–51	4	1.23	NCM L2009.263.21
Aylsham, Norf	899x924	?9	7.15	TAR 2002 T204
Alfrison area, E Sussex	c.899–946	2	3.63	TAR 2007 T661
E Meon, Hamps	C9–12	7+		TAR 2006 T18
Little Chesterford, Essex	c.900	2	2.84	2010 T790
Wymondham, Norf	?939x?956	5+	4.21	TAR 2007 T685
Nr North Owersby, Lincs	c.965	4	4.90	Num Circ 1989, p. 255
Henley area, Oxon	980s	3	3.23	TAR 2007 T432
Beechamwell, Norf	c.991–997	2	2.465	TAR 2009 T31
Westfield, E. Sussex	c.991–997	16+ &bullion	17.09	2009 T122
Unprovenanced, 2 lumps	c.991–997	6+	10.28	York Coins, June 2011
Great Barton	978–1016	48+	79.48	Num Circ 1958,102-4
Unprovenanced	978–1016	5	3.86	eBay, May 2012
Bedale, N. Yorks	C10	2+		TAR 1998-9 No. 326
High Risby, Lincs	C10–12	2+ & bullion		2010 T688
Stalbridge, Dorset	?1089–92	4	3.70	TAR 2005 T342
Isley cum Langley, Leics	lC12–eC13	5	4.30	2010 T518
Huggate, E Yorks	c.1279	37	52.80	TAR 2006 T598
Willingate, Essex	Post-1353	20+	33.16	TAR 2005 T153
Market Rasen area, Lincs	?1420–50	?8		TAR 2002 T42
Bristol area	c.1648	24+		TTRCAR 1996-7 No. 32

Abbreviations used:
Num Circ   *The Numismatic Circular*
TAR   Treasure Annual Report
TTRCAR   Treasure Trove Reviewing Committee Annual Report

fragment of an Arabic dirham from the Cuerdale hoard 'partly melted in a crucible hence its deformed shape' and a penny of Edward the Elder, also in the British Museum, as possible evidence for this practice, commenting that 'this method of testing a sample of coins would normally leave no trace on the rest of the parcel'.[74] Such fused coin groups are still relatively rare, but it will be of interest to see whether future finds help to refine any favoured distribution chronologically or spatially, or if it helps provide clues to their functional use.[75]

Finally, if stray-find ingots mark out the wider Danelaw as utilizing bullion in much the same way as in Scandinavia and the Irish Sea province, so too does the increasing number of Arabic dirham coins now known to have been circulating in Viking Age England. Dirhams are well known in Scandinavian coin hoards where their presence, often in some numbers, attests to the penetration of the Russian river systems (in particular the Volga), primarily by Swedish adventurers.

There had long been links with the Arabic world, as the celebrated gift of an elephant named Abu l'Abbas by the Abbasid caliph Harun al-Rashid to Charlemagne in 802 showed.[76] Evidence of Anglo-Saxon contacts is far more sparse, although illustrated in the discovery of a handful of eighth-century gold *dinar* coins, for instance those from Wickhampton in Norfolk and Brandon in Suffolk, and most famously by the gold mancus of King Offa in which his name in Roman script is set within a blundered Arabic inscription, copied from a dinar of AH 157 (AD 773–4).[77] While mechanisms therefore existed for Arabic coins to reach England, it was only with the appearance of the Viking Great Army and settlers that the numbers of silver dirhams rose to an appreciable level.[78] A number have now been found in East Anglia through metal-detecting, and show the dissemination and use of this most foreign currency type within the Danelaw. Equally interesting, four Norfolk sites (Barton Bendish, Oxborough, Shipdham and

---

[74] Archibald, 'Testing', 54. The quotation about the dirham is taken from N. M. Lowick, 'The Kufic Coins from Cuerdale', *British Numismatic Journal* 46, 1976, 19–28 at 28.

[75] A fused group of coins and hacksilver has been recovered from Kaupang in Norway. Containing at least twelve fragmented coins, only two are identifiable, being Abbasid dirhams of 782/3 and 750–816. The lump appears to date to the second half of the ninth century or early tenth century. The small pieces of hacksilver present also help to show, along with similar single-find hacksilver fragments from stratified deposits of the first half of the ninth century on the site, that the practice was developing in Scandinavia in the ninth century: M. A. Blackburn, 'The Coin Finds', in *Means of Exchange*, ed. Skre, 29–74 at 32–4. Like that from Great Barton in Suffolk, it may be that this lump is simply an interrupted melt, but given the fused coins from elsewhere, we certainly need to look for the practice more widely.

[76] R. Hodges, 'Charlemagne's Elephant', in *Goodbye to the Vikings? Re-Reading Early Medieval Archaeology*, ed. R. Hodges, London 2006, 72–9; P. E. Dutton, *Charlemagne's Mustache and Other Cultural Clusters of a Dark Age*, New York and Basingstoke 2004, 189–90.

[77] L. Webster and J. Backhouse, *The Making of England Anglo-Saxon Art and Culture AD 600–900*, London 1991, cat. no. 148c. The Wickhampton coin, of 764/5, is now NCM 1990.202.2. The Brandon coin, of 784/5, is recorded on the online Corpus of Early Medieval Coins (hereafter EMC) as 2007.0235.

[78] R. Naismith, 'Islamic Coins from Early Medieval England', *Numismatic Chronicle* 165, 2005, 193–222.

Sparham) have yielded cut dirham fragments,[79] the presence of which at Torksey Blackburn compared to their common use as bullion on contemporary ninth-century Scandinavian sites like Kaupang.[80]

Hoard evidence suggests that dirhams first began to enter England in substantial numbers from the second half of the ninth century and continued into the early tenth. Indeed, the pattern of English finds is similar to that of Scandinavia, suggesting that until *c*.925 England was part of the same network connected with the caliphate via Scandinavia and Russia, but with a sharp decline in dirhams minted after *c*.910.[81] The presence of many dirhams in hoards that also contained hacksilver reinforces their nature as Viking bullion, and the fact that such hoards were deposited in Scotland and Ireland until *c*.950–70 reflects their continued participation in a Scandinavian economic sphere. This contrasts with the situation, revealed by coin hoards at least, from the southern Danelaw: Blackburn pointed out that St Edmund memorial issue coins demonstrate that by *c*.915 'there was an organised money system in the Danelaw, from which non-local coin was effectively excluded'.[82]

While the memorial issue had perhaps been replaced *c*.917 when the 'many people who had been under the rule of the Danes both in East Anglia and Essex submitted' to Edward the Elder (*Anglo-Saxon Chronicle* 'A' *s.a.* 917), the new East Anglian issues appear not to have had any genuine East Anglian moneyers named on them, and they continued to use the lighter Danelaw weight standard of coins. Indeed, Blackburn suggests Edward may never have truly established his authority in the kingdom.[83] Some turmoil is suggested in the region after his death, judging by three hoards that seem to have been buried at this time (Morley St Peter, *c*.924; Framlingham Earl, Norfolk, *c*.920–4; and Brantham, Suffolk, *c*.924).[84] We might recall that this is perhaps the same time the backward-facing beast and knotwork brooches come into vogue (above, p. 237). However, despite this non-West Saxon outlook, the hoards are all of English-only coinage, with no hacksilver. We therefore see an interesting contrast between silver hoards in southern and eastern England and that in the north, where bullion use as part of the 'dual economy' lived on into the middle of the tenth century. The conclusion would seem to be that eastern England witnessed a visibly intense period using Scandinavian forms of economic exchange in the late ninth and early tenth centuries that must have existed side by side with the production and use of an English tradition of coin production. The corollary is that there must have been an equally intense period of Scandinavian occupation and settlement to have generated this non-English usage.

---

[79] Barton Bendish (HER 17212) has yielded four fragments, Shipdham (HER 42644) and Oxborough (unlocated) two each and Sparham (EMC 2011.0010) one.
[80] Blackburn, 'Winter Camp', 229–30.
[81] Naismith, 'Islamic Coins', 198–202.
[82] Blackburn, 'Expansion and Control', 134.
[83] Ibid., 137–8.
[84] McK. Clough, *Museums in East Anglia*, Sylloge 26, 3–45; *Treasure Trove Reviewing Committee Annual Report 1994–5*, 11 no. 15 and *Treasure Trove Reviewing Committee Annual Report 1996–7*, 17 nos. 20 and 21; *Treasure Annual Report* 2003, 165, no. 390.

CONCLUSIONS

In our search for the material correlates of Viking activity and settlement, it has been argued that those items relating to deeper-seated cultural practices are the most reliable. Thus, items relating to religion and belief are both distinctive and least likely to have been adopted by the native, Christian, Anglo-Saxons. That most of those examples are known have been found in East Anglia provides support for their presence in the region, a picture emphasized when looking at the evidence for economic activity. It has been shown that East Anglia continued to mint coinage even at the height of Viking campaigning, during Eadmund's reign, and during the dark days of his successors Æthelred and Oswald. Despite this, there is good evidence for an active, if short-lived, bullion economy that is more usually associated with the hoarding activity seen in the north and north-west of England. Together, they provide a powerful indication of foreign, Viking, cultural practices at work, habits that were unlikely to be adopted by an indigenous population.

If ingots, dirhams and Thor's hammers soon made way for a politically-advantageous monetized Christian kingdom under Guthrum, issuing coins under his baptismal name Æthelstan,[85] arguably less susceptible to such quick change were dress codes and fashion. This initial core of Viking settlers inevitably maintained contacts with their Scandinavian homelands, ultimately giving the access to markets that encouraged economic development and the expansion of urban centres like Thetford and Norwich. It also allowed new stylistic developments in Scandinavian metalwork designs to transfer across the North Sea. Undoubtedly the English also adopted and absorbed some of these foreign influences. We have, after all, scraps of evidence like the tenth-century Old English letter containing the admonishment of an unknown author:

> *I tell thee also, brother Edward ... that you do wrong in abandoning the English practices which your fathers followed, and in loving the practices of heathen men who begrudge you life ... you despise your race and your ancestors, since in insult to them you dress in Danish fashion with bared necks...*[86]

Such bared necks were still sported by Duke William's Normans in the Bayeux Tapestry a century later, and it is hard not to think of some wayward teenage son coming home with the Early Medieval equivalent of a mohican. However, the ideas behind the use of ingots for trade or amulets of pagan belief were very clearly imported and relied on immigrants to use (and lose) them so widely. The rising number of finds, representing only those items lost by their owners, attest to the presence of a non-English population that surely also influenced the subsequent adoption and use of new styles of dress accessories.

---

[85] Blackburn, 'Expansion and Control', 135–6.
[86] *EHD* I, no. 232.

In conclusion, the Viking settlement first proposed by Margeson on the basis of metalwork is becoming clearer and allowing us to pose new questions about the nature of Anglo-Saxon society in that crucial period that saw the formation of the English state. Brooches, ingots or Thor's hammers may not, in themselves, help us to identify individual early Viking settlers. However, they do demonstrate the clear impact Viking forms of culture exerted in East Anglia, even while the West Saxon state was rolling back its political influence.

ACKNOWLEDGEMENTS

I would like to thank Lesley Abrams, James Graham-Campbell, John Hines, Andrew Rogerson and Gareth Williams for kindly reading draft versions of this paper and for making many helpful comments and suggestions. I should also like to thank Mark Morgan, Chris Mycock, Ester Oras, Linzi Simpson and Gabor Thomas for providing me with other references and information. Needless to say, any errors or misinterpretations are my responsibility alone. Mark Blackburn's legacy is clear from the references contained above, and his untimely death has left early medievalists with a large hole to fill. This paper is dedicated to his memory from one museum curator to another.

---

[79] Barton Bendish (HER 17212) has yielded four fragments, Shipdham (HER 42644) and Oxborough (unlocated) two each and Sparham (EMC 2011.0010) one.
[80] Blackburn, 'Winter Camp', 229–30.

— Chapter 13 —

STONE BUILDING IN ROMANESQUE EAST ANGLIA

Stephen Heywood

INTRODUCTION

The lack of freestone in East Anglia is an often quoted fact that is sometimes linked to the widespread use of round west towers on churches, which do not need large quantities of ashlar for corners. This assumption fails to recognize that the many other areas without freestone did not choose to build round towers and that East Anglia is remarkably close to the limestone belt and has an extensive coastline and network of inland waterways. This would have made the supply of stone relatively easy, as demonstrated by the Normans with shiploads arriving principally from the quarries at Caen and Barnack.[1] The marked lack of its use before the arrival of the Normans was not only for reasons of expense, as might be supposed, but because there was no particular need for stone in a region where all buildings since the departure of the Romans were of timber. This was owing to the fact that, following the successive waves of invasion from Scandinavia, East Anglia was essentially part of a North Sea centred community dominated by Scandinavia.[2] By the eleventh century, it was part of the Danish empire where the tradition and craft of building was based on timber.

TIMBER-FRAMED CHURCHES

The evidence of such buildings is naturally sparse owing to the organic nature of the material. Most evidence of timber buildings of the eleventh century is in the form of excavated post holes. However, there is one surviving timber church, dated by dendrochronology to between 1063 and 1100, in eastern England at Greensted-

---

[1] The Barnack quarries were out of use by the sixteenth century.
[2] The issue of migration is the subject of much debate. See S. Margeson, 'Viking Settlement in Norfolk: a Study of New Evidence', in *A Festival of Norfolk Archaeology*, ed. S. Margeson, B. Ayers and S. Heywood, Norfolk and Norwich Archaeological Society, 1996, 47–57. For a recent analysis on a wider scale: H. Härke, 'Anglo-Saxon Immigration and Ethnogenesis', *Medieval Archaeology* 55, 2011, 1–28. See also Chapters 1 and 12 in this book.

PLATE 1
Greensted-next-Ongar, Essex, church of St Andrew.

next-Ongar in Essex.[3] This consists of walls of upright logs split in halves and joined together with tongues that were jointed into a sill beam which was set in a trench. This has been replaced with brick plinths in recent times (Plate 1).

We learn from documentary sources that the cathedral of East Anglia was a mere timber chapel at Elmham[4] and that the shrine of St Edmund at Bury was a 'very large building constructed of wooden planks'.[5] From this alone it is highly unlikely that any parish church in East Anglia was built of stone before the arrival of the Normans.

Excavated evidence of eleventh-century timber churches in the region has been found at Thetford, Brandon, and at three sites in Norwich. The first of the Norwich churches was excavated on the site of the north-east bailey of the castle and a complete post-in-trench plan was uncovered with evidence of two earlier churches on the site. The most recent plan had a narrower flat-ended chancel as opposed to the earlier plans which had undifferentiated chancels.[6] At St Martin-at-Palace in Norwich the post holes and trenches of two late Anglo-Saxon timber churches were within the later medieval shell of the extant building. The excavation also revealed the characteristic late eleventh- or early twelfth-century striped foundations of the first masonry replacement building associated, in all probability, with the early

---

[3] See C. E. Hewett, *English Historic Carpentry*, Chichester 1980, 5–13.
[4] ... *in vico qui Elmham dicitur in sacello ligneo...* *The First Register of Norwich Cathedral Priory*, ed. H. W. Saunders, Norfolk Record Society 11, 1939, f. 1.
[5] *construxit per maximam miro ligneo tabulato ecclesiam*, Abbo of Fleury, 'Passio Sancti Eadmundi' in *Memorials of St Edmund's Abbey*, ed. Thomas Arnold, 3 vols, Rolls Series, 96, 1890-6, I, 19.
[6] B. Ayers, 'Excavations within the North-East Bailey of Norwich Castle, 1979', *East Anglian Archaeology* 28, 1985, 23–25.

PLATE 2 Urnes, Norway, stave church (Miriam Heywood).

medieval east wall with its long-and-short quoins.[7] Also close to the castle, another collection of post holes in a cemetery site was identified as being a church.[8] At Thetford, a small eleventh-century timber post-in-trench two-cell church was replaced with a stone church in the early twelfth century which was then enlarged to the west shortly afterwards.[9] At Brandon the most complete example of post

[7] O. Beazley, 'Excavations in St Martin-at-Palace Church, 1987', in O. Beazley and B. Ayers, 'Two Medieval Churches in Norfolk', *East Anglian Archaeology* 96, 2001, 1–63.

[8] E. Propescu, 'Norwich Castle: Excavations and Historical Survey, 1987–98. Part One: Anglo-Saxon to c.1345', *East Anglian Archaeology* 132, 2009, 135.

[9] C. Dallas, 'Excavations in Thetford by B. K. Davison between 1964 and 1970', *East Anglian Archaeology* 62, 1993, 79–94.

PLATE 3 Urnes church. Interlace on north nave wall (Miriam Heywood).

hole evidence of a timber church in the region was revealed.[10] It was constructed of posts and planks set in trenches. It consisted of a nave and narrower chancel and in addition a western porticus. There was possible evidence of an altar at the eastern end of the nave and opposing doorways into the nave. Very little excavation of the interior of churches has taken place in the region but it is highly probable that evidence of timber predecessors exists as the sites of parishes and their churches were well established by the eleventh century.[11]

A degree of evidence comes from excavations in Scandinavia which reveal similar techniques of post-in-trench walls. At Lund the existence of three stave churches has been found through excavation – Santa Maria Minor excavated from 1911,[12] St Clemens partly excavated in 1932, and another unidentified church in Lund excavated in 1961.[13]

The surviving early twelfth-century church at Urnes, in Norway, is the only relatively unrestored stave church of the period (Plate 2). Its famous interlace decoration (Plate 3) carved into the external timber walls is found in numerous sites in East Anglia, mainly in miniature form on metalwork and jewellery. The main

[10] For Brandon, R. Carr, A. Tester and P. Murphy, 'Middle-Saxon Settlement at Staunch Meadow, Brandon', *Antiquity* 62, 1988, 371–7.
[11] J. Blair, 'Introduction: from Minster to Parish Church', in *Minsters and Parish Churches, The Local Church in Transition. 950–1200*, ed. J. Blair, Oxford University Committee for Archaeology, Monograph 17, 1988, 1–30.
[12] 'Stave churches' is the term used uniquely for Scandinavian timber churches which date from the eleventh century and later. Very few survive in their original state and they are characterized by having principal posts set within the structure with the external walls forming aisles. This technique is similar in principle to the medieval aisled hall or barn of which several timber-framed examples survive in eastern England.
[13] E. Gustafsson and M. Weidhagen, 'Investigations in Hammarlunda Church', in *Res medievales Ragnor Blomqvist kal. Mai. mcmlxviii oblata*, ed. A. W. Matencson, Archaeologica Lundensia III, 1968, 154–68, at 154. Also with plans, K. J. Conant, *Carolingian and Romanesque Architecture, 800–1200*, Pelican History of Art, 3rd edn, Harmondsworth 1974, 78.

difference from East Anglian examples of timber churches, which can be interpreted from excavations, is that the principal posts support the roof structure and do not form the external walls which create narrow aisles surrounding the nave.[14] The plan is basilican with a projecting two-part rectangular chancel at lower levels. The posts are joined with arches forming tall narrow bays and carrying cushion capitals decorated with carving.

Well recorded evidence has been revealed in the floor of the round-towered church of Hammarlunda in Scania.[15] The Romanesque masonry church of c.1150 has an aisleless nave, a narrower chancel consisting of a choir and a distinct apse (Plate 4). In the floor there was a clay surface associated with the masonry church, and beneath this a layer of coarse sand. Beneath were two series of well defined post holes with remains of the posts still *in situ* in some cases (Hammarlunda II). The earlier post holes of Hammarlunda I were found directly below and beside them and were clearly destroyed by fire. The posts were not associated with the walls which stood slightly further to the north and south in the positions of the present masonry walls as at Urnes. The posts supported the roof in the typical manner of stave churches, a type which has not yet been found in East Anglia or in England. The dating is quite firmly fixed by the finds. A coin from the reign of Harald Hein (c.1075–80) was found near the bottom of a Hammarlunda II post hole and a mid eleventh-century gilded bronze clasp associated with Hammarlunda I.

CHURCHES OF STONE AND MORTAR

Despite the fact that no stave churches, i.e. with internal principal posts, have yet been found in East Anglia, the region was essentially Scandinavian or at least with a Danish ruling class until 1042 with the death of Harthacnut. The preference for stone in building starts in royal circles where we learn that Cnut paid for the mud walls of the monastery at St Benet's at Holme in about 1020 to be replaced with stone,[16] and also where we are told that the same king paid for a new stone church to house the shrine of St Edmund.[17]

In Scandinavia, however, stone churches are rarely earlier than the middle years of the twelfth century. King Cnut may have been responsible for a stone church at

---

[14] P. Anker, 'L'église d'Urnes', in *L'Art Scandinave*, Zodiaque, 28 La Nuit des Temps series, La-Pierre-qui-Vire, 1969, I, 207–31, pls 100–15, 205–6 and 223.

[15] Gustafsson and Weidhagen, 'Investigations in Hammarlunda Church', 154–68.

[16] *Chronica Johannis de Oxenedes*, ed. H. Ellis, Rolls Series, London 1859, 292. For a discussion of this text, T. Pestell, *Landscapes of Monastic Foundation: The Establishment of Religious Houses in East Anglia, c.650–1200*, Woodbridge 2004, 142–5.

[17] See Hermann, 'Liber de Miraculis Sancti Eadmundi', in *Memorials of St Edmund's Abbey*, I, 84–5. It transpires that Cnut built a separate church in stone and the translation of St Edmund's relics took place in 1032 as noted as a feast day in the Bury Psalter calendar (Rome, Biblioteca Apostolica, reg. lat. 12, fo. 8r). The timber church remains standing until Baldwin begins building the new abbey church in 1081 as recorded in the Gesta Sacristarum (Arnold, *Memorials II*, 289). The arguments are fully discussed in E. Fernie, 'Abbot Baldwin's Church and the Effects of the Conquest', in *The Effect of the Conquest on the Abbey of Bury St Edmunds*, ed. Tom Licence, forthcoming.

PLATE 4 Hammarlunda church, Scania, Sweden.

Roskilde (Sjaelland, Denmark), of which foundations have been discovered, and nearby the more certain remains of St Jorgensbjaerg, where coins of c.1040 had been deposited. The cathedral of Roskilde (1060–1076), of which some remains have been found beneath the present building, was also of stone.[18] This and other indications of small churches of stone in Denmark and at Lund were the beginnings of building in stone in Scandinavia but they are exceptions, as has been shown, with the stave church remaining the norm until the middle years of the twelfth century. Inspired by Lund cathedral, which was under construction from 1123 and consecrated in 1145, parish churches were rebuilt in stone and at Hammarlunda and others the round western tower was included (Plate 4). Further afield, an early interesting mention of the use of stone is made by Thietmar of Merseburg, who refers to the early eleventh-century church of Heeslingen near Bremen, where he remarks on the use of stone and says that it is rarely used in these parts.[19] The very fact that the use of stone is a remarkable occurrence, emphasized by the chroniclers, reinforces the view that most churches were of timber before the arrival of the Normans.

[18] Anker, 'L'église d'Urnes', II, 33–47.
[19] ... in aeclesia, quam post de lapidibus qui in hac terra pauci habentur, Thietmar of Merseburg, Chronicon, book II, Ch. 26, ed. J. M. Lappenberg, Monumenta Germaniae Historica, Scriptores, iii, Hanover 1839, 756–7. This church at Heeslingen near Bremen had a round tower which was struck by lightning and replaced in the later ninteenth century. Thietmar says that the church was built by Abbess Hathui (973–1013) but it is unlikely that the surviving church which had the round tower is of this early date and the field stone masonry is indistinguishable from other mid twelfth-century buildings in the area. See F. Oswald, L. Schaefer and H. R. Sennhauser, Vorromanische Kirchenbauten, Munich 1966–71, 410.

With the arrival of the Normans in East Anglia, as elsewhere in the country, there was a massive increase in church building and rebuilding. The techniques of stone construction were very much a characteristic of Norman building with abundant supplies of high quality limestone and with major buildings such as the abbey of Jumièges and Rouen cathedral already established by the mid eleventh century.[20] This culture of building in stone was imposed on the Anglo-Scandinavian population. It is no surprise that a building profession composed of carpenters was at sea when it came to building with flint, ashlar and lime. The use of archaic techniques in conjunction with new imported decorative forms suggests that builders were looking to existing stone buildings such as Cnut's new stone shrine at Bury and St Benet's at Holme, which had also been rebuilt in stone, or other churches just outside the region such as St Benet's in Cambridge,[21] and possibly just beyond the Fens to the early major foundations of Peterborough, Ely, Crowland, Ramsey and Thorney,[22] as well as the surviving church at Barnack of c.1000.[23]

The Taylors' magisterial volumes on Anglo-Saxon architecture list many churches which were evidently built after the Norman Conquest.[24] The existence of obvious post-Conquest features such as billet and chevron ornament, ashlar facing and dressing, double bell openings within containing arches, cushion capitals and richly decorated doorways are found next to features identified as belonging to Anglo-Saxon culture such as double-splayed windows, long- and short-quoins, rubble dressings, and tall narrow tower arches. In East Anglia this debate is further disturbed by the existence of the round western tower which is a distinctive feature of the medieval architecture of the region. Nowhere in England is the so-called Saxo-Norman overlap so marked as in East Anglia. The most thorough and considered recent book on round-towered churches in East Anglia, by Stephen Hart, finds twenty-five churches with round towers which are *probably* of Anglo-Saxon date.[25]

Given the premise that building in stone was virtually unknown or not practised in East Anglia before the Normans, these buildings must belong to the period of Norman consolidation (approx. 1070–1140). Without going into a case by case argument, it is worthy of note that double-splayed windows have been shown to be far more common in East Anglia than elsewhere in England.[26] Many more have been identified since the Taylors' survey. The window type has wide splayed embrasures to both sides of the wall and they are circular or of a normal arched shape. The method of construction means that the frames for glazing or other barrier had to be built in during the building of the wall and in the case of the

---

[20] E. Fernie, *The Architecture of Norman England*, Oxford 2000, 91–6.
[21] See notes 16 and 17, above; for St Benet, Cambridge, H. M. and J. Taylor (vols I and 2) 1965 and H. M. Taylor (vol. 3), *Anglo-Saxon Architecture*, Cambridge 1978, I, 129–32.
[22] For these early Fenland foundations, Pestell, *Landscapes of Monastic Foundation*, 131–8.
[23] See E. Fernie, *The Architecture of the Anglo Saxons*, London 1983, 139–41.
[24] Above, note 21.
[25] S. Hart, *The Round Church Towers of England*, Ipswich 2003, 166.
[26] S. Heywood, 'The Double-Splayed Window: An Early Medieval Norfolk Masons' Technique', in *An Historical Atlas of Norfolk*, ed. T. Ashwin and A. Davison, 3rd edn, Chichester 2005, 62–3.

circular windows permanent centring of basketwork was used. Evidence of basketwork can be seen at Roughton and Hales and surviving frames are visible at South Lopham and Houghton-on-the-Hill. The great majority of these windows have been blocked and no doubt contain their original frames which could be useful for dating as well as having an intrinsic interest. The fact remains, however, that they are common from the late eleventh century to the mid-twelfth century. It is of interest and possible relevance that the standard windows of the mid-twelfth century in former southern Denmark and north Germany were double-splayed, and that in the round towered church of Neukirchen in Malente Kreis there are circular double-splayed windows in the west wall of the nave flanking the tower.

The tower of Hethel church with its rubble quoins on megalithic bases, round double-splayed windows and non-radial Roman brick voussoirs has been dated by dendrochronology to between 1104 and 1140. This was based on an oak sample from a put-log hole in a lintel at mid height of the tower. Of course, with this tiny piece of wood, there is less certainty that it came from a recently felled tree.[27] The long- and short-quoins at Debenham in Suffolk and St Martin-at-Palace in Norwich can be shown to be of twelfth-century dates.[28] The Debenham example has a fine west tower with striking long-and-short quoins. The tower arch, however, has typical Norman hollow chamfered imposts and, exceptionally in this case, with incised chevron ornament. A building which epitomises this mixture of architectural languages is Herringfleet, on the Norfolk/Suffolk border, which has double bell openings with triangular heads within billet-moulded containing arches in the French fashion, yet not recessed to take advantage of them (Plate 5).[29] Similarly, the perfectly built, slightly battered, round tower at Haddiscoe has chamfered stringcourses in limestone, and a bell stage with scalloped capitals to the bell openings, yet the openings are triangular headed and surrounded with stripwork. The stripwork, however, is decorated with a typical Norman billet moulding (Plate 6). The contemporary doorway into the church has chevron ornament, roll moulding and other high Romanesque decoration, along with a sculpture of a seated priest in a niche above the doorway. In the interior there is an elegant tall narrow tower arch. All these things can be no earlier than 1130.

So commonplace and so well advanced in date is this peculiar mixture of styles that there is an argument for the so-called overlap becoming an autonomous cultural signature of the region. This is strongly suggested by the decoration flanking the western tower arch at Guestwick where the Anglo-Saxon Romanesque technique of stripwork composed of three half shafts is used. It is developed and enhanced by using three half shafts, rather than the more typical half shaft and

---

[27] For Hethel, P. Thomas and T. Pestell, *All Saints, Hethel: A Report on the Standing Archaeology*, unpublished report, 2003, Norfolk Historic Environment Record No. 9523. For dendrochronology see ibid., Appendix 1, p. 43.

[28] For Debenham, H. M. and J. Taylor, *Anglo-Saxon Architecture*, 192, and for another view, see N. Pevsner and E. Radcliffe, 'Suffolk', *Buildings of England*, 2nd edn, 1974, 185. For St Martin-at-Palace, above, note 7.

[29] H. M. and J. Taylor, *Anglo-Saxon Architecture*, 296.

PLATE 5 Herringfleet church.

PLATE 6
Haddiscoe church.

pilaster, and by recessing the feature, making a more sophisticated and emphasized embellishment.[30] The decoration which surrounds the eastern tower arch is small half rolls flanking a triangular sectioned strip, also an interpretation of the Anglo Saxon decoration. This is within an early Norman building with axial tower showing that this archaic technique has been taken and improved upon.

By far the most obvious indication of a regional style is the round western tower which is ubiquitous and the rule for churches with western towers in the region until the later twelfth century.[31] However, it continues to be used in diminishing

---

[30] For Guestwick, S. Heywood, 'VI. Interpretation and Dating', in A. Rogerson and P. Williams, 'The Late Eleventh-Century Church of St Peter, Guestwick', in 'Three Norman Churches in Norfolk', *East Anglian Archaeology* 32, 1987, 75–9.

[31] S. Heywood, 'The Round Towers of East Anglia', in *Minsters and Parish Churches*, ed. Blair, 169–77; S. Heywood, 'Round-Towered Churches', in *An Historical Atlas of Norfolk*, ed. Ashwin and Davison, 60–1.

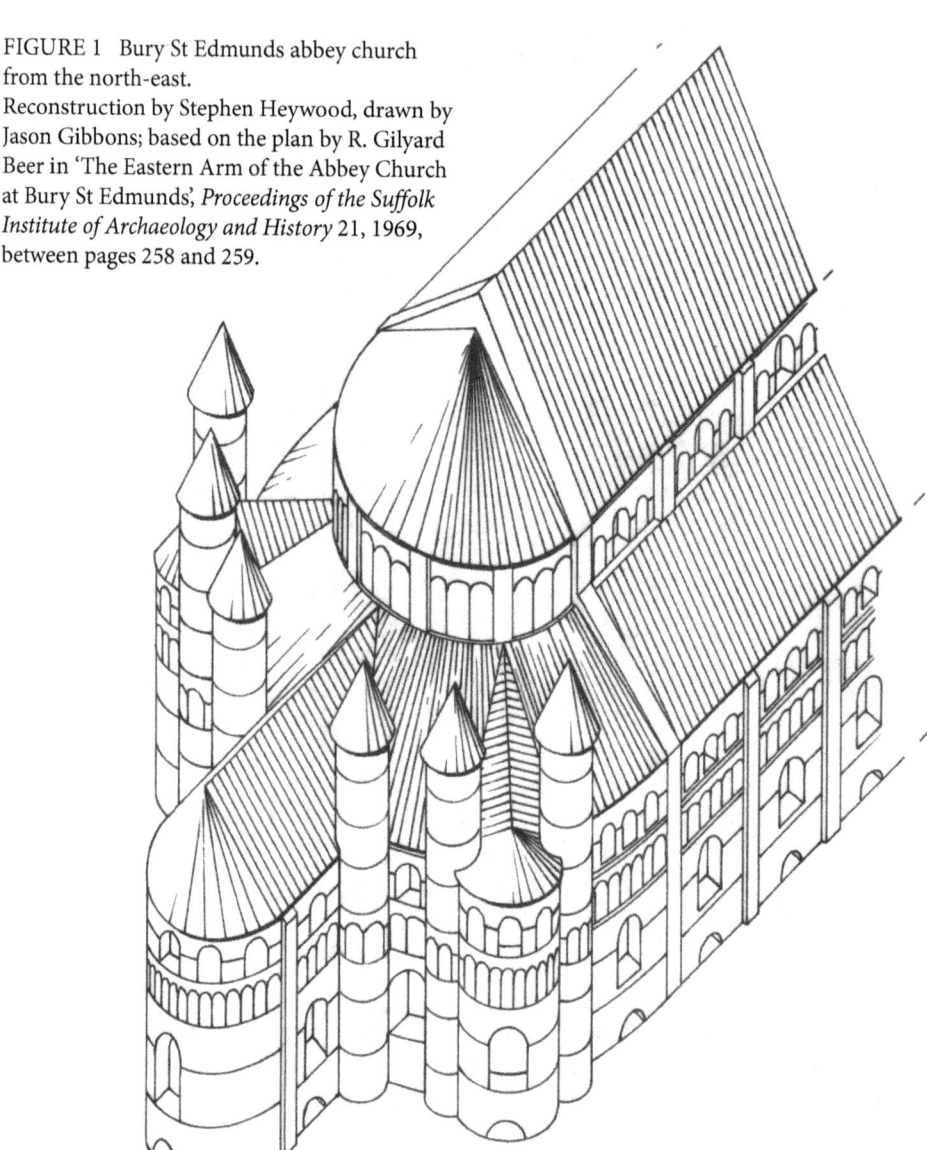

FIGURE 1 Bury St Edmunds abbey church from the north-east.
Reconstruction by Stephen Heywood, drawn by Jason Gibbons; based on the plan by R. Gilyard Beer in 'The Eastern Arm of the Abbey Church at Bury St Edmunds', *Proceedings of the Suffolk Institute of Archaeology and History* 21, 1969, between pages 258 and 259.

numbers until the end of the Middle Ages. It is far more common in East Anglia than in any other region bordering the North Sea.

The sources and iconographic context for the round tower are the two great churches of the region erected by the Normans: the abbey church of Bury St Edmunds (from 1081) and Norwich cathedral (from 1096). The storeyed radiating chapels are in form similar to the round towers, especially at Bury St Edmunds where the chapels are simple circular projections (Figures 1 and 2). This reference to a major church in the design of a parish church has been observed most famously

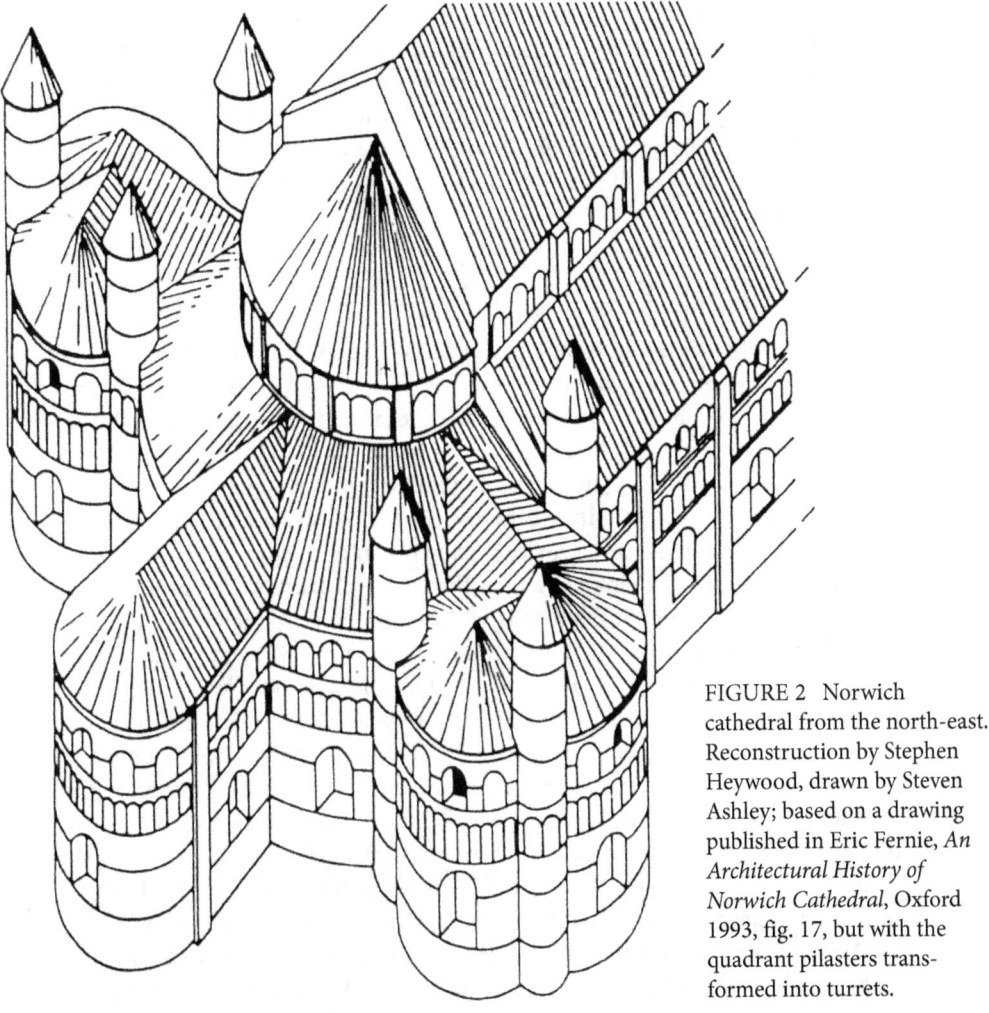

FIGURE 2 Norwich cathedral from the north-east. Reconstruction by Stephen Heywood, drawn by Steven Ashley; based on a drawing published in Eric Fernie, *An Architectural History of Norwich Cathedral*, Oxford 1993, fig. 17, but with the quadrant pilasters transformed into turrets.

in copies of the Holy Sepulchre in Jerusalem.[32] The feature which confirms the origin of the round tower is the highly distinctive quadrant pilaster: a filet of masonry in the angles between a round tower and the west wall of the nave to which it is attached. This is found on about 30 per cent of East Anglian round towered churches and on the radiating chapels of Bury and Norwich. On these major buildings the pilasters were carried up to form turrets which could not be replicated for simple parish church towers. The tower of Haddiscoe Thorpe church provides

[32] See R. Krautheimer, 'An Introduction to an Iconography of Medieval Architecture', *Journal of the Warburg and Courtauld Institutes* 5, 1942, 1–38. See also S. Heywood, 'Towers and Radiating Chapels in Romanesque Architectural Iconography', in *Architecture and Interpretation: Essays for Eric Fernie*, eds. J. Franklin, T. A. Heslop and C. Stevenson, Woodbridge 2012, 99–110.

particularly significant quadrant pilasters which may have been the result of first hand observation. The pilasters rise up beyond the angle, against the tower, and terminate with two pieces of ashlar forming a semi cone, undoubtedly referring to the conical roofs of the former turrets accompanying the radiating chapels on the great churches. The pilasters are further emphasized by being topped with *prokrossoi*. The tower itself has blind arcading which is a further reference to the radiating chapels.

CONCLUSION

The predilection for round towers originated with copying the great churches of Bury and Norwich. The type was so popular that the connection with the great churches may have become less important and more to do with the neighbouring parish.

Other regions bordering the North and Baltic seas have small groups of round towered churches: for example, Schleswig Holstein in former Denmark and Lüneburg Heath in north Germany; Scania, south Sweden, also part of the eleventh-century Danish empire; and in the Orkney Islands.[33] The earliest round towers were without doubt the turrets which adorned Carolingian and Ottonian great churches such as those that existed at Saint-Riquier (*c*.790) and which survive at St Michael Hildesheim (1010–33) and at Möllenbeck on the Weser (dated to the tenth century), which has a pair of round towers at its west end decorated with plain blind arcading at its bases and very similar to the East Anglian single towers.[34] The great churches of East Anglia are very much part of the northern European taste for the turreted skyline and, in the case of Bury, the western transept is also a reference to the northern empire. The round towers of East Anglia, seen in this context, are a very evident part of a North Sea culture which comes from the migration of peoples and the constant traffic of trade across these waters.

All the regions which have round western towers border the North or Baltic seas and it is obvious that sea passages had a lot to do with the dissemination of the distinctive type. More difficult to answer is where did the form originate? The East Anglian towers have a local source which is an iconographic reference to two great churches. Also they are more numerous by far. Although local, the design of the great churches in their sizes, and certain features such as the turrets and the west transept, are definite references to the Holy Roman Empire with its huge eleventh-century buildings such as Speyer cathedral and St Michael, Hildesheim. The abbey and the cathedral are buildings on an international scale. Although the earliest single round western towers of which there is evidence are Heeslingen near Bremen and Johannisberg near Hersfeld, the number of towers in East Anglia by the third quarter of the twelfth century and their closer relationship in time with

---

[33] For Orkney round towers, E. Fernie, 'St Magnus Church, Egilsay', in *St Magnus Cathedral*, ed. B. Crawford, Aberdeen 1988, 140–61.

[34] See Oswald, Schaefer and Sennhauser, *Vorromanische Kirchenbauten*.

the Romanesque towers in Sweden, Denmark, North Germany and Orkney makes East Anglia the most likely source.

The gradual replacement of timber churches with stone was happening in East Anglia from the early eleventh century with major buildings and royal patrons. The all round change to stone probably happened with the construction of the abbey at Bury (from 1081) and Norwich cathedral (from 1096). The masonry churches in Schleswig Holstein and Scania are not, in the main, earlier than the 1140s.

There is an argument that the early Norman churches of East Anglia constitute a regional style of their own, bound together not only with the round tower but also the ubiquitous use of double-splayed windows, the use of stripwork around bell openings in particular and the reference to Anglo-Saxon practice with triangular headed openings and tall, narrow, tower arches.

The continuing relationship with Scandinavia is very well illustrated by one of the former cloister capitals from Norwich cathedral which is decorated with Urnes interlace (See Plate 2, p. 86, this volume). The form occurs at the eponymous church in central Norway and on the best preserved of the stave churches and the decoration is carved in timber (Plate 3). Its appearance in stone at Norwich represents the region-wide shift in materials and the subsequent domination of stone building in both regions. Building in timber continues in both regions, however, through to the nineteenth century, in East Anglia mainly in domestic contexts, but as regards churches, the accepted materials for their construction had changed from timber to stone by the mid twelfth century. The influence of English architecture on Scandinavia is well attested and continues well into the twelfth century with the church of St Swithun in Stavanger in south Norway, which is not only dedicated to an English saint but is unmistakeably of Anglo-Norman inspiration in its architecture.[35]

There is an obvious to and fro of trade and ideas circulating around the North and Baltic Seas. As regards the round western tower, East Anglia was the most probable disseminator acknowledging, however, the more general use of round towers in the Empire at earlier times. Nevertheless, its specific origins were local – the radiating chapels of the two great churches at Bury and Norwich which not only inspired the form but also promoted architecture in stone.

---

[35] C. Hohler, 'The Cathedral of St Swithun at Stavanger in the Twelfth Century', *Journal of the British Archaeological Association*, 3rd ser., 27, 1964, 92–119.

— Chapter 14 —

ROMANESQUE EAST ANGLIA AND THE EMPIRE

Richard Plant

THE ROMANESQUE architecture of East Anglia is marked by a number of regional characteristics: the great length of some its major churches and the inventive pier forms used in those churches among others.[1] Moreover, a number of great churches have a plan type which has no parallels in Normandy, and is mirrored in only a few parts of Romanesque Europe.[2] On the face of it the use of a west transept at Bury, Ely and Peterborough seems to be one of the clearest examples of an architectural type drawn from across the North Sea, from the Holy Roman Empire where most comparable examples are to be found. The means and reasons for this transmission, however, are harder to evaluate; it is always difficult to determine who might be responsible for a design, and medieval texts are usually silent on the sources of buildings, and hard to interpret even when they are not.[3]

Before moving on to these buildings it is worth discussing a number of smaller buildings whose characteristics seem to owe something to lands around the North Sea, both to establish contexts, and to illustrate some problems of interpretation. These buildings have the advantage of featuring either unusual west ends, or unusual transept forms, both relevant for our discussion.

Langford (Essex) is, as far as is known, unique among post-Conquest churches in England in having had a western and an eastern apse, though only the western one survives.[4] This plan is almost always found at major churches, and most often

---

[1] B. Cherry, 'Romanesque Architecture in Eastern England', *Journal of the British Archaeological Association* 131, 1978, 1–29.
[2] J. P. McAleer, 'Le problème du transept occidental en Grande-Bretagne', *Cahiers de civilisation médiévale* 34, 1991, 349–56.
[3] The most discussed English example is in Hereford, where a building was claimed by William of Malmesbury to follow the palace chapel at Aachen. Usually it has been argued that this claim refers to the now destroyed Bishop's Chapel there, but also, because the two buildings are very unlike, that it did not, or that William was mistaken. For a summary see E. Fernie, *The Architecture of Norman England*, Oxford 2000, 233–6.
[4] *Victoria County History: Essex* I, London 1903, 443, 521 and 525; H. Laver, 'Langford Church', *Transactions of the Essex Archaeological Society*, new ser. 10, 1906, 10–13.

found in the Holy Roman Empire. There were, however, examples in Anglo-Saxon England, most notably at Canterbury cathedral.[5] There the western apse seems likely to have been derived from the Empire, especially as other aspects of the design, such as the flanking stair turrets find parallels there. Langford itself remains inexplicable; we cannot know whether the inspiration was in the Anglo-Saxon past or from across the North Sea, nor the function of the apse, nor who made the decision to have it built.

A second church with a unique feature for England is the ruined church at North Elmham, once believed to be the Anglo-Saxon cathedral, now viewed as a church for the personal use of the bishop of Norwich and probably built by Bishop Herbert Losinga (bishop 1091–1119).[6] The church had the only continuous transept known from our period in England, a continuous transept being a transept the length of which is uninterrupted by north-south arches. Usually this type of transept is seen as referring to the early Christian churches of Rome, and in particular to Old St Peter's, as well may be the case here. However, it is found at a number of churches in the Empire, as are other unusual elements of the building; the towers in the angles between the nave and transept, and the semi-circular stair vice attached to the substantial west tower. Each finds parallels in the Empire, the former in churches of the Hirsau school, the latter in a number of churches in the Mosan region, in what is now Belgium, such as Hastière-par-dela (Namur).[7] The form of the stair vice might reasonably be assumed in this case to be the choice of the mason, which would imply that he at least had knowledge of architecture in the Empire. The reference to Rome would probably be the choice of the patron, though his motivation is hard to determine, but might include his own submission to the Holy See, or a statement about his diocese, newly settled in the city of Norwich.[8]

Round towers attached to the west end of the nave, such as those at Haddiscoe and Hales in Norfolk, have been extensively discussed in earlier literature. This is clearly an architectural type which belongs to the North Sea world, having a distribution from Norway to Flanders, taking in the Orkneys and northern Germany (where the type may have originated) and Denmark, though the largest concen-

---

[5] K. Blockley, M. Sparks and T. Tatton-Brown, *Canterbury Cathedral Nave: Archaeology, History, and Architecture*, Canterbury 1997, 18–23, 106–11. Another may have been at St Oswald's, Gloucester, C. Heighway and R. Bryant, 'A Reconstruction of the 10th Century Church of St Oswald, Gloucester', in *The Anglo-Saxon Church: Papers on History, Architecture and Archaeology in Honour of Dr H. M. Taylor*, ed. L. A. S. Butler and R. K. Morris, London 1986, 188–95.

[6] S. Heywood, 'The Ruined Church of North Elmham', *Journal of the British Archaeological Association* 135, 1983, 1–10; Fernie, *Architecture of Norman England*, 236–8.

[7] H. E. Kubach and A. Verbeek, *Romanische Baukunst an Rhein und Maas*, 3 vols, Berlin 1976, 4th vol., *Architekturgeschichte und Kunstlandschaft*, Berlin 1989, I, 354–6, and A. Dierkens, *Abbayes et chapitres entre Sambre et Meuse (VIIe-XIe siècles)*, Sigmaringen 1985, 149–61.

[8] C. Harper-Bill, 'Losinga, Herbert de (d.1119)', *Oxford Dictionary of National Biography*. Online ed. <http://www.oxforddnb.com/view/article/17025>.

tration is in East Anglia.⁹ It is hard to assign a precise mechanism whereby an architectural idea like the round tower would have circulated the North Sea. One suggestion has been that they were introduced to East Anglia by tenth-century German missionaries, though most, if not all, of the English examples are post-Conquest. Other suggestions have been that the round shape was suitable for baptism, though there are some examples where this was almost certainly not the case, or that they were a convenient shape to build in areas with little good stone for building. Finally the prestige of the Holy Roman Empire, where the earliest examples were found, might be a factor. The question would be easier to address if we knew the first instance of a round-towered church in East Anglia, so that the local prototype could be related to its continental model, if any, and patterns of reception in the region assessed, but we do not know which building was first.[10]

More striking are the west ends of some of the great churches of the region. The trend in most parts of England, following Canterbury cathedral, was for a two-tower façade, though other simple types are found. The eastern part of England has four major Romanesque churches which have complex and massive western structures; Lincoln, Bury St Edmund's, Ely and Peterborough. The western block at Lincoln, usually dated to the late eleventh century, is *sui generis*. It is, or was, a two-bay deep block, with niches alternating with deep recesses on the south and, most visibly, west walls. The military aspects of the block have caused much recent discussion, and it has even been proposed that it was constructed as a separate structure from the church.[11] The stepped arrangement of the tall recesses on the western front has frequently been compared to a triumphal arch, a similarity that would have been accentuated by the sculpted frieze which runs across the façade.[12] While this may have been carved *in situ* some time in the middle of the twelfth century, the stones it was carved into might have previously carried a still more Roman-looking bronze-lettered inscription.[13] Certain aspects of the structure can be related to the west transepts of East Anglia; width, the frieze and the triple arched façade, perhaps indicating an adherence to Roman prototypes.

Ely, Bury and Peterborough differ from Lincoln in that they have transepts at the west end of the church. Transepts can be quite varied in form: they are spaces

---

[9] S. Heywood, 'The Round Towers of East Anglia', in *Minsters and Parish Churches. The Local Church in Transition 950-1200*, ed. J. Blair, Oxford 1988, 169-77; E. Fernie, 'The Church of St Magnus, Egilsay', in *St Magnus Cathedral and Orkney's Twelfth-Century Renaissance*, ed. B. Crawford, Aberdeen 1988, 140-61; Fernie, *Architecture of Norman England*, 218-19. An example to the south of the North Sea is at Echinghem (Nord-Pas-de-Calais).

[10] See further Stephen Heywood's essay in this volume.

[11] R. Gem, 'Lincoln Minster: Ecclesia Pulchra, Ecclesia Fortis', *British Archaeological Association Conference Transactions: Medieval Art and Architecture at Lincoln Cathedral*, Leeds 1986, 9-28; D. Stocker and A. Vince, 'The Early Norman Castle at Lincoln and a Re-evaluation of the Original West Tower of Lincoln Cathedral', *Medieval Archaeology* 41, 1997, 223-33.

[12] A. Quiney, '"In Hoc Signo": The West Front of Lincoln Cathedral', *Architectural History* 44, 2001, 162-71.

[13] Most recently on the frieze, P. Dixon, *Lincoln Cathedral: The Romanesque Frieze*, Lincoln 2009, especially for the possibility of an inscription, 15.

PLATE 1 Peterborough abbey church (now cathedral), west front.

that run transversely to the nave of the church, with or without crossing arches (the latter are called continuous transepts, such as that at North Elmham), either the full height of the main vessel of the church, or lower but with the entrance higher than the openings of the nave arcade in which case they are called low transepts. There are other variants, but that these were all understood as comparable features in the Romanesque period is apparent from the use of a church with one type of transept as a model for a church with a different type, a number of which are discussed below.

West transepts as part of a building that also has transepts at the east end (as opposed to buildings like Old St Peter's which was occidented) are comparatively rare in Romanesque Europe, with the vast majority being in the Empire, especially the western part. The appearance of three in England and two more in Scotland might therefore seem to be a clear case of the architecture in Britain following that of the Empire, and it would seem unlikely that the three in eastern England, at least, are unconnected with each other. The west transept at Peterborough is clearly the latest of the three English examples, and must surely derive its inspiration from one or both of Ely and Bury; it can therefore be dealt with first.

The west front of Peterborough abbey, now cathedral, consists of an exceptionally tall porch of three arches rising to the full height of the building, fronting a rather modest transept (Plate 1). This is narrow in its east-west direction compared with the five-bay north-south length; the bays of which correspond to the aisles of the nave support towers. The whole western complex is part of a rethink: the initial early twelfth-century design had planned for a shorter nave and a two-tower façade. The western transept was constructed during the last quarter of the twelfth century, and before completion was augmented by the addition of the porch.[14] There are no chapels or otherwise architecturally defined altar spaces

---

[14] L. Reilly, *An Architectural History of Peterborough Cathedral*, Oxford 1997, 87–111.

PLATE 2 Ely cathedral, west front, lower parts.

in the transept, though there is what looks to be a thirteenth-century piscina in the south arm, set into a wall with cut back blind arcading. This represents a functional reduction from the Ely and Bury transepts, both of which have architecturally defined chapels. The porch has its closest parallel at Lincoln in which diocese it lay, while the paired towers over the transept may be seen as an attempt to bring it into line with other English great churches.[15]

The west transepts at Ely and Bury are difficult to interpret: ruination and alteration have changed them in quite fundamental ways. In some respects they were similar: both had an axial tower, and neither had a western choir, which was the norm with western transepts on the Continent. Both had chapels on two storeys at the ends of the transepts, but otherwise they were structurally very different. That at Ely survives better, though only as the south arm and crossing, while the western transept at Bury is entirely ruinous. The Ely transept is also more straightforward: while the north arm survives only as a stub, the crossing (with later medieval reinforcements) and south arm survive (Plate 2).[16] The south arm is for all of its length as high as the nave, and projects internally over 10 metres beyond the aisles.[17] On the eastern side of the projecting part are the (reconstructed) chapels. Neither the lower nor the upper chapel were connected to the nave, the

[15] Reilly, *An Architectural History*, 103–6.
[16] E. Fernie, 'The Architecture and Sculpture of Ely Cathedral in the Norman Period', in *A History of Ely Cathedral*, ed. P. Meadows and N. Ramsay, Woodbridge 2003, 92–111, especially 103–4.
[17] Dimensions from E. Fernie, 'Observations on the Norman Plan of Ely Cathedral', *British Archaeological Association Conference Transactions: Medieval Art and Architecture at Ely Cathedral*, Leeds 1979, 1–7.

upper being reached by passages in the terminal wall of the transept.[18] The southeastern and south-western corners of the transept have projecting polygonal stair turrets. On both the interior and exterior of the transept there is carved geometric ornament, and the south and west walls of the interior and the exterior have tiers of blind arcading. Passages run through the thickness of the wall: three open to the interior, and a passage which runs behind the second level of arcading on the exterior seems once to have opened outwards.[19]

While this level of elaboration contrasts with the rather austere nave, nothing suggests that construction of the transept was discontinuous, at least for its lower levels, with that of the nave. The west bay of the south nave aisle also has blind arcading. None of the decorative elements preclude a date in the 1120s for the beginning of work, a date supported by dendrochronology, and the masonry of transept and nave aisle course through.[20] The upper parts of the transept and the tower, however, are clearly Gothic, dating from the time of Bishop Geoffrey Ridel (1174–89).[21] More problematic is the western porch, or Galilee. This is a thirteenth-century structure, projecting some 13 metres from the façade, but early modern histories of the cathedral claimed to have detected a predecessor.[22] However, above the vault some blind arcading and chip-carved decoration continues, precluding anything very substantial projecting from the west wall.

Bury is completely ruinous, and was a much more eccentric structure than Ely. Much has collapsed or been pulled down, all the facing stonework has been robbed, and even had the building survived, our understanding of it would be impeded by collapse and fire in the fifteenth century (Figure 1, Plate 3). Interpretation has been further hampered by houses which were built into the remains, but renovation of those houses allowed access in the1990s, and our understanding has been greatly improved by the minute detailing of the remains by J. P. McAleer.[23] In addition there is an unusual amount of documentary information preserved about the construction of the church.[24] The church had three portals, corresponding in alignment

---

[18] McAleer, 'Problème', 352.
[19] The evidence for this is the rather crude blocking – more visible inside the passage – between the shafts.
[20] Fernie, 'Architecture and Sculpture', 103–4.
[21] J. Maddison, 'The Gothic Cathedral: New Building in a Historic Context', in *A History of Ely Cathedral*, ed. Meadows and Ramsay, 113–41 especially 114–19.
[22] W. Stevenson, *A Supplement to the First Edition of Mr Bentham's 'History and Antiquities of the Cathedral and Conventual Church of Ely'*, Norwich 1817, 'Addendum' 2, 'Supplement', 60. Pagination is not continuous.
[23] J. P. McAleer, 'The West Façade-Complex at the Abbey Church of Bury St Edmunds: A Description of the Evidence for Its Reconstruction', *Proceedings of the Suffolk Institute of Archaeology* 30/2, 1998, 127–50; J. P. McAleer, 'The West Front of the Abbey Church', *British Archaeological Association Conference Transactions: Bury St Edmunds Medieval Art, Architecture, Archaeology and Economy*, Leeds 1998, 22–33. Also useful are E. Fernie, 'The Romanesque Church of Bury St Edmunds Abbey', *Bury St Edmunds*, 1–15; A. B. Whittingham, 'Bury St Edmunds Abbey. The Plan, Design and Development of the Church and Monastic Buildings', *Archaeological Journal* 108, 1952, 168–87.
[24] Much of it compiled in M. R. James, 'On the Abbey of St Edmund at Bury', *Publications of the Cambridge Antiquarian Society* 7, 1895.

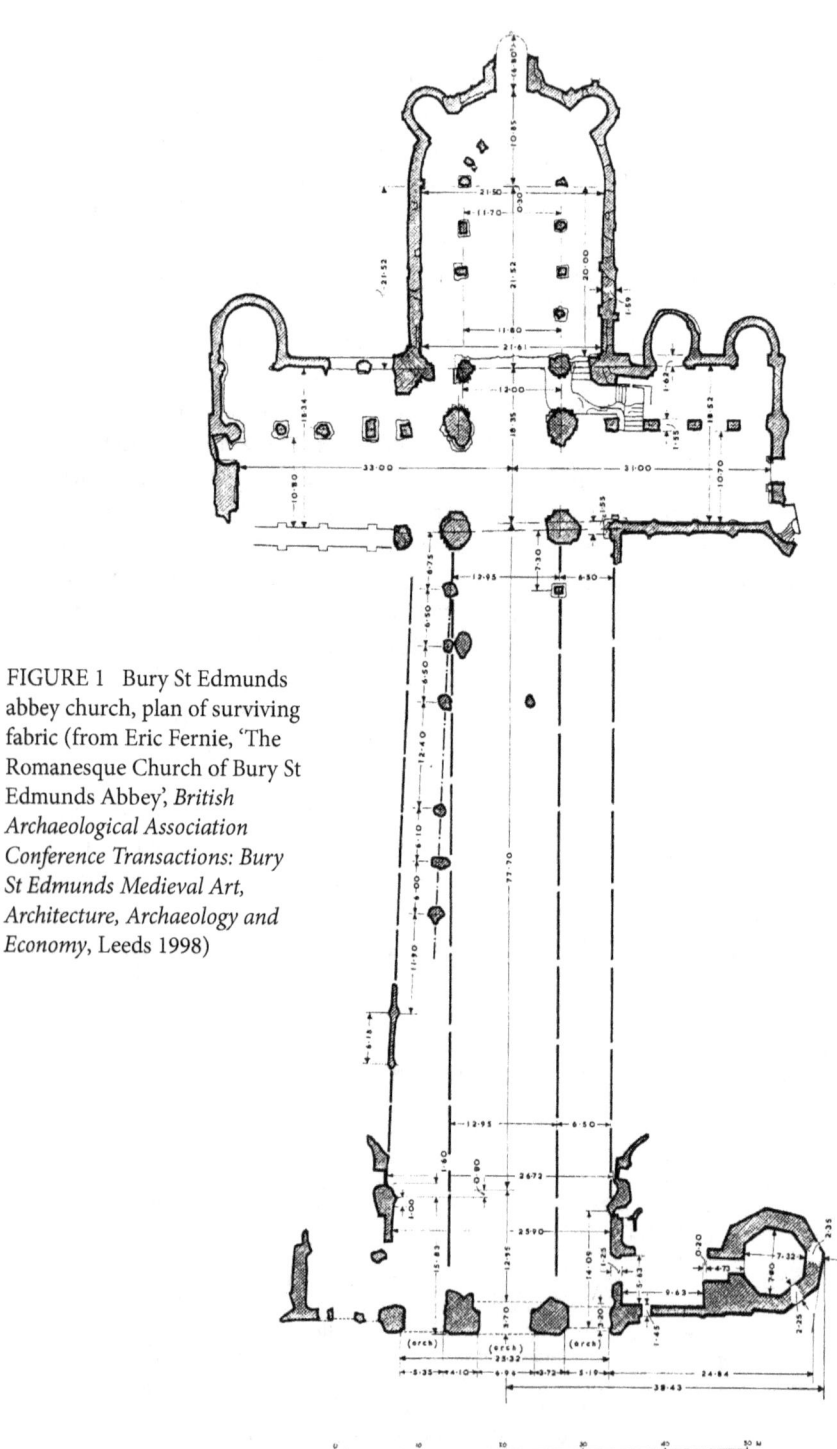

FIGURE 1 Bury St Edmunds abbey church, plan of surviving fabric (from Eric Fernie, 'The Romanesque Church of Bury St Edmunds Abbey', *British Archaeological Association Conference Transactions: Bury St Edmunds Medieval Art, Architecture, Archaeology and Economy*, Leeds 1998)

PLATE 3 Bury St Edmunds abbey church, remains of west front.

to the nave aisles, set within deep porches. While these were less imposing perhaps than the Lincoln recesses to which they might owe a debt, the resemblance to a Roman triumphal arch might have been stronger. This façade also seems to have had a sculpted frieze, fragments of which survive in the Moyses Hall Museum, another point of comparison with Lincoln though it is hard to know which is earlier. Flanking and above the central porch were a pair of stair turrets of which the north one survives in part, and above them a tower, though the evidence for this comes only from documentary sources. North and south of the central triplet of arches the façade is harder to reconstruct, but continued with a section fronting double-storeyed chapels and ended with a large octagon at the south end which was matched by one at the north, now vanished.

The interior is even more problematic. The eastern face of the west wall had three tall recesses in it, perhaps taller than those on the western face, and the central one was possibly apsidal. Nothing remains of the eastern side of the crossing, even the position of the crossing piers has to be inferred from remains of the nave gallery. Despite the great width of the façade, the western transept itself was only as wide as the nave aisles. Beyond the line of the aisles, however, were chapels on two storeys, screened from the transept by arcades. These chapels had a rectangular nave two bays wide and two long, and an apse. On the north the lower chapel was dedicated to St Denis, the upper to St Faith, and on the south the lower was dedicated to St John and the upper to St Catherine.[25] The upper chapels were considerably lower in height than the lower ones. There is enough masonry remaining to show that they were groin-vaulted. Beyond these there were the large octagons, of uncertain purpose and of uncertain height, though they were described as towers (*turris*) in medieval sources.[26]

It would be useful for our understanding of the buildings to know which came first, the transept at Ely or that at Bury, but this, unfortunately, is impossible. It is tempting to see the Bury design, more eccentric in respect of Anglo-Norman tradition as the first, which the design of Ely then normalizes, but the documentary evidence does not give sufficient information, and stylistic analysis is impossible at Bury. Both buildings were begun at about the same time, in the early 1080s, but neither was completed until the late twelfth century, as the documents at Bury and fabric and documents make clear at Ely. At Ely it is the upper sections of the transept and the tower which were delayed; at Bury (at least) the western tower and the completion of the octagons.[27] It is not absolutely clear in either case whether the west transept was planned from the outset, though there is no pressing reason to think otherwise at Ely. Bury is a slightly different story: changes of plan are evident around the western crossing, probably indicating an increase of length of the church as a whole, which might have taken place in the first decade of the twelfth century.[28] Furthermore the construction of the west front necessitated the removal of the parish church of St Denis, built by Abbot Baldwin (1065–97) where the later chapel of St Denis, attached to the west transept, stood.[29] This was during the period of Abbot Anselm (1121–48), and it was also during his period that two of the chapels attached to the west transept were dedicated, before 1142.[30] Whether the parish church had to be destroyed solely because the abbey church was of greater length, or because of the greater width or the greater length caused by the transept, or a combination of these factors, is impossible to say. In brief if the west transepts were planned at the outset of each building, then the planning was more or less contemporaneous, they were built at the same time, and intermediate stages in the process are (unlike Peterborough) impossible to reconstruct.

Before moving on to considering the sources and meanings of these structures, it is worth enumerating the features at each of these churches which are, or have been considered to be, outside the Anglo-Norman mainstream. These are, for both churches: western liturgical complexes in general, western transepts in particular, and western axial towers. Many more features are specific to Bury: the transept enclosed within the nave aisle walls, the recesses on the inner and outer faces of

---

[25] Whittingham, 'Bury St Edmunds', 174.
[26] James, 'On the Abbey', 153–4.
[27] For the west tower, Jocelin of Brakelond. *Chronicle of the Abbey of St Edmunds*, ed. and trans. D. Greenway and J. Sayers, Oxford 1989, 10, 63–4; James, 'On the Abbey', 153.
[28] Fernie, 'Romanesque Church'; S. Heywood, 'Aspects of the Romanesque Church of Bury St Edmunds Abbey in their Regional Context', *Bury St Edmunds*, 16–22.
[29] James, 'On the Abbey', 162.
[30] Whittingham, 'Bury St Edmunds', 171.

the west wall, the chapels constructed beyond the transept, and finally the octagons at the end of the western massif.

The western massifs at Ely and Bury are more elaborate than any in Normandy, though these could be quite complex.[31] Another possible source is in the architectural tradition of Anglo-Saxon England, in which the west end of the church was more important, liturgically speaking, than it was after the Conquest. Sir Alfred Clapham proposed that Ely itself was the source for the west transepts at Ely.[32] This he derived from the Anglo-Saxon Chronicle (*sub anno* 1036) describing the burial of Alfred Ætheling (d.1036) at Ely at the west end by the tower in the south *porticus*.[33] There is no archaeological information about Anglo-Saxon Ely. A parallel may be provided by the cathedral of Sherborne. This had square chambers projecting north and south of the west tower of a church that also had eastern transepts.[34] If in plan the arrangement might have looked like a western transept, these chapels only communicated to the adjacent volumes through small openings, and the first floor of the tower once contained a chapel, the western arcade of which survived until the nineteenth century.[35] If the idea of complexes of chapels at the west end is inherited from an Anglo-Saxon tradition, the form they took is not.

The use of Anglo-Saxon architecture as a source has also been used to provide a symbolic explanation for the massif at Bury and (to a lesser extent) Ely. The use of an axial western tower, seemingly more common in Anglo-Saxon than Anglo-Norman architecture, has been interpreted as a sign of the presence of the relics of a great Anglo-Saxon saint – St Edmund at Bury, St Etheldreda at Ely – with the transept only built as a necessary abutment for it.[36] However, if the association were a strong one, one would especially expect it to be found at post-Conquest Durham where the late Anglo-Saxon cathedral had an axial western tower, and the relics of the major saint of the North. The presence of a Romanesque axial tower at Hereford cathedral (without a western transept) also dilutes the claim for unusualness of the feature.[37] Finally, the designer at Peterborough evidently did not regard the tower as the most significant element of the design, adopting the western transept without it.

---

[31] J. Le Maho, 'Tours et entrées occidentales des églises de la base vallée de la Seine (IXe–XIIe siècle)', in *Avant-nefs et espaces d'accueil dans l'église entre le IVe et le XIIe siècle*, ed. C. Sapin, Paris 2002, 281–95.

[32] A. W. Clapham, *English Romanesque Architecture before the Conquest*, Oxford 1930, 80.

[33] "aet þam west ende, þan styple ful gehende, on þam suð portice". *Porticus* is a somewhat ambiguous term, E. Fernie, *The Architecture of the Anglo-Saxons*, London 1983, 71–2. It was also used to describe the chapels of St Denis and St Faith at the west end of Bury St Edmunds, James, 'On the Abbey', 161–2.

[34] J. Gibb, 'The Anglo-Saxon Cathedral at Sherborne', with an appendix by R. Gem, *Journal of the British Archaeological Association* 135, 1975, 71–110.

[35] Gibb, 'Anglo-Saxon Cathedral at Sherborne', 76–77 and fig. 2.

[36] A. Gransden, *A History of the Abbey of Bury St Edmunds, 1182–1256*, Woodbridge 2007, 86–7; McAleer 'West Front', 28–9

[37] M. Thurlby, 'Hereford Cathedral: the Romanesque Fabric', *British Archaeological Association Conference Transactions: Medieval Art and Architecture at Hereford Cathedral*, Leeds 1995, 15–28.

Similar sorts of symbolic readings have been applied to the most unusual feature of the Bury design, the flanking octagons. McAleer has tentatively interpreted them as a recollection of the rotunda built for St Edmund by King Cnut, duplicated for reasons of symmetry, and with the south one acting as a baptistery next to the chapel of St John.[38] Peter Fergusson has recently put forward the view that the western complex at Bury was intended to recall Old St Peter's in Rome.[39] The peculiar octagons would, in Fergusson's interpretation, find their source in the late-antique rotunda, dedicated to St Andrew, which was attached to the south transept of old St Peter's, again duplicated for symmetry.[40] The font at St Peter's was at the end of the opposite transept. This was in one of what Richard Krautheimer called the exedrae, lower annexes at the ends of the transept screened from the main vessel, which could have inspired the odd placement of the chapels at Bury.[41] Fergusson's interpretation has as its focus the tower to the west of the monastic enclosure and its enclosing atrium, which recalls the atrium to the east at St Peter's (where the apse is to the west), and its gate tower and chapel, S. Maria in Turri or S. Maria ad Gradus.[42] Fergusson proposed that these and the west front were all the work of Abbot Anselm, who was himself from Rome. While this may be questionable for the west block since, for reasons discussed above the date is unclear, the connection to the church of St Peter is plausible.

Evocation of Early Christian monuments has been proposed for a number of monuments in Anglo-Norman England, though this has usually been on the grounds of overall size as at, for example, Winchester,[43] Durham,[44] and Ely and Bury. In terms of architectural features the spiral columns used in a number of Anglo-Norman churches, most notably at Durham, have been said to evoke the structure around the shrine of St Peter.[45] There is not therefore any need to make special pleading for the use of Rome as a source of inspiration, nor would there be for Ely, also possessor of the relics of a major Anglo-Saxon saint and having St Peter as the co-dedicatee (with the Virgin Mary) of the church. St Peter was (naturally) the dedicatee of Peterborough. If this is the case then the west transept on its own

---

[38] McAleer, 'West Front', 29.
[39] P. Fergusson, 'Abbot Anselm's Gate Tower at Bury St Edmunds', in *Architecture, Liturgy, Identity: Liber Amicorum Paul Crossley*, ed. Z. Opacic and A. Timmerman, Turnhout 2011, 25–33.
[40] R. Gem, 'The Vatican Rotunda: A Severan Monument and its Early History, c.200 to 500', *Journal of the British Archaeological Association* 158, 2005, 36–7.
[41] R. Krautheimer, *Corpus basilicarum christianorum Romae*, 5 vols, V, Rome 1977, 251–3.
[42] Krautheimer, *Corpus*, 175–6, 261–71.
[43] R. Gem, 'The Romanesque Cathedral of Winchester: Patron and Design in the Eleventh Century', *British Archaeological Association Conference Transactions: Medieval Art and Architecture at Winchester Cathedral*, Leeds 1983, 1–12.
[44] M. Thurlby, 'The Roles of Patron and Master Mason in the First Design of the Romanesque Cathedral of Durham', in *Anglo-Norman Durham 1093-1193*, ed. D. Rollason, M. Harvey and M. Prestwich, Woodbridge 1994, 161–84.
[45] E. Fernie, 'The Use of Varied Nave Supports in Romanesque and Early Gothic Churches', *Gesta* 23, 1984), 107–17; idem, 'The Spiral Piers of Durham Cathedral', *British Archaeological Association Conference Transactions: Medieval Art and Architecture at Durham Cathedral*, Leeds 1980, 49–58.

would be the bearer of this particular architectural meaning, a point to which we shall return. Ely, however, also had its own gate tower in the early twelfth century; the tower of St Peter 'at the entrance of the church of Ely' was struck by lightning in 1111.[46] Sadly there is no way of knowing whether it stood in the same relation to the church as that at Bury, though none of the later gates do.

Were the use of a western transept as part of a church that also had an eastern transept a novel formulation then we might leave it there. However, the majority of churches with transepts at both the east and west of the building were, or are, in the Empire, and these were among the most prestigious buildings of the realm. In this area they are almost always associated with churches that have apses at either end, a Carolingian development. Perhaps the best known example of this was at Fulda, from around 800, where the connection with Rome and its liturgical practices was made explicit in contemporary sources.[47] From this develop churches that are sometimes described as bipolar, having both choir and transept at east and west ends.[48] As a group these buildings have a poor rate of survival, so that the most famous is the heavily reconstructed St Michael in Hildesheim[49] (Plate 4). The earliest example, however, may well have been the cathedral in Cologne, the predecessor to the current Gothic cathedral (Figure 2). The date of this building is controversial, with starting dates in the ninth and tenth centuries both proposed.[50] There is a consensus, however, that the building acted as a model to other great churches in the last quarter of the tenth century. Among these was the monastery at Memleben in Saxony,[51] which perhaps in turn provided a model for St Michael in Hildesheim, and a group of buildings in the western part of the Empire, including the cathedrals of Verdun and Liège.[52] Other bipolar churches of the region include St Lebuinius in Deventer,[53] St Gertrude in Nivelles (which still stands),[54] and

---

[46] 'turris sancti petri, que est in porta Helyensis ecclesie sita'. The quote is from *Liber Eliensis*, ed. E. O. Blake, Camden 3rd series, xcii, London 1962, 264; *Liber Eliensis: A History of the Isle of Ely from the Seventh Century to the Twelfth*, trans. J. Fairweather, Woodbridge 2005, 317.

[47] Charles B. McClendon, *The Origins of Medieval Architecture*, New Haven 2005, 158–61.

[48] Edgar Lehmann, 'Zu Querschiff, Vierung und Doppeltransept in der karolingisch–ottonischen Architektur', *Von der Kirchenfamilie zur Kathedral, und andere Aufsätze*, Berlin 1999, 149–56, esp. 152–5.

[49] H. Beseler and H. Roggenkamp, *Die Michaeliskirche in Hildesheim*, Berlin 1954; J. Cramer, W. Jacobsen, and D. von Winterfeld, 'Die Michaeliskirche' in, *Bernward von Hildesheim und das Zeitalter der Ottonen*, ed. M. Brandt and A. Eggebrecht, Hildesheim 1993, I, 369–82.

[50] K. G. Beuckers, *Der Kölner Dom*, Darmstadt 2004, 14–27, for a summary of dating and sacral topography; the arguments over the date are presented at length in A. Wolff (ed.), *Die Domgrabung Köln: Altertum – Frühmittelalter – Mittelalter*, Cologne 1996.

[51] M. Untermann, 'Memleben und Köln' in *Form und Stil: Festschrift für Günther Binding zum 65. Geburtstag*, ed. S. Lieb, Darmstadt 2001, 45–55.

[52] H. G. Marschall, *Die Kathedrale von Verdun*, Saarbrucken 1981, esp. 53–55 and 65–92; M. Otte (ed.), *Les fouilles de la Place Saint-Lambert à Liège*, 4 vols, Liège 1984–92; Lex Bosman, 'Der Dom zu Köln als Vorbild der Kathedrale Bishof Notgers in Lüttich', *Kölner Domblatt* 56, 1991, 245–58.

[53] Kubach and Verbeek, *Romanische Baukunst*, I, 187–192; IV, 141–2.

[54] Kubach and Verbeek, *Romanische Baukunst*, III, 860–76; X. Barral i Altet, *Belgique Romane*, La Pierre-qui-Vire 1989, 75–122.

PLATE 4 Hildesheim, church of St Michael.

St Trond.[55] They were quite a varied group: Cologne (at least as far as can be told from the image of the building in the Hillinus Codex[56]) had transepts lower than the body of the main vessel, as is the west transept at St Gertrude. Others, such as St Michael in Hildesheim, had transepts to full height. St Michael also has towers over the east and west crossings, while the Hillinus Codex shows round (wooden?) towers in the same positions at Cologne. Others (such as St Gertrude) had none, while Deventer, with a full height western crossing, had a tower in front of the west wall, perhaps over a western choir. Both Liège cathedral and Verdun cathedral had square western choirs.

Indeed the main obstacle in earlier scholarship to viewing these buildings as the source for the English churches is the lack of a western choir at the latter buildings.[57] This may be partly a question of perception, however. There is one Cologne church, St Kunibert, which has a western transept without a western choir, but it is later than the English buildings. However, the western block of St Pantaleon in Cologne can also be interpreted as a western transept (Plate 5). The western block was the result of the patronage of the Empress Theophanu (960–91), and although the exact date is disputed, it was built around the year 1000. The structure, which was added to an earlier aisleless building, consists of a square central bay

[55] Kubach and Verbeek, *Romanische Baukunst*, II, 1029–1035.
[56] Cologne Diözesanbibliothek, MS 12, fol. 16v. 1007/8. H. Simon, 'Architekturdarstellungen in der ottonischen Buchmalerei. Die Alte Kölner Dom in Hillinus-Codex', in *Form und Stil*, ed. Lieb, 32–44.
[57] McAleer, 'Problème', 354.

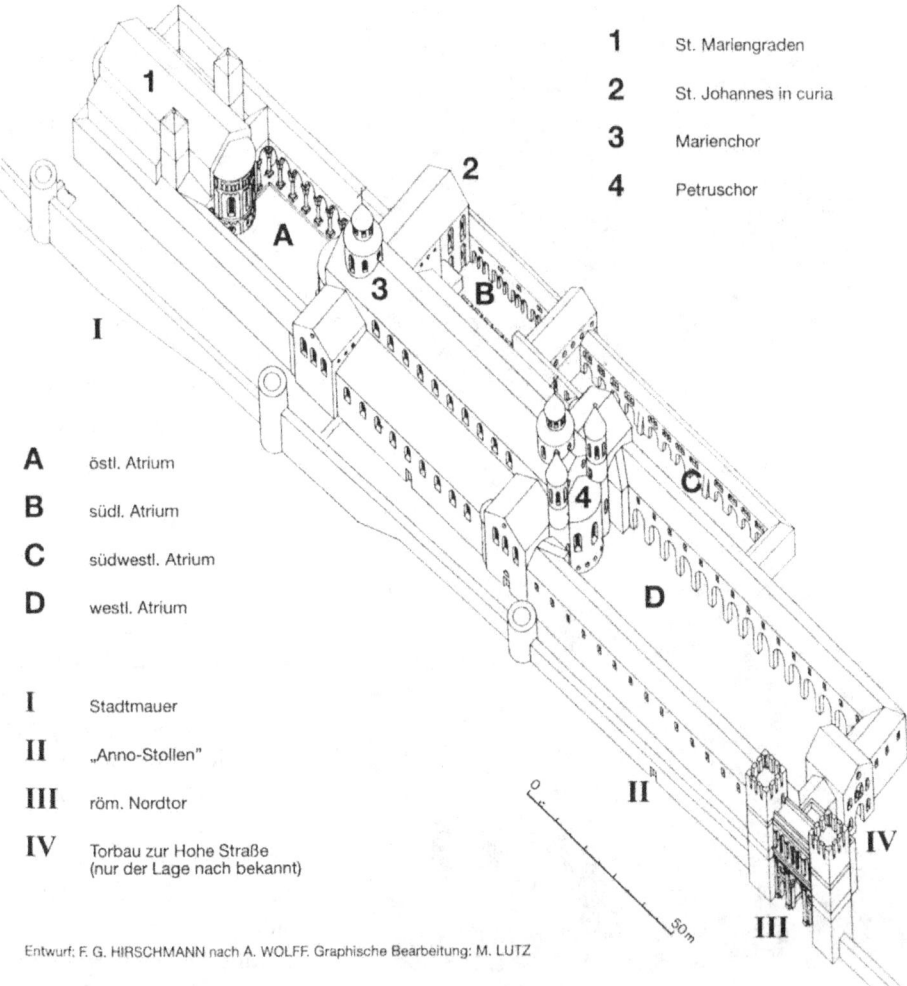

FIGURE 2   Cologne cathedral, reconstruction of cathedral c.1100 (from Frank G. Hirschmann, *Stadtplanung, Bauprojekte und Grossbaustellen im 10. und 11. Jahrhundert: Vergleichende Studien zu den Kathedralstädten westlich des Rheins*, Monographien zur Geschichte de Mittlealters, 43, Stuttgart 1998).

with galleries on three sides. The entrance is though a deep porch to the west, under the western gallery, while the arms to north and south are arranged as chapels on two stories, with niches for altars in the east walls.[58] This has generally been inter-

---

[58] F. Mühlberg, *Köln: St Pantaleon und sein Ort in der karolingischen und ottonischen Baukunst*, Cologne 1989. Details of liturgical arrangements, C. Kosch, *Kölns Romanische Kirchen: Architektur und Liturgie im Hochmittelalter*, 2nd edn, Regensberg 2005, 87–99; S. Ristow, *Die Ausbgrabungen von St. Pantaleon in Köln: Archäologie und Geschichte von Römischer bis ins Karolingisch-Ottonische Zeit*, Bonn 2009; doubts about the date in U. Lobbedey, *Die Ausgrabungen im Dom zu Paderborn 1978/80 und 1983*, 4 vols, Bonn 1986, I, 175–6.

PLATE 5 Cologne, church of St Pantaleon, interior of west block looking north west.

preted in German scholarship, probably because of its connection to imperial patronage, as a *westwerk*, a rather unhelpful term, which defines clearly neither form nor function.[59] The second obstacle to viewing it as a transept is that it has no clear lateral space. However, a number of Anglo-Norman churches had platforms in their eastern transepts: Winchester still does and Ely did until some point in the twelfth century. At the church at Jumièges, begun in the first half of the eleventh century these platforms extended as far as the crossing.[60]

A source of inspiration across the North Sea might also be preferred because other aspects of the western complex at Bury can also be paralleled in the Empire. The back-to-back recesses of the west wall find parallels (in single form rather than the three at Bury) at Wimpfen-in-Tal, and the destroyed building to the north of Magdeburg cathedral, once interpreted as the palace of Otto the Great, and at present interpreted as a church.[61] While these are rather widely spread examples, the best comparable examples to the chapels on two storeys separated from the transept were or are at buildings where two sets of transepts are found: St Michael in Hildesheim,

[59] Briefly discussed with further bibliography in R. Plant, 'Architectural Developments in the Empire North of the Alps: The Patronage of the Imperial Court', in *The White Mantle of Churches*, ed. N. Hiscock, Turnhout 2003, 45–6.
[60] Fernie, *Architecture of Norman England*, 93–6.
[61] Wimpfen: H. Wischermann, *Romanik in Baden-Württemburg*, Stuttgart 1987, 240; Magdeburg: B. Ludowici, 'Archäologische Quellen zur Pfalz Ottos I. in Magdeburg: erste Ergebnisse der Auswertung der Grabungen 1959 bis 1968 auf dem Magdeburger Domplatz', in *Ottonische Neuanfänge: Symposion zur Austellung Otto der Grosse, Magdeburg und Europa*, ed. B. Schneidmüller and S. Weinfurter, Mainz 2001, 71–84; R. Kuhn, 'Die Kirchen des Magdeburger Domhügels', in *Aufbruch in die Gotik: Die Magdeburger Dom und die Späte Stauferzeit*, ed. M. Puhle, I, Mainz 2009, 39–53.

PLATE 6
Hildesheim, church of St Michael, east transept looking north east.

(Plate 6) where there are chapels on three levels in both east and west transepts, and (probably) at St Lebuinus in Deventer, though the arrangement at St Pantaleon is obviously analogous.

It is also clear that some, if not all, of the double transept buildings in the Empire were making some reference to Old St Peter's. This is most obviously true at the prototype Cologne cathedral, which had its high altar, dedicated to St Peter, at the west end. The western apse was flanked by round towers, as was the case at Rome, the church had, by the middle of the eleventh century at least (the date is once again controversial) pairs of aisles flanking the main vessel, again as at Rome, and to the east of the eastern apse was an atrium linking the cathedral church to the eleventh-century church of S. Maria ad Gradus, a dedication replicating that at Rome.[62] The association with the church of the Apostle was evidently understood at some of the followers. In the cathedral of St Lambert at Liège, for example, relics of the titular saint of the church were kept in the western choir, as they were at St Peter's. This association would make the plan with a western transept a most appropriate form for the two great churches of East Anglia, housing the relics of major Anglo-Saxon saints.

The evocation of sacred places or topographies in the medieval architecture of the Empire was extensive, and has a correspondingly extensive literature.[63] The impact of the architecture of the Empire beyond its borders has been less widely acknowledged. In the case of the churches discussed above, the mechanisms whereby the architectural schemes were transmitted remains unclear, but discussing them in their North Sea context helps illuminate their purpose.

---

[62] Helmut Fussbroich, 'St Maria BV ad Gradus' in *Köln: Die Romanischen Kirchen Von den Anfängen bis zum Zweiten Weltkrieg*, ed. H. Kier and U. Krings, Cologne 1984, 557–61.

[63] Plant, 'Architectural Developments in the Empire', 49–51 summarizes some, with further literature.

— Chapter 15 —

ALL IN THE SAME BOAT?
EAST ANGLIA, THE NORTH SEA WORLD AND THE 1147 EXPEDITION TO LISBON

Charles West

INTRODUCTION[1]

In May 1147, a substantial fleet of around two hundred ships, composed for the most part of contingents from Flanders, northern Germany and England, set sail from the southern English port of Dartmouth, where it had gathered. After putting in at the Portuguese coast for food and water, it assisted the Portuguese king Afonso in a seventeen-week siege of the city of Lisbon, held at the time by one of the *taifa* rulers of al-Andalus, which ended successfully with the city's capture in October. Most of the fleet then sailed on, arriving eventually on the shores of Syria, but its subsequent achievements were probably less distinguished, and in any case certainly more obscure, as our major – though not unique – source for its activities, an eyewitness text known as the *De Expugnatione Lyxbonensi* ('On the Storming of Lisbon'), does not cover the events that followed the city's fall.[2]

This expedition has not exactly been neglected by historians, but its discussion has been largely confined to histories of Portugal, where it is usually guaranteed at

---

[1] I should like to thank Liesbeth van Houts, Simon Loseby, Susan Raich, and Christopher Tyerman for their helpful comments on an earlier draft of this chapter.
[2] *De Expugnatione Lyxbonensi: The Conquest of Lisbon*, ed. and trans. C. W. David, with a foreword by J. Phillips, New York 2001. The other major source is the so-called Lisbon Letter, edited in its various versions by S. Edgington, 'The Lisbon Letter of the Second Crusade', *Historical Research* 69, 1996, 328–39. A number of annals and chronicles preserve briefer and in general less insightful accounts, including Henry of Huntingdon's *Historia Anglorum*, the *Annales Elmarenses*, continuations of Sigibert's world chronicle, a fragment associated with Guibert of Nogent known as the 'Little Chronicle of Count Baldwin', and Helmold of Bosau's *Chronica Slavorum*. The only near-contemporary Portuguese narrative is provided by the (not entirely trustworthy) *Indiculum Fundationis monasterii sancti Vincenti*, in *Portugaliae Monumenta Historica, Scriptores*, ed. A. Herculano, Lisbon 1856, 90–93, which was written in the 1180s. For documentary evidence, see the material discussed in A. Virgili, 'Angli cum multis aliis alienigenis: Crusade Settlers in Tortosa (Second Half of the Twelfth Century)', *Journal of Medieval History* 35, 2009, 297–312.

least passing mention, and to studies of the crusading movement.³ There it has often received more extended consideration, treated as one element of the Second Crusade, the Latin West's response to the fall of Edessa in December 1144. These two contexts seem natural and self-evident; to discuss the expedition in a book on East Anglia and the North Sea world may appear by comparison somewhat eccentric. Nevertheless, I would like to suggest that to do so is not merely justifiable, but actually permits a better grasp of the episode's particularities than does seeing it simply as a footnote to the Second Crusade or a milestone in early Portuguese history. Viewed from this perspective, the expedition serves to demonstrate how medieval East Anglia's links to its North Sea world mattered, not just to the history of East Anglia or the North Sea, but within a broader European frame too.

THE DARTMOUTH EXPEDITION AND THE SECOND CRUSADE

To describe the Dartmouth expedition as a footnote to the Second Crusade in fact rather understates its role in the recent revival of interest in the latter. This revival, most closely associated today with the work of Jonathan Phillips, avowedly takes inspiration from a seminal article by Giles Constable, written in 1953.⁴ Constable argued that in spite of its superficially disparate appearance, the Second Crusade was actually a well managed combined assault against the enemies of Christendom, targeting from the outset not only the Arab leaders in Syria, but also the pagan Wends in the north, and al-Andalusian territories in the Iberian peninsula. Although lacking the drama of the First Crusade and the glamour of the Third, the Second could nevertheless be appreciated as a properly systematic attempt to extend the frontiers of Christendom.

The Dartmouth expedition formed a crucial element of Constable's argument. Against those who assumed that the fleet had initially been bound for Jerusalem, and was only diverted or distracted into its Portuguese adventure, Constable proposed that the siege of Lisbon had been pre-planned as part of a wider strategy – in other words, that the fleet arrived at Lisbon by design, not by accident. It is a testimony to the influence of Constable's arguments that the capture of Lisbon is now routinely described as one of the few successes of a generally disastrous crusade.⁵

---

3 As an example, see S. Lay, *The Reconquest Kings of Portugal: Political and Cultural Reorientation on the Medieval Frontier*, Basingstoke 2009, 95–102.
4 G. Constable, 'The Second Crusade as Seen by Contemporaries', *Traditio* 9, 1953, 213–79. For discussion and restatement of this article's chief point, see J. Phillips, 'Papacy, Empire and the Second Crusade', *The Second Crusade: Scope and Consequences*, ed. M. Hoch and J. Phillips, Manchester 2001, 15–31; J. Phillips, 'Saint Bernard of Clairvaux, the Low Countries and the Lisbon Letter of the Second Crusade', *Journal of Ecclesiastical History* 48, 1997, 485–97; and J. Phillips, *The Second Crusade: Extending the Frontiers of Christendom*, New York 2007, xxiv–xxviii.
5 See, for example, Phillips, *The Second Crusade*, 136, and similar comments in his foreword to the *De Expugnatione*; cf. S. Edgington, 'Albert of Aachen, Saint Bernard and the Second Crusade', in *The Second Crusade*, ed. Hoch and Phillips, 54–70, at 60; and S. Lay, 'Miracles, Martyrs and the Cult of Henry the Crusader in Lisbon', *Portuguese Studies* 24, 2008, 7–31, at 7.

The vision of the Second Crusade as Bernard of Clairvaux's enterprise that underpins most of the recent scholarship on the topic is fully in harmony with the widespread tendency of much recent crusading historiography to analyse all post-1096 religiously-inspired war from a top-down, pope-oriented perspective (the so-called 'pluralist' school).[6] Yet influential though it may be, this is not a vision without its critics. At a general level, quite how institutionalized the crusades were in the twelfth century has been brought into question. Christopher Tyerman, for example, has suggested that in an important sense there were no crusades in the twelfth century, merely episodic and disjointed attempts to repeat the success of the expedition of 1096.[7] If Tyerman and others are right, then attempts to classify the numerous religiously-influenced outbreaks of organized violence as part of or separate from the crusading movement in the twelfth century are in themselves misconceived, since any attempt to see crusade prior to the thirteenth century as a technical term, and thence to use it to categorize post-1096 holy war as crusading or not, is anachronistic.

The radical implications of this challenge to the nature of crusading historiography is not my concern here, but it does provide a general framework for a reconsideration of the association of the Dartmouth expedition with the other constituent elements collectively classified as the Second Crusade. This association rests in particular on four propositions: that St Bernard, who is usually understood to have acted as the mouthpiece of the papacy, was directly involved in planning the Dartmouth expedition; that Lisbon was intended as the expedition's destination from the beginning, and so can be understood as part of the Crusade's distinctive aim to expand Christendom in all directions; that there were papal legates on board the fleet; and, finally, that contemporaries themselves perceived the Dartmouth expedition as an integral part of the Second Crusade. On close investigation, none of these connections withstands scrutiny.[8]

The evidence for Bernard's direct involvement in the expedition rests chiefly on a letter he addressed to King Afonso. The letter is however far from unambiguous, and in any case, a detailed recent study by Alan Forey has thrown the letter's authenticity into doubt.[9] Already in 1953 Constable himself acknowledged that there were problems with it, but Forey has convincingly shown that because of a very suspicious transmission – it is preserved only in early modern copies associated with known forgers – it simply cannot be taken as reliable evidence.[10] Other

---

[6] See C. Tyerman, *The Debate on the Crusades, 1099-2010*, Manchester 2011, particularly 216–246, for an overview of recent historiography.

[7] C. Tyerman, 'Were There Any Crusades in the Twelfth Century?', *English Historical Review* 110, 1995, 553–77. Compare here the important comments in J. Gilchrist, 'Papacy and the War against the Saracens, 795–1216', *International History Review* 10, 1988, 174–97.

[8] Much of the following further develops arguments formulated by J. France, 'Logistics and the Second Crusade', in *Logistics of Warfare in the Age of the Crusades*, ed. J. Pryor, Aldershot 2006, 77–93; and by C. Tyerman, *God's War*, London 2006, 308–17.

[9] A. Forey, 'The Siege of Lisbon and the Second Crusade', *Portuguese Studies* 20, 2004, 1–13.

[10] Constable, 'The Second Crusade', 261, n.175. Phillips has accepted this correction: see his *Second Crusade*, 139, n.20.

evidence for Bernard's personal involvement is scarcely any more conclusive. For example, the observation that he had met some of the Flemish participants is really only an elaboration of the fact that one or two Flemings who took part in the expedition had, amongst other witnesses, attested donations undertaken in Flanders involving Bernard.[11] Bernard might have glad-handed them in the throng, or he might not. In any case, we should note that our major source includes a speech which states that the fleet had mustered and set sail 'without the urging of any preacher'.[12] This is not to gainsay the overarching role of Bernard's preaching tour in promoting the Latin West's response to the fall of Edessa, whose general importance is widely acknowledged, nor does it mean that we should cease to try to sniff out Bernardine theological influence; it is merely to observe that there is no convincing evidence that Bernard had a direct hand in planning, or even that, 'predisposed to be receptive' to Iberian initiative, he and Pope Eugenius III in some way facilitated an attack on Lisbon.[13]

Bernard's letter has also served as the main proof adduced to show that Lisbon was the expedition's pre-meditated destination. With the letter so weakened as evidence, this idea too seems much less attractive. As Forey and others have noted, not a single source states that Lisbon was the initial target, and Pope Eugenius III's silence on the matter, while he issued bulls for assaults on Tortosa and the Baltic, is surely deafening. In fact, our major source, the *De Expugnatione*, includes a long speech from a Portuguese bishop whose entire purpose is to persuade the fleet to stay in Portugal. That this speech shows indications of literary reworking, whether by the original author of the *De Expugnatione* or by the copyist of the single extant manuscript, is beside the point.[14] What matters is that whoever was responsible for the text we have today was happy to give the impression that the Dartmouth fleet's Portuguese adventures were contingent, not definitively pre-meditated or pre-arranged.

The idea that there were papal legates on board the fleet is based largely on arguments about the author of the *De Expugnatione* put forward in an influential article by Harold Livermore. Proposing that the R. who identifies himself as the work's author was a cleric named Raol, a priest in the entourage of the East Anglian Glanville family, Livermore went on to suggest that Raol was himself the representative of the papacy, on the basis that he possessed a fragment of the True Cross,

---

[11] Phillips, *The Second Crusade*, 141–2. The charter is in *De oorkonden der Graven van Vlaanderen*, ed. A. Verhulst and T. De Hemptinne, Brussels 1988, 152, no. 92.

[12] Phillips's quotation from this speech (*The Second Crusade*, 146) omits this clause (*De Expugnatione*, 72).

[13] Phillips, *The Second Crusade*, xxvii, for the phrase. On Bernard's theological influence, see J. Phillips, 'Ideas of Crusade and Holy War in *De Expugnatione Lyxbonensi*', in *Holy Land, Holy Lands, and Christian History*, Studies in Church History 36, ed. R. Swanson, Woodbridge 2000, 123–41, arguing that the theology of *De Expugnatione*, at least in its current form, reflects Bernard's ideas.

[14] See the detailed analysis in E.-D. Hehl, *Kirche und Krieg im 12. Jahrhundert*, Stuttgart 1980, Appendix I, 'Kanonistische Vorlagen in der Predigt des Bischofs von Porto zu den Kreuzfahrern', 259–61.

was personally very wealthy, and associated himself with kings.[15] Every step of this argument can however be questioned.[16] Leaving aside the questions of the author's identity, and whether it was the author himself who possessed the relics (for the text actually attributes them to an anonymous cleric), it is far from certain that relics of the True Cross were rare enough in the mid twelfth century to be exclusive to papal representatives.[17] The notion of Raol's personal wealth is based on a charter donating land and, supposedly, money, to a newly-founded priory outside Lisbon immediately after the siege. This man may or may not be the same as the author of our text, but in any case, the charter does not really attest to the donor's personal wealth. The land in question could have been acquired in any number of ways after a military conquest, and closer inspection reveals what has been interpreted as a cash donation of 200 marks of silver – certainly a princely sum – as actually part of a penalty clause, condemning anyone breaking the terms of the donation to an enormous fine.[18] Whether the foundation charter's assertion that it was witnessed by kings can be relied upon is an issue I must leave to those more expert in Portuguese diplomatic, though retouching of foundation charters is hardly unusual elsewhere in Europe, and the charter has some inconsistencies with other accounts.[19]

Finally, the argument that contemporaries saw the Dartmouth expedition of 1147 as an integral part of the Second Crusade can only be partially justified. It is certainly true, as Constable emphasized, that the Saxon chronicler Helmold of Bosau describes the crusading effort as being split in three directions, against Muslims in Spain, Muslims in the Holy Land, and Slavs in north-eastern Europe.[20] But Helmold wrote in the 1160s and 1170s, not the 1140s, and so had the benefit of hindsight. In any case, his description of the Lisbon expedition strongly implies that the Dartmouth expedition was not originally intending to put in there at all, since, like the *De Expugnatione*, he describes how the Portuguese had to persuade the fleet when it moored offshore to assist.[21] It seems more likely that Helmold was simply grouping contemporary events together to try to make sense of the past, as

---

[15] H. Livermore, 'The "Conquest of Lisbon" and Its Author', *Portuguese Studies* 6, 1990, 1–16. The reference to Raol's personal wealth is repeated in Phillips, *The Second Crusade*, 136–7; Raol as papal legate in idem, 162. Similar arguments are expressed in Phillips's foreword to the *De Expugnatione*.
[16] Even the identification of Raol is uncertain, given that the father of the dedicatee, Osbert, was a certain Roger, another R.: see R. Mortimer, 'The Family of Rannulf de Glanville', *Bulletin of the Institute of Historical Research* 54, 1981, 1–16; for further caution, see also Lay, 'Miracles', 15, n.20.
[17] A. Frolow, *La relique de la vraie Croix, recherches sur le développement d'un culte*, Paris 1961. For a concrete example of how these relics circulated at just this time, see *Chronique de Saint-Pierre-le-Vif de Sens, dite de Clarius* ed. and trans. R.-H. Bautier and M. Gilles, Paris 1979, 184–6.
[18] As is evident from inspection of the facsimile helpfully printed by Livermore, 'Conquest', 5.
[19] For example, the *Indiculum Fundationis* states that it was the king who built the cemetery churches, rather than the crusaders; and interestingly, it states that the 'German' priest was called Roard. See Lay, 'Miracles', for a discussion of how the siege, and its Christian victims, were used in later medieval Portuguese history-writing.
[20] Helmold of Bosau, *Chronicle of the Slavs*, tr. F. Tschan, New York 1935, 216.
[21] Ibid., 220.

chroniclers do: Helmold's text does not prove that the master organizers had a grand plan, or for that matter that there were really any master organizers at all.

Our conclusion must therefore be that the adventurers who set sail from Dartmouth in early 1147 had not been briefed by Bernard or anyone else to besiege Lisbon; they had simply heard of the troubles affecting Outremer, and intended to go to help there, until they were persuaded first by the bishop of Oporto, then by King Afonso himself, that their assistance in Portugal would be just as valuable and, in every sense, rewarding a use of their time and energies.[22] This perspective brings into question how far we should conceptualize the Second Crusade as a whole, which begins to look more like a group of essentially autonomous responses to a developing situation that were certainly stimulated by Bernard's preaching tour, but not organized or determined by him.

More relevant for our present purpose, however, is that uncoupling the Dartmouth expedition from the 'Second Crusade', and understanding it instead as one of several essentially autonomous responses to reports of crisis in the east, also carries important implications for how we perceive the expedition itself. Specifically, there are several questions which can be side-stepped if the expedition is classified as part of an organized crusade, but which become more pressing if it is viewed differently. The most glaring of these is the issue of precisely how the Dartmouth expedition was arranged. If the direct involvement of the pope or St Bernard cannot be seen in any surviving source, how did almost 200 ships come together to create a fleet capable of assaulting and conquering a sizeable, well defended port on the Atlantic coast of Portugal?

THE DARTMOUTH EXPEDITION'S OATH

Most recent historiography tends to stress the involvement of a number of leading figures, and this is not entirely without support in the evidence. The *De Expugnatione*, here as often our most detailed source, makes reference to 'four constables' under whom it places the Anglo-Norman contingent and of whom the most important was Hervey of Glanville, to a Flemish castellan named Christian of Ghistelles to whom the author attributed command of the Flemings, and to a Rhineland count named Arnold of Aershot, who was in charge of the men from the Holy Roman Empire.[23] It does not, however, include a claim that these figures actually organized the expedition in the first place, and it shows them offering strikingly little by way of leadership once the expedition was underway. On a variety of important questions, in fact when any decision of genuine importance had to be taken, these individuals were ignored, and a general meeting of all the participants was held – a noisy affair which, according to the *De Expugnatione*, rather unnerved the properly refined aristocratic sensibilities of King Afonso, who was

---

[22] That they indeed went on to Syria is shown by the *Annales Elmarenses*, in *Les Annales de Saint-Pierre de Gand et de Saint Amand*, ed. P. Grierson, Brussels 1937, 111.
[23] *De Expugnatione*, 52–4.

informed that the expedition had not yet 'decided on anyone on whom authority should be conferred to make answer for all'.[24]

Far more important than aristocratic leadership in providing the necessary coherence to the fleet was the swearing of a collective oath at Dartmouth prior to sailing. This oath, subsequently invoked on a number of occasions in the course of the expedition, established the basic guidelines of how the fleet was to operate both during the journey and on disembarkation.[25] There were to be regular religious services, brawling was prohibited, the fair distribution of any spoils arranged, and, perhaps most interestingly, a number of judges were elected as the chosen representatives of the fleet's participants to resolve any disputes. There are enough parallels to this oath in other comparable instances to reassure the reader that the *De Expugnatione* was not wholly making them up.[26] But there are enough differences to confirm its specificity, too. The crusading army of King Louis VII, camped at Metz in 1147, swore 'laws necessary for securing peace and other requirements on the journey', but not only were these laws not in fact kept, they were also very clearly hierarchically imposed.[27]

Reflecting the interpretation of the expedition as part of the Second Crusade, and perhaps too an assumption that elites were always in charge in some way in the Middle Ages, some historians have been tempted to seek connections between the Dartmouth oath and, once again, St Bernard of Clairvaux.[28] There is certainly no doubt that Bernard had strong views on the nature of friendship and mutual obligation, and saw armies as corporate entities. Yet to view this particular association (or *coniuratio*, in the Latin) as an indication of Bernardine influence seems a little forced.[29] The oaths in question were not taken simply as a spiritual bonding exercise, but in response to the challenge of how to create a composite community where none had existed before, and in the absence of any obvious alternative.

Though it is not impossible that Bernard's deputies were present at Dartmouth, informing the decisions taken in ways consistent with the great Cistercian's theological priorities, when viewed without the lenses of crusading faith, the oaths resemble most of all the establishment of a merchants' guild, or the creation of an urban commune.[30] Just as in the case of the communes, the Dartmouth oath was

---

[24] Ibid., 98 ('sed nondum deliberatum cui responsionis officia committerent'); cf. similar meetings, 126, 166, 176.
[25] The oath is detailed in ibid., 56; for later references to it, see 100, 104, 118, and 166.
[26] Cf. S. Reynolds, *Kingdoms and Communities in Western Europe, 900–1300*, Oxford 1984, for a tour de force exposition of the pervasiveness of 'horizontal' bonds in medieval Europe.
[27] Odo of Deuil, *De profectione Ludovici VII in orientem*, ed. and trans. V. Berry, New York 1948, 20: these *leges* were enacted by the king.
[28] For example, for Constable, 'Second Crusade', 238, the oath 'shows the influence of St Bernard and of the rule written for him by the Templars…'; cf. Phillips, 'Saint Bernard', 495.
[29] The argument has also now become circular: for example, J. Brundage, 'St Bernard and the Jurists', in *The Second Crusade*, ed. Hoch and Phillips, 25–34, uses the Lisbon material as evidence for Bernard's attitudes.
[30] On this, useful overviews from a European perspective are provided by G. Dilcher, 'Historiographische Traditionen, Sachprobleme und Fragestellungen der Erforschung der mitte-

intended 'to ensure protection, security and equality in law'.[31] Indeed, similar issues are covered, and in much the same way, as in oaths for guilds and other urban associations. For example, the celebrated Flemish Saint-Omer guild regulations, which may have been put together as early as the 1120s, also contain clauses about priests, clothing, exclusionary meetings, specific compensation for injuries, and discussion of the duties of elected officials, and they arrange payments to merchants' wives when the merchants are away – perhaps to keep the women indoors and honourable, much as arranged at Dartmouth.[32] Little of this, in fact, would have surprised the inhabitants of later Italian communes.[33]

In view of who made up a substantial proportion of those on the expedition, little of it should surprise us, either. Near-contemporary sources stress not the aristocratic element, but quite the reverse, the low social status of those involved. And the *De Expugnatione* gives us more details. It does not tell us anything more about who made up the Flemish element, but we do hear of the people from Hastings, Ipswich, Bristol, and Southampton, towns on the southern and eastern coasts of England that were growing at just this time. Significantly, as the *De Expugnatione* continues, the grand 'army of the Holy Roman Empire' turns into the more revealing 'men of Cologne'.[34] That the urban component was considerable, if not predominant, is further suggested by the behaviour of those participants who remained in the Iberian peninsula, who apparently settled in the towns, not the countryside. Even the inducements offered to the expedition by King Afonso, which included a remission of trading tolls, carry the same implications: this was an offer designed to appeal to traders.[35] Finally, the very fleet itself implies the involvement of urban merchants. Most similar naval expeditions in the twelfth and thirteenth centuries seem to have been connected with towns, and the evidence for boat ownership points in the same direction. Such boats' design had, conveniently enough,

---

lalterlichen Stadt', *Stadt und Recht im Mittelalter*, ed. P. Monnet and O. Oexle, Göttingen 2003, 73–95, though it is perhaps a little over-enthusiastically neo-Weberian; and F. Opll, 'Das Werden der mittelalterlichen Stadt', *Historisches Zeitschrift* 280, 2005, 561-89. Important studies include E. Ennen, *Die europäischer Stadt des Mittelalters*, Göttingen 1972, particularly chapter 4; K. Lilley, *Urban Life in the Middle Ages, 1000–1450*, Basingstoke 2002, and the enormous and invaluable D. Palliser (ed.), *Cambridge History of urban Britain*, vol. I, Cambridge 2000.

[31] A. Verhulst, *The Rise of Cities in North-West Europe*, Cambridge 1999, 126. The comparison was first made, according to Charles David, by none other than Pirenne himself in personal correspondence (*De Expugnatione*, 57, n.5).

[32] G. Espinas and H. Pirenne, 'Les coutumes de la gilde marchande de Saint-Omer', *Le Moyen Age* 14, 1901, 189–96, though caution is required concerning the date, given that the text is itself undated and the manuscript is fourteenth-century.

[33] The restrictions on clothing are perhaps particularly interesting in this light: cf. D. O. Hughes, 'Sumptuary Law and Social Relations in Renaissance Italy', in *Disputes and Settlements: Law and Human Relations in the West*, ed. J. Bossy, Cambridge 1983, 69–99, for strong, albeit later, Italian parallels. On civic collaboration in northern Italy, see G. Raccagni, *The Lombard League, 1167–1225*, Oxford 2010.

[34] On the towns, see Palliser, ed., *Cambridge Urban History*, vol. I, particularly the section on East Anglia by B. Brodt, pp. 639–56.

[35] For settlement, see Virgili, 'Angli'. On the toll, see *De Expugnatione*, 112.

begun to change in the eleventh century, with the addition of deeper keels which made merchant ships more capable of long-distance, blue water travel.[36]

The fact that urban participation on the expedition was by no means restricted to the English further supports the notion that this oath bears some relation to urban contexts, since the evidence for the collective activities of urban communities in north-west continental Europe is both somewhat earlier in date and less ambivalent in nature than the English material, and so provides perfect context for the Dartmouth expedition.[37] For example, the Flemish towns had already mounted a determined common resistance to a newly appointed count in 1127, while Cologne, whose 'extraordinary capacity for group formation' has been remarked on elsewhere, has an urban seal that dates from almost exactly the same time as some of its citizens travelled to Dartmouth, in turn just a few years before its merchants began to win privileges from the Holy Roman Emperor.[38] Some of the parallels between the Dartmouth oath and certain aspects of Cologne's urban organization are rather striking. By the mid twelfth century, the Rhineland city was divided into twelve parishes, all of which had civic functions and elected officers, and we have lists of members of these parishes, strongly resembling guilds, that happen to date to the 1140s.[39] Significantly, two of these 'parishes' were not in origin ecclesiastical units at all, but purely civic districts, called *parrochiae* simply by force of habit.[40] All this resonates very strongly with the agreement at Dartmouth to consider each boat a 'parish'. One is led to wonder exactly whose idea the oath at Dartmouth was: for all that the meeting point was an English port, doubtless chosen for the convenience of winds or currents, the agreement has a strong continental flavour to it.

So, even if we do not need to see the communal oath as a *specifically* urban form of organization – all sorts of communities swore collective oaths in the Middle

---

[36] For comparative evidence on merchants owning ships, see P. Strait, *Cologne in the Twelfth Century*, Gainesville 1974, 25 (based on Lambert of Hersfeld's chronicle). On ship design, see R. Unger, 'Warships and Cargo Ships in Medieval Europe', *Technology and Culture* 22, 1981, 233–52, and R. van de Noort, *North Sea Archaeologies: A Maritime Biography, 10,000 BC to AD 1500* Oxford 2011, 172–4.

[37] An overview is given by K. Schulz, *'Denn sie lieben die Freiheit so sehr': kommunale Aufstände und Entstehung des europäischen Bürgertums im Hochmittelalter*, Darmstadt 1992. For guilds, see I. Gadd and P. Wallis (ed.), *Guilds and Associations in Europe*, London 2006, particularly the article by D. Keene, 'English Urban Guilds, 900–1300: The Purposes and Politics of Association', 3–26.

[38] For Flanders, see in general Verhulst, *Rise*, particularly 119–48. For Cologne's seal, see Strait, *Cologne*, 62; for the quote, see M. Groten, 'Von den wunderbaren Grösse Kölns oder: Was war das Besondere an der Kölner Stadtverfassung des 12. Jahrhunderts?', *Mitteleuropäisches Städtewesen im Mittelalter und Neuzeit*, ed. W. Janssen and M. Wensky, Vienna 1999, 41–62, at 43.

[39] For an account of the duties of these parishes dating to around 1150, see K. Beyerle, 'Die Anfänge des Kölner Schreinswesens', *Zeitschrift für Rechtsgeschichte: Germanistische Abteilung* 51, 1931, 318–509. The guild lists are reproduced in facsimile in R. Höniger (ed.), *Kölner Schreinsurkunden des zwölften Jahrhunderts: Quellen zur Rechts- und Wirthschaftsgeschichte der Stadt Köln*, 3 vols, Bonn 1884–94, vol. 2; for a discussion, see H. von Lösch, *Die Kölner Kaufmannsgilde im zwölften Jahrhundert*, Trier 1904. Thankfully these remarkable 'Schreinsurkunden' survived the 2009 collapse of the Cologne archive.

[40] Niederich and Airsbach: Strait, *Cologne*, 47.

Ages, as Susan Reynolds has rightly stressed – in this particular case it seems unnecessary to search for any inspiration behind it beyond the direct, personal, previous experience of many of the participants.[41] Although the urban resonances of these oaths have been noticed before, the theme has never been developed, perhaps because historians of the crusades and historians of urbanism are specialists in rather different fields, but perhaps also because the role of the non-noble in holy wars tends to be understated in much recent crusading historiography.[42] Seen from this angle, the Dartmouth expedition appears less as the third wing of St Bernard's grand Christian offensive, and more as a semi-improvised association of men from the towns, who organized themselves as townsmen usually did by the twelfth century, with remarkable success.

THE DARTMOUTH EXPEDITION AND THE NORTH SEA WORLD

What connected men from towns and coastal hinterlands from eastern and southern England, Flanders, and the Rhineland, what brought them together to swear this oath in the first place? The answer is surely obvious: the North Sea, and the trading networks that were developing across it. True, direct archaeological proof for extensive North Sea trade before the later twelfth century is thin on the ground; yet that such trade existed, and that it was relatively intense by the twelfth century, is undeniable.[43] So too is it that it involved precisely the kinds of people who met at Dartmouth. Texts such as the Billingsgate tolls, the Koblenz tolls, and the Law of the Lorrainers, prove that it was people from Flanders, the Rhineland, and England, and particularly eastern England, who were engaged in trade of various kinds of goods already from the early eleventh century.[44] If this were not

---

[41] D. C. Douglas, *Social Structure of Medieval East Anglia*, Oxford 1927, provides a still useful study of these countryside communities.

[42] See note 6 above.

[43] For the lack of clear archaeological proof of trade before the very late twelfth century, see A. Vince, 'The Use of Pottery to Chart Trade Routes in the North Sea and Baltic Areas', in *Cogs, Cargoes, and Commerce: Maritime Bulk Trade in Northern Europe, 1150–1400*, ed. L. Berggren, N. Hyble, and A. Landen, Toronto 2002. For the evidence afforded by coins, J. Huffmann, 'Documentary Evidence of Anglo-German Currency Movement in the Central Middle Ages: Cologne and English Sterling', *British Numismatic Journal* 65 (1995), 32–45, and B. Cook, 'Foreign Coins in Medieval England', *Local Coins, Foreign Coins*, ed. L. Travaini, Milan 1999, 231–84; and for an unpublished Andernach hoard of c.1050 that included a number of English coins, A. Reverchon, *Metzer Denare vom 10 bis 13 Jahrhundert: Untersuchungen zu den Währungsräumen zwischen Maas und Rhein*, Trier 2006, 464.

[44] For eastern England's economic connections with Flanders in particular, see the chapter by E. Oksanen in this volume, pp. 174–87. The Law of the Lorrainers is edited by M. Bateson, 'A London Municipal Collection of the Reign of John', *English Historical Review* 17, 1902, 483–511, 707–30; see J. Huffman, *Family, Commerce and Religion in London and Cologne: Anglo-German Emigrants, c.1000–1300*, Cambridge 1998, for a general discussion. For the Koblenz tolls, T. Kölzer, 'Der Koblenzer Zoll im 11 und 12 Jahrhundert: eine diplomatisch-palaeographische Nachlese', *Rheinische Vierteljahrsblatter* 66, 2002, 39–73.

enough, we should know that these were people used to living with each other, as well as trading with one another, from the evidence for diasporic merchant communities, which records men from Ipswich, amongst other English towns, living in Cologne in the 1150s, and plenty of men from Cologne resident in England, and particularly eastern England, at around the same time.[45]

Accompanying the intensification of trade across the North Sea were more concerted efforts to exploit the sea's resources, probably in part a response to the demand of the trading towns developing along its coasts. Recent archaeological investigations, using fish bone evidence, have proposed an 'AD 1000 fish event horizon', the point at which marine fish began to form a larger part of urban or proto-urban diets than fresh-water fish across the North Sea littoral.[46] Documentary traces of this shift can be found in eleventh-century English evidence, for example in the herring renders recorded in Domesday, which came from precisely the English counties best represented in the Dartmouth expedition. Sea fishing as a livelihood could be expected to promote international contacts, and there is some evidence to suggest that this was the case, with fishing fleets from Germany and Antwerp apparently coming to Yarmouth, for instance, on a regular basis in the early twelfth century.[47]

In the absence of any further evidence, the only reasonable conclusion to draw is that it was from these fishing and trading networks that the idea of putting together a fleet came. Doubtless the wealthier elements, and perhaps even some of the lesser aristocracy who were seeking to tap the growing prosperity of the North Sea trade, played a leading role; nevertheless, the 'international' character of the fleet is powerful witness to its comparatively unhierarchical nature. Huffman has observed that 'This venture shows both the interregional cooperation and interaction created by crusading...'.[48] Yet this statement might be better reversed, to suggest that the channels of communication routinely maintained for trade and mercantile information might also be used, on occasion, for preparing holy war.

Of course, it may be that for the social coherence of the North Sea world to find the particularly striking expression that this chapter proposes it did in 1147, favourable political circumstances were required, and the conditions had to be right. In the 1140s, the North Sea was unusually peaceful. The count of Flanders, Count Thierry, had enjoyed good relations with England since he began his rule, snatching Flanders from Henry I's greatly feared nephew, William Clito. But he also had cordial relations with the Holy Roman Empire, as the son of the duke of Upper Lotharingia; and he maintained good links too with King Louis VII, on whose expedition to Jerusalem he participated. England's rulers, caught up in civil

---

[45] Huffmann, *Family*, 83 for Adam of Ipswich; and 162 for eastern England in general.
[46] Van de Noort, *Archaeologies*, 86–9.
[47] J. Campbell, 'Domesday Herrings', in *East Anglia's History: Studies in honour of Norman Scarfe*, ed. C. Harper-Bill, C. Rawcliffe, and R. Wilson, Woodbridge 2002, 5–18, with further references. The counties are Norfolk, Suffolk, Kent, Sussex and Surrey.
[48] Huffmann, *Family*, 235.

war, also had strong North Sea connections of their own at this time. Matilda was, after all, a former empress who had spent much of her youth in Rhineland cities, as well as the granddaughter of a Flemish princess; King Stephen was count of Boulogne by marriage.[49] This propitious North Sea conjuncture was to be short-lived, not least because King Henry II's accession, and the accompanying creation of an Angevin empire, gradually oriented England's politics, if not its economics, more towards the Atlantic coast, and after 1154, the North Sea became a more politically tense region.

However, it is not clear how important the high politics really was for the North Sea network manifested by the fleet at Dartmouth. After all, it was also Henry II who was the first Anglo-Norman king to grant merchants of Cologne formal trading privileges. In fact, in the course of the thirteenth century, the North Sea trading network would gain institutional coherence, with the consolidation in England of the Cinque Ports, and on a larger scale, of the Hansa, a trading cooperative which for a time dominated trade in the North Sea and its increasingly busy adjunct, the Baltic.[50] And there is evidence, albeit less evocative in nature than the *De Expugnatione*, to show that the North Sea community had already mounted expeditions of a strikingly similar nature in an earlier generation, and would do so again later, too. Amidst many fleets mentioned by Albert of Aachen's account of the First Crusade is one that arrived in the eastern Mediterranean in 1106, with representatives from England, Flanders, Antwerp and Denmark, again without recognizable aristocratic leadership.[51] Similarly, in 1189 a fleet composed of contingents from Germany, Flanders and England would meet again at Dartmouth, and again stop off in Portugal, en route to the Holy Land.[52]

CONCLUSION

The Dartmouth expedition is surely best viewed as testimony to a latent but persistent potential built up by trading connections across the North Sea, a testimony whose full nature can only be appreciated when untethered, even if only momentarily, from the typological classifications and papal-centred approach of much crusading historiography. That potential should perhaps not surprise us, for unlike the Mediterranean, that benchmark of interactions across water, and notwithstanding the occasional conflict over trading privileges, the communities inte-

---

[49] For Matilda's period in Germany, see M. Chibnall, *Empress Matilda: Queen Consort, Queen Mother and Lady of the English*, Oxford 1991, 22–44. On Stephen, see E. King, *King Stephen*, New Haven and London 2010.

[50] D. Kirby and M.-L. Hinkkanen, *The Baltic and North Seas*, London 2000, is a good general introduction. On the Cinque Ports – important but not of direct concern here – see the forthcoming work of Susan Raich.

[51] Albert of Aachen, *Historia Ierosolimitana – History of the Journey to Jerusalem*, ed. and trans. S. Edgington, Oxford 2006, Book X, c.1, p. 718.

[52] For subsequent expeditions to Portugal, see Lay, 'Miracles'. On the 1189 fleet in particular, Tyerman, *God's War*, 413–14.

grated into the North Sea network were fundamentally rather similar to one another in cultural terms.[53]

Indeed, the *De Expugnatione* demonstrates that in spite of the different languages spoken amongst the Dartmouth fleet – the division between the Anglo-Normans on the one hand, and the men of Cologne and Flanders on the other, was particularly important – and quite apart from a shared interest in the defence of Christendom (and personal enrichment), all the participants evidently spoke a similar language of political organization, and did so fluently enough to make a success of a composite endeavour against stiff odds. That alone implies a basic similarity in values across the North Sea, or at least across the urban network which had developed around the sea. The expedition is therefore excellent evidence for how the North Sea could bring people closer together, as it had in earlier periods, and would again later, too.[54]

Nevertheless, this network of interests did not at all obliterate local identities. And for present purposes, perhaps the most interesting aspect of the Dartmouth expedition is how it reveals a North Sea world in which East Anglians were active participants. Our chief source singled out men from Norfolk and Suffolk – the former well known for its 'county patriotism' – as significant elements of the expedition.[55] But it also paid special attention to the vital role played by Hervey of Glanville, whose family's connections to East Anglia are well known, in keeping the expedition together at a crucial moment, and to the bravery in battle of 'seven youths' of Ipswich, distinguished by their bravery in battle. And, moreover, the *De Expugnatione Lyxbonensi* itself was addressed to an East Anglian cleric, and its unique and roughly contemporary manuscript was preserved in East Anglia until one of Norwich's better known sons, Archbishop Matthew Parker, donated it to Corpus Christi College, Cambridge, where it remains today. The major source for this particular manifestation of the North Sea world can therefore be considered as an East Anglian perspective on the event.[56]

I began by suggesting that this volume, on East Anglia and the North Sea world, is the best means of approaching the Dartmouth expedition, a context better suited

---

[53] For the conflict between Ghent and Cologne over wine in the later twelfth century, see Verhulst, *Rise*, 138–9. On conceptualizing the Mediterranean, see D. Abulafia, 'Mediterraneans', in *Rethinking the Mediterranean*, ed. W. Harris, Oxford 2005, 64–93.

[54] See M. Carver, 'Pre-Viking Traffic in the North Sea', in *Maritime Celts, Frisians and Saxons*, ed. S. McGrail, London 1990, 117–25; and S. Lebecq, *Marchands et navigateurs frisons du haut Moyen Age*, Lille 1983, for studies of the earlier period, and J. Roding and L. van Voss (eds), *The North Sea and Culture (1550-1800)*, Hilversum 1996, for studies of the later.

[55] See D. Crouch, 'From Stenton to MacFarlane: Models of Societies of the Twelfth and Thirteenth Centuries', *Transactions of the Royal Historical Society* 6th ser., 5, 1995, 179–200, with further references.

[56] Corpus Christi College, Cambridge, MS 470, where the text occupies ff. 125–46. For the East Anglian provenance of Hervey de Glanville and his family, see Mortimer, 'The Family of Rannulf de Glanville' and Henry of Huntingdon, *Historia Anglorum*, ed. and trans. D. Greenway, Oxford 1996, for the editor's comments at pp. xxiii–xxv. For the manuscript's history, including Matthew Parker's donation of it, Livermore, 'The "Conquest of Lisbon" and its author'.

to elucidating the specifics of the event than subordinating it to a story about papal or Cistercian attempts to co-ordinate Christendom. But what I hope has also become apparent is that if the North Sea World sheds light on the Dartmouth expedition, the reverse is equally true. The Dartmouth expedition shows quite how natural a history of East Anglia and the North Sea world should be to write, for it leaves little room for doubt that ordinary East Anglians in the twelfth century would have seen themselves as part of that world.

---

[49] For Matilda's period in Germany, see M. Chibnall, *Empress Matilda: Queen Consort, Queen Mother and Lady of the English*, Oxford 1991, 22–44. On Stephen, see E. King, *King Stephen*, New Haven and London 2010.

[50] D. Kirby and M.-L. Hinkkanen, *The Baltic and North Seas*, London 2000, is a good general introduction. On the Cinque Ports – important but not of direct concern here – see the forthcoming work of Susan Raich.

[51] Albert of Aachen, *Historia Ierosolimitana – History of the Journey to Jerusalem*, ed. and trans. S. Edgington, Oxford 2006, Book X, c.1, p. 718.

[52] For subsequent expeditions to Portugal, see Lay, 'Miracles'. On the 1189 fleet in particular, Tyerman, *God's War*, 413–14.

— Chapter 16 —

THE *LIBER CELESTIS* OF ST BRIDGET OF SWEDEN (1302/3–1373) AND ITS INFLUENCE ON THE HOUSEHOLD CULTURE OF SOME LATE MEDIEVAL NORFOLK WOMEN

Carole Hill

For I telle the forsothe rygth as I spak to Seynt Bryde ryte so I speke to the, dowtyr, and I telle the trewly it is trewe euery word that is wretyn in Brides boke, and be the it xal be knowyn for very trewth.[1]

NORWICH WILLS and other texts, such as Margery Kempe's book, just quoted, make a clear statement of just how well disseminated were the written revelations of St Bridget of Sweden in fifteenth-century Norwich, even among those who could not read, as Margery (1373–1438?) herself makes clear. Furthermore, she goes so far as to state that Christ has given her parity with Bridget in the matter of personal revelation: '... right as I spoke to Saint Bridget right so I speak to thee'. Indeed, Margery saw her own role in authenticating Bridget's voice as Christ-ordained: '... by thee it shall be known for very truth'. Thus did Margery comprehend her call to live out Bridget's example and teachings. For the wife and daughter of a burgher from the port of Bishop's Lynn these were extraordinarily confident claims. But, as we shall see, they were precepts lived out domestically by other women less bent on sainthood than Kempe, but convinced, like her, of their moral authority and spiritual duty of care for their households and children.

Why should this be? The answer provides the hook from which hang many aspects of cultural and spiritual life in and around medieval Norwich. The establishment of the city as a base from which international trading had developed from its earliest Anglo-Scandinavian times, and the resultant prosperity, provided both the means and the conduit for a cross-fertilization of ideas, technology and evolving

---

[1] *The Book of Margery Kempe*, ed. S. B. Meech and H. E. Allen, Early English Text Society, original series 212, London and New York, 1940 (reprint Woodbridge 1997), ch. 20, p. 47, lines 31–5.

religious observance. In particular, the close ties with towns in the Low Countries, Germany and other centres of commerce around the Baltic left traces in Norfolk still visible today. The surviving rood screens depicting the Holy Kin of Christ are evidence of an imported and thriving cult that imbued marriage, family, and especially motherhood, with an elevated spiritual status.[2] Devotion to St Anne, the legendary grandmother of Jesus, experienced by itinerant Norwich merchants in city churches throughout Belgium, Germany and beyond, found an enthusiastic response among the much-married mercantile elite, who came home and commissioned representations of the saint in their own parish churches.[3] Similarly, the cult of St Elisabeth of Hungary (1207–31), another saint with experience of marriage and children, promoted the practise of the seven corporal works of mercy as promulgated in the twenty-fifth chapter of Matthew's Gospel. It has been shown that such charitable activity was embraced by Norwich women, not merely financially but by personal long-term engagement, and was perceived as sacrificial and redemptive.[4] Within this *milieu* of service to the body appeared the shadowy groups of women, unique to Norwich, living lives of lay spiritual poverty under a self-imposed rule, like the early beguines.[5]

Culturally, therefore, from the thirteenth century the ground had been prepared for the reception in Norwich of the revelations of St Bridget of Sweden. Her story and teachings reinforced the established cult of St Anne and demonstrated that married non-virgins could aspire to sanctity and share pragmatic resolutions to the trials that beset all women.[6] It is also fascinating to note that the rosaries bequeathed by the better-off wives and widows of Norwich aldermen to their kinswomen were often made of prized amber beads gleaned from the Baltic's shores, closing the circle, as it were, with their heavenly sponsors from beyond the sea.[7]

Bridget was a married Swedish noblewoman, Birgitta Birgersdotter, a mother of eight children and from her early forties a widow living as a vowess, who after a twenty-four-year sojourn in Rome died there in 1373.[8] This meant she was living under a rule of life committed to chastity, obedience and prayer (but not poverty), independently, not in a conventual foundation. A monastic life may have been her ultimate goal once the enclosed double order she wished to establish had received

---

[2] For example, at Houghton St Giles and Ranworth St Helen. See Carole Hill, 'St Anne and Her Walsingham Daughter', in *Walsingham in Literature and Culture from the Middle Ages to Modernity*, ed. Dominic Janes and Garry Waller, Farnham 2010, 99–111.

[3] The Norwich School glass of St Peter Mancroft church, Norwich, contains depictions of St Anne teaching the Virgin to read and St Elisabeth of Hungary feeding the poor and leprous. St Anne was alleged to have had three marriages; St Elisabeth became a Franciscan tertiary in widowhood.

[4] Carole Hill, *Women and Religion in Late Medieval Norwich*, Royal Historical Society, new series, Studies in History, London 2010, 118–66.

[5] Norman P. Tanner, *The Church in Late Medieval Norwich, 1370–1532*, Toronto 1984, 130–1.

[6] For the cult of St Anne in Norwich, Hill, *Women and Religion in Late Medieval Norwich*, 17–60.

[7] White amber was especially valued and carried an extra premium for the importing merchant dealing in amber.

[8] Claire L. Sahlin, *Birgitta of Sweden and the Voice of Prophecy*, Woodbridge 2001, ch. 1, 13–33, for a full biography.

papal approval. In the event she died before the first postulants were received into the mother house in Vadstena, Sweden, in 1384.⁹ During Bridget's time in Rome she became a figure of power and authority, the correspondent and chastiser of kings, queens and princes of the Church, but, inevitably, of increasing controversy.¹⁰ Women, even aristocratic women, were not meant to go public. Bridget's many children, and her 700-plus revelations, mainly of the Blessed Virgin Mary, made her an exemplar for Margery Kempe's own aspirations to sainthood through manner of life, pilgrimages, and the recording of her own revelations in her spiritual autobiography written in the English vernacular. With a metaphorical fanfare of trumpets, Bridget's writings had demonstrated to western Christendom (and women in particular) that a married woman with children could achieve holiness, become like her, a *sponsa Christi*, in a one-to-one unmediated relationship with Christ.¹¹ In addition, in the public and political arena she had achieved international status and recognition (even notoriety), unknown for a widowed mother not a queen.

The aim of this chapter is not to provide an exegesis or an analysis of St Bridget's extensive canon. Simply it will attempt to show signs of the influence of her teachings in Norfolk, firstly as a marker of women's growing literacy and the attraction to the spiritual life of a vowess among Norwich women. Secondly, it will illustrate how knowledge of Bridget's revelations and her high view of the maternal role may have permeated the moral framework underpinning the running of some Norfolk households. Thirdly, it will highlight Norwich's special link with St Bridget and the bringing about of her canonization, which might to some extent account for a special regional receptivity to her writings and the assimilation by Margery Kempe and others of Brigettine wisdom.

From the late twelfth into the thirteenth century there had been a steady increase in married female saints and holy women in Europe, some manifesting their sanctity and union with God through their recorded revelatory visions and ecstatic utterances, all concerned with apostolic poverty.¹² Their auditors and editors, as with Bridget, were mainly male clerics, often of some status. For the most part such women were French, German or from the Low Countries, which countries constituted Norwich's closest and oldest trading partners. It should be no surprise that the spiritual life of the beguine, Marie de Oignies (b.1177), for example, became known to a friar in the busy port of Bishop's Lynn two hundred years later.¹³ It may be more surprising that the Carmelite, Alan of Lynn (b.c.1348),

---

⁹ Ibid., 17. Forty-six nuns and eighteen brothers formed the founding community.
¹⁰ Ibid, ch. 5, 'Doubts, Derision and Denunciation', 136–68.
¹¹ *The Liber Celestis of St Bridget of Sweden*, ed. Roger Ellis, Early English Text Society original series 291, Oxford 1987.
¹² For example, Dorothea of Montau, and the Blessed Angela de Foligno, who were married and mothers of eight and nine children respectively, and also documented visionaries. See, for example, C. Mazzoni, *Angela of Foligno's Memorial*, Cambridge 1999. Nor should we forget St Elisabeth of Hungary (1207–31), who though not a visionary author, was a married saint with children, whose cult prioritized and promoted sacrificial charitable works and chastity in widowhood.
¹³ *The Book of Margery Kempe*, ed. Barry Windeatt, London 1985, Introduction, 18–19.

should become an indexer of St Bridget's work so relatively soon after her death and speedy canonization, which was not, inevitably, without its detractors.[14] It is interesting to note that Bridget died in 1373, the same year as Julian of Norwich's (1342–1416?) first revelations and the year of Margery Kempe's birth. It is tempting to speculate that Margery might have found this synchronicity with Bridget very significant, in a special way affirming her adherence to the Swedish saint as a model of spiritual receptivity as well as literary evangelism in the recording of her own revelations.[15] Or it may have been merely a device of Margery's hagiographer.

So, first, how may medieval Norfolk women's literacy be assessed, and, indeed, their attraction to the life of a vowess, the two not unconnected?[16] Elements of literacy were gained at varying levels, according to experience, need and status, and not least, access to books and literate clergy.[17] Margery Kempe's access to Bridget's text and other works through the good offices of her reading priest, attests to the value of the latter.[18] As demonstrated by Norman Tanner, there was a rise in numbers of graduate clergy in Norwich, which, arguably, was enormously influential on the calibre of educational 'mentoring', as well as spiritual direction, available to women within the parishes and beyond in the friaries.[19] The Norwich Carmelites, for example, had a growing library and in 1420/1 enclosed an anchoress, Emma Stapleton, who, on the detailed orders of their prior-provincial, Thomas Netter, was tutored by several Carmelite academics of international status.[20] But it is also apparent from Margery's book that reading skills or actual possession of Bridget's text was not a prerequisite of women of lesser social standing than the anchoress Emma for such inculturation to take place.

The elite status of the singular English Brigettine foundation at Syon, in Isleworth, Middlesex, founded in 1415 by Henry V, perhaps speaks more of the pious aspirations of the nobility and literate governing classes than those of Margery Kempe's standing. Never one to be deterred on that account, she says at the end of her book that she, like others, went there on pilgrimage for the plenary

---

[14] Ibid., ch. 9, 56, n.4; *The Book of Margery Kempe*, ed. Meech and Allen, ch. 62, 152–4. See also, J. Hogg, 'Adam Easton's *Defensorium Sanctae Birgittae*', in *The Medieval Mystical Tradition: Exeter Symposium VI*, ed. M. Glasscoe, Cambridge 1999, 213–40.

[15] *Book of Margery Kempe*, ed. Meech and Allen, ch.39, 94–6.

[16] See Mary Erler, *Women, Reading, and Piety in Late Medieval England*, Cambridge 2002, especially chapters 1–4.

[17] For example, Margaret Paston's use of a clerical amanuensis to write her letters, though she could probably read. See Joel Rosenthal, *The Piety of Margaret Paston*, New York 2010, 4–5.

[18] Margery records her attempts at setting up two small businesses, both of which failed, so basic reckoning skills may have been present which did not constitute 'literacy': reading and writing skills at that stage of her life, *Book of Margery Kempe*, ed. Meech and Allen, ch. 2.

[19] Tanner, *The Church*, 29. Tanner shows that between 1370 and 1449, only twelve out of 158 beneficed clergy in Norwich were graduates, while between 1450 and 1499 this had risen to twenty-three out of seventy-one, and rose again to twenty-five out of sixty between 1500 and 1532. See ibid., n.204. The friars, too, offered an alternative source of guidance outside the parish.

[20] For further discussion of Emma Stapleton see Carole Hill, 'Julian and Her Sisters: Female Piety in Late Medieval Norwich', in *The Fifteenth Century* 6, ed. Linda Clark, Woodbridge 2006, 176, n. 65.

indulgence offered at Lammas tide.[21] The foundation kept various redactions of Bridget's text, and the dissemination of versions of it was rapidly increased with the advent of the printing press. Nearer home, Margery's interest in Bridget was highly stimulated by prolonged access to a specialist. Her own desperate desire for vowess status (in her case, while still married, echoing Bridget's married virgin daughter, Catherine of Vadstena), her attempts to record her own revelations and her later public struggle for her errant son's soul, all attest to Brigettine influence mediated by the Carmelites in Bishop's Lynn.[22] And if Mrs Kempe responded to the saint's *Vita*, and expressed it on what was to become an international platform of pilgrimage, we can reasonably argue that other women were similarly open to such cultural exposure, if expressed in ways more elided to their domestic situation: the household and family. Bridget was a great exemplar for all mothers of troublesome sons.

In the next generation, the Norwich widow, Dame Margaret Purdans of St Giles's parish, who died between 1481 and 1483, is an interesting example as something is known about her life and circumstances, apart from her book ownership and significant interest in St Bridget's revelations.[23] Her husband, Richard (d.1436) who would appear to have been many years her senior, was appointed to the front rank of the ruling elite of the city by 1403, possibly before Margaret was born (Purdans had been married to his first wife, Emma, for twenty-five years). When Margaret was a young wife Richard's political life was fraught with tensions and intrigue caused predominantly by the ex-mayor, the combative and manipulative Thomas Wetherby and his faction, who tried to fix the election of his successor to exclude Alderman Purdans, the popular choice. Despite Wetherby's best efforts, Richard Purdans became mayor (1433–4), making Margaret a woman with precedence in the city. These were turbulent times.[24] But for most of her adult life she was a widow and vowess and head of her own household. She and Richard enjoyed a long affiliation to the parish church of St Giles (she left it six bequests). Their memorial brass, presumably ordered, overseen and paid for by Margaret, can still be seen in the central aisle, facing east at the chancel steps, in company with their contemporaries, another aldermanic couple, Robert (d.1432) and Christian Baxter.

Around 1428/9, the man who became Dame Margaret's long-term spiritual mentor, Sir Richard Fernys (d.1464), priest and hermit, inhabited a hermitage in the churchyard of St Giles. It was the aforementioned alderman and former mayor, Robert Baxter, who in 1432 left Fernys the huge sum of £40 to go on pilgrimage

---

[21] *Book of Margery Kempe*, ed. Meech and Allen, Bk.ii, ch.x, 245–6. It may be that Margery could read at this late stage of her life. See R. Krug, *Reading Families: Women's Literate Practice in Late Medieval England*, Ithaca, NY 2002, 153–206.

[22] Ibid, ii, ch.i, 222.

[23] Norfolk Record Office, NCC, Reg. Caston ff.163v–5r (Purdaunce); will written 10 July 1481, proved 12 July 1483.

[24] See Phillipa Maddern, *Violence and Social Order: East Anglia 1422–1442*, Oxford 1992, *passim*.

for his soul to both Rome and Jerusalem.²⁵ Most of all, Margaret's extensive, long-pondered and redrafted will reveals much about her piety, her books, and her network of like-minded friends. As Mary Erler has demonstrated, this group reciprocated friendship, money, and prayerful support over many years, including the exchange of books between themselves and also from the lay to the professed or reclusive woman.²⁶ We can only speculate on how these relationships, as well as the circulating literature, may have been catalysts for the evolving role of the anchoress, for example, or how well travelled was Margaret Purdans's English Book of St Bridget in her lifetime. We cannot know how many years she possessed it or with whom she shared it, but manuscripts in various redactions had been in circulation for over sixty years when Margaret died. As Tanner has remarked, it is significant that the works of Walter Hilton, St Catherine of Sienna, and St Bridget of Sweden were the only works by mystics documented as being in current private ownership in late medieval Norwich, and they were owned by lay women.²⁷

Apart from her English book of St Bridget, which she bequeathed to the nuns at Thetford, Dame Margaret Purdans also owned a book entitled *Le Doctrine of the Herte*, a guide to living under a rule, which she left to her deceased daughter's sister-in-law, Margaret Yaxley, a nun at Bruisyard abbey in Suffolk, a foundation of the Poor Clares. Already on loan to Sister Margaret, on her decease, Dame Margaret instructed, it was to pass to the convent community. In addition to gifts of money to Carrow priory and Joan Elys, a nun there, Dame Margaret also left another 'English book' (*unum librum anglicanum*) to the house.²⁸ It would be nice to know what it was. Margaret Purdans owned at least four more books, two of them psalters. Significantly, one of her executors, John Steyke, rector of St Laurence, Norwich, from 1480 to 1484, was a great bibliophile, whose own extensive library contained the texts of the English mystical writers Walter Hilton and Richard Rolle, and clearly shared something of Margaret's own spiritual interests. She also owned 'A Book of Hilton' which she bequeathed to Alice Barly, sister of John Barly, priest at St Michael Coslany and fellow of Gonville College, Cambridge. Unsurprisingly, Margaret also left a legacy of 10s to the brothers and sisters of Syon, the Brigettine house at Isleworth.

More women of the status and pious inclination of Dame Margaret were choosing the vocation of chaste vowess in widowhood, rather than the customary remarriage negotiated by their male relatives in order to consolidate family land-

---

[25] Norfolk Record Office, NCC, Reg. Surflete fol. 86v (Baxter). He asked that Fernys 'make a pilgrimage for me to Rome going round there fifteen times in a great circle', before proceeding to Jerusalem. Baxter was also one of four former mayors who left bequests to groups of women living a life of holy poverty in city parishes.
[26] Erler, *Women, Reading and Piety*, 68–84.
[27] Tanner, *The Church*, 112.
[28] The nun, Joan Elys, was the daughter of Margaret's friends and contemporaries, Alderman Robert Elys and his wife. Elys had an interest in educating boys with potential for the priesthood: Ab. C. Reg. Morton 2 (1486–1500), fol. 23v (Elys). Joan Elys attracted other bequests from her parents' friends. Robert Grond, clerk, left her 6s. 8d.: Norfolk Record Office, NCC, Reg. Gelour fol.189 (1477).

holdings and property, and possibly improve their inheritance prospects. There are hints in the terminology of Margaret's will that perhaps indicate elements of unease with her son, William. Her widowed son-in-law, Richard Yaxley, is written of with every sign of tender affection as 'My beloved son'. William is not. It is clear in the wills of some Norwich widows who were deploying money in charitable works that the prospect of a thus diminishing inheritance base did not find favour with their sons and heirs. For example, Elizabeth, widow of John Yaxley, serjeant-at-law, who lived her last years in the precincts of Carrow nunnery, held letters of obligation binding her son, Antony, to enact her charitable bequest to William Hammond, a disabled beneficiary whom she had supported for many years.[29] Her will (c.1530) expressed the hope that her son would remember the kindness shown to him in his own need, but she also instructed her executors to enforce her letters of obligation at law if her son did not comply with her wishes. Antony Yaxley was going to do the right thing if his mother had any say in the matter.

The fourteenth-century *Book of Vices and Virtues*, known in many vernacular redactions throughout Europe, defines widowhood as the fourth state of chastity.[30] Vows undertaken by numbers of widows in fifteenth-century Norwich were customarily authorized and made visible by the ceremony of licensing by a bishop and the bestowal of a designated robe and ring. St Bridget's book gave great validation to women who chose this way of life. But though it was the path chosen by the saint, she took a pragmatic view that chastity came in different guises at varying cost. She opined 'for some women keep chastity (but they love it not) for they have no great stirring', while others should 'covet not to high virtue that is above their strength', because that amounted to spiritual 'pride and presumption'.[31] For her, a dedicated chastity for the wrong reasons, such as natural inclination to celibacy, or achieved at great human cost *against* inclination, therefore vulnerable to failure, carried no special spiritual merit and amounted to cheap grace. Christ revealed to her: 'Therefore, your daughter, whether she be wife or virgin still, she pleases me if her will and desire be to me'.[32] Bridget did, therefore, acknowledge the validity of other ways to sanctity to the extent that the role of continuing motherhood laid on women the greatest spiritual responsibility of all: the salvation of their children.

The public role of the vowess, who thus retained sole control of her household and finances, unlike the life of other pious married lay women, was rooted in sexual abstinence and the single life, after the model promoted by St Jerome and others. Bridget recorded that the Virgin Mary said to her: 'This greeting belongs to St Jerome, who left false thinking and came to true wisdom, despised worldly worship

---

[29] Norfolk Record Office, NCC, Reg. Platfoote fols 104–8, at f. 105. She, like Margaret Purdans, made provision for her servants (f. 107). Elizabeth may have been the wife of John Yaxley, Richard Yaxley's son by his first wife, Rose Goldwell, and therefore related to Margaret Purdans by marriage as her step-granddaughter-in-law.

[30] *The Book of Vices and Virtues*, ed. W. N. Francis, Early English Text Society, original series 217, Oxford 1942, 250.

[31] Ellis, *Liber Celestis*, Bk iv, ch. xx, 277, lines 9–10, 20–1 (my translation).

[32] Ibid., Bk iv, ch. xxi, 316.

and won God. That was a blessed Jerome! And they are blessed that follow his teaching. He was a lover of widows; he was a mirror of good livers; he was teacher of all truth and cleanness.'[33] The Brigettine order thus promoted Jerome's teaching for the guidance of pious widows. To this end, Symon Wynter, who was part of the Brigettine community at Syon at Isleworth, Middlesex, was commissioned in the 1440s to write Jerome's life.[34] Bridget of Sweden, it seems, believed in achievable goals supported by dependence on God. For her, as for Julian of Norwich, it was 'the will to Christ' that counted, rather than marital status versus 'born-again' virginity.

St Bridget's maternal concern for her daughter's virginity or lack of it leads us to the influence her writings may have had on women heads of households in Norfolk as arbiters of spiritual wholeness and morality, either in chaste widowhood or in their husband's repeated absences. It is clear that some women such as Margery Kempe, Margaret Paston (1420?–1484), Elizabeth Yaxley and possibly Margaret Purdans, had difficulties, like Bridget, managing 'difficult' sons, which could give rise to life-long tension at best, hostility at worst. To quote Bridget's visions: 'And then cried the fiend, "Alas! I can neither find the sins, nor have mind of the time that he sinned in." Then said the angel, "The prayers of his mother and her tears and her great mourning for his sin ... got him contrition of his sin and grace to shrive him of them: and therefore they are out of your mind (memory).".[35]

Bridget's son, Karl, whose degenerate life caused her great grief while he lived and extreme anxiety after his death, was a model of what might be achieved by the determined and faithful mother. Bridget describes a vision in which the Virgin revealed to her that by her direct sponsorship of Karl's soul on his deathbed and his mother's unceasing intercession for him, they had together pulled him through to salvation, unrepentant and lacking in grace though he had been in life. Mary informed Bridget that she had assumed the role of spiritual midwife to Karl's soul in his death throes, delivering him as a new-born soul into eternal life, so that the 'fiends had no power then to touch his soul'.[36]

The weight placed by Bridget on this interpretation of her visions could be carried to pragmatic extremes by her devotees. We observe this in what seem to us the ruthless and uncharitable actions of Margery Kempe towards her own sick son when she refused to visit or help him until he was confessed, absolved and returned to the Church.[37] She feared his leprous appearance was the result of sexual incontinence, about which she had warned him before he left home, to the point of ill-wishing him if he disobeyed her. Once repentant, Margery takes credit for her son's

---

[33] Ibid., Bk iv, ch. xxi, 278, lines 18–22 (my translation). For Jerome in the *Liber*, see also Bk vi, ch. xx.
[34] The dowager duchess of Clarence, widow of John Beaufort, was the commissioning benefactor, G. R. Keiser, 'St Jerome and the Brigettines: Visions of the Afterlife in Fifteenth-Century England', in *England in the Fifteenth-Century*, ed. D. Williams, Proceedings of the 1986 Harlaxton Symposium, Woodbridge 1987, 143–52, at 143.
[35] *Liber Celestis*, ed. Ellis, Bk vii, ch. xiv, 478 (my translation).
[36] Ibid., 477 (my translation).
[37] *Book of Margery Kempe*, ed. Meech and Allen, Bk ii, ch. i, 221–2.

conversion and return to health, spiritual and physical, before he left Lynn to work and marry in Germany.

In this instance she surpassed St Bridget's own achievements in Karl's lifetime in much the same way that she out-wept the Magdalen, and outran the Virgin in the role of handmaid of the Lord. 'So long she (Margery) prayed that he was clean delivered of the sickness and lived many years after and had a wife and child ... blessed must God be'.[38] It happens that we are certain of Margery's knowledge of St Bridget's exemplary behaviour with her own wayward son. In the case of the 'filial management skills' of Margaret Paston we cannot prove the influence of the saint's injunctions to mothers, except by her responses to family crises, particularly as a widowed parent after the death of John Paston I in 1466.

In 1471/2, the Paston letters indicate the deteriorating relationship between Margaret Paston and her sons, John III and his younger brother, Edmund, blamed by both men on the interference of James Gloys, a priest in their mother's employ.[39] Significantly, and not for the first time, matters had come to a head over issues of reckless sexual misconduct combined with what Margaret undoubtedly saw as a loss of family reputation and public virtue, as well as the loss of spiritual capital, for which she in particular bore the responsibility. On this occasion she had summarily dismissed the alleged instigator, Gregory, manservant to the young Edmund, despite the latter's evident chagrin and letters of angry protest to his mother. Margaret had heard that Gregory had admitted a prostitute to her natal manor of Mautby to service himself and (at the least, one imagines) two working ploughmen, who had witnessed Gregory's cavortings in the 'rabbit-warren-yard' and asked to join in. The woman subsequently spent the night with them in the stables.[40]

This was a year of recurring pestilence in Norfolk with the consequent mortality and labour shortages. Despite that and Edmund's vehement defence, Mrs Paston was having none of it: Gregory was straightway discharged from duty. Retaining him in her family's service was no more an option for her than had been the retention of her excellent steward, Richard Calle, following his clandestine marriage to her daughter, Margery, two years before.[41] On that calamitous occasion, Margaret had refused to have her daughter in her house, and asked her friends to likewise decline to receive Margery. Bishop Walter Lyhert of Norwich (d.1472) was virtually under siege by Margaret Paston, being both visited and formally petitioned by her in an attempt to prove the marriage invalid. After interviewing all parties, pending his formal judgment of the case, the bishop placed Margery Calle in the household of Roger Betys and his wife for two weeks or so, where, Margaret informed her son John II, Margery would not 'be suffered there

---

[38] Ibid., 223 (my translation).
[39] *The Paston Letters and Papers of the Fifteenth Century*, ed. N. Davis, Oxford 1971, 635, letter no. 395, Edmund to John III.
[40] Ibid., 635, no. 395. In essence Edmund's (Gregory's?) defence was that nothing happened 'within my modyres place', and asked his brother, John III, to take Gregory into his own employment.
[41] Ibid., 341–3, no.203. For the Calles, see also no. 203, 343, lines 51–6; no. 203, 343, line 62; no. 203, 342–3.

to play the brothel'. Lyhert wisely felt that a cooling-off period would be beneficial, but it changed Margaret's attitude not an iota.

The later sexual misconduct of Edmund's manservant and ploughmen, and possibly Edmund himself, was perceived as resulting in the casting of noisome miasmas of sin about the household at a time of vulnerability and not to be tolerated. Margaret Paston was possibly steeled by earlier experience of spiritual danger: the fact of a clandestine marriage held implications of destruction of family 'worthship' in society at all levels with lasting repercussions both pragmatic and spiritual. Wilfulness and disobedience to parental authority were held to be damaging enough. But the debasement of the sacrament of marriage incurred substantial spiritual damage that could stain them all unless Margaret could prove the marriage null and void, which she made every effort to do. She wrote to update her son, John II, but also to emphasize her concern for the eternal spiritual credit of her family:

> As to the divorce that you wrote to me of, I understand what you meant, but I charge you upon my blessing that you do not, nor cause any others to do what should offend God and your conscience; for if you do or cause it to be done, God will take vengeance thereupon and you should put yourself and others in great jeopardy. For understand it well, she shall full sorely repent her lewdness hereafter, and I pray God she must so.[42]

The bishop subsequently found the marriage a true one and the outcome for the Calles was years of estrangement from the Paston *familia*. A year after the event Margaret was writing to John II: 'As for your sister, I can send you no good tidings of her. God make her a good woman.'[43] I think St Bridget and Margery Kempe would have loudly applauded her stand, though the direct influence of the Brigettine text on Margaret would be hard to prove. Little documentary evidence survives of her access to books other than those which were required for the celebration of the Mass, but we should be cautious about ruling it out. There may be additional reasons to support a belief that Norfolk women had a special exposure to the mindset of Bridget's revelations.

Norwich had a unique connection with the saint because of a talented 'local boy made good'. Cardinal Adam Easton was born around 1330, possibly in the village of Easton, just outside Norwich, and probably schooled at the cathedral's cell, St Leonard's priory, Mousehold, Norwich. He eventually became a monk at the city's Benedictine cathedral priory where he was a contemporary of Thomas Brinton, who in the 1390s was appointed bishop of Rochester. Both able and gifted

---

[42] Ibid., no. 203, 343, lines 68–74 (my translation). See also no. 208, 351 (my translation). Margery died about ten years after her marriage and predeceased her mother. Margaret did soften enough to leave bequests to the Calle children.

[43] Davis, *Paston Letters*, no. 208, p. 351.

students, they were sent from the priory to study at Gloucester College, Oxford around 1360.[44] Easton became a well known preacher and defender of orthodoxy and was recalled from his studies and employed to refute the preaching friars in Norwich who were growing in influence with the laity to the financial disadvantage of the Benedictines and some city parishes.

Easton's later career in Rome and rise to the cardinalate in 1381 was eventful. During a disrupted, dramatic and highly traumatic period in a Rome enmeshed in a schismatic papacy, probably some time between 1385 and 1389, Easton wrote his *Defensorium Sanctae Birgittae*, probably while in prison at the order of Pope Urban VI.[45] Its purpose was to refute dissenting voices criticising the plans for Bridget's speedy canonization, promoted by Boniface IX, and accomplished in 1391. Attacks on her authenticity had begun in her lifetime. A Perugian opponent recorded his opinion that it was implausible that Christ dictated anything to Bridget, and was unlikely to promulgate anything through a woman, whom the apostle (Paul) did not permit to speak in church.[46] Easton responded to this anonymous attack in his *Defensorium*. Much criticism of the canonization was entangled in the politics surrounding competing papal claims and adversarial court networks. None the less, religious teaching by a woman, written or spoken, was technically forbidden and liable to lead to accusations of heresy, madness, or both, as Margery Kempe later discovered. For the same reason, Julian of Norwich made a disclaimer at the beginning of her own book.[47] It is interesting to note that Boniface did not give undue weight to Bridget's visionary experiences in his argument for her canonization. Such happenings among female religious remained a matter for suspicion rather than validation. Jean Gerson, her most influential and weighty critic, was still condemning Bridget's revelations as the dangerous delusions of a haughty woman at the Council of Constance in 1415.[48]

There is no evidence that Adam ever met Bridget, but he did meet her pious daughter, Catherine of Vadstena, who was key to the establishment of the double Brigettine mother house in Sweden in 1384.[49] After enduring years of imprisonment and torture, Adam Easton, the sole survivor of a group of six imprisoned cardinals, eventually died in Rome in 1397 fully restored to his office and estate of cardinal. His burial place and prestigious memorial can still be seen in his ancient church of St Cecilia in Trastavere, Rome. Easton's bequest of his library of 288 books to his mother house in Norwich was a tremendous boost to the priory collection. The books, loaded into six barrels, duly arrived in the city in 1407. Whether his gift contained any Brigettine material is unknown, but in view of Easton's preoc-

---

[44] Tanner, *The Church*, 31.
[45] Hogg, 'Adam Easton's *Defensorium Sanctae Birgittae*', 226.
[46] Sahlin, *Birgitta of Sweden*, 154, n.68.
[47] *Julian of Norwich: A Book of Showings*, ed. Edmund Colledge and James Walsh, 2 vols, Toronto 1978, I, Short Text, 220, lines 14–24.
[48] Sahlin, *Birgitta of Sweden*, 162, who explores this more extensively.
[49] The date when forty-six nuns and eighteen brothers took formal vows in the now established Order of St Bridget.

cupations in his last active years, it would be remarkable if his library was denuded of any trace of the saint's revelations. Only four texts identified as belonging to this bequest survive, none of them related to this last campaign.[50]

The Benedictine cardinal Easton and Carmelite friar, Alan of Lynn, it could be argued, embody in their divergent lives and ministries many possibilities for the dissemination of Bridget's teaching in Norfolk, but perhaps the Carmelite mediation of her work is now easier to distinguish because of Margery Kempe's book. Even today a fifteenth-century rood screen panel depicting St Bridget survives at Horsham St Faith, a priory church on the northern periphery of Norwich. Uniquely in Norfolk this shows the saint receiving her vision of the Godhead, seated writing her book. Eamon Duffy has shown the attachment to the prayers called the 'Oes of St Bridget' (although wrongly attributed), which focused on Christ's life and Passion.[51] The popularity of Bridget's revelations expanded exponentially after William Caxton translated them into the vernacular and printed them in the 1490s, and thus made available to a new and less-sophisticated audience books of hours suitably illuminated with detailed block-prints of the eponymous saint.

Clearly, the osmotic effect of St Bridget's teachings on Norwich and Norfolk mothers can never be verified statistically. But it seems to me of related significance that many fifteenth-century aldermanic couples in Norwich had a son or daughter in professed religion, often locally among the Norwich orders of friars and particularly at the city's only nunnery at Carrow.[52] Some Norwich mothers were taking their religious responsibilities very seriously indeed. This is also reflected on rood screen panels at Fritton St Margaret, Norfolk, displaying the Bacon family, confidently saint-sized and all in postures of supplication, which exhibit the same priority, with one son shown to be a cleric and the leading daughter fingering a sizable rosary. Such a family pattern was not a universal given. The nurturing of professed religious in the family was patently not evident in fifteenth-century Bristol, for example, another city with similar access to shipping and busy interna-

---

[50] The barrels were transported from London to Norwich at the cost of 12s. (Norfolk Record Office, Communar's Roll 1407–8, DCN 1/12/41 – third paragraph of the roll). Of the surviving four texts, two are in the Parker Library at Corpus Christi College, Cambridge (MS74, MS180), one in the Bodleian Library (MS Bodley 151), and one in France (Avignon, Bibl. de la Ville, MS 996).

[51] Eamon Duffy, *Marking the Hours: English People and their Prayers 1240–1570*, Newhaven and London 2006, 80 and n.36.

[52] For example, Margaret Wetherby, whose daughter, Alice, was a nun at Carrow, and was bequeathed 10 marks by her mother and appointed co-executrix: Norfolk Record Office, NCC, Reg. Brosyard f. 83 (1458); Thomas Welan (barber) and his wife, Joan Barbour, left legacies to their daughter Isabell Welan, nun at Carrow: Reg. Brosyard f. 159 and f. 206 (1459, 1460); John Folcard (d.1464), alderman, and his wife did well in that their son, Thomas (d.1461), was rector of Heigham and their daughter, Margery, a nun at Carrow, and like some other nuns, attracted bequests from her parents' circle as well as her own parents and brother (Reg. Brosyard f. 252). See also W. Rye, *Carrow Abbey, otherwise Carrow Priory, near Norwich, in the County of Norfolk, Its Foundation, Buildings, Officers and Inmates, with Appendices*, Norwich 1889, Appendix 9, xiii–xxix.

tional trading on the waterfront.[53] In this as in other areas of cutting-edge religious practice, the women of Norwich had a marked particularity.[54]

In regional studies it is seldom that Julian of Norwich is heard mentioned in the same sentence as St Bridget, despite the coincidence of Julian's illness and 'shewings' taking place in the year that Bridget died. True, the saint does not figure specifically in Julian's books as an overt influence. But the fact that Julian felt impelled to record her own revelations in the vernacular as an exercise of prophetic and teaching ministry for the guidance of her 'even Christians' in the years following Bridget's death and canonization surely does reflect, even exceed, her example. The two women were over-lapping contemporaries, both with access to books and their owners, both female visionaries who recorded their experiences, as they believed, in obedience to God's will. Julian, too, had probably known motherhood and widowhood.[55] She did not suddenly appear or write in a cultural or spiritual vacuum.

It might, however, be argued that Julian's attitude to spiritual parenting, as encapsulated in her writing on the motherhood of Christ towards his children, bears the same imprint of striving towards salvation through incarnational piety as Bridget's and which the saint made so specifically a maternal imperative.[56] Julian, like Bridget, makes a strong connection between Christ's redemptive motherhood and the concept of his humanity being provided only by the flesh of his mother, the Blessed Virgin Mary. So it is that the Virgin mother features so much in Bridget's spiritual 'conversations', and for some time in the visualizations of her imitator, Margery Kempe. God as the parent who corrects a child out of great love that they might grow in grace is an analogy made by Julian, echoing Bridget's view on the subject of a mother's ultimate responsibility for her child's soul, and prefiguring Margery's intransigence with her own sick son.[57]

It may be that the medieval households of Norfolk owe more to Adam Easton's six barrels of books than can now be known. What is certain is that the city of Norwich was the hub of circles of women with long-standing affiliations to those vowed to solitary or monastic lives, such as Margaret Purdans and her friends, women characterized by book ownership and exchange, and charitable works. Some, it must be said, had errant sons, and could identify with Bridget's domestic concerns and be receptive to her spiritual advice. The vitality of religious aspiration in fifteenth-century Norwich demonstrated by the wide-ranging expressions of incarnational piety which were embraced by lay women, surely marks it out as fertile ground for St Bridget's revelations both in precept and in practice.

Cardinal Adam Easton and Brother Alan of Lynn were both clearly instrumental

---

[53] S. J. Adams, 'Religion, Society and Godly Women: The Nature of Female Piety in a Late Medieval Urban Community', unpublished PhD thesis, University of Bristol 2001, *passim*.
[54] For a fuller exploration of this see Hill, *Women and Religion, passim*.
[55] Grace Jantzen, *Julian of Norwich*, London 1987, 25, who follows Clifton Wolters and Benedicta Ward in this opinion based on internal evidence of the text.
[56] Colledge and Walsh, *A Book of Showings*, Pt. 2, ch. 60, 594–600.
[57] Ibid, Pt.2, ch. 60, 594–5, lines 9–16; ch. 61, 601, lines 15–21; *Book of Margery Kempe*, Bk 2, ch. 1.

in their divergent ways in mediating St Bridget's text throughout Norfolk. The Benedictine, by writing his *Defensorium* in Rome, arguably produced the catalyst that ensured Bridget's canonization so soon after her death and the widespread dissemination of her writings. The Carmelite, on home ground, by his personal spiritual direction and his specialized knowledge of the saint furthered knowledge of her text, we have seen, among aspirant women engaged in commerce and domesticity in Lynn. The inescapable irony of the unity of common purpose of the Benedictine cardinal and the Carmelite friar would doubtless have amused Bridget, whilst being a mark of her own authenticity.

— Chapter 17 —

FLEMISH INFLUENCE ON ENGLISH MANUSCRIPT PAINTING IN EAST ANGLIA IN THE FOURTEENTH CENTURY

Lynda Dennison

THIS CHAPTER CRYSTALLIZES earlier research:[1] it examines Flemish influence on manuscript painting in East Anglia during the 1340s and the years immediately following the Black Death of 1348–9 as a contribution to understanding East Anglia's place within its North Sea world. At this time manuscript painters working in this region appear to have been especially receptive to foreign influences, particularly those from Flanders. This contrasted with the first thirty years of the fourteenth century when English illuminators had been receptive to artistic currents from Paris and northern France. It is well established that manuscript painting in East Anglia – specifically Norwich – throughout the 1330s had been dominated by Italian influences.[2] Although certain iconographic elements were conveyed to the North from Duccio and his workshop, both Bolognese and Sienese influences saw the appropriation of Italian painting techniques for the modelling of the flesh and draperies and an embryonic experimentation with three-dimensional form, the former especially well demonstrated by the Ormesby and

---

[1] For which see L. Dennison, 'The Artistic Context of Fourteenth Century Flemish Brasses', *Transactions of the Monumental Brass Society* 14, 1986, 1–38. See also, L. Dennison, 'The Stylistic Sources, Dating and Development of the Bohun Workshop, *ca.* 1340–1400', unpublished PhD dissertation, University of London, 1988, reference to specific chapters of which will be cited in the following discussion.

[2] Ideas first expressed in O. Pächt, 'A Giottesque Episode in English Mediaeval Art', *Journal of the Warburg and Courtauld Institutes* 6, 1943, 51–70, with Norwich as a more specific location, recently reinforced by a number of writers, including C. Hull, 'Abbot John, Vicar Thomas and M. R. James: the early History of the Douai Psalter', in *The Legacy of M. R. James*, ed. L. Dennison, Donnington 2001, 121–6; S. Panayotova, *The Macclesfield Psalter*, London 2008, 23–8, and L Dennison, 'The Technical Mastery of the Macclesfield Psalter: A Preliminary Stylistic Appraisal of the Illuminators and their Suggested Origin', *Transactions of the Cambridge Bibliographical Society* 13/3, 2006, 253–88. See also P. Binski and D. Park, 'A Ducciesque Episode at Ely: The Mural Decorations of Prior Crauden's Chapel', *England in the Fourteenth Century, Proceedings of the 1985 Harlaxton Symposium*, ed. W. M. Ormrod, Woodbridge 1986, 28–41.

Macclesfield Psalters.[3] This Italianate 'episode', a term earlier coined by Otto Pächt,[4] was at its peak in the 1330s in Norwich although on the wane by 1340 by which time English illuminators were becoming open to different artistic impulses. These are best explained by reference to Flemish art of the period, the stylistic interchange between Flanders and England that is the subject of this chapter. It will touch on the careers of three English illuminators, and one Flemish artist who was working in England in the period immediately post-dating the Black Death. All four artists, however, are united in sharing stylistic characteristics with works in other media, principally monumental brasses which, along with illuminated manuscripts, will be central to this paper.

The style of the first artist lay in the indigenous English tradition of the pre-Black Death period of the broad, cusped, border motifs of the Ormesby Psalter, a manuscript with an indisputable provenance in Norwich and in all likelihood copied and decorated there. A connection with the Ormesby Psalter is evident from this artist's apparently first extant work, a Psalter datable to around 1340,[5] but contrasting with the Ormesby Psalter is an approach to three-dimensional form. The inclusion of a bizarre architectural frame surrounding the miniature depicting the *Judgement of Solomon* (Plate 1a) constitutes a new departure in English illumination.[6] This extraordinary engagement with three-dimensional form is combined with the Italianate lessons absorbed from the Ormesby and Macclesfield Psalter artists. These fanciful canopies are remarkably similar to those which surround the full-page miniatures in the Flemish *Romance of Alexander* (Plate 1c), produced between 1338 and 1344, at a centre in Flanders, possibly at Tournai.[7] The protracted execution of the *Alexander* precisely coincided with the period of England's concentrated activity in the Low Countries at the outset of the Hundred Years' War

---

[3] For the Ormesby Psalter, Oxford, Bodleian Library, MS Douce 366, see S. C. Cockerell and M. R. James, *Two East Anglian Psalters at the Bodleian Library*, Roxburghe Club, Oxford 1926; L. F. Sandler, *Gothic Manuscripts 1285-1385*, A Survey of Manuscripts Illuminated in the British Isles, ed. J. J. G. Alexander, 2 vols, London 1986, no. 43, henceforth cited as Sandler *Survey*, followed by the catalogue number in question. For the Macclesfield Psalter, Cambridge, Fitzwilliam Museum, MS 1-2005, see Panayotova, *Macclesfield Psalter*; Dennison, 'Macclesfield Psalter' and C. de Hamel, in Sotheby's, *The Library of the Earls of Macclesfield Removed from Shirburn Castle, part 3: Western Manuscripts, London, 22 June 2004*, London 2004, 28-51; and *The Cambridge Illuminations*, exhibition catalogue (Cambridge, Fitzwilliam Museum), ed. P. Binski and S. Panayotova, Cambridge 2005, 187-8, no. 78.

[4] Pächt, 'Giottesque Episode'.

[5] Oxford, Bodleian, Douce MS 131, see Sandler, *Survey*, no. 106. For comparison of the respective Beatus pages in the two Psalters, Dennison, 'Bohun Workshop', figs 7 and 8, with discussion. For a description of Douce 131.

[6] These structures also serve as frames for the historiated initials. For further discussion and illustrations, see L. Dennison, 'The "Fitzwarin Psalter and its Allies": a Reappraisal', in *England in the Fourteenth Century: Proceedings of the 1985 Harlaxton Symposium*, ed. W. M. Ormrod, Woodbridge 1986, 50-1; Dennison, 'Macclesfield Psalter', 261-2.

[7] Oxford, Bodleian Library, MS Bodley 264. See M. R. James, *The Romance of Alexander. A Collotype Facsimile of MS Bodley 264*, Oxford 1933. This manuscript is discussed in Dennison, 'Artistic Context', 16, 20; see also Dennison, 'Bohun Workshop', 140-2.

with France. It is thus worth considering that the transmission of Flemish influence may have been facilitated by political, economic and social factors. Before initiating the Hundred Years' War Edward III looked to the Low Countries for support, leading to the Anglo-Flemish alliance in 1339–40. During several of the Flemish campaigns Edward had his headquarters at Antwerp and Ghent, the latter where Queen Philippa held court.[8] Lionel, later duke of Clarence, was born at Antwerp in 1338 and John of Gaunt in Ghent in 1340.[9]

Although this precocious artist appears to have initiated his career in Norwich in the years around 1340, identification of his hand in a foundation charter of the University of Cambridge, dated 1343, may suggest that he gravitated from Norwich to Cambridge.[10] The iconography of the charter does not lend itself to excursions into three-dimensional space. His next work, however, datable to around 1345, offered greater scope – as its opening miniature demonstrates (Plate 1b). It is a Psalter, now in Brescia, with a calendar of the Ely diocese, a factor which further reinforces his departure from Norwich to the area of Cambridge.[11] In this manuscript the artist's handling of three-dimensional structures remain complex, although less painterly than those in the Douce Psalter (Plate 1a), arguably executed when he was in closer proximity to Italian influences, to which Norwich illuminators were especially sympathetic. The ownership of the Brescia Psalter is not precisely known, but this artist's broadly East Anglian sphere of operation is resolved by his appearance in the first campaign in a Psalter, now in the Vienna National Library, commissioned by the Bohun family of Pleshey, Essex.[12] Although still manifesting an interest in spatial elements, the structures in the Vienna Psalter have become more rationalized.[13] Given that these characteristically Flemish forms manifest themselves most overtly in his apparently first work which has close

---

[8] This is discussed at greater length in Dennison, 'Bohun Workshop', chapter 3. For further discussion of political contacts between the two countries, see H. S. Lucas, *The Low Countries and the Hundred Years' War (1326-47)*, University of Michigan, Ann Arbor, MI 1929.

[9] M. McKisack, *The Fourteenth Century, 1307-1399*, Oxford 1959, 267; A. Strickland, *Lives of the Queens of England, from the Norman Conquest*, new edn, 6 vols, 1864–5, I, 386.

[10] On Luard *33a, see Dennison, 'Fitzwarin Psalter', 56, 64, 65, fig. 22, and Dennison and Rogers, 'Elsing Brass', 183, plate 6b.

[11] On this Psalter, Brescia, Biblioteca Queriniana, MS A. V. 17, see Dennison, 'Fitzwarin Psalter', 50, 51, 52, 53, 54, 55, 56, 62, and Dennison and Rogers, 'Elsing Brass', 182, 183, 184, 185, plate 4a. For a description of the manuscript, see Sandler, *Survey*, no. 109.

[12] Vienna, Österreichische Nationalbibliothek, Cod. 1826*, for which see M. R. James and E. G. Millar, *The Bohun Manuscripts: a Group of Five Manuscripts Executed in England about 1370 for Members of the Bohun Family*, Roxburghe Club, 200, Oxford 1936, 33–46, plates xxxix–lvi; Dennison, 'Fitzwarin Psalter', *passim*; Sandler, *Survey*, no. 133; *Age of Chivalry. Art in Plantagenet England 1200-1400*, exhibition catalogue (London, Royal Academy of Arts), ed. J. J. G.. Alexander and P. Binski, London 1987, no. 687, with further bibliography. See also Dennison, 'Bohun Workshop', *passim*.

[13] To be noted is the attempt at recession in David's throne in the Vienna Psalter which is more convincing spatially than in his presumed earlier work, the Brescia Psalter, for illustrations of which see Dennison, 'Fitzwarin Psalter', fig. 9 (Brescia), fig. 21 (Vienna).

a.

b.

FLEMISH INFLUENCE ON PAINTING IN EAST ANGLIA 319

c.

PLATE 1 (*left and above*)
a. *(left)* Oxford, Bodleian Library, MS Douce 131, Psalter, fol. 96v, detail of miniature. (By permission of The Bodleian Libraries, The University of Oxford)
b. *(left)* Brescia, Biblioteca Queriniana, MS A. V. 17, Psalter, fol. 7r, Psalm 1, detail of miniature.
c. *(above)* Oxford, Bodleian Library, MS Bodley 264, 'Romance of Alexander', fol. 51v, miniature. (By permission of The Bodleian Libraries, The University of Oxford)

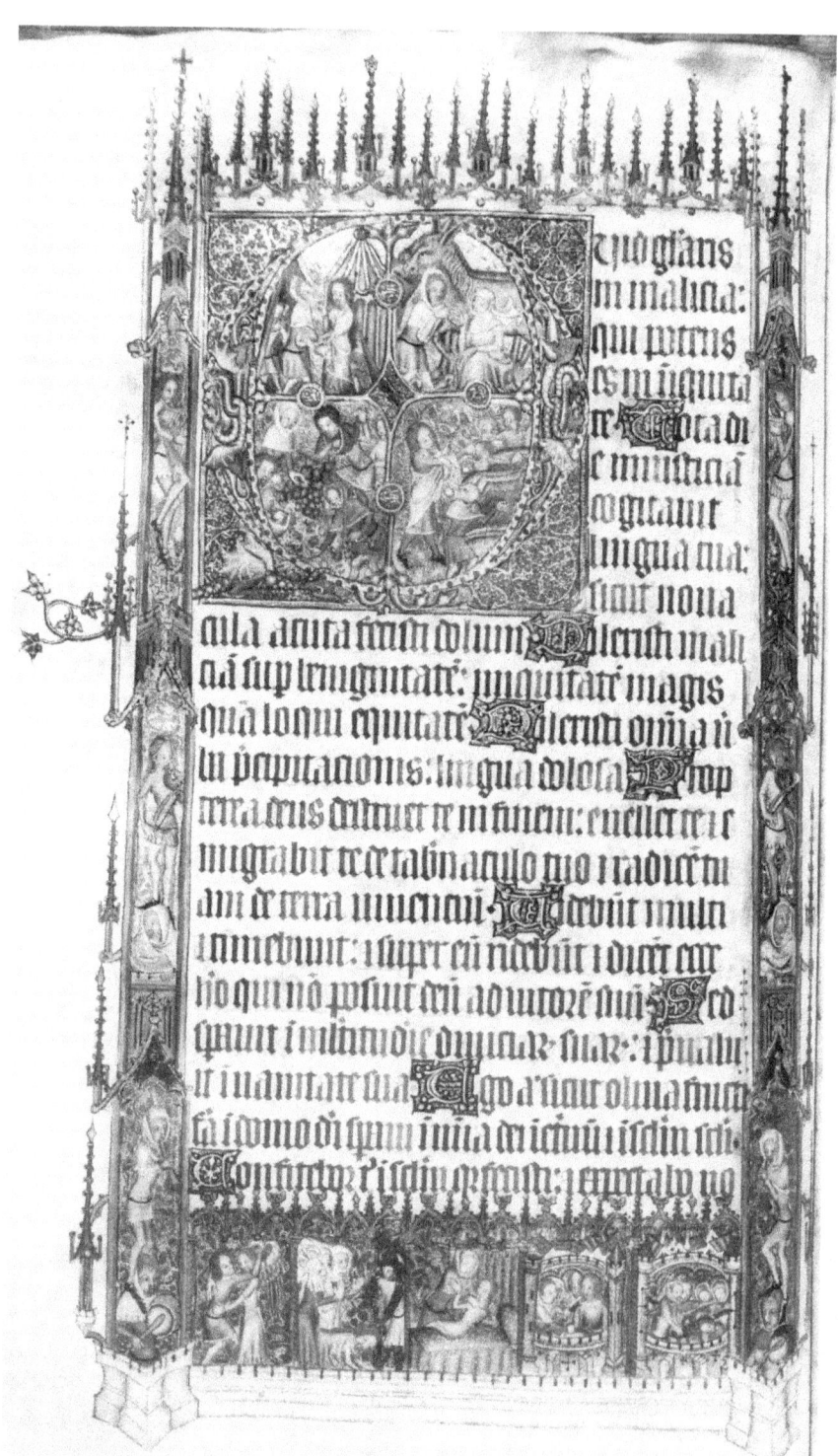

PLATE 2 (*left and above*)
a. (*left*) Oxford, Exeter College, MS 47, Psalter, fol. 33v, Psalm 51, initial and border. (By kind permission of the Rector and Scholars of Exeter College in the University of Oxford)
b. (*above*) Church of St Mary Magdalene, Newark, Nottinghamshire, Alan Fleming, brass rubbing. (© Monumental Brass Society)

a.

b.

PLATE 3
a. Cambridge, Fitzwilliam Museum, MS 38-1950, Psalter, fol. 29r, detail, Psalm 26, miniature. (© The Fitzwilliam Museum, Cambridge)
b. St Margaret's Church, King's Lynn, Robert Braunche, detail, brass rubbing (© Monumental Brass Society)

PLATE 4 a. *(Note: Plate 4b overleaf)*
The Hague, Rijksmuseum Meermanno-Westreenianum, MS 10. A. 14, Missal, fol. 143v, Crucifixion miniature. (By permission of the Rijksmuseum Meermanno-Westreenianum)

PLATE 4 b.
Paris, Bibliothèque nationale, MS latin 765, Fitzwarin Psalter, fol. 14r, Crucifixion miniature. (By permission of the Bibliothèque nationale de France)

a.

b.

c.

d.

PLATE 5
a. Oxford, Bodleian Library, Lat. liturg. f. 3, Book of Hours, fol. 118v, detail, minor initial.
(By permission of The Bodleian Libraries, The University of Oxford)
b. Cambridge, Fitzwilliam Museum, MS 38-1950, Psalter, fol. 49v, detail, minor initial.
(© The Fitzwilliam Museum, Cambridge)
c. London, British Library, MS Royal 13 D. 1*, Psalter, fol. 20v, Psalm 68, detail, border.
(© British Library Board)
d. Leça do Balio, Estêvão Vasques Pimentel, detail, heads of Christ and two Apostles, brass rubbing. (© Monumental Brass Society)

a.

b.

PLATE 6
a. Oxford, Bodleian Library, MS Auct. D. 4. 4, Psalter-Hours, fol. 234r, detail, initial of the Evangelist Matthew. (By permission of The Bodleian Libraries, The University of Oxford)
b. Leça do Balio, Estêvão Vasques Pimentel, detail, the Evangelist Matthew, brass rubbing. (© Monumental Brass Society)

PLATE 7
a. Brussels, Bibliothèque royale de Belgique, MS 6426, Antiphonary, fol. 26r, detail, initial of the Nativity of Christ. (By permission of the Bibliothèque royale de Belgique)
b. Lübeck cathedral, Bishops Burchard von Serken and Johann von Mul, detail, background pattern of grotesques and butterflies, brass rubbing. (© Monumental Brass Society)

PLATE 8
a. Brussels, Bibliothèque royale de Belgique, MS 6426, Antiphonary, fol. 188r, detail, pen initial of female drollery. (By permission of the Bibliothèque royale de Belgique)
b. Oxford, Bodleian Library, MS Bodley 264, 'Romance of Alexander', fol. 108r, detail, initial of female drollery. (By permission of The Bodleian Libraries, The University of Oxford)

affiliations with the border structures in the Ormesby Psalter, it is likely that his first encounter with these progressive elements took place in Norwich. Broadly speaking, surviving evidence indicates that in the period leading up to the 1340s Norwich was in the vanguard of development in terms of manuscript painting.[14]

The style of this avant-garde illuminator raises the question of an association with works in other, but related, media executed in East Anglia, such as stained glass, discussion of which has taken place elsewhere.[15] There, comparison was made between the figure style in the Vienna Psalter – the artist's most mature work – datable to the late 1340s, and the stained glass of the Ely Lady Chapel, of 1348–9, where there is close correspondence between the figures in contemporary dress.[16] An identical style is also evident in the monumental brass to Sir Hugh Hastings at Elsing, Norfolk, and a related one at Wimbish, Essex; Sir Hugh died in 1347.[17] All three media exhibit figures with a pronounced déhauncement in which the style is one of refined elegance. Indeed, the analogies are so profound as to suggest the design of the one hand in all three media.[18] As this illuminator cannot be identified in works assignable to the 1350s, and the Vienna Psalter – his final work – was terminated abruptly, in all likelihood he succumbed to the devastating outbreak of Black Death of 1348–9, corresponding to the sudden termination of the Ely glass campaign.[19]

The Vienna Bohun Psalter shows evidence of a further illuminator who makes an even briefer appearance but who has a similar fascination for these exceptional architectural structures which first occur in English illumination around 1340. His hand has been identified in other manuscripts, principal of which is the Fitzwarin Psalter, now in the Bibliothèque nationale.[20] It is instructive to compare the architectural structures on the *Crucifixion* page in the Fitzwarin Psalter – one of an extensive prefatory cycle by this artist – with those in the Bodleian *Alexander*, raised in the context of the other Vienna Psalter artist (Plates 4b and 1c). Admittedly, the Flemish miniaturist shows greater understanding in the rendering of three-dimensional space: his architectural framework recedes convincingly into space, whereas that in the Fitzwarin Psalter is more awkwardly achieved. The artist has resorted to two dimensions in order to represent the vaulting, and not modelling in recession as in the *Alexander* – but nevertheless there is a fundamental agreement with the

[14] A consensus reinforced by the emergence of the Macclesfield Psalter into the public domain; see Dennison, 'Macclesfield Psalter', 267–73; Panayotova, *Macclesfield Psalter*, 20–8.
[15] Dennison and Rogers, 'Elsing Brass', 184, 187, 193, plates 2, 3b, 4b; see also plate 3b in connection with plate 4a (Brescia Psalter).
[16] Ibid., plates 2, 3a, 3b, 4b.
[17] This is discussed in ibid., 172, 174, 182–6.
[18] Parallels between the three media are discussed in ibid., *passim*.
[19] On the Ely stained glass in question, see D. King, in *Medieval Art in East Anglia 1300–1520*, exhibition catalogue, ed. P. Lasko and N. J. Morgan, Norwich 1972, no. 33.
[20] Paris, Bibliothèque nationale, MS lat. 765. For discussion, Dennison, 'Fitzwarin Psalter', 42–66. See also F. Wormald, 'The Fitzwarin Psalter and its Allies', *Journal of the Warburg and Courtauld Institutes* 6, 1943, 71–9; Sandler, *Survey*, no. 120; N. Rogers, 'The Original Owner of the Fitzwarin Psalter', *Antiquaries Journal* 69, part 2, 1989, 257–60.

structures in the Flemish manuscript. Further evidence of a close relationship between English and East Anglian illumination at this date is provided by one of the illuminators in a Flemish Missal, now in The Hague,[21] whose miniature of the Crucifixion compares closely in the handling of the architectural surrounds which are blocky in nature and witness to a similar modelling of the architectural forms in light and dark tones (Plates 4a and 4b).

It is with Tournai, the likely centre of production for the *Alexander*, that the question of Flemish monumental brass production comes to the fore as it is in this medium, agreeing with the *Alexander*, where sophisticated versions of these complex architectural frames are evident. From the middle of the fourteenth century these impressive monuments were being transported to England, their final resting place predominantly down the eastern coast of England. It can be demonstrated that they were to become exceedingly influential on English manuscript painters of the East Anglian region.[22]

It is without question that the production of illuminated manuscripts, which had become focused in East Anglia at this time, was catastrophically affected by the 1348-9 outbreak of the Black Death, with the result that the Vienna Bohun Psalter – to take a key example already mentioned – was curtailed.[23] The manuscript, in an unfinished state, was apparently passed to another member of the Bohun family who procured other artists to illuminate for them at Pleshey castle, Essex, where the Vienna Bohun Psalter was probably completed.[24] Indeed, the recovery in production of 'luxury' manuscripts in England was due largely to the Bohun family, who employed at least two illuminators in their castle at Pleshey, Essex.[25] Two of these artists will be central to the following discussion.

Almost immediately after the completion of the Vienna Psalter a further Psalter, now in Exeter College, Oxford, commissioned for the sixth earl, Humphrey de Bohun, was begun by two illuminators,[26] one of whom can be identified as John de Tye, an

---

[21] The Hague, Rijksmuseum Meermanno-Westreenianum, MS 10. A. 14, for discussion of which, see L. Dennison, 'The Dating and Localisation of the Hague Missal (Meermanno-Westreenianum MS 10 A 14) and the Connection between English and Flemish Miniature Painting in the Mid Fourteenth Century', in *Corpus of Illuminated Manuscripts* 11–12, Low Countries Series 8, ed. B. Cardon, Leuven 2002, 505–36, where further bibliography is cited.

[22] For discussion of this phenomenon in relation to the decoration in manuscripts, see Dennison, 'Artistic Context', *passim*.

[23] Dennison, 'Fitzwarin Psalter', *passim*.

[24] See Dennison, 'Bohun Workshop', chapters 4 and 11, 250–52. See also my discussion in L. Dennison, 'Oxford, Exeter College MS 47: The Importance of Stylistic and Codicological Analysis in its Dating and Localization', *Medieval Book Production: Assessing the Evidence, Proceedings of the Second Conference of the Seminar in the History of the Book to 1500, Oxford, July, 1988*, ed. L. L. Brownrigg, Los Altos Hills, CA 1990, 42, 44, 45, 46, 47, illustrations 2, 4.

[25] Their careers are traced in Dennison, 'Bohun Workshop'.

[26] Oxford, Exeter College, MS 47 where they were engaged in the first campaign, for which see Dennison, 'Bohun Workshop', chapter 4, for background concerning the formation of the partnership, and chapter 11, 250–52. My arguments for dating the various campaigns in this manuscript are also contained in L. Dennison, 'Oxford, Exeter College MS 47', 41, 42, 44, 45, 46, 47, 57, illustrations 1, 3, 5, 6, 7, 19, 22. See also Sandler, *Survey*, no. 134.

Austin friar.[27] Like the Vienna Psalter, it was later completed for another member of the family.[28] Despite the essential difference in conception between the two media, a clear relationship exists between the Flemish brass to Alan Fleming, at Newark in Nottinghamshire, of c.1360,[29] and the two surviving pages of major decoration in the Exeter Bohun Psalter, executed at Pleshey castle by John de Tye. (Plates 2a and 2b). The borders on either side of the manuscript text are composed of architectural motifs and the artist, like the brass engraver, has created an illusion of height by graduating the shafts inwards towards the top. This is an original way of handling an illuminated page in an English manuscript. These structures, with buttressed pinnacles at the outer side are, in turn, divided into further sections which serve to accommodate standing figures, exactly paralleling those in the brass. As in the later Wycbold brass,[30] there is a solid architectural base and an upper section decorated with an elaborate array of pinnacles. The illuminator has thus created a freestanding architectural structure to surround the text and historiated initial, closely similar to that in Flemish brasses. There is no precise precedent for these forms in extant English manuscript painting or stained glass and their occurrence in the Exeter Psalter may well have been occasioned by the importation of Flemish monumental brasses, such as that to Alan Fleming, at a period which marks the zenith of the Hanseatic League's power. The economic and political closeness of communities on either side of the North Sea would have facilitated artistic interchange of this kind.[31]

John de Tye collaborated with another artist in the production of most of the Bohun manuscripts (they had earlier come together for the final campaign in the Vienna Psalter). This second hand can be assigned most of the illumination in the Bohun Psalter, now in the Fitzwilliam Museum, which on stylistic grounds is some ten years later than the first campaign in the Exeter College Psalter (c.1370) in which they also both participated.[32] All the miniatures in the Fitzwilliam Bohun Psalter are surrounded by a complex array of slender turrets and pinnacles with flying buttresses at the sides of each structure, some of which show interior vaulting of the type noted in the brasses. For instance, a miniature from the Fitzwilliam

---

[27] This friar is mentioned in the will of Humphrey de Bohun, sixth earl of Hereford and Essex, who died in 1361, and to whom he bequeathed £10 to pray for him, for which see J. Nichols, *A Collection of All the Wills, Now Known To Be Extant, of the Kings and Queens of England*, London 1870, 50. It is undoubtedly the same friar who is mentioned in a special dispensation granted by Bartholomeus Venetus, for which see F. Roth, *The English Austin Friars 1249-1538, I: Sources*, New York 1961, 223 (document 559).

[28] For discussion, Dennison, 'Oxford, Exeter College, MS 47', *passim*. See also Dennison, 'Bohun Workshop', chapters 4, 7, 8 and 11.

[29] For discussion of the Fleming brass, H. K. Cameron, 'Flemish Brasses to Civilians in England', *Archaeological Journal* 139, 1982, 422–6, plates xliii, xlvi–xlviii.

[30] For a reproduction of this brass, Dennison, 'Artistic Context', plate II(A), and for discussion, H. K. Cameron, 'The 14th-Century School of Flemish Brasses: Evidence for a Tournai Workshop', *Transactions of the Monumental Brass Society* 11, part 3 (1972, for 1970), 62–3, 79, 81.

[31] See discussion in connection with notes 8 and 9 above.

[32] Cambridge, Fitzwilliam Museum, MS 38-1950. As postulated in Dennison, 'Bohun Workshop', chapters 6, 7, and 11. See also Dennison, 'Oxford, Exeter College, MS 47', 41, 47, 48, and Sandler, *Survey*, no. 139.

Bohun Psalter can be compared with a detail from the scene of the 'Peacock Feast' on the Braunche brass at Lynn, of 1364 (Plates 3a and 3b).[33] In each, the effect is elegant and courtly: the women wear fashionable gowns, with tightly fitting bodices which follow the smooth lines of their bodies and small hoods which expose neat side plaits. The musical instrument played by the figure on the extreme right in the brass is of a type played by the figure in the upper left of the miniature.

Some fifteen years earlier this artist executed the border decoration in the fragmentary Psalter, of c.1355–60, probably the first extant manuscript in which the two Bohun artists collaborated.[34] The margins are filled with birds, but mainly butterflies, reminiscent of those found between the trefoils in the background pattern on Flemish brasses, such as in the brass to Bishops Burchard von Serken and Johann von Mul in the cathedral of Lübeck of c.1350.[35] A single page, containing Psalm 68, has a rectangular border with figural illumination by this artist, the lower portion of which depicts the head of Christ, flanked by the heads of the Four Evangelists, whose hair is delineated in a calligraphic pattern of undulating lines (Plate 5c). In two of the heads a highly characteristic curl of hair forms in the centre of the forehead and falls forward, or is pushed back over the head; equally distinctive, and apparent in three of the heads, is the prominent wave of hair on either side of the head in the approximate position of the ear, although the ear itself remains covered. These features compare closely with the row of heads, representing Christ and the Twelve Apostles, in the upper frame of the Flemish brass to Frei Estêvão Vasques Pimentel at Leça do Balio in Portugal of c.1336.[36] (Plates 5c and 5d). It is in the calligraphic linearity of the illuminator's style where the correspondence with the brasses is paramount. The specific relationship between the engraver of the Leça brass and the style of the miniaturist under discussion is secured by comparison of the heads in the brass and those in the Bohun manuscript in the Fitzwilliam Museum, highlighted in an earlier context (Plates 5b and 5d).

---

[33] For discussion of the Braunche brass, H. K. Cameron, 'The Fourteenth-Century Brasses at King's Lynn', *Archaeological Journal* 136, 1979, 158–62.

[34] British Library, MS Royal 13 D. I*. The manuscript is described in full in G. F. Warner and J. P. Gilson, *British Museum, Catalogue of Western Manuscripts in the Old Royal and King's Collections*, 4 vols, London 1921, II, 109. Also described in Sandler, *Survey*, no. 131. Further discussion of the part played by the two Bohun artists in this manuscript and evidence for the suggested dating is in Dennison, 'Bohun Workshop', principally chapters 4 and 11. See also Dennison, 'Artistic Context', 8–9, 12, plates II(B), IV(B), X(C), Dennison, 'Oxford, Exeter College, MS 47', 46, 47, illustration 8 and Dennison, 'Flemish Miniature Painting in the Mid Fourteenth Century', 505, 506, 507, plates III 1A, D, III 3A, III 4A.

[35] For discussion and illustration of this brass, see principally H. K. Cameron, 'The Brass of c.1350 in Lübeck Cathedral to Bishops Burchard von Serken and Johann von Mul', *Transactions of the Monumental Brass Society* 13, part 5, 1984, 363–80. See also, Dennison, 'Artistic Context', 8, 9, 12, 16, 28, figs 2, 10, (A) (B), 12 (A) (B), Plate VI (D).

[36] For discussion of this brass see, principally, H. K. Cameron, 'The Memorial to Dom Frei Estêvão Vasques Pimentel, a Unique Brass at Leça do Balio, Portugal', *Transactions of the Monumental Brass Society* xii, part 5 (1984), 363–80. See also Dennison, 'Artistic Context', 8–9, plates IV (A), (C), (D), V (B), fig. 8 (A),(B) and Dennison, 'Flemish Miniature Painting in the Mid Fourteenth Century', 506, 507, plate III 1C.

FLEMISH INFLUENCE ON PAINTING IN EAST ANGLIA   333

In the light of such powerfully close analogies it can be postulated that this second Bohun illuminator, who was working in England, is Flemish in origin. His hand cannot be identified in English manuscripts datable to before 1355 although it occurs in two books, both of which are indisputably Flemish, the one a Book of Hours in the Bodleian Library, Oxford,[37] the other an Antiphonary in the Royal Library in Brussels.[38] The Flemish Hours contains heads in initials which relate closely to those by this artist in the Bohun manuscripts (Plates 5a and 5b). Furthermore, the type of the angel of the Annunciation in the Flemish Hours compares with the Evangelist Matthew on the Leça brass.[39] The Evangelist on the Leça brass, in turn, compares favourably with the St Matthew in the Bohun Psalter-Hours, now in the Bodleian (Plates 6a and 6b), substantially illuminated by this Flemish artist.[40] There is no internal evidence for dating the Flemish Hours although a date in the 1340s is suggested by its style. The artist's emigration to England probably occurred in the early 1350s.[41] Parallels between the Flemish manuscripts cited and those of the Flemish brasses, imported to England, speak for the same hand in both media – suggestive possibly of similar practices on both sides of the Channel.[42]

The Flemish Antiphonary by the same Bohun artist has borders filled with butterflies, as in the British Library fragment, produced in England, and historiated initials containing a background of diaper; the initials have canopies of exactly the same type as those in the Flemish Hours, now in the Bodleian. A significant feature is the manner in which the letter forms mutate into the distended mouths of curious winged beasts; additional ornament is then accommodated in the space created (Plate 7a). Creatures of a closely related breed occur in the ground of the Serken and Mul brass, (Plate 7b) which in turn compare with a type appearing thirty years

[37] Oxford, Bodleian Library MS Lat. Liturg. f. 3. For a brief description and further bibliography, see O. Pächt and J. J. G. Alexander, *Illuminated Manuscripts in the Bodleian Library*, Oxford, I: *German, Dutch, Flemish, French and Spanish Schools*, Oxford 1966, no. 299. See also, Dennison, 'Artistic Context', 9, 11, 12, 16, 29, plates III (D), V (D), XII (B), (C), (D), XIII (B), XIV (A) (the borders and not the miniature), fig. 5(A), (B) and Dennison, 'Flemish Miniature Painting in the Mid Fourteenth Century', 506, 507, plates III 2A, D, III 3B, III 4B.

[38] Brussels, Bibliothèque Royale Albert Ier, MS 6426. For a description of this manuscript, J. Van den Gheyn, *Catalogue de manuscrits de la Bibliothèque royale de Belgique*, 1: *Écriture sainte en liturgie*, Brussels 1901, no. 664; C. Gaspar and F. Lyna, *Les principaux manuscrits à peintures de la Bibliothèque royale de Belgique*, 1, 2 vols, 2nd edn, Brussels 1984, no. 142, plate lxxiii d. See also Dennison, 'Artistic Context', 9, 12, 16, 24, plates V (C), VI (C), X (A), (B).

[39] For this comparison, Dennison, 'Artistic Context', plate V(B) and (D).

[40] Oxford, Bodleian Library, MS Auct. D. 4.4. For the comparison, Dennison, 'Artistic Context', plate 5 (A), (B). For discussion of the Bohun Psalter-Hours in the current context, ibid., 8, 9, where further bibliography is given. See also Sandler, *Survey*, no. 138 and Dennison, 'Oxford, Exeter College', 47, 48, fig. 14.

[41] In published literature I have referred to this artist as the Flemish Bohun Hand. Further discussion of the stylistic relationship between the Flemish Hours and Flemish brasses of the period is contained in Dennison, 'Artistic Context', 9, 11–12, 16.

[42] This is supported by evidence from England, for discussion of which see Dennison and Rogers, 'Elsing Brass', *passim*.

or so later in the Flemish Bohun illuminator's repertoire – although also employed earlier in his English career – in a fragment of a Bohun Book of Hours, now in Schloss Pommersfelden, Germany, of c.1380.[43] These forms, once created, were perpetuated by illuminators and brass engravers alike. They are applied by the Flemish Bohun Artist throughout his career, both in Flanders and England, spanning approximately forty years, from c.1345 to c.1385. Of added significance, many of the marginal motifs of the Flemish illuminator relate to those in the Bodleian *Romance of Alexander*, raised in an earlier context, as comparison between the drolleries from the *Alexander* and the pen drawn initials in the Antiphonary indicates (Plates 8a and 8b).[44] A close relationship thus exists between the style of the main, as well as subsidiary, decoration in Flemish brasses and illuminated manuscripts, factors which have repercussions on both sides of the Channel.

There is tangible evidence, therefore, to postulate an artistic connection between Flanders and East Anglia in the period from around c.1340 to c.1370, a first wave of influence manifesting itself in the ten years leading up to the Black Death, with its likely genesis in Norwich, although conveyed certainly by one illuminator to other parts of East Anglia. The Black Death clearly had a devastating impact on manuscript production in England (and probably in Flanders too), with the result that when it was again revived under the patronage of the Bohun family, around 1355, it was necessary to import a Flemish artist to their castle at Pleshey, Essex, where the two Bohun artists worked. This could have had advantages in both directions, given that the political and economic upheavals in Flanders can hardly have been conducive to settled artistic activity there. The surviving examples of fourteenth-century Flemish monumental brasses are situated, in the main, down the eastern coast of England, from Newcastle-on-Tyne to St Albans, transportable no doubt via the networks of the Hanseatic League. It is surely significant that at precisely the period marking the importation of Flemish brasses to England the two Bohun artists, one English, the other Flemish (they first collaborated c.1355–60), were producing miniatures indisputably influenced by these monuments, especially those to Robert Braunche at Lynn and Alan Fleming in Newark. There can be little doubt that the Flemish Bohun Artist evolved out of the milieu of Tournai illuminators and engravers of the 1340s and migrated to Pleshey, Essex in the 1350s.[45] The decorative linearity and complexity of these Flemish brasses must have been of considerable fascination for artists native to England. The fact

---

[43] Pommersfelden, Schönbornische Bibliothek, MS 2934 (348). For an illustration of the letter forms in question, see Dennison, 'Artistic Context', fig. 7(A), (B), and for discussion of this manuscript, see ibid., chapter 7 and 266–7. For a description of the book, see also Sandler, *Survey*, no. 137.

[44] Drolleries of this type have clearly been adapted from those made current by Jean Pucelle, active in Paris from c.1315–34 and perpetuated by his followers; they also occur in the Leça brass. For further discussion and illustration, Dennison, 'Artistic Context', 16, 20, plates X (C), (D) and fig. 8 (A), (B).

[45] For further discussion of this artist's likely Tournai origins, Dennison, 'Artistic Context', 12, 16, 20–21.

that these Flemish brasses were being exported widely over Europe goes some way to explain the complex transfer of a style from one centre to another – a vexed question for art historians. Therefore, it is possible to resolve, to some extent, enigmatic issues of this kind by the assessment of parallels between one medium and another. Indeed, manuscripts and brasses can be seen to support the provenance and dating of the two media. Flemish influence in England, specifically in East Anglia in the period, can thus be accounted for by the presence there of Flemish artists, as well as Flemish artifacts.

— INDEX —

Aachen (Germany), Charlemagne's chapel, 76, 270 note 3
Abbeville (France), 193
Åbo Akademi (in Turku, Finland), 162
Abrams, Lesley, 230
Adam de Walsokne (Norf.), brass, 95
Adam Easton, Cardinal, 310–11, 313
Adam Horn (from Cley, Norf.), 213
Adam of Bremen, 160
Ælfwald, king of the East Angles, 228
Æthelberht I, king of the East Angles, 137
Æthelberht II, St, king of the East Angles, 112, 137, 138
Æthelberht, king of Kent, 16, 122, 226
Æthelred, king of the East Angles, 137, 149, 150, 245, 253
Æthelstan, king of the East Angles, 17, 137
Æthelweard, king of the East Angles, 137
Afonso, king of Portugal, 287, 289, 292, 294
Agnes, widow of Nicholas Sotherton, 76
Alan of Lynn, Carmelite, 303–4, 312, 313
Alan Fleming, brass, Newark (Notts.), 321, 331, 334
al-Andalus, 287, 288
Albarella, U., 78
Aldeburgh (Suff.), 210, 213
Aldwulf, king of the East Angles, 228
Alfred Ætheling, brother of King Edward the Confessor, 279
Alfred the Great, king, 52, 83, 146, 150, 244
Alfriston (East Sussex), 251
Alice Barly, 306. See John, brother of
Amiens (France), 193
amphorae, 58
Amsterdam (Netherlands), 71, 79
Anglo-Saxon Chronicle, 52
animal husbandry, 78
Anjou, 167
Anne Lovell, 109–10. See Francis Lovell (Sir), husband of
Anne, St, 302
Anselm, abbot of Bury St Edmunds, 278, 280
Antoine Vérard, French publisher, 112
Antony Yaxley, son of Elizabeth Yaxley, 307
Antwerp (Belgium), 78, 188, 297, 298, 317
Arabic links, 252

arable land, 49, 51, 70
Archibald, Marion, 129, 250
Armentières (France), excavation, 224
Arnold of Aerschot (Belgium), 292
Arrhenius, Birgit, 31
Astill, Grenville, 69
Atlantic Ocean, 3–4, 5, 6, 7, 13, 127, 206, 298
Attleborough (Norf.), 98, 99, 240, 241
Augustine, St, missionary, 122, 128
Austria, 82, 92
Avignon (France), 92
Axel (Netherlands), 192, 193
Aylsham (Norf.), 251
  screen painting, 109

Babingley (Norf.), 240, 241
Bäckby (in Mälar region of Sweden), 29, 32
Bacon, family, 312
Bacon, Robert, Cromer fisherman, 206, 216
badgers, 160, 162, 163
Baldwin, abbot of Bury St Edmunds, 278
Baldwin IX, count of Flanders, 184
Baltic Sea, 6, 7, 13, 14, 23, 29, 32, 40, 61, 71, 73, 77, 79, 82, 86, 117, 152, 156, 157, 159, 164, 188, 189, 190, 193, 195, 196, 199, 200, 214, 249, 268, 269, 290, 298, 302
Bamburgh (Northumberland), 10
Banks, Sir Joseph, 214, 216
Barfleur (France), 193
Barham (Suff.), 223
barley, 181
Barnack (Cambs.)
  church, 262
  stone, 256
Barrington (Cambs.), 36
Barton Bendish (Norf.), 251, 252
Bassett, Steven, 60, 61
Bawsey (Norf.), 249
Bayonne (France), 196
Beachamwell (Norf.), 127
bear, 155, 159, 161, 162, 163
Beatrice of Valkenburg (d.1272), 91
beaver, 153, 155, 159, 162, 163, 164, 168–9
Beccles (Suff.), 184
Bedale (N. Yorks.), 251
Bede, 2, 8, 16, 17, 18, 19, 53

Bedford (Beds.), 52
Bedfordshire, 38, 52
Beechamwell (Norf.), 251
beguines, 77
Belgium 44, 60, 62, 120, 139, 224, 302. *See also* Low Countries
Beonna, king of the East Angles, 137, 145
Beornferth, East Anglian moneyer, 145
Beornwulf, king of the Mercians, 17
Beowulf, poem, 17
Bergen (Norway), 68, 73, 188, 192, 205, 207, 211
Bergen-op-Zoom (Netherlands), 188
Bernard of Clairvaux, St, 289–90, 292, 296
Bertha, Frankish princess and queen of Kent, 226
Bertram of Hamburg (Meister), 97
Beverley (E. Yorks.), 80
Billingford (Norf.), 249, 250
Binham (Norf.), priory, 9
'bircarlians', 162
Birka (Denmark), 160, 161
Black Death, 92, 95, 315, 316, 329, 334
Black Sea, 152, 160
Blackbourne, river (Suff.), 59
Blackburn, Mark, 248, 250, 252, 255
Blackwater, river (Essex), 47
Blair, John, 61
Blakeney (Norf.), 172, 207, 208, 213, 216
Blankenberge (Belgium), 192, 193
Blaydes Saith (Hull), 71
Blomefield, F., 77
Bloodmoor Hill, Carlton Colville (Suff.), 221
Bohemia, 82, 97, 98
Böhme, Horst Wolfgang, 22
Bohun, family, 94, 317, 330, 331–2. *See* Humphrey de Bohun
Bohun Book of Hours, 334
Bohun Psalter, 331–2, 332, 333, 334
Bologna (Italy), 315
Boniface IX, pope, 311
Boniface, St, 164
Bordeaux (France), 188, 193, 195, 196, 202
Boss Hall (Ipswich), 40
Boston (Lincs.), 66–7, 68, 172, 177, 180, 183, 208, 209, 214
    Guildhall, 71
Bothnia, Gulf of, 162
Botolph, St., 11
Boucicaut Master, 105, 109
Boudicca, queen, 16, 58
Boulogne (France), 193, 298
bracteates, 19
Brandon (Suff.), 252, 257, 258–9
Brantham (Suff.), 253
Braudel, Fernand, 3–4

Breckland (Norf.), 59, 169
Bremen (Germany), 65–6, 79, 192, 193, 196
Brescia Psalter, 317, 318–19
brick, 80, 200–1
Bridget of Sweden, St, 13, 301–14. *See also* Catherine of Vadstena, daughter of; Karl, son of
Brihtwulf, ealdorman of Essex, 52
Bright, Henry, 49
Brill (Netherlands), 196
Brinkum (Lower Saxony), 65
Bristol, 209, 212, 215, 216, 251, 294, 312–13
Britnell, Richard, 198
Brittany, 167, 199
Broadland, marshes, 49
Brodetopp (Sweden), altar frontal, 90
Bromholm Psalter, 92
brooches, 19, 30–1, 32–7, 56, 232, 233–8, 255
Broughton Lodge, Willoughby-on-the-Wolds, (Notts.), 30, 31
Brownsword, Roger, 33
Bruges (Belgium), 74, 77, 179, 184, 188, 192
Brugmann, B., 28, 29
Bruisyard abbey (Suff.), 306
Brussels (Belgium), 111
Buckinghamshire, 133, 134
bullion, 244–53
Burchard von Serken, bishop of Lübeck, 327, 332, 333
Bures Hamlet (Essex), 60
Bures St Mary (Suff.), 60
Burgh Castle (Norf.), 236
Burnham (Norf.), 208, 213
Bury St. Edmunds (Suff.), 10, 76, 174, 177
    abbey, 13, 85, 257, 262, 266, 267, 268, 269, 270, 272, 273, 274, 275–8, 279, 280, 284
    St Catherine, chapel of, 278
    St Denis, chapel of, 278
    St Faith, chapel of, 278
    St John, chapel of, 278, 280
    See also Anselm, Baldwin, abbots of
    battle of (16 October 1173), 11, 174
butchers, 170
Bylaugh (Norf.), 243
Byzantine Empire, 126, 144
    coins, 127, 144

Caen (France), 193
    abbey of Saint-Etienne, 84
    stone, 84, 256
Caister (Norf.), castle, 105
Caius, John, 212
Calais (France), 188, 189, 190, 193, 194, 197, 200
Cambridge (Cambs.), 95

St Benet's, church, 262
University of, 171, 317
Cambridgeshire, 8, 36, 38, 134, 135, 139, 150, 177, 178, 180, 181, 182
Canterbury (Kent), 75, 130, 146, 147, 148
  archbishop, 181
  cathedral, 271, 272
Carausius, Roman emperor, 134
Carolingian Empire, 147
Carrow (Norwich)
  priory, 306, 307, 312
  Psalter and Hours, 88–9
Carus-Wilson, E. M., 205, 212
Carver, Martin, 47, 61
Castle Acre (Norf.), 167, 168
  priory, 9, 168
Castle Rising (Norf.), 167
cat, 159, 161, 164
Catherine of Siena, St, 306
Catherine of Vadstena, daughter of St Bridget, 305, 311
Cats (Netherlands), 192
Cattermole, A. M., 235–7
cattle, 179
Cawston (Norf.), screen painting, 109
Cecil, Lord, 209
Cecilia Beaupre, prioress of Crabhouse, 101
Ceonwulf, king of Mercia, 138
Cerisy-la-Forêt, abbey (Normandy), 85
Chalons-sur-Saône (France), 127
Champion, Tim, 63–4
Channel, English, 57, 60, 62, 127, 139, 179, 180, 219, 225, 226, 229
Chapel Hill, near Markshall (Norf.), 132
Charlemagne, emperor, 252
Charles I, king, 210
Charles II, king, 211
cheese, 171
Chessell Down, Isle of Wight, 36
Childs, Wendy R., 212
Christian I, king of Denmark, 214
Christian IV, king of Denmark, 213
Christian of Ghistelles, 292
Cinque Ports, 298
Clapham, Sir Alfred, 279
Clare (Suff.), 167
Clark, Grahame, 18
Clark, William (of Southwold), 215
Clarke, Helen (née Parker), 68
Clenchwarton (Norf.), 70
Cley (Norf.), 208, 213
Cnut, king of Denmark and England, 8, 83, 260, 280
Coddenham (Suff.), 40, 126, 131, 134, 221, 223
cogs, 63, 64–7, 76, 178

coinage, 58, 120–36, 137–51, 226, 227, 229, 232, 244–6, 248, 250–4
Coke, John, 210, 216
Colchester (Essex), 52, 127, 195, 198
Colkirk (Norf.), 244
Colne, river (Essex), 47
Cologne (Germany), 92, 116, 127, 199, 294, 295, 297, 298, 299
  cathedral, 281, 282, 283, 285–6
  church of St Kunibert, 282
  church of St Pantaleon, 282, 284, 285
Colton (Norf.), 233, 234
Congham (Norf.), 235, 236
Constable, Giles, 288–9
Constance, Council of, 311
Constance, duchess of Brittany, 183
Constantine the Great, Roman emperor, 134
  See Helena, mother of
Constantine III, Roman emperor, 122
Constantius III, Roman emperor, 121–2
Copenhagen (Denmark), 214
cordwainers, 171
Cornwall, 208
Crabhouse (Norf.), priory, 101. See Cecilia Beaupre, Joan Wiggenhall, Matilda Talbot, prioresses
Crispus, Roman emperor, 134
Cromer (Norf.), 206, 208, 213
Crondall (Hants.), hoard, 124, 127, 128, 131, 132, 133, 134
Crowland (Lincs.), abbey, 262
Crusades, 288
  First, 298
  Second, 14, 288–9, 291
Cuerdale (Lancs.) hoard, 245, 246, 252
curriers, 171
Cuyp, Aelbert, 49

Damme, river (Belgium), 197
Danelaw, 52, 150, 242, 245, 246, 252
Danes, 52, 62, 83–4. See also, Vikings
Danzig (Poland), 195–6, 202
Dartford (Kent), 33
Dartmouth (Devon), 14, 287, 288–9, 291, 293, 295, 296, 298–300
Davis, R. H. C., 52
Deben, river (Suff.), 59, 61
Debenham (Suff.), church, 263
deer, 168, 173
Deira, kingdom, 131
Delort, Robert, 153
Denmark, 44, 47, 50, 56, 84, 139, 143, 144, 205, 206, 214, 215, 226, 261, 263, 269, 271, 298. See also Christian I, Christian IV, Cnut, Erik VII, Hans I, Harald Hein, kings of

Denver (Colorado), Art Museum, 100, 101
Dersingham (Norf.), 208
Desborough (Northants.), 221
Deventer (Netherlands), 192
    church of St Lebuinus, 281, 282, 285
diatoms, 71
Dieppe (France), 193
Diksmuide (Belgium), 192
dirhams, 252-3, 254. See also Arabic links
Ditchingham (Norf.), 246
dog, 161
doggers, 205, 206, 208, 210, 211, 215
Domburg (Netherlands), 227
Domesday Book, 44, 50, 180, 182, 297
Donington (Lincs.), 243
Dordrecht (Netherlands), 69, 188, 193, 196
Dorestad (Netherlands), 127, 147, 227
Douai (France), 184
    Psalter, 92
Douce Psalter, 317, 318-19
Dover (Kent), 179, 184
    Straits of, 5
Dronrijp, Frisian hoard, 127
Dublin (Ireland), Temple Bar West, 239, 242
Duccio di Buoninsegna, 315
Ducklington (Oxon.), 164
Duffy, Eamonn, 312
Dumville, David, 52
Dunkirk (France), 192, 193, 213
Dunwich (Suff.), 12, 184, 205, 210, 213
Durham, cathedral, 85, 279, 280
Dyrhólaey (Iceland), 206

Eadbald, king of Kent, 130
Eadberht, king of Northumbria, 145
Eadnoth, East Anglian moneyer, 145
Eadwald, king of the East Angles, 137, 138, 145
East Angles, 8
    kingdom of, 9-10, 16-17, 38-43, 60, 61, 120, 131, 137-8, 218, 248
    See also, Wuffingas, kingdom of; Ælfwald, Æthelberht I, Æthelberht II (St), Æthelred, Æthelstan, Æthelweard, Aldwulf, Beonna, Eadwald, Edmund (St.), Oswald, Rædwald, Sigeberht, kings of
East Harling (Norf.), 109
East Meon (Hants.), 251
Easton (Norf.), 310
Edessa (now Turkey), 288, 290
Edgar Ætheling, 164
Edinburgh (Scotland), 79
Edix Hill (Cambs.), 36
Edmund of Gotland, merchant, 172
Edmund, St, king of the East Angles, 8, 10, 17, 42, 83, 112, 137, 145, 149, 245, 253, 254, 257, 260, 279, 280
Edmund, son of Margaret Paston, 309-10
Edward the Elder, king, 84, 150, 252, 253
Edward the Confessor, St, king, 112
Edward I, king, 91
Edward III, king, 71, 167, 207, 317
Edward IV, king, 204
Efe, East Anglian moneyer, 145
Elbing (Poland), 195
Eleanor, daughter of King Edward I, wife of Henry, count of Bar, 91
Elbe, river, 39
Elisabeth of Hungary, St, 302
Elizabeth I, queen, 213
Elizabeth, widow of John Yaxley, 307, 308. See Antony, son of
elk, 157
Elmham (Norf.), 257. See also North Elmham
Elsing (Norf.), 95, 329
Ely (Cambs.), 60, 94
    abbey/cathedral, 85, 95, 180, 262, 270, 272, 273, 274-5, 278, 279, 280, 281, 284, 317
    Lady Chapel, 329
    See also Geoffrey Ridel, bishop of
Emma, wife of Richard Purdans, 305
Emma Stapleton, anchoress, 304
Empingham, (Rutland), 32, 33, 34, 35, 36
Erik VII, king of Denmark, 207
Eriswell (Suff.), 25, 28, 29, 39
Erler, Mary, 306
ermine, 160, 162, 164, 165, 167
Ervynck, A., 78
Esbjerg (Denmark), 10
Essex, 8, 22, 36, 41, 46, 52, 53, 56, 57, 58, 59, 62, 125, 127, 133, 134, 135, 139, 163, 177, 180, 181, 182, 184, 185, 189, 193, 253, 317
    kingdom of, 52, 60, 61
Estonia, 23, 29
Etheldreda, Saint, 279
Everitt, Alan, 45-6
Etaples (France), 193
Eugenius III, pope, 290
Evison, Vera I., 57
Exeter College, Oxford, Psalter, 320-1, 331
Exton (Rutland), 243
Eye (Suff.), 167
Eyke, near Woodbridge (Suff.), 134

falcons, 162
Fastolf Master, illuminator, 105
Faustina II, Roman empress, 249
Felix, St, bishop of the East Angles, 85, 227
Fennoscandia, 161, 162, 173
Fens, the, 37, 47, 49, 60, 163, 168, 180, 262

Fergusson, Peter, 280
Fernie, Eric, 76
ferret, 169
Finland, 23, 29, 79, 157, 161, 162
Finnmark, 161, 162, 173, 215
fish, 10, 67, 179, 190, 198, 204–16, 297
Fitzwarin Psalter, 324, 329–30
Flanders, 11, 12, 13–14, 70, 79, 92, 94, 95, 97, 98, 105, 112, 117, 170, 174–87, 190, 192, 193, 196, 197, 200, 201, 227, 271, 287, 290, 296, 298, 299, 315–35
    counts of, 74. *See* Baldwin IX, Philip, Thierry of Alsace, William Clito
Flemings, 174, 189, 190
Flitcham with Appleton (Norf.), 249
Forey, Alan, 289, 290
Foss Way, 24
Fornham (Suff.), battle of. *See* Bury St Edmunds
fox, 160, 161, 163, 164, 172, 173
Fox, Harold, 46
Framlingham (Suff.), church, 111
Framlingham Earl (Norf.), 253
France, 91, 92, 101, 105, 112, 120, 127, 139, 151, 167, 196, 202, 226
    northern, 57, 60, 62, 76, 79, 82, 117, 127, 135, 193, 224, 227, 315
Francis Lovell (Sir), 109. *See* Anne Lovell, wife of; Thomas Lovell, uncle of
Franks, 61, 120, 132, 145, 151
free peasantry, 50–1
Freshwater (Isle of Wight), 248
Freya, goddess, 159
Friesland, 70, 193
Frisia, 11, 13, 39, 41, 44, 50, 120, 127, 135, 136, 144, 145, 147, 227
Frisians, 21
Fritton St Margaret (Norf.), rood screen, 312
Frösö (Jamtland, Sweden), 159
Fulda (Germany), abbey, 281
fur, 152–73

Gaimster, D., 79
Galbert of Bruges, 181
Galloway, J., 78
Gannon, Anna, 144
Gardiner, Mark, 176
Gascony (France), 189, 190, 199, 200
Geahčeváinjárga (East Finnmark), 157
Gene in Ångermanland (Sweden), 32
Geneva (Switzerland), 36
Genghis Khan, 11
Geoffrey de Mandeville, earl of Essex, 183–4
Geoffrey, duke of Brittany, 183
Geoffrey Ridel, bishop of Ely, 275
Germany, 13, 22, 37, 44, 58, 61, 79, 82, 83, 86, 92, 97, 98, 101, 105, 112, 116, 117, 120, 179, 188, 190, 193, 195, 200, 202, 226, 232–3, 263, 269, 271, 287, 297, 298, 302, 309
Ghent (Belgium), 77, 184, 317
Giese, Georg, 80
Gilbert de Coye-la-Forêt, marbler, 97
Gilchrist, Roberta, 76
Gildas, 18
Giles the Painter of Bruges, 91
Gimingham (Norf.), 169
Gipping, river (Suff.), 40, 47, 59, 223
Glasgow (Scotland), Burrell Collection, 91
Gloucestershire, 133
glovers, 171
goat hair, 164
Gokstad ship, 65
Gorleston Psalter, 92, 93, 169
Gosford (Woodbridge Haven) (Suff.), 193
goshawks, 162
Gothia, 11
Gotland, 172, 192
grain, 181, 185–6, 190, 198
Gravelines (France), 193
Graveningen (Netherlands), 193
Great Barton (Suff.), 234, 251
Great Chesterford (Essex), 39
Great Dunham (Norf.), 233
Great Witchingham (Norf.), 242
Great Yarmouth (Norf.), 11, 13, 171, 184, 189–90, 191–2, 193, 194, 195, 196, 197–8, 199, 200, 202, 208, 210, 211, 212, 216, 297
Greenland, 6
Greensted-next-Ongar church (Essex), 256–7
Grimsby (Lincs.), 208
Groß Strömkendorf (Germany), 77
Guestwick, church (Norf.), 263
Gummersmark, Jutland, 35, 36
Guðmundsson, Jón lærði, 215
Gundrada, wife of William I de Warenne, 182
    See Oosterzele family
Gungnir (Odon's spear), 239
Guthrum, Danish chieftain, 52, 83, 150, 245, 254
Guy Marchant, French publisher, 112

Hackluyt, Richard, 207, 209
Haddiscoe, church (Norf.), 263, 265, 271
Haddiscoe Thorpe, church (Norf.), 267–8
Hadleigh Road (Ipswich, Suff.), 40
Hague (The) Missal, 323, 323
Hales (Norf.), church, 263, 271
Hálogaland (Norway), 215
Hamburg (Germany), 189, 192, 193, 196

Hammarlunda (Scania, Sweden), church, 260, 261
Hampshire, 139
Hans I, king of Denmark, 209
Hans Holbein the Younger, 109–10
Hanseatic League, 5, 74, 79–80, 155, 156, 157, 161, 189, 195, 196, 197, 198, 199, 205, 209, 298, 331, 334
Harald Hein, king of Denmark, 260
Harderwijk (Netherlands), 192, 193
hares, 161, 162, 163, 164, 173
Harford Farm, Caistor St Edmund (Norf.), 221
Hart, Stephen, 262
Harthacnut, king of England and Denmark, 260
Harwich (Essex), 193, 196, 208, 213
Hastière-par-dela, church, Namur (Belgium), 271
Hastings (Sussex), 294
Hastings, Sir Hugh, brass, 95, 97, 329
Haughley (Suff.), 167
Heckington (Lincs.), 126
Heddal (Norway), altar frontal, 89–90
Hedeby (Denmark/Germany), 245
Heeslingen, church, near Bremen (Germany), 261, 268
Helena, mother of Constantine the Great, 132
Helgö, island (Sweden), 29, 31, 32
Helmold of Bosau, Saxon chronicler, 291
Henley (Oxfords.), 251
Henry I, king, 297
Henry II, king, 174, 180, 182, 183, 184, 186, 298
Henry III, king, 169, 171–2
Henry V, king, 171, 206, 207, 208, 304
Henry VII, king, 209
Henry VIII, king, 209
Henry, the Young King, son of Henry II, 174, 180
Henry Buckston, falconer of King's Lynn, 212
Henry, count of Bar, 91
Henry de Trith-Saint-Léger (France), 94
Henry Mundeford, 103. *See* William Mundeford
Henry of Huntingdon, 179
Henry Piers, glazier, 103
Heraclius, Byzantine emperor, 125, 129
Heraclius Constantine, Byzantine emperor, 129
heraldry, 152, 165
Herbert Losinga, bishop of Norwich, 84, 85, 271
Hereford, cathedral, 279
herring, 11, 188, 194, 198, 201, 297
Herringfleet (Suff.), church, 263, 264

Herteig, Asjbørn, 68
Hertfordshire, 50, 57, 58, 139, 163, 164
Hervey of Glanville, 292, 299
Heslop, T. A., 98, 101
Hethel (Norf.), 263
Heywood, Stephen, 58
Hills, Catherine, 56, 57
High Risby (Lincs.), 251
Hildesheim (Germany), church of St Michael, 268, 281, 282, 284–5
Hindringham (Norf.), 233, 247–8
Hines, John, 226
Hirsau (Germany), church, 271
Historiae Norvegiae, 161
Hobbema, Meindert, 49
Hodges, Richard, 21
Holland, 70, 188, 190, 192, 193, 194, 195, 196, 197, 200
Holy Roman Empire, 85, 268, 270–86, 292, 294, 297
Holywell Row (Suff.), 33
Hondecoeter, Melchior de, 49
Horsham St Faith (Norf.), rood screen, 312
Houghton-on-the-Hill (Norf.), church, 263
Hoxne (Suff.), hoard, 16, 124
Huffman, H., 297
Huggate (E. Yorks.), 251
Hull (E. Yorks.), 68, 69, 71, 74, 80, 196, 207, 209, 212, 214, 215, 216
river, 69
Hulst (Netherlands), 193
Humber, estuary, 20, 24, 37, 147
Humphrey de Bohun, earl of Hereford and Essex, 330
Hundred Years' War, 316–17
Huntingdonshire, 177
Hutcheson, Andy, 77
Huxley hoard (Cheshire), 246
Hythe (Kent), 184
Hywel Dda, laws of, 168–9

Iberia, 197
Iceland, 6, 13, 199, 204–16
Iceni, 8, 16, 58
Icknield Way, 38
ingots, silver, 246–50, 253, 254
Ipswich (Suff.), 10, 11, 13, 39, 40, 41, 58, 61, 138, 143, 146, 147–8, 148, 149, 167, 184, 189, 192, 193, 194, 195, 196, 197–8, 199, 200, 202, 208, 218–29, 294, 297, 299
Boss Hall, 221, 228
Buttermarket (St Peter's Street/Greyfriar's Road excavation), 40, 219–25, 227
Hadleigh Road cemetery, 227
Ware, 58, 60, 220, 246

INDEX 343

Ireland, 84, 128, 246, 253
Irish Sea, 6, 246, 252
Iron Age, 58
Iser (Belgium), 193
Isle of Wight, 36, 37
Isleworth (Middx.), 304, 306, 308
Isley cum Langley (Leics.), 251
Italy, 82, 92, 148, 315

James I, king, 215
James Gentleman (of Southwold), 215
James Gloys, priest in service of Margaret Paston, 309
Jansson, I, 242
Jarrow (Tyne and Wear), 168
Jean Gerson, 311
Jerome, St, 307–8
Jerusalem, 288, 297, 306
    church of the Holy Sepulchre, 267
Joan Elys, nun of Carrow priory, 306
Joan Wiggenhall, prioress of Crabhouse, 101
Johann von Mul, bishop of Lübeck, 327, 332, 333
John Barly, priest of St Michael Coslany, Norwich, 306. *See* Alice, sister of
John Crome, 49
John de Norweye, goldsmith, 94
John de Ramsey, mason, 94–5
    see also Richard le Machun, probable father of
John de Tye, illuminator, 330–1
John, duke of Bedford, 105
John Fastolf (Sir), 105
John Fincham the younger, 112–16
John, king, 177, 184
John Mundeford, 103, 105. *See* William Mundeford
John I Paston, 309. *See* Margaret, wife of
John Salmon, bishop of Norwich, 92, 94, 97
John Steyke, rector of St Laurence, Norwich, 306
John Wighton, 102–3, 105–7, 109
Johannisberg near Hersfeld (Germany), church, 268
Johnessone, Andrew, Dutch merchant, 196
Jones, Evan T., 205, 209, 210, 211
Jordan Fantosme, 9, 174–6, 180, 186
Jordanes, 160
Jörmungandr (serpent), 12
Julian of Norwich, 304, 308, 311, 313
Jumièges, abbey (Normandy), 262, 284
Jutland, 19, 25, 28, 39, 145, 192

Kalmergården (Denmark), 235
Kampen (Friesland), 192, 193, 196
Kaupang (Norway), 245, 252

Karelia region (Russia), 162
Karl, son of St Bridget of Sweden, 308–9
Kenninghall (Norf.), palace, 111
Kent, 18, 19, 35, 36, 37, 41, 46, 53, 83, 121, 124, 125, 133, 134, 135, 139, 143, 145, 148, 181, 183
    See Æthelberht, Eadbald, kings of; Bertha, queen of
Kershaw, Jane, 232, 233, 235
Keswick (Norf.), 249
King, Chris, 76, 77
King's Lynn (Norf.), 13, 67, 67–8, 68, 77, 80, 95, 97, 101, 116, 117, 172, 177, 178, 184, 189–90, 191–3, 194, 195, 196, 197–8, 199, 200, 202, 207, 208, 210, 212–13, 213, 214, 215, 216, 301, 303, 305, 309, 314, 332
    chapel of St Nicholas, 95
    church of St Margaret, 95–6
    Greyfriars, 81
    Stockfish Row, 213
    Thoresby College, 68
Knyvett family of Ashwellthorpe, 111
Kołobrzeg (German Kolberg, Pomerania), 153
Kortegene (Netherlands), 192
Krautheimer, Richard, 280
Kuusisto, castle (in Turku, Finland), 162

La Hougue (France), 193
Lakenheath (Suff.), 25
lamb, 172
Lambert de Beguin, 77
Lanfranc, archbishop of Canterbury, 11
Langford (Essex), church, 270, 271
Lapscheure (Belgium), 192
Lark, river (Suff.), 59
Lavenham (Suff.), 9
Lea, river (Herts.), 52
Leagrave (Bedfords.), 52
Leahy, Kevin, 231, 235
leatherworkers, 170
Leça de Balio (Portugal), brass, 325, 326, 332, 333
Ledbroc of Gothland, 172
Leeds, E. T., 56
Leicestershire, 24
Leland, John, 206–7
Licinius I, Roman emperor, 132
Liège (Belgium), cathedral, 281, 282, 286
Lille (France), 184
Limbourg brothers, 105, 109
Lincoln (Lincs.), 69, 230
    cathedral, 272, 278
Lincolnshire, 8, 50, 51, 125, 133, 134, 139, 177, 180, 231

Lindsey, 131
Linton Heath (Cambs.), 36
Lisbon (Portugal), 14, 287–300
Little Chesterford (Essex), 251
Livermore, Harold, 290
Lombaertsijde (Belgium), 193
London, 9, 39, 40, 47, 52, 60, 68, 69, 71, 72, 75, 76, 79, 81, 92, 94, 95, 97, 118,121, 130, 134, 146, 147, 156, 171, 172, 177, 183, 184, 189, 190, 197, 198, 207, 209, 212, 213, 216
   Fleet river, 71
   the Steelyard, 80
   Trig Lane, 73
Louis VII, king of France, 293, 297
Loveluck, C., 227
Low Countries, 79, 137, 141, 176, 178, 184, 188, 189, 190, 192, 193, 196, 197, 198, 199, 200, 201, 202, 203, 302, 303. *See also* Belgium, Flanders, Netherlands
Lowestoft (Suff.), 195
Lübeck (Germany), 67, 73, 74, 192, 195, 327
   See also Burchard von Serken, Johann von Mul, bishops of
   cathedral, 325
   Große Petersgrube, 73
Lucilla, daughter of Roman emperor Marcus Aurelius, 249
Lul, East Anglian moneyer, 138, 145
Lull, 164
Lund (Sweden), 259, 261
Lüneberg Heath (Germany), 268
lynx, 159, 161

Macclesfield Psalter, 92, 169, 316
Magdeburg (Germany), destroyed church in, 284
Magna Carta, 184
Magnus Eriksson, 162
Magnus 'Island man' (of Southwold), 215
Magnus Maximus, Roman emperor, 132
Magnússon, Skúli, treasurer of Iceland, 216
Maine (France), 167
Malcolm III (Canmore), king of Scots, 164
Mammen (Denmark), 159
Margaret, St, queen of Scots, 164
Margaret, wife of John de Norweye, goldsmith, 94
Margaret Calle, daughter of Margaret Paston, 309–10
Margaret Paston, 308, 309–10. *See* John I, husband of; Edmund, son of; Margaret Calle, daughter of
Margaret Purdans, 305–7, 308, 313. *See also* Richard Purdans, husband of: William, son of; Richard Yaxley, son-in-law of

Margaret Yaxley, nun of Bruisyard abbey, 306
Margery Kempe, 196, 301, 303, 304, 305, 308, 308–9, 310, 311, 313
Margeson, Sue, 231, 232, 255
Marie de Oignies, beguine, 303
Market Rasen (Lincs.), 251
Marsham (Norf.), screen painting, 109
marten, 159, 160, 162, 163, 164, 173
Martin, Edward, 59
Martin Gray (of King's Lynn), 215
Martin Schongauer, 109
Martina, St, 116
Master of the Magdalen Legend, 111
Matilda, Empress, daughter of Henry I, 298
Matilda Talbot, prioress of Crabhouse, 101
Matthew Paris, 11
Matthew Parker, archbishop of Canterbury, 299
Mautby (Norf.), 309
McAleer, J. P., 280
meat, 179
Medemblik (Netherlands), 193
Mediterranean Sea, 3, 58, 61, 127, 144, 160, 176, 188, 226, 298
Méhun-sur-Yèvre, abbey (France), 85
Melchior Broederlam of Ypres, 102
Melton Constable (Norf.), church, 116, 117
Memleben, abbey (Saxony, Germany), 281
Mercia, kingdom, 17, 41, 52, 143, 145, 148
   See Beornwulf, Ceonwulf, Offa, kings of
Merovingians, 125, 131
Merton (Norf.), 132, 134
   church of St Peter, 87
Metcalf, Michael, 143
Methwold (Norf.), 169
Metz (France), 293
Meuse, river, 45
Middelburg (Netherlands), 190, 192, 194, 196
Middlesex, 57
Midlands, 57, 180
migration, 200–1, 230–55
milk, 179
Milne, Gustav, 72
Mitchell, A. R., 210
mole, 164
Möllenbeck (Germany), church, 268
Monnikerede (Belgium), 192
Montfoort (diocese, Utrecht), 103
Montivilliers (France), 201
monumental brass, 95, 107
Morley St Peter (Norf.), hoard, 247, 253
Mosan region (Belgium), 271
Mucking (Essex), 22, 36
Muiden (Netherlands), 193
Mundham (Norf.), 29, 30, 31, 32, 33

Neilsen, Karen Høilund, 37
Nene, river, 178
Netherlands, 44, 48, 78, 82, 97, 148, 224, 226
    See also Low Countries
Neukirchen in Malente kreis (Germany), church, 263
Newcastle-upon-Tyne (Northumberland), 334
Newfoundland, 209, 216
New Buckenham (Norf.), 167
New Shoreham (Sussex), 65
Nicholas, David, 181
Nicholas Heyward, glazier, 107, 109. See also William Heyward, brother
Nicholas Sotherton, citizen of Norwich, 76 See also Agnes, widow of
Niedersachsen (Germany), 70
'Nietap', Frisian coin type, 127
Nieuwpoort (Belgium), 179, 193
Nivelles (Belgium), church of St Gertrude, 281–2
Norfolk, 8, 8–9, 24, 29, 32, 58, 59, 71, 82–118, 134, 135, 139, 141, 143, 177, 180, 181, 182, 184, 185, 195, 231, 299, 303, 309
Normandy, 85, 167, 177, 193, 196, 201, 270, 279
North Creake (Norf.), 235, 236
North Elmham (Norf.), 83, 271, 273. See also Elmham
North Owersby (Lincs.), 251
North Sea
    definition, 1–2, 5–7, 13–14, 44–8, 77, 81, 82–3
    weather, 2–3, 12
Northampton, 177
Northamptonshire, 36, 38, 150, 177
North Tuddenham (Norf.), church, 105, 109
Northumbria, kingdom, 41, 131, 145, 164, 250. See also Eadberht, king of
Norway, 13, 20, 21, 23, 31, 39, 44, 88, 89, 94, 97, 98, 105, 157, 163, 172, 188, 192, 193, 194, 196, 198, 200, 205, 269, 271
Norwich (Norf.), 9, 11, 39, 47, 62, 71, 74, 75, 76, 79, 92, 94–5, 95, 97, 117, 170–1, 189, 230, 254, 257–8, 271, 301, 302, 303, 304, 306, 307, 312, 313, 315, 316, 317, 329, 334
    Aviva Insurance, Marble Hall building, 117
    Briton's Arms, 77
    Carnary College, 76
    castle, 167
    Castle Museum, 29, 30, 48
    cathedral, 65, 84–6 (Despencer Retable), 97–8, 102, 266–7, 268, 269
    friary, 91
    Guildhall, 116
    guild of St George, 105
    'le Welleyard', 94
    Millennium Library site, 249
    St Andrew, church of, 112, 114
    St Giles, church and parish of, 305
    St Gregory, church of, 107, 108
    St Laurence, church of, 306
    St Leonard's priory, Mousehold, 310, 311
    St Martin-at-Palace, church of, 257–8, 263
    St Mary the Less, parish, 94
    St Michael at Plea, 98, 102
    St Michael Coslany, church of, 306
    St Peter Hungate, churchyard, 77
    St Peter Mancroft, church and parish, 94, 104–05, 105 (Toppes Window, 105), 107
    St Stephen, church of, 112, 113, 116
    St Vedast, church of, 84
    Society of Artists, 48
    Strangers Hall, 76
    William of, sculptor, 94–5
    See also Herbert Losinga, John Salmon, Walter Lyhert, bishops of
Novgorod, principality of, 162, 163, 176
Nydam (Denmark), 25, 29

oats, 181
Odense (Denmark), 161
Odin, 238–9, 245
Offa, king of Mercia, 17, 137, 138, 139, 145, 146, 252
Olaf, St, king of Norway, 88–9, 116
Old Buckenham (Norf.), 248
Ommundrød in Vestfold (Norway), 31
Oosterzele, family, 182
Orford (Suff.), 184, 210
Orkney Islands, 268, 269, 271
Ormesby Psalter, 92, 315–16, 316, 329
Orwell (Suff.), 190, 208
Orwell, river (Suff.), 61, 218, 220, 222, 227
Ostend (Belgium), 192, 193
Oswald, king of the East Angles, 137, 149, 150, 245, 254
Ohthere, Viking adventurer, 233
otter, 153, 160, 161, 163, 164
Ouse, river, 52, 68, 178
Outwell (Norf.), church of St Clement, 112, 115, 116
Oxborough (Norf.), hoard, 125, 126, 252
Oxford (Oxfords.)
    church of Greyfriars, 91
Oxfordshire, 38

Pächt, Otto, 316
Pada, coin type, 135, 136

346 INDEX

Paglesham, (Essex), 36
pantiles, 48
parchment makers, 171
Paris (France), 98, 315
   church of Saint-Jacques-l'Hôpital, 95
   Cluny Museum, 95, 97
   Sainte-Chapelle, 76
Parkhurst, Anthony, 209
Parsons, David, 230
Paston, family, 105. See also Edmund, John, Margaret
Patching (W. Sussex), hoard, 125
Paterson, Caroline, 231, 235
peat digging, 10
pendants, 164
Penn, K., 28, 29
Perth, 79
Pestell, Tim, 29
Peterborough (Cambs.), 134, 243
   abbey, 262, 270, 272, 273, 273–4, 279–80, 281
Philip, count of Flanders, 180, 184
Philip II Augustus, king of France, 184
Philip of Namur, regent in Flanders, 184
Phillips, Jonathan, 288
Phythian-Adams, Charles, 46
Picards, 174
Pietro Torregiano, 109
pine marten, 156
Pippin III, king of the Franks, 145
Pleshey (Essex), 317, 330, 334
Poitou, 167
Poland, 86
polecat, 160, 161
Poringland (Norf.), 98
Portugal, 287–8, 298
pottery, 78
Procopius, *De Bello Gothico*, 226
Provence, 127
Pulham St Mary (Norf.), 98

Quentovic (France), 10, 127

rabbit, 71, 152, 156, 164, 168, 169, 170, 171, 172. See also warrens
Rædwald, king of the East Angles, 9, 16, 17, 61, 62, 83, 129
Ragnarok, 12
Ralph Diceto, 11
Ramsey (Cambs.) abbey, 177, 262
Ranworth (Norf.), church, 107, 109
Raol, proposed East Anglian author of *De Expugnatione Lyxbonensi*, 290–1
Rau, A., 25, 28, 29
reindeer, 157, 161
Rendlesham (Suff.), 47, 60, 126, 127, 132–3, 134, 246, 251
Renesse (Netherlands), 192
Repton (Derbs.), 240, 242
Reynolds, Andrew, 222
Reynolds, Susan, 296
Rhine, river, 45, 120, 127, 179, 227
Rhineland, 14, 79, 91, 188, 224, 227, 296
Ribble, river (Lancs.), 245
Ribe (Denmark), 145, 239
Richard I the Lionheart, king, 184
Richard III, king, 209
Richard Fernys, Sir, priest and hermit, 305
Richard le Machun, probable father of John de Ramsey, 94
Richard of Cornwall, king of the Romans, 91
Richard Fouler (of Cromer), 213
Richard Purdans, mayor of Norwich, 171, 305. See also Emma, Margaret, wives of; William, son of; Richard Yaxley, son-in-law of
Richard Rolle, 306
Richard Yaxley, son-in-law of Richard and Margaret Purdans, 307
Rigold, Stuart, 141
Roach-Smith, C., 56
Robert Baxter, mayor of Norwich, 305–6
Robert Braunche, brass, King's Lynn, 95–6, 322, 332, 334
Robert de St Edmund, goldsmith, 94
Robert, earl of Leicester, 174
Robert Mundeford, 103, 105. See William Mundeford
roe deer, 162
Roger Betys, 309
Roger of Howden, 186
Roman period, 16, 83, 120–1
Romance of Alexander, 316, 319, 329–30, 334
Romans, 160
Rome, 302, 306, 311
   church of St Cecilia in Trastavere, 311
   church of St Peter, 271, 273, 280, 285–6
Rømersdal (Denmark), 240
roofs
   crown post, 59
   queen post, 59
Roskilde (Denmark), 260–1
Rotterdam (Netherlands), 190, 196
Rouen (France), 98
   cathedral, 262
Roughton (Norf.), church, 263
round-towered churches, 11, 44, 58, 86, 256–69
Russia, 14, 79, 152, 159, 163, 164, 172–3, 253
Rutland, 24

Rye (Sussex), 184
rye, 181
Saami, 157, 159, 161, 162, 173
sable, 161, 162, 163, 165
saddlers, 171
Saffron Walden (Cambs.), 183
Saham Toney (Norf.), 249
St Albans (Herts.), 57, 134, 334
St Andrews (Fife), 79
St Benet's at Holme (Norf.), abbey, 260, 262
St Ives (Hunts.), 172, 177
St Jorgensbjaerg (Denmark), 261
Saint-Omer (France), 184
    abbey of Saint-Bertin, 182
    guild regulations, 294
    Psalter, 92
Saint-Denis (France), 97
    parish church, Bury St Edmunds, 278
Saint-Riquier, abbey (France), 268
Saint-Trond (Belgium), church of, 282
Saint-Valéry-sur-Somme (France), 193
Salle (Norf.), church of St Peter and St Paul, 9, 102, 103, 103–5
salmon, 162
salt marshes, 180
Sandlings (Suff.), 61, 62
Sangatte (France), 193
Saul, A., 198
Saxlingham Nethergate (Norf.), church of St Mary the Virgin, 90
Saxons, 5, 18–19, 83
Saxony, 39
Scandinavia, 17, 19, 21, 22, 23, 24, 25, 28, 29, 31, 32, 41, 56, 58, 61, 78, 79, 82, 85, 117, 147, 148, 151, 152, 157, 160, 161, 172–3, 226, 230, 252–3, 256, 269
    influence on place-names of East Anglia, 51–2
Scania (Sweden), 268, 269. *See also* Skåne
Scarborough (N. Yorks.), 201, 208
sceattas, 139, 140, 141–5
Scheldt, river, 45, 78
Schiedam (Netherlands), 196
Schleswig-Holstein, 11, 39, 75, 268, 269
Schloss Pommersfelden (Germany), Book of Hours, 334. *See also* Bohun
Scole (Norf.), 249
Scotland, 128, 199, 208, 253, 273
Scull, Christopher, 29
scutiform pendants, 19
seals, 162
Seine, river, 120
Sejlflod (Denmark), 28
Sherborne (Dorset), cathedral church, 279
's-Hertogenbosch (Netherlands), 69
Shipdam (Norf.), 252

shoemakers, 171
Siberia, 14
Siena (Italy), 92, 315
Sigeberht, king of the East Angles, 83, 227
Sigtuna (Sweden), 160, 161
siliquae, 122, 123
silver, 179
Silverdale (Lancs.), 246
Sindbæk, S. M., 249
Skagerrak, 5
Skåne, Skånia (Sweden), 195, 201, 240. *See also* Scania
skinners, 170
Skuldelev fjord (Denmark), 65
Sleaford (Lincs.), 24
Slepeldamme (lost settlement, Netherlands), 192, 193
Sluis (Netherlands), 192, 193
Smart, Veronica, 150
Snetterton (Norf.), 33, 34, 35, 36, 37
Snorri Sturlusson, 238, 239
Sogn og Fjordane (Norway), 19
Soignies, abbey (Belgium), 85
Somerset, 48
Southampton (Hants.), 39, 40, 79, 294
South Lopham (Norf.), 240
    church, 263
Southwold (Suff.), 210, 213, 215
Spain, 127, 199. *See also* Iberia
Sparham (Norf.), 253
Speyer (Germany), cathedral, 85, 268
Spong Hill (Norf.), 22, 173
Springthorpe (Lincs.), 249
squirrels, 155, 157, 160, 162, 163, 164, 165, 172, 173
Staecker, J., 242
Stalbridge (Dorset), 251
Stamford (Lincs.), 150, 172, 177, 183
Stannard, family, 49
Stark, James, 49
Stavanger, church of St Swithun, 269
Stavoren (Friesland), 193
Stenton, Sir Frank, 50, 52
Stephen, king, 298
Stettin (Poland), 195
Stirling, 79
stockfish, 163, 188, 205, 207, 208, 211, 213
Stockholm (Sweden), 160, 162
Stour, river (Suff.), 47, 60, 62
Stralsund (Germany), 65, 192
Suffolk, 8, 30, 33, 53, 57, 58, 59, 62, 120, 134, 135, 139, 141, 143, 177, 180, 181, 182, 184, 185, 193, 231, 299
Surlingham (Norf.), 234
Sussex, 56
Sutton Hoo, ship burial, 9, 17, 41, 41–2, 60,

61, 83, 120–1, 124–5, 126, 127, 128, 129, 136, 164
Svear, 160
Swallowcliffe Down (Wilts.), 221
Sweden, 23, 29, 31, 32, 44, 56, 84, 86, 157, 159, 269
Switzerland, 120
Symon Wynter, member of Syon community, 308
Syon, Brigittine house (Middx.), 304, 306, 308
Syria, 288

Tacolneston (Norf.), screen painting, 109
Tamworth (Staffs.), 10, 47
Tanner, Norman, 304, 306
Tanngnjost (goat that pulled Thor's chariot), 238
Tanngrísnir (goat that pulled Thor's chariot), 238
tanners, 171
Tarrant Rushden (Dorset), 251
tawyers, 171
Taylor, H. M. and J., 262
Thames, river, 52, 53, 56, 72, 81, 133, 149
Theophanu, empress, 282
Thetford (Norf.), 11, 83, 84, 167, 169, 240–1, 254, 257, 258
   Cluniac priory, 111, 117
   Dominican friary, 97
   nuns of, 306
   St Nicholas Street, 241
Thierry of Alsace, count of Flanders, 297
Thietmar of Merseburg, 261
Thøfner, Margit, 82, note 1
Thomas Brinton, bishop of Rochester, 310
Thomas Goldbeater, 107
Thomas Howard, third duke of Norfolk, 109–11, 117
Thomas Lovell (Sir), 109. *See also* Francis Lovell (Sir), nephew
Thomas Netter, Carmelite prior-provincial, 304
Thomas Rudd (of Cromer), 213
Thomas Wetherby, mayor of Norwich, 305
Thor, 12, 238–9
Thor's hammer, 238–43, 254, 255
Þorláksson, Helgi, 210, 213
Þorleifsson, Björn, Danish governor of Iceland, 214
Thorney (Cambs.), abbey, 262
Thornham Parva (Suff.), 97
Þorsteinsson, Björn, 204, 206, 208, 209, 212, 213, 214
Tilbeorht, East Anglian moneyer, 144
timber-framed churches, 256–60
Tissø (Denmark), 239, 242

Tobias Gentleman of Southwold, 210
Tøftom in Grimsdalen (Norway), 161
Tønsberg (Norway), 192
Torksey (Lincs.), 240, 242, 245, 250, 253
Tortosa (Spain), 290
Tournai (Belgium), 97, 111, 316, 330, 334
Trave, river (Lübeck), 73
tremissis, 120, 127, 131, 132
Trendgården (Denmark), 242
Trent, river, 24
Trinovantes, 58
Trondheim (Norway), 69, 192
Tune in Alsike (Sweden), 31
Tunstead (Norf.), 169
Turku (Finland), 162
Two Emperors, coin type, 132, 135, 136
Tyerman, Christopher, 289
Tys, D., 227

Ufford (Suff.), 133
Ullna (in Uppland, Sweden), 239
Urban VI, pope, 311
Urnes (Norway), church, 258, 259–60, 269
Ursula, St, 116
Utrecht (Netherlands), 69
   ship, 65

Vadstena (Sweden), religious community, 303, 305
Vågen (Norway), 68
Valentinian I, Roman emperor, 132
Valkyries, 243–4
Van de Noort, Robert, 7, 70
Vanimundus, moneyer, 135, 136
Veer (Netherlands), 196
Veeckman, J., 78
Verdun (France), cathedral, 281, 282
Verhaege, Frans, 78, 79
Viborg (Denmark), 161
Vienna Psalter, 317, 329–30
Vierck, Hayo, 226
Viken (on Lovö in Uppland, Sweden), 29, 30
Vikings, 5, 6, 13, 17, 42, 50, 83–4, 89, 137, 149–51, 156, 159, 161, 172, 230–55
Vindolanda, Roman Fort (Northumberland), 246
Visigothic kingdom, 127, 144
Vlaardingen (Netherlands), 196
Vlissengen (Netherlands), 196

Wadden Sea, 70
Walberswick (Suff.), 210, 213
Waldercome (Netherlands), 193
Wales, 128, 168
Walpole St Peter (Norf.), 251
Walraversijde (Belgium), 80

Walsoken (Norf.), 251
Walsingham (Norf.), 75
Walter Hilton, mystical writer, 306
Walter Lyhert, bishop of Norwich, 309–10
Walton (Suff.), 61
Warenne, family, 167–8, 169, 183. *See* Gundrada, William I de; William V de
warrens, 169–72
Warwickshire, 38
Wash, the, 20, 24, 177, 186
Watling Street, 52
weavers, 174–5
Wedmore, treaty of (879), 52
Welland, river, 178
Wellingham (Norf.), 116
Wells (Somerset), archdeacon of, 185
Wells-next-the-Sea (Norf.), 210, 213–14
Wends, 288
Weser, river (Germany), 65, 268
Wessex, kingdom, 41, 52, 53, 56
Westfield (E. Sussex), 251
Westman Islands (Iceland), 208, 215
Westminster, 213
    St Peter's chapel, 76
West Dereham (Norf.), 249
West Heslerton (N. Yorks.), 32
West, Stanley, 237
West Stow (Suff.), 36, 163, 173
Wetheringsett (Suff.), 36, 37
wheat, 181
Whitby (N. Yorks.), 201, 208
White Sea, 163
Wickham Market (Suff.), 243
Wickham Skeith (Suff.), 249
Wickhampton (Norf.), 252
Widsith, poem, 17
Wiggenhall St Mary Magdalen (Norf.), 101
Wiggenhall St Peter (Norf.), 105
Wigræd, East Anglian moneyer, 144
wild boar, 164
William Cade of Saint-Omer, financier, 182–3
William Caxton, 312
William Clito, count of Flanders, 297
William de Bittering, 95
William de Mandeville, earl of Essex, 184
William I de Warenne, 182. *See* Gundrada, wife of
William V de Warenne, 183
William Hammond, 307
William Heyward, glazier, 107, 109. *See* Nicholas Heyward, brother
William of Norwich, sculptor, 94–5

William Mundeford, 103. *See* Montfoort; Henry, John (sons of); Robert
William, son of Richard and Margaret Purdans, 307
William Sporle, Norwich pelter, 171
William Yslond, Bristol merchant, 215
William I the Conqueror, king, 11, 254
Williams, N. J., 213
Williamson, Tom, 231
Willingate (Essex), 251
Wilton (Norf.), cross-pendant, 129, 130
Wimbish (Essex), 329, monumental brass
Wimpfen-in-Tal (Germany), church, 284
Winchelsea (Sussex), 184
Winchester (Hants.), 10, 177
    Bishop's Palace, 168
    cathedral, 280, 284
windmills, 49
wine, 178, 180
Wismar (Germany), 195
Wissant (France), 176, 193
Witmen, coin type, 132–3
Witnesham (alias Westerfield) (Suff.), 36
Wiveton (Norf.), 249
    church, 65
woad, 178, 193
wolves, 161, 163
Woodbridge (Suff.), 127, 134. *See also* Gosford
woodland, 152, 162
wool, 67, 175, 179, 180, 185, 190, 194–5, 196, 198
Worlaby (Lincs.), 164
Worstead (Norf.), screen painting, 109
wrist-clasps, 19, 20–1, 23–9, 56
Wuffa, supposed grandfather of Rædwald, 17
Wuffingas, kingdom of, 60, 61, 62. *See also*, East Angles, kingdom of
Wulfstan, Viking adventurer, 233
Wycbold brass, 331
Wymondham (Norf.), 251

York, 40, 76, 121, 150, 230
    Minster, 98
    Vale of, 246
Yorkshire, 24, 50, 51, 53, 56, 57, 131, 139, 180, 201
Ypres (France), 78, 102, 177, 184

Zeeland (Netherlands), 70, 188, 190, 192, 193, 194, 196, 197, 200, 201
Zierickzee (Netherlands), 192, 196

www.ingramcontent.com/pod-product-compliance
Lightning Source LLC
Chambersburg PA
CBHW052056300426
44117CB00013B/2148